MW01627280

ENGAGED RESISTANCE

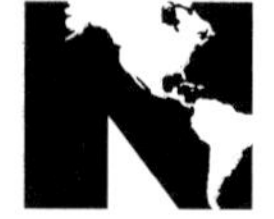

THE WILLIAM & BETTYE NOWLIN SERIES
in Art, History, and Culture of the Western Hemisphere

ENGAGED RESISTANCE

AMERICAN INDIAN ART, LITERATURE, AND FILM FROM ALCATRAZ TO THE NMAI

DEAN RADER

University of Texas Press Austin

Printed in the United States of America
Second paperback printing, 2012

"How to Write the Great American Indian Novel" reprinted from *The Business of Fancydancing*, © 1992 by Sherman Alexie, by permission of Hanging Loose Press.

Requests for permission to reproduce material from this work should be sent to:
Permissions
University of Texas Press
P.O. Box 7819
Austin, TX 78713-7819
www.utexas.edu/utpress/about/bpermission.html

♾ The paper used in this book meets the minimum requirements of ANSI/NISO Z39.48-1992 (R1997) (Permanence of Paper).

LIBRARY OF CONGRESS CATALOGING-IN-PUBLICATION DATA

Rader, Dean.
Engaged resistance : American Indian art, literature, and film from Alcatraz to the NMAI / Dean Rader. — 1st ed.
p. cm. — (The William and Bettye Nowlin series in art, history, and culture of the Western Hemisphere)
Includes bibliographical references and index.
ISBN 978-0-292-72399-3 (cloth : alk. paper) — ISBN 978-0-292-72696-3 (pbk. : alk. paper)
1. Indian arts—Political aspects—United States—History. 2. Government, Resistance to—United States—History. 3. Indians of North America—Politics and government. 4. Indians of North America—Ethnic identity. 5. Indian ethics—United States—History. 6. Indian art—United States—History. 7. American literature—Indian authors—History and criticism. 8. Indigenous films—United States—History. 9. Indians in motion pictures—History. 10. Indians of North America—Intellectual life. I. Title.
E98.A73R23 2011
323.1197—dc22

2010047370

ISBN 978-0-292-73482-1 (E-book)

For my family

CONTENTS

ACKNOWLEDGMENTS

THIS BOOK HAS, literally, taken me from coast to coast: from Ocean Beach and Alcatraz in California to the National Museums of the American Indian in Battery Park, Manhattan, and Washington, D.C., on that other coast. It required stops in Utah, Oklahoma, Arizona, New Mexico, Mississippi, Georgia, Nebraska, Minnesota, Michigan, Oregon, Washington, and Connecticut—even Hawaii. The list of people who have provided assistance along the way is staggering. I will forget to name many of them here, and for that I apologize, but there are many whose advice, guidance, and cooperation have been unforgettable.

Grateful acknowledgments go out to Amanda Williford at the National Parks Archive in San Francisco and to Emily Moazami at the Cultural Resources Center of the National Museum of the American Indian in Suitland, Maryland, both of whom were especially helpful in regard to archival matter and image preparation. I also want to thank Rick Romagosa at the *San Francisco Chronicle*, Sean Campbell from the Buffalo Bill Historical Center, Robert Hershon of Hanging Loose Press, Pat Dobbs at the Crazy Horse Memorial, Sarah Cucinella-McDaniel at the Denver Art Museum, Trysha Le at HarperCollins, Courtney Wagner at the American Folk Art Museum, Christy Cox at FallsApart Productions, Chris Hamilton-Emery from Salt Publishing, Russ Bodnar at the Chaco Canyon National Historical Park, Craig Glassner at Alcatraz, Elizabeth Archuleta, Ilka Hartmann, Jordan James, Tyler Anderson, Paul Chaat Smith, and a host of others for providing images, texts, and the permission to include them. A special note of gratitude is reserved for Christina Steiner, an attorney in Los Angeles who specializes in public-art issues. She was exceedingly gracious with her time and expertise.

I also want to thank many of the individual writers and artists I write about in the book for making their work available, in particular Jaune Quick-to-See Smith and her husband, Andy Ambrose. Both gave me a great deal of their time, answering a number of questions and providing me with high-quality work. Also, I'm grateful to Neal Ambrose Smith, who was exceedingly helpful with Jaune's image library. I am grateful to Edgar Heap of Birds, who was also extremely helpful and generous. Valerie Red-Horse was both kind and responsive when I asked for film stills from *Naturally Native*.

A number of friends, colleagues, and fellow scholars have been invaluable in the writing, researching, and revising process. Joanna Brooks, LeAnne Howe, P. Jane Hafen, Jonathan Silverman, William Nericcio, Greg Barnhisel, Scott Andrews, Craig Howe, Harvey Markowitz, Joseph Bauerkemper, Peter Novak, Eric Gary Anderson, Gwen Griffin, Carolyn Kastner, Denise Cummings, Janice Gould, Molly McGlennen, Robert Warrior, and Janet McAdams have all, at some point, read at least part of this book. I am grateful to all of them for their feedback and insight.

Portions of this book debuted elsewhere, oftentimes in radically different form. A good bit of Chapter 5, "Word as Weapon," appeared under the same title in *MELUS: Multi-Ethnic Literature of the United States* 27 (Fall 2002): 216–224, and small segments from the chapters on Jaune Quick-to-See Smith's map paintings and Sherman Alexie's films appeared in "Engaged Resistance in American Indian Art, Literature and Film," *Peace Review* 15 (2003):

179–186.) I presented a much shorter version of Chapter 9, on public art, at the 2009 Native American Literature Symposium, and a dramatically condensed version of Chapter 1, on Alcatraz, at the 2009 Modern Language Association Convention. I presented a portion of Chapter 4, on *Skins* and *Naturally Native*, at the 2010 Society for Film and Media Studies conference in Los Angeles. Thanks to Joanna Hearn and Michelle Raheja for their assistance here. Also, I test-drove some of the material in this book on my blog, *The Weekly Rader*, in 2008, 2009, and 2010. Thanks to those of you who posted comments (both positive and negative!).

A book like this is not cheap to put together. To this end, I remain eternally grateful to the University of San Francisco's fabulous Faculty Development Fund, which defrayed parts of the permissions costs for the 100-plus images and texts reprinted here. I would also like to thank John Pinelli, the executive director of the Office of Business Affairs in the College of Arts and Sciences. His office has been great. I am also indebted to Jennifer Turpin, the dean of the College of Arts and Sciences, and to Peter Novak, the associate dean for the Arts and Humanities. Most of this book was researched while on a yearlong sabbatical and was written the following year while on fellowship. My deepest thanks go out to the Humanities Advisory Board at USF for naming me the National Endowment for the Humanities chair for 2008–2009. The extended research and writing release made the timely completion of this work possible.

Thanks also go out to my colleagues in the English Department at USF as well as to our program assistant, Kimberly Garret. Thanks also to the great staff at the Gleeson Library at USF.

When I joined the faculty at the University of San Francisco, my Native American Literature class was the first such course offered there. Since 2001, I have taught hundreds (maybe thousands) of students many of the texts in this book, and I remain impressed and inspired by their interest in and respect for Native creative discourse. I want to thank two students in particular, Danny Kambur and Dan Finnegan, who served as my research assistants in 2008 and 2009.

I also want to thank everyone at the University of Texas Press, including my fantastic editor Theresa May and the endlessly patient Sarah Hudgens and Victoria Davis, my manuscript editors. Thanks to Kaila Wyllys and Derek George for help with all of the images and design issues. I remain in the debt of Kip Keller, a fabulously talented copy editor (I am curious about how he will edit this sentence) who caught many things I missed and who was graciously patient with my unorthodox project.

In 2007, as I was beginning to write this book, my dissertation director, Frederick Garber, passed away. My first graduate seminar with him focused on the intersection of art, literature, and film; it is impossible to think of this book without also thinking of the multigenre approach I learned from Fred. I cannot thank him enough for his wisdom, patience, support, and generosity. I dedicate this book to his memory.

Lastly, I'm inexpressibly grateful for the support of my family. Thanks to Ginger Rader, Gary Rader, Barbara Rader, Amy Rader Kice, Adam Kice, Genie Ramsey, and Mick Ramsey. My son, Gavin, was born a few weeks before the first version of this manuscript was due at the press. Words, even the most engaging ones, resist expression at how lucky I was and am that my wife, Jill Ramsey, made the completion of that (and this) project doable.

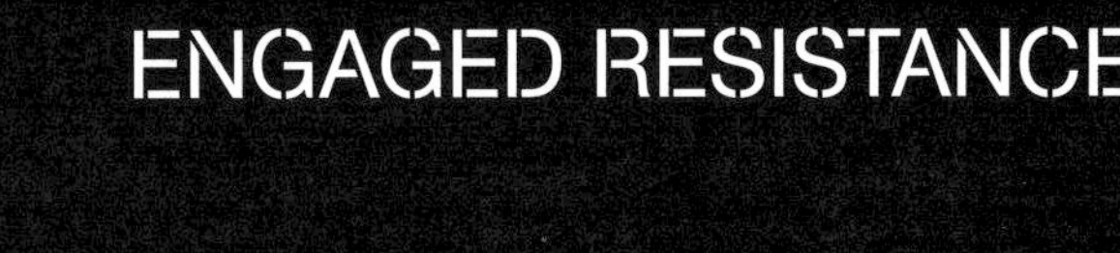
ENGAGED RESISTANCE

PROLOGUE

I HAVE NEVER BEEN a huge fan of lengthy introductions to scholarly books. With eleven chapters, this book is long enough as it is. So, instead, I offer this short prologue—with its roots in oral discourse—in hopes that the chapters both stand and speak for themselves. Also, since there are many intertextual and intrachapter paths connecting ideas, genres, and themes, I prefer to let the reader map her own way through the terrain of this text without me laying out a route that is either overdetermined or too pedestrian.

This is a book about texts. It addresses, of course, many other things, but its main goal is to provide some new ways of looking at, thinking about, and making sense of recent American Indian art, literature, and film. It takes as its controlling metaphor the notion of engaged resistance, which I see as a fundamentally indigenous form of aesthetic discourse that engages both Native and American cultural contexts as a mode of resistance against the ubiquitous colonial tendencies of assimilation and erasure. American Indian writers, filmmakers, and artists participate in engaged resistance through creative work and cultural production as a means of defiance but also as a source of connection to tribal ways of telling stories, representing images, and animating the world.

In his now-famous essay "Toward a National Indian Literature: Cultural Authenticity in Nationalism," Acoma writer Simon Ortiz makes a strong case for the importance of creativity and language in American Indian resistance: "It is entirely possible for a people to retain and maintain their lives through the use of any language. There is not a question of authenticity here; rather it is the way that Indian people have *creatively* responded to forced colonization. And this response has been one of resistance; there is no clearer word for it than resistance" (10; emphasis added). Protecting indigenous identity is inseparable from protecting indigenous cultural values, and, for Ortiz, these have survived in large part because of the ability of Native creative productions like literature and art to resist erasure, bind communities, and articulate a discourse of survivance.

Engaged Resistance: American Indian Art, Literature, and Film from Alcatraz to the NMAI is a contextual examination of the many ways that American Indian languages—both visual and verbal—respond to and resist American cultural machineries by framing how Native artists, writers, and filmmakers participate in engaged resistance that engenders and defends Native identities. Since Ortiz articulated the role of language and creativity in Native resistance in 1981, virtually no one in either the academic world or the mainstream press has looked closely and comprehensively across disciplines at the aesthetic texts American Indians have made as they "creatively responded to forced colonization." This book seeks to fill that gap.

Three main engines drive *Engaged Resistance*. First, the book demonstrates that Native-produced texts like poetry, fiction, movies, paintings, and sculpture are fundamental products and processes of American Indian sovereignty. Second, it explores how Native cultural expression comprises a strategy of aesthetic activism fashioned by Natives for both Native and Anglo publics. Third, the study moves across genres, situating Native art, literature, and film in context and in conversation with one another to create a cross-genre discourse of resistance, what I refer to as "indigenous interdisciplinarity." Within these frameworks, *Engaged Resistance* poses and responds to a new constellation of questions about Native cultural productions, such as: What work does Native aesthetic resistance do? What is the role of resistance in Native cultural identity? To what degree are creative forms of aesthetic activism also ethical stances? What can aesthetic modes of resistance accomplish that legal or political options cannot? How do these cinematic, literary, and artistic texts fit within the larger sweep of Native studies? When Native art, literature, and film are read together, what sort of contextual conversations emerge across genres? And why are creative forms of resistance so important to Native peoples?

Part of the project of this book is to expand the notion of resistance beyond mere defiance to include simple notions of strength and substantiality. *Résistance* in French connotes power, an inability to be torn asunder or ripped apart. The pièce de résistance is the main course of a meal, a prize item, or the most important part of an event. Too often, the discourse of resistance gets pigeonholed as crankiness or recalcitrance, but from a cultural and etymological perspective, resistance is, at its core, about more than rebuttal. It's about ability, capacity, energy, and authority. For me, aesthetic resistance is a demonstration of fortitude and an ultimate form of engagement. My project moves away from considering these issues solely from the vantage point of formal criticism, opting instead to explore the ethical values and ethical strategies of Natives themselves—as embodied in art, film, and literature—whose themes assert survivance, renewal, hope, egalitarianism, autonomy, and engagement. Ultimately, I argue that for these artists, forging their own artistic language is not simply an aesthetic but also an ethic—not merely an idea but an assertion of Indian autonomy.

As Sherman Alexie and others have argued, critical responses to Native American discourse tend to focus on the same themes—the oral tradition, nature, myths, and storytelling. These approaches, while valid, can encourage a perspective of isolation and provincialism in regard to the effects and aspirations of Native texts by relegating Indian creativity to the past. Few scholars address how American Indian texts interact with current mainstream American culture or how they work in the two different (and often antagonistic) worlds of Native and Anglo realities. This project examines provocative Native texts that access both worlds through the door of resistance. It may seem contradictory at first to think of resistance as a door or window, but there is a long history of Native activism that is ameliorative.

More recently, Native writers, artists, and filmmakers have turned that spirit of resistance to realms of creative expression and cultural production in their attempts to contravene Hollywood images; correct incorrect histories; counter decades of captivity, romance, and Wild West novels; refashion public perceptions of Indians; participate in the linguistic coding of American discourse; and reshape the social, geographic, and cultural map of America. "We find it effective to challenge the white man through our use of the mass media," asserts Hock E Aye Vi (Edgar Heap of Birds), "the survival of our people is based upon our use of expressive forms of modern communication. The insurgent messages within these forms must serve as our present-day combative tactics" (*I Stand in the Center*, 30). As Heap of Birds correctly notes, the new battlefields exist on screens, online, in the media, and—perhaps most importantly—in how the presence and absence of Indians in these spaces gets downloaded onto America's cultural hard drive. This book chronicles examples of engaged resistance that capture the public's imagination, gives a creative language to resistance, and shows how Native texts engage with American culture in order to change it.

Engaged Resistance also foregrounds sites of resistance that confront easy assumptions about Indians, assimilation, and tribal expression, and it discusses indigenous texts that have catalyzed resistance into powerful change, such as the Indian occupation of Alcatraz from 1969 to 1971, and in particular, the poems, paintings, and public documents produced during the occupation. By painting on the exterior walls of prison buildings, riffing on antiquated treaty laws, comparing the decrepit state of the then-defunct Alcatraz to Indian reservations, and writing poems about the justice of Natives' seizing government land, these activists made a profound statement about the sophistication and determination of Native resistance. I argue that Alcatraz marks a movement away from cultural segregation in favor of cultural engagement, enabling Natives to reclaim identity on their own terms. By "cultural segregation," I mean not only reservations but also various other ways of marginalizing Indians and even rendering them invisible or dead. The occupation of Alcatraz enables not only reclamation of identity but also public, visible, rhetorically sophisticated performances of this reclamation for both Native and non-Native audiences.

The various modes of engaged resistance seen in the cultural expressions produced on Alcatraz serve as a microcosm for the rest of the book, not simply as a framing mechanism but also as a model of indigenous interdisciplinarity. While much has been much written about Native fiction, and somewhat less about traditional Native arts, little has been said about recent, edgy Native cultural production. The rest of the book works through myriad genres and a vast array of topics in order to paint in broad strokes a polyvalent portrait of recent American Indian aesthetic resistance. The chapter on Salish artist Jaune Quick-to-See Smith's stunning series of paintings of U.S. maps looks at the way Smith uses the iconography and semiology of maps to remind the viewer of land reclamation, broken treaties, name changes, and relocation. Sticking with cartographic metaphors, I also sketch a broad map of the new Native American novel (dating from 2001). This chapter places nine novels in conversation with one another, ultimately suggesting that together they can be a mechanism for preserving nonlinear, historical modes of storytelling, tribalography, and identity formation. In a chapter designed to be particularly pedagogical, I go übertextual and devote the entire space to Leslie Marmon Silko's popular and influential story "Storyteller." I read the story as an example of compositional resistance, and I frame the chapter around how one might teach the theories in the book via Silko's text. If the chapter on the new Native novel is a sweeping macro study, this chapter on "Storyteller" stands as a focused micro study.

I also devote two chapters to poetry, which, as most scholars of Native studies know, gets very little critical attention. In one chapter, I show how three writers (Alexie, Louise Erdrich, and Wendy Rose) use the lyric poem as a modern weapon to combat the colonizing gestures of American media, in particular, visual culture. In another, I argue that American Indian poetic genre bending and genre blending enact what I call compositional resistance. Perhaps the most theoretical piece in the book, this chapter suggests poetic genre is a metanarrative that Indian poets seek to deconstruct through their inventive and irruptive engagement with and resistance to genre. In both chapters, I argue that poetry, usually seen as an abstract or distancing genre, becomes a means of aesthetic activism that asserts cultural sovereignty.

Similarly, in two distinct but complementary chapters, I look at both popular and independent Native films in an attempt to show how recent movies participate in but also subvert standard Hollywood genres and constructs. In one chapter I posit that two nearly opposite films (*Naturally Native* and *Skins*) locate resistance in similar places, and in another chapter, I read Alexie's two movies, the wildly popular *Smoke Signals* and the far less popular *The Business of Fancydancing* against and through each other by way of Gerald Vizenor's theory of "postindianism." When placed in context, Alexie's two movies offer a balanced and interdependent form of engaged resistance, and when the two film chapters are read together, they provide a brief history of resistance in recent Native film.

In the two final chapters, I focus on art projects—Native public art and the National Museum of the American Indian (NMAI)—in an attempt to show how dynamic Native aesthetic production asserts claims on "public" space and structures. American Indian public art is an area that has received almost no critical attention, but it is a topic ripe for analysis. Here, I trace the history of public sculptures and statues of Indians—especially on federal lands and buildings—and explore the complicated boundaries of resistance and assimilation these objects indicate. I also draw attention to contravening artists who abrogate flat and facile Indian images. Finally, I return to the beginning by offering a reading of the new NMAI through the lens of the occupation of Alcatraz. The NMAI is replete with art, film, and literary texts and functions as the standard for publicly accessible Native interdisciplinary work. I argue that despite its shortcomings, we can read it as an aesthetic (and activist) text.

This is a book about texts, which also means there are many writers, artists, concepts and genres it does not cover. It is not, for example, a history of Indian resistance (though it positions itself as a kind of history of recent Native aesthetics). It is also not a biography of important Native American figures (though it does, at times, home in on certain artists and writers). It is neither a tribalography nor a study in nationalism (though it contains elements of both of these projects). It is not a monograph of critical theory (though it both pulls from theoretical perspectives and advances its own theories of reading and interpretation). It is also not a book about music, drama, or dance, despite the obvious merits of all three genres. I opt instead to focus on the genres of Native discourse most commonly written and talked about. I look forward to future studies that will do what I have been unable to.

Rather than hitching its wagon to one theoretical horse, *Engaged Resistance* employs a wide-ranging assortment of critical and theoretical methodologies. Neither Native writers nor Native tribes have ever been particularly wed to monolithic ways of looking at the world. Indian communities have distinguished themselves by making polyvocality, multiplicity, and interactivity part of their ontology. This book takes this synthetic approach to reading and being in the world and applies it to reading and being in these texts—all of which invite the reader or viewer inside. Indeed, it acknowledges that American Indian creative texts are created for an audience. All the texts I write about here intend to be read, digested, enjoyed, discussed, and used. Poems, movies, paintings, and novels are made for people, about people. They are human endeavors. The critical approaches I take in this book try to accentuate that humanity, underscoring not just how Native texts engage American culture but equally (and even more importantly) how they engage Native cultures.

If this book situates Native texts in conversation with one another, it also, at least to some degree, contextualizes my conversation with other writers and critics, some of whom I would like to honor here. First, I want to acknowledge Paula Gunn Allen's notion of the "word warrior," which she deploys in *The Sacred Hoop*. Though she uses that term more evocatively than prescriptively, her grouping of writers who weaponize words to defend Native self-determination has resonances in these pages. I am also indebted to LeAnne Howe's collative theory of tribalography. For Howe, tribalography is, at its core, interdisciplinary and multigeneric. Combining personal and tribal experiences, she argues, enables her and other Native writers to tell particularly inclusive stories to both Native and non-Native audiences.[1] Two of the Ws—Robert Warrior and Craig Womack—have also informed my approaches. In Warrior's case, his articulation of sovereignty within literary texts is critical to my readings. Similarly, Womack's theory of "Red Stick" criticism ("the assumption that Indian viewpoints cohere, that Indian resistance can be successful . . . that subverting the literary status quo rather than being subverted *by* it constitutes a meaningful alternative") has influenced how I think about successful forms of resistance (*Red on Red*, 12). More than once I avail myself of the concept of "reinventing the enemy's language," the title of Joy Harjo and Gloria Bird's fine anthology of Native women's writing, which chronicles how Indian writers have made a new language out of imperialist discourse.[2]

I also talk frequently about survivance, a term given a specifically Native meaning by Gerald Vizenor.[3] It finds its most frequent utilization in the final chapter (on the NMAI), but it works its way into many other chapters as well, especially because of its emphasis on activism, creation, and invention. Lastly, I like talking about the "cultural work" a text does. Coined by Jane Tompkins, the term refers to the actual influence a text has within a context. In order to better understand how a text affects people, Tompkins argues, we must move away from the elite master texts and see literature "as attempts to redefine the social order," because these marginal texts offer better "examples of the way a culture thinks about itself" (*Sensational Designs*, xi). In these pages I alter her term, stretching it to fit the expanse of nonliterary texts.

A brief word about my own terminology. I often distinguish between "contextual resistance" and "compositional resistance." The former refers to modes of resistance on the thematic level, while the latter denotes resistance on the structural one. By "compositional," I mean how the text is composed: the materials the artist uses, the organization or plot structure of a film or novel, or the inversions of Western poetic genres. Conversely, "contextual resistance" occurs when a text's message indicates defiance, even if its formal qualities do not. A perfect example: many of the poems written during the Alcatraz occupation assert sovereignty, reclamation, even revolution, but are rendered in very traditional rhyme and meter. All of the Native-produced texts I examine here embody one of these forms of resistance—many engage both.

I also use the phrase "aesthetic activism" to describe a manner of political and social activism that finds representation in the artistic realm. Unlike marches, sit-ins, or other forms of physical protest, aesthetic activism implies social action on the plane of artistic discourse, such as poetry, painting, and film.[4] Similarly, I ground much of my study in my theory of interdisciplinary activism—a form of aesthetic activity that gains its strength, significance, and synthetic energy from Native cultural expression's embrace of the polyvocal and multigeneric. We see examples on the writerly level in figures like Howe and Alexie, who work across genres but also in larger projects, like the occupation of Alcatraz and the NMAI, that rely on the semiotic, the symbolic, and the literary. As for terms like "Romanticism," "postmodernism," "metanarrative," and "modernism," I intend their standard literary and theoretical definitions. A concept that arises often—perhaps in every chapter—is semiotics. My use of it has roots in its linguistic past, but in general I intend its visual associations—the study of the signifier (the sign) and the signified (the meaning of the sign). One last word on this topic: I use Native American, American Indian, and Native interchangeably, though I evince a preference for "Indian." In this manner, I take my cues from other Indian writers and critics who have paved the way for this study and the putative vocabulary of this field.

Also taking a cue from Native structures is the very structure of the book itself. Influenced by the patterns and composition of Native texts, *Engaged Resistance* is designed to be circular. By this, I mean it can be read in just about any order: from the last chapter to the first, or spiraling out from the middle. Whatever the starting place, the same pattern of generic subject matters will be encountered in the chapters. I like the way the various genres speak to one another this way. Film becomes an entrée to poetry, and fiction an entrée to art. Rather than making the works feel disjointed, this structure, in my eyes at least, augments the ability of Native texts to signify across boundaries, genres, and chapters of American history.

Speaking of history, *Engaged Resistance*, ultimately, tells a story. It tells a story of creation and defiance, resistance and participation, engagement and survivance. It is a historical narrative. It chronicles creative expression in the era since 1969, when American Indian creative discourse began in robust ways to speak truth to power. As mentioned above, this book never pretends to be a comprehensive historical study, but it does function—both in scope and scale—as a kind of genealogy of Indian aesthetic activism. It focuses a lens on a historical moment to show how that moment has shaped how we see Native cultural production. To this end, I offer a series of detailed snapshots of the diversity of important and innovative work being done by both well-known and lesser-known Native writers, artists, and directors. I want to historicize and contextualize the kinds of conversations that these revolutionary artists are having with the key narratives that compose American and Native American high, popular, and tribal cultures. Unlike histories that purport to show a linear progression of events, this history moves back and forth within time and across genres. Its manner and direction of historicity take their cues from the novelists, winter counts, and mapmakers it describes. This study narrates these histories by attempting to map the healing power of art; the possible interplay among literary, artistic, and cinematic texts; the necessity of creative expression for oppressed peoples; the ecstatic joy of perseverance; the proactive, procreative resistance to colonialism; and the significant contribution of Native artists to the wide record of human achievement.

Well, so much for a short prologue. The good news, though, is that I now get to write in the final sentence of this piece what LeAnne Howe says at the end of many of hers: *Whee, that's enough. I can tell you no more today!*

1.

ENGAGED RESISTANCE

ALCATRAZ

This time we fight not with bows and arrows / But with pencils and books

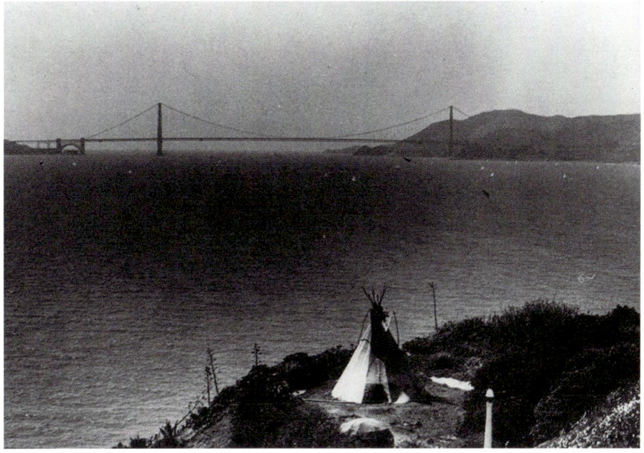

FIGURE 1.1. *Teepee on Alcatraz c. 1970. According to Ranger Craig Glassner, the teepee belonged to actor and activist Peter Coyote. Courtesy of the U.S. Department of the Interior, National Park Service. Photo by John Slavicek.*

STANDING ROCK, THE DAKOTAS, DECEMBER 1890. Snow and more snow. Almost no food. September and October had been unusually hot and dry. Crops were scarce, bison more so. For the Sioux, there was little reason for optimism.

In February of that same year, the United States government had violated a treaty with the Great Sioux Reservation of South Dakota, dramatically shrinking its land by adjusting reservation boundaries. Of course, land was not all that was taken away. Families were forced into parcels of acreage where they lived in substandard housing, and were made to farm and raise livestock. But the dry summer and autumn made this next to impossible. Children were sent to boarding schools, and ceremonies were essentially squelched. It would be an understatement to say that basic spiritual and religious autonomies were in jeopardy. They were under assault.

In order to "assist" the Sioux's adjustment to their new living conditions, the Bureau of Indian Affairs (BIA) sent agents to simultaneously help and surveil the tribes. It was these agents who first became worried about the rumors of frenetic dances that were bringing Indians of various tribes together. Eventually, these agents became downright terrified by the dances themselves.

The dance in question was the Ghost Dance, a religious and healing movement that originated among the Tovusidokado in Nevada in December 1888. The Ghost Dance was initiated by the charismatic and visionary Jack Wilson, also known as Wovoka, a Northern Paiute who claimed to have been endowed by God himself with miraculous powers. Preaching a message of cleansing, renewal, and rebirth, Wovoka claimed that proper performance of the Ghost Dance would, among other things, raise Indians up into the sky, at which point the earth would swallow all whites and return the land to its Native inhabitants. At a time of almost no hope, this dance was the most engaging, most rational, most ecstatic remedy.

Word of the dance and the movement's message spread across the region like nothing previous. In fact, Kicking Bear (Minneconjou) paid a visit to Wovoka in Nevada, and the dance made such an impression on him that he shared it with Sitting Bull (Hunkpapa) upon his arrival in Standing Rock in October 1890. The Lakota embraced the dance. Performances not only flourished but also increased—so much so that by December, BIA agents were petrified. So they went after Kicking Bear. He was removed from Standing Rock, but the dances continued. A misguided and ill-informed BIA agent named James McLaughlin described the Ghost Dance as "demoralizing, indecent, disgusting," characterizing it as an "absurd craze" (Liggett, "Wounded Knee"). Fearful that the increasing popularity of the dance would scare off or potentially harm white settlers, McLaughlin called for backup. Thousands of troops from the U.S. Army arrived in mid-December, and on the 15th, Sitting Bull himself was taken into custody for refusing to stop the Ghost Dance. Mistakenly assuming that Sitting Bull was the leader of the movement, McLaughlin was sure that his removal would lessen its fervor. He was wrong. Indians resisted Sitting Bull's arrest. Shots were fired. Several U.S. soldiers and Lakota, including Sitting Bull himself, were killed. During the brief exchange of gunfire, the Lakota bravely wore ghost shirts—garments painted with symbols—they believed were impervious to bullets. They, too, were mistaken.

Many historians call into question what they see as foolish mystical Christian overtones of the Ghost Dance and a naïve faith in the ghost shirts, but it is literally impossible to imagine the complexity and the despair of 1890. It is also shortsighted to focus on the failures of the movement itself. It stands as one of the first performative pan-Indian acts of resistance.

SAN FRANCISCO, CALIFORNIA, MARCH 9, 1964. Fog and more fog. Undeterred by the weather or the ominous waves, five Bay Area Sioux named Allen Cottier, Walter Means, Garfield Spotted Elk, Richard McKenzie, and Mark Martinez set out for Alcatraz Island in an attempt to claim it as Indian land. In 1963, the federal General Services Administration (GSA) acquired the responsibility for Alcatraz (which had closed as a prison in March of the previous year) as excess land. Belva Cottier, Allen's wife, knew of a little-used provision in the Sioux treaty of 1868, which entitled the Sioux to claim surplus government land and facilities.[1] It was under this provision that the five Sioux men, adorned in ceremonial clothing and carrying "claim sticks," declared the recently abandoned Alcatraz as Indian land.

By their own admission, it was a stunt. The men were on and off the island in about an hour. However, two additional pieces of information are of note. One, before they were removed, the men performed a ceremonial dance. Second, they read a typewritten proclamation in which they justified taking control of Alcatraz and offered to purchase it—for forty-seven cents an acre. The amount is both funny and ingenious.

The Indian Claims Commission Act, enacted in 1946, gave the government the right to purchase Indian land. And so it was that just before this first attempt to claim Alcatraz, the government, under the jurisdiction of this act, tried to buy around sixty-five million acres of land from various California tribes. The offer: forty-seven cents an acre.

The "invasion" was big enough news that it was covered in the pages of the *San Francisco Chronicle* and the *San Francisco Examiner*. Seventy-four years after Wovoka, performative pan-Indian resistance had been resurrected.

SAN FRANCISCO, CALIFORNIA, NOVEMBER 9, 1969. Ten a.m., Pier 39. Five boats chartered to ferry nearly seventy-five Indians to Alcatraz are missing. Several members of the media and almost a hundred confused Bay Area Indians stand around the Embarcadero waiting for transportation to the island. Worse, a TV crew is already on Alcatraz, hoping to film the Indians' disembarkation. The boats are nowhere to be found.

A couple of weeks previous, in a turn of events both suspicious and tragic, the San Francisco American Indian Center burned to the ground. The center had served as a meeting place, an employment agency, and the best local spot for health and legal aid for around thirty thousand Indians in the Bay Area, many of whom had wound up in Oakland because of termination policies that did away with many reservations and relocated Indians to urban areas. After the fire, a group of Indians started planning a serious reclamation of Alcatraz, not simply as a symbol of persistence but also as a kind of locus for Indian-related issues and services. Determined to take the island and to do so publicly, the organizers, led by Richard Oakes (Mohawk) and Adam Nordwall (Red Lake Chippewa), got savvy. Well ahead of time, they alerted the media to their plan. They also drew up very specific demands, in a proclamation that is smart, acerbic, and, most importantly, funny. It remains one of the most important Indian documents of the second half of the twentieth century.

According to Troy Johnson's excellent account of the morning, Nordwall had students keep the media occupied while he searched for a vessel (*Occupation of Alcatraz*, 57). Nordwall happened to run into Ronald Craig and impressed upon him the significance of the occasion. Before he knew it, Craig had his three-masted boat the *Monte Cristo* loaded up with a feisty crew of fifty Indians bound for Alcatraz.

Accounts of the entire day vary, but what is consistent is the following: the *Monte Cristo* was going to have a difficult, probably impossible, time docking on the island. When actually landing on Alcatraz seemed unlikely, Oakes dove into the icy waves and began swimming. Within minutes, four other men were also in the water. "We were supposed to get dressed up in all of their 'television' costumes," Oakes said, "and just make a pass around the island, to symbolically claim Alcatraz" (quoted in Johnson, *Occupation of Alcatraz*, 58). But the men were tired of symbols; they wanted action.

Eventually, after fighting the cold water, the breaking waves, and the strong undertow around the rocks at the base of the island, all five made it ashore. The first thing the Indian men did was to claim Alcatraz "by right of discovery."

Within two hours, the coast guard—"their warriors," according to Oakes (quoted in Johnson, *Occupation of Alcatraz*, 59)—picked them up and returned them to the mainland.

SAN FRANCISCO, CALIFORNIA, NOVEMBER 9, 1969. Six p.m., Fisherman's Wharf. After reconvening at the temporary headquarters of Indian Center, around one hundred Indians agreed to return to Alcatraz that same night; they enlisted the help of a fishing boat, the *New Vera II*, to deliver the insurgents to Alcatraz for three dollars a head. When the captain pulled alongside of the docking pier at Alcatraz, people began throwing sleeping bags, tents, and other supplies onto the dock. Fearful of being charged with aiding a federal crime, the captain of the boat pulled away, but not before fourteen souls clamored out of the *New Vera II* and onto the recently claimed Indian land, formerly known as Alcatraz.

Fourteen young American Indians, most of whom were still in college in and around San Francisco, occupied Alcatraz for nineteen hours. Even though it signified largely in the symbolic realm, claiming the island for "Indians of All Tribes" was the first major instance of pan-Indian resistance in the twentieth century. The occupiers read from their proclamation, in which they formalized their claim to Alcatraz by right of discovery. After a brief meeting with the press, the group was escorted back to San Francisco, peacefully.

SAUSALITO, CALIFORNIA, NOVEMBER 20, 1969. Two a.m., No Name Bar. Almost one hundred Indians are in and around the bar, waiting for closing time. They have tried to mingle with the local crowd so as not to attract too much attention. A little after two, they will climb aboard three boats that await them at the docks just down the pier. They will move slowly across the dark water, eastward, toward the former prison, Alcatraz, that sits a

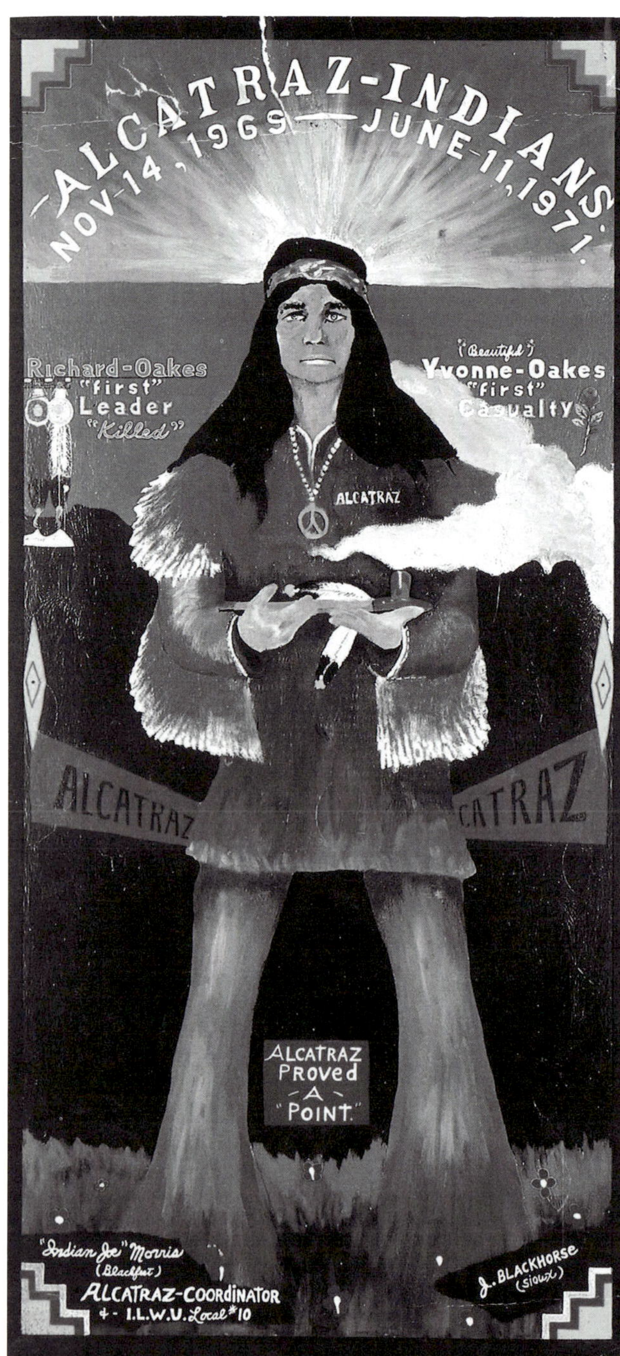

FIGURE 1.2. *"Indian Joe" Morris,* Modern Militant Indian, or Alcatraz Proved a Point, *1972. Oil on board, 48 × 108 in. An iconic painting. Courtesy of the U.S. Department of the Interior, National Park Service.*

little over a mile between them and the city and county of San Francisco. When they disembark, the island's deputy caretaker will greet them. His name is Glenn Dodson, and he will welcome the landing party. He will wink at Oakes and confide that he is one-eighth Indian. The adventurers will celebrate with a ceremony—a victory powwow. Singing. There will be drums. They will move into comfortable quarters. They will take over the island. They will paint on the buildings. They will name the island and themselves. They will warn anyone trying to approach the island to stay away, for they are approaching Indian land.

The Indians of All Tribes will occupy Alcatraz Island until June 11, 1971, when GSA officials will remove the remaining occupiers. While on the island, the Indians will write poems, sing songs, issue proclamations, and adorn the facades and structures with visual symbols of their occupation. There will be tragedy, death, and dishonor. There will be solidarity and survivance. But by the end, Alcatraz will have proved a point.

The Indian occupation of Alcatraz from 1969 to 1971 is one of the most important instances of American resistance since the American Revolution. It is also one of the most underreported and underexamined. It stands as the longest occupation of any federal facility in the history of the United States, and it is one of the few examples of resistance that actually engendered change. The Indians were never awarded Alcatraz, nor were they given everything they asked for, but their ideas, their determination, and their autonomy were taken seriously on a national stage. This chapter takes a close look at the art, literature, and proclamatory discourse produced on the island, which helped give voice and vision to the occupation, lending it the intellectual and artistic credibility Natives needed in order to articulate a sovereign position and communicate with the American populace. Indeed, perhaps no other project embodies the notion of engaged resistance more than this occupation. Over the course of their time on the island, the occupiers bonded with their surroundings, making it their own. They courted the mainstream press, they wrote poems, they performed ceremonies, and they issued proclamations and manifestos. In short, they courted a readership. At the same time, the determined defiance of the occupation began to articulate what Indian autonomy might mean.

Let me be clear at the outset: this study does not pretend to be a history of the occupation or of Indian resistance; rather, it attempts to place the artistic work done by the occupiers in context, and it aspires to alter how we read the various texts of the Alcatraz occupation as well as the text of Alcatraz itself. This study is less concerned with the question, Did the Alcatraz occupation fail? and more interested in such questions as, Why is Alcatraz important for Native aesthetics? What cultural work can Indian occupation paintings, proclamations, and poems do? How can American Indian creative discourse both resist and engage the American public?

To answer these questions and others, I will read the three main forms of cultural production the Alcatraz occupation engendered—public proclamations, poems, and paintings—through the lens of aesthetic activism. For eighteen-plus months on the island, the occupiers relied on language (both visual and verbal) to help create a sense of place and to construct a nuanced perspective of Indian self-determination and self-articulation. These aesthetic projects, then, served dual functions of center and circumference. They established a place, and they constructed a vantage point from which to show us how to see it.

Proclamations and Manifestos: The Discourse of Discovery

No documents fulfilled these place- and perspective-establishing functions better than the occupation's proclamations and manifestos. Their genius should not be undersold. Much has been made of the various declamatory documents within the small globe of Alcatraz studies, but no one has examined these texts from a literary or rhetorical perspective. Even more interesting is the fact that most critics have focused on the lacunae between what the documents asked for and what the Indians received; few have unpacked the cultural work the various texts actually did; and no one has looked closely at the symbolic discourse of these documents and how they paved the way for later works of art and protest.[2] What the authors of these documents understood was that the occupation was, at its heart, a rhetorical project. And as Charles Morris and Steven Browne note, "social movements [are] definitely *rhetorical*: that is, movements for reform are intrinsically bound up with the management of symbolic resources . . . movements are by their nature rhetorical" (*Readings on the Rhetoric of Social Protest*, 2). As I demonstrate in the remaining pages in this section, the authors of the main treaty-based documents marshaled the linguistic, historical, and cultural symbols of Indian-white relations in order to persuade through what I call "rhetorical resistance." By this, I mean a form of indigenous resistance that grounds itself in an aesthetic of argumentation and appeal.

Until now, these documents have been ignored by the body of the already meager scholarship devoted to Native American protest rhetoric. For example, two of the most influential essays in the field, by Randall A. Lake, disregard Alcatraz altogether in favor of more incendiary topics like the American Indian Movement (AIM) and Wounded Knee.[3] But the main three documents I turn to now—the original Alcatraz reclamation proclamation (hereafter referred to as the "Alcatraz Proclamation"), the "Occupation Manifesto," and the "Declaration of the Return of Indian Land"—remain unrivalled in American history for their focus, humor, anger, and rhetoric.

The most important single written text to emerge from the occupation is the original Alcatraz Proclamation, which catalyzed the seizure of the island and established its discourse (Fig. 1.3). "The proclamation," writes Troy R. Johnson, Alcatraz's most prolific chronicler, "drawn up to announce the group's plans reflected serious intentions, sarcastic humor, and hope for the future of Indian people" (*Occupation of Alcatraz*, 53). Some might wonder how a proclamation can carry both sarcasm and seriousness, but the document's ability to simultaneously embody Indian humor and the deep cultural associations of the earnest, liberating history of American proclamations makes it powerful. Indeed, like much of Indian tradition and culture itself, the proclamation is a twinning of opposites: humor and determination, despair and hope, cooperation and defiance.

The dualities of human existence

The history of proclamations in the Western world—both literal and metaphorical—is rich. Traditionally, it involves the party in power proclaiming some sort of law or edict to the masses. When made by a king or president, a proclamation is a binding executive issuance, and it carries the weight of authority, government, and execution. The most famous proclamations, such as the Emancipation Proclamation, the Royal Proclamation of 1763,

proclamation:

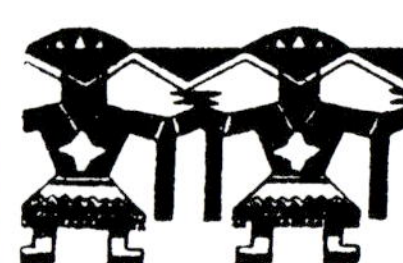

To The Great White Father And All His People

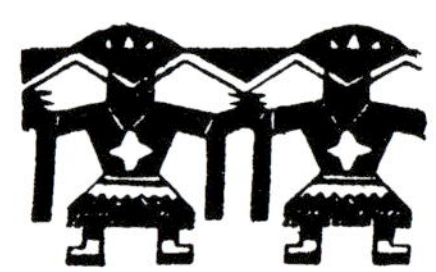

We, the native Americans, re-claim the land known as Alcatraz Island in the name of all American Indians by right of discovery.

We wish to be fair and honorable in our dealings with the Caucasian inhabitants of this land, and hereby offer the following treaty:

We will purchase said Alcatraz Island for twenty-four dollars (24) in glass beads and red cloth, a precedent set by the white man's purchase of a similar island about 300 years ago. We know that $24 in trade goods for these 16 acres is more than was paid when Manhatten Island was sold, but we know that land values have risen over the years. Our offer of $1.24 per acre is greater than the 47 cents per acre the white men are now paying the California Indians for their land.

We will give to the inhabitants of this island a portion of the land for their own to be held in trust by the American Indian Affairs and by the bureau of Caucasian Affairs to hold in perpetuity - for as long as the sun shall rise and the rivers go down to the sea. We will further guide the inhabitants in the proper way of living. We will offer them our religion, our education, our life-ways, in order to help them achieve our level of civilization and thus raise them and all their white brothers up from their savage and unhappy state. We offer this treaty in good faith and wish to be fair and honorable in our dealings with all white men.

We feel that this so-called Alcatraz Island is more than suitable for an Indian reservation, as determined by the white man's own standards. By this we mean that this place resembles most Indian reservations in that:

1. It is isolated from modern facilities, and without adequat means of transportation.
2. It has no fresh running water.
3. It has inadequate sanitation facilities.
4. There are no oil or mineral rights.
5. There is no industry and so unemployment is very great.
6. There are no health care facilities.
7. The soil is rocky and non-productive; and the land does not support game.
8. There are no educational facilities.)
9. The population has always exceeded the land base.
10. The population has always been held as prisoners and kept dependent upon others.

Further, it would be fitting and symbolic that ships from all over the world, entering the Golden Gate, would first see Indian land, and thus be reminded of the true history of this nation. This tiny island would be a symbol of the great lands once ruled by free and noble Indians.

What use will we make of this land?

Since the San Francisco Indian Center burned down, there is no place for Indians to assemble and carry on tribal life here in the white man's city. Therefore, we plan to develop on this island several Indian institutions:

1. A CENTER FOR NATIVE AMERICAN STUDIES will be developed which will educate them to the skills and knowledge relevant to improve the lives and spirits of all Indian peoples. Attached to this center will be traveling universities, managed by Indians, which will go to the Indian Reservations, learning those necessary and relevant materials now about.

2. AN AMERICAN INDIAN SPIRITUAL CENTER which will practice our ancient tribal religious and sacred healing ceremonies. Our cultural arts will be featured and our young people trained in music, dance, and healing rituals.

3. AN INDIAN CENTER OF ECOLOGY which will train and support our young people in scientific research and practice to restore our lands and waters to their pure and natural state. We will work to de-pollute the air and water of the Bay Area. We will seek to restore fish and animal life to the area and to revitalize sea life which has been threatened by the white man's way. We will set up facilities to desalt sea water for human benefit.

4. A GREAT INDIAN TRAINING SCHOOL will be developed to teach our people how to make a living in the world, improve our standard of living, and to end hunger and unemployment among all our people. This training school will include a center for Indian arts and crafts, and an Indian restaurant serving native foods, which will restore Indian culinary arts. This center will display Indian arts and offer Indian foods to the public, so that all may know of the beauty and spirit of the traditional INDIAN ways.

Some of the present buildings will be taken over to develop an AMERICAN INDIAN MUSEUM, which will depict our native food & other cultural contributions we have given to the world. Another part of the museum will present some of the things the white man has given to the Indians in return for the land and life he took: disease, alcohol, poverty and cultural decimation (As symbolized by old tin cans, barbed wire, rubber tires, plastic containers, etc.) Part of thie museum will remain a dungeon to symbolize both those Indian captives who were incarcerated for challenging white authority, and those who were imprisoned on reservations. The museum will show the noble and the tragic events of Indian history, including the broken treaties, the documentary of the Trail of Tears, the Massacre of Wounded Knee, as well as the victory over Yellow Hair Custer and his army.

In the name of all Indians, therefore, we re-claim this island for our Indian nations, for all these reasons. We feel this claim is just and proper, and that this land should rightfully be granted to us for as long as the rivers shall run and the sun shall shine.

Signed,

Indians of all Tribes
November 1969
San Francisco, California

PAGE 10 THE MOVEMENT JANUARY 1970

FIGURE 1.3. *The original Proclamation in its entirety, as it appeared in* The Movement, *January 1970. Courtesy of the U.S. Department of the Interior, National Park Service.*

and the Proclamation of Rebellion, point toward liberation, but subtextually, they exude circumscription and enumeration. A masterpiece of inversion and reversal, the Alcatraz document plays with not only the discourse of proclamations but also the history of petitions. Even more interesting, though, is its deconstruction of the larger body of federal documents of issuance and order. Take, for example, the opening sentences and their cagey evocation of everything from the Preamble of the Constitution to the diaries of Columbus to the Louisiana Purchase to the Emancipation Proclamation. The use of the royal "We" makes the piece sound presidential and regal, lending an air of legitimacy and collaboration. Similarly, claiming the land by right of discovery—itself a concept established in papal decrees and U.S. law—suddenly gives the Indians' claim the very same legal support enjoyed by Anglo conquerors of the New World.[4]

What those documents lack, and this one has in spades, is a sense of humor. If readers aren't laughing at the "right of discovery" line, it is impossible to miss the dark comedy in the Indians' extension of a treaty. The desire to be "fair and honorable . . . with the Caucasian inhabitants," along with the offer to purchase Alcatraz "for 24 dollars ($24) in glass beads and red cloth," is too funny and too painfully ironic to dismiss. On one hand, there is no mistaking the anger being expressed, but on the other hand, the document contains a level of play even Jacques Derrida could have appreciated:

> We will give to the inhabitants of this island a portion of that land for their own to be held in trust by the American Indian Affairs and by the bureau of Caucasian Affairs to hold

> in perpetuity—for as long as the sun shall rise and the rivers go down to the sea. We will further guide the inhabitants in the proper way of living. We will offer them our religion, our education, our life-ways, in order to help them achieve our level of civilization and thus raise them and all their white brothers up from their savage and unhappy state.

If the reader is any kind of student of American history, I need not unfold the many layers of this passage, except to say that the document rises above anger and achieves the level of art. Its nearly biblical cadence and vocabulary, its appropriation of the language of unfair treaties, its indirect mockery of the Bureau of Indian Affairs (BIA), its searing indictment of American's most cherished metanarratives of religion and values—even its parody of mythic Native American descriptions of time—point to self-awareness and self-identity that is both resilient and revolutionary.

But it doesn't stop there. The next section turns that black comedy on the reservation system itself, noting how the dilapidated facilities of Alcatraz are shockingly similar to those on reservations:

> We feel that this so-called Alcatraz Island is more than suitable for an Indian reservation, as determined by the white man's own standards. By this we mean that this place resembles most Indian reservations in that:
>
> 1. It is isolated from modern facilities, and without adequate means of transportation.
> 2. It has no fresh running water.
> 3. It has inadequate sanitation facilities.
> 4. There are no oil or mineral rights.
> 5. There is no industry and so unemployment is very great.
> 6. There are no health-care facilities.
> 7. The soil is rocky and non-productive; and the land does not support game.
> 8. There are no educational facilities.
> 9. The population has always exceeded the land base.
> 10. The population has always been held as prisoners and kept dependent upon others.

The observations are so insightful, so laser-like in their accurate critique of reservation realities, that they make the serious demands that follow actually sound reasonable. "Alcatraz's pre-existing reputation as a cruel place," observe Carolyn Strange and Tina Loo, "offered an opportunity for activists to dramatize the plight of Indian people; paradoxically it also presented the *possibility* to reimagine the place as the home for American Indian rebirth and self-determination" ("Holding the Rock," 60; emphasis added).

The move in the document from assertion to litany tropes in unexpected but effective ways, linking despair with possibility. Possibility and reasonableness were, after all, at the heart of the occupation. In 1969, claims that "militant Indians" had taken over a federal facility in San Francisco could have sounded scary; in general, protests of oppression can come off as plaintive; requests for ecological centers can seem weird; painting graffiti on a water tower may frighten some. In writing about the rhetorical tightrope that the great Paiute writer and activist Sara Winnemucca Hopkins found herself walking, Malea Powell makes an insightful observation about what, exactly, is at stake for Native rhetors: "Winnemucca and others like her faced difficult rhetorical circumstances in which they had to weigh carefully the price of convincing Euro-American audiences of the worthiness of their 'cause' against the risk of both alienating their own people and reinscribing dominant ideas about the dependency of Native peoples" ("Princess Sarah," 64).[5]

As Winnemucca and figures like Pequot politician and pastor William Apess discovered, appeals to a person's human nature—her good humor and common sense—even if the content of the appeal is notably other, can be utterly likeable. It can, as in the case of President Nixon, elicit sympathy. Ultimately, one cannot separate the occupation from the texts it engendered, especially this most seminal text. So it is particularly important that this proclamation, which many people saw, including President Nixon, set the stage for the larger theater. The language of treaties, like the language of proclamations, resides in a limbo-like place in the American psyche. Americans both know and don't know the precise language of such documents, despite their importance in American history. However, even if Americans are not familiar with the precise wording, they possess, as part of their cultural memory, the tone and tenor of treaty language. The best example of this occurs in the final full paragraph of the proclamation: "We feel this claim is just and proper, and that this land should rightfully be granted to us for as long as the rivers run and the sun shall shine." A send-up of the now stereotyped phrase that Andrew Jackson supposedly wove into many different treaties with Indian tribes, indicating how long the Indians would have right to their land, this redeployment of infantilizing treaty language provides the perfect icing on the Alcatraz cake.[6]

The ability of this document to mobilize the language of the enemy against the enemy is a classic rhetorical move; in this case, a Janus-faced gesture that harks back to the era of treaties and forward to a time when poets and fiction writers would ironize treaty discourse as linguistic tropes. In *Blood Narrative*, Chadwick Allen notes that "American Indian activists and writers tend to redeploy treaty discourse as metaphor and metonymy . . . [and] typically foreground the generalized contents and surface features of a treaty, including the physical characteristics of the document itself as well as the rhetorical and literary style, figures of speech, and narrative devises" (20). To be sure, Allen is correct, but for the authors of this document, such language is more than metaphor; it is also proof the Indians know their history, their legal terminology, the slipperiness of treaty-speak. It authenticates the document while indigenizing proclamatory discourse. Moreover, the proclamation establishes one of the first pan-Indian attacks on the aftereffects of conquest and the domino effects of the colonial project. In his recent study of the Red Power movement, Sean Kicummah Teuton (Cherokee), makes a similar argument: "The document was a watershed for American Indians. With humor and irony, it expressed a clear analysis of colonialism" (*Red Land, Red Power*, 6).

Teuton is on point, but more than offering an analysis of colonialism, the proclamation inverts the ethos of colonialism by turning its condescending language back on itself. In the voice of Indians of All Tribes, the document speaks truth to power for the Indians of all tribes. Regarding this point, one of the smarter decisions was to issue the proclamation authorlessly.[7] Signed by "Indians of All Tribes," the document suggests unity and collectiveness, despite its essentially revolutionary trajectory. At its heart, the proclamation, like the Proclamation of Rebellion forged by the early American revolutionaries eager to separate from the British Crown, is about autonomy and self-determination. The Alcatraz version pulls from and calls on both Native and Anglo voices of the past in order to establish a place and vision for the present. The less rhetorically moving (and less successful) Occupation Manifesto tries to pick up where the proclamation leaves off.

It, too, is authorless, though it clearly comes from the collective voice of the Indians on the island. Just as the Alcatraz Proclamation draws on the language of earlier decrees and edicts, it attempts to capitalize on the political and social associations of the manifesto, which has its roots in the Latin-Italian terminology of the evidentiary—like the manifest of a ship or something clearly obvious like the destiny of a culture to inhabit all of the land between two oceans. Even so, Americans have never been keen on manifestos, which still carry a European and renunciatory connotation. This particular document came on the

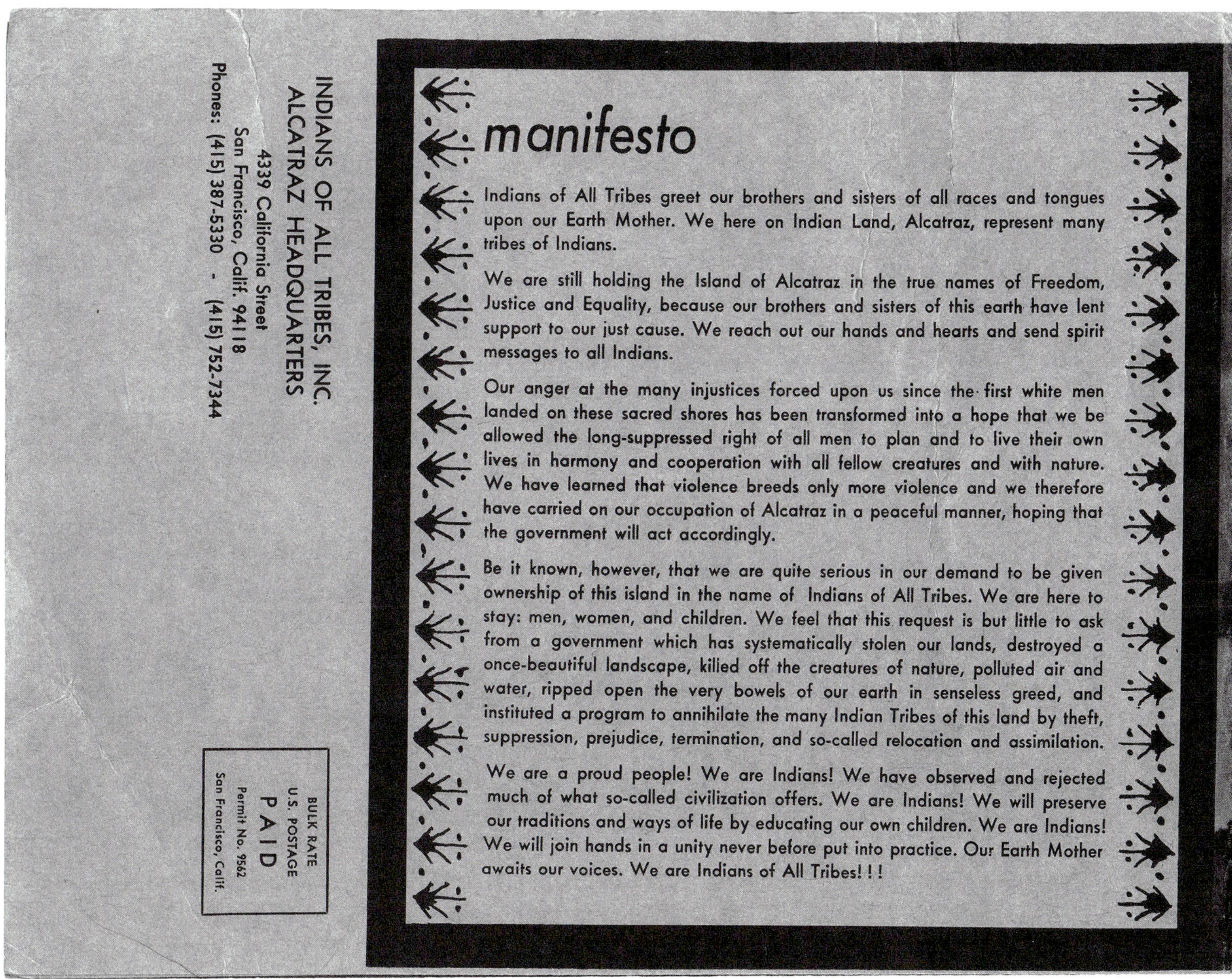

manifesto

Indians of All Tribes greet our brothers and sisters of all races and tongues upon our Earth Mother. We here on Indian Land, Alcatraz, represent many tribes of Indians.

We are still holding the Island of Alcatraz in the true names of Freedom, Justice and Equality, because our brothers and sisters of this earth have lent support to our just cause. We reach out our hands and hearts and send spirit messages to all Indians.

Our anger at the many injustices forced upon us since the first white men landed on these sacred shores has been transformed into a hope that we be allowed the long-suppressed right of all men to plan and to live their own lives in harmony and cooperation with all fellow creatures and with nature. We have learned that violence breeds only more violence and we therefore have carried on our occupation of Alcatraz in a peaceful manner, hoping that the government will act accordingly.

Be it known, however, that we are quite serious in our demand to be given ownership of this island in the name of Indians of All Tribes. We are here to stay: men, women, and children. We feel that this request is but little to ask from a government which has systematically stolen our lands, destroyed a once-beautiful landscape, killed off the creatures of nature, polluted air and water, ripped open the very bowels of our earth in senseless greed, and instituted a program to annihilate the many Indian Tribes of this land by theft, suppression, prejudice, termination, and so-called relocation and assimilation.

We are a proud people! We are Indians! We have observed and rejected much of what so-called civilization offers. We are Indians! We will preserve our traditions and ways of life by educating our own children. We are Indians! We will join hands in a unity never before put into practice. Our Earth Mother awaits our voices. We are Indians of All Tribes! ! !

INDIANS OF ALL TRIBES, INC.
ALCATRAZ HEADQUARTERS
4339 California Street
San Francisco, Calif. 94118
Phones: (415) 387-5330 - (415) 752-7344

BULK RATE
U.S. POSTAGE
PAID
Permit No. 9562
San Francisco, Calif.

FIGURE 1.4. *The Alcatraz Manifesto from the back cover of the* Indians of All Tribes Bulletin, *1970. The purpose of this publication was to keep both Anglos and Natives informed of news on the island, to solicit donations, and, as the manifesto indicates, to serve as a platform for the demands and concerns of the occupiers. Courtesy of the U.S. Department of the Interior, National Park Service.*

heels of Vine Deloria, Jr.'s *Custer Died for Your Sins: An Indian Manifesto* (1969), so the association was in the air—particularly in regard to the pleas of Indians.

Unlike Deloria's manifesto, one of the most important Indian books of the last century, the Alcatraz version suffers from earnest clichés and nearly purple prose. Here, the authors opt for drama rather than comedy, and the effect is diminished. Immediately upon reading the proclamation, one senses urgency and history. It feels historical, important. The manifesto bites with fewer teeth in part because it does not incorporate the language of significant American documents. Where the proclamation attacks the vacuousness of treaty language and the fatuous discourse of American supremacy, the manifesto merely declares. Where the proclamation is rhetorical, the manifesto is informative.

Even so, the manifesto contains some fine passages. The second paragraph's reference to justice, freedom, and equality, and its assertion of a "just cause," recall Thomas Paine's *Common Sense*, and it draws a direct link between the revolutionary act of taking Alcatraz from the government with the act of seizing the American colonies from the British. Moreover, the final paragraph energizes the document, transforming it from complaint into a call to arms by skillfully using a classic Native American linguistic technique—repetition—to lend the closing an incantatory momentum. On some level, the internal "success" of the manifesto is far less important than what its existence suggests. A manifesto differs from a proclamation in that the former seeks to set out intentions and principles as opposed

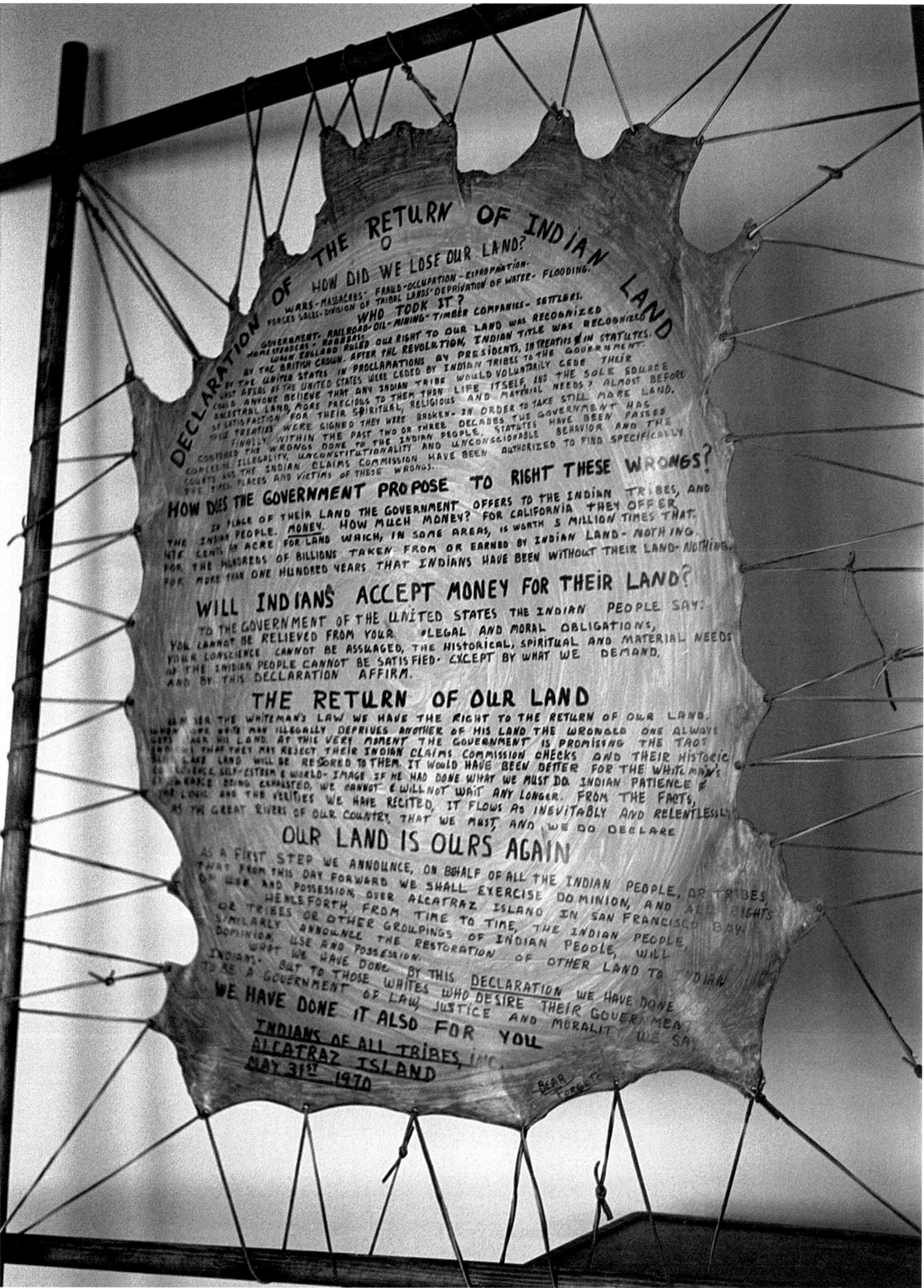

DECLARATION OF THE RETURN OF INDIAN LAND
HOW DID WE LOSE OUR LAND?
WARS-MASSACRES- FRAUD-OCCUPATION-EXPROPRIATION-
FORCED SALES-DIVISION OF TRIBAL LANDS-DEPRIVATION OF WATER- FLOODING.
WHO TOOK IT?
GOVERNMENT- RAILROAD-OIL-MINING-TIMBER COMPANIES- SETTLERS.
HOMESTEADERS - ROBBERS.
WHEN ENGLAND RULED OUR RIGHT TO OUR LAND WAS RECOGNIZED
BY THE BRITISH CROWN. AFTER THE REVOLUTION, INDIAN TITLE WAS RECOGNIZED
BY THE UNITED STATES IN PROCLAMATIONS BY PRESIDENTS, IN TREATIES & IN STATUTES.
VAST AREAS OF THE UNITED STATES WERE CEDED BY INDIAN TRIBES TO THE GOVERNMENT.
COULD ANYONE BELIEVE THAT ANY INDIAN TRIBE WOULD VOLUNTARILY CEDE THEIR
ANCESTRAL LAND, MORE PRECIOUS TO THEM THAN LIFE ITSELF, AND THE SOLE SOURCE
OF SATISFACTION FOR THEIR SPIRITUAL, RELIGIOUS AND MATERIAL NEEDS? ALMOST BEFORE
THESE TREATIES WERE SIGNED THEY WERE BROKEN- IN ORDER TO TAKE STILL MORE LAND.
FINALLY WITHIN THE PAST TWO OR THREE DECADES THE GOVERNMENT HAS
CONFESSED THE WRONGS DONE TO THE INDIAN PEOPLE. STATUTES HAVE BEEN PASSED
CONFESSING ILLEGALITY, UNCONSTITUTIONALITY AND UNCONSCIONABLE BEHAVIOR AND THE
COURTS AND THE INDIAN CLAIMS COMMISSION HAVE BEEN AUTHORIZED TO FIND SPECIFICALLY
THE TIMES, PLACES AND VICTIMS OF THESE WRONGS.
HOW DOES THE GOVERNMENT PROPOSE TO RIGHT THESE WRONGS?
IN PLACE OF THEIR LAND THE GOVERNMENT OFFERS TO THE INDIAN TRIBES, AND
THE INDIAN PEOPLE. MONEY. HOW MUCH MONEY? FOR CALIFORNIA THEY OFFER
47¢ CENTS AN ACRE FOR LAND WHICH, IN SOME AREAS, IS WORTH 5 MILLION TIMES THAT.
FOR THE HUNDREDS OF BILLIONS TAKEN FROM OR EARNED BY INDIAN LAND- NOTHING.
FOR MORE THAN ONE HUNDRED YEARS THAT INDIANS HAVE BEEN WITHOUT THEIR LAND- NOTHING.
WILL INDIANS ACCEPT MONEY FOR THEIR LAND?
TO THE GOVERNMENT OF THE UNITED STATES THE INDIAN PEOPLE SAY:
YOU CANNOT BE RELIEVED FROM YOUR LEGAL AND MORAL OBLIGATIONS,
YOUR CONSCIENCE CANNOT BE ASSUAGED, THE HISTORICAL, SPIRITUAL AND MATERIAL NEEDS
OF THE INDIAN PEOPLE CANNOT BE SATISFIED- EXCEPT BY WHAT WE DEMAND,
AND BY THIS DECLARATION AFFIRM.
THE RETURN OF OUR LAND
UNDER THE WHITEMAN'S LAW WE HAVE THE RIGHT TO THE RETURN OF OUR LAND.
WHEN ONE WHITE MAN ILLEGALLY DEPRIVES ANOTHER OF HIS LAND THE WRONGED ONE ALWAYS
GETS BACK HIS LAND. AT THIS VERY MOMENT THE GOVERNMENT IS PROMISING THE TAOS
INDIANS THAT THEY MAY REJECT THEIR INDIAN CLAIMS COMMISSION CHECKS AND THEIR HISTORIC
BLUE LAKE LAND WILL BE RESTORED TO THEM. IT WOULD HAVE BEEN BETTER FOR THE WHITEMAN'S
CONSCIENCE, SELF-ESTEEM & WORLD-IMAGE IF HE HAD DONE WHAT WE MUST DO. INDIAN PATIENCE &
FORBEARANCE BEING EXHAUSTED, WE CANNOT & WILL NOT WAIT ANY LONGER. FROM THE FACTS,
THE LOGIC AND THE VERITIES WE HAVE RECITED, IT FLOWS AS INEVITABLY AND RELENTLESSLY
AS THE GREAT RIVERS OF OUR COUNTRY, THAT WE MUST, AND WE DO DECLARE
OUR LAND IS OURS AGAIN
AS A FIRST STEP WE ANNOUNCE, ON BEHALF OF ALL THE INDIAN PEOPLE, OR TRIBES,
THAT FROM THIS DAY FORWARD WE SHALL EXERCISE DOMINION, AND ALL RIGHTS
OF USE AND POSSESSION, OVER ALCATRAZ ISLAND IN SAN FRANCISCO BAY.
HENCEFORTH, FROM TIME TO TIME, THE INDIAN PEOPLE,
OR TRIBES OR OTHER GROUPINGS OF INDIAN PEOPLE, WILL
SIMILARLY ANNOUNCE THE RESTORATION OF OTHER LAND TO INDIAN
DOMINION, USE AND POSSESSION.
WHAT WE HAVE DONE BY THIS DECLARATION WE HAVE DONE
INDIANS. BUT TO THOSE WHITES WHO DESIRE THEIR GOVERNMENT
TO BE A GOVERNMENT OF LAW, JUSTICE AND MORALITY WE SAY
WE HAVE DONE IT ALSO FOR YOU
INDIANS OF ALL TRIBES, INC.
ALCATRAZ ISLAND
MAY 31ST 1970
BEAR FORGETS

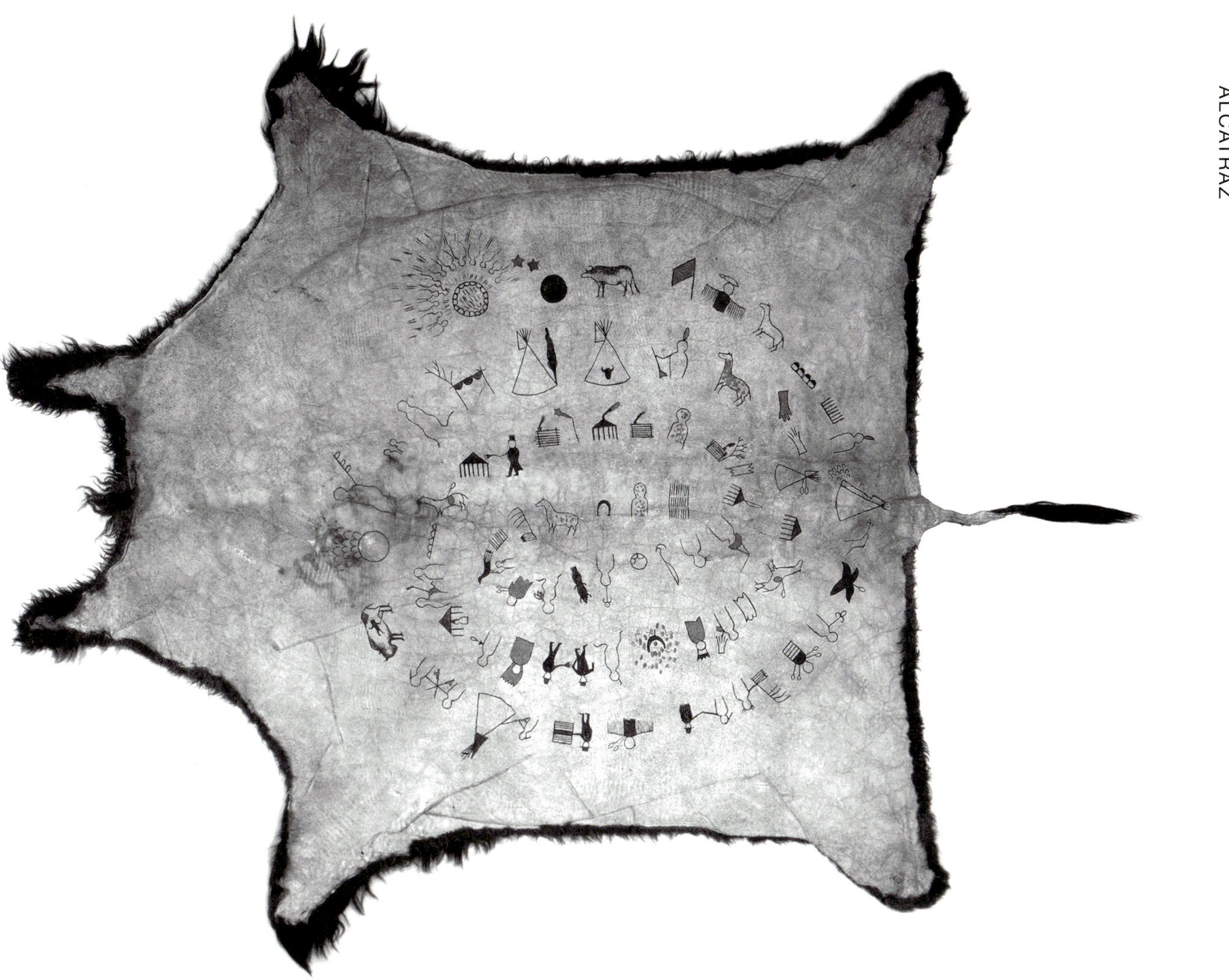

to declaring an edict. Here, the Indians probably intuited they would not be able to stay on the island permanently, so they invested in documents, long-tested Western political genres, and the power of language in order to lay the political and cultural groundwork for autonomy in the minds and hearts of the people, who might thereby see them through an entirely new lens.

Along with a manifesto and a proclamation, the Indian occupiers also issued a "Declaration of the Return of Indian Land" (Fig. 1.5). Though it has taken a backseat to the other two documents, this plea for the return of stolen lands remains one of the more striking texts produced on the island, in part because of its focus. Whereas the manifesto was largely about righting general wrongs, this declaration lays down ethical, moral, and legal arguments for the return of land to Native tribes. It also establishes a moral stance that Indians and Indian land cannot be bought. In the second section, the declaration notes that in the early years of the "discovery" of the Americas, Indians retained ownership of their land, but the remainder indicts the machinery of American capitalism not simply for taking tribal lands but also for profiting from such seizures at the expense of tribes and peoples. Like the manifesto, this text lacks the rhetorical pressure and humor of the proclamation, but it is effective on two important levels.

First, it asserts a legal and moral right to claim Alcatraz via the terminology of both law and religion: "On behalf of all the Indian people or tribes . . . We shall exercise dominion, and all rights of use and possession over Alcatraz Island . . . Henceforth, from time to time, the Indian people similarly announce the restoration of other land to Indian dominion use

FIGURE 1.5. (facing page) The Declaration of the Return of Indian Land. *The text lays out a legal and moral justification for claiming Alcatraz and also for returning stolen Indian land. Photo by Ilka Hartmann, © 2010.*

FIGURE 1.6. (above) *Winter Count by Shunka Ishnala (Lone Dog), Yanktonai, c. 1870. Courtesy of the National Museum of the American Indian, Smithsonian Institution. Photo by Janine Sarna Jones.*

and possession." One doesn't normally associate the concept of territorial "dominion" with Native American beliefs, but in this case, that term, used twice, evokes both the first chapters of Genesis and legal statutes governing such concepts as the plenary right of dominion. This line of argument dovetails with similar tacks taken in the proclamation, and, in fact, it was these very assertions that swayed lawmakers to give the occupiers a great deal of what they asked for. This rhetoric of land dominion—what Kiowa writer N. Scott Momaday calls "a land ethic"—actually ties in with the main thrust of the proclamation, which makes a moral case for returning land to the Indians of All Tribes.[8]

Second and, for the purposes here, more importantly, the text utilizes classic and nearly sacred Native documentary icons: the stretched hide and the winter count. Because this document was never printed and distributed, unlike the manifesto and proclamation, it has not garnered the same attention, but it stands as one of the most beloved pieces of art-text from the occupation, and it is commonly seen in photographs as a visual marker of the days spent on the island.[9] In this sense, the declaration very much resembles a winter count, a Plains Indian mode of marking and recording time (Fig. 1.6). Tribal historians would mark each year (or winter) that passed on a stretched animal hide, creating a pictographic calendar of both time and endurance. Granted, this text does not schematize years like a traditional count, but it does mirror a historical pictorial textuality that is part of Indian memory.

In his discussion of Chief Eagle's painting *Winter Count*, Chadwick Allen makes a similar observation, arguing that the creators of the declaration "mobilized the force of the winter count tradition to assert a distinctly indigenous perspective on American Indian History" (*Blood Narrative*, 171). Though the declaration and the proclamation belong to different categories, the hide establishes an important authenticity through its semiotic authority. Thus, when the Indians merge the semiotic power of the hide with the historical resonances of declarations, they transform mere rhetoric into a resistance of polyvalent engagement.

Though it is not technically a proclamation, the Permanent Resident card of "Indian Joe" Morris remains for me one of the most salient texts of engaged resistance from the occupation. I discovered it in 2010, just before this book went to press. I had returned to the National Park archives to confirm some dates, and I found Morris's card in a folder among some items he had donated to the archive. More of a micro- than a macrotext, this little card both counters the legitimacy of traditional "American" documents and advances forms of Indian identity. In Chapter 6, I discuss how Navajo poet Ester Belin undermines standard forms by recasting how we see governmental officialness. Morris's card (and the fact that he kept it all these years) speaks to the degree to which the occupiers sought to puncture the puffed-up persona that is government bureaucracy. We tend to think of a resident card not just as a form of identification but also as a source of identity. In this case, the card is a private certificate for a public stance, reinforcing the notion that the personal is the political. Ultimately, the residence card's power lies in its symbolism: it indicates arrival and a sense of belonging.

As I discuss below, the occupiers of Alcatraz often garrisoned the symbolic power of iconography as a semiotic weapon in the larger cultural battle over Indian identity, Indian sovereignty, and Indian autonomy. Part of the assertion both in the proclamation and the declaration is that past is present. Time is a hoop, circling back. Traditions are not just relics from history; they are active practices that draw on the power of language to effect change and put the world in right relation. These documents fuse the visual and the verbal, the oral and the written, the spoken and the drawn, just as they fuse present and past, engagement and resistance. And like the poems written on the island, they set the stage for the intellectual arrival of Indian aesthetic activism.

FIGURE 1.7. (facing page) *Permanent Resident Card of "Indian Joe" Morris. Courtesy of the U.S. Department of the Interior, National Park Service.*

ALCATRAZ PERMANENT RESIDENCE

Name JOSEPH MORRIS

Tribe BLACKFEET

Walter Hatch

Security Chief

The Poetry of Protest, the Protest of Poetry

Just as the declamatory documents from Alcatraz interact with the discourse of their particular genres, poems about Alcatraz overtake the language and systems of Western poetry. Indian poets invent and reinvent poetic genres all the time; not surprisingly, many of the poems produced during the occupation are fine examples of this technique.[10] But, more important, these texts assert an indigenous resistance that merges both tribal and pan-Indian gestures, creating a new vernacular that has antecedents in two different but complementary worlds and worldviews. These Native writers often marry phrases or images drawn from their tribes with the spirit of the Alcatraz resistance. Additionally, like much of the painting on the island, these poems evince a notable aesthetic that walks a fine line between beauty and bitterness, as in these opening lines from "The Indian Question," by Dorothy Lonewolf Miller (Blackfoot), written on December 3, 1969, only a few days into the occupation:

> Why won't you give us the Island—
> What is it that you fear?
>
> Why don't you try to set things right
> Now that we are here?
>
> Why won't you give us our land and schools
> And let us begin to build?
>
> Are you ashamed of what you've done—
> Of what you spoiled and killed?
>
> —(JOHNSON, *ALCATRAZ: INDIAN LAND FOREVER*, 23)

Like the proclamation and the declaration, "The Indian Question" utilizes classic rhetorical strategies; in this case, the rhetorical question. But the poem also employs formal poetic techniques like couplets, end rhymes, and a relatively consistent rhythmic foot. Lonewolf, a registered nurse, became the poet laureate of the occupation, penning at least a dozen finely wrought verses.

Clearly, this poem is asking to be read as a poem, as opposed to an essay or a manifesto, raising the question, what can poetry or art do that nonaesthetically driven texts cannot? Or, to ask the same question a different way, how do poems, along with paintings and treaty documents, help complete a circle of aesthetic activism? Johnson argues that the poems "capture the passion of the movement as spoken and written by those most intimately involved in it," and to be sure, they do a fine job of serving as both documentary and exclamatory evidence (*Alcatraz: Indian Land Forever*, ix). But even more is at stake. These poems perform two important duties. First, they reinforce Indian poetry as indigenous performative texts that eschew abstracted reality for a lived reality of their own, and second, they remind us of the ability of such texts to create a sense of place, especially within and among contested spaces.

Of the three main forms of aesthetic activism produced on the island—painting, proclamations, and poems—poems were the least visible to those on the outside, but writing them was among the favorite and most popular activities on the island.[11] On occasion, a poem would appear in one of the publications put together by the occupiers and their supporters in San Francisco, and it frequently functioned as a kind of incantatory call to action (Figs. 1.8 and 1.9). To the Indians at Alcatraz, writing, reciting, and passing around poems proved to be one of the most effective forms of community making. Because of poetry's orality, it lends itself to interaction and exchange.

FIGURE 1.8. (facing page) *"An Indian's Song," one of the poems Dorothy Lonewolf wrote while on the island. Courtesy of the U.S. Department of the Interior, National Park Service.*

AN INDIAN'S SONG

Stand firm, my brothers on the Rock
Do not despair!

Be brave, my brothers on the Rock
Our spirit's there!

Walk tall, my sisters on the Rock
Stand up with your men!

Grow fast, my children on the Rock
Learn our ways again!

O, Indians of Alcatraz
Lift up your eyes!

Lone Wolf, Blackfoot
December 4, 1969

ALCATRAZ MEDICINE

Wo hai -- Wo hai -- Wo hai!

Some fur, glass beads, a thong of hide
And the tips of an Eagle's wing --
Will make me a man again!

Wo hai -- Wo hai -- Wo hai!

Hot fire, strong meat, a ring of stone
And the smile of a Blackfoot girl
Will make me a man again!

Wo hai -- Wo hai -- Wo hai!

Brave men, strong wind, a bright red dawn
And my brothers on Alcatraz
Will make me a man again!

Wo hai -- Wo hai -- Wo hai!

Long thoughts, wise words, a warrior band
And great dreams of Indian Land
Will make me a man again!

Wo hai -- Wo hai -- Wo hai!

Strong wind, dark night, the sound of waves
On the sacred rock of Alcatraz
Will make me a man again!

Wo hai -- Wo hai -- Wo hai!

Long years, barren land, the smell of death
All fade on the winds of Alcatraz
And make me a man again!

Lone Wolf, Blackfoot
November 29, 1969

Poetry also has a long history of serving as a kind of storehouse for collective memory and as a catalyst for collective action. One argument this book advances is that contemporary American Indian artists and activists are always already involved in nonlegal, non-policy strategies to right a virtual catalogue of wrongs. In the America of late capitalism, the battlegrounds have shifted from land to ethos; thus, the weapons Indians amass must be commensurate with the context of the enemy. In the case of Alcatraz, the poet-occupiers knew what was at stake:

Alcatraz, death buffalo of the sea
  I want to revive you that my children may ride you
Into the stampede of freedom and hope
  For their minds and bodies.

This time we fight not with bows and arrows
  But with pencils and books

—(JOHNSON, *ALCATRAZ: INDIAN LAND FOREVER*, 9)

The anonymous author of this poem understands that one attacks symbols through symbolic language, or what Julia Kristeva calls "signifying practice"—a term she uses interchangeably with "poetic language."[12]

For many, the struggle for Alcatraz was also the struggle for articulation. The act of poetry has always been an act of naming. Though it oversimplifies the situation to reduce it to the "public perception" of Indian sovereignty, self-determination, and agency, it is important to remember that the occupation intends an audience, and it intends an outcome. What kind of outcome can one expect from the writing of rhymed and metered poetry? One might be surprised:

Throughout the cold and winter nights—
We tended to our fires,
We drew our blankets close around
And watched the waves crash higher.

Though the cold waves beat on Alcatraz
Indian hearts are stout,
For white men think we'll go away—
But we'll live this winter out!

For the North Wind is our Brother;
We share his bitter shock;
Aii—we are warriors of Alcatraz,
And we hold the Rock!

—(DOROTHY LONEWOLF MILLER, "WE HOLD THE ROCK!" QUOTED IN JOHNSON, *OCCUPATION OF ALCATRAZ*, 49)

As Johnson notes, "We hold the Rock" became the catchphrase for the new residents of Alcatraz, and the poem itself served as a rallying cry, a call to arms for the occupiers. This short rhymed poem (sometimes called "Alcatraz Rain"), with its Dickinsonian dashes and its neat quatrains, feels of another century. Which may lead some to ask: Why this poem? Why would participants in an act of rebellion, transgression, and revolution be drawn to a rather conventional, even conservative poem?

FIGURE 1.9. (facing page) *"Alcatraz Medicine" by Dorothy Lonewolf. Note how this poem combines both Western poetic techniques (rhyme and meter) and aspects of Native oral performance (repetition and incantation). Courtesy of the U.S. Department of the Interior, National Park Service.*

The answer might lay, oddly enough, in formal discourse itself, poetry's heightened, recuperative language—what Navajo poet Luci Tapahonso calls "words of healing, words of holiness" ("Dít'óódí," in *Blue Horses Rush In*, 34). Oddly enough, the German philosopher Martin Heidegger also locates in poetry the ability to connect to the sacred in a destitute time: "To be a poet in a destitute time means: to attend, singing, to the trace of the fugitive gods. This is why the poet in the time of the world's night utters the holy" (*Poetry, Language, Thought*, 94). For many Native peoples, there are blurry (if any) distinctions between poetry and prayer, prayer and song, song and poem. In other words, this poem connected with people because of its exalted language, because its intricate form and exhortations of endurance stand in contrast to the bleakness of Alcatraz, which resembled (if only symbolically) reservation life. Poems, after all, occupy both the symbolic and the realistic realms, and "We Hold the Rock!" populates and expands both worlds. On one hand, it chronicles the harsh conditions on the island, deromanticizing the mythology of the occupation. But on the other hand, it strategically symbolizes Indian perseverance. The waves crashing against the island might suggest the tidal flood of white soldiers and settlers. Living out the winter may be a metaphor for surviving the long winter of colonization. The reference to blankets could be a dark and mocking reference to smallpox blankets, which the Indians also outlived. The final stanza, with its communal language and its battle cry, announces that within the struggle lies victory, permanence, survivance.

Like a prayer or a song, a poem carries immediacy, a now-ness, that a narrative can't replicate. In her excellent study of resistance literature in Third World countries, Barbara Harlow argues that "poetry and the poems of organized resistance movements struggle to preserve and *even to redefine* for the given historical moment the cultural images which underwrite collective action" (*Resistance Literature*, 82; emphasis added).[13] This poem plays with so many flammable cultural images, it is no wonder it caught fire. Few things burn hotter than the passion of collective resistance, especially when those involved believe they have the power to reframe discourse and redefine identity.

No stranger to the efforts of liberation, Native Americans have woven sovereignty and tradition into the tapestry of tribal and pan-tribal consciousness. Lonewolf drapes her emphatic poem "The Rocks of Alcatraz" in this garment, clothing the Alcatraz present in the shared material of the past:

> The wild pony stomp of Crazy Horse
> Thunders just over the hill
> For brave men tried to fight and die
> And defy the white man's will!
>
> O, our fires burn bright
> Throughout the night
> On the rocks of Alcatraz!
>
> The wild chant of Blackfeet men,
> And the cries of their women, too,
> Join with the songs of the Navajo
> The Cherokee and Sioux!
>
> O, our children play
> In the Indian way
> On the rocks of Alcatraz!

For we are the men who were wild and free
And now dawns our new day—
We Indians know, we Indians feel
The old brave Indian way!
    For brave strong men
    Lead us again
        On the rocks of Alcatraz!

—(JOHNSON, *ALCATRAZ: INDIAN LAND FOREVER*, 47)

Written on November 27, 1969, the poem is fresh with the energy of the project. By drawing direct connections between a hero of Native history and the heroic struggle of those on the island, Lonewolf places the Alcatraz fight within the vast sweep of indigenous resistance. She also canonizes that fight. What's more, the poem enacts one of the first poetic instances of pan-Indianism, linking the Blackfeet, Navajo, Sioux, and Cherokee through a common project, a gesture that runs throughout one of the most famous poems of the occupation, "Alcatraz Visions" (Fig. 1.10).

Through protest, the poem arrives at endorsement; through tradition ("The old brave Indian way"), it positions the future ("And now dawns our new day"); through resistance, it marshals engagement. In her fine study of contemporary American Indian poetry, Robin Riley Fast makes the argument that this merging of old and new is de rigueur for Native writers: "Contemporary Native poets express and assess mixed cultural influences variously. While they may associate the tensions and fluidity of borderland experience with creativity, they are often engaged in reclaiming or affirming aspects of traditional culture—

FIGURE 1.10. *"Alcatraz Visions," as it appeared in one of the occupation newsletters. Courtesy of the U.S. Department of the Interior, National Park Service.*

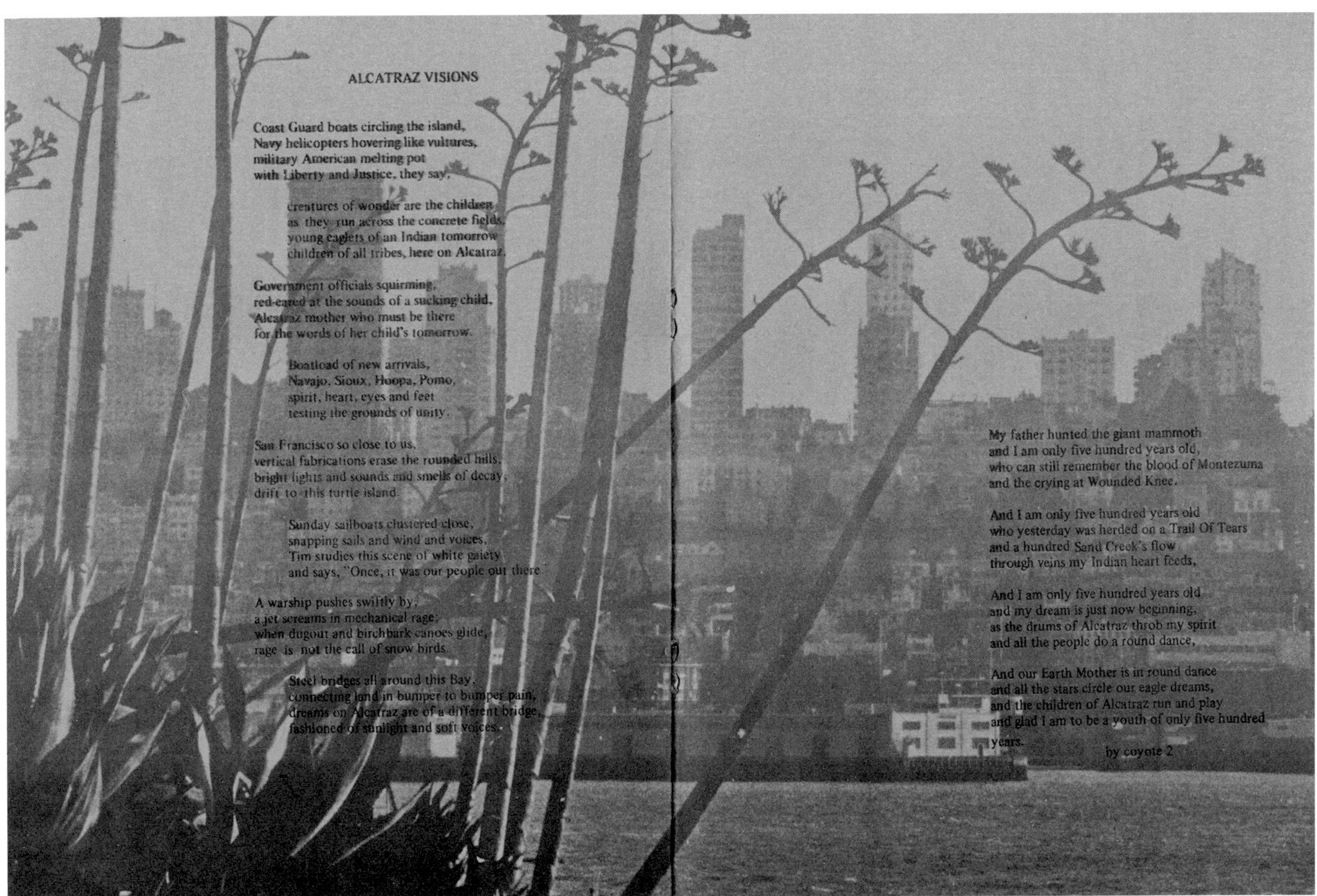

ALCATRAZ VISIONS

Coast Guard boats circling the island,
Navy helicopters hovering like vultures,
military American melting pot
with Liberty and Justice, they say,

    creatures of wonder are the children
    as they run across the concrete fields,
    young eaglets of an Indian tomorrow
    children of all tribes, here on Alcatraz.

Government officials squirming,
red-eared at the sounds of a sucking child,
Alcatraz mother who must be there
for the words of her child's tomorrow.

    Boatload of new arrivals,
    Navajo, Sioux, Hoopa, Pomo,
    spirit, heart, eyes and feet
    testing the grounds of unity.

San Francisco so close to us,
vertical fabrications erase the rounded hills,
bright lights and sounds and smells of decay,
drift to this turtle island.

    Sunday sailboats clustered close,
    snapping sails and wind and voices,
    Tim studies this scene of white gaiety
    and says, "Once, it was our people out there.

A warship pushes swiftly by,
a jet screams in mechanical rage;
when dugout and birchbark canoes glide,
rage is not the call of snow birds.

    Steel bridges all around this Bay,
    connecting land in bumper to bumper pain,
    dreams on Alcatraz are of a different bridge,
    fashioned of sunlight and soft voices.

My father hunted the giant mammoth
and I am only five hundred years old,
who can still remember the blood of Montezuma
and the crying at Wounded Knee.

And I am only five hundred years old
who yesterday was herded on a Trail Of Tears
and a hundred Sand Creek's flow
through veins my Indian heart feeds,

And I am only five hundred years old
and my dream is just now beginning,
as the drums of Alcatraz throb my spirit
and all the people do a round dance,

And our Earth Mother is in round dance
and all the stars circle our eagle dreams,
and the children of Alcatraz run and play
and glad I am to be a youth of only five hundred
years.

by coyote 2

even as they acknowledge and participate in the change that is inevitably part of all living cultures" (*The Heart as a Drum*, 7). For example, in her powerful poem "The Rock of Our Foundation: Mother Earth," Cheryl Anne Payne (Bautnuq Punguk) masterfully captures the larger metaphor of Alcatraz—the reclamation of Indian Land.

> The symbol of Alcatraz stands for
> All Native people and all Native lands
> Stolen and abused
>
> Alcatraz was desecrated and disrespected
> Left for dead
>
> But the Native People danced and sang life back into
> The Rock of our foundation:
> Mother Earth
>
> —(JOHNSON, *ALCATRAZ: INDIAN LAND FOREVER*, 86)

The contested space of Alcatraz becomes a metaphor for the more complex contact zone of North America, and the only act that resuscitates the Rock (and Indian land) is ceremony—and, of course, this poem itself. Indeed, as Paul Chaat Smith and Robert Warrior note, Indian Alcatraz became "a reservation-like piece of real estate . . . that represented the incarcerated spirit of Indians everywhere" (*Like a Hurricane*, 34).

To reclaim Alcatraz is to reclaim all land previously taken by the very people who constructed the prison there and who saw removal as part and parcel of Manifest Destiny. But the poem also suggests that Alcatraz serves as a symbol for Indians themselves. Like Alcatraz, hundreds of Indian tribes were "desecrated and disrespected / Left for dead," which is to say that the poem's metonymic power extends beyond land to people as well. The poet-occupiers of Alcatraz danced life back into Mother Earth, but they also danced life back into Indian resistance. The poem and the occupation animate Native past and present.

Lonewolf's and Payne's poems not only mobilize language into action, but also serve to establish a sense of place—in this case, the "borderland experience" (in Fast's terms) and the "frontier" (in Louis Owens's) of holding the Rock. Native oral expression has always fused people and land, either through ceremony or story, and once again, in moments of extremis, Native verbal artistry became the string that circumscribed place and the flag that waved above it. So interconnected is language and landscape that, as Leslie Silko notes, it is often unclear which came first, a natural landmark or the story about it. "Narratives," writes Silko, "linked with prominent features of the landscape . . . delineate the complexities of the relationship which human beings must maintain with the surrounding natural world if they hope to survive in this place" ("Interior and Exterior Landscapes," 37).[14] More even than the proclamations, the poems of Alcatraz do the important work of transforming the craggy barrenness of Alcatraz into home. Native tribes had inhabited Alcatraz long before the military or Al Capone; so when the poet-occupiers laid linguistic claim to the Rock, they not only averred a right to the land, they participated in the world-making power of language to root the authors of the poems to the place that is the source of the poem.

Connection through landscape and language is particularly important for contested spaces like reservations, borderlands, and the frontier, which Louis Owens describes as "a space of extreme contestation" ("'The Song Is Very Short,'" 58). Indeed, there is a rich tradition of Native literature that explores the tensions surrounding border conflicts, reservation life, and the removal to alien lands. The poems of the Alcatraz occupation participate in this tradition of location and grounding through the acts of naming the contested space of "Alcatraz" and articulating the border between Indian and non-Indian land. Redrawing borders, reframing arguments, and redirecting conversations needs language—in this case, poetry—to bring the past into relation with the present and to replace the discourse of Alcatraz with the ceremonial discourse of the Indians of All Tribes. Such a project, though, entails more than simply setting up shop. As the poems show, the occupiers used symbolic language to convert occupation into lived interactive experience—what Momaday refers to as "ethical appropriation": "The native American ethic with respect to the physical world is a matter of reciprocal appropriation: appropriations in which man invests himself in the landscape, and at the same time incorporates the landscape into his own most fundamental experience" ("Native American Attitudes to the Environment," 80).

The Indian investment in Alcatraz is often discussed in symbolic terms, which is not inaccurate, but tells only one story. The inhabitants went to great lengths to bring Indianness to Alcatraz and, even more importantly, to import Alcatraz into Indian worldviews. In Payne's "The Rock of Our Foundation: Mother Earth," Momaday's theory is literalized:

> The layers and layers of concrete could not
> stop the flowing of spirit between the Land
> and her People
>
> We danced the Spirit back into the Land
>
> —(JOHNSON, *ALCATRAZ: INDIAN LAND FOREVER*, 86).

Later in the poem, Payne suggests that such an interchange enables the Indians to claim Alcatraz and make it a source of residence and relation: "Yes, we made Alcatraz ours again / We brought back our connection to that 'Sacred Rock'" (87).

Lonewolf demonstrates a similar process in her poems "Alcatraz Medicine" and "Buffalo Song," companion poems written on November 29 and 30. In the former, Alcatraz conveys a form of healing: "Strong wind, dark night, the sound of waves / On the sacred rock of Alcatraz / Will make me a man again" (quoted in Johnson, *Alcatraz: Indian Land Forever*, 91). Similarly, in "Buffalo Song," the occupation engenders renewal:

> Our young men stand brave and tall
> And Alcatraz will never fall!
>
> And once again, sweetgrasses grow
> And once again, the bear, the buffalo!
>
> Ah hai—Ah hai—Ah hai!
>
> —(89)

Both texts appropriate the landscape of Alcatraz into the larger sweep of Native ceremony, and both see the island as a means of renewal.

On the other hand, Peter Blue Cloud's *haibun* (a poetic form that combines haiku and prose) "Alcatraz Is Not an Island" appropriates the accoutrements of Alcatraz into an Indian-centered dance of victory:

> We dance the fog back to the ocean
> And we dance the stars into being.
> Our voices mock the whiteman's fog horn

And soon the fog horns are forgotten,
As are the lights of the surrounding cities.

—(JOHNSON, *ALCATRAZ: INDIAN LAND FOREVER*, 57)

Here, Native ceremony supplants the non-Native infrastructure of Alcatraz, enacting an inversion of the colonial project and delivering a modern version of Wovoka's Ghost Dance to the island. The poem ends with a vision of Indian unity brought about by the dance: "All tribes and unity are the words of the drum and all tribes in unity are the dancers. The ancient dream of Indian unity is begun" (57). For the poet-occupiers, Alcatraz, then, ceased to be simply a locale. These poems ceremonize the rock into Indian Land.

War Paint on the Walls: Alcatraz's "Graffiti" and the Semiotics of Place-Names

If the poet-occupiers invoked the power of verbal expression to name the island, the painter-occupiers staked their claim through the equally powerful mode of semiotics. Over the course of the occupation, the Indians created more than two hundred paintings on walls, buildings, doors, signs, and facilities, and those that remain stand as the most enduring visual evidence of the Indian occupation. These paintings can serve to reinforce an observer's stance about the occupation. Those who see the project as having been unlawful will most likely see the paintings as graffiti; those who think of the occupation as having been necessary will find the images celebratory; those who see the takeover through a lens of anarchy, sedition, or subversion will likely view the works as desecration and defacement; and those who see the occupation as a project of positive resistance and self-determination will understand that the marking of the infrastructure of Alcatraz was a gesture of independence, autonomy, and self-naming.

As with the proclamations and poems, it is useful to consider how the paintings work as tools of engaged resistance—how they interact with both Anglo and Native traditions, how they reach out for an audience, how they rely on the associative force of visual naming to articulate and establish resistance. Momaday's notion of ethical appropriation can certainly be applied to the built environment as well as the natural one, meaning that the establishment of a sense of place requires a reciprocal arrangement with the surroundings. The occupiers lived in the barracks, held meetings in the buildings, arrived on the docks, and held powwows in the courtyards. They also understood the significance of the occupation, so they marked Indian land with Indian symbols, Indian phrases, and Indian images. These paintings endure as a kind of visual diary of Alcatraz's Native history—a diary that the occupiers lived and interacted with every day. Like cave paintings, winter counts, and petroglyphs, these paintings write a people to a place; they inscribe history with humanity.

what are semiotics?

Despite its theoretical baggage, semiotics is largely about humanity, or at least about how humans perceive and receive symbols and signifying practices. In traditional semiotics, one distinguishes between the sign or signifier (the thing itself, in this case, the paintings on Alcatraz's facilities) and the signified (the message the signifier sends).[15] In their fascinating reading of the semiotics of Pueblo pottery and revolt, Patricia W. Capone and Robert W. Preucel borrow from Charles Sanders Pierce, "who considered the sign relation as consisting of the object, the sign, and the interpretant" to argue that pueblo pots "shape popular revitalization discourse" ("Ceramic Semiotics," 101, 111).[16] In their reading of pottery semiotics, Capone and Preucel argue that artists decorated their pots with maps, icons, wind directions, and linguistic symbols in order to enact what they call "an 'iconography of resistance'" (111). My reading of the paintings on the facades of buildings, on water towers, on walls, and, most provocatively, on other signs asserts that the artist-occupiers also re-created an iconography of resistance that has been part of Native aesthetic production for centuries.

Indeed, at the outset of the occupation, a decision was made to change the semiotics of Alcatraz. In December 1969, the occupation's leaders met to lay out both long- and short-term plans for the physical plant of the island. The more ambitious, long-range plans involved building new structures and addressing the water shortage, but in every scenario, there was unified interest in changing the iconic visual markers from those signaling a U.S. governmental facility to ones proclaiming the land to be American Indian inhabited territory. Part of that transformation relied on what we might call "Native semiotics," whose signifiers would overwrite the previous signifiers of the prison and the government. Notes from the minutes taken at the meeting stress that it is "important to use traditional Indian art ideas as basic to the architectural structures so as to be authentic (*Gathering of All Indian Tribes*, 1). Indian iconography, then, began to crop up around the island, both internally and externally, such as the small petroglyphic image pictured in Figure 1.11.

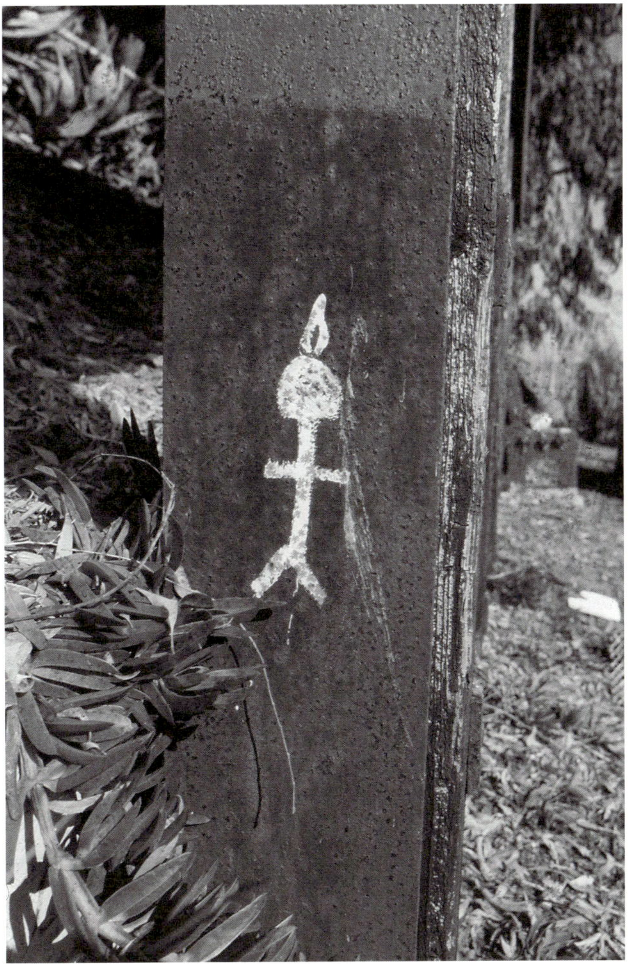

If the proclamatory documents confront the discourse of treaty language and governmental declarations, and the poems take on the machinery of poetic genre and the language of conquest, the paintings attack the symbols of imprisonment, domination, and erasure that have helped evacuate Indians from mainstream American consciousness. When placed alongside the documents and the poems, the paintings form the third branch of a kind of trinity of aesthetic resistance, marking the most comprehensive project of its kind. In other words, the paintings are not separate from these other genres; they are part and parcel of one another, interdependent and intersymbolic.

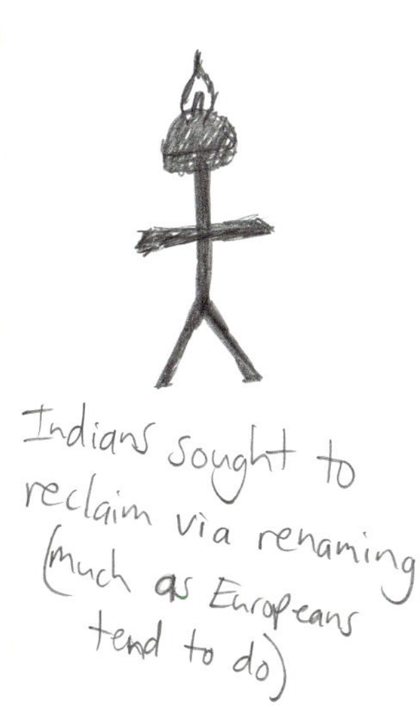

For most Indians, names and symbols carry special significance. They mark boundaries, they identify clans, and they articulate identity. Robert A. Rundstrom makes the case that the "graffiti" on the island was the Indians' way of "placemaking," transforming the non-Indian site of Alcatraz into a thoroughly Indian space. Indeed, there may be no better way of establishing place, of situating, than naming that place. "Placenames are elemental," writes Rundstrom, "to the panhuman experience, often preceding other aspects of the placemaking process" ("American Indian Placemaking," 189). For Rundstrom, the graffiti is about Alcatraz, but as with the poems and other documents, such projects are also about Indian land, broadly conceived. Converting Alcatraz to Indian land didn't just reclaim Alcatraz for the Indians, it also inverted all Indian place-names that were replaced by "Manhattan," "New York," "California," "San Francisco," "Texas," "Washington, D.C.," "Georgia," and the countless other instances of whitewashing.

Though local markers do crop up now and then around the island, the most prominent place name is "Indian Land." Certain designations appeared in particular kinds of places. For example, tribal affiliations and tribal phrasings tend to be localized—in rooms, on interior walls—and most of the prominent spaces were marked with signs expressing more global concerns: Indians of All Tribes, Indian Land, Peace, and Red Power. In Ilka

FIGURE 1.11. *A neopetroglyph on the island. Courtesy of the U.S. Department of the Interior, National Park Service.*

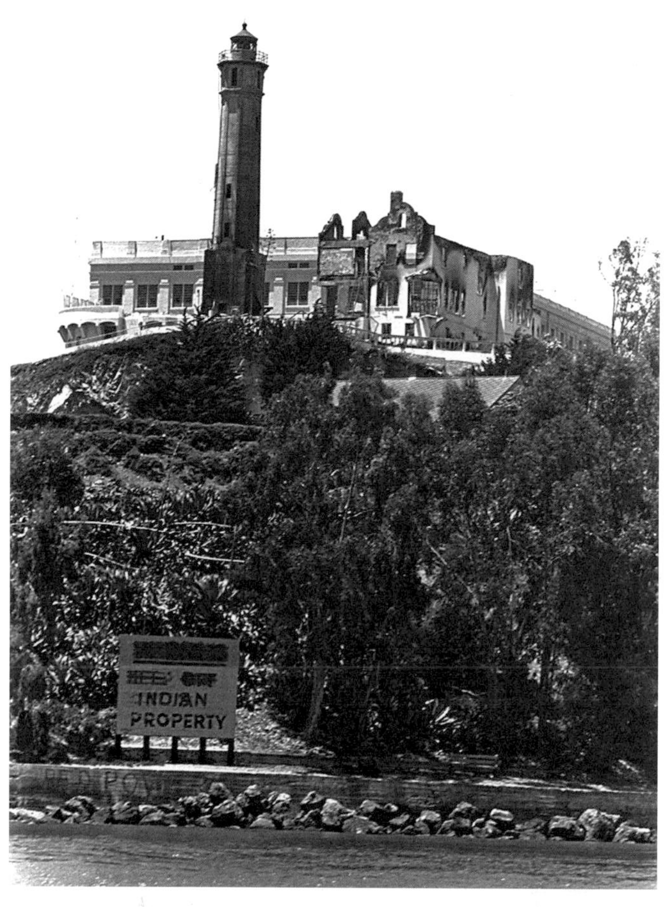

1.12

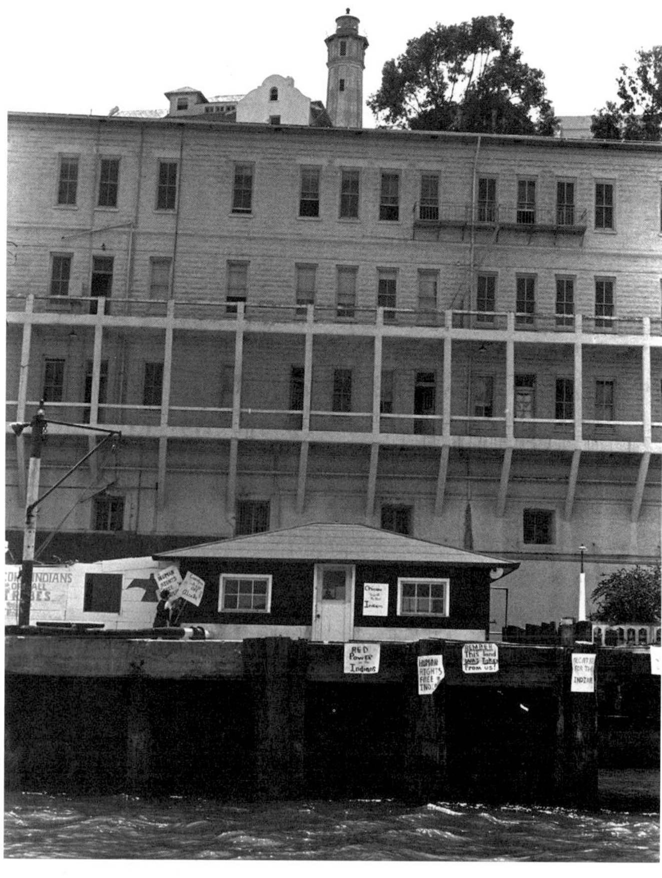

1.13

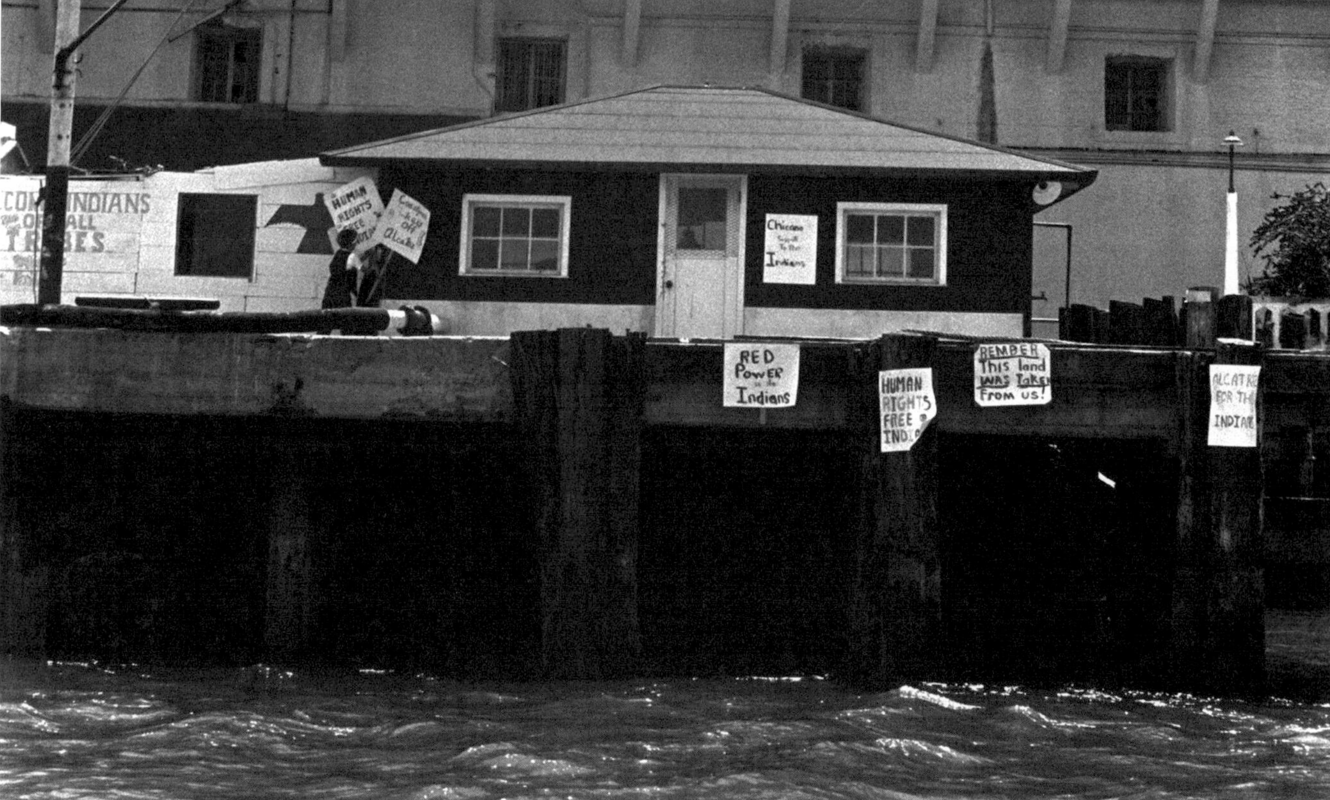

1.14

Hartmann's wonderful photos of the dock signs (Figs. 1.13 and 1.14), one gets a sense of the competing sloganizing on this newly acquired land, like billboards going up in a new state. The occupiers wanted to advertise. They wanted to start over. They wanted, like Adam, to name. Because they knew who they were as people, they began by naming their new land, that which had been acquired. Some signage veers from slogans to the merely prosaic (Fig. 1.15) or straightforward (Fig. 1.16). Nonetheless, to go to such trouble to label a place means one has an intended outcome and, connected to this, an intended audience, or to invoke the language of Capone, Preucel, and Pierce, an "interpretant." Some scholars have argued that these signs were messages to the media and governmental agents, both of whom read, scrutinized, and interpreted the occupation. But, I think the messages go beyond external signification. Clearly, identity is also internal. No one needed to interpret those signs more than the occupiers themselves. At their core, the signs attempt to right a

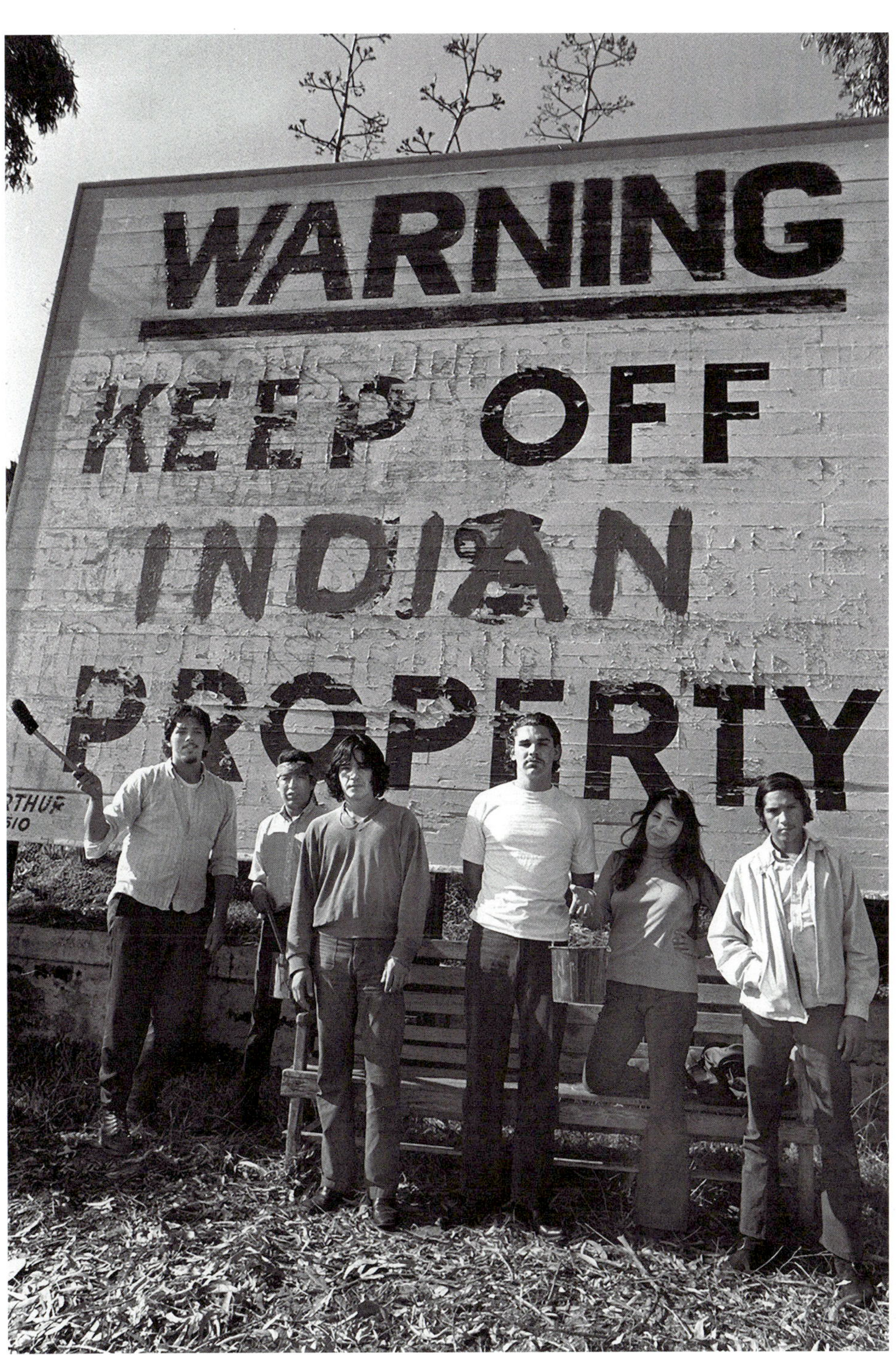

FIGURE 1.12. (facing page) *Signs announcing the bold act of the occupiers. New arrivals and passing vessels from all over the world were greeted by these messages. Naming (and claiming) the island became part of the placemaking for Indian Alcatraz. Note "Red Power" painted on the retaining wall below the wooden sign. Photo by Ilka Hartmann, © 2010.*

FIGURE 1.13. (facing page) *Handmade signs along the dock, indicating new ownership of the island. Labeling the new space was part placemaking, part public relations. Photo by Ilka Hartmann, © 2010.*

FIGURE 1.14. (facing page) *Dock sign detail.* *Left to right:* Welcome Indians Of All Tribes; Human Rights Free Indians; Coast Guard Keep Off Alcatraz; Red Power To The Indians; Chicano Support To The Indians; Human Rights Free Indians; Remember, This Land Was Taken From Us; Alcatraz For The Indians. *Photo by Ilka Hartmann, © 2010.*

FIGURE 1.15. (left) *Portions of former signifiers left visible, making it clear the occupiers were writing over the previously authoritative text. Photo by Vince Maggoria, 1969. Courtesy of the* San Francisco Chronicle.

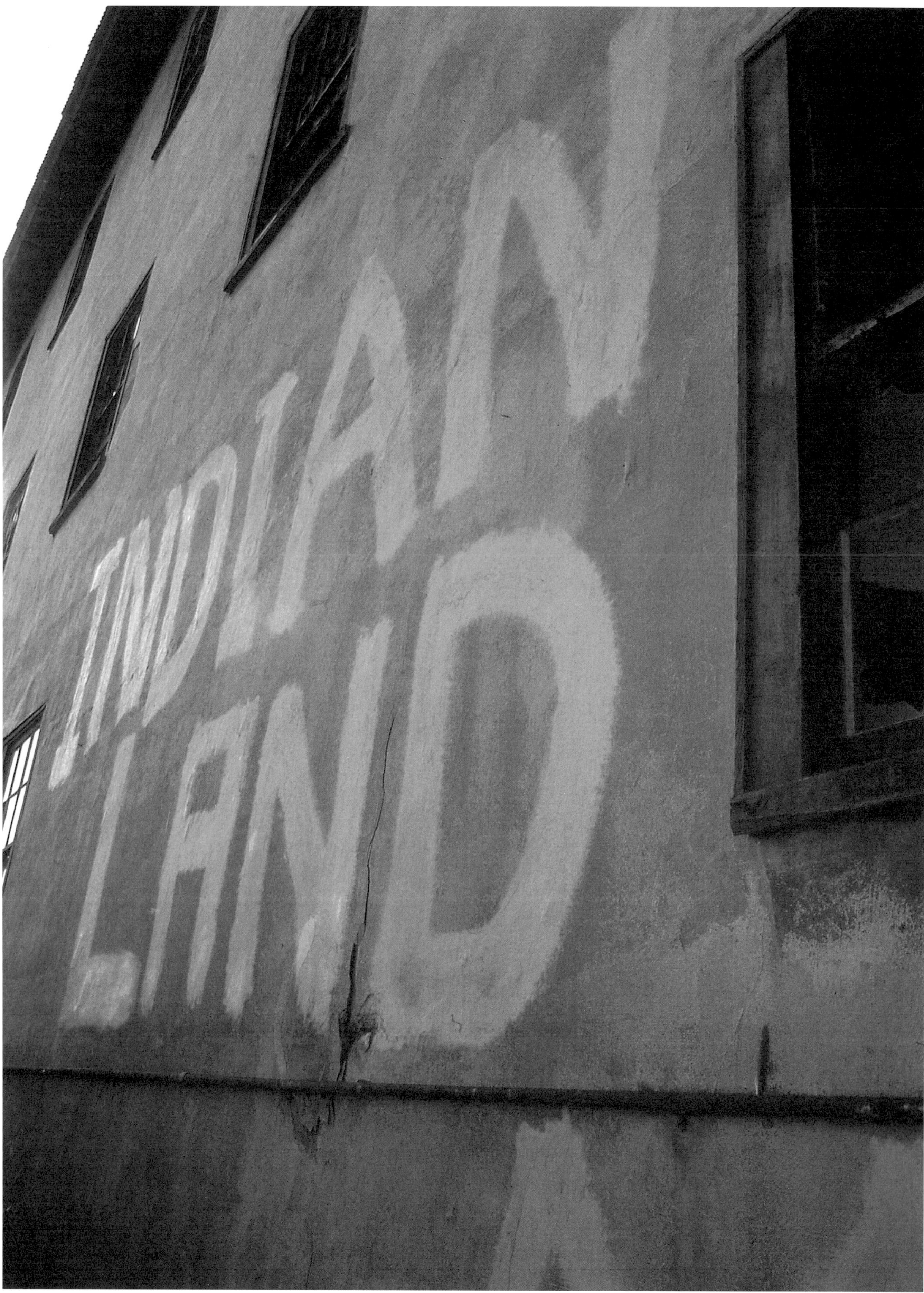
INDIAN
LAND

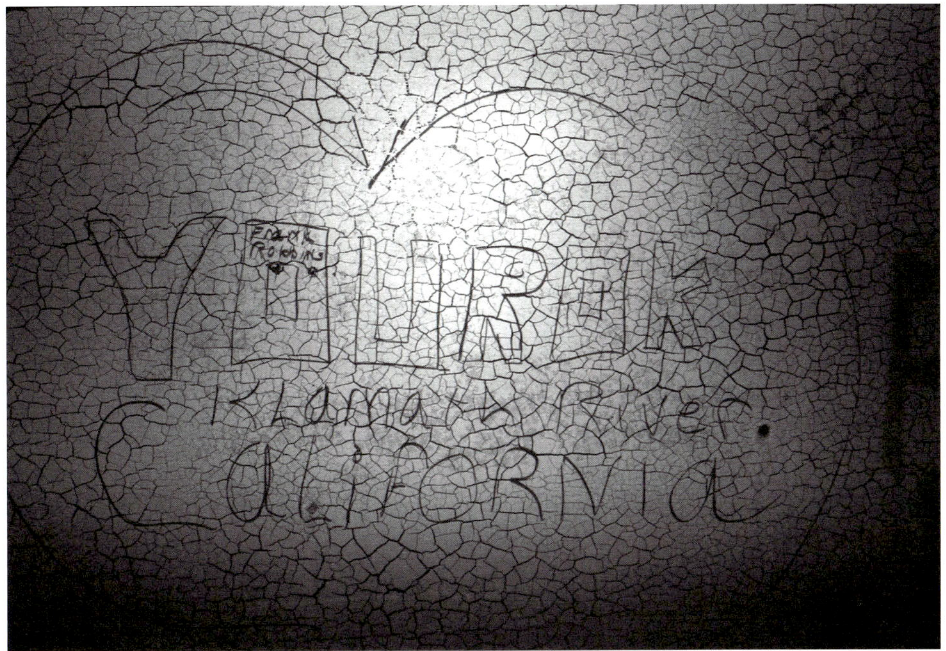

FIGURE 1.16. (facing page) *"Indian Land," one of the more popular slogans for the occupiers. Courtesy of the U.S. Department of the Interior, National Park Service.*

FIGURE 1.17. (top) *Drawing on the inside of one of the barracks, denoting the Youroks. Courtesy of the U.S. Department of the Interior, National Park Service.*

FIGURE 1.18. (bottom) *An interesting blend of a tribal-specific greeting (the Navajo Ya-ta-hey) and Pan-Indian sentiment (Red Power). Courtesy of the U.S. Department of the Interior, National Park Service.*

wrong, to refocus attention from the transgressive government and orient it toward their own sovereign society.

As I suggest above, this happens on large and small scales. For example, inside the barracks were tribally specific rooms, such as those for the Sioux and Pomo. To this day, there are several instances of tribal affiliations inscribed on walls and doors of the barracks, as with the Yurok painting (Fig. 1.17) and the Navajo "*Ya-Ta-Hey!*" (Fig. 1.18).[17]

On the other hand, grand gestures like painting the smokestack (Fig. 1.19) were unmistakable, large-scale statements of intent. The message of peace to all painted in bold red letters on a big chimney evokes Christmas. Given that the occupation extended over two Christmas seasons, perhaps the Indians celebrated the new gift of their land. Much like the smokestack, the water tower (Fig. 1.20) serves as a focal point for the visual plane but

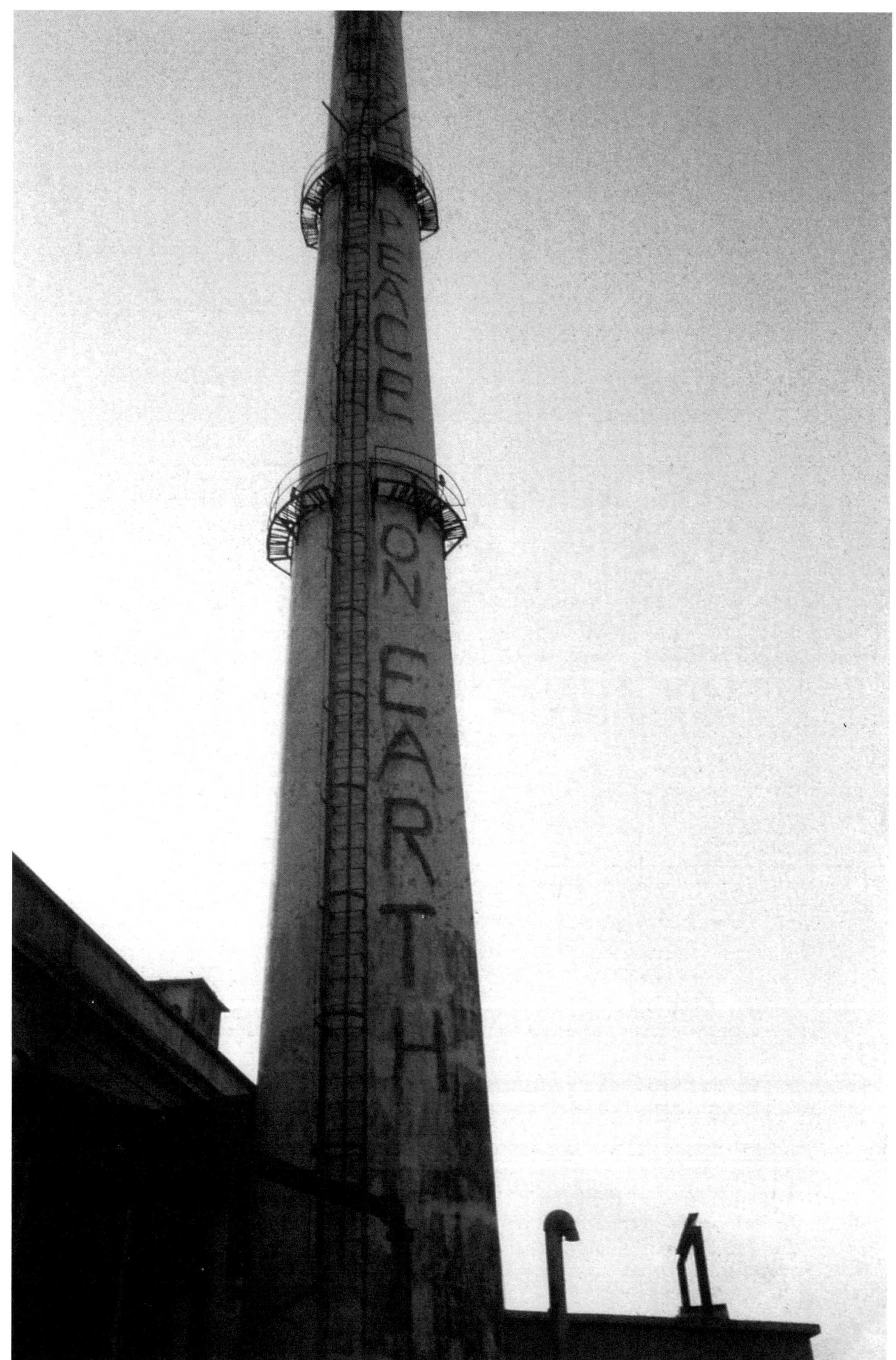
PEACE ON EARTH

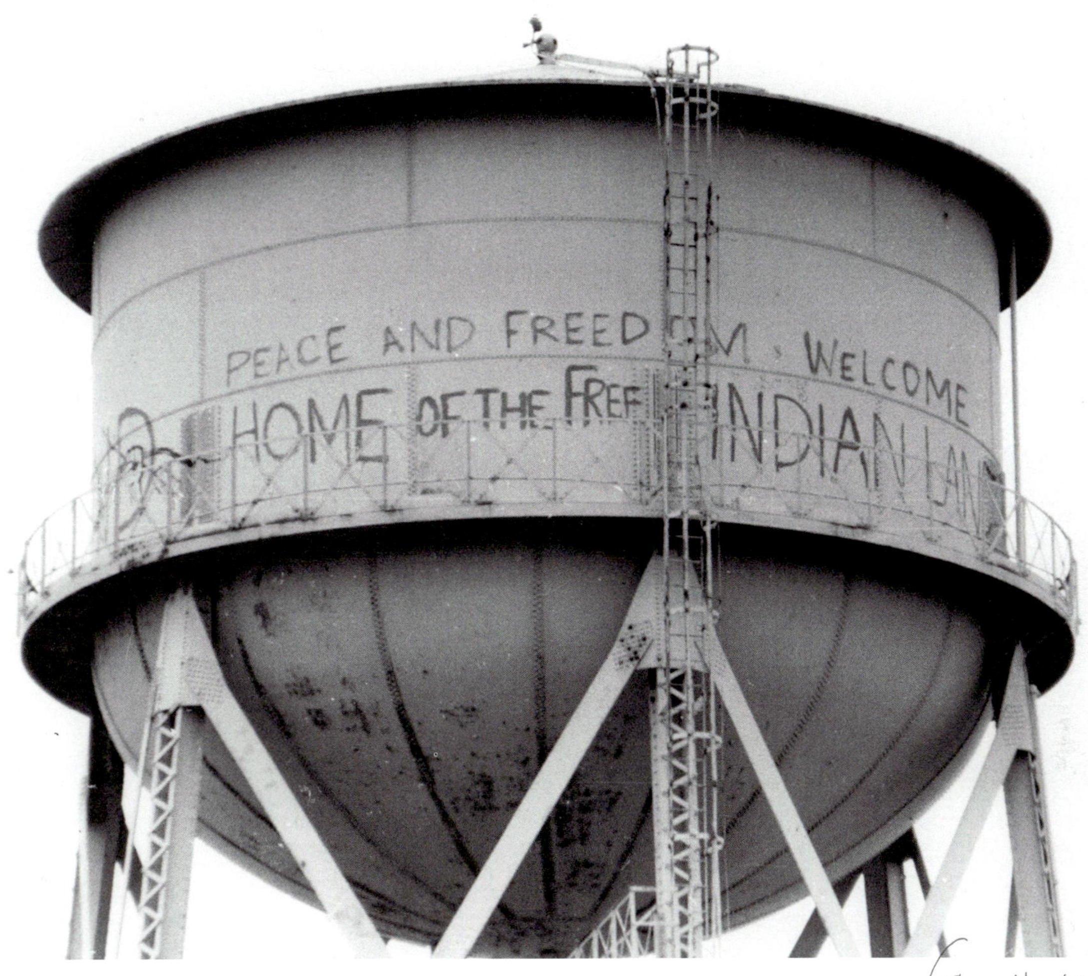

also for the contextual one. In fact, the painting of the water tower holds particular interest because of the role water towers and grain elevators often play in community identification. Anyone who has lived in or visited a small American town knows how common it is to paint the local water tower with either the town's name or, as in Yukon, Oklahoma, identifying information such as "Home of Garth Brooks" or "State Football Champions, 1988." The Alcatraz water tower's message of peace and welcome does similar work: it announces the identifying principles of the occupation (peace and freedom), and it catapults the island's new identity as "Indian Land" up into the sky for everyone to see.

Nothing says Indian Alcatraz, though, like the famous welcome sign above the main entrance to the old barracks (Figs. 1.21 and 1.22). Still the first thing tourists see as they step off the boat and onto the island, the sign is a loaded semiotic text that, along with the water tower, has come to stand as a visual remnant of the occupation (Fig. 1.23). As Rundstrom notes, "The shadowy remains of the words written on the barracks building and the water tower persist today as the most tangible expressions of Alcatraz as an Indian place" ("American Indian Placemaking," 189). In both instances, a gesture of reception, of salutation, is given prominence through placement and scale. Also, both signs signal a transfer of power from the government to the Indians. Control of utility structures like water towers indicates ownership and proprietary involvement that goes beyond mere squatting. Converting the official governmental sign above Alcatraz did similar work through an

FIGURE 1.19. (facing page) *Perhaps a Native version of the Washington Monument. The "Peace on Earth" smokestack did major semiotic work. The paint has since worn completely off. Courtesy of the U.S. Department of the Interior, National Park Service.*

FIGURE 1.20. (above) *A Native version of the small-town and suburban tradition of painting municipal markers on the local water tower. The faintest traces of the words are still visible. Courtesy of the U.S. Department of the Interior, National Park Service.*

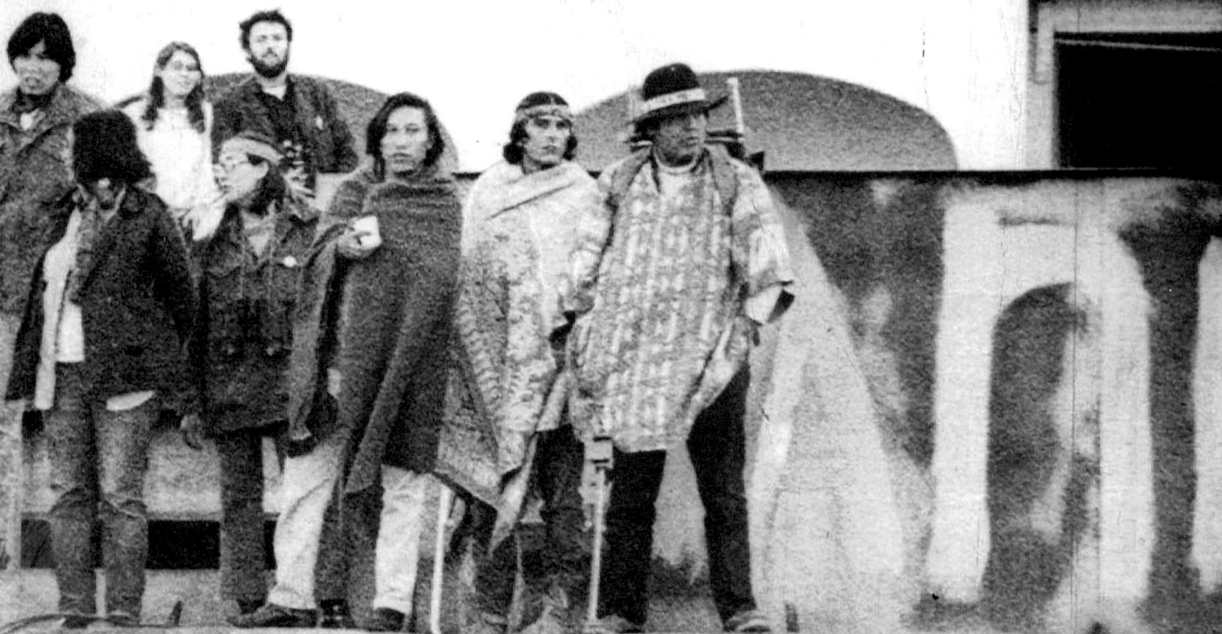
INDIANS
WELCOME
UNITED INDIAN
PROPERTY
ALCATRAZ ISLAND AREA 12 ACRES
1½ MILES TO TRANSPORT DOCK
ALLOWED ASHORE
WITHOUT A PASS
INDIAN LAND

inversion of the discourse of federal naming: the simple act of erasing the bureaucratized language of sanctioned governmental semiotics. In short, it endows the Indians with the same authority as the more sterile but sanctioned federal sign. More importantly, though, the Indian version embodies the dialogic nature of the occupation: welcome (engagement) and assertion (resistance). The same interplay animates the "Ya-Ta-Hey!" painting. The performative aspect of the Navajo language bridges "Red Power" and "Peace." For some, these two ideologies are at odds with each other, but for the occupiers, they are two sides of the same shield. War paint on and war paint off: same person, same identity.

But identity is a complex business. In this case, the semiotics of the graffiti signifies both engagement and resistance. The water tower might welcome, but other signs caution

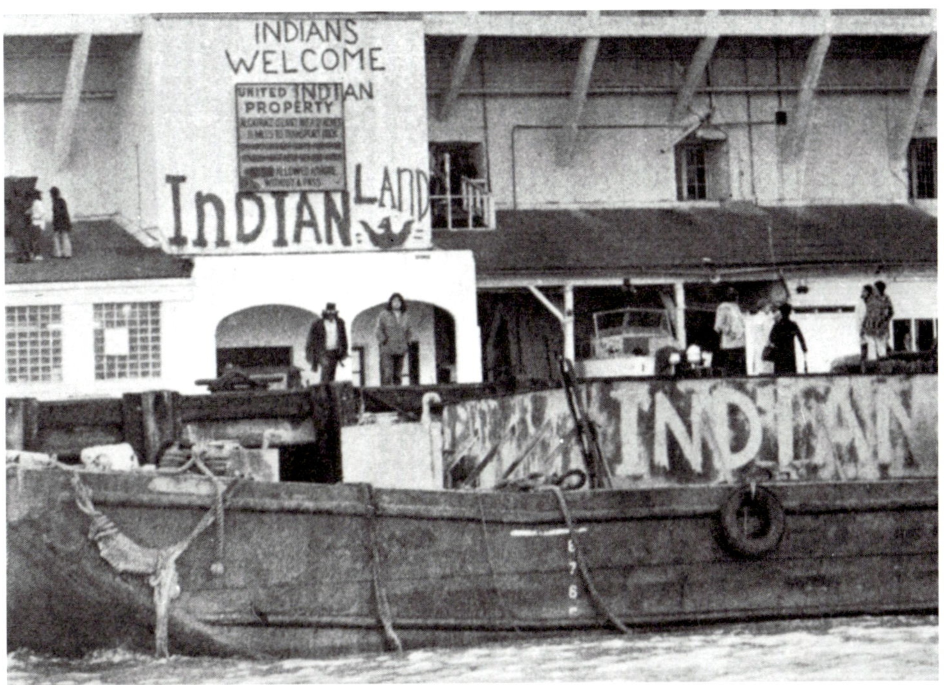

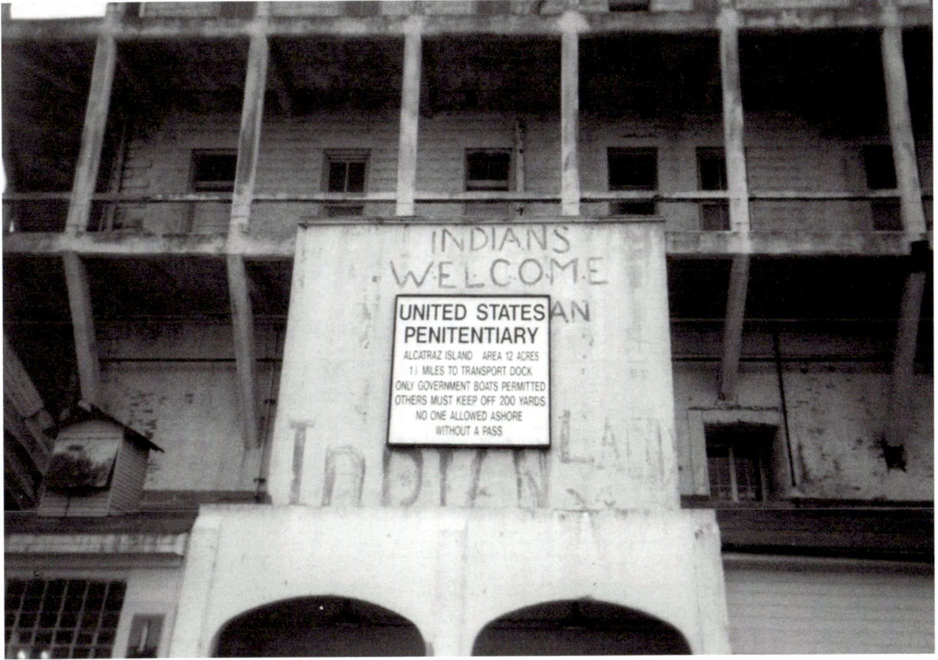

FIGURE 1.21. (facing page) *The exclusionary language of the Alcatraz sign converted to a message of inclusion on Indian Land. The pan-Indian gesture "United Indian Property" is also of import. Photo by Vince Maggoria, 1970. Courtesy of the* San Francisco Chronicle.

FIGURE 1.22. (top) *Wide-angle shot of the sign, 1970. Courtesy of the U.S. Department of the Interior, National Park Service.*

FIGURE 1.23. (bottom) *The sign in 2003. Note that the "United Indian Property" sign is gone. Photo by the author.*

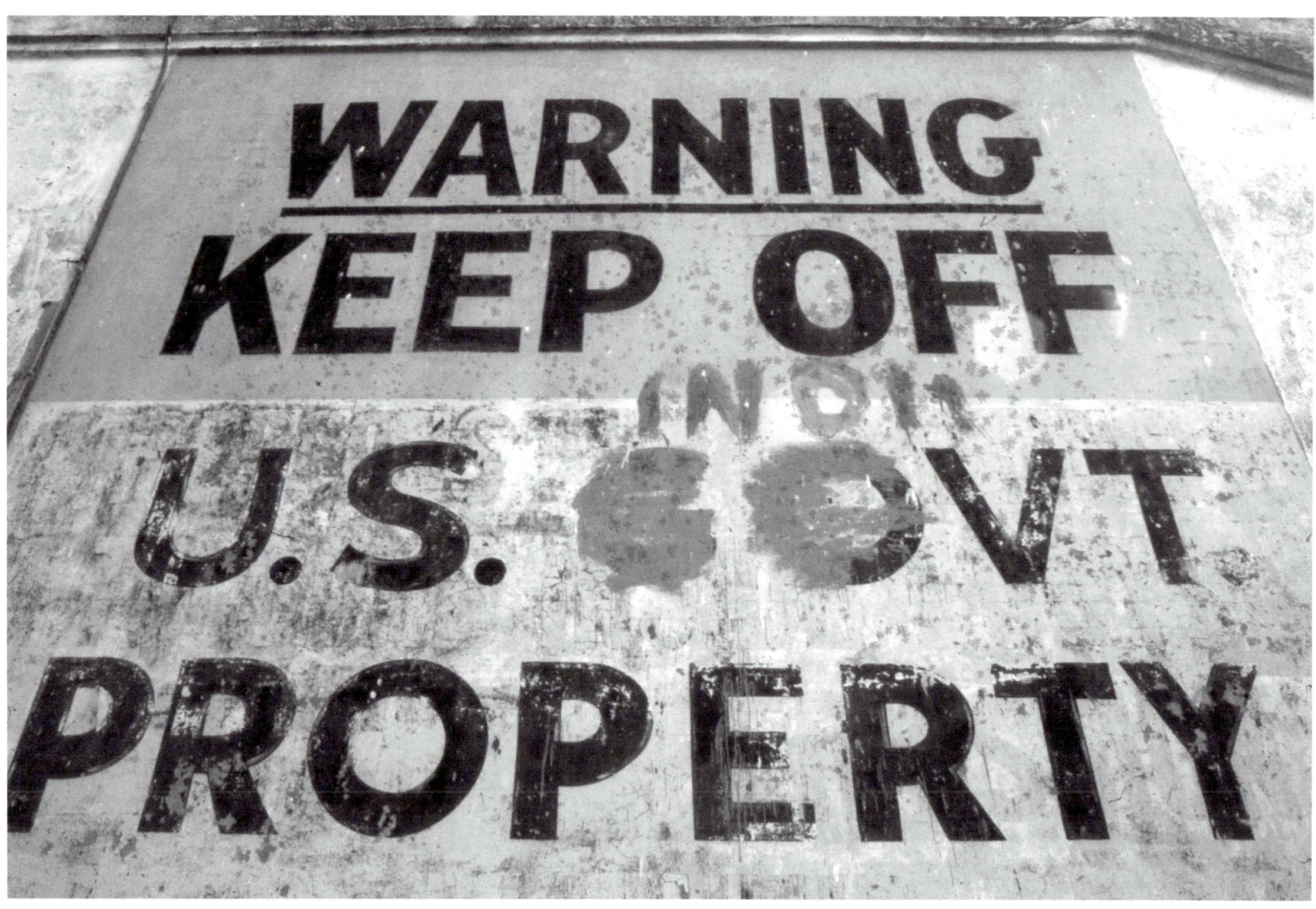

FIGURE 1.24. *One of the iconic signs cautioning would-be trespassers. This seems to be more about converting governmental signifiers than actually urging people to stay away. Courtesy of the U.S. Department of the Interior, National Park Service.*

FIGURES 1.25 and 1.26. (facing page) *Minimodes of placemaking. More private than public, these functioned much as posters or art prints would in a home: they defined belief and reinforced vision. Courtesy of the U.S. Department of the Interior, National Park Service.*

FIGURE 1.27. (facing page) *As though painted in blood. This room, which belonged to Oakes, contains many loaded signifiers. Courtesy of the U.S. Department of the Interior, National Park Service.*

(Fig. 1.24). In the case of the large repurposed admonition, this was often one of the first written messages people would see when approaching Alcatraz from the Fisherman's Wharf dock. Its play on standard "Keep Off / Private Property" signs, popular with white ranchers and landowners, suggests there might be some sort of reprisal for trespassing. Similarly, some of the most common phrases marking the halls of Alcatraz are references to George Armstrong Custer, the American ~~general~~ Lt Col who led his troops to slaughter at the Battle of the Little Bighorn. For the occupiers, as for many Indians, Custer stands as a symbol not simply of American racism and violence but also of Indian triumph. Throughout the barracks, phrases referencing Custer's defeat are intertwined with mottos of Indian assertion. For example, in room 4 of building 64, the following phrases are painted into the walls: "We discovered America," "Our land, we will not give it up," "Power to all of us," "Indian Power," "Custer was white." Three phrases, "We the Indians discovered America," (Fig. 1.25) "Custer was white," and "Custer had it coming" (Fig. 1.26), appear most frequently inside the buildings. Each of these responds to popular stereotypes and American myths about Indian civilization, Indian passivity, and Indian indigeneity. One of the most compelling images, the combination wall-and-door painting of an Indian profile and the phrase "Taken by Oakes" (Fig. 1.27), makes a semiotic connection between the radiant Indian head profile and American coins, dollars, and even the haloed head of Jesus. The sloppily scrawled "Taken By Oakes" seems to have been drawn in blood. When taken together, the iconic and the verbal signifiers lay claim to the Indian land, its purchase, reversing the centuries of indigenous displacement, when countries seized land by right of discovery.

In this same vein are the larger assertions of pan-Indian authority, most notably the various permutations of "Red Power" seen around the island (Figs. 1.28 and 1.29). Of

Again, the Alcatraz occupiers utilize Euro/American iconography & text to send a message: We're taking this shit back

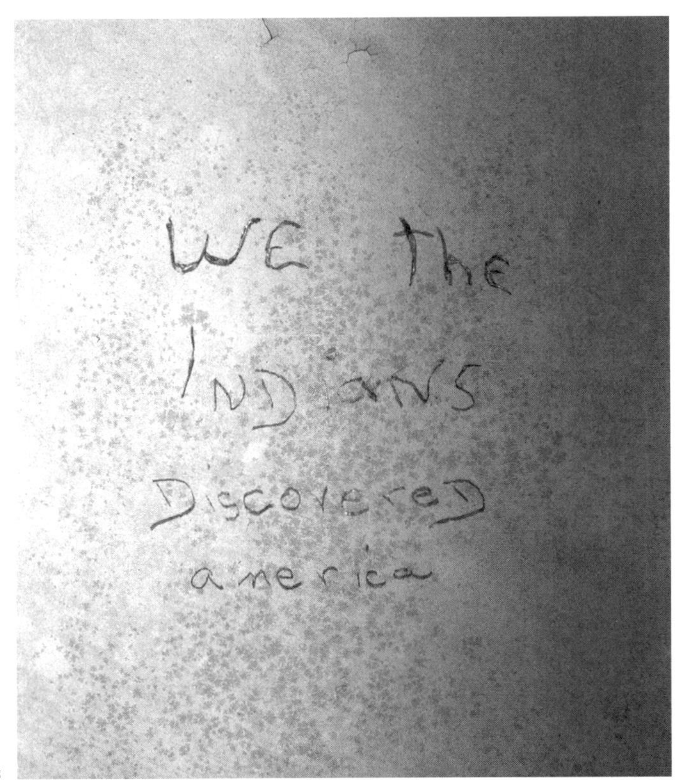
WE the
INDians
Discovered
america

1.25

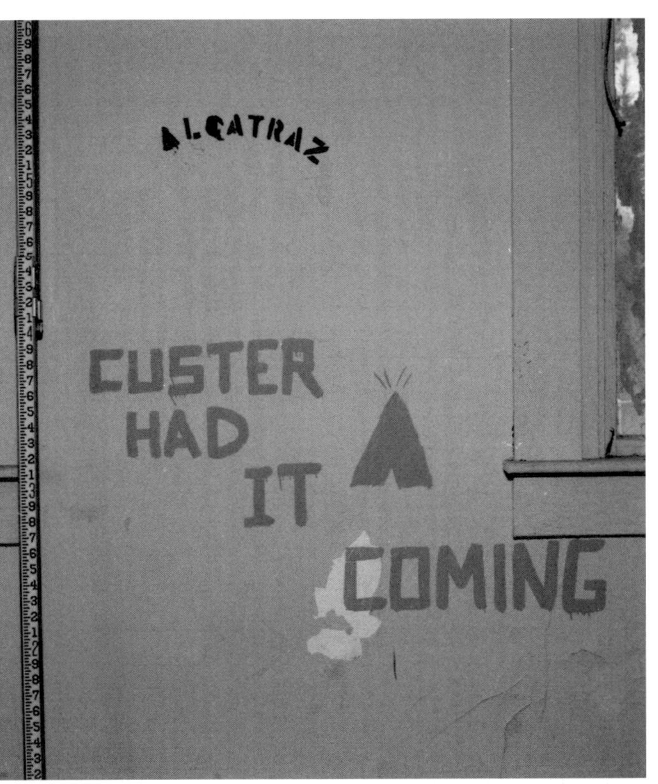
ALCATRAZ
CUSTER
HAD
IT
COMING

1.26

1.27

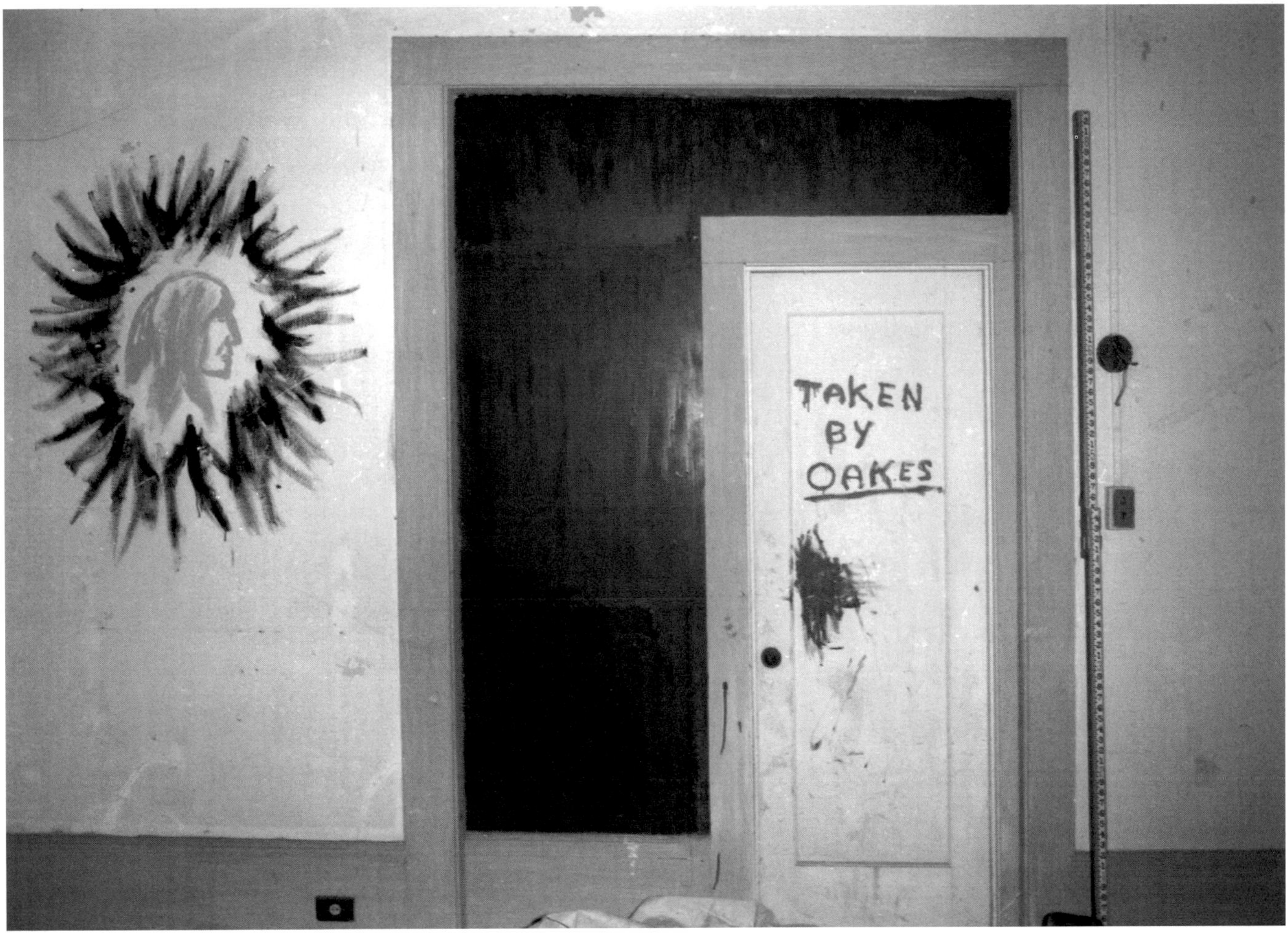

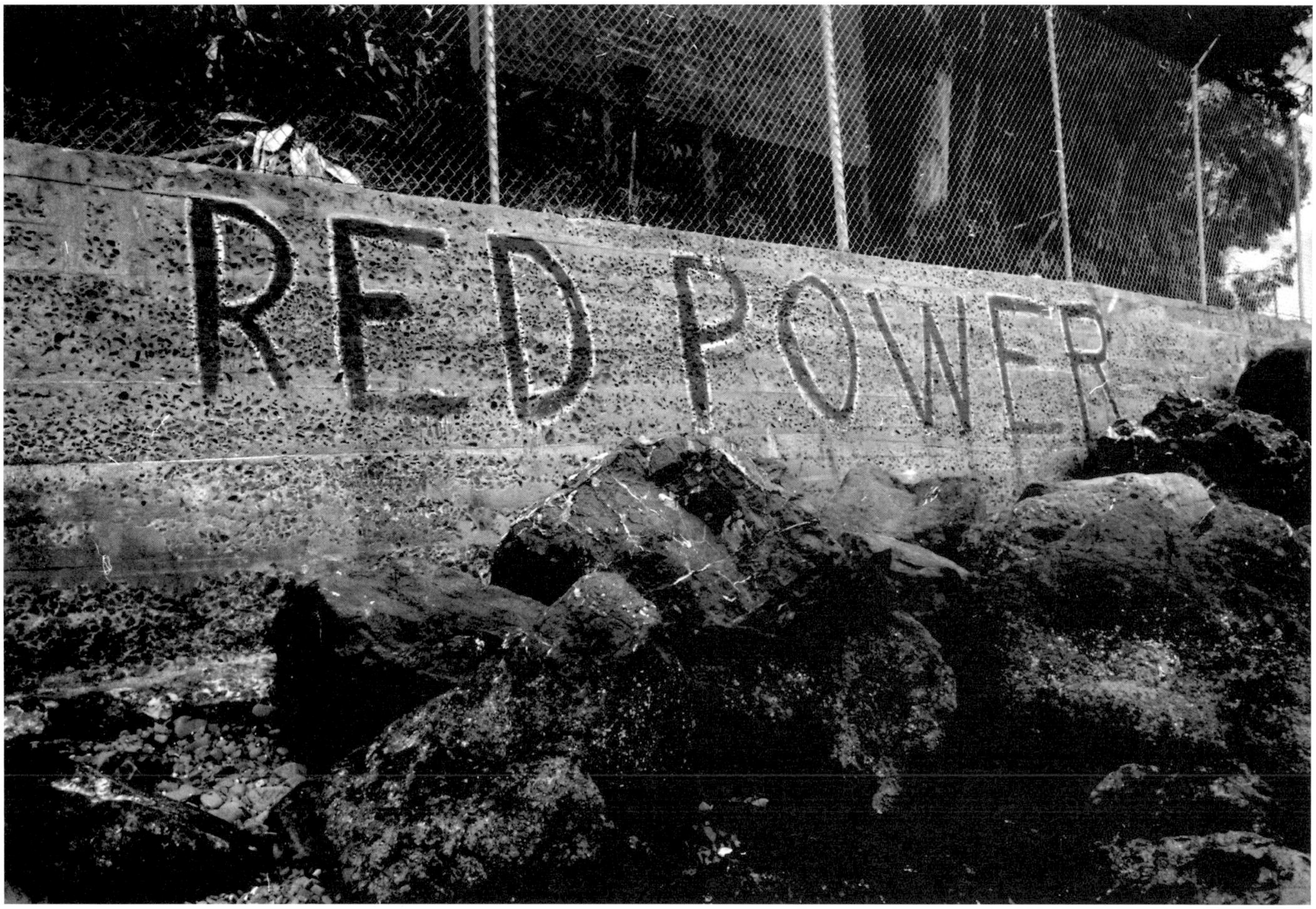

1.28

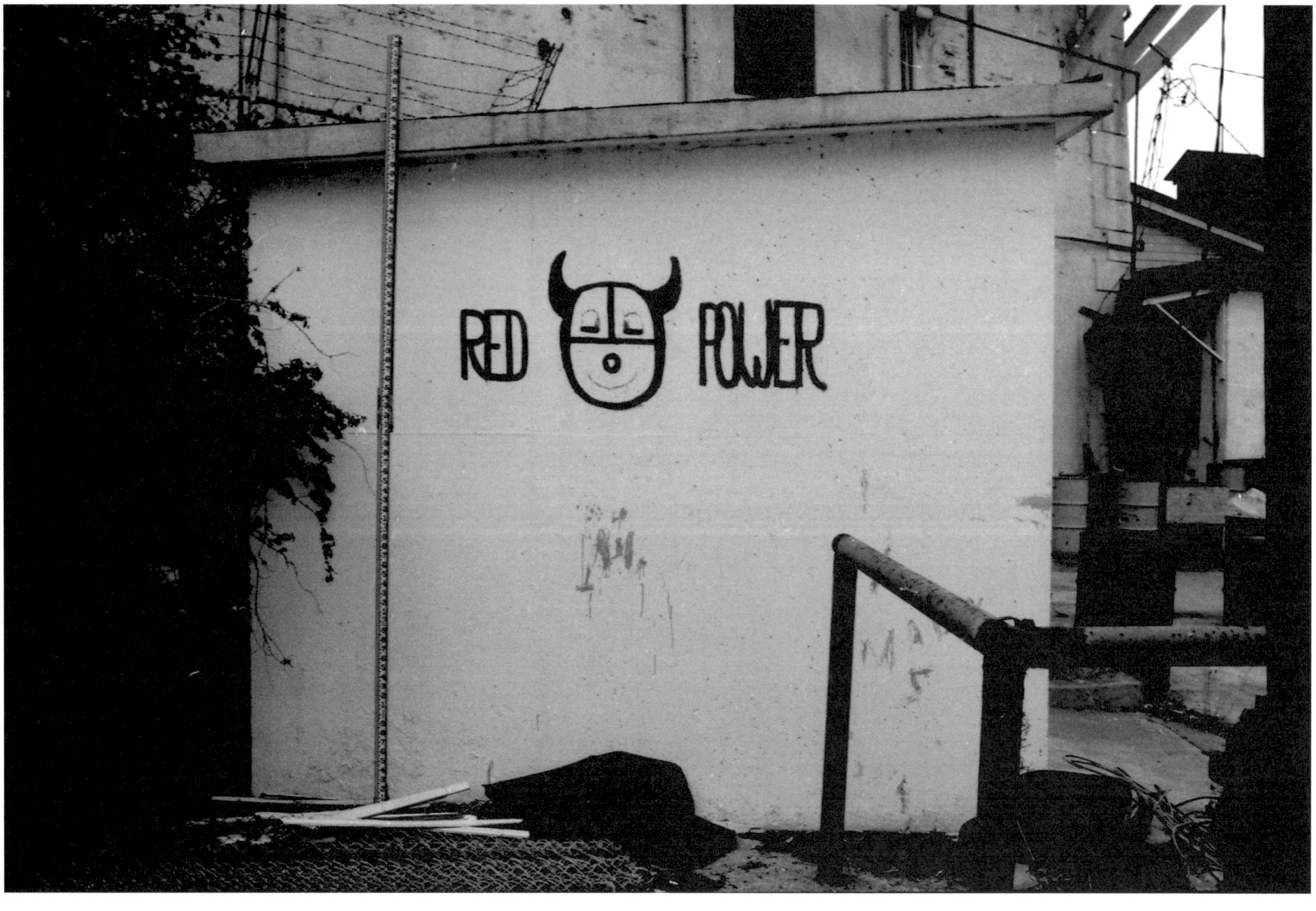

1.29

course, the term plays off the Black Power movement that rocked the 1960s and 1970s, but the occupiers made it their own. While the associations may not have been intentional, most of the Red Power phrases are painted in red, reinforcing Alcatraz's redness, both literally and metaphorically. Additionally, the associative qualities of red—anger, war, aggression, blood—attend whatever cultural work the linguistic connotations and denotations might be doing. That said, the images here skew toward the soft side. The first painting (Fig. 1.28) is outlined in white, sort of tucked away against a wall, at knee level, nearly obscured by stones. The font is neither threatening nor violent. On the contrary, the painting seems a part of the environment in which it is situated. Similarly, its counterpart (Fig. 1.29), the endearing painting on the side of the building (the painting still exists, though it has faded) appears to be almost an afterthought. The small, unassuming font coupled with a sweet, smiley (almost sleepy) face evokes a kinder, gentler Red Power than the one that presumably seized the island. Yet again, the aesthetic texts of Alcatraz unite seemingly opposite gestures (here, warmth and aggression) to counter prevailing assumptions of Indian sovereignty, facility, and authority.

These dueling yet complementary forces found their most sophisticated realization in the occupiers' subversive deconstruction of an American eagle sculpture above one of the main entrances (Fig. 1.30). Typically, such a sculpture—an American eagle, its wings outstretched, gripping the icon of the American penal system with its talons—is signifier enough because it embodies so many sacred American values. On Indian Alcatraz, though, American symbols had no truck. The occupiers abrogated standard patriotic principles by transforming the eagle into a kind of tchotchke. Draped around the eagle's neck hangs a homemade sign, "This land is my land," and taped to that is a classic portrait of Geronimo holding a gun. A fine example of mixed signification, the sign can mean many things. On one hand, through the reference to Woody Guthrie's song of peace, the sign reinforces the various inscriptions of peace found on the island. Invoking the notion of reciprocity that is part of Indian place making, the sign invites interchange and a rejection of Manifest Destiny. On the other hand, the American government might have been the audience for the sign, which could be taken as a reminder to federal officials that while the land of the eagle is American land, Alcatraz is Indian land. Still another reading of the sign makes it an invitation, a greeting card, to the occupiers, letting them know that this land is their land. Somehow, the casualness of the sign and the lyrics undermines the authority and triumphalism of the eagle. In this reading, the eagle, perched above the doorway, becomes the inversion of fetishized Indian petroglyphs and those howling coyotes sporting bandanas—a humorous stereotype of American symbolism.

Geronimo's defiant visage adds another layer of resistance here. His stern expression, his posture of resistance, his refusal to be appropriated or mocked stand in stark contrast to what the eagle has become. Just as the documents and the poems make Native traditions and history part of their artillery, so too does Geronimo's mythos become part of the weaponry of this piece. Geronimo's face stands in for the countless, faceless thousands who were eradicated, imprisoned, and removed by the same federal ideology that created Alcatraz. Any way you look at it, the décor of the eagle becomes a sculpture, an assemblage of resistance.

At a later point in the occupation, the sign and photo were taken down, and someone painted, in large red letters across the shield, the word "free." This simple word performs as demand, statement, label.[18] In its simplicity lie layers of complexity. Even so, setting the cell block free liberated the entire island.[19] "In two deft moves," writes Rundstrom, "the island, the cell house, the symbolic power of the eagle and flag, and a popular national anthem all had been appropriated. In addition, the spirit of a prison and a people had been marked for freedom in one stroke of placemaking" ("American Indian Placemak-

FIGURE 1.28. (facing page) *Large "Red Power" sign, now gone. Courtesy of the U.S. Department of the Interior, National Park Service.*

FIGURE 1.29. (facing page) *"Red Power" sign with an image that bears a strong resemblance to a Hopi kachina. The sign is at present partially preserved behind Plexiglas. Courtesy of the U.S. Department of the Interior, National Park Service.*

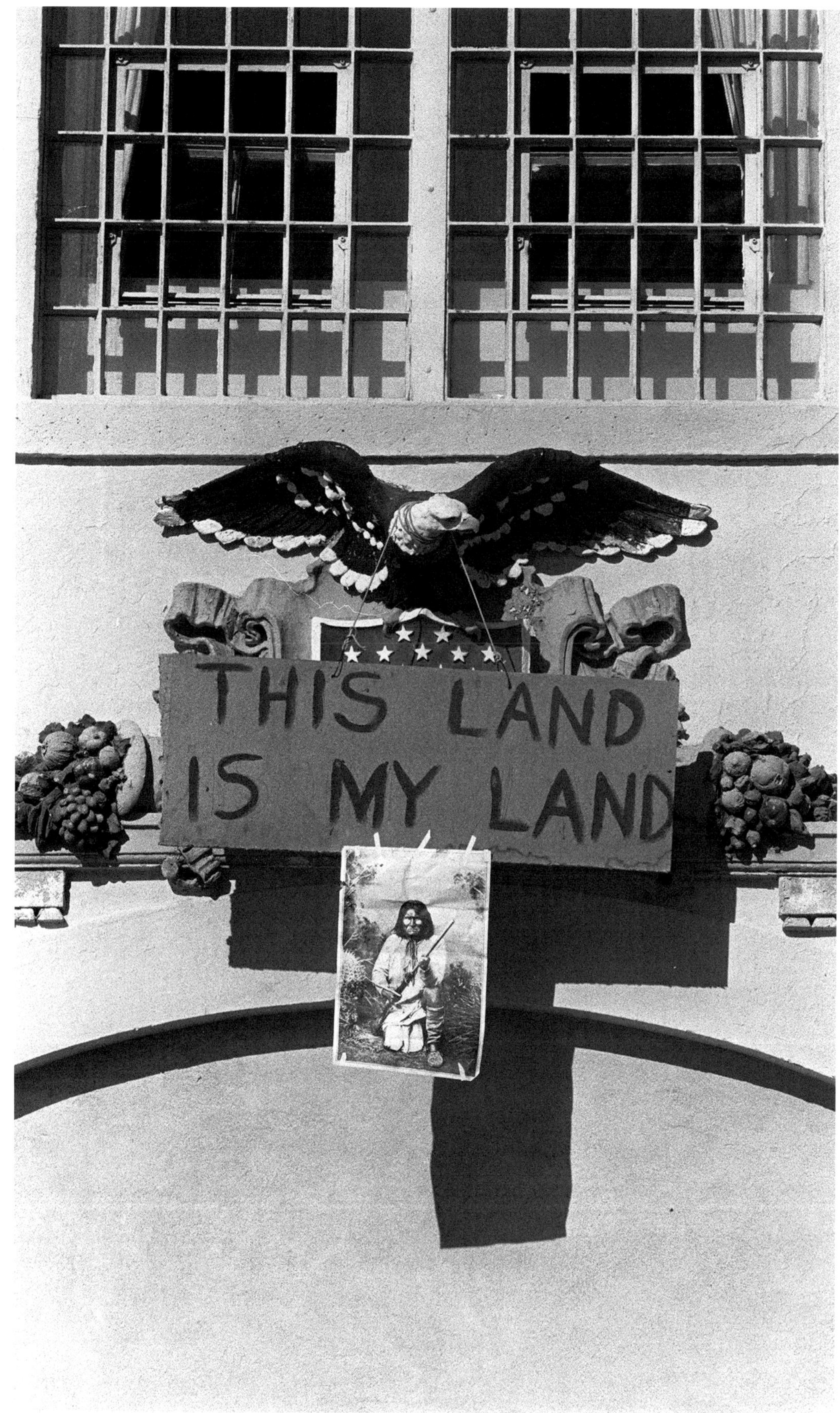

FIGURE 1.30. (right) *The most interesting and complex example of Alcatraz placemaking. Photo by Vince Maggoria, 1969. Courtesy of the* San Francisco Chronicle.

FIGURE 1.31. (facing page) *Another example of "graffiti" maintained by the National Park Service, 2003. It is remarkable that these examples of "defacement" are being preserved. Photo by author.*

FIGURE 1.32. (facing page) *The main building on the day of the fire that effectively ended the occupation. Photo by Vince Maggoria. Courtesy of the* San Francisco Chronicle, *© 1971.*

ing," 191). As Michel Foucault argues in *Discipline and Punish*, prisons have always been about control and surveillance. They often function as the machinery of power and subjugation. The subversions the occupiers performed on the eagle, then, become a metonym for the entire occupation. It dismantles, through visual and verbal performative language, the cultural and historical machinery of colonial control and cultural incarceration. The freedom of authority then rested in the hands of the Indians.

The most common "final" image of Alcatraz, the era's visual symbol of resistance and defiance—a closed fist—reinforces this notion of authority (Fig. 1.32). The semiotics of that stark fist tell us that the Indians will endure beyond Alcatraz, that their defiance will outlast the coast guard that removed them from the island. It reminds the viewer that the new boss is the same as the old boss; Indians have been removed from their land for centuries. Even so, Indians never disappear. They always survive.

When the coast guard removed the last of the holdouts on June 11, 1971, the government was unable to remove sentiment for the occupation from American consciousness. Across the country there was support. Donations and visits from rock stars like Bob Dylan, Janis Joplin, and Credence Clearwater Revival; the radio program *Radio Free Alcatraz*, which was broadcast in New York, Los Angeles, and San Francisco; and the hundreds of letters and telegrams that flooded the offices of local, state, and federal officials (including President Nixon) attested to the support of even mainstream Americans. What's more, Alcatraz gave birth to the more aggressive manifestations of Indian activism that would later drive the Red Power movement and the American Indian Movement. Without question, the occupation of Alcatraz was the antecedent for the occupation of the Bureau of Indian Affairs in Washington, D.C., in 1972 and for the standoff at Wounded Knee a year later. Indeed the best studies of Native Activism—Smith and Warrior's *Like a Hurricane: The Indian Movement from Alcatraz to Wounded Knee*; Johnson, Nagel, and Champagne's *American Indian Activism: Alcatraz to the Longest Walk*; and Teuton's *Red Land, Red Power*—locate the origination point of such activism in Alcatraz. Unlike most narratives of resistance, the occupation's mythology was matched by its reality.

Two important paintings that Indian Joe Morris completed during the occupation speak to this mythology. In the first (Fig. 1.33), an Indian chief with an impressive headdress straddles Alcatraz as though he

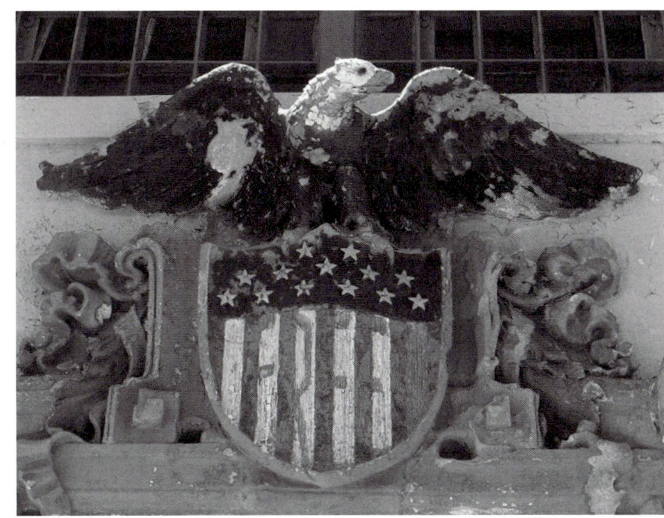

1.31

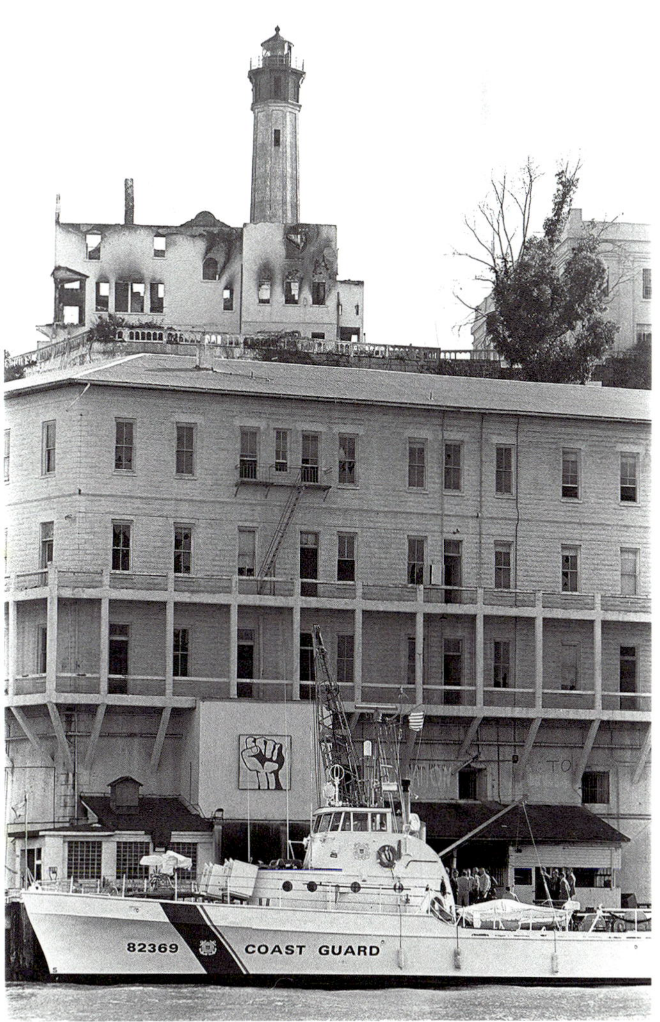

1.32

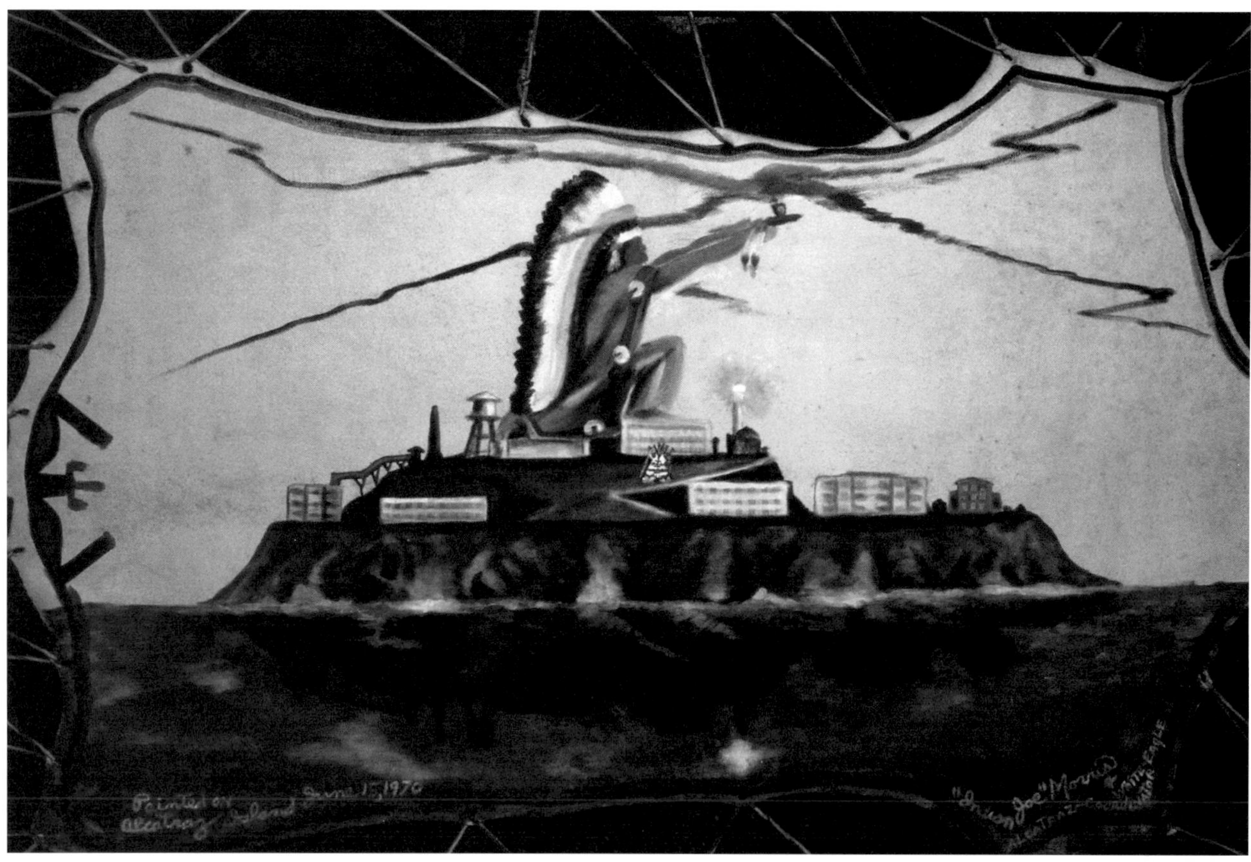
Painted on Alcatraz Island June 15, 1970
"Indian Joe" Morris

1.33

Richard Oakes
Joe Bill
David Leach
Fred Shelton
John White Fox
Ross Hardin
Kay Many Horse
John Martell
Rick Evening
14 Eagle Feathers Represents 14 Braves That defied the United States Armed Forces on Nov. 14, 1969 by
taking Alcatraz Island and returning it to
The Rightful Owners — the
American - Indian.

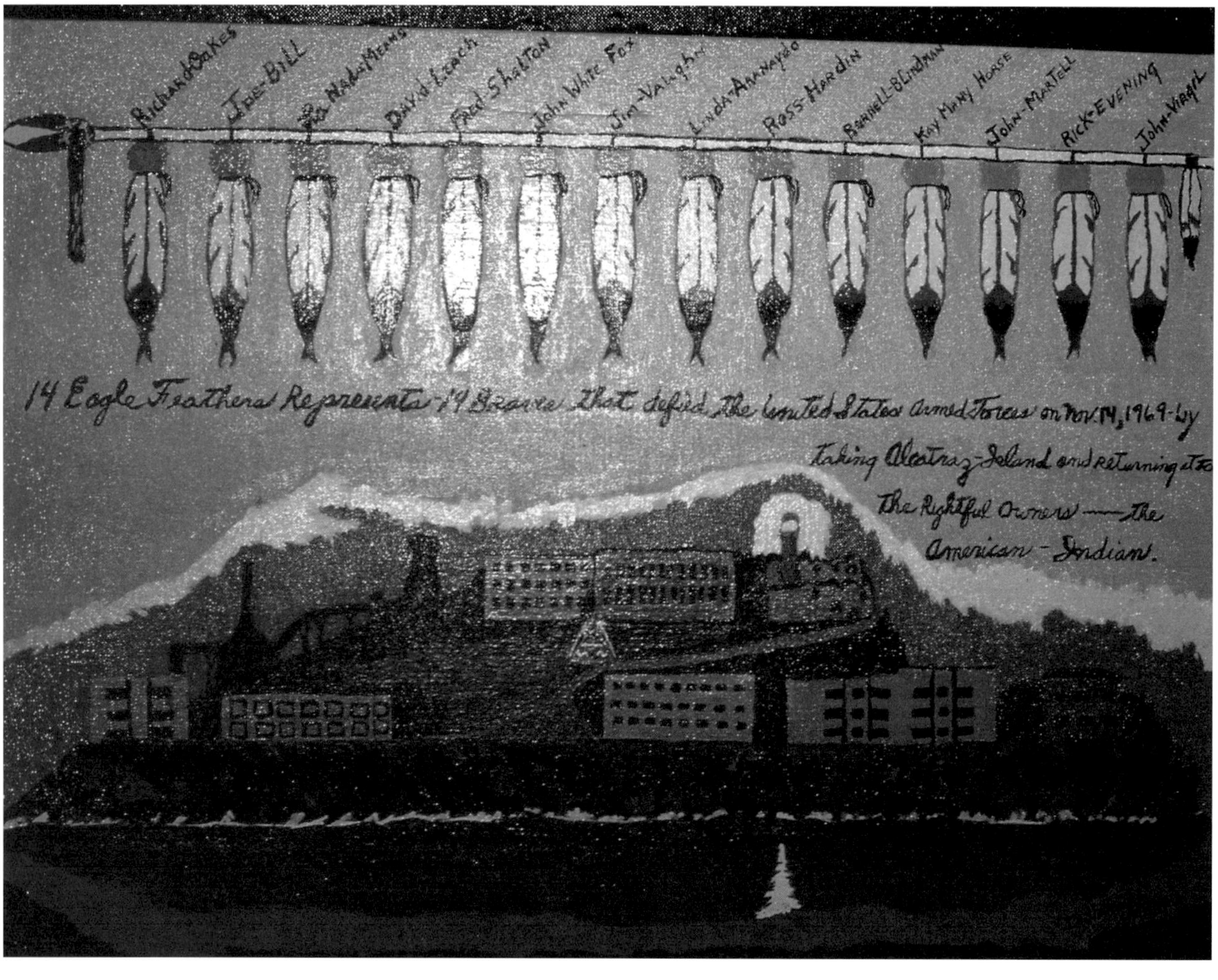

1.34

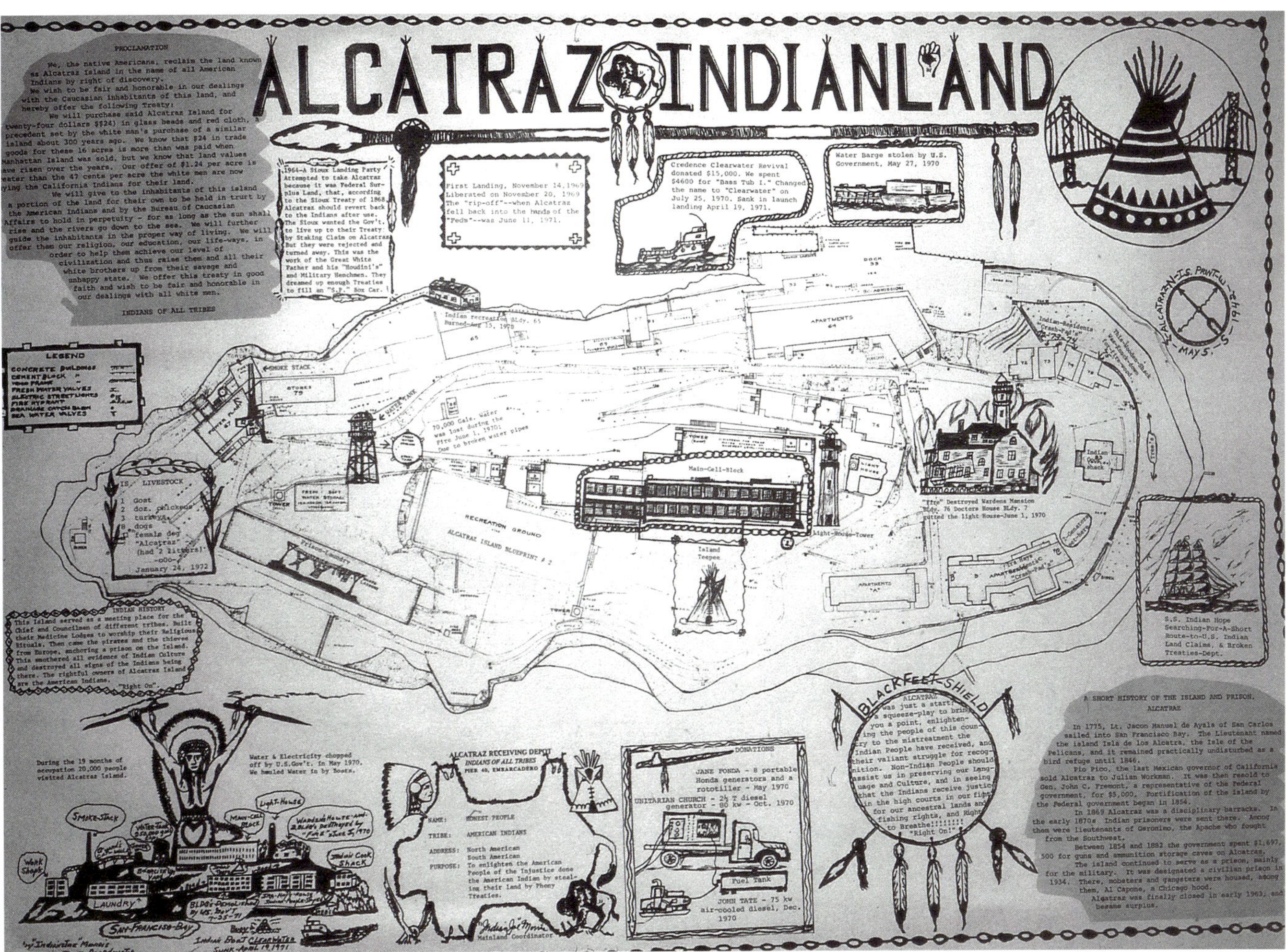

were both conqueror and god. And yet, as we have seen before, the same Indian enacts a gesture of peace (and also perhaps prayer) through a ceremonial extension of the peace pipe. The heavens crack. The waves crush themselves against the rocks. The lighthouse candles up in the dark. Amid the buildings stands a small teepee, just in front of the main rectangular structure. Striped in white and red, the teepee's triangular shape seems particularly animated when set against the drab rectangles of the governmental buildings. In the sky, the bolts of lighting or smoke make a nexus at the pipe, as though the island and the Indian and the pipe are some great omphalos, centering the elements, and we are forced to consider that the chief may be neither god nor conqueror but sentry, watching over Indian land both here and elsewhere, both now and in the future.

Even more famous (and more mythic) is Morris's canonization of the first inhabitants of the island, who arrived on November 14, 1969 (Fig. 1.34). Again, Morris invokes traditional Indian icons; this time, eagle feathers and a spear to honor, in his words, "14 Braves that defied the United States Armed Forces on Nov. 14, 1969 by Taking Alcatraz and Returning it to the Rightful Owners—the American Indian." Morris goes on to memorialize each person by painting his or her name above a feather. Like the Indian chief in the previous painting, the Native symbology looms over the island, which appears to be vacant, even sleepy, except for the lighthouse, which continues to glow.

For many, Alcatraz's symbology functioned as a map of Indian resistance, a cartography of activism that showed (and continues to show) others where to go and how to get there; in fact, Morris must have intuited Indian Alcatraz's future significance when he created his

FIGURE 1.33. (facing page) *Joe Morris,* Jim Blackhorse—"Chief" Richard Oakes, *1970. Oil on cardboard. The piece evokes peace more than war. Courtesy of the U.S. Department of the Interior, National Park Service.*

FIGURE 1.34. (facing page) *Joe Morris,* 14 Feathers over Alcatraz, *c. 1971. A tribute to the fourteen "braves" who dove into the water to claim Alcatraz. Courtesy of the U.S. Department of the Interior, National Park Service.*

FIGURE 1.35. (above) *Joe Morris,* Alcatraz Indianland, *c. 1971–1972. Less a map of place than experience, it tells many stories. Courtesy of the U.S. Department of the Interior, National Park Service.*

stunning map (Fig. 1.35). To my mind, this is one of the most impressive pieces of aesthetic activism that emerged from the occupation. Part time line, part historical narrative, part directional map, part scrapbook, the map chronicles in both written and visual language the island's resistance cartography. Resembling many eighteenth- and nineteenth-century Indian maps, Morris's painting tends toward a circular visual narrative linking people to a place, thereby predicting Leslie Marmon Silko, and his use of Indian mapping as a mode of resistance presages Jaune Quick-to-See Smith. Like Smith, he also understands the connection between iconography and story. To map Indian Alcatraz is to map history and the future, signifier and signified, engagement and resistance, occupation and survivance.

Even though almost all of the visual markers of the occupation have been worn away by wind, water, and fog, Alcatraz as a symbol continues to live on. The "Indians Welcome" sign still greets visitors, and a great four-part video, *We Hold the Rock*, runs during visiting hours in its own small theater. With live footage of Richard Oakes reading the proclamation and Indians leaping into the water, it does important cultural work by bringing this aspect of the prison's history into the consciousness of mainstream America. In November 2009, the fortieth anniversary of the occupation was celebrated in numerous ways in the Bay Area. But beyond these examples, the island still educates. Between the remaining uneroded signs of the occupation and the commitment of present head ranger Craig Glassner to keep alive the Native history of Alcatraz, thousands of tourists stuffed on buttery crab from Fisherman's Wharf and dreamy squares of Ghirardelli chocolate learn a little something about Alcatraz and their country every time they step off the ferry and onto Indian land, proving Helen C. Becker was right:

> So once again the world will know
> Of proud people they could not kill
> Then as a united army
> We will walk beyond Alcatraz.
>
> —("KEEPERS OF THE FLAME," JOHNSON, *ALCATRAZ: INDIAN LAND FOREVER*, 95)

Like the Ghost Dance, the Alcatraz occupation inspires not so much through "results" as through performative symbolism, which catalyzes past practice and future endeavors. Through its commitment to symbolic action and subversive semiotics, the interdisciplinary activism of the Alcatraz occupation not only galvanized Indian support for issues of sovereignty and self-governance, but also located, in Indian aesthetic practice, the real possibility of renewal, relation, and revolution.

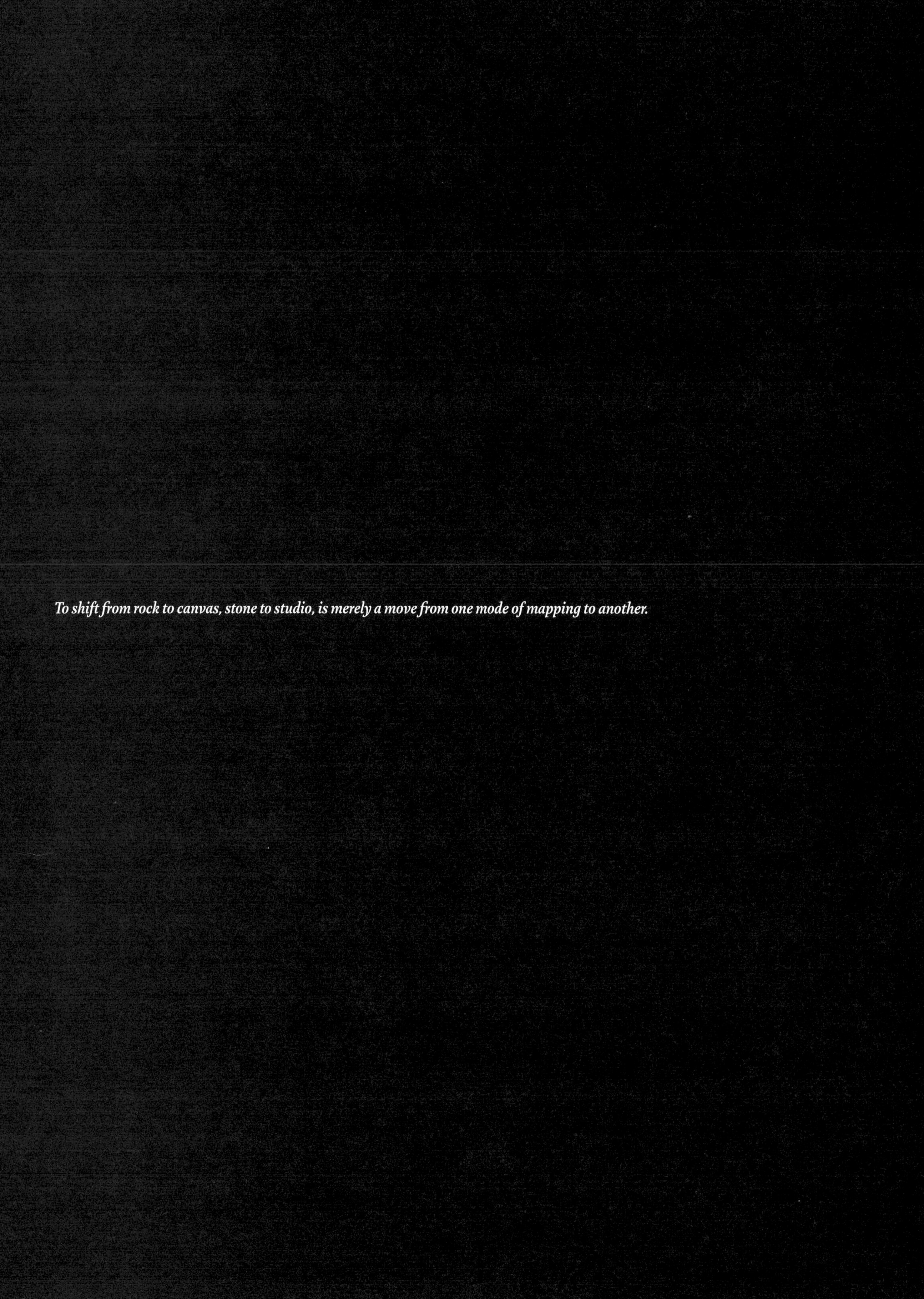

To shift from rock to canvas, stone to studio, is merely a move from one mode of mapping to another.

2.

THE CARTOGRAPHY OF SOVEREIGNTY

JAUNE QUICK-TO-SEE SMITH'S MAP PAINTINGS

Beneath the map imposed by science is a map in the blood.

ABSENCE AND DISPLACEMENT are the provenances Chickasaw writer Linda Hogan attempts to chart in "Map," a mythic poem in her mythic collection, *The Book of Medicines*:

> This is the map of the forsaken world.
> This is the world without end
> where forests have been cut away from their trees.
> These are the lines wolf could not pass over.
>
> —(37)

One of the many provocative aspects of the poem is the difficulty of re-presenting that which has been either neglected or erased. Here and in the remainder of the text, Hogan muses over the inefficacy of language: how can words imported by men from different lands, alien cultures, adequately name the animals and landscapes, borders and boundaries of this land? She asks, as maybe we all do, to what degree do the original names for things linger in memory and embodiment? How does one map the invisible?

For Native Americans, maps tend toward different uses from those created by and for traditional Western peoples. "Native American maps are pictures of experience," writes Mark Warhus in *Another America: Native American Maps and the History of Our Land*. "They are formed in the human interaction with the land and are a record of the events that give it meaning" (3). That indigenous connection to land, residence, and experience automatically subjectifies Native maps, converting them into creative documents that blend both perspective and place. Not surprisingly, Native maps can also be political statements, assertions of belonging and reciprocity. In her essay "Poems as Maps in American Indian Women's Writing," Janice Gould argues that poetic "cartography is a way for Native poets to know and affirm our integration of identity with place. . . . This mapmaking is important to our concept of sovereignty as Indian nations, and to our concept of self-discovery as Indian individuals" (25). Like Gould and Hogan, Flathead-Cree-Shoshone artist Jaune Quick-to-See Smith is interested in the semiotic and political work of maps and mapmaking, particularly in regard to Indian country. Her astonishing series of map paintings—fourteen in all—is one of the great projects of recent American art; yet, to date, there has been no comprehensive examination of these pieces as either aesthetic or political texts.

This chapter seeks to rectify that oversight through a reading of these paintings as models of engaged resistance. By forcing viewers to rethink "objective" texts like maps, by replacing Anglo place-names with Indian names, and by redrawing traditional boundaries, Smith advances a semiotic sovereignty that indigenizes the lower forty-eight by fundamentally reframing the broad, contradictory canvas that is America.

"Maps are pictures," observes Gerald Vizenor, "and some native pictures are stories, visual memories, the source of directions, and a virtual sense of presence" (*Fugitive Poses*, 170). To be sure, Quick-to-See Smith's pictures tell stories, though not always the stories people want to hear. They often, as Vizenor suggests, tell stories of inversion. One of the stories maps tell is of the collaboration between the verbal and the visual.[1] Pictographically, maps represent a space, and linguistically, language narrates that space. Maps without words feel like songs without lyrics. The words tell us how to interpret the symbolic field. They alpha and omega the visual narrative. Like Gould, Vizenor locates in mapping the semiotic toolbox of sovereignty, which for him is all about communicative action made manifest. In "Visual Cartography," he posits that mapmaking is one of the totemic creations, and he endows authentic Native mappery with the power to stave off the advances of colonialism and dominance: "Native virtual cartography is much more than the base lines and cardinal directions of territory" (*Fugitive Poses*, 173). For him, Native maps actuate "the virtual cartography of native survivance and sovereignty" (178). This chapter tells stories about the stories that Smith's Native cartography tell: reappraisals and revisions of the larger narrative of America and American Indian sovereignty.

Since Robert Allen Warrior made sovereignty an important concept in American Indian studies, the term has both gathered and lost momentum. In recent years, it seems to have been lapped by "nationalism," though I am predicting a comeback from the former. To his credit, Warrior deftly avoids defining sovereignty in *Tribal Secrets: Recovering American Indian Intellectual Traditions*, but a consensus definition has emerged.[2] Gould defines it as a "declaration of a necessary inner dignity, power and trust, as well as a declaration—however difficult—of unbroken connection to our Mother Earth" (25). For Gould, sovereignty is fundamentally, inextricably linked to land—an important concept in regard to mapping. Vizenor, on the other hand, defines it more theoretically: "Native sovereignty is sovenance, the immanence of visions, and transmotion in artistic creations. Sovereignty, moreover, is practical, reciprocal, and theoretical" (*Fugitive Poses*, 178).[3] When I use the term in this chapter and throughout the book, I imply a combination of these definitions with an acknowledgment that sovereignty is largely about self-determination, autonomy, and capability. Within my framework of aesthetic activism, sovereignty means the ability of artists, writers, and filmmakers to tell their own stories in their own words, in their own language—whether that language is verbal or visual.

No contemporary Indian artist is better at this than Jaune Quick-to-See Smith. Born on the Confederated Salish and Kootenai Indian Reservation in Montana in 1940, Smith now resides in New Mexico. But the subject of her art extends beyond Indian country. Along with Fritz Scholder, T. C. Cannon, Jimmie Durham, George Morrison, Rick Bartow, and Duane Slick, Smith is considered one of Native America's most important painters, despite the fact that her exhibition profile has not been commensurate with either her reputation among artists and critics or the quality and scope of her work. Among more mainstream artists, Smith is perhaps most commonly compared to post—abstract expressionists like

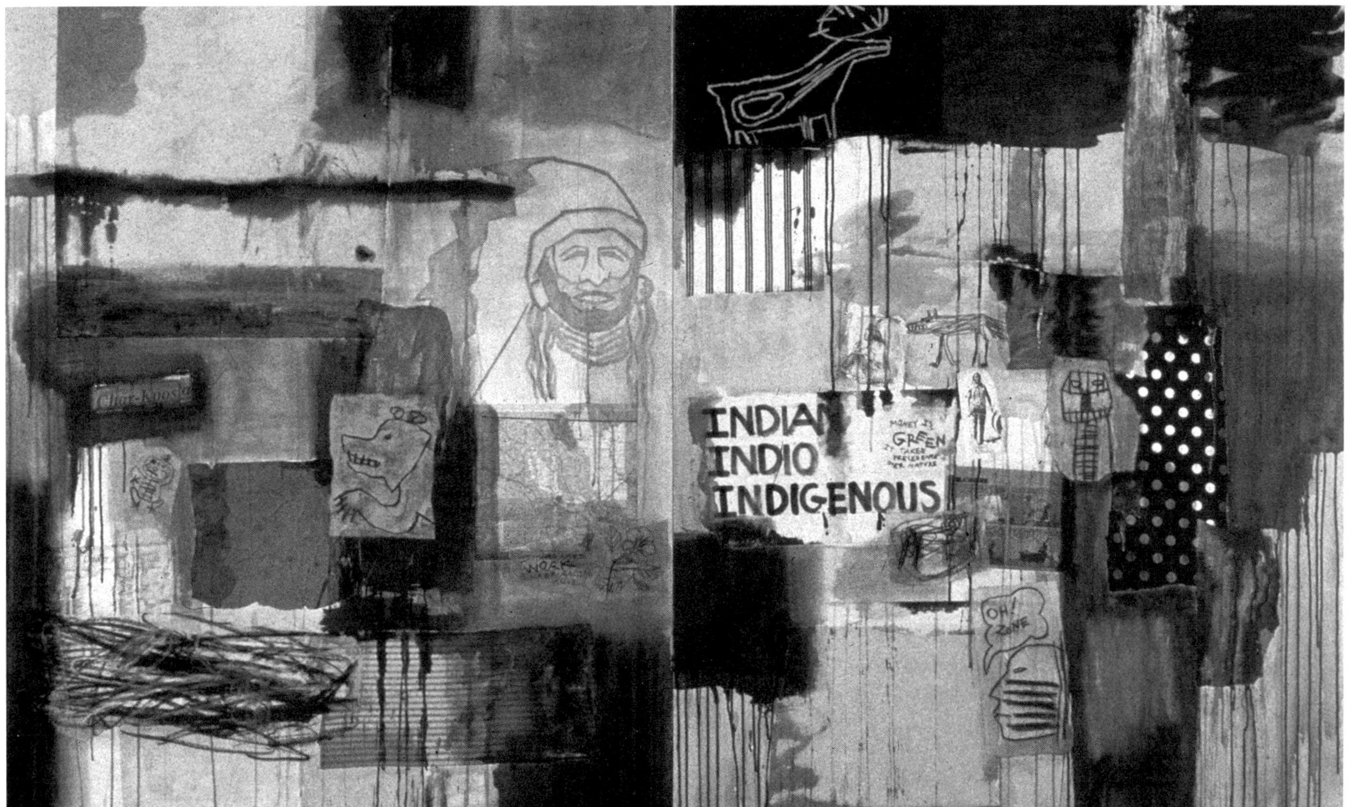

Jasper Johns and Robert Rauschenberg; however, her work remains less canonized than theirs—a problem that no doubt has as much to do with politics as it does with race, since the three share a great deal aesthetically. For example, all three artists create large pieces in which color, everyday objects, and culturally significant images enter into conversation with one another in provocative and arresting ways. Additionally, all three artists are drawn to maps. Johns and Smith play with representations of the lower forty-eight more conventionally, while Rauschenberg was interested in mapping America's spatial and cultural planes, as in a piece like *Persimmon*. All three artists devote a great deal of their work to a visual cartography of American icons. Where Smith departs from her more famous predecessors—and, for that matter, from most of the Native American gallery art in places like Santa Fe and Sedona—is in her devotion to Native identity and Native sovereignty.[4]

In a piece like *Indian, Indio, Indigenous* (Fig. 2.1), for example, Smith employs a Rauschenbergian field to make statements about indigenous America. She affixes boxes, photos, sticks, and bits of paper to the canvas (as Rauschenberg did so famously), playing on the other significations of media by blending representations of Indians, Indian stereotypes, and the often-appropriated and romanticized petroglyph. An example of what she calls a "narrative landscape," this piece becomes a map of stories told to fill what has been emptied. Smith asks us to bear in mind the materials, methods, and methodologies of colonization, indigenous histories, and identity.

Unlike artists who seem primarily interested in shocking their audiences, Smith wants to engage hers. "I like to bring the viewer in with a seductive texture," she claims ("Subversions/Affirmations," 113). In fact, the formal qualities of her paintings often mirror their thematic arcs. She employs paint, collage, artifacts, newspapers, and photographs to create a combination of representational and abstract images that illustrate the extent to which contemporary Native life is fundamentally interwoven with the destruction of the environment, governmental oppression, and the pervasive myths of American cultural identity.

FIGURE 2.1. *Jaune Quick-to-See Smith,* Indian, Indio, Indigenous, *1992. Oil and collage on canvas. 60 × 100 in. Courtesy of the artist.*

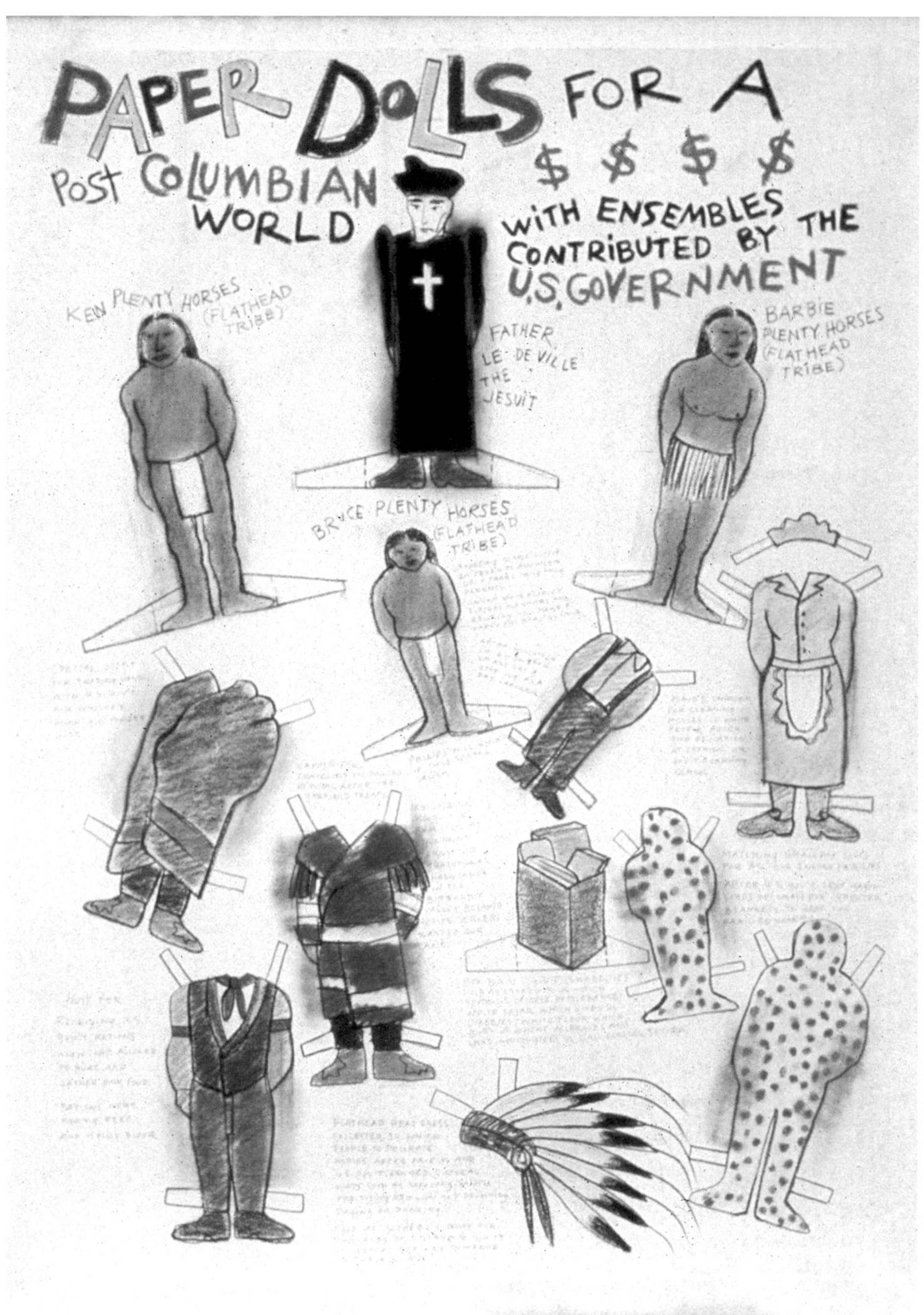

FIGURE 2.2. *Jaune Quick-to-See Smith,* Paper Dolls for a Post-Columbian World with Ensembles Contributed by the U.S. Government, *1991. Pastel and pencil on paper. 40 × 29 in. Courtesy of the artist.*

By employing a familiar artistic grammar, Smith welcomes us into her pieces by using striking juxtapositions and aesthetically pleasing colors and formations. What's more, her favorite subjects—America and American Indian imagery and narrative—feel immediately accessible to us. For better or worse, we are used to seeing iconic Indian images on display. Smith engages our comfort with objectification. One senses that Smith's paintings want to be looked at. They want to communicate. They invite us into their uneasy home.

And uneasy they are. To call Smith a political painter is to say nothing. All art is political. However, what distinguishes Smith's work from that of contemporary mainstream American museum art is its foregrounding of otherwise ignored political issues. Would Willem de Kooning have made the subject of one of his paintings the troubling use of Indians as sport mascots? Would Jeff Koons do a piece on smallpox blankets? Would Cindy

Sherman create a photographic series on poverty and death on Indian reservations? Even more importantly, would any of the Native or Anglo painters whose work is lapped up in Santa Fe and Taos be brave enough to create a work like *Paper Dolls for a Post-Columbian World with Ensembles Contributed by the U.S. Government* (Fig. 2.2)?

On the other hand, it would be a mistake to equate Smith with incendiary artists like Robert Mapplethorpe or Andres Serrano, who intentionally turn the artistic space into a moment of visual shock. There are no penises in Smith's work. No crucifixes. No naked children. No sperm, no shots of Klansmen. No urinals. But in a piece like *Paper Dolls*, Smith shows that the enactment and reenactment of "discovery" functions as an allegory for power and violence—an allegory that continues to be inscribed not just orally but visually. Smith's interest in American popular culture and the American culture of space, mastery, and dominance puts her directly in the tradition of the most important American Indian orators, warriors, and writers. As with others discussed in these pages, her language functions as a mode of engaged resistance against the near-totalizing forces of American cultural inscription and representation.

Like Sherman Alexie, Leslie Marmon Silko, Edgar Heap of Birds, and Joy Harjo, Smith engages in both compositional and contextual resistance. Her pieces are not paintings, they are not sculptures, they are not essays, they are not journalism, they are not public relations; yet her work draws from each of those fields. Thus, the form her work takes challenges the formal assumptions and expectations of an aesthetic that was created and is maintained by a kind of Anglo elitism and cultural hegemony that stand in opposition to Native expression. The forging of her own artistic language is not simply an aesthetic, but also an ethic. Her work is both a measure and a means of sovereignty.

The *State Names* Series

Nowhere do we see this commitment to the semiotics of sovereignty more than in the map paintings. Here, her vision of art as aesthetic activism finds its most salient form. Though it is hard to think of these pieces as a formal "series," they share a great deal. Begun in 1992 and extending well into the new millennium, these representations of maps have evolved along with Smith's politics, highlighting both new and old points of interest on her political journey. "Smith's map paintings," writes Julie Sasse, "are among the first works where [Smith] makes wryly humorous, outspoken political declarations that resonate with the injustices inflicted upon Native peoples in America" (*Jaune Quick-to-See Smith,* 7). Sasse is spot on here. Smith's use of humor breaks down traditional defenses, making her canvases invitations rather than obstructions. To be sure, the map of the lower forty-eight states is familiar territory. For many, it is a comfortable, patriotic, unassailable icon of freedom, Manifest Destiny, and dominance. But for Smith, it is a symbol of authoritarianism, a visual treaty, an imposed, colonialist overlay. "My life's work involves examining contemporary life in America and interpreting it through Native ideology," says Smith. "I sometimes use maps as a point of departure for the political treatment of Native people" (University of New Mexico, *Jaune Quick-to-See Smith*, 2). The use of maps as a site of Native ideology distinguishes her maps from Jasper Johns's famous but innocuous paintings of the United States. Whereas Johns's maps merely present the states in a unique but essentially unaltered perspective, Smith's maps mark both states and states of violence. Johns empties out his states; Smith fills hers up. Smith's paintings become a kind of contested space where contemporary and traditional Native issues take the foreground—not unlike the contested geographic spaces of early America. For her, the canvas doesn't simply evoke, but it provokes.

Though all of Smith's work explores these issues, her maps function particularly well

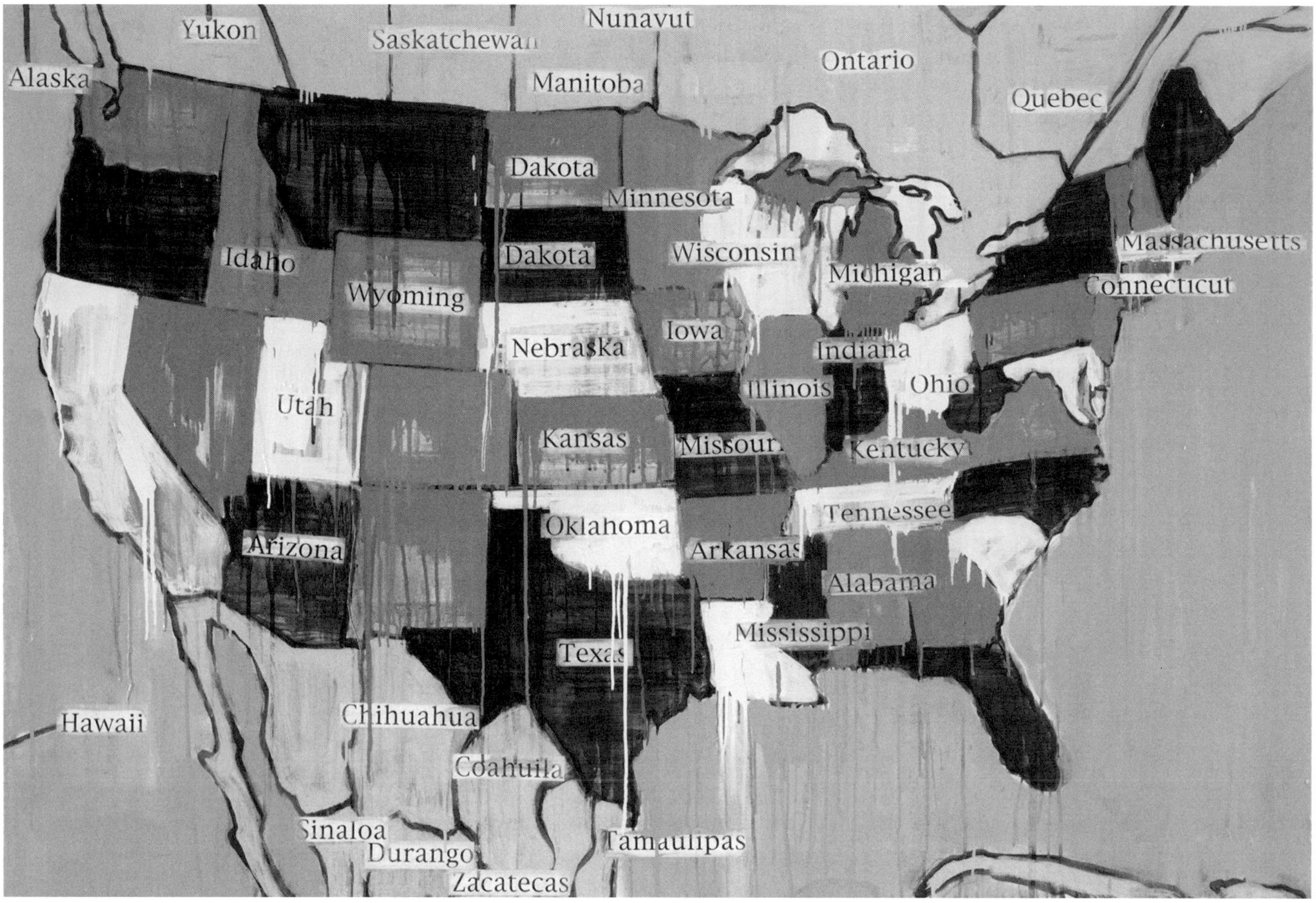

2.3

2.4

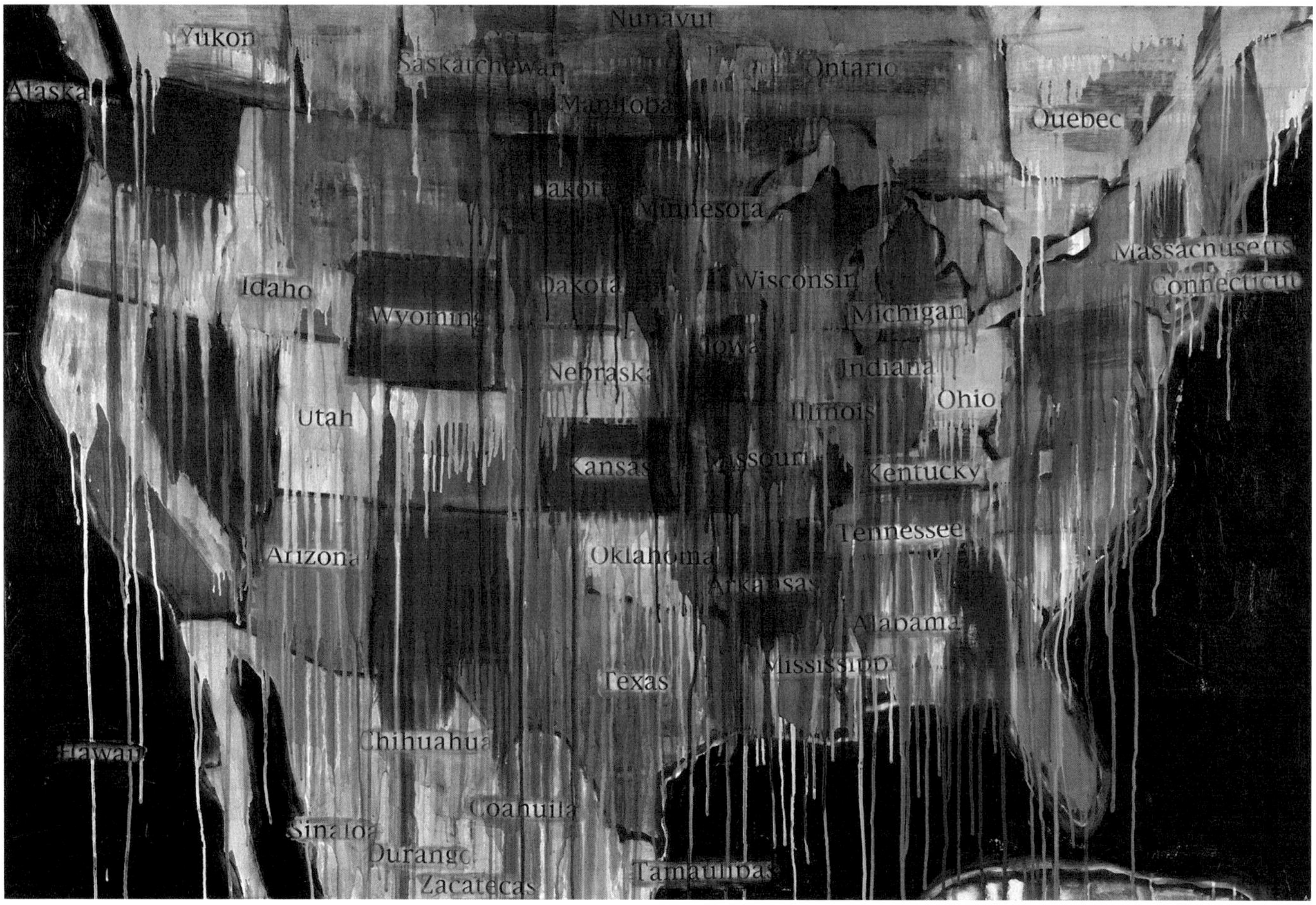

as sovereign sites of engaged resistance because they force us to reconsider visual demarcations of identity. Take the understated *State Names II* (Fig. 2.3) for example. Fundamentally pleasing to look at, the painting engages the viewer on all levels. Its realist aesthetic disarms, perhaps even charms, through its use of recognizable detail. The artist does not overly abstract the U.S. map; she represents its states and borders faithfully, ensuring that we see her piece first and foremost as a map (as opposed to a painting). At first glance, it appears to be an homage to Johns's maps, but then you notice that about half the states are missing names. Where is "Oregon"? "Washington"? "Florida"? "New York"? And wait, there is no "New Hampshire"! Look again, though, and see "Manitoba" and "Chihuahua." What gives? Eventually, the viewer probably figures out that he is looking at a map of states whose names are either Indian names or are derived from Indian names. All of a sudden, the painting transforms into a map of presence and absence. Absent are the anglicized place names of conquest and removal; present are the names of those who were removed and those who resisted. The strong, nearly primary colors of the clearly defined states neither overtly challenge the viewer nor placate her. Nothing is surprising but what is missing. Less a critique than a missive, *State Names II* asks the viewer to consider the daily practice of language, the seemingly invisible history of the nomenclature of the United States, and the ignored languages whose vocabularies are responsible for the ontology of American identity.[5]

The companion painting to *State Names II*, the cleverly titled *State Names I* (Fig. 2.4), works on the same thematic premise but makes a more forceful visual statement. Whereas *State Names II* resembles a child's map or one of those wooden puzzles in which each state is its own piece, its predecessor moves cultural mapping into darker terrain. Gone are the finely demarcated boundaries, gone are symmetrical repetitions of state colors. A surprising amount of white paint that has dripped vertically down the canvas obscures a great deal of the written text. Those tributaries of paint carry with them the colors of all the states as they run headlong into an ocean of near blackness. At first, the painting appears to be constructed entirely of wax, and the flaming candle that is this country has burned itself down to a nub. But then it becomes clear that the long sinewy drips are not wax but paint. Visually, the effect is hard to describe. It is staggering, confusing, and absolutely beautiful. Thematically, it tells a different story from the one in *States Name II*. Smith tropes the whitewashing of America by literalizing how whiteness has permeated, covered, even seeped into the fabric of Native land. That *State Names II* resembles a patchwork quilt is no coincidence; in fact, I would argue that the obfuscated nature of *State Names I* enacts a dialogic pairing with *State Names II*, creating a kind of diptych of American presence and Indian absence, and Indian presence and American absence.

Read together, the two paintings have a great deal to say about Native presence and absence. In *States Names II*, Native names exist, whereas the later Anglo overlays do not, calling attention to the absence of American names on a current map of America. Similarly, not even the white paint of *State Names I* can blanche Native America of its linguistic roots; even if the false state borders stay, the authentic names that predate them also preempt them.

Echo Maps and Tribal Maps

A similar project—the three-painting series *Echo Map I*, *Echo Map II*, and *Echo Map III* (Figs. 2.5, 2.6, and 2.7)—excises anglicized place names in favor of odd images and repeated salutations from different languages. The first two integrate popular greetings like *hola* and *allo* as well as foreign-language newspaper clippings (mostly in Spanish) into the individual states. Like Louise Erdrich situating a John Wayne western on a reservation or Sherman

FIGURE 2.3. (facing page) *Jaune Quick-to-See Smith,* State Names II, *2000. Oil and mixed media on canvas. 40 × 72 in. Courtesy of the artist.*

FIGURE 2.4. (facing page) *Jaune Quick-to-See Smith,* State Names I, *2000. Oil and mixed media on canvas. 40 × 72 in. Courtesy of the artist.*

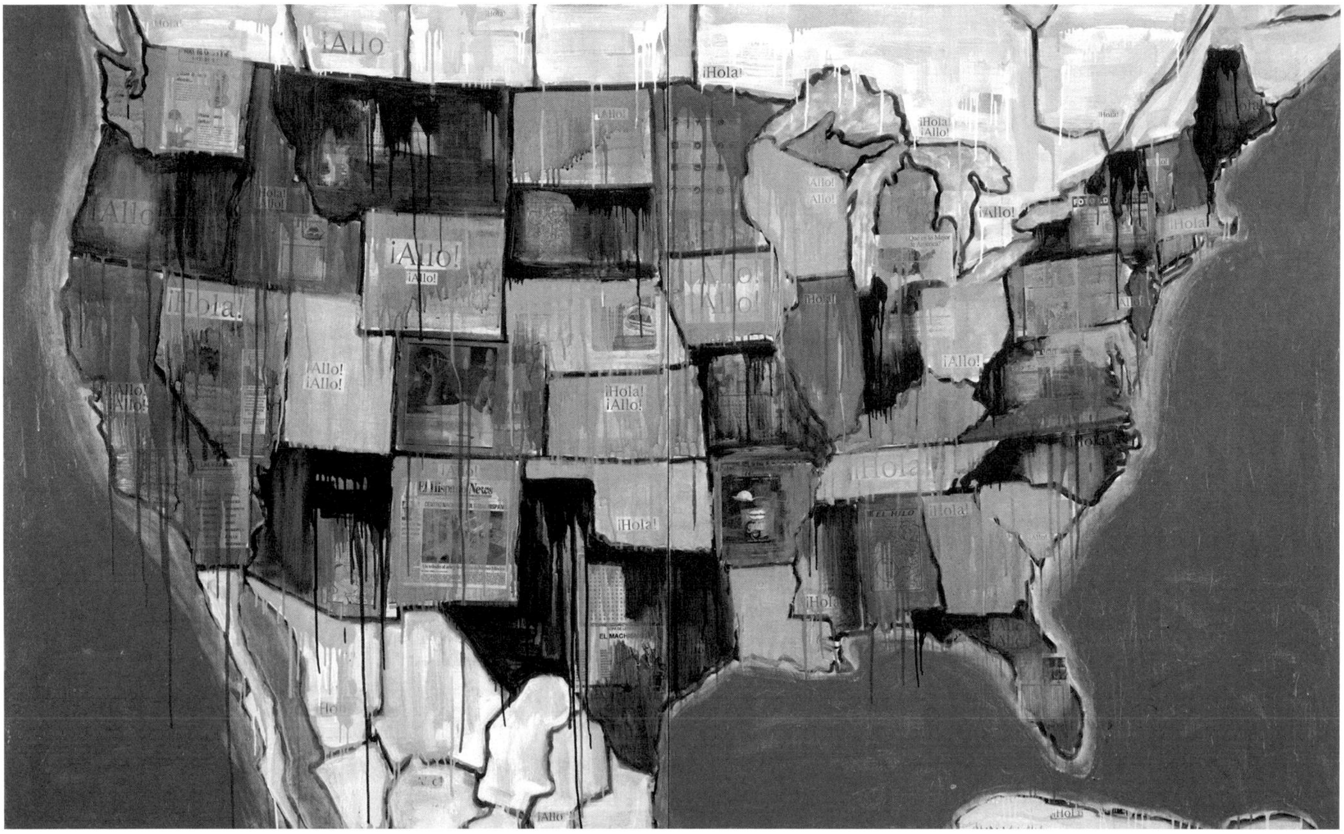

2.5

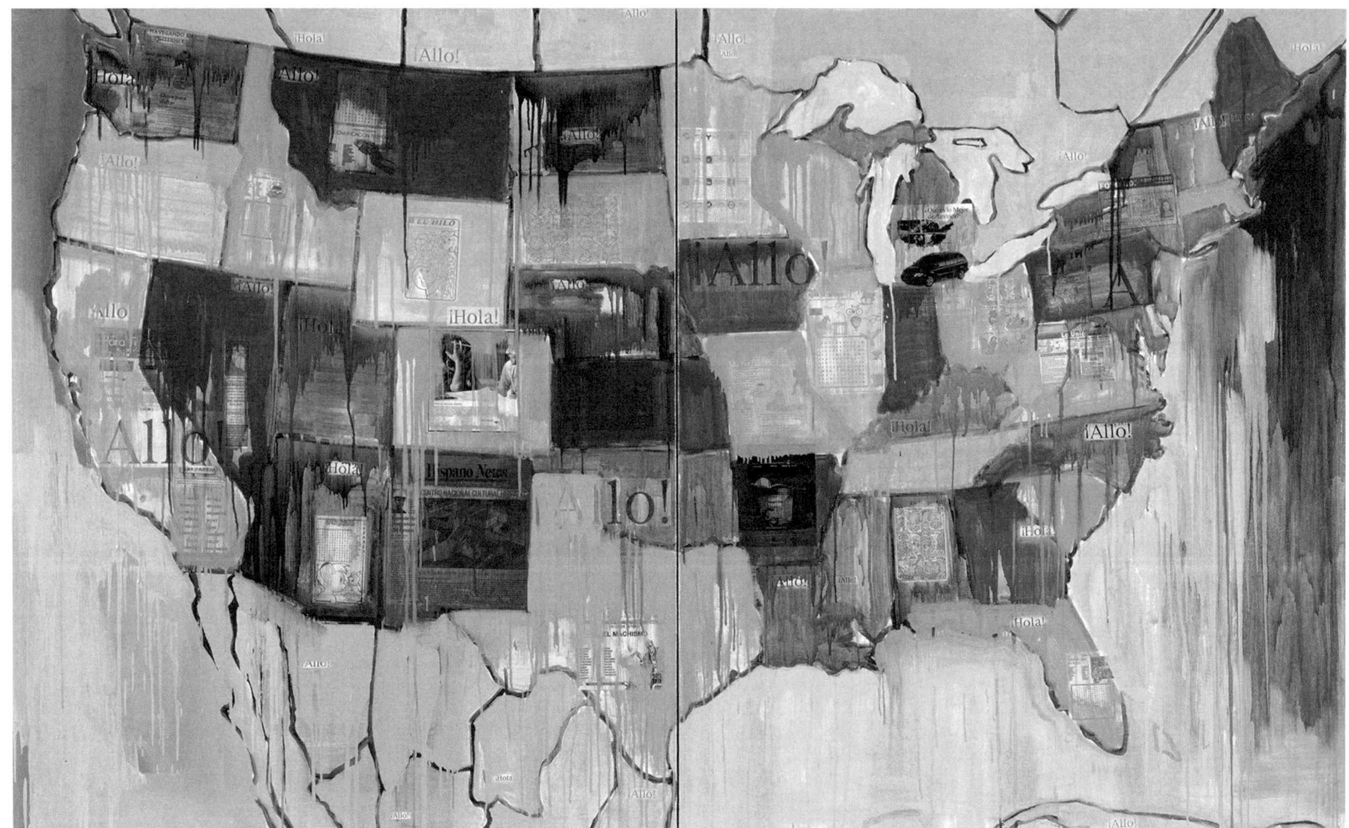

2.6

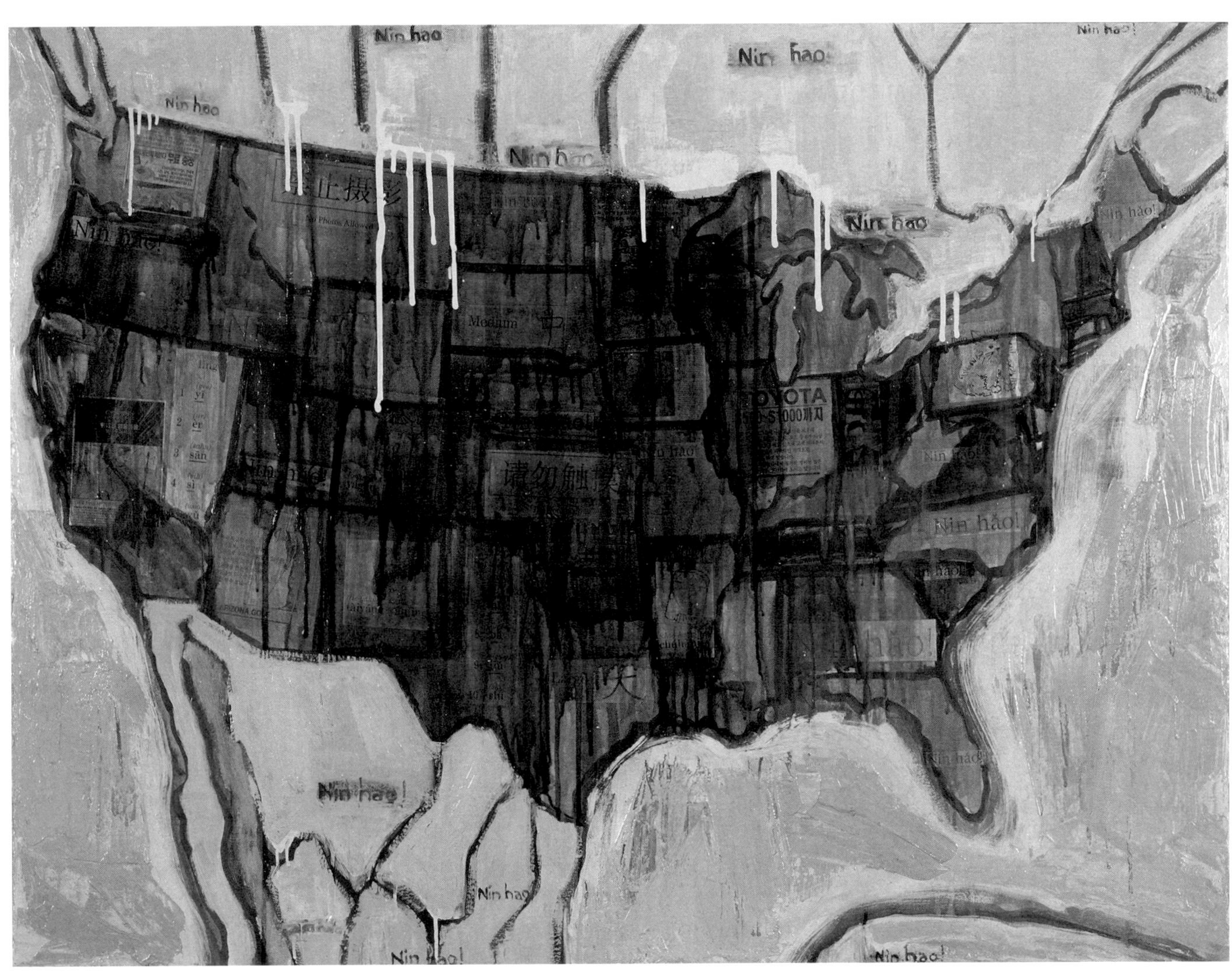

FIGURE 2.5. (facing page) *Jaune Quick-to-See Smith,* Echo Map I (Allo), *2000. Oil, collage, and mixed media on canvas. 60 × 100 in. Courtesy of the artist.*

FIGURE 2.6. (facing page) *Jaune Quick-to-See Smith,* Echo Map II (Allo), *2000. Oil, collage, and mixed media on canvas. 36 × 48 in. Courtesy of the artist.*

FIGURE 2.7. (above) *Jaune Quick-to-See Smith,* Echo Map III (Nin Hao), *2000. Oil and mixed media on canvas. 36 × 48. Courtesy of the artist.*

Alexie placing Fred Astaire in an Owl Dance, Smith's paintings participate in the aesthetics of juxtaposition. Using non-American phrases to label America forces the viewer to reconsider America's American-ness. As Smith herself has said, these map paintings provide a unique platform for social and political commentary about America. Because they operate within a connotative field of creativity, paintings provide a site of discourse that is less expository and more suggestive than prose. That said, Smith masterfully conflates connotation with denotation, making her map paintings fine examples of visual rhetoric.

One argument the paintings make is that we can no longer associate America exclusively with English. For centuries a mélange of languages, America has now officially reached the point that it must let otherness through its cultural door. Though *allo* functions primarily as a greeting in French, "allo-" is also a Greek-derived combining form used to mean "different" or "other" in English compounds, a duality that works well with the bimodal semiology of the paintings. Anyone who has spent any time in the U.S. states bordering Mexico knows that non-Anglo discourse has now become part of the social fabric of the United States, part of its interior identity. So why should it not, these maps assert, become part of its external coding? Additionally, this series reminds the viewer that the lingua franca of the United States is an imported language, a language of immigrants. English was invented elsewhere and, therefore, enjoys no claim to this land. English became American, but it is not indigenous.

That the maps echo raises other questions, most notably, what the echoes mean. Maps, of course, are themselves objects of unchartable repetition: visual echoes in weather reports, in glove boxes, on news programs, in textbooks, and in classrooms. In a great ironic twist, Smith's maps use their visuality as an aural reminder that voices do not exist in a vacuum; language is concatenated by repetition and renewal. The speech act does the opposite work of borders, which circumscribe boundaries and arrest movement. Language, the ultimate form of transmotion, peoples America as much as any other measurable characteristic. In this case, the maps echo a greeting, a salutation, a welcoming—in short, cordiality. Any number of concepts or words could be echoed across the states, but Smith chooses the most unlikely of linguistic gestures—that of engagement—for her cartographic discourse. Remarkably, Smith makes the tropes of language and indigeneity hospitable.

Smith takes this troping one step further in the wonderful *Tribal Map* and *Tribal Map II*. Here, she subtly changes cartographic language, thereby altering identity and classification. If, say, Arizona were known not as "Arizona" but rather by the various names of its indigenous tribes, then it would become a different entity, not simply a differently named space. Even more provocative is the possibility of doing away with states altogether and conceptualizing the land we think of as America only as a collection of Native tribes. This neo-diptych annuls the colonial or governmental overlay. It determines the destiny of land, culture, and people. The maps feel old, but we know they are new. In fact, the colors may remind us of maps of so-called red and blue states, but the many shades suggest both connection and difference. Are the colors random or part of a plan?

Ultimately, what emerges from the paintings is the bizarre paradox of state borders but no state names. Why create a map that erases the names imposed by the government but does not erase the borders established by the same government? In my mind, this detail comes out of Smith's desire to both engage and resist. On one hand, she acknowledges a legal fact: the lower forty-eight have random boundaries that we did not create. On the other hand, she refutes the claim that non-Native boundaries circumscribe Native realities. "Maps are not neutral documents that contain facts and figures," argues Elizabeth Archuleta (Yaqui/Chicana). "In the past, colonial regimes named, organized, constructed, and controlled space and place through the imperialistic practice of mapmaking. Maps are virtual realities that represent for the colonizers permanent and visible markers of

FIGURES 2.8 and 2.8A (facing page) *Jaune Quick-to-See Smith,* Tribal Map *and* Tribal Map II, *2001, Oil, collage, and mixed media on canvas. 80 × 120 in. Courtesy of the artist.*

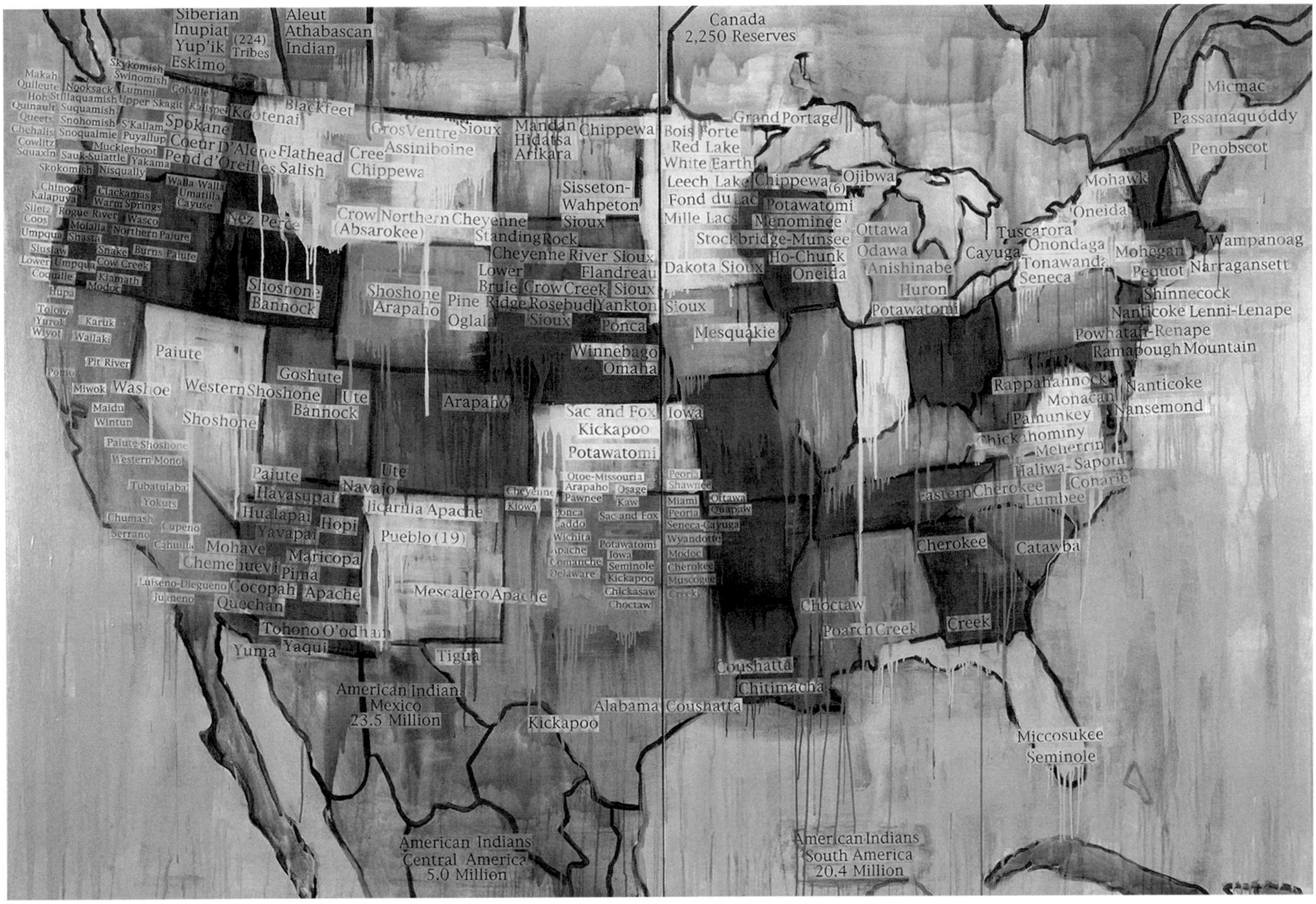

2.8

2.8A

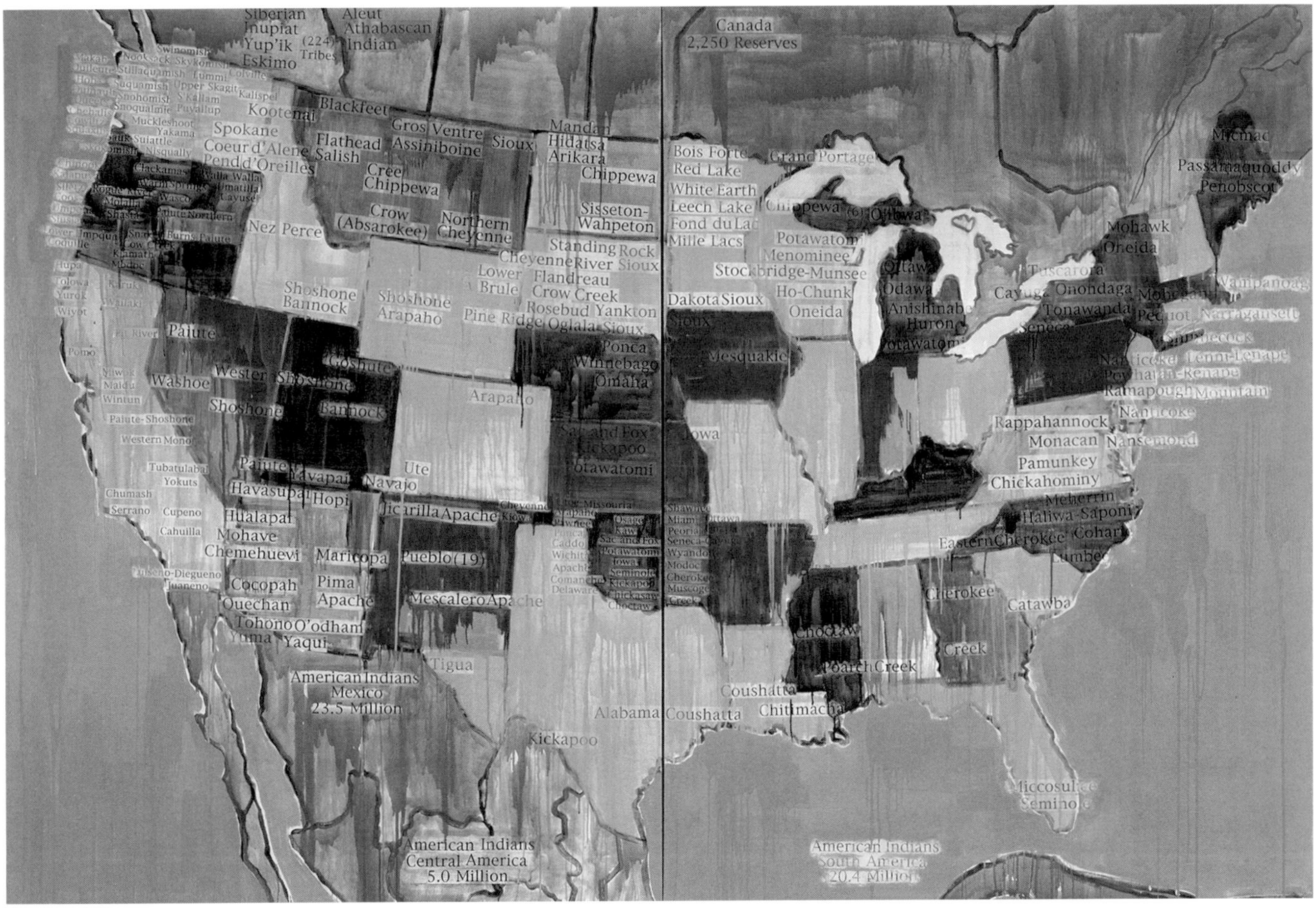

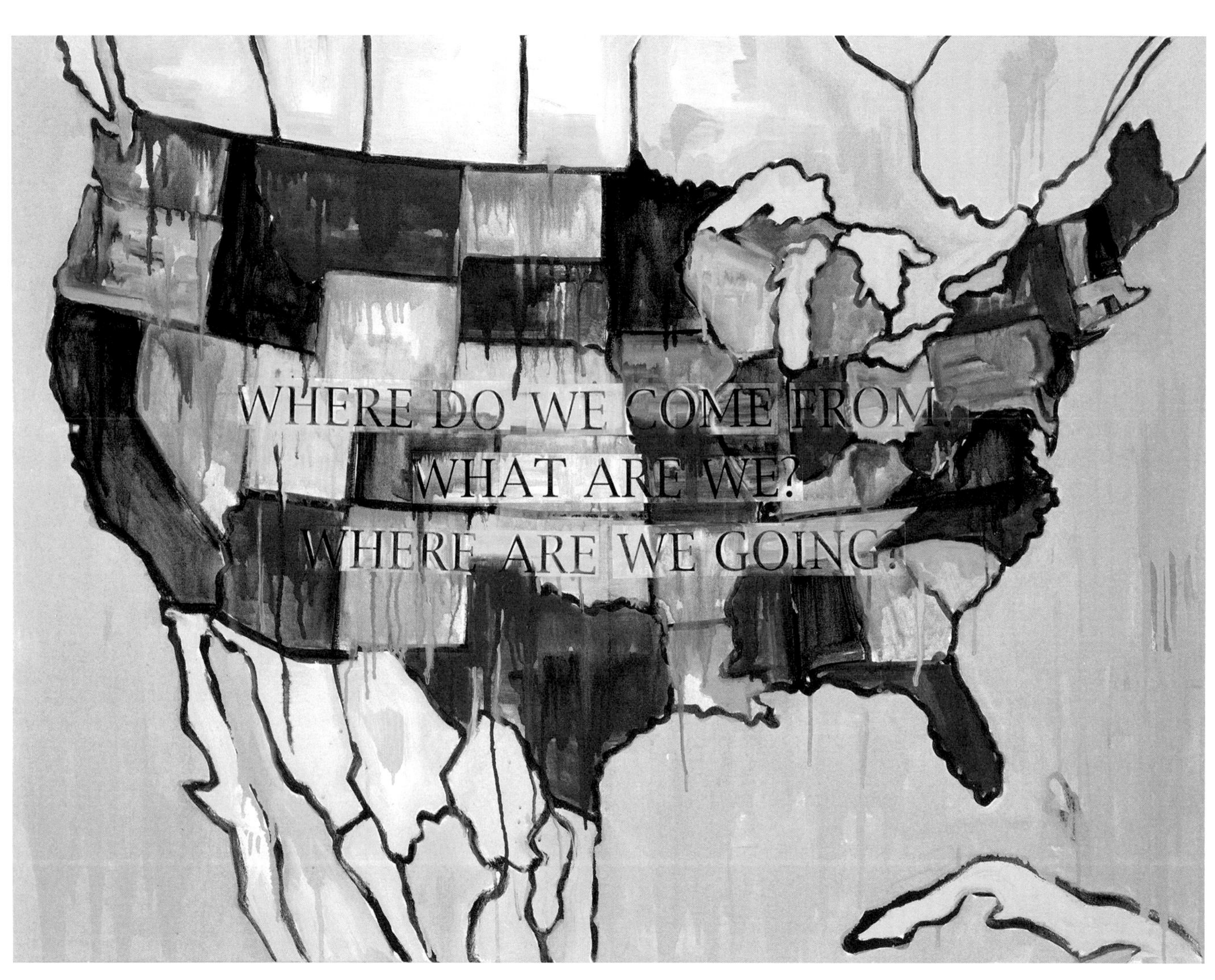

FIGURE 2.9. *Jaune Quick-to-See Smith,* Where Do We Come From?, *2000. Oil and mixed media on paper. 45.75 × 33.75 in. Courtesy of the artist.*

conquest, domination, the triumph of civilization, and the subjugation of nature. Maps are also myths designed to conceal Indigenous ways of knowing and connecting with their homelands" ("Gym Shoes, Maps, and Passports," 436). In her tribal maps, Smith unveils the indigeneity that colonialism and the documents of imperialist practice have tried to cover up. Tribal names transgress boundaries here, the way they do not in standard maps. They reclaim space and reorder realities. They reach out into the ocean and across state lines. Thus, the borders, the cultural machinery that allocates land, may frame space, but that framing mechanism does not extend into language. Only the original inhabitants of a space, those who invited the language spoken on that land, can determine its name and its destiny. Anything else is window dressing.

K. Johnson Bowles, the director of the Longwood Center for the Visual Arts and the curator of an important show by Smith in 2001, likens *Tribal Map* to the large map of the United States that hung in her classroom as a girl. At 80 inches by 120 inches, its scale would, indeed, mirror that of one of the classic pull-down maps ubiquitous in the pre-PowerPoint years. For Bowles, the experience of standing in front of this piece created a confusing mixture of nostalgia and displacement: "The colors are the same as remembered from a map in Mrs. Sills' fifth grade class in Durham, North Carolina—burnt oranges, pinks, mauves, lime greens, light blues. But instead of words like North Carolina, Virginia, and South Carolina, I read the names of Indigenous tribes of North America densely collaged onto the map" ("Stop. Look. Listen.," 1).

Bowles's astute observation about the map's colors—their apparent innocuousness—underscores my earlier point about Smith's seductiveness. Almost impressionistic in their color palette, the pastels of the map are so comforting, so reassuring, that we walk easily into her terrain. But as Bowles quickly realizes when she reads the names on the map, that early nostalgia changes to "loss and bewilderment" (1). Traditionally, we look to maps to help us, to put us on the right path, to turn loss and bewilderment into orientation, but here, Smith shows us what it might feel like, if just for a second, to see Indian land through Indian eyes. How dislocating it must have been to suddenly refer to mountains, rivers, and lakes not by their original names but with the disconnected language of the conqueror. According to Julie Sasse, *Tribal Map* makes an important symbolic statement about the symbology of maps: "Once the dominion of hundreds of Indian tribes, the land that distinguishes the map of the United States is now carved into tidy geometric parcels, the product of politics, war, and Manifest Destiny. Smith's argument for exposing the map symbol for what it really is cannot be denied" (*Jaune Quick-to-See Smith*, 8). The map symbol, like the eagle symbol above the Alcatraz cell house, stands for authority. To be sure, maps have demonstrated tremendous resilience as colonial constructs. Smith knows that one can fight icons only with icons, so she outmaps the maps.

Where Do We Come From?

The impossibility of denial is at the heart of another map painting from the same era, the less evocative but more interrogative *Where Do We Come From?* (Fig. 2.9). Like the previous paintings, this one enters into dialogue not only with the canon of American mapmaking but also with the canon of Johns's maps. Notice here, though, how the interplay between the visual and the textual swerves the semiotics away from mere information and converts it into a combination of question and contemplation. If maps, at their core, signify placement and location, then one of their key functions is the cartography of identity. What happens, though, if the textual signifier of the map is replaced with questions? Instead of the outlines and colors serving as the primary field—what I call a foretext—they function instead as backdrop or context for the questions Smith poses, suggesting that the construct

"United States" is merely set design for the larger issue of Indian identity. In typical maps, state and city names fit neatly inside the parcels of states, but here the text superimposes itself on top of states, stretching, Manifest Destiny—like, from Massachusetts to Nevada, South Carolina to Arizona. In effect, Smith recalibrates the semiotic machine of the map, making it do different cultural work, altering it from a chart of Anglo incursion into a palette of Indian interrogation. As part of his reading of aboriginal maps, David Turnbull acknowledges the sometimes-totalizing effect that maps can have on indigenous cultures: "Maps, like theories, have power in virtue of introducing modes of manipulation and control that are not possible without them. They become evidence of reality in themselves and can only be challenged through the production of other maps or theories" (*Maps Are Territories*, 54). In the case of this painting, Smith collapses Turnbull's poles of meaning in one text—it is both map and theory.

Indian Map and *Memory Map*

Smith's first foray into map painting came in 1992, when she found herself responding to Columbus's quincentenary. She understood then the kind of power that maps hold in the popular imagination, especially in regard to theories of nationalism. Her response to the hemisphere-wide celebration of the Columbian project was *Indian Map* (Fig. 2.10), a phenomenally complex and gorgeous canvas that inverts the symbology of American claims on identity, land, and representation. One of the first things to notice is the color. Though the map includes earth tones and deep blues, the dominant shade is red, underscoring the Indianness of the space the painting demarcates. But again, Smith refuses to provide the expected place names; instead, she allows photographs, newspaper clippings, and other memorabilia to signify tracts of land. Almost every inch is covered with either photos or headlines. In fact, it is difficult to know where to begin decoding this painting; there is so much information, all of it in dialogue with itself. In the bottom-right corner, where Georgia would be, Smith gets in a dig at Manifest Destiny ("From Sea to Shining Sea"); over Ohio and West Virginia, an ironic reference to white encroachment ("Pilgrim's Progress"); between Mexico and Texas, a play on identity and citizenship ("Patrolling the Borders"); on top of Washington, D.C., she makes a statement about government and ethics ("The Bad Boys"); and over northern California and Nevada, a darkly comic twist on how Indian land was "purchased" from tribes ("Get away with the best deal of this century"). As is often the case with a Smith painting, image accompanies text. Pictures of Indian leaders (Chief Joseph on the border of the United States and Canada, icons of classic Indian portraiture, and images from newspaper articles and advertisements, all Indian-related) help drive home the point that people, actual people with faces, inhabit these spaces and participate in the daily drama of the United States. According to Sasse, Smith's use and positioning of Chief Joseph is key, since it serves "as a sobering reminder of this leader's resistance to White encroachment" (*Jaune Quick-to-See Smith*, 8). But, Smith refuses to confine such symbolism to Chief Joseph. The map bleeds with the color and iconography of resistance.

In its color, the map might be largely monochromatic, but its larger signification is pluralistic. Images, words, ideas, and symbols interact with one another in a cacophony of semiotic interpenetration. In fact, so multivalent is *Indian Map* that it holds within its fuzzy borders an infinite number of possible readings: map as evidence of Indian presence; map as actuation of Indian sovereignty; map as catalogue of transgression; map as billboard for indigenous survivance; map as visual history of empire; map as visual history of Native resistance to empire; map as fictional blueprint of colonization; map as visual poem of Native ubiquity; map as fluidity; map as mutability; map as ultimate text of activism. In this painting and others, Smith abrogates the map's traditional utility as a kind of flowchart

which indigenous symbology erases American symbology, relegating to the background the diagram of colonization. While the borders between states find clearer definition here than in some of her other paintings, those distinct borders remain part of the backdrop, while several petroglyphic symbols occupy or extend into almost every state, transforming the painting from a map of land to a map of 40,000 years of human habitation. The past that the petroglyphic figures connote usurps the contemporary notion of America that the bordered states denote.

Visually, Smith makes an ironic statement about American ideas of spatiality by arranging her symbols in a grid (Fig. 2.12)—the layout of choice for almost every American city. I see both artistic and thematic similarities in this piece and in LeAnne Howe's *Shell Shaker*, in which Howe creates a narrative matrix of historical and contemporary indigenous narratives. The present not only tries to impose itself on the past, but it also tries to configure that past to track back to the present. Both Howe and Smith create a fabulous tension between order and chaos. The colored states of Smith's world, with their imperfect borders, look messy, while the symmetrical grid of symbols organizes and arranges the compositional space. The overlay also provides compositional structure to the painting, making Native semiology feel patterned and the United States random. In effect, Smith negates the newness of the U.S. map; its relevance becomes open for debate.

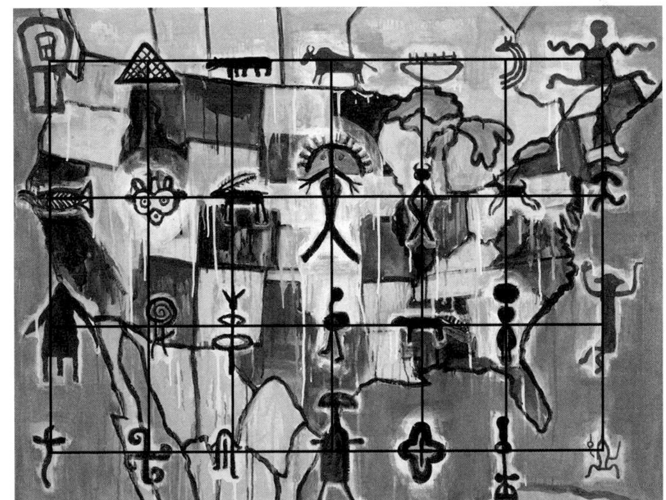

FIGURE 2.12. *Petroglyphs creating a grid that also embodies indigenous polarities.*

That organization arises not simply out of painterly balance but also out of indigenous reconciliation. In her essay on ritual reversal in the peyote hunt among the Wirikuta, Barbara G. Myerhoff argues for the symbolic importance of polarity. "Polarity reaffirms continuity," she writes. And to drive her point home, she quotes Alan Watts: "'Polar opposites are therefore inseparable opposites, like the poles of the earth or of a magnet, or the ends of a stick or the faces of a coin'" ("Return to Wirikuta," 233). Not only does Smith's grid pattern suggest a matrix of polarities, but the indigenous symbols fused to the American map also create a new level of polarity—a world in which Anglo and Native symbologies form two poles of competing and commingled worlds.

Through the creation and reversal of these poles, *Memory Map*, along with the rest of Smith's map paintings, enacts what Barbara Babcock calls "symbolic inversion," which she defines, in part, as "any act of expressive behavior which inverts, contradicts, abrogates, or in some fashion presents an alternative to the commonly held cultural codes, values and norms, be they linguistic, literary or artistic, religious or social and political" (*The World Upside Down*, 14). I would add "spatial" to that list of adjectives, but its absence suggests the degree to which mapping has been internalized as objective. Smith not only "inverts" the map of the United States, but also contradicts and abrogates the linguistic and symbolic machinery that makes a map a blueprint for conquest. In some cases, her symbolic inversion finds expression through deconstruction; in other paintings, through reconstruction. But in all cases, her maps are about instruction.

The *Browning of America* Series

In a similar painting, *The Browning of America II* (Fig. 2.13), Smith moves away from the grid, deconstructing the infrastructure of borders. But she retains the primacy of indigenous symbols. Note also how the national borders remain—suggesting the painting is less about empire and more about nationalism.

For me, the two most important distinctions between this painting and *Memory Map* are the absence of state borders and the piece's color palette. In fact, the two details work symbiotically to create an entirely different visual effect in the former, despite its many technical similarities to the latter. Many of Smith's map paintings resemble quilts, the states stitched together in bold colors. But here, the tactile component has gone the way of state names and borders. Instead, the United States is rendered like the wall of a cave painting. Its flat color plane, painted a deep terra cotta—a mixture of brown and red—takes the metaphor of *Memory Map* one step further. This aesthetic detail turns what might otherwise be little more than a painting with political overtones into a political tableau. In effect, Smith turns the liminal space of the United States into a tabula rasa, except for the petroglyphs. Before states, before state names, before borders, and before federalism, this space was inhabited, inscribed, and marked by people who remain part and parcel of its ontology. The list of names off the Atlantic seaboard signifies a host of invasions and invaders who crossed the threshold onto Indian land, but Smith's careful positioning of them in the margins relegates their power to the peripheries. Their one-dimensional signs, with their Arabic letters, pale, both literally and metaphorically, against the awe-inspiring symbolic field. This map may not tell us where we are going, but it tells us where people have been, and it tells us where people are.

Maps distinguish themselves from pictures in their objectivity. Like science or journalism, they are supposed to be neutral, value free, and so they carry a putative authority. But, what happens when that authority is called into question? What do Smith's map paintings say about the larger empirical project for which maps function as a tool? Smith's maps alter traditional modes of understanding by forcing the viewer to reconsider how objectivity and subjectivity accompany two seemingly dissimilar texts—maps and paintings. To illustrate, I offer a personal anecdote. The companion painting to *The Browning of America II* is *The Browning of America* (Fig. 2.14), which also happens to be the background image for my laptop and for the computer I work on in my office—making it the only image on my desktop. I get a lot of questions about the piece, and I find that I have a hard time talking about it casually; discussions of it generally involve an unsolicited and probably uninvited explanation or lecture. This is also the same computer that I take on every airline flight. Not long ago, while I was returning to San Francisco, a man sitting next to me on the plane inquired about the painting. "What is that on your wallpaper?" he asked. I didn't understand the reference at first, but then I remembered that "wallpaper" is PC lingo for "desktop." I was surprised by my response. "It's a map," I said. "That's an unusual looking map," he said. "Yeah it is," I responded. "I mean, it's actually a painting. A painting of a map. A kind of, you know, imagined map." "Yeah," he said. "I wasn't sure if it was a painting or a map." We had a very brief discussion about paintings versus maps before going back to our respective tasks.

But our talk intrigued me.

His question, my response, and his subsequent comments made me think of how narrowly we tend to conceive of maps and how the multiperspectivism of Smith's map paintings challenges our narrow conceptions of what maps are. For my fellow passenger, the piece would have to be a painting or a map—one is objective, the other subjective. It couldn't be both. As I indicated previously, there is a kind of assumed objectivity associated with maps.[6] Elsewhere in this book, I make other connections between Native representations of land, landscape, and place (as in the discussion of Silko's "Storyteller," for instance) and literary and cinematic representations of land, landscape, and space (in the section on the film *Skins*). But the visual has always enjoyed less leeway than the verbal. Perhaps that is the reason Smith's canvases surprise so.

FIGURE 2.13. (facing page) *Jaune Quick-to-See Smith,* The Browning of America II, *2000. Oil, collage, and mixed media on canvas. 36 × 48 in. Courtesy of the artist.*

FIGURE 2.14. (facing page) *Jaune Quick-to-See Smith,* The Browning of America, *2000. Oil, collage, and mixed media on canvas. 36 × 48. Courtesy of the artist.*

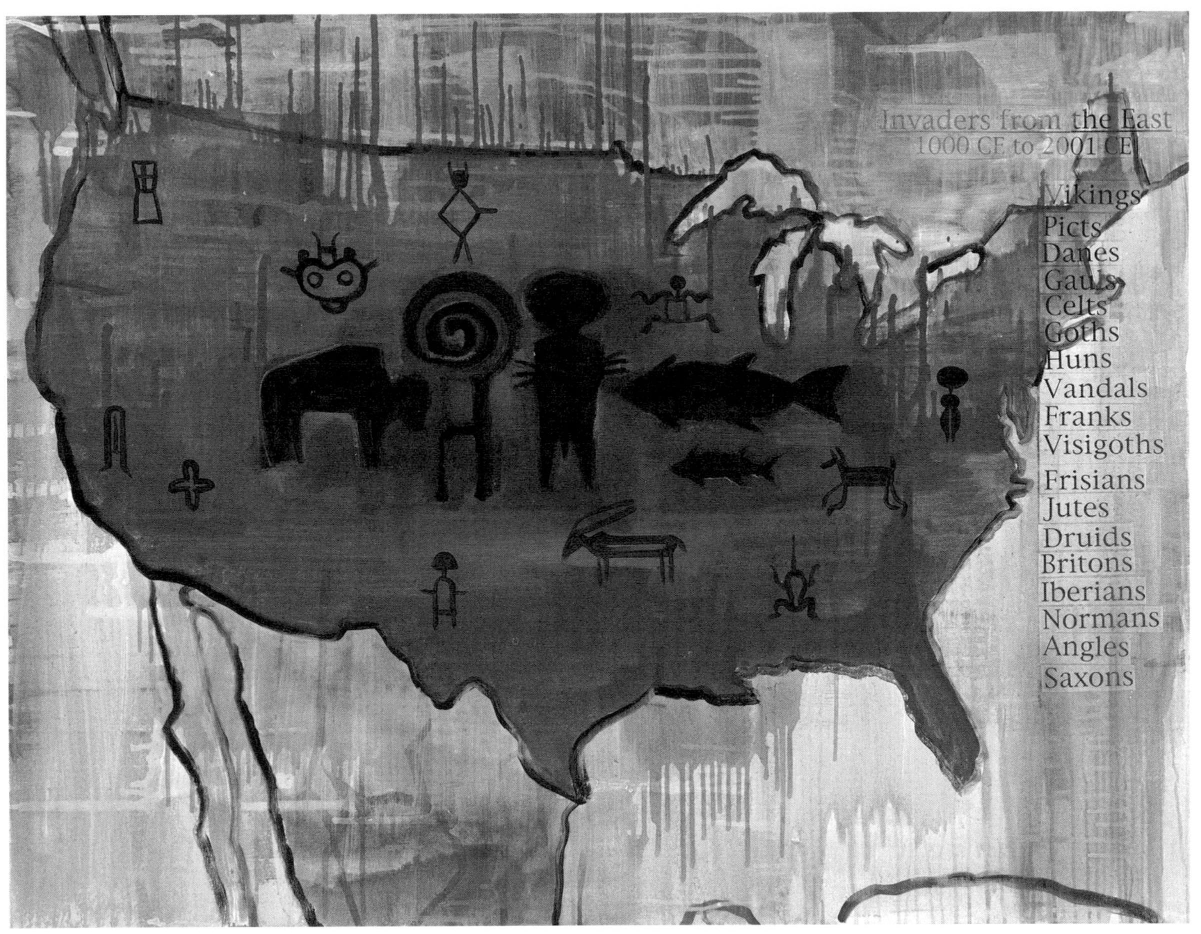

Invaders from the East
1000 CE to 2001 CE
Vikings
Picts
Danes
Gauls
Celts
Goths
Huns
Vandals
Franks
Visigoths
Frisians
Jutes
Druids
Britons
Iberians
Normans
Angles
Saxons

Gauls
Franks
Frisians
Druids
Iberians
Saxons

2.13

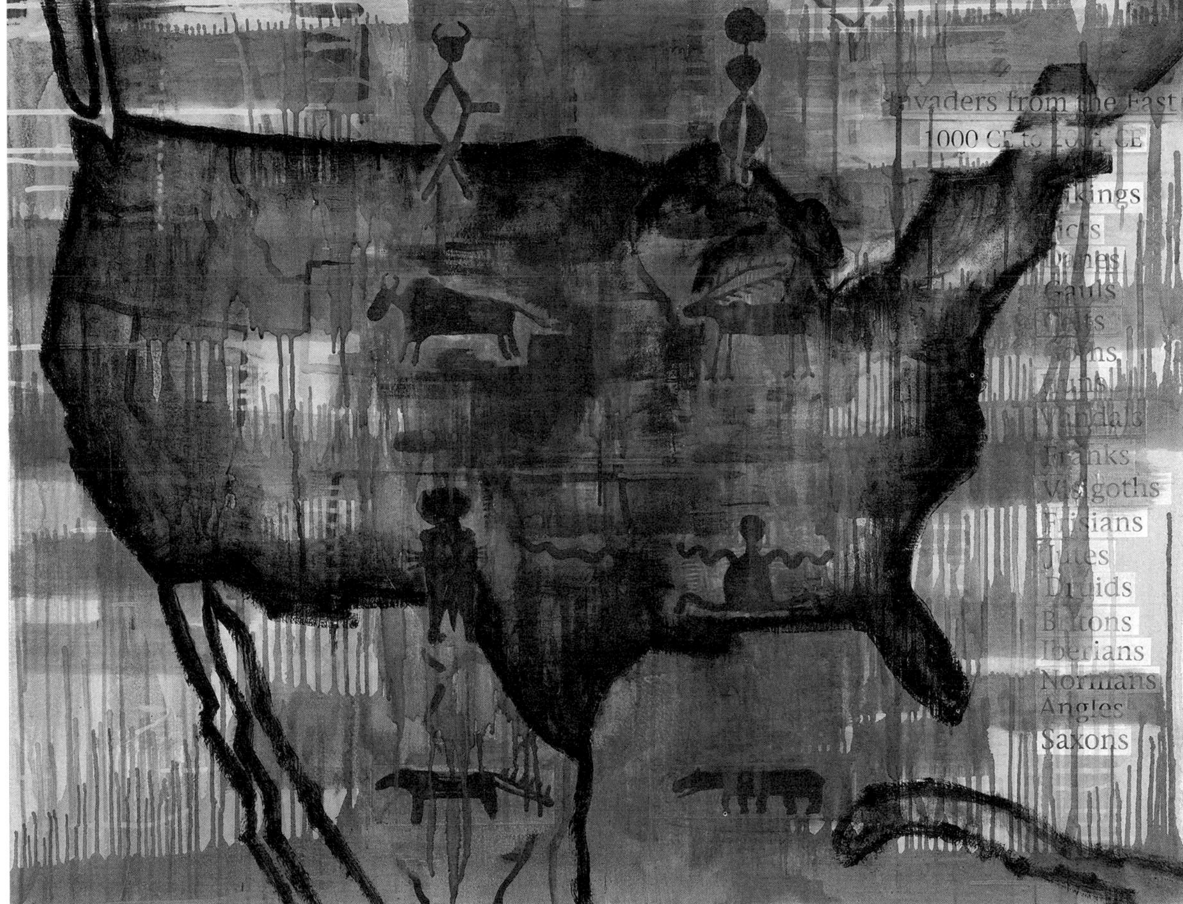

2.14

To me, the paintings in the *Browning of America* series operate as maps in a way that Johns's paintings of the United States do not. Johns offers a realistic cartographic representation of the lower forty-eight states as we have come to identify them. In fact, formally speaking, Johns's paintings are more maplike than Smith's. But if maps are designed to help us navigate a place, we need more than words and colors. In many ways, Smith's maps predict tools such as Google Maps and the visually annotated maps of the digital era that narrate as well as chart space. In the case of *The Browning of America*, one of my favorite paintings of the twenty-first century, the map also narrates a mythic history. The canvas looks more like an excavated parchment than a detailed map—some areas are darker and hazier than others. Most striking, of course, are the drawings. Daubed across the landscape of a browned America, figures that seem to have come from petroglyphs hover like spectral shadows over various regions of the country. A large armless human straddles the borders of Texas, Arizona, and Mexico; a human who looks to be either flying or doing the splits splays herself and her wavy, snakelike arms over Alabama, Louisiana, Mississippi, and Missouri; a stark bison or buffalo seems to erase all borders between Nebraska and Wyoming; a faint, almost ghostly elk fades into the background of the lower Great Lakes region; otherworldly mammals appear to be migrating across the Gulf of Mexico and Mexico itself; and, most bizarrely, rising out of the bottom right-hand corner of the painting as though in pursuit of the animal in the Gulf, a creature that looks like the Loch Ness monster lurches toward Florida and the rest of the tasty United States. These characters not only mark but also animate the landscape, moving it from map to vision; the figures simultaneously inhabit and imbue land. They inscribe the reality that space is lived.

For me, this painting oozes contextual resistance by completely unwriting the traditional text of mapping. For one, it suggests the degree to which humans, animals, and the mythical visions of both are woven into the land and space of the United States. "Beneath the map imposed by science is a map in the blood," writes Gould in response to the Hogan poem that begins this chapter, "that takes us back to a more original knowing—that we are not a separate creation" ("Poems as Maps," 29). For Hogan, Gould, and Smith, poetic and aesthetic cartographies don't just map space, but also lay out a diagram of how that space has been inhabited. In keeping with Gould's point, the borders between the individual states in Smith's painting seem less important than the interplay between animal, human, and vision. As I suggest in the chapter on the new Native novel, identity is both formed and forged through dialogical relation. Part of the work in this painting is an attempt to chart the dialogical history of this land's embodied animus.

Furthermore, Gould's recognition that Native maps forge "a more original knowing" gets visually calculated through the antiqued texture of the painting, a technique that reminds the viewer of the fact that Native tribes have been inhabiting and imagining these spaces for a very, very long time and that they have, despite countless incursions (as represented by the column of Anglo names anchored off the East coast), maintained semiotic sovereignty. Last, the foretext of noticeable crimson streaks that trickle from the upper Midwest down through Oklahoma and Missouri before appearing to bleed through Texas marks vistas of violence that themselves cannot be an unimagined part of this land. Ultimately, these components articulate not just a symbolic inversion but also an ontology of resistance. The painting, then, converts the whitewashing of Native America that "normal" maps typically do and instead advances Smith's own red cleansing of America. Because it marks its own space, determines its own boundaries, and applies values and life to the land and the history of occupation and removal from the land, *The Browning of America* establishes not only a kind of aesthetic sovereignty but a sort of spatial one as well. To circumscribe space, to inhabit it, to visually create and envision it, is to make it, is to be it.

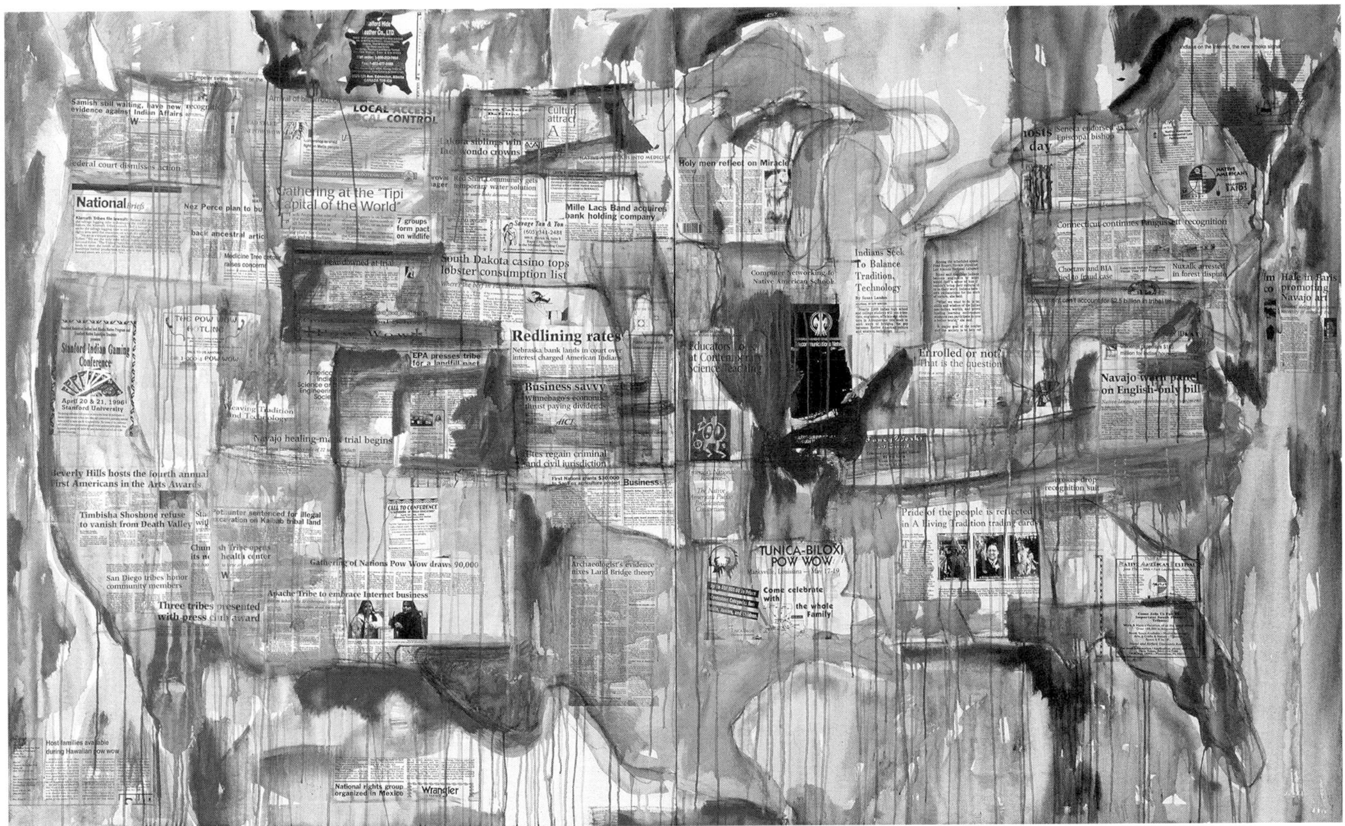

Indian Country Today

As provocative as all the aforementioned pieces are, Smith's *Indian Country Today* (1996; Fig. 2.15) remains, for me, her most impressive piece of work and one of the most important pieces of American art in the last forty years. In this piece, Smith creates yet another visual-lexical map, yet this one features newspaper clippings about Native issues—most of which are state specific—pasted into each individual state. As with *Indian Map*, there is too much information in *Indian Country Today* to parse it all here, but suffice it to say that the subjects of many of the stories focus on the gamut of experience—celebrations, powwows, Indian laws, language issues, casinos, economic issues, and the tension between tradition and technology.

One of the main assertions of the National Museum of the American Indian (NMAI) is that Indians are still present in the United States. *Indian Country Today* makes a similar point in a similar way—just on a smaller scale. The NMAI draws from myriad media to help tell the story of historical Native America and contemporary Native America. It relies on artifacts and texts to construct a multifaceted narrative about Indian survivance; here, Smith relies less on paint and more on news clippings to create a discourse of identity. In other map paintings, the paint tends to occlude much of the textuality of the artwork, but in *Indian Country Today*, the news takes precedence over the map. For readers who may not be aware of it, *Indian Country Today* is also the name of the largest Indian newspaper in the United States, so the title of Smith's canvas carries a double meaning. On one hand, it calls attention to a major national newspaper run by Indians, which generally does a fantastic job keeping its readers apprised of tribal life all across the United States. On the other hand, the various stories function as mininarratives, vignettes of Native experience that help prove the point that the land parceled out on this map is, in fact, Indian country today.

FIGURE 2.15. *Jaune Quick-to-See Smith,* Indian Country Today, *1996. Acrylic and collage on canvas. 60 × 100 in. Courtesy of the artist.*

One of the colonial functions of maps is to narrate dominance; they tell stories of acquisition and ownership. It is a mistake to assume that maps are purely informational. At their core, they are political. "Mapping is, of course, an intensely political enterprise," observes Louis Owens, "an essential step toward appropriation and possession. Maps write the conquerors' stories over the stories of the conquered" (quoted in Vizenor, *Fugitive Poses*, 170). What I love most about Smith's map paintings, and this one in particular, is how, with great artistic care and with attention to aesthetic detail, she reverses this trend. She imprints the stories of Indians over the storytelling device of America. For a century, America has deployed the map of the lower forty-eight to illustrate the metanarrative of Manifest Destiny, but Smith reminds us that America remains Indian country both pragmatically and geographically. Instead of the interior spaces of the states being empty, except for an occasional state capitol and major city, Smith populates her map with voices and accounts of Indians in Indian country.

An interesting effect of the news clippings is the subtext of authority and objectivity they lend the painting. They endow it with a documentary quality that vivifies a typically vacant space. In fact, all of Smith's paintings, but *Indian Country Today* in particular, can be seen as an artistic form of what William Stott would call "social documentary." For Stott, social documentary "educates one's feelings" and "encourages social improvements" in regard to "conditions neither permanent nor necessary," such as the Depression, police brutality, racial discrimination, or, in the case of Smith, Indian removal, termination policies, and the eradication of indigenous cultures (*Documentary Expression*, 19, 21).[7] For Stott, aesthetic projects take on the role of documentary when they concurrently activate emotion and intellect in order to catalyze social change. Smith's canvases work on both levels—they inform and move, startle and stir.

Creek poet Joy Harjo makes a similar observation about *Indian Country Today*, likening it to an expose:

> *Indian Country Today* is not a neat patchwork quilt. It is, however, a patchwork of guilt. There are no easy boundaries or lines in this nation. How do you concurrently illustrate the original concept of sovereign tribal nations who held lands in common and overlap from other tribal nations? Which U.S. law has attempted to erase with treaties, compacts, and lies and new boundaries made by these U.S. Laws? The map shifts and twists with each lie, though the boundaries of states and the U.S. are always neatly marked by cartographers who illustrate the lie. The boundaries are false and they drip in shame. Forming this nation of nations are phrases and questions that have gone into forming what is called the U.S. of America. Words are powerful and create the reality of the world in which we live.
>
> —("CREATION STORY," 65–66)

Like Owens, Harjo understands how easily stories and lies get inscribed into the public consciousness, how frequently they get written into national narratives of subjugation and relegation. Both Harjo and Smith reinvent the enemy's language. They engage the discourse of mastery but resist its discourse of dominance. Through the two-pronged approach of words and image, Smith attacks that discourse from multiple perspectives, calling into question the objectivity and finality of the atlas of empire.

Smith discredits the atlas of empire through a nuanced understanding of the semiotics of representation. Without question, both culturally and geographically, the United States is a text. The semiotics of geography and represented space must not be overlooked. To read the United States is to explicate the narrative of boundaries, borders, and bodies. We are comfortable doing this lexically, but perhaps not so much visually. In regard to poetic cartography, Gould notes the impossibility of making a perfect map: "No map can really tell us all we need to know, and a map made of language—as all maps are—must necessarily be an imperfect rendering despite the poet's attempts to mark the way" ("Poems as Maps," 33). So complex is our visual and cultural notion of Indian space that one map is not enough. Smith must paint many. Each map gets at a different nuance; each one peels another layer off the American onion.

In his fine poem "Atlas," near the beginning of his wonderful collection *Shapeshift*, Navajo poet Sherwin Bitsui imagines back to 1868: "In the cave on the backside of a lie / soldiers eye the birth of a new atlas" (7). Like Harjo, Bitsui is interested in unearthing the many untruths buried deep beneath American maps. Smith's map paintings ask us to rethink the lie we have been sold, the bill of goods we have been handed, the flinty parcel of land we have been given. To help us, she illustrates what a cartography of truth—the semiotics of sovereignty—might actually look like. Herself a visionary and a soldier in the long war of self-determination, it is Smith who gives birth to a new atlas.

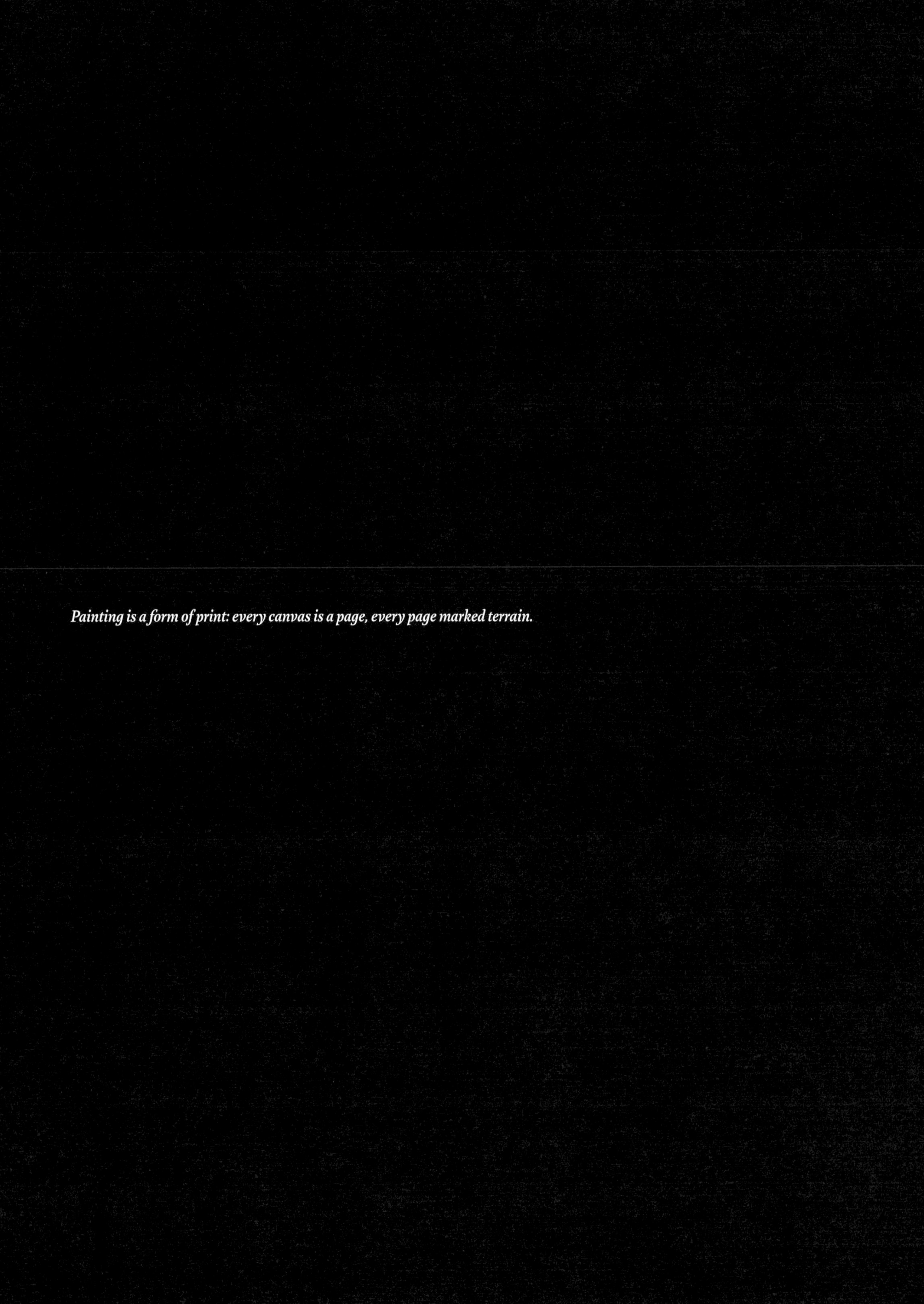

Painting is a form of print: every canvas is a page, every page marked terrain.

3. THE NEW AMERICAN INDIAN NOVEL

A USER'S MAP

We have changed a lot,
but we still know how to fight.

"TO BEGIN TO WRITE about something called 'the American Indian novel,'" Louis Owens cagily observes, "is to enter a slippery and uncertain terrain" (*Other Destinies*, 1). When talking or writing about the progression of the American Indian novel, most critics begin their discussion with N. Scott Momaday's 1969 masterpiece *House Made of Dawn*, citing its Pulitzer Prize and its inauguration of the so-called Native American Renaissance. Frequently, such readers employ cartographic metaphors to illustrate the importance of Momaday's book—how it altered the "landscape" of Native literature, how it was a "compass" for other writers, how it put Indian writing on the "map." Indeed, in her introduction to a 1999 issue of *Modern Fiction Studies* devoted to Native American fiction, Nancy J. Peterson begins her essay with just such a claim: "The acclaim given to *House Made of Dawn* (and Momaday's next published work, *The Way to Rainy Mountain*) not only provided Momaday well-deserved recognition, but, just as importantly, it helped to put Native American literature and Native American authors on the American cultural map" ("Introduction," 1). Such terminology suggests not simply a charting of cultural terrain, but also a peopling of that terrain and a need for a reading and writing population to move from literary place to literary place. Without question, the map of Native literature has expanded since Momaday's novel and Peterson's essay. Like America and Native America, it has become more complex, more diverse, and harder to circumscribe. Despite its many limitations, this chapter attempts an early sketch of what a map of the American Indian novel in the twenty-first century might look like and how a reader might navigate the topography of Native novels in what we should think of as the post-Renaissance era.[1]

We are now post-Renaissance not simply because of a new millennium but also because we have passed the "rebirth" of Native writing. In fact, we have passed adolescence and moved well into adulthood. Michael Dorris's 1979 claim that there is no such thing as a Native American literature seems from another age. In fact, we know Native American literature exists because in some circles that term is now out of fashion. The movement away from pan-Indian literature toward nationalism reveals the degree to which Native literature has staked its claim in a new time and a new place.

Though poetry, short stories, and nonfiction have certainly made their mark, there is no denying that the American Indian novel remains the most visible landmark on the landscapes of Native writing and mainstream American culture. Devon A. Mihesuah (Choctaw) reaffirms this observation in her essay on being an "unpopular" writer: "When *AIQ* [*American Indian Quarterly*] put out a call for opinions as to what works by Indigenous authors have most influenced readers, the responses were more than depressing. What I got were lists that featured 98 percent fiction writers" ("Finding Empowerment through Writing and Reading," 98). Granted, she does not distinguish between fiction writers and novels, but Mihesuah does talk about how, under her editorship, most of the submissions to *AIQ* focused on *House Made of Dawn* and Leslie Marmon Silko's *Ceremony*. To be sure, many syllabi for classes in Native American literature comprise readings that are entirely or nearly entirely drawn from novels. So even within the scholarly community of Native studies, the novel reigns supreme.[2] To map that kingdom, then, is, as Owens says in the epigraph, both slippery and uncertain, not only because Native novels can be complex, but also because they carry such authoritative weight both within and without Native studies.

Owens's excellent *Other Destinies: Understanding the American Indian Novel* (1992) was perhaps the first comprehensive study of the American Indian novel read through a Native lens, and it still stands as one of the best books devoted to Native fiction. Influenced by both Russian theorist Mikhail Bakhtin and Anishinaabe writer Gerald Vizenor, Owens positions the American Indian novel among the provenances of identity and culture. Borrowing from scholar James Clifford, Owens argues that "novels by Native American authors might be thought of as 'local narratives of cultural continuity and recovery,'" tribally based texts that tell the stories of an individual and a community. "American Indian novelists," Owens continues, "are revising fundamentally the long-cherished, static view of Indian lives and cultures (or noncultures) held by people around the world" (28). It is exactly this belief—that the Native novel is a window into the magic, power, mystery, and realities of American Indian culture—that has attracted so many readers, scholars, and teachers.

As readers of this book might know, Ojibwe author David Treuer argues the complete opposite in his recent and highly publicized manifesto *Native American Fiction: A User's Manual* (2006). Treuer urges devotees of the Native novel to stop reading them through a cultural lens and start looking at them, first and foremost, through a literary lens. Toward the end of his chapter on Louise Erdrich's *Love Medicine*, Treuer makes a case for noncultural criticism: "It is so tempting for me to read *Love Medicine* as a cultural proof, and for a long time I did . . . But to make it divine (and isn't that what we ask of culture today) is to destroy its humanity. To treat it as culture is to destroy it as literature" (68–69). From Treuer's perspective, seeing Native novels as cultural documents not only gives the illusion of tribal understanding and Indian verisimilitude, but also undermines what critics used to refer to as a writer's "genius."

The subtitle for this chapter plays off Treuer's but goes in a different direction. A user's manual connotes a utilitarian objective, perhaps even a step-by-step guide for decoding Native literary texts. A map, on the other hand, is less of a how-to and more of a where-to. It is more speculative and less proscriptive than a guide, and it suggests a special connection rather than a linear one. This chapter proceeds in that vein, noting cross-connections and webs of intersections.

This chapter's cartography draws from both Treuer's and Owens's studies of Native novels in hopes of creating an abbreviated atlas of the American Indian novel in the early days of the new millennium. To this end, I look only at novels published after 2000: *Perma Red*, by Debra Magpie Earling (2002); *A Pipe for February*, by Charles H. Red Corn (2005); *The*

Plague of Doves, by Louise Erdrich (2008); *Shell Shaker*, by LeAnne Howe (2001); *The Translation of Dr. Apelles: A Love Story*, by David Treuer (2008); *Drowning in Fire*, by Craig Womack (2001); *The Last Report on the Miracles at Little No Horse*, by Louise Erdrich (2001); *Flight*, by Sherman Alexie (2007); and *Miko Kings*, by LeAnne Howe (2007). Since my project involves mapping rather than surveillance, cartography not cataloguing, it is important to state at the outset that I do not intend to offer even remotely exhaustive interpretations of these books. Unlike the chapter on "Storyteller," this one is far from telescoping; in fact, it is its polar opposite: a tracking shot, a charting of trends, movements, and strategies that might offer some sort of direction for those attempting to navigate their way through the Native novel in the first decade of this new era, all the while keeping close to my own meridian of engaged resistance. Also, since most of these novels have only recently been published, virtually no peer-reviewed sources exist for these books. What secondary sources lurk out there in the desolate suburbia of literary criticism tend to be reviews, and those tend to be online. So while I hope in these remaining pages to show new Native novels as being in dialogue with one another, I regret that I am less able than I would like to enter into a similar scholarly dialogue. Without question, though, as these novels make their way into classrooms and libraries, that will change.

"Before 1968, only nine novels by American Indian authors had been published," notes Owens (*Other Destinies*, 24). If those nine novels were pre-Renaissance, this chapter maps nine novels published in the post-Renaissance era of the twenty-first century in hopes of providing a Janus-faced criticism, a mirror (sometimes a reverse mirror) of invention and revolution. Nine novels are a lot to diagram in one chapter, so to make that nearly impossible task more manageable, I read the books in groups or, more often, in pairs. This strategy not only shows the thematic byways connecting the novels, but also underscores the degree to which Native writing functions as a community. Taiaiake Alfred begins his study of indigenous identity by laying out tenets of fundamental indigeneity. For Alfred, what "makes an individual 'indigenous' is his or her situation within a community . . . To know indigenous people, those seeking knowledge must interact with indigenous communities, in all their past and present complexity" (*Peace, Power, Righteousness*, xvi, xvi–xvii). I am less interested in reading new Native novels as silos dotting the literary landscape than in situating these books within the community of Native noveling. More interesting than decoding each book as an autotelic text is to show it in conversation with other texts. It is through this community of knowledge seeking and novel writing that we can best chart the unfurling growth of the Native novel.

The Past Is Always Present: *Perma Red, A Pipe for February,* and *The Plague of Doves*—Three Tribalographies

At first glance, it would appear impossible to find three American Indian novels more different from one another. One, a first novel by an unknown writer that sold and was reviewed surprisingly well; the second, by an even more unknown independent writer whose novel was published by a university press to virtually no reviews or acclaim; and a much-heralded novel by one of America's best-loved authors. What connects the work of writers Debra Magpie Earling (Salish), Charles H. Red Corn (Osage), and Louise Erdrich (Ojibwe)—utterly distinct writers from utterly distinct tribes—is an interest in revisiting specific past transgressions in hopes of either explaining or resolving the tribal present. In short, all three of these novels also function as important texts of tribalography.

In her autobiographical essay "My Mothers, My Uncles, Myself," Choctaw writer LeAnne Howe unfolds what, for her, tribalography means: "My obligation . . . is that I must learn more about my ancestors, understand them better than I imagined. Then I must be able to render all our collective experiences into a meaningful form. I call this process 'tribalography'" (214–215). Two years later, in a follow-up essay, "The Story of America: A Tribalography," Howe expands her definition of tribalography: "Native stories, no matter what form they take . . . seem to pull all the elements together of the storyteller's tribe, meaning the people, the land, and multiple characters and all their manifestations and revelations, and connect these in the past, present, and future milieus . . . I have tried to show that tribalography comes from the Native propensity for bringing things together" (42). The main motif connecting Howe's two descriptions of tribalography—the connection of past and present, the ability to synthesize historical and tribal events of the past with what is happening now—is already expanding. Though none of the three writers featured here is Choctaw, the need to bring things together into a meaningful form crosses tribal boundaries. The remainder of this section will read these three novels through a tribalographic lens in an attempt to show that localized narratives of the past can contextualize—even if they don't explain—episodes of the present.

Of the nine books under study in this chapter, these three are the most traditional in theme and narrative strategy. They focus on family trauma, identity, and the complicated tensions between Indians and whites. What sets these books apart from other historical novels, such as Erdrich's *Tracks*, is that they do not take place during the nineteenth century but rather in the "in-between" decades of the 1920s, 1930s, and 1940s. Framed by the mythic past and the metapresent, these novels take place in neither yet shed light on both, serving as connective tissue between parts of the historical body. In the case of *Perma Red* and *A Pipe for February*, there are clear autobiographical overtones: the main character, Louise, is based on Earling's Aunt Louise, and a lovely photograph of two members of Red Corn's family graces the cover of his book. Yet just as these books are not merely family histories, they are not autobiographies either. This differentiates them from novels like *Winter in the Blood*, of which Owens writes: "[James] Welch delves into an Indian past, re-membering, putting together the fragments of that past into a significant whole which confers identity and meaning upon the protagonist" (*Other Destinies*, 147). *The Plague of Doves*, *A Pipe for February*, and *Perma Red* distance themselves from such a narrative because their protagonists are not individuals but communities. In them, the reader learns more about a town, a place, or a tribe than about any one person, so when the reader either sees or imagines a future history unfolding, it is into an unresolved, even invisible present. Like Howe and Alfred, these writers see the circularity of past and present as necessary for a more inclusive notion of indigenous identity.

Unlike Welch in Owens's reading, none of these authors seems interested in assembling the "fragments of [the] past" into a cohesive whole or into the promise of a "better" future. What makes these books interesting as literature and as cultural windows is how they merge conventional storytelling with unconventional dénouements. Mapping these sites of authorial resistance, then, may provide us with a chart of how Native storytellers see history and the contemporary intersecting at the ground zero of tribal identity.

Like canonical novels such as Erdrich's *Love Medicine* and Susan Power's *The Grass Dancer*, these novels take the past as their points of departure, but they never assume that what is past stays in the past, despite both narrative and cultural pressure to understand the many transgressions buried there.[3] *The Plague of Doves* loops around the unsolved murder of an Anglo farming family that lived just off the reservation border in Pluto, North Dakota; *Perma Red* traces the history of intertribal, domestic, and interracial violence; while *A Pipe for February* explores suspiciously recurrent Osage "suicides" that have now come to be known as the "Osage murders." Though the plots of these novels never directly address issues of conquest per se, a refusal to be victimized by acts of internal or external violence becomes a powerful subtext.

For example, in *The Plague of Doves*, when a group of Indian men are about to be wrongfully hanged for the family's murder, they sing an Ojibwe resistance song:

> They began high—Cuthbert's voice a wild falsetto that cut the air. Asiginak joined him and Holy Track felt almost good, hearing the strength and power of their voices. And the words in the old language:
>
> These white men are nothing
> What they do cannot harm me
> I will see the face of mystery
>
> They sang the song twice before the Buckendorfs shook themselves and prepared the wagon.
>
> —(78–79)

That act of resistance burns itself into the memory of Mooshum, a boy at the time, and the only survivor of the hanging. Even though he never leaves his community, and even though he lives side by side with the vigilantes and their descendants his entire life, he never lets himself be defined by the near hanging, nor does he allow himself to forget the Indians' defiance. Such events almost never manifest in his day-to-day routine—whom he loves, what he eats—nevertheless, violence's nearness to that life means he is always haunted. Later in the novel, an aging Ojibwe judge perfectly articulates the intensity of proximate violence: "Nothing that happens, nothing, is not connected here by blood." William Faulkner understood as well as any American novelist the long, deep pull of blood and its inability to forget and forgo, but where Faulkner's vision homed in on families, Erdrich—Faulkner's Native counterpart—has spent her career exploring not just families but also entire communities and tribes.

The hanging scene embodies two major tropes each of these novels wrestles with in order to make sense of the past: the web of words and the web of geography. Both connect characters to one another and to their communities. The characters' inability to dissociate themselves from land, people, and places or from stories and language binds them to a zone of proximity. For example, later in life, after both he and the descendants of those killed and those who did the killing have had decades to internalize and remake the past, Mooshum asks Neve Harp, one of the matrons of Pluto, how either side could live knowing the town was stolen from the Ojibwe: "What you are asking is how was it stolen? How has this great thievery become acceptable? How do we live right here beside you, knowing what we lost and how you took it?" (84). The text of their conversation refers to Pluto, just inside the boundaries of the reservation, but the intentionally vague "it" suggests something else may have been stolen as well—the past, innocence, peace, trust, and respect. How both parties have been able to live together without those values is an even more provocative question.

Red Corn poses similar questions in *A Pipe for February*, in which a group of young, well-educated Osages try to deal with their newfound wealth (from oil money) and with the spate of "suicides" among wealthy members of the Osage community. On one hand, the influx of cash and moneyed sophistication into Pawhuska, Oklahoma, pulls them away from both their traditional weltanschauung and their Native languages. Fluent in English and Osage, the characters take afternoon tea, underwrite Olympic athletes, invest in real estate, and travel around the world. But as the deaths become more and more suspicious, it is clear that the magnetism of the Anglo world might also be lethal. Therein lies the tension in the novel—are the Anglos who help make the Osage rich also the ones responsible for killing them? Is a neighbor an enemy? How can one tell? And if one does suspect foul play, what are the realistic options?

As the death toll increases, its reality becomes harder to process. It is easier to retreat into the world of high tea, dancing, and gourmet dinners, but for others, for whom the scenario feels anchorless and without moorings, maintaining connections with the living manifestations of Osage tradition is the only recourse. Such is the case for John Grayeagle, the novel's protagonist, who is at home neither in the flashy new Anglo world nor in the mysterious world of Osage tradition. However, a reacquaintance with Wah-she-u-tse, an Osage elder and a keeper of traditional stories, who speaks only in Osage (which Red Corn indicates through italics), offers Grayeagle a level of wisdom he gets nowhere else. "There are people who want to harm us," Wah-she-u-tse tells Grayeagle. "It could be they want to harm us so they can have our money or our land. It could be they want to harm us for oil. It could be they want to harm us because they do not like Osages . . . They tell us that our children are dying from accidents. We know this is not true" (122). At first, Wah-she-u-tse, his odd ways, and his allegiance to the less-marketable Osage language feel more distant to Grayeagle than the happy-go-lucky Anglos he hangs out with, but over time, he begins to see a pattern emerge through the kaleidoscope of past and present, and it connects him to a larger spectrum of Osage history and temporality.

That pattern reveals a buried pipe, which becomes a metaphor for the importance of land and tradition, and a series of stories about the Osage past, which shed light on the bicultural present. In *The Plague of Doves*, years of intermarriage between Anglos and Ojibwe complicate the boundaries—both racial and geographic—between "Indian" and "white," but for the Osage in *A Pipe for February*, the boundaries remain distinct, for the moment. One can feel them becoming blurrier and blurrier all the time—hence, the reality check for Grayeagle and his friend Molly, who, speaking in Osage, gets to the crux of Osage identity and its value system:

> The man who spoke was a good man and I respect him. Still, one thing he said was not right. It will take more than white teachers to make us think like white people . . . It is true we sound like white people when we speak their language, and yet before we learned the language of the white people, we spoke Osage and our thoughts are Osage thoughts.
>
> Things in the mind and things in the heart make people what they are, and I know we were born with hearts that are Osage. That does not change. (230)

Molly perfectly articulates W. E. B. Du Bois's concept of "double consciousness" here—the sense of two-ness, of being divided, always seeing one's self or selves through the eyes of the other. For Mooshum and the Ojibwe, that meant assimilation and perhaps even acquiescing, but for Grayeagle and Molly, a cultural trinity of language, land, and ontology emerges to circumscribe identity and establish a moral compass. That connection to language keeps them connected and, like the pipe—the symbol of their own making—anchored to the land. Ultimately, it is that ontological rooting that engenders action. Earlier in the book, Wah-she-u-tse staked out his own moral imperative: "I am an old man. If I could find these people I would fight them. Maybe I am too old and I would be unable to kill them. Still, I would fight them. . . . Together, we would kill them. We have changed a lot, but we still know how to fight. We still know how to die if necessary" (122). The novel ends when Grayeagle and his friend track down the white men who have been killing the Osage in a kind of murder-for-profit scheme, but they find only the hit men. Who pulls the strings behind the operation remains a mystery—as do the full ramifications of these events on the present psychology of the tribe and even the mindset of the state of Oklahoma.

Whereas *The Plague of Doves* flies all the way up to the present, allowing us to hear, in a plurality of voices, what it means to be both white and Indian and living in a zone of past violence and current resentment, Red Corn offers no such closure for the Osage. The story simply stops. As readers, we get no authorial translation of the past onto the here and now, no contemporary voices from Pawhuska telling us how things are going—none, that is, except Red Corn's. Is his reworking of the past a warning call to the present? Is his novel a way of telling us that nothing ever really changes? One wonders whether Red Corn intends his book as a cautionary tale—the oil of the 1920s as a trope for today's intoxicating technology, a diversion that draws us away from what really matters. In an otherwise conventional novel, the rhetorical indeterminacy comes off as neither arbitrary nor experimental, but as wholly mimetic. In other words, maybe the novel does comment on contemporary Osage realities, and that comment is that Osage epistemological practices are still unfolding, still evolving, always unwritten and unwritable.

Like *A Pipe for February* and *The Plague of Doves*, *Perma Red* tells the story of a small Indian town reeling from unexplained murders and the mounting tensions between whites and Indians. But the unknown acts of violence—terrible as they are—can't compare with the known acts, most of them enacted upon lovers by lovers. Set on the Flathead reservation of Montana in the 1940s, *Perma Red* tracks Louise White Elk through a series of dysfunctional relationships that nearly leave her dead on more than one occasion. Unlike Red Corn's Pawhuska, where the Osage live like royalty, in Flathead, "life on the reservation is wretched," writes reviewer Peter Lewis. "Maltreatment and poverty are handmaidens to bad behavior and worse choices."

Written as a kind of paean to Earling's Aunt Louise, who was murdered at twenty-three, Earling's original manuscript was rejected by publishers because it was too violent. Indeed, even in its more sanitized, published version, brutality never leaves Louise's side. At almost every turn, she is cursed, stabbed, beaten, seduced, or assaulted—or, all too often, some combination thereof. Twice, she is left for dead. In each instance, the transgressors are either local lovers or her own husband, the notorious Baptiste Yellow Knife. In *A Pipe for February*, elders who speak Osage are an antidote to violence, but in Earling's world, the novelized Indian mysticism is bad magic and provides utterly no recourse. Just about the only elder in touch with traditional ways is Louise's mother-in-law, who holds a grudge against her and her family; so not even tradition provides succor here. Knowing the Native tongue does nothing, staying on Native land brings no renewal, marrying an Indian man offers no sense of wholeness or healing, sleeping with white men engenders no sense of hybridized strength, and avoiding alcohol doesn't seem to keep her out of trouble. Like the Ojibwe and Osage in Erdrich's and Red Corn's novels, proximity is the character's undoing, but unlike them, that proximity provides no exit strategy for Louise.

Also unlike the other two books, *Perma Red* contains virtually no likable characters. Louise is tough and determined and sexy and passionate and, at her best, full of self-generating resistance. But she is also weak and desperate and foolish and maddening. The closest she comes to agency is in her strategic marriage to Yellow Knife, which she sees as a possible entrée into a family in which "the old ways" are the present ways: "She knew she was now part of the oldest kind of marriage, a marriage of blood power. She wondered if what she really felt for Baptiste was only urgency to reclaim what Baptiste had taken from her. She did not feel romance for Baptiste Yellow Knife. She sensed Baptiste could change her" (123). What Baptiste has taken from Louise is the belief that Louise is her own agent: her sense of worth, of efficacy, of belonging. Later in the novel, she thinks she might be able to reclaim a little bit of these things through Charlie Kicking Woman, a hapless reservation sheriff, ridiculed by the white policemen and his fellow Indians. Like Louise, he is paralyzed by his position, tied up and gagged by the tight straps of the reservation, its strangling history, and its strangling present.

Earling experiments with a storytelling technique that makes Kicking Woman come off as particularly sympathetic, despite his ineffectuality. Like *The Plague of Doves*, *Perma Red* is narrated by different characters with different points of view. The Louise chapters are told by a third-person omniscient narrator, while the Officer Kicking Woman chapters are told in the first person, by Charlie himself. Thus, the reader finds herself identifying with Charlie, whereas Louise always feels distant, both unknown and unknowable. In a novel about proximity, in a novel about Perma Red (Louise's nickname), the reader never gets particularly close to her, though she is also never too far on the periphery—certainly not for Charlie, who wants Louise more than anything. Ultimately, it is Charlie, not Louise, who finally enacts the most forceful act of resistance, and because we have witnessed so much badness through his eyes, we cheer him on.

Toward the end of novel, two white men take Louise for an ominous ride. We realize that one of the men was responsible for some previous murders, including that of Louise's sister, and we realize that they are about to kill Louise, a realization she comes to herself. In her own act of defiance, she grabs the steering wheel and forces an accident, which throws her from the car and traps one of the men, Harry Stoner, within the mangled automobile. The smell of gasoline is strong. As Charlie goes to save him, he is visited by a vision and says to himself, "I can save the whole Flathead nation" (277), after which, he sets the car and Stoner on fire. For Charlie, who has never been a great sheriff, this is his crowning act of justice. In this manner, Charlie resembles Rudy in both the novel and film version of *Skins*—a tribal police officer driven more by his own desires than an ethic of law and order. For both men, though, important moments of personal and tribal justice merge through acts of vigilantism. In a world where tribal police have little power to effect change, enacting justice requires them to abandon the Western conception of policing and adopt local, even trickster-based, value systems. For Charlie and Rudy—as for the occupiers of Alcatraz—transgression equals justice.

Aside from her decision to grab the steering wheel, Louise's great act of resistance is her refusal to die. Beaten, thrown from a racing car, and nearly frozen, she stubbornly resists the fate of so many Salish women before her. That said, the final scene of the novel doesn't show her leaving the reservation or returning to school or even embracing "the old ways." Rather, Earling closes her novel with Louise eagerly stepping toward Baptiste Yellow Knife, who, we are supposed to believe, may have righted himself and who has come to claim his wife. Will things be different for Louise and Baptiste? Will he kill her, as Earling's Aunt Louise was killed? Will they become two drunks who never leave Flathead? The reader never finds out.

As with *A Pipe for February*, the reader also never knows what these events in the past mean for the present, and to a certain degree, the same holds true for *The Plague of Doves*. In each of the novels, the reader is left not with easy morality or revisionism but with the indeterminate reality of small-town lives strangled by an inability to either fully forget or fully remember. In *The New York Times Book Review*, Michiko Kakutani writes of *The Plague of Doves*: "It's a place where intimacy breeds feuds and gossip and long-simmering resentments, but also understanding and maybe even forgiveness, a place where the roots of neighbors' family trees are often mysteriously twisted together, and where the younger generations find themselves reprising—or expiating—the actions of their elders." Though she is speaking of the small town in Erdrich's novel, it could be any of them—or all of them.

As tribalographies, these novels do important cultural work because they illustrate for both Native and non-Native readers the circularity and simultaneity of individuals and tribes participating in the act of becoming. In her tribalographic reading of Navajo writer Irvin Morris's *The Glittering World*, Howe talks about the importance of atemporal synthesis for community making. "In essence," writes Howe, "he is saying identity is determined by his history and the future . . . Morris's stories transcend his own memories to include those of his relatives and tribal community" ("Story of America," 42). Earling, Erdrich, and Red Corn ask their novels to do exactly the same work, honoring not only their tribal pasts but also their cosmic futures. The other honor is that their novels serve as the most delightful invitation to participate as well in this most important and most inclusive process of community making.

Two Novels, Four Stories: Narrative Twinning in *Shell Shaker* and *The Translation of Dr. Apelles*

If little external data connected the previous three novels, it would appear, upon initial inspection, that David Treuer's *The Translation of Dr. Apelles* and LeAnne Howe's *Shell Shaker* are equally dissimilar. One is wacky, irreverent, and wholly concerned with Indian identity and tribal politics, while the other is a metafictional layering designed to convince readers that Indian fiction is not Indian reality. One uses painstaking research to ensure the accuracy of the Indian history presented, while the other inserts subtle clues to help the reader doubt the reliability of the historical Indian narrative. Despite the thematic and storytelling differences—or perhaps because of them—there are advantages to reading these two wildly popular novels alongside each other. Though they take different tacks, both books jump back and forth between nearly mythological Indian stories of the past (the 1730s for *Shell Shaker* and a little later for *Apelles*) and frustratingly relatable love stories in the present. Neither book uses the past as a catapult to the present (as Alexie does in *Flight*), but rather as a way to animate epochs as parallel planes of simultaneity. Because the books never assume a linearity from past to present, the plot lines that occur in the present also do important work backward, helping contextualize not past events, but how we read and interpret those events.

In the case of *Shell Shaker*, two seemingly unrelated plots, separated by 250 years, converge in the present. To get there, Howe's novel jumps back and forth from the eighteenth century to the 1990s, drawing both literal and metaphorical parallels between past transgressions and present criminality, past sacrifices and present realizations, past passions and present passions. In the novel, both panels of time are flanked by the murder of a tribal leader—Red Shoes in the eighteenth century, and Redford McAlester in the late twentieth. Through the actions of the leaders, Howe tells the stories of the people around them and of the people their decisions ultimately affect—people whose actions have also shaped eventual outcomes. "In writing *Shell Shaker*," Howe explains, "I wanted to remain faithful to some of the historical events in the eighteenth century that continue to influence the Choctaw present. Daniel Boorstein [*sic*; Boorstin] has labeled these kinds of events as 'pseudo-events,' meaning that there is agreement that something happened in history, but a disagreement as to its significance, or how it plays out within a specific cultural group" ("Interview with LeAnne Howe").

Howe's novel, then, is a kind of public-private working-out of that disagreement and its significance. Simply telling a story of the past without including the tribal echoes in the present would be to give only part of the story. Similarly, unpacking the scandals, pressures, and problems of the tribal present without pinpointing specific incidents in the past would be a bit like showing up with shells and no shaker. Representing the dual (and dueling) strains of Choctaw tribal intricacies as parallel (as opposed to perpendicular) narratives holds both a mirror and a lamp up to Choctaw decisions and determination: "It's just the trappings of time that have changed," Auda explains to Red toward the end of the novel (200). Auda goes on to realize that she is reliving the past, or at least refracting its events in the present day: "Auda sits in silence, remembering a struggle that began so long ago.

Here they are shedding skins, becoming a reflection of what they once were. She sees it all happening again" (200). Drawing that line from the eighteenth century to the twentieth drives home the point that the Choctaw endure. No matter what tragedies irrupt time and place, the Choctaw survive.

Similarly, Treuer's parallel narratives in *The Translation of Dr. Apelles* juxtapose the historical and the contemporary. In the here and now, Dr. Apelles, an Indian scholar of unstated tribal affiliation, is a researcher and translator who spends most of his days working at RECAP (Research Collections and Preservations), an archive, library, and research facility. He spends Fridays, though, translating an obscure Indian tale, "a document for which he himself is the only remaining key" (24). That tale, which, the reader is led to believe, is rendered as a classic frame narrative (à la *The Scarlet Letter* and "The Custom-House") within the larger story of Dr. Apelles, reveals itself to be a lushly mythical folktale of two Indian foundlings—Bimaadiz and Eta—who fall in love with each other despite personal, communal, and cultural tragedies. As the novel uncoils, the two narrative strands grow more closely together. Bimaadiz and Eta come to resemble Dr. Apelles and his coworker, Campaspe, who also fall for each other. Where Treuer's novel parts from Howe's, though, is with the revelation that the historical segment of the novel is not history but fiction. Apelles has made up the story all along. If the reader doesn't figure this out, she will learn along with Campaspe that what Apelles has been translating is his own life, his love for Campaspe, and the unfolding of their relationship: "once I started reading I couldn't stop," she tells Apelles, "and I was surprised! I had no idea. *the* translation is really *your* translation. it is your story. and to see myself there . . . to see me as you see me. how thrilling" (309). The text, then, is the author, and the author-translator-reader distinction collapses on all levels. Such play extends to every aspect of the novel. In fact, a savvy reader may recognize the Bimaadiz-Eta story as a translation of Longinus's classic tale of Daphnis and Chloe, confirming that one can never trust any translation, any rendering of "Native America" to be a documentary of Native Americans.

Yet despite the different stances Treuer and Howe take in regard to the "truthfulness" of Native American history, they do share a belief in the importance of translation in the larger narrative that we might classify as Native American history. Treuer functions as a kind of professor, sending a warning shot across the bow of any reader likely to take heavily translated texts of Native history at face value. His obvious targets are readers who swallow *Black Elk Speaks* as a sacred text full of Indian truth and wisdom. His less obvious ones might be those authors and readers who believe that literary constructions (*Ceremony*, *Love Medicine*, *House Made of Dawn*) by writers trained in the Western tradition are windows into authentic Indian experiences and culture. *The Translation of Dr. Apelles* helps make the point that the reader has to maintain a critical distance between the texts of Native Literature and the unscripted lives of Native American people. Douglas Robinson makes a similar observation in his review, noting that "the whole question of the reliability of the translator from Native American languages is central to the novel." "To what extent," asks Robinson, "can we trust an English story that claims to be an 'authentic Native American myth'? Is it really that myth, or has it been assimilated to English literary conventions, or, worse (or perhaps better?), invented out of the whole cloth?" ("The Translator as Lover"). For Treuer, literature is literature. Life, on the other hand, is not nearly so neatly constructed. Literature is a translation of living, a translation that is also an interpretation.

Howe makes a similar assertion in *Shell Shaker*, though for her, an inversion occurs. Remarkably, *Shell Shaker* not only demonstrates how present events can help construe the inscrutable past for us, but also shows the reader that the present actually translates the past. In her smart reading of *Shell Shaker*, Patrice Hollrah correctly picks up on the importance of translation and history: "As a history professor Auda understands that history is a narrative, and who tells the story will determine what people believe. She understands that history can be distorted" ("Decolonizing the Choctaws," 82). One has to wonder if the "she" Hollrah speaks of here is Auda or Howe? Does it even matter? If Native history is a vast text, as yet unexplained in many regards, our present desires, sins, and dreams can become a kind of Rosetta stone, unlocking the glyphs of past traumas, the script of history's lacunae. Indeed, it would appear that Auda's troubled relationship with Redford is a destined cipher needed to complete the incompleteness of Red Shoes's personal and tribal endeavors. For Howe, as for Treuer, past and present are intertext: the author is the translator here to decode the hidden codes.

Another correspondence is the way in which both authors see translation as a form of subversion and resistance—especially regarding readers' and writers' assumptions about gender. In particular, more attention needs to be paid to the role of women in these translations. Both novels position men as pillars in their respective spaces, whether it is a research library or Mississippi in 1738. Men appear to be at the center, the axis around which the rest of characters rotate. But in fact, the women not only perform the translations of the story, but also, ultimately, translate the men. When the men can't make peace, it is the women of the Inholahta Choctaw who pick up that baton. When Redford McAlester lets down the tribe, it is Auda who restores order and her sisters who help ensure his return to Nanih Wayiah—the Choctaw home mound in Mississippi. It is through Auda and Shakbatina that the lives of Red and Redford have meaning. The same holds true for *Dr. Apelles*. The "translation" of Dr. Apelles is yet another trick; it is not a translation by Dr. Apelles but of him. The text that is his life, his living inscription, doesn't exist until it and he have a reader. In fact, ultimately, his life is the indecipherable text, the "document for which [she her] self is the only remaining key." She is Auda to his Redford. She makes his life, otherwise meaningless, meaningful.

The twinning narratives of Treuer and Howe stand as two important iterations of American Indian literary intertext but from two opposite extremes. In the case of Howe, the contemporary narrative finishes the story started by Shakbatina and Red Shoes in the 1700s. Since the moment Shakbatina was scarified, Choctaw consciousness—like Shakbatina's painted body—was split in two. It is not until the novel's final page, when some other narrator appears, some amalgamation of present and past, that the narratives experience both thematic resolution and tribalographic concord. Like Shakbatina, Dr. Apelles splits himself in two, never to realign until, through Campaspe, theory meets practice, self meets alter-self, writer meets reader. Though nothing like a tribalography, *Dr. Apelles* nonetheless embodies how Native identities become bifurcated through misreading, miswriting, and mistranslation. Finally, one wonders whether the two novels are themselves twin narratives—an example of intertext on the grandest scale, conjoined opposites that ultimately complete each other's incompleteness.

Passing and the Invention of Identity in *Drowning in Fire* and *The Last Report on the Miracles at Little No Horse*

"To pass is to sin against authenticity," asserts Henry Louis Gates, Jr., in "The Passing of Anatole Broyard," "and 'authenticity' is among the founding lies of the modern age" (*Thirteen Ways of Looking at a Black Man*, 207). According to Gates, Broyard, an African American man who passed as white, "was a connoisseur of the liminal," one who lived in the shadowy, undefined world of no boundaries and fluid identity. In *Drowning in Fire* and *The Last Report on the Miracles at Little No Horse*, Craig Womack and Louise Erdrich challenge traditional notions of identity and authenticity through utterly unique explorations of passing. Rather than writing novels of racial passing, they opt for more complex and perhaps even subtler forms of passing—those involving gender and sexual orientation. Josh Henneha, the main character of *Drowning in Fire* (and, the reader is to assume, an alter ego of Womack), is a young Creek man in 1970s and 1980s Oklahoma who tries to hide (but is consumed by) his attraction to other men. Erdrich's protagonist, Father Damien Modeste, is really a former nun named Agnes who has spent eighty years passing not only as a priest but also as a man. Both novels take up the already unwieldy mantle of Native identity and carry it that much further by shouldering the additional burdens of gender and queerness. In so doing, they offer new perspectives on the standard questions of authenticity and identity that frame so much of indigenous discourse.

If there is a trope connecting both novels and their thematics, it is fluidity. Father Damien and Josh float and flow in and out of both personal and private spaces, genders, and orientations. The liminality that Gates excavates in Broyard requires no such digging in *Drowning* and *Last Report*—it itself is a floating text.[4] Despite the many cultural, geographic, and religious boundaries designed to colonize Damien and Josh, both defy being written by a larger, more rigid grammar. Interestingly, it is through Native cultural practices that they find both the language and the norms of antiassimilationism. Put more bluntly, they resist through engagement.

For Womack, and for Josh, coming to terms with queerness, is a simultaneous coming to terms with Creek-ness.[5] Both embrace personal, tribal, and communal codes, but both feel risky. In "Canonizing Craig Womack," Michelle Henry correctly cites Womack's debt to Beth Brandt's concept of "presenting oneself" in his characterization of Josh and Jimmy, a fellow teenage boy and the object of his desire: "'Presenting oneself' has to do with communal activity, in which a queer Native affirms her or his position in the community" (39). Josh finds less hostility in Creek culture for two-spirits than in the dominant Oklahoma Anglo culture. Josh and Jimmy's friends, for example, have a particular fondness for antigay terms like "fag," and, not surprisingly, Josh finds nothing in mainstream culture or in mainstream humanity that helps give voice to his hidden language of desire. Womack (and Josh) locate a metonym for that boundless, borderless, and proud desire in the flight of an eagle: "It was the first time I'd seen an eagle outside the zoo. The wind currents under their wing tips had lifted them as they effortlessly rose up on columns of air, and I knew by their movement that I had seen other worlds beyond words, other languages inside circles of motion. I wanted to learn that language" (187). Without question, Josh wants also to rise, effortlessly, into his queerness with the same pride and openness of the eagle. It is perhaps the eagle, its freedom (not confined in a zoo), and its circles of motions (likely a reference to fellow Creek Joy Harjo's "Eagle Poem") that set him on a path to learn the language of reciprocal, sanctioned love.

I suspect there is also an ironic subtext to this passage, most notably using the eagle—America's symbol of colonialism, its predatory nature—against mainstream American heterosexist and anti-Indian values. By making the eagle his own symbol of Creek-ness and queerness, he also reinvents the enemy's semiotic language.[6] Henry avers that, for Josh, "identity is not about fitting into or subverting a Eurocentric 'queer theory' of their sexuality but about affirming their place within the Creek and Indian community" (40). Henry's final observation about affirmation is spot on, but *Drowning in Fire*, like Womack's scholarly book *Red on Red*, subverts Eurocentric theories of human interpretation—concepts like "normal," "straight," "savage," "civilized," and "legal." Of course, Josh and Jimmy are not consciously subverting queer theory—they haven't read Judith Butler's *Gender Trouble*—but Womack has, and as an author of both the book and his own identity, he absolutely has an interest in subversion.

And subversion remains one of the traits that endow his work with power.

One wonders whether a desire to subvert what we would call the hegemonic system—

but what Father Damien Modeste would not have words for—motivates her. It is possible Erdrich intends for Father Damien some means of transgression; the question is, is transgression subversive? It is pretty clear that someone like Sor Juana de la Cruz had subversion in mind when she passed as a man to enter a university, but it is less clear here. Either way, a more motivating factor than subversion seems to be connection. Father Damien wants to belong. He wants to make a difference. One of the great ironies of the novel is that this experience of belonging comes via what some might see as double inauthenticity. Passing as a man and as a man of the cloth is no small feat, but doing so and also becoming part of a community of Ojibwe does, in retrospect, strike most people (including students) as radical.

Where it does not feel radical is among the Ojibwe. In a scene of great tension, due to the dramatic irony Erdrich has created, Damien is confronted, in an usually nonthreatening way, by his long time friend Nanapush, during a game of chess: "Are you a female Wishkob? My old friend thought so at first, assumed you went and became a four-legged to please another man, but that's not true. Inside that robe, you are definitely a woman . . . So you're not a woman-acting man, you're a man-acting woman" (231). In the white world, there are only derogatory categories and names for Father Damien, but among the Ojibwe, the terms that might describe him are value free. They are accepted categories of gender identification beyond the confining dichotomy so thoroughly a part of Western language and Western worldviews. "Nanapush's conjectures," writes Deirdre Keenan of this conversation, "reveal the Ojibwe assumption of third and fourth gender categories, as well as additional categories, which include gay men and, by implication, lesbians. They also reaffirm Damien's accepted status within the Two Spirit tradition among the Ojibwe at Little No Horse" ("Unrestricted Territory," 7). Keenan astutely notes how Nanapush's questions are a silent acceptance of her uniqueness (in fact, he later admits that to do what she has done must have required not only the blessing of the spirits but a great deal of strength and sacrifice). Categorization, then, in the Ojibwe language and social system is inclusive, whereas for Father Damien and for Josh, it is exclusive.

In reading these novels alongside each other, one gets the feeling that the states of being Womack and Erdrich explore are also influenced by geographic states—Oklahoma and North Dakota. As residents of frontier states, contact zones, Josh and Father Damien stand in for the Creek and the Ojibwe while also struggling to find a comfort zone in American culture, to decide on a classification that eludes racism and relegation—an identity that floats above and across whatever might limit it. Of course, encoded in these systems are questions of authenticity. Is Father Damien a real "man of God?" Is Josh a "real Indian?" Is either living his or her true truth? What both Womack and Erdrich suggest is that personal stances of authenticity are related to public value systems. It is not so much who a person pretends to be or even is but, rather, who accepts his or her persona, public or private? For both Womack and Erdrich, it is the tribal culture that embraces the "presented self"—the self that is enacted into being.

In the vast dialogic map of the new American Indian novel, the line connecting *Last Report* and *Drowning* with *Dr. Apelles* and *Shell Shaker* is a thoroughfare of twin narratives. Whereas the last two merge past and present, the first two merge public and private. Father Damien and Josh construct twin narratives for themselves, two narratives for one story. But ultimately, like Howe and Treuer, they must merge the two stories of self into one cohesive identity. In the film *The Business of Fancydancing*, Seymour Polatkin discovers that queerness is less fraught with personal and communal ghosts than Indianness, but he understands that the interplay of both make him who he is. Though Father Damien does not have to accommodate her sexual identity within an ancestral local tribal system, she does have to contextualize it within the Ojibwe she lives among, within the performative context of being a priest, and within her own private context of being an Anglo woman in America. To pass is not to sin against authenticity, but to hold it up as the fiction it truly is. Authenticity, the handmaiden of assimilation, is little more than a call to conformity. Womack, never known for his eagerness to assimilate, titles the chapter of *Drowning in Fire* in which Josh gives in to his burning desire for Jimmy "The Spirit of Resistance." What he finds in this "spirit" is also what Father Damien discovers: whatever authenticity might mean, its manifestation in identity just might be best experienced through engagement.

Time Traveling, Time Telling: *Flight*, *Miko Kings*, and Indian Invention

A confession: science fiction has never resonated with me. At its best, science fiction can help create palatable metaphors that better dramatize social issues facing modern society—race, gender, our relationship to technology, and the threat of surveillance. But most of the time, it comes off as either overdetermined allegory or ham-handed manifesto. At its worst, it comes off as a sophomoric oversimplification of complex issues. In my experience, the exceptions prove the rule. Both *Miko Kings*, by LeAnne Howe, and *Flight*, by Sherman Alexie, have a great deal in common with science fiction, but to be sure, they are—in the parlance of the genre—the good cyborgs.

In my reading, *Flight* and *Miko Kings* are fine examples of the indigenous version of science fiction—what I will call "Indian invention." I have manufactured this term to distinguish the tropes and figurations of Native novels from the Western notions of "science" and "fiction" that frame the mainstream examples of that genre. The Indian invention novel draws from all of the motifs of science fiction that make it fun, fanciful, and forward looking, but, unlike the "science" and "fiction" components of sci-fi, Indian invention tropes are neither scientific nor fictional. They arise out of the diversity of Indian narrative—its humor, its disregard for the laws of physics, its trickster traditions, and its sense of circular and unending time. The novels of Indian invention play with creation stories, shape-shifters, coyotes, and all that is atemporal, creating a new genre that takes indigenous aesthetics to new planes. Predecessors might include Thomas King's *Green Grass, Running Water* and even Howe's *Shell Shaker* and Alexie's *Reservation Blues*, but no novels do this work better than *Miko Kings* and *Flight*.

Flight, Sherman Alexie's short, sassy novel about Zits, an angry adolescent boy shipped from foster family to foster family, is among his most endearing and most fun. With an epigraph from Kurt Vonnegut and an obvious debt to *Slaughterhouse-Five*, it is also his most overtly fantastic. Zits becomes an unwitting time traveler, suddenly and surprisingly inhabiting the bodies of people who happen to be playing key roles in specific historical events—an FBI agent infiltrating an AIM-like group of activists in the 1970s, a mute Indian boy at the Battle of the Little Bighorn, an Anglo-Indian tracker who helps save a white child after an Indian raid, and a white flight instructor who unknowingly trains a terrorist. The hyperjumping first occurs when Zits is about to open fire on a random group of people in a random bank in contemporary Seattle. Driven to this act of "justice" by Justice, a boy Zits befriended (Justice had busted him out of jail), Zits gets transported back in time at the moment he pulls the trigger on the people in the bank. In subsequent eras, he gets beamed over to an alternate history at similarly climactic moments. Each crisis bleeds into an epiphany, each instance of terror goes some distance toward scaring Zits straight: "I hear screaming. I realize it is me screaming. I hear weeping. I realize it is me weeping. I close my eyes" (106). And zap, off he goes to 1960 as a white FBI agent; then zap, to 1876 as a white soldier; then zap, to the future as an airline pilot unknowingly training a terrorist.

As with Billy Pilgrim's temporal displacements in *Slaughterhouse-Five*, Zits's various embodiments enable not only sympathy but also symbiosis. The novel reads like a postmodern version of *A Christmas Carol* in which Zits inhabits the ghosts of his (and others') past and future. And yet, there are also remnants of trickster tropes—Zits as shape-shifter, Zits with no control over his actions, Zits as the personification of good and evil, Zits as both teacher and student, Zits as antihero, Zits as comic. "There, in comic discourse," writes Gerald Vizenor, "the trickster is being, nothingness and liberation; a loose seam in consciousness; that wild space over and between sounds, words, sentences and narratives" (196). Alexie doubtless makes Zits a loose seam in time; and Alexie, the master tailor of absent-present, threads patches of epoch and transgression through the narrative.

That narrative's relation to American Indian storytelling traditions was, surprisingly, completely ignored by the reviewers of *Flight*. Zits's role as storyteller, the novel's community of voices, and its circular notion of time all take a back seat to the seemingly monolithic "science fiction" influence. It could be that most mainstream reviewers had not read *Shell Shaker*, *Green Grass, Running Water*, *Grass Dancer*, or *Miko Kings*, but surely most had read *Love Medicine*, Silko's *Almanac of the Dead*, or *House Made of Dawn*. Surely the tradition of Native circular narrative has become part of American literary consciousness. Even more surprising was the dearth of references to communal storytelling. As Treuer notes in his reading of Native American fiction, polyvocality has become a touchstone of the Native novel. Indeed, most of the books I write about in this chapter feature a plurality of voices, as do many canonical American Indian novels. Polyvocality frames *Flight* as well, but here Alexie and Zits go trickster on Native narrativity by playing with reader expectations, the cachet of ethnography, the lexicon of Native literary criticism, and the scholars interested in each. Although there are a number of different voices from the present and the past, they are all the same voice—that of Zits. Like any good trickster tale, *Flight* both mirrors and mocks. It plays with Western allegorical texts the same way it riffs on other contemporary American Indian texts. *Flight* is an homage and a springboard—just like Zits himself—a wacky wagon of engagement and resistance.

Though it is less frenetic than *Flight*, LeAnne Howe's *Miko Kings* has much in common with Alexie's genre- and era-crossing novel. Like *Flight*, *Miko Kings* offers an original spin on a classic popular genre (the sports novel). It incorporates polyvocality, and it highlights an Indian character able to journey through time. The novel is too complicated, too layered, to capsulate easily here, but suffice it to say that Howe creates frames within frames, stories upon stories, rendered not just by a typical novel's narrator but also through letters, diary entries, and photographs. One segment of the novel tells the intertwined stories of Lena Coulter, a Choctaw writer, and Ezol Day, a progressive, artistic Choctaw postal clerk who lived in the early 1900s and who travels across the decades to visit Lena. When she was alive, Ezol was in love with a star player on the Miko Kings, the actual Choctaw baseball team that dominated the Indian leagues and even defeated their archrival, the Seventh Cavalrymen from Fort Sill, Oklahoma. The story of Choctaw baseball, its connection to Choctaw culture, and American baseball's roots in Choctaw "base and ball" are the subjects of the second strain of Howe's novel. Ezol appears in both sections—she is the Zits of *Miko Kings*—connecting history and voice. Like Zits, she functions as the book's moral compass. She not only understands the tribal impulses to play baseball, she also presages how Choctaw baseball will influence how the tribe moves forward into the future. Once the future arrives, she is needed by Lena so that the true story of the Choctaw (and baseball) can be told.

Zits travels through time so that he can live a better life, but the main reason for Ezol's temporal traverse is so that others (those in the future in particular) might live a better life. Both characters translate the meaning of time travel, but to different audiences. Ezol speaks to Lena, but Zits speaks directly to the reader. Cautionary tales both, and one wonders exactly whom Howe and Alexie intend for the heads-up. Authorial intent is truly a slippery business, but given the abundance of historical data in *Miko Kings* and given the pop-culture vibe of *Flight*, it seems to be that both novels are pitched at a general audience. Howe wants to educate hers about Choctaw culture and the true origins of baseball; Alexie hopes to broaden and problematize stereotyped notions of Indian identity. What is amazing is how differently the authors go about their tasks and how well they do them.

Whereas Zits's sci-fi beaming from historical film set to film set feels random (it is never clear what his ultimate point of arrival will be, unless it is his own present), Ezol appears to have intentionally selected Lena and Ada, Oklahoma, as her cross-dimensional destination. Yet both Howe and Alexie are interested in more than play and prophecy: Zits and Lena—and, to a certain degree, Ezol—need healing, unification, integration. Lena, who has traveled the world but never felt centered, longs for information about her family and the Choctaw, a substantive root fastening her to a people and place. And, as a writer, she wants her own storytelling to intersect with Choctaw storytelling, but at present, all aspects feel fragmented. Near the novel's end, Lena asks Ezol the reason for her groundlessness, to which Ezol responds: "Because when your mother died, you had no other real ancestors to turn to . . . I may not have been your blood grandmother—but I should have been. And I have always been with you in spirit. That is the true story I came to tell" (221). As it turns out, it is Lena's ability in the present to write about the past's line through to the future that brings everything into right relation. "As you know," Ezol tells Lena, "I continually occupy myself with patterns and questions. The interpretation of time, the speed of love, the velocity of a meteor shower, or the time it takes for a small white ball to fly from the pitcher's hand across home plate. These things still interest me. As you have always interested me, my girl" (221). Home plate is a double metaphor here. A place of arrival and completion that is both inside and outside of time, rooted to a place but with connections across all space.

Zits also wants to cross home plate, but moving from foster home to foster home makes him feel as if he is in a rundown between first and second base. Like Lena, he seeks some form of amalgamation, a composite of his time-trekking selves and his present self. Here is Zits after he has time-warped back to the present, standing in the bank, guns in hand: "I don't understand how time works anymore . . . I want to tell him that I fell through time and have only now returned. I wasn't to tell him I learned a valuable lesson. But I don't know what that lesson is. It's too complicated, too strange. Or maybe it's really simple" (162). One lesson might be that Indian invention allows for reason beyond reason, that indigeneity creates its own time-space continuum. In *Miko Kings*, Lena informs the reader that Ezol is the author of an essay on Choctaw time in which she argues "that universal time in space could not exist because there are no universal verb tenses . . . Her paper is elegantly reasoned, addressing fundamental questions around Choctaw expressions of space and time" (38). Zits may not be Choctaw, but he still benefits from a pan-Indian, transhistorical experience beyond what Vizenor calls "linear methods of perception," which have "denied a theater for tribal events in mythic time" (*Fugitive Poses*, 11). Given nothing by society, Zits comes to inhabit a Native theater in mythic time; in fact, he is a player on various stages in that theater, an active, participating ventriloquist of himself and others.

Na tohbi—"something white"—is the Choctaw concept Howe invokes to describe the place that Hope Little Leader, Ezol's love interest, disappears into while on the pitcher's mound. Ezol also talks about it, as does Shakbatina in *Shell Shaker*. On the mound, Hope looks up into the light and vanishes, Zits-like, moving through time and space. A vision maker himself, Hope turns back time and takes it with him into a vision. Though Alexie doesn't frame Zits's dislocations in such a tribally specific way—Zits doesn't have a tribe, after all—he experiences something similar, turning back time, inhabiting the here and here, the there and there. Fundamentally antithetical to Western notions of linear time, this ability is, at its core, defiantly trickster-esque: being and nothingness, here and thereness, absence and presence, present and past. Alexie's playing field is the theater of history; Howe's is the playing field itself. *Miko Kings* makes not only an argument for time travel, but also a compelling case that Indians, not Abner Doubleday, invented baseball: "How plausible is it that white people, who live by the clock and sword, would invent a game without time, one that must be played counter-clockwise?" (42).

While the Miko Kings play base and ball as a means of physical and spatial engagement with Choctaw-ness, the game also becomes a collective act of resistance. According to Adrienne Lynn, "playing ball at the turn of the 20th century had an urgency well beyond game and sport: It was both a form of resistance to the dominant culture, and a form of survival" ("Baseball Novel Explores Role of the Game," 1). As Ezol notes, baseball's counterclockwise structure works against the grain of Western temporality and directionality. Whereas sports like basketball, football, soccer, and hockey move in a line, back and forth, baseball turns in a circle. It is also a game that sets its own ending, "past time," as Ezol says, since there is no clock. For the Choctaw, base and ball was ritualized play that facilitated both community and commerce. "Don't confuse our ancient game with the one that's been assimilated into America's consciousness," warns Ezol, "We played the game to collaborate with other tribes, the stars, and with the great mystery" (43–44).

On the spiraling web that is the dialogic map of the American Indian novel, *Flight* and *Miko Kings* appear at the center. Without question, both novels explore important concepts of authenticity, gender, and identity, which link them to *Drowning in Fire* and *Last Report*. One can even imagine Zits flashing back to animate the aging body of Father Damien. And just as these two novels discover how cultural values can shape and galvanize identity, so too does *Miko Kings* locate in baseball personal meaning for Lena, Hope, and Ezol as well as tribal cohesion for the Choctaw. Additionally, the time-traveling characters of Zits and Ezol—and their epiphanies—seem to carry on intertextual conversations with the past and present narratives of *A Pipe for February*, *The Plague of Doves*, and *Perma Red*. *Miko Kings* absolutely works as a tribalographic text, collating past, present, and future. Similarly, *Flight* and *Miko Kings* are connected to *Dr. Apelles* and *Shell Shaker* through the metaphor of twinning; they are connected to each other through Zits's split personalities and Ezol's twin significance in the present and the past. The effect these novels create becomes rather startling. Smaller conversations between books lead to a larger discourse on the micro level among all of these books—and among all Native American fiction.

The map that these novels populate and illustrate functions a bit like Red Corn's buried pipe—a Native-made symbol connecting times beyond time. The pipe also links these books through the active metaphors of breath and voice, exchange and inspiration. Like pipes, maps are passed from person to person, generation to generation, their essence drawn in and returned. This map points in many directions and to many eras, directing us toward the places we have always known we were heading toward and returning to.

Red on the page cuts away to red on the screen; the reel rolls.

4. THE CINEMATICS OF ENGAGEMENT, THE POLITICS OF RESISTANCE

NATURALLY NATIVE AND *SKINS*

We've been dealing with the feds for a hundred years. We can handle them now.

THE DAY I BEGAN working on this chapter, I received an e-mail from a student in Italy who asked for advice about top graduate programs in American Indian film, including leading scholars in contemporary Native film studies. I generally receive two or three such queries a year, from both international and domestic students seeking guidance about where to go to study American Indian film. Of course, at present, there are no graduate programs devoted entirely to Indian film, and her question provided a timely, even if coincidental, entrée into larger questions about the state of Indian film in the United States. For example, there are no leading critics of Native film who write for major publications or websites; there are only a couple of books that discuss Indian cinema (and those tend to focus on representation). And as yet no Native filmmakers have had the same level of mainstream success with Native film as directors like Spike Lee or John Singleton have enjoyed for African American film. This is not to say that Indian cinema is deficient but rather to suggest that the reception of Indian film is not yet as sophisticated or as progressive as the films themselves.

Film shares much with literature and the visual arts, but it occupies a special place in the American popular imagination that books and these other genres don't enjoy. Since the rise of the studio system in the 1940s and 1950s, movies, along with popular music, have provided the slideshow and the sound track for how America sees and hears itself. Important film critics like Bill Nichols, André Bazin, Thomas Schatz, Gerald Mast, and others have demonstrated how successful Hollywood has been in shaping and framing American attitudes toward just about everything. "American cinema," writes Bazin, "has been able, in an extraordinarily competent way, to show American society just as it wanted to see itself" ("On the *politique des auteurs*," 251). And because visual texts like television and movies are public experiences, they also become a sort of lingua franca of cultural expression. We often have no idea what books others have read or what painters our neighbors know, but we can be pretty sure most people have a shared canon of American movies and television shows. We can, for instance, feel confident that many people over forty have seen *The Searchers* (1956), episodes of *The Lone Ranger* (1949–1957), *Stagecoach* (1939), and *Dances with Wolves* (1990), which means we can also assume that attitudes about Indians have been absorbed by Americans, either consciously or not, through overlapping narratives of cinema and television. Thus, many people have written about the representation of Indians in popular Hollywood films and television programs because everyone knows, instinctively, how influential such visual texts can be.

Linked to this issue is the disturbing fact that because movies and television have traditionally resided within the realm of popular culture, there has not been a particularly strong push to take films seriously as cultural documents. Outside of small film-studies circles, no real impetus has emerged to encourage people to interrogate their movies. Because movies, television, cartoons, comics, and pop music are fun, accessible, ubiquitous, and easy, decades went by with almost no one giving these sorts of texts much thought as to their influence. For years, Americans consumed westerns like cotton candy, and almost no one asked any questions about their cultural nutritional value. Can these movies reinforce racist ideas? Do they reflect American ideals of colonialism and white ascendancy? Do they marginalize ethnic groups? Are Indians really like the ones depicted on the screen?

But now things have changed.

Most people acknowledge popular culture as a significant force of ideology. Most are now aware of the troubling representations of Indians in classic westerns. My students, for example, actively laugh at the campiness of *The Searchers*. They are so turned off by the film's overt racism that they can't even engage it on a textual, political, or historical level. They find it dated and ridiculous, the opposite of dangerous. So when contemporary American Indian filmmakers move in this arena, they confront an unusual kind of double consciousness. On one hand, they are expected to do their part to erase the negative memories of past celluloid transgressions, and on the other, there is pressure to do right by Indians in the here and now.

Enter *Naturally Native* and *Skins*.

The reader may be puzzled at the choice to narrow in on these two movies over more canonical texts like *Harold of Orange* (Richard Weise, 1984) and *Powwow Highway* (Jonathan Wacks, 1989) or strong recent films like *Waterbuster* (J. Carlos Peinado and Daphne Ross, 2006) and *Four Sheets to the Wind* (Sterlin Harjo, 2007). It's true that neither *Skins* (Chris Eyre, 2002) nor *Naturally Native* (Jennifer Wynne Farmer and Valerie Red-Horse, 1998) are the first or the best Indian movies, but they remain two of the most interesting cinematic texts and two of the most important.

Initially, the movies appear so different from each other that it hardly seems worth pairing them, but in truth, they have a great deal in common. The two films share an interest in problematizing Native stereotypes, changing the representation of Indians on the big screen, and tracing a specific Native family as it confronts issues endemic to Native communities. Also, despite their differing styles and approaches, both *Skins* and *Naturally Native* are ultimately texts of defiance—dynamic examples of resistance that Native families have enacted for the last five hundred years.

Though I read these texts first and foremost as cultural documents, I will also pay attention to them as films, since their structure as cinematic texts contributes to their architecture of resistance. Elements of editing, music, pacing, casting, and cinematography distinguish celluloid from literature, painting, and sculpture; so even though these terms don't necessarily have correlatives in indigenous discourse, any good reading of indigenous film must address them. Normally, I agree with Robert Allen Warrior's assertion that "critical interpretations of [Indian] writings" should "proceed primarily from Indian sources," (*Tribal Secrets*, xvi), but movies problematize notions of writing. In the case of contemporary film, purely indigenous sources (whatever that might mean) are, frankly, impossible to distinguish from nonindigenous sources (whatever that, too, might mean). But as Warrior notes in his foreword to Beverly Singer's useful *Wiping the War Paint off the Lens: Native American Film and Video*, Native film resides both in the "broader context of American film" and "within the larger context of American Indian life" (ix). Indeed, so many people are involved in the funding, casting, set construction, filming, and editing of movies, it is hard to determine which aspects of a particular movie are "Native" and which are simply "film." Furthermore, technology plays such a prominent role in feature films these days that any movie of any significant length is, by its very nature, a bicultural, hybrid text, regardless of who writes, acts, or directs. Thus, I would like to offer a reading of *Skins* and *Naturally Native* that embodies the complexity of cinematic production, keeping one eye pressed to the camera and the other trained on Native America. While the latter eye will pay attention to issues of identity, sovereignty, and resistance, the former will incorporate the discourse of film itself—the "frame" and the "lens"—as metaphorical filters through which we may view these texts.

Since no scholarly work has been done on either of these films—except for a few pages in Elise Marubbio's *Killing the Indian Maiden: Images of Native American Women in Film*—I have had to rely solely on the reviews (around ten in all) for a critical context. However, almost none were helpful. Most are short, capsule reviews that do expository rather than interpretive work. And though I can't be sure of this, I do not believe any of the reviews were penned by Native critics. Film theory has not proved particularly useful either, at least not as an entrée to these two indigenous projects. As mentioned previously, I agree with Warrior that readings of Native texts should take as their mirror or lamp, window or lens, key or busted door, Native methodologies. But as yet, no comprehensive American Indian film theory exists, and reading *Naturally Native* and *Skins* through the projection of preceding films (even Native ones) implies a derivation that would be inaccurate. I also want to avoid lumping these two movies into the larger category of "ethnic cinema," since, obviously, the issues and approaches of African cinema, Bollywood, and Asian filmmaking—to name just a few—reside in different provenances than either of these two projects.

So while I am not suggesting that these films are islands (or reservations) isolated from the larger community of film and critical discourse, I do want to call attention to a dearth of critical infrastructure supporting recent Indian films made by Indian directors. As I explain in the chapter on Sherman Alexie's movies, almost all film scholarship involving Native cinema focuses on representation; only a handful of articles actually try to offer complex readings of new films by living Indian filmmakers.[1] In writing about Joy Harjo's poetry, Craig Womack argues that Native literary texts "deserve to be judged by their own criteria, in their own terms, not merely in agreement with, or reaction against, European literature and theory" (*Red on Red*, 242–243). Though I feel a critical responsibility to pull from as many sources as possible in order to distill smart and inclusive interpretations of these movies, I find that relying on non-Native sources potentially dilutes the indigeneity of the films and leaves me vulnerable to what I call the "trap of receptive determinacy."

Typically, I use this term in regard to primary sources—films or artworks that tell the reader how to read them—but there is also an interpretive trap that critics can fall into when they place their texts within a rigid framework that clamps the text to a fixed analytical point, denying it freedom of recursive or thematic movement. This chapter tries to step over and around that trap. It reads *Skins* and *Naturally Native* as activist Indian texts and as documents of Indian resistance—counternarratives that call into question the injustices and ineptitudes of the American cultural and legal machinery. The films utilize the cinematic space to tell their own stories, on their own terms, within the space of popular and visual culture. As a critic, then, I try to read them as such, without the finery or filter of non-Native sources to cloud the screens. As an interpretive gesture, I hope this approach underscores the degree to which the films stand as examples of cinematic sovereignty.

When Resistance Meets Engagement: *Naturally Native* as Lens

Naturally Native tries to do more cultural work than any other film I know—Indian or otherwise. It addresses nearly every imaginable Indian hot-button issue while introducing themes like Native capitalism and entrepreneurship, for which no button exists. It is also the only movie I have seen that actually shows a healthy married Indian couple in their thirties seducing each other. No matter how many times I watch or screen *Naturally Native*, I remain intrigued, impressed, beguiled, and fascinated by the mélange of issues, themes, plots, subplots, and messages. Is the movie about identity? Entrepreneurship? Finding romance? Making ends meet for a family of four in suburban Los Angeles? Returning to one's home reservation? How drinking can strain a marriage? How three sisters negotiate and maintain a relationship and a friendship? The many obstacles Indians face when, say, getting a loan or landing a meaningful role in Hollywood? How casinos can save the day? For better or worse, *Naturally Native* is about all of these and more. Because the film works hard to zoom in on the complicated issues Indians deal with daily while also panning wide to show the broad spectrum of the macro issues of Indian people, it does the cinematographic work of a lens, bringing both big and small aspects of Native issues into focus. *Naturally Native* homes in on issues facing urban Indians, training its camera tightly on the face of a Native family—particularly its women.

Released in 1998 and directed by Valerie Red-Horse (Cherokee) and Jennifer Wynne Farmer, *Naturally Native* is the first movie written by, directed by, and starring Indian women. The movie tells the story of the Lewis sisters, Vickie (Red-Horse), Tanya, (Irene Bedard [Inupiat Eskimo and Métis]), and Karen (Kimberly Norris [Colville—Salish-Kootenai—Cherokee]), who try to start their own cosmetics line, called Naturally Native, based on ancient tribal recipes and mixtures that Vickie learned from their biological father before he died. Despite a solid business plan and some expertise from Karen, who recently earned an MBA, the sisters keep getting turned down for the small-business loan they need in order to jumpstart the company. Because the sisters were removed from the reservation after the death of their mother and raised by a foster family in the Los Angeles suburbs, the sisters have no tribal-registration documentation nor a Certificate of Degree of Indian Blood (CDIB), so they are ineligible for loans from federal programs. To add insult to injury, they also meet resistance from a firm that refuses to invest in Naturally Native because of moral opposition to immoral gaming at the "damned casinos."

But venture capital works in mysterious ways.

In addition to all of the firsts listed or implied above, *Naturally Native* is also the first feature-length film to be entirely funded by a casino—owned by the Mashantucket Pequot Tribe of Connecticut—and to be sure, the casino plays a major role in the film, even as a kind of trickster deus ex machina. Thanks to the success of the casino, the sisters' tribe, the Viejas Band of Kumeyaay Indians of California, not only underwrites their business but also provides a homecoming that gives all three sisters a connection to a place and a people they lacked their entire lives.

If *Naturally Native* seems all over the place, it is. But, that doesn't make it an ineffective movie or an unimportant project. For all of the reasons mentioned above, it remains a milestone for Native filmmaking, and it has become a standard cinematic text for introductory classes in American Indian literature and Native American studies. The movie was screened at the second Native American Literature Symposium, where there was also a roundtable discussion of the film; so it has entered the canon of teachable Native texts,

FIGURE 4.1. (facing page) *Promotional photo of,* left to right, *Kimberly Norris (Karen Lewis), Irene Bedard (Tanya Lewis), and Valerie Red-Horse (Vickie Big Hawk)—the sisters of* Naturally Native. *© Photofest.*

FIGURE 4.2. (facing page) *The sisters sorting through Vicki's herb garden to find the right ingredients for the* Naturally Native *products. © Photofest.*

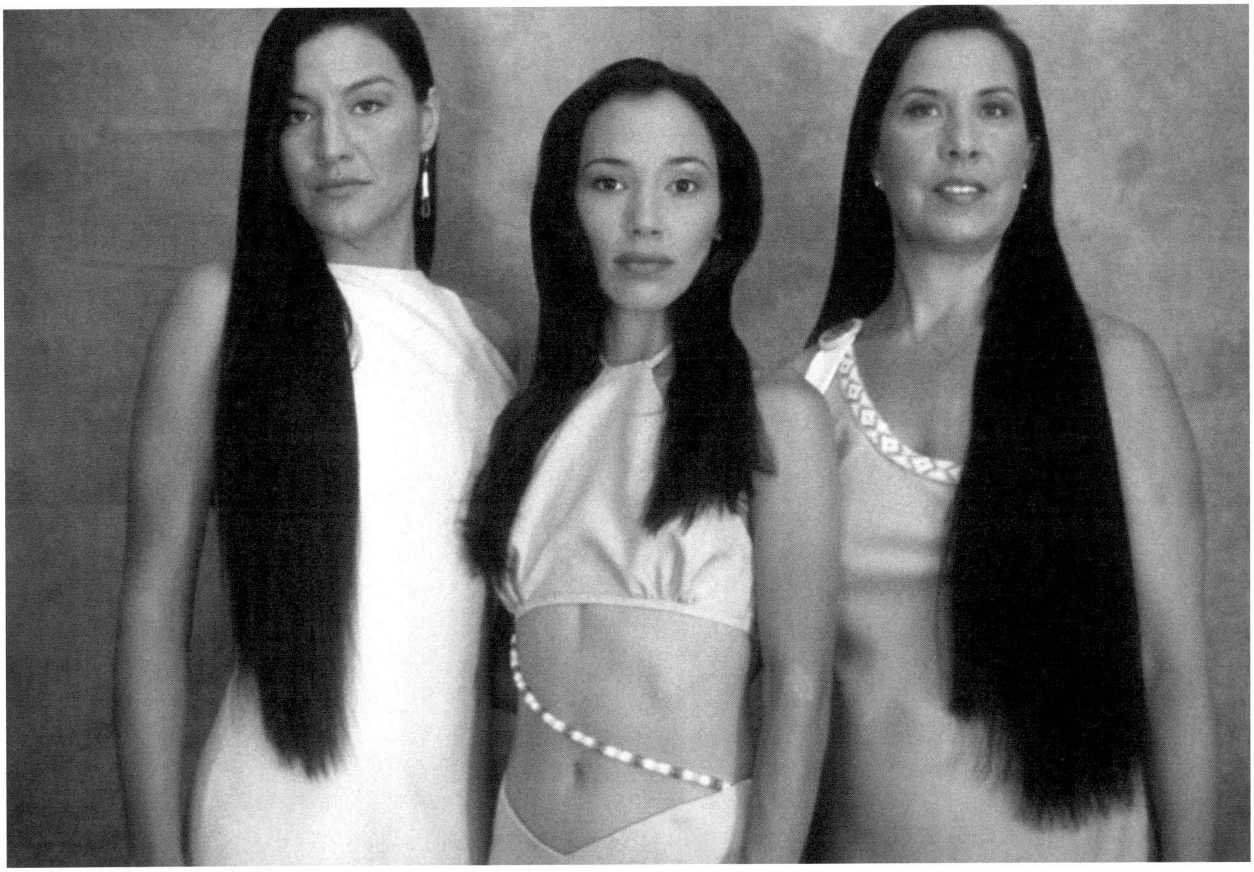

4.1

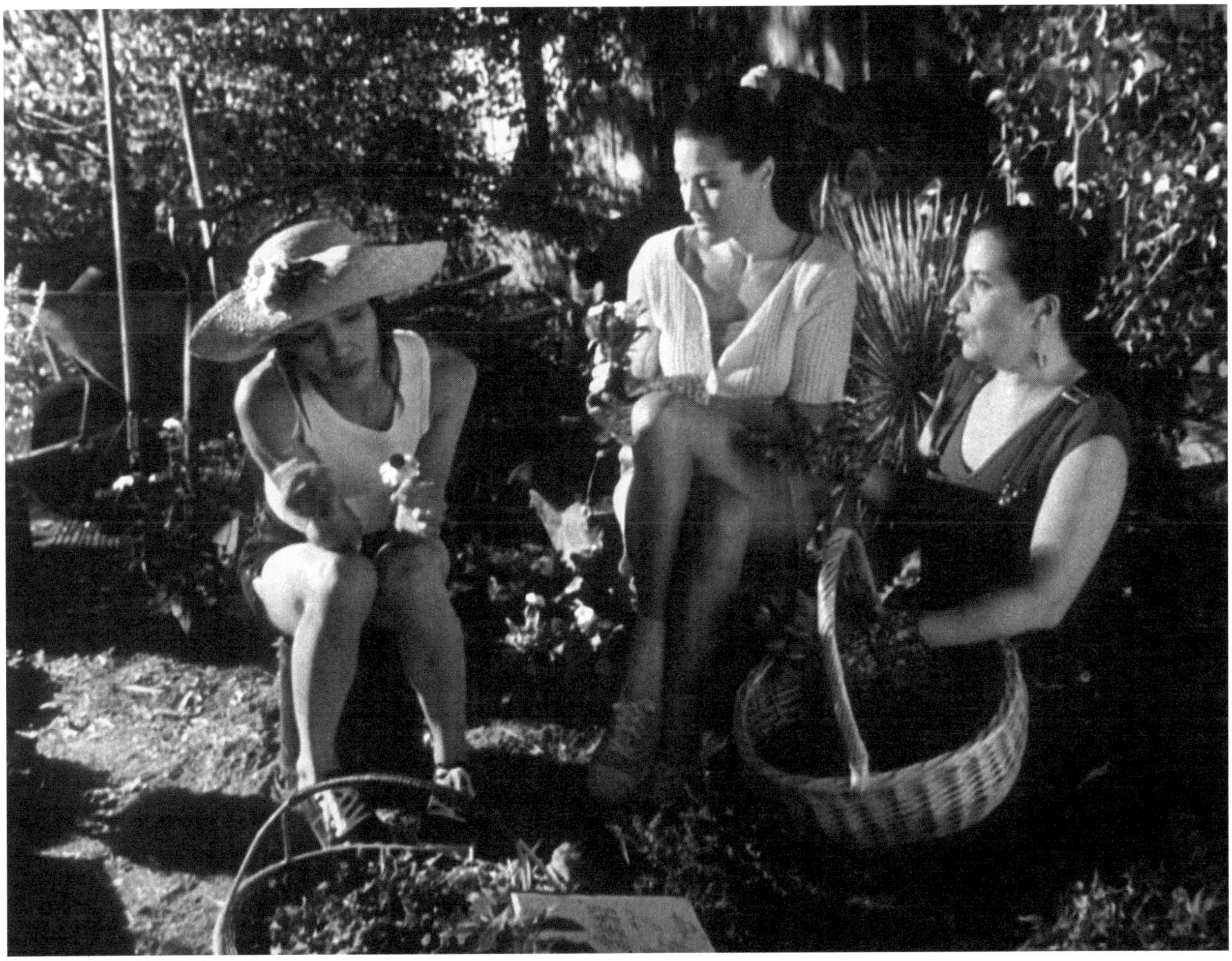

4.2

despite the fact that it never entered national theaters. Even though *Naturally Native* did well at many film festivals, winning a Special Jury Prize at the Dreamspeaker Film Festival and an Audience Award at the Santa Clarita Film Festival, it was never picked up for nationwide release. Like the film's cosmetic project called Naturally Native, the cinematic *Naturally Native* failed to receive the full embrace of the mainstream Anglo system. This enables the movie to offer a metacommentary on the film itself: both Naturally Native products ultimately have to rely on Indian-based options to fund and consume their products. To be sure, *Naturally Native* takes a pro-Indian, pro-casino stance, but contextualizes that stance within the non-Indian framework of middle-class America. In different ways, the film keeps asking the same question—how do Indian families maintain Indian identities while also living the American suburban dream of normalcy.

Red-Horse locates one of the best examples of this tension in her opening two scenes. Opening scenes are often the most memorable moments of movies, not only because films are compact but also because in theaters and in screenings, someone else controls when things start and how the narrative begins. There is always anticipation. Even now, the first blasts of light and shade when a movie starts still feel somewhat magical. How *Naturally Native* and *Skins* open could not be more different, and these establishing shots set the cinematic and thematic stage for the rest of each film. In *Naturally Native*, this happens over two scenes that take place twenty-six years apart. First, in 1972, a black-and-white photo of three young Indian girls appears on-screen, while a voice-over of male and female voices discusses the difficulty of placing all three sisters together in a foster home, in part because there are three children but primarily because people are afraid of "problems" associated with Indians. Flash forward to 1998 and a large house in suburban LA, where about twenty people of all ethnicities are gathered around a swimming pool for a celebratory party. We learn that Karen, the middle sister, has just earned her MBA. To commemorate the event, Vickie's husband, Steve Blackhawk (Pato Hoffman [Quechua]), captures the event on film with their home-video camera, including shots of their fussy teenage daughter, who complains about her brother. In fact, as viewers we see what the handheld camera sees, as though we are in on the party, part and parcel of the celebration.

In this second scene, we are treated to a dunking of Karen, a short lecture on dream catchers, a sisterly conversation about a cute boy, a longer lecture on alcohol, and some questions about tribal affiliation. With their swimming pool, barbeque grill, video camera, sibling complaints, and MBA celebration, both the scene and the setting feel more like a television sitcom (on the order of *The Brady Bunch* or *Charles in Charge*) than a serious feature film—until, of course, the viewer realizes that almost no images of happy, healthy, cul-de-sac Indian families exist in pop culture. In fact, every time I teach this film, some of my students admit that they have never seen an Indian family—in person or on television or in film—situated within the typical Anglo family setting we tend to associate with suburban households and family television programming.

If the opening photo and voice-over focus on Indianness, the suburban, post-MBA pool-party scene downplays that Indianness, opting for familiarity over otherness. Much of the movie seesaws back and forth, demonstrating how Indians are like every other American suburban family but also calling attention to Indian-specific problems. On one hand, Vickie's daughter throws a fit about the brother tagging along to a friend's party; on the other, Steve lectures his son about the Indian mascot on the son's baseball uniform. Tense husband-and-wife talks about the evils of alcohol punctuate marital discussions about bills and mortgage payments. Whenever Vickie is tempted to drink a little wine, Steve initiates the Indian-and-alcohol conversation, which, bizarrely, always leads to some sort of erotic activity.

In one nonerotic scene that comes off as entirely too forced, Vickie helps her daughter with a spelling lesson. As the sisters discuss strategies for a small-business loan after being initially denied, Vickie and her daughter say and spell the following words: "harmony," "persist," "equality," "obstacle," and "visionary." The effect of these moments contributes to a kind of schizophrenia in which seemingly mundane moments become both normal and instructional at the same time. If the movie fails, it is because it tries too hard to drive both points home.

That said, there are important scenes in *Naturally Native* that both push the business plotline along and offer insight into the practical roadblocks of being Indian. These scenes work because they feel more like a story and less like a lecture. On their first visit to the fictional YEA—an organization that funds small businesses run by minorities and women—the sisters run into the buzz saw of federal regulations and bureaucracy. While the YEA representative (played by Max Gail, most famous for his role as "Wojo" on *Barney Miller*) likes the proposal and is sympathetic to the business venture, he is handcuffed by the need for enrollment identification. "Normally you would be the easiest for us to fund," he tells the sisters, "but you must be federally recognized through the BIA. Unless you can show you are a member of a federally recognized tribe, we can't do anything." When the women explain they are California Morongo on their mother's side and Viejas on their father's but raised by a foster family off the reservation, all he can do is explain the need for CDIBs.

For those familiar with the endless and contradictory BIA bureaucratic regulations and the federal requirements for tribal enrollment, this scene feels particularly real. Moreover, for the many viewers who know nothing about enrollment numbers or CDIBs, the sisters' exchange functions as a real-world example of the unusually antiquated and fundamentally racist policies in place regarding American Indian citizenship and identity. Vickie reminds the YEA agent of the disturbing history of the Nazis' numbering of the Jews and later fumes over the reality that the BIA's flowchart does little to reassure anyone that Indians can get humane treatment. "BIA falls under the Department of Interior," she exclaims to Karen and Tanya, "forests, parks, and Indians!" Here, Red-Horse as director dramatizes a number of confluences facing Natives, especially on the West Coast, including the problem with enrollment numbers, CDIBs, the need to belong to federally recognized tribes, the power the BIA has over Indian identity and resources, and the hurdles many California "landless Indians" and rancherias face today. In short, she reveals one of the great contradictions facing many native communities—federal policies actually prohibit Indians from benefiting from federal policies.

The scene ends with the agent offering to put their paperwork through as "Hispanic" in order to get around the legal restrictions, but Karen refuses, saying simply, "We're not Hispanic." The subtext here is that Hispanics don't have regulations requiring them to prove a degree of Indian blood—nor does any other ethnicity. A larger, more insidious subtext permeating this scene has to do with institutional policies that work against what we might think of as Native capitalism. One wonders how many hindrances, both intentional and merely systemic, inhibit or simply discourage Natives from entering fully into the American economic system—another marker of mainstream American success.

Similar contradictions surface when the sisters seek funding from a private investment firm. As noted above, they get turned down yet again, but this time because their Morongo-Viejas identities link them with casinos and gambling. For this "family organization," Indian gaming reeks of immorality, despite the 1988 Indian Gaming Regulatory Act, which legalized Indian casinos. After a heated back-and-forth between Vickie and the firm's loan representative about the nuances of gambling, addiction, and morality, Karen not so accidentally knocks the man's coffee in his lap. The hot coffee on his crotch, the hot Indian women in his office, and the heated exchange about morality and business ethics prompt him to say what the viewer senses he has been thinking for the past several min-

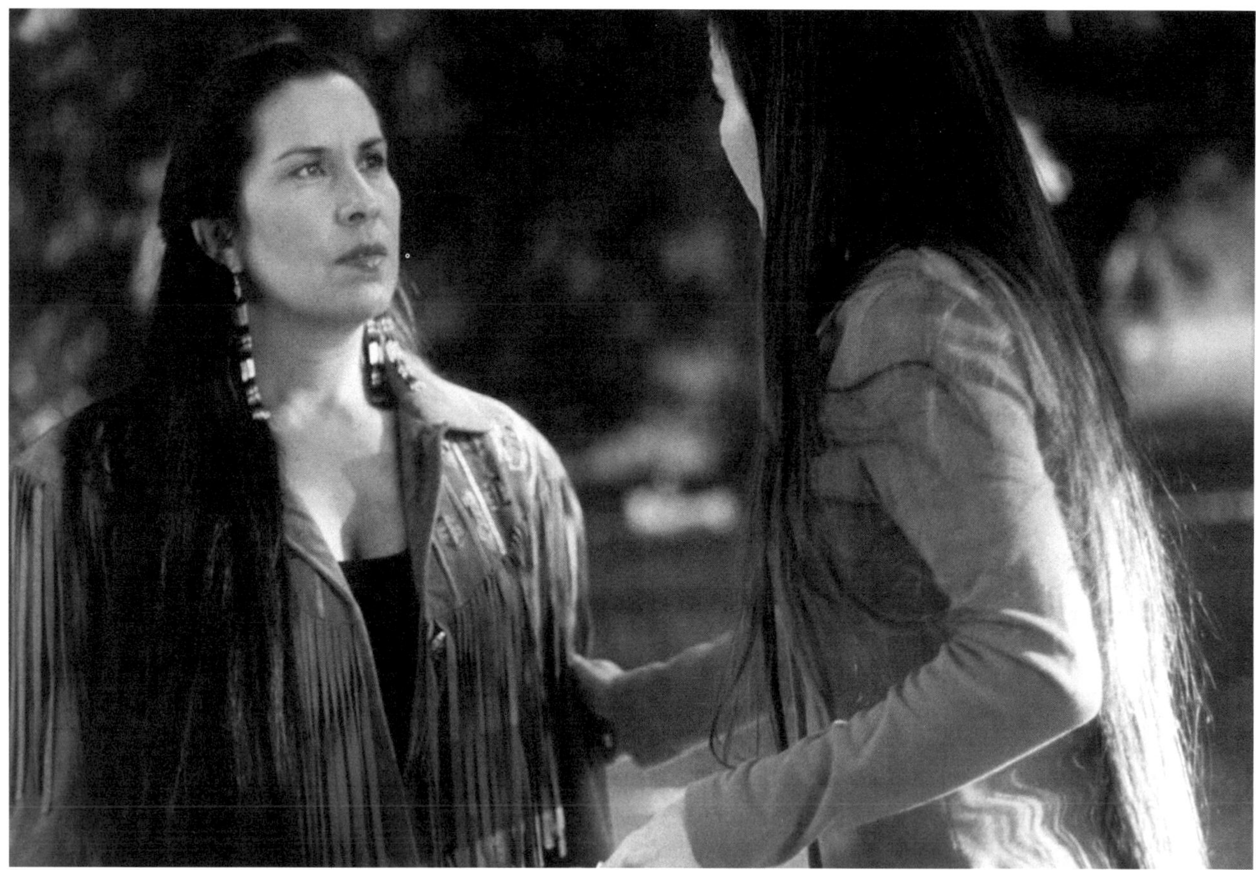

FIGURE 4.3. *Trouble in the Indian world too. Vickie gets lectured at a powwow when another Native woman thinks the sisters are trying to pass as Kumeyaay to profit from casino revenues. © Photofest.*

utes, but in this case, it is directed at Karen: "You stupid little Indian bitch!" In response to this, Vickie decks him with a wicked left hook, and the scene ends.

It is a fine moment.

The dramatics of the segment play a bit broad, but nothing seems out of the realm of possibility. These events prove to be important forms of resistance for the sisters and for the film itself. Just as they refused to capitulate by checking the "Hispanic" box for the purposes of the loan, so too do they refuse to renounce sovereign Indian rights in regard to casinos and what is or is not ethical behavior. They also refuse to let a white man insult their gender or ethnicity. I am a big fan of Vickie punching the investor; it caught me by surprise. So much of the movie models controlled resistance and playing by the rules that when Vickie responds physically, outside the system, it lends the movie a much-needed edge. Moreover, it presages Rudy's justice seeking outside the system in *Skins*, although things play out on a much larger scale there. Here, things play out in the semiotic realm, and Red-Horse has fun with the confluence and juxtaposition of uncommon images—most notably, of an Indian woman in a boardroom, taking a posture of strong defiance against the model of the white, capitalist, patriarchal system.

At its best, *Naturally Native* creates scenes (like the one above) not seen on-screen before, as it takes well-known stereotypes and lends them its own brand of Indian inversion. The best of this kind occurs when the sisters visit Madam Celeste (Mary Kay Place), an Indian wannabe who leads spiritual exercises in what she imagines are Native traditions. A friend of Karen's from business school, Madam Celeste claims to visit sweat lodges and is an active participant in a "talking medicine circle." The women visit her to see whether she might have interest in partnering with them on their venture to market Naturally Native, but she has other things in mind. Before they begin their meeting, though, she insists on burning sage, to the puzzlement of the sisters. But that's not all. Before anyone can speak, she transitions into a sort of caricatured chant that both begins and ends with loud "Ho!" scaring the sisters and more than a few audience members. After her performance, with which Madam Celeste is clearly pleased, Vickie asks her whether she is Indian. Her response is priceless. "Yes," she says confidently, "I was in a previous life." And to Karen: "I knew we'd be drawn together; spirit of our ancestors." In a movie in need of levity instead of forced sitcom hijinks, this plays as a truly funny scene. Place seems to enjoy being ridiculous, and here the over-the-top-ness plays as parody rather than didacticism.

What is not parody is Madam Celeste's proposal. She wants to use the sisters' Indianness to legitimize her scam of sweats, vision quests, and faux-Indian hocus-pocus, so she asks them to endow her business with authenticity by attaching their Indian brand to her product. There is no question that the sisters could have made money for their own business by being mascots for Madam Celeste, but again they refuse. Despite the scene's broad play, its message becomes one of the film's more nuanced moments. In all their other attempts to get funding, the sisters' Indian status has worked against them, but here their Indian status is a potential gold mine, and an aspect of Indianness still works against them. The Anglo fetishization of Native spiritual renewal, the trappings of the New Age movement, and the desire for authentic Native healing have transformed private tribal rituals and traditions into public commodities. Vickie's admonition to Madam Celeste not to profit from sacred ceremonies lacks the wallop of a punch, but it carries a moral reprimand that hits just as hard. By the end of the scene, though, the movie has gone a long way toward making its point that almost no aspect of being Indian gets any cultural or financial purchase in the Anglo world.

Part of the important cultural work the movie performs involves training its lens on the various aspects of contemporary Indian life—both obvious and more occluded—that might not otherwise come into view for the average moviegoer. The movie screen has not traditionally been a space filled with complex Indian characters living out their lives free of buckskin and head feathers and yet still living as "real Indians." In one of the few reviews of the film, David Claudio Iglesias praises the fact that Red-Horse's project "addresses weighty contemporary issues, including sports mascots, alcoholism, date rape, biracial dating and the quackery surrounding the commercialization of Native spiritual practices by non-Indian . . . *Naturally Native* portrays Natives as urban and contemporary, and reflects the reality of the modern Native American family living off-reservation" (60). Though his comments don't make evaluations or judgments, Iglesias gets everything right. For him, the film's ambition is a virtue—he likes the menu of issues the film puts on its plate. On the other hand, some critics panned the film for piling on too much at the buffet of Indian concerns. "Each sequence tackles a new issue," quips Glenn Lovell in his review for *Variety*, "turning into another major confrontation, and this gives the narrative a jerky, erratic quality" (73). Ironically, Lovell also reads the film correctly, but his take suggests no particular sympathy for the film's project. As a relatively new concept, the mainstream full-length Indian film has an astonishing amount of ground to cover. Of the many egregious transgressions and racist policies, which does the responsible but aspiring filmmaker ignore?

Two issues the critics miss but Red-Horse does not include the disturbing legacy of the Celluloid Maiden and the role of the casino in contemporary Indian society. Though these tropes may appear to be worlds apart, both address important preconceived notions of sovereignty and self-determination. M. Elise Marubbio defines the "Celluloid Maiden" as a "young Native woman who dies as a result of her choice to align herself with a white colonizer" (*Killing the Indian Maiden*, 4). For Marubbio, the Celluloid Maiden is a construct that helps perpetuate imperialist ideology despite the lack of any real connection between the invented Hollywood Indian maiden and living women: "No concrete relationship exists between the Celluloid Maiden and actual Native American women; rather, the figure works as a colonial rhetorical strategy to promote a national American identity defined against a raced and "savage" Other" (5). Red-Horse has said that the sisters' difficulties in finding funding for their cosmetics line is a complex metaphor for her own difficulty in landing meaningful roles in Hollywood ("Production"). Frustrated by the limited opportunities and the limited parameters for what a leading lady might look like, she decided to do that work herself. While *Naturally Native* does many things well, it signifies most saliently in the area of gender and indigeneity. The film completely rewrites the Hollywood script for what Indian women do, think, feel, and become. "This is the first film I've appeared in," says Bedard, "that I didn't have to wear buckskin" (quoted in Red-Horse, "Production").

An article of clothing Bedard's character does wear in the film is a cheeky T-shirt that has the phrase "They're Real" emblazoned across the chest. The shirt goes without comment in the film and in any of the reviews, but this small detail contributes to the larger process of killing the Indian Maiden. Just as Tanya flaunts her sexuality, so too does Vickie, who experiments with lingerie when her husband tells her how much he would like to see her wear it. So often, films, television, history, and pulp fiction show Indian women seduced, subsumed, and ultimately sacrificed for the Anglo male ego or the colonialist project, but *Naturally Native* allows each of the women to exert control over her own sexuality. Vickie gets to have steamy Jacuzzi sex with her attractive and loving pony-tailed husband; Karen, a virgin, has agency over her body and her sexual identity; and Tanya, fends off a would-be rapist and ultimately makes a conscious choice about dating an Indian man who has been smitten with her for years. Much of the subtext surrounding the Indian Maiden is that she, like Indians in general, can't help but succumb to the potent and powerful figure that is America, that is Manifest Destiny, that is the American jeremiad. Tied up in all of these narratives are the most disturbing assumptions about racial and sexual domination. Granted, it is just a movie, but *Naturally Native* does what it can to undermine this dynamic. "This film," asserts Marubbio, "perhaps more than any other, demands that the viewer question the violence behind the Celluloid Maiden figure without fully enacting the figure. The young woman does not die!" (223). Anyone who has read much literary or film criticism knows how rare it is to get an exclamation point in a university press book; so that particular punctuative indicator speaks as loudly as any other icon about how important this point is to Marubbio and, by extension, to Native women and their communities.

But what if those communities include casinos? How many exclamation points will we find at the end of sentences supporting Indian gaming? If films can be punctuation marks, then *Naturally Native*'s grammatical signifier would be one big exclamation point. As encouraging as the film's stance is on gender and sexual autonomy, it is exactly that enthusiastic about the recuperative role of the casino for Indian country. Given the fact that the main funder for *Naturally Native* was the casino of the Mashantucket Pequot, one wonders what options Red-Horse had with the script. She certainly couldn't be critical of casinos, but to what degree was there an assumption that the casino would play such a large role in the movie? Ultimately, it functions as a main character, a secret protagonist that rides in on a big concrete horse to save the day.

If there is any doubt about the centrality of the casino to the project, one need only pay attention to the textual bookends framing the movie. To wit: the first words to appear on the screen as the film opens are "The Mashantucket Pequot Tribal Nation." Here, in this most sacred visual site, where one might expect to find traditional producer iconography like the Paramount logo or the Universal rotating-planet imagery, one sees instead an Indian tribe. And on the other end, in the final text at the end of the film before the credits roll, an instructive paragraph appears on the screen: "In 1988, Congress passed the Indian Gaming Regulatory Act recognizing the right of Sovereign Indian Nations to operate gaming

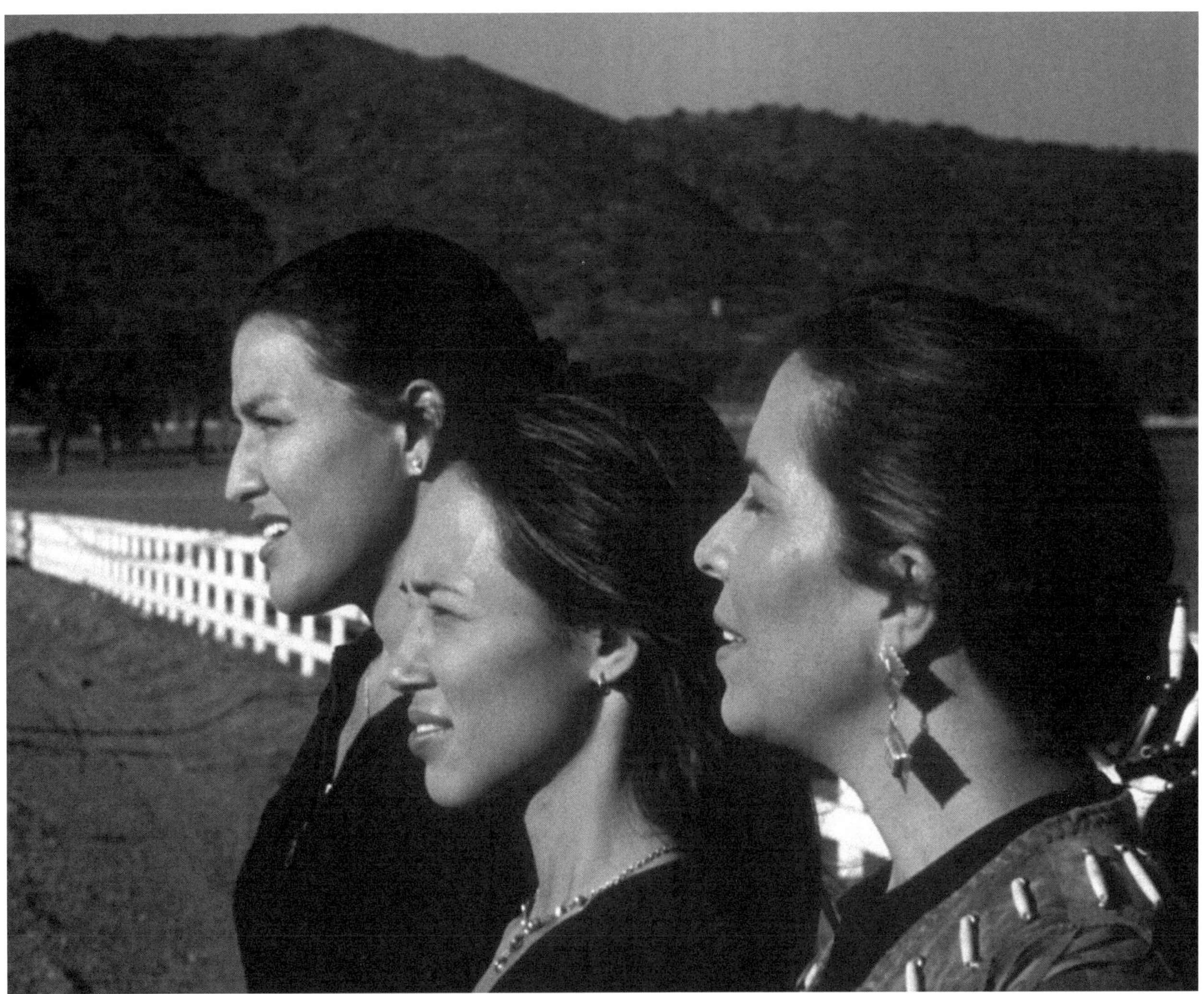

facilities. A decade later, the number of American Indian families on public assistance has been decreased dramatically . . . down to 0% on many reservations." The former text foregrounds the financial and cultural support of the tribe, and the latter indicates that Indian casinos do what the government has been unable to do—make real differences in the lives of Indian people.

This is certainly the case in the film. When, for instance, the sisters meet roadblock after roadblock on the uphill path of trying to secure financial assistance, they are prepared to pull over to the side of the entrepreneurial road. But little do Karen and Vickie know that Tanya has contacted the Viejas tribe to see whether it might be able to help. As it happens, flush with money from a casino, the tribe has just set up a small-business division, designed to help members of the Viejas tribes with start-ups. The scene when the sisters return to the reservation is touching because the tribe both encourages and welcomes them. For the first time, they are treated warmly and with respect. When they ask one of the tribal leaders (Charlie Hill) whether they need roll numbers, he replies, "We don't need any numbers. We're family here. We know who you are. And that's better than any roll number, right?" That personal connection undergirds the decision by Chairman Anthony Pico (Floyd Red Crow Westerman [Dakota]) to award them a loan of $50,000. What is more, he offers the casino's marketing department for marketing assistance and informs the sisters that the casino gift store and those at two other casinos will carry their product. So the casino functions as a bank, an advertising agency, and a retail outlet.

FIGURE 4.4. *The sisters staring in amazement at the large new casino on their home reservation. © Photofest.*

Even more interesting is the casino's embodying of engaged resistance. During his meeting with the sisters, the chairman receives an urgent phone call informing him that the "feds have just shown up and they want to shut down the casino." When Vickie asks whether that is legal, Chairman Pico's response is genius: "We've been dealing with the feds for a hundred years," he deadpans. "We can handle them now." It is a great line in a strong scene. Again, where agencies like the BIA fall short—in protecting Indian autonomy and looking out for its people—the casino prevails. In fact, the film either textually or subtextually aligns the casino with great Indian warriors of the past, like Red Cloud, Geronimo, and Tecumseh, as it fends off the U.S. government, protects its homeland, and stands its ground. In a world where Indians seem to have few resources, the casino, *Naturally Native* argues, is a bastion of hope.

Ultimately, *Naturally Native* stands as a hopeful project. It does for Indian women what its plot claims the casino can do for Indian nations: understand their problems and give them support. Without coming off as either angry or bitter, it dramatizes specific instances of resistance, especially within the context of American capitalism, while engaging in pan-Indian forms of community and tribally specific motifs of return and renewal. As for Indian identity, that is much better, despite Madame Celeste's claim to the converse, than locating Indianness in a past life.

When Engagement Meets Resistance: *Skins* as Frame

Like *Naturally Native*, *Skins* opens with scenes from a handheld video camera, but not of a San Fernando Valley suburban pool party. In fact, the first six minutes of both films have little in common. Instead of focusing on a happy family get-together, *Skins* begins with documentary footage depicting the brutality of life on the Pine Ridge Reservation in South Dakota. Flyover vistas of the barren hills cut to shots of dusty trailers, cemeteries, and hungry dogs. A jangly blues guitar drones in the background, lending auditory effects to the visuals. As the sound track softens, it merges with a voice-over by Bill Clinton from a visit to the reservation in 1999. Images of President Clinton and a host of Sioux morph to shots of Mount Rushmore and throngs of happy tourists. Another voice-over, this one informing viewers that within sixty miles of the great tourist destination lies the poorest county in the United States—Pine Ridge. Shots of signage ("Wounded Knee" and "Bigfoot Surrenders") fade to a catalogue of images hard to describe and harder to forget: Indians receiving food stamps; two Indian men drinking; two more Indian men fighting; police booking a wasted Indian; policemen escorting a flag-covered coffin in the back of a pickup; and police putting an intoxicated Indian man into a caged vehicle, where he looks like a kept animal. This time, the voice-over rattles off a litany of Pine Ridge statistics that underscore the images:

- 40 percent of residents live in substandard housing.
- The average yearly earning of the residents of Pine Ridge is $2,600.
- 75 percent unemployment on the reservation.
- The life expectancy on Pine Ridge is fifteen years less than the national average.
- Death by alcohol is nine times the national average.

Cut to a shot of a drunk tank, where at least sixteen Indian men lie on the floor of a cell, passed out, nearly on top of one another. At first, it appears to be a cage in a zoo or a kennel, the bodies are packed so close together, but soon enough, the viewer discerns that the incarcerated are all men, all inebriated, all Indian. Then, in another flyover shot, are more scenes of houses, but they are in no particular order and show no particular signs of life.

Finally, the director card, "A Film by Chris Eyre." The movie has barely begun, but already the audience is exhausted.

At just over two minutes, the opening montage may not be long, but it is powerful. It is also two minutes of film that could not be more different from the opening two minutes of *Naturally Native*. Whereas one begins in upper-middle-class suburbia, the other opens in the nation's poorest county (what the *New York Times* calls "a windswept slum"). Whereas one shows affluent, successful, happy Indians, the other shows dispossessed, incarcerated, beleaguered Indians. Whereas one depicts sober Indians in control of their lives, the other depicts drunken Indians helpless in theirs. Whereas one positions itself clearly as a "movie," the other positions itself as "reality." Whereas *Naturally Native* functions as a lens, zeroing in on certain hot-button issues, *Skins* works like a frame—a wide-angle shot, free of filter and affect—that shows a people and a place with unflinching verisimilitude.

With a nod to cinema verité, Eyre (Cheyenne-Arapaho) combines documentary-style naturalism with clever uses of flashback and montage to frame Pine Ridge and its inhabitants in all of their contradictions. The picture inside that frame? Bleak.

Eyre's film, released in 2003, remains one of the more desolate feature films about American Indian life. Based on the 1995 novel by poet, fiction writer, and former journalist Adrian C. Louis, the film version of *Skins* holds admirably to its literary namesake. Louis has never been known for pulling punches—his fantastic poem "Dust World" is a classic example—and Eyre does him proud, though the celluloid version of the main protagonist, Rudy Yellow Shirt, is far and away more sympathetic than his doppelganger in the novel. Still, the film's romance-free exploration of life on Pine Ridge in all its hopelessness, self-destruction, and despair emerges, in many ways, as heroic in its commitment to mimetic representation.

Like *Naturally Native*, *Skins* explores the internal tensions between siblings. The film tracks Rudy (Eric Schweig [Inuit]), a tribal police officer, and his brother Mogie (Graham Greene [Oneida]), a notorious but lovable drunk, whom Rudy simultaneously busts and saves. The two love each other, clearly, but each is a bit embarrassed by the other. Rudy feels constant shame from Mogie's lack of ambition, his chronic intoxication, and his inability to be anything but a cliché and a statistic. On the other hand, to Mogie, Rudy is humorless and square, a sellout, a company man who turns on his own people. One of the many unfortunate aspects of Rudy's job is the unenviable task of arresting his fellow Sioux, including his brother Mogie. Though *Skins* follows both brothers, it is primarily Rudy's story, meaning we see Pine Ridge and Mogie through his eyes. Because his perspective on the reservation frames how we sit it, Pine Ridge looks softer than it might be otherwise, and Mogie less offensive. Officer Kicking Woman from Debra Magpie Earling's *Perma Red* is cut from the same cloth as Rudy. Ineffectual but good-hearted men, both seem destined to save their fellow townspeople from themselves, even if they have no idea how to fill out their own existences. *Naturally Native* is an optimistic tale about frustration; *Skins* is a pessimistic story of desire.

Not surprisingly, the screenplay leads the viewer to believe that the brothers desire nearly opposite things—and on one level that is true—but over the course of the film, it becomes clear that both men long for some kind of connection, a meaningful existence, a sense that they have contributed to something. If Mogie feels he has made a contribution, it is through his humor, which can enliven and animate an otherwise gloomy terrain. His most engaging trait, humor, connects him to his community, and even in his most desperate moments, his ability to laugh in the face of utter hopelessness becomes his best claim to a well-lived life. His ability to recognize and call out the absurd aligns him with trickster characters in both literature and film, as does his willingness to play the fool, the clown prince of Pine Ridge. Rudy's desire on the other hand, does not seek the same outlet as

Mogie's. He buries his beneath concepts like duty and pride, and when mixed with other emotions like contempt, despondency, and anger, it becomes clear (though surprising) which is the darker of the two.

That perfect storm of personal and tribal ineffectualness leads Rudy down a path even darker than his own emotional landscape. After falling and hitting his head on a rock, Rudy awakes to a new kind of consciousness, one we are to believe is informed by Iktomi, the spider trickster spirit who has stalked him his entire life. From an early childhood trip to the outhouse when he was bitten by a spider on his testicles, to the present, when Iktomi surfaces at the most inappropriate times, the film draws a map of Rudy's life as a testing ground for Iktomi's duality of purpose: foolishness and insight, bravery and stupidity, truth and consequence. Fed up with the cycle of violence, self-destruction, and alcoholism he knows are killing the people closest to him, the postepiphany Rudy takes matters into his own Iktomi-influenced hands. Turning his back on the system—as the system has turned its back on his people—Rudy becomes a vigilante. Desperate for justice and mindful that justice via the government and the reservation simply isn't in the cards, Rudy goes old-school.

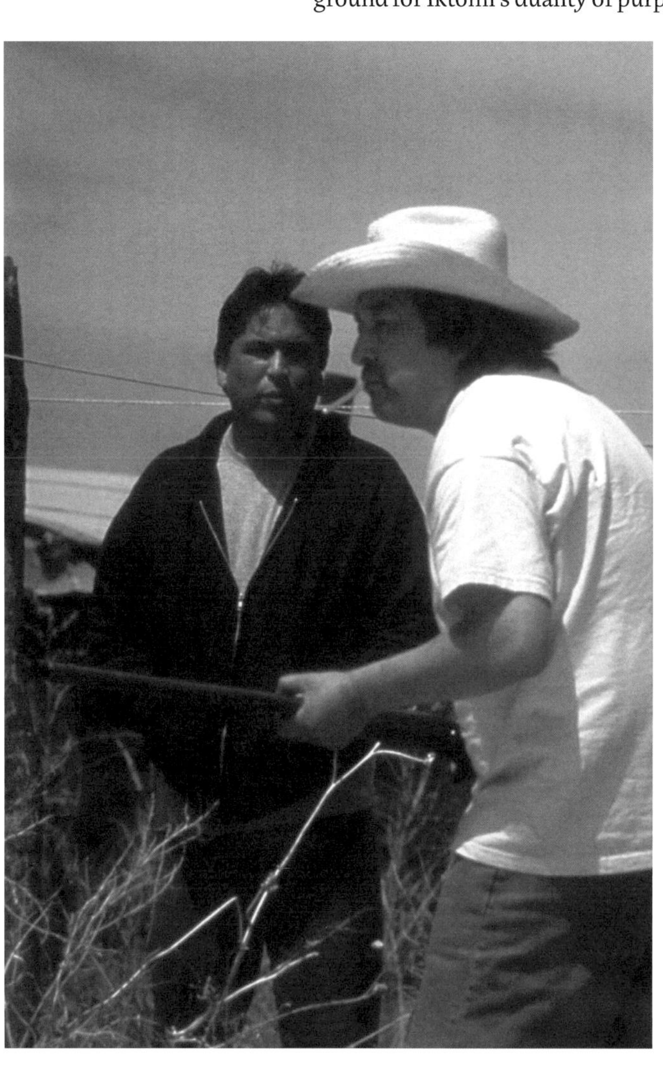

FIGURE 4.5. *Brothers Rudy (Eric Schweig,* left*) and Mogie (Graham Greene) in* Skins. © *Photofest.*

When he discovers that two shiftless locals are responsible for killing a friend of his, he goes after the boys while disguised as the dead man's ghost. Though he doesn't kill them, he breaks their legs and probably even scares them straight. Buoyed by what appears to be success on this front, he turns his attention to the real culprit in the community—alcohol. Unable to do anything about the rampant alcohol abuse and addiction on the reservation, he decides to cut the supply off at the source. He burns down a liquor store just over the South Dakota—Nebraska state line, where Mogie and many other Indians from Pine Ridge go to drink. Fool Iktomi once, shame on you; fool him twice, shame on him. And the shame falls, in fact, on Rudy because Mogie happens to be hiding in the liquor store when Rudy sets the building on fire. A savvier reader of Iktomi tales would know how often the trickster gets tricked, but Rudy's rage blinds his judgment, and consequently, it is Mogie, not Rudy, who gets burned.

A similar rage motivates Officer Kicking Woman in *Perma Red*. Like Rudy, Kicking Woman engages in vigilantism. Toward the end of *Perma Red*, instead of saving Harvey Stoner, the man who tried to kill Louise, Kicking Woman ignites Stoner's wrecked car, which is dripping with gasoline, until it and Stoner explode. In both cases, the acts of resistance take form through fire, an efficient mode of purgation and renewal. "There was only this one duty before me," Kicking Woman tells the reader, "this one responsibility." On his daily beat, Rudy sees countless Indians crossing the state line to get drunk, and there is no question that he thinks if he can remove the store, he will mitigate the problem. The illuminated Rudy no doubt sees eradicating the store as his duty, his responsibility. Eyre himself sympathizes with this perspective. In his director's commentary for *Skins*, he notes that this particular liquor store sells over four million cans of beer a year—in a town that has a population of

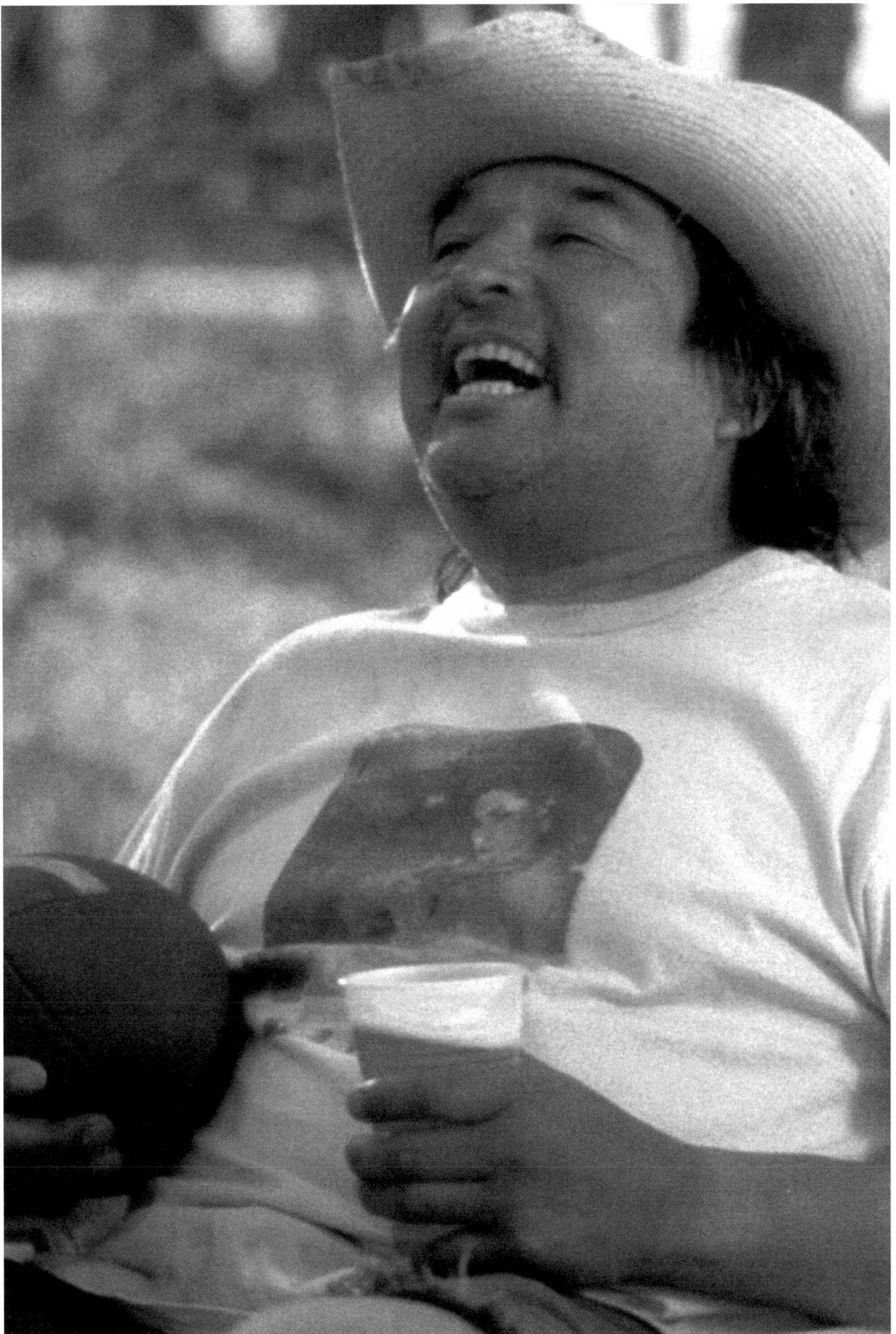

twenty. He calls these stores "merchants of death," and one knows well that if they didn't exist, at least some of the problems on the reservation wouldn't either. Not surprisingly then, the viewer sides with Rudy when he commits arson—especially after that opening montage. It is the right thing to do.

Until you see Mogie burning alive.

Is it Iktomi who tricks Rudy into thinking his rage and retribution can actually make things right, or is it, as Roger Ebert suggests in his review, merely a metaphor for larger forces of ineptitude and helplessness on the reservation? "His protest," writes Ebert, "direct and angry, is as impotent as every other form of expression seems to be."

FIGURE 4.6. *Mogie with his three favorite things: a football, his Madonna T-shirt, and a beer. © Photofest.*

Though Mogie lives, the viewer (along with Rudy) discovers soon enough that Mogie's liver, fried by a lifetime of abuse, is in worse shape than the store Rudy torched. His condition is terminal, though Rudy never communicates this to Mogie; instead, he spends the rest of the movie trying to make right as many things as possible. Part of that reconciliation means coming to terms with his own family history. *Skins* and *Naturally Native* veer back on similar paths in this regard, since both projects attempt to work through how a toxic past can continue to poison the present. In the case of the Lewis sisters, their alcoholic mother and deadbeat father left them without a sense of place or belonging and, most importantly, without identity. Mogie and Rudy endure almost too much identity. Having never really left the reservation, they are reminded every day of their harsh childhood. Through flashbacks and hazy memories, Eyre re-creates recollective mile markers on Rudy's developmental highway: an abusive and alcoholic father, an ineffectual mother handcuffed by her situation. Rudy, Mogie, Vickie, Karen, and Tanya each deal with dysfunctional parents and how that dysfunction contributes to the always already dysfunctional construct of what Thomas Builds-the-Fire calls, in *Smoke Signals*, "the crime of being an Indian in the twentieth century." As Rudy knows well, at Pine Ridge, dysfunction begets dysfunction, even within (perhaps especially within) families. Mogie, for example, can't even raise his own son. He makes his sister do it, and even then, he still forgets the boy's birthday. Were they to meet, Mogie's son and the Lewis sisters would find they have more in common than they might expect.

In both films, the concatenation of familial noxiousness gets ignored by the critics in favor of the plot-driven story lines, particularly in *Skins*. However, when read alongside *Naturally Native*, with its politics of paternal neglect, *Skins* becomes a provocative exploration of familial survivance and resistance. While Native literary texts have done an exemplary job of mapping the importance of families within the tribal system—think of Louise Erdrich's novels as well as those of LeAnne Howe, Eric Gansworth, and Susan Power—Native cinema has not yet taken on this topic with as much aplomb. Part of the problem is film's temporal compression: anyone with siblings, parents, or children knows how complicated and entangled family drama can be. Sherman Alexie nods toward some of these issues in parts of *Smoke Signals*, but, for good reason, his main story belongs to Thomas and Victor and their filmic journey south. *Naturally Native* and *Skins* take up this mantle from different perspectives and turn it into a major narrative strain. Flashbacks tell us that both Mogie and Rudy held promise as boys and that they were close, no doubt because of their family climate. After Rudy is bitten on the testicles by the spider, it is Mogie who carries him back to the house. We also find out that both were standout football players together in high school and that Mogie, in particular, excelled. Though Eyre is unable to vocalize it, the film connotes a strong bond between the two boys, perhaps as a kind of barrier against their father's alcoholism and their mother's weakness. In some ways, Rudy turns into his mother—good-hearted but weak—so he hides behind the authority of the tribal police force and its metaphorical backbone. Mogie becomes their father: angry, bitter, and neglectful, spending more time drinking with Verdell Weasel Tail (Gary Farmer) than being with his son. And yet something about both men keeps them from spiraling too far downward.

For Rudy, like Officer Kicking Woman, his sense of duty fuels his vigilantism. Unlike his parents, Rudy wants to make things right, and he has discovered that working within the tribal police system, which is the American legal system, simply perpetuates a cycle of dependency, punishment, and dehumanization, without any real measures of rehabilitation or renewal. So when he acts on his own, outside "the law," those actions carry shades of both engagement and resistance. Rudy refuses to sit on the metaphorical sidelines while the never-ending game of Pine Ridge's implosion goes back and forth in front of him. To relinquish responsibility is to give in to the system, is to turn his back on his

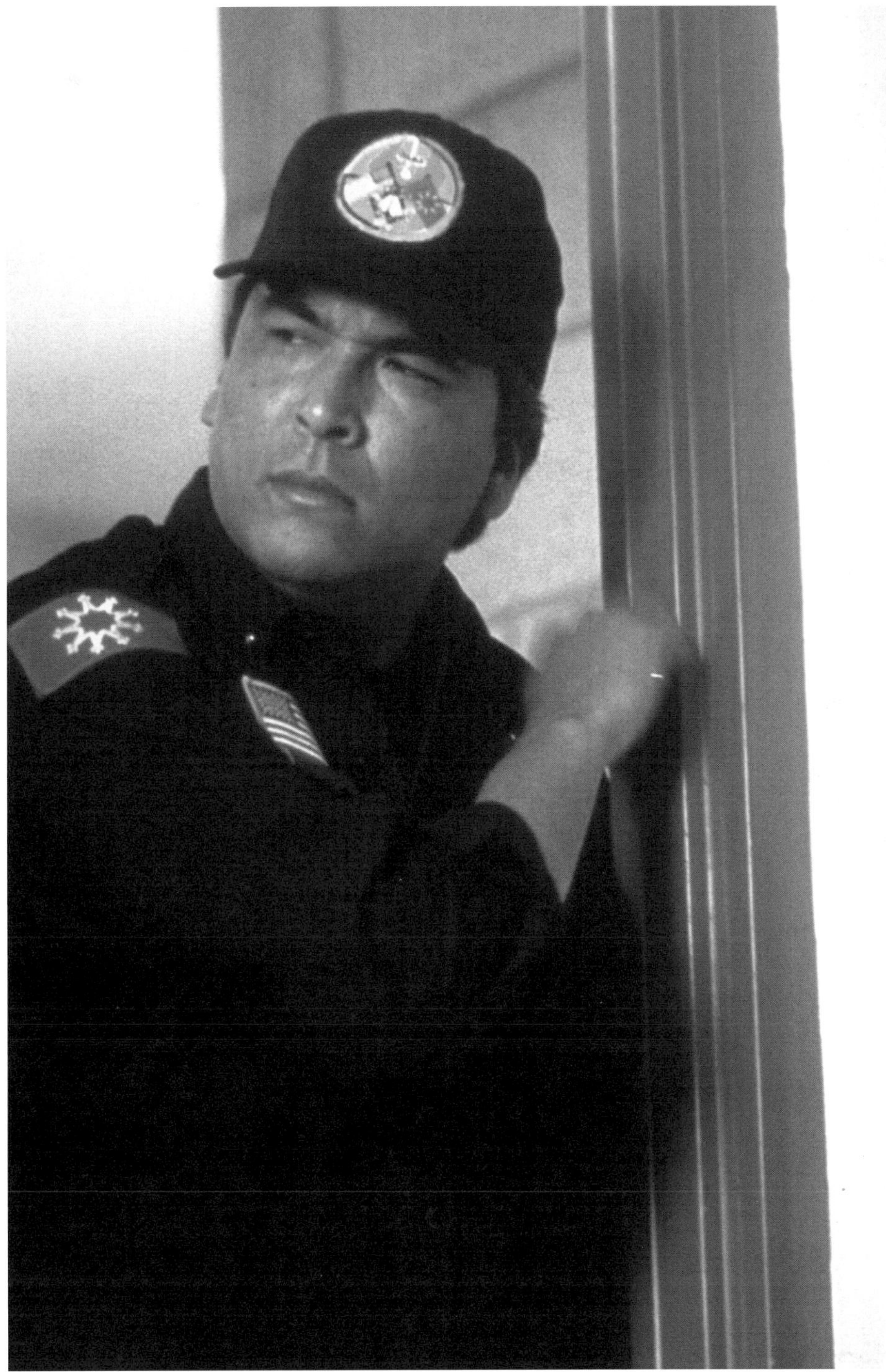

tribe. Of course, his vigilantism turns into an imperfect retaliatory approach, but in a world of limited options and even fewer resources, what tenable choices does he have? There is also a sense in which his actions are Iktomi-driven, a fact acknowledged by Eyre himself. Indeed, the first nondocumentary scene in the film shows Rudy in a bathroom, wiping off his face paint after an act of vigilantism while a large black spider crawls across the sink. That scene cuts to the outhouse, to that fateful morning when Iktomi seems to have tagged him, marked him for life. In the director's commentary, Eyre talks about how, for him, the movie is largely about how Rudy embraces the trickster spirit of Iktomi, how Rudy not only mirrors Iktomi's stupidity and wisdom, but actually becomes a trickster

FIGURE 4.7. *Rudy in his tribal police uniform. He functions as a counterbalance to Mogie, and yet doesn't. © Photofest.*

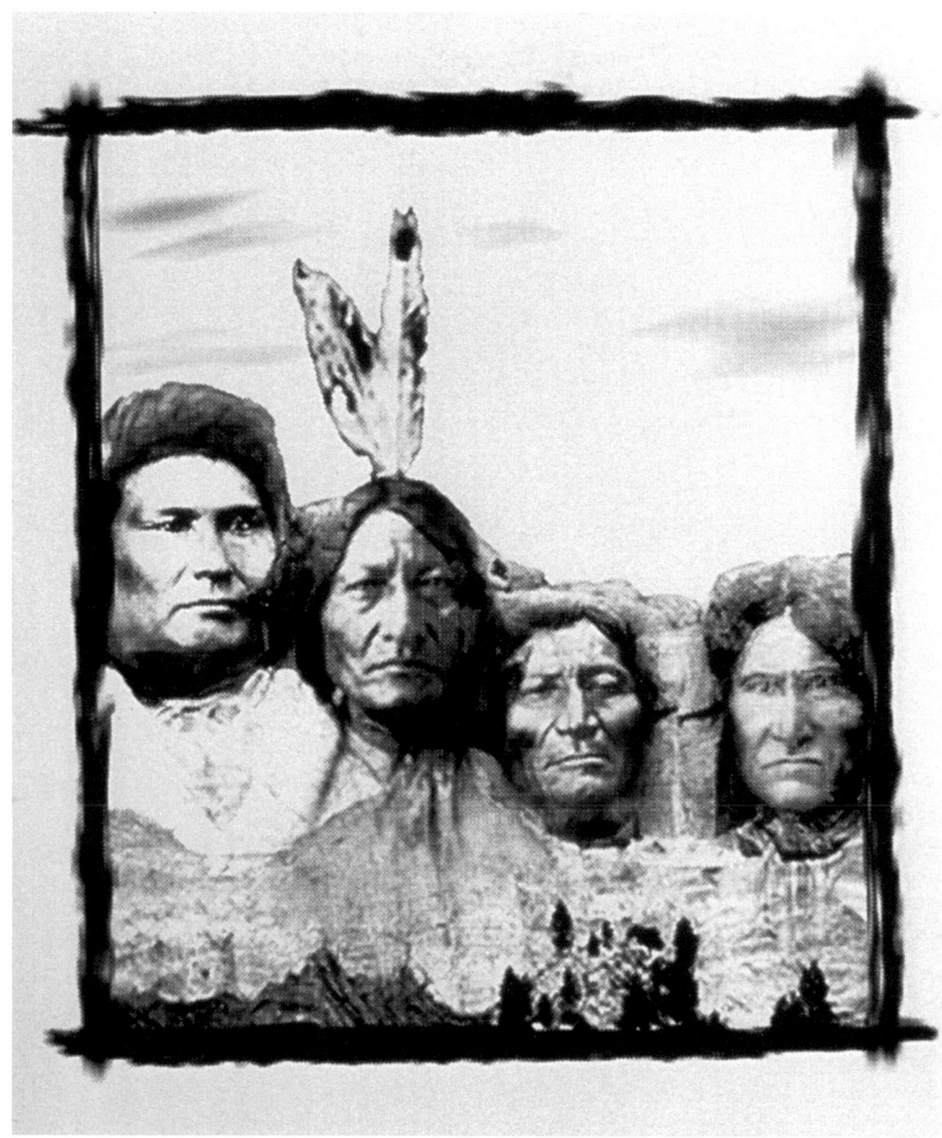

FIGURE 4.8. The Real Founding Fathers, *from the shirt Rudy brings for Mogie. © Photofest.*

himself. That level of full-on engagement and literalization of Native narrative transforms Rudy's actions from mere human reaction to an embodiment of Native world making. Even more significantly, the trickster ubiquity imbues his behavior with the long history of indigenous proactivity.

That said, Rudy's resistance may not come entirely from Iktomi. His most persuasive source is Mogie, who functions as Rudy's conscience of protest. Mogie bucks the system any chance he gets, even the governmental system, despite his status as a veteran. In fact, one of Mogie's longtime dreams is to blow off the nose of Mount Rushmore's George Washington. If *Skins*'s indigenous icon of resistance is Iktomi, its main American counterpart is Mount Rushmore—Mogie's symbolic foil. Profoundly offended by the monument, Mogie urges Rudy to remove the appendage as a symbolic act of protest and Indian autonomy. To its credit, *Skins* does a fine job of reminding viewers that the mere existence of Mount Rushmore is a desecration—the Black Hills it calls home are, after all, sacred to the Sioux. But like some sort of bizarre anthropomorphic panopticon, the carved faces stand guard, doing surveillance over Pine Ridge and its unruly inhabitants. As an homage to Mogie, Rudy performs two different but related Mount Rushmore–based gestures late in the film. First, when Mogie is hospitalized after the liquor store fire, the most mourned casualty of which is his beloved Madonna T-shirt, Rudy buys him a new T-shirt bearing the image of the iconoclastic "Real Founding Fathers" of Mount Rushmore. Supplanting the faces of Washington, Lincoln, Jefferson, and Roosevelt are the visages of Chief Joseph, Sitting Bull, Geronimo, and Red Cloud. By replacing Madonna with Indians, Rudy acknowledges a symbolic replacement of prominent Anglo iconography with just as significant Indian iconography. Rudy knows this gift is perfect not simply because it is a cool shirt but also because it signifies an acknowledgment by Rudy of Mogie's spirit of resistance.

But the real act of protest comes at the end of the film when, after Mogie dies, Rudy searches for an appropriate way to honor his brother, whose life was too short, too miserable, and too broken but whose bravery and humor in the face of addiction and trauma were, nevertheless, courageous. Wounded three times in Vietnam and the recipient of three Purple Hearts, Mogie is no coward, though he too often turns to alcohol as a palliative. Indeed, Mogie seems a victim of the system—used by his country in a foreign war, forgotten by his country afterward, and taunted by his country as his own community suffers in the shadow of Mount Rushmore. But, unlike his father, he never acts out that rage and frustration against his own son. It is all internalized or, at the right moment, directed harmlessly and mockingly toward Rudy (who probably needs it). Those memories of his brother motivate Rudy to celebrate his brother's life and mourn his death in a way commensurate with Mogie's better angels—Rudy desecrates a desecration.

As this book argues, resistance in the symbolic field can be as powerful as resistance on the battlefield. Rudy, emboldened as a cultural warrior, seems to intuit this as well. After purchasing a large container of red oil-based paint, Rudy drives to Mount Rushmore. It is late at night, and all the tourists and park rangers are away. He hikes up the mountain and, while standing on top of Washington's rounded head, cracks open the vat of paint, only to find another spider crawling along the lid. Buoyed by the spirits of both Iktomi and his brother, Rudy launches the paint high into the air, and it comes down just below Washington's left eye. In a moment of exultation and renewal, Rudy raises his arms to the heavens in a gesture of completion and victory.[2] He enacts a form of conquest, a personal and tribal triumph. The next morning, when the sun rises over the Black Hills, we see a truly arresting image: the alabaster George Washington crying a big fat red tear.

From another angle, the long streak of red paint resembles a scar, an infliction whose symbolism carries a host of connotations, perhaps the most ironic of which asks which is the bigger "scar on the landscape": the slash of paint or Mount Rushmore. Also, red paint on the face of George Washington no doubt reminds many readers of past instances of imaginative resistance, such as the time Russell Means painted Plymouth Rock red. Rudy's reddening of America's whitewashing does similar work to Means's, as does the graffiti on the buildings of Alcatraz. On one hand, some might consider these instances of defacement, even vandalism. But on the other hand, one can read these acts of defiance as performances of engagement with the surrounding iconography, an alteration of the semiotics of a hostile landscape. The Treaty of Fort Laramie (1868) gave the Black Hills to the Lakota, but just a few years later, after the Black Hills War of 1876, the United States reclaimed the entire area. A few decades after that, Mount Rushmore was conceived to promote tourism in the Dakotas, but even then it was not without controversy. Indian resentment toward what Means has called a "shrine of hypocrisy" reached its zenith on July 4, 1971, when he and other members of AIM occupied Mount Rushmore.[3] In my mind, Eyre's film serves as the mainstream sequel to Means's first run. If, in the postmodern era, everything is a simulacrum, if the screen of visual culture is the arena in which anything of import transpires, then Eyre's project fights representational fire with representational fire. Rudy brings a new level of symbolic and synesthetic authority to

Red Power, and *Skins* helps frame the discourse that makes such a contravention feel not like transgression but liberation.

One could make the argument that movies like *Naturally Native* (which never saw theatrical release) and *Skins*, which saw limited release, will never be seen by as many people as see Mount Rushmore in one year. But part of what makes these movies promising is who will see them—students, writers, professors, scholars, reviewers, and Indians themselves. Thanks to the "Rolling Rez Tour," Eyre's groundbreaking promotion in which he drove a big bus to various reservations to screen the film, an unusually wide range of people got to see the movie and talk about it in settings where that would not have otherwise been possible.

Eyre has said that Rudy's rouging of George Washington is, to him, like counting coup—an act of shaming. For most Plains Indians, counting coup involved some sort of physical interaction with an enemy, such as landing an arrow or hitting a combatant with a "coup stick." It was considered particularly brave if a warrior touched an enemy with his hand and escaped, proving both his superior fighting skills and his superior ethics. Counting coup shamed the enemy but did not kill him. Perhaps in Eyre's movie, itself an act of counting celluloid coup, other Indian artists will find a model for future aesthetic activism and a language for symbolic resistance both smart and just.

Naturally Native and *Skins*: Lens and Frame, Engagement and Resistance

Though there seems to be a silent assumption in the world of Native American studies that *Naturally Native* is naïve and optimistic, while *Skins* is bleak and hyperrealistic, both categorizations do the movies a disservice. Focusing on the formal shortcomings of movies that were shot in around twenty days for very little money may not be the best way into the films. It also doesn't matter particularly that in the very few reviews of either movie, neither came out particularly well. *Skins* garnered a well-written positive review from Jonathan Curiel at the *San Francisco Chronicle* and strong acclaim from Roger Ebert, but the *New York Times* was critical and the *Village Voice* was brutal. *Naturally Native* was not written about in very many publications of note, only the *Los Angeles Times*, which gave the movie a favorable review; the industry publication *Variety* was less than kind. More importantly, as I suggest early in this chapter, is the cultural work the movies perform. They dramatize different but wholly complementary modes of resistance to and within American systems, often using humor and symbolic action as accoutrements. They also locate in Indian families the interdependent support mechanism for individual autonomy, which almost always turns around and functions either tribally (in the case of *Naturally Native*) or globally (in the case of *Skins*).

When compared to *Smoke Signals* and *The Business of Fancydancing*, *Naturally Native* and *Skins* seem to take themselves more seriously. Though it contains serious scenes, *Smoke Signals* positions itself as a comedy, while *Fancydancing* asks to be read as an experimental, even postmodern film. *Skins*, Eyre's follow-up to *Smoke Signals*, goes the more mimetic route and, by featuring some funny scenes but positioning itself as a drama, almost reverses the pattern established in *Smoke Signals*. Similarly, *Naturally Native* comes off as primarily rhetorical despite its desire to eschew alterity. It wants to be mainstream. At times, the Lewis sisters seem as if they could be grown up Indian versions of the girls from *The Brady Bunch*—still living in the same suburban-LA house, still involved in hijinks. *Fancydancing*, with its spliced scenes of dancing, its metacommentary, its self-referentiality, and its queer subtext couldn't be farther from such a project. For me, this doesn't signal Native films' inconsistency by any means; rather, it indicates a richness of vision, a diversity of stories, and a cinematic polyvocality that demands to be taken seriously.

Finally, all these films resist what Amanda J. Cobb calls the Hollywood "comfort zone," which she defines as "anything outside of the 19th century" ("This Is What It Means," 226). Instead, like the National Museum of the American Indian, these projects share a desire to represent Native American presences by engaging contemporary problems and contemporary solutions. "No single film," writes Jacqueline Kilpatrick in *Celluloid Indians*, "can be expected to undo the misinformation about Native Americans that has accumulated over many generations" (232). True. But a plurality of films can help reinscribe the here and now; they can frame the present; they can train a lens on the strategies of coping, love, compassion, humor, and resistance that define Indian activism. Activist texts take many shapes, but they also share many tenets. Here, *Skins* and *Naturally Native* question the legitimacy of fundamental U.S. policies (the reservation system, CDIBs), the organization and structure of the capitalist system, the symbolic violence of mascots and monuments, and the denial of Indians' basic human rights. In the final passage of *Conquest*, Andrea Smith closes her study by quoting Jean Ziegler: "We know what we don't want, but the new world belongs to the liberated freedom of human beings. There is no way, you make the way as you walk" (191). In this new world of Indian activism and aesthetic sovereignty, Red-Horse and Eyre are making the way down the rez road, the Hollywood road, the pop-culture road, showing us Indian America in all of its contradictions and conflicts. The past will always write itself in its own way and in its own time, but it takes people like Red-Horse and Eyre to write and right the present.

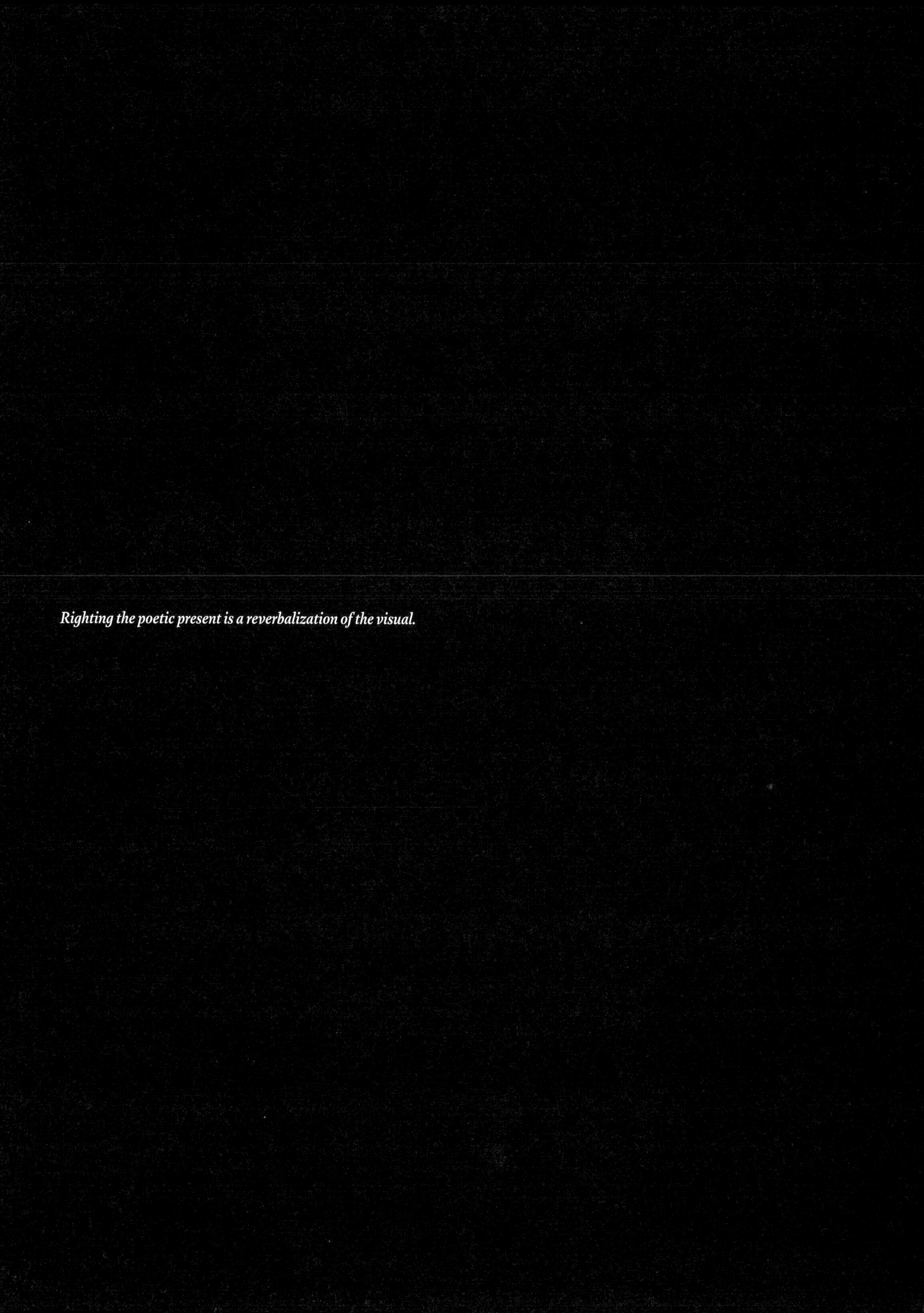

Righting the poetic present is a reverbalization of the visual.

5. WORD AS WEAPON

VISUAL CULTURE AND CONTEMPORARY AMERICAN INDIAN POETRY

No words flashed across the screen at the reservation drive-in, no words promising either of us top billing.

WHAT WOULD THE land mass we call the "United States" be like without Anglos?

If Wovoka's Ghost Dance had transpired as he hoped, such a concept would not be mere fantasy but reality. In Sherman Alexie's *Indian Killer*, Marie Polotkin, a Spokane college student, tries to explain to her wannabe-Indian professor (for whom the Ghost Dance stands as a "beautiful, and ultimately desperate act") that Wovoka's vision was more than mere "symbolism" and "metaphorical beauty." For her and for Wovoka and his followers, the Ghost Dance attempted to bring about a form of radical justice that would rid the earth of all white people: "Don't you see? If the Ghost Dance had worked, you wouldn't be here. You'd be dust" (313).

Indeed.

Though the Ghost Dance steered clear of violence, its followers believed that the mystical combination of dance, chant, and religion would bring to pass a cleansing in which "white people and their culture [would] be destroyed by a natural cataclysm" (Mooney, *Ghost Dance Religion*, viii). From the Ghost Dance to the Maya power song "They Came from the East" to the Iroquois's anti-Anglo spell "Magic Formula" to the Yana's "Curse on People that Wish One Ill," Native communities have invested language with the ability to control identity and destiny. As scholar and linguist John Bierhorst argues, the "belief that words in themselves have the power to make things happen . . . is one of the distinguishing features of Native American thought" (*The Sacred Path*, 3). When Wovoka and his followers performed the Ghost Dance, they trusted that their singing would "make things happen." If words, performative language, could reach their full potential, then, like a great spell, the unified chorus of Indians would be able to act as an inverted Yahweh: they would speak all white people out of being.

The Ghost Dance continues to serve as a provocative vision of confrontation and a complex example of how Native America sees language as a viable weapon to protect cultural identity and sovereignty. When physical resistance becomes implausible, linguistic resistance becomes necessary; stories can be told about the white devil (Handsome Lake), power songs sung, spells invented, and myths constructed. Not surprisingly, Native American communities have emerged with a relationship to language that most contemporary Anglos do not and cannot understand. That so many Ojibwe, Choctaw, Laguna, Navajo, Cherokee, Modoc, Creek, and countless other clans and communities produce important poets surprises no one. It is what is supposed to happen.

To sustain the transformative power of charged oral expression, many contemporary writers from these tribes have turned to the lyric poem as a mode of both connection and defiance. Like its oral ancestors, the lyric has sought the dual catalyzation of author and reader, but has not really cultivated a reputation as a viable space for protest, especially in the United States. While lyric poetry in English has not been without its private contrivances or tropes of conquest, for the most part, its ontology has been one of engagement. In its essence, the lyric project seeks relation and transformation, as Edward Hirsch rightly argues: "Reading poetry is an act of reciprocity, and one of the great tasks of the lyric is to bring us into right relationship with each other" (*How to Read a Poem*, 4). For Native writers, poetry functions not only as a relationship but also as a gesture of power that transforms reality for authors, readers, and their communities. In fact, in her study of contemporary American Indian poetry, Robin Riley Fast echoes Hirsch, arguing that Native writers participate in a dialogic poetics that modifies the world for speaker and listener, writer and reader. According to Fast, this "dialogic exchange" enacts a "concept integral to Native oral cultures—that of language's efficacy, its power to change the world" (*The Heart as a Drum*, 214). Through the unusual and provocative conflation of public and private significations, performative powers, and subtexts of relation and confrontation, the contemporary American Indian poem has become a unique and effective form of simultaneous engagement and resistance.

This chapter looks closely at poems by three contemporary Native writers—Louise Erdrich (Ojibwe), Sherman Alexie (Spokane—Coeur d'Alene), and Wendy Rose (Hopi-Miwok)—in an attempt to understand how these authors use the lyric poem as a mode of defiance that also participates in the cultural history of Native oral discourse. Like traditional indigenous power songs, the American Indian lyric poem functions as a weapon of contention, revolution, and continuation. However, as I argue in the chapters on film, the world has changed, and so have the spaces where the struggles for Indian identity take place. There are no Trails of Tears or Sand Creeks in late-twentieth-century or early-twenty-first-century America; the sites of cultural colonialism and erasure have shifted from the expanse of the Great Plains to the expanses of television, movie, and computer screens. Whereas place names, broken treaties, and raids robbed Indians of cultural identity a century year ago, westerns, team mascots, comics, Tonto, and other caricatures try to dilute Indian sovereignty and appropriate Native cultural identity. Visual culture—movies and television in particular—has erected new one-dimensional Native identities.

So effective have the modern media been in altering how Indians see themselves that many Native writers talk about growing up sympathizing with cowboys and ridiculing the Cheyenne and Arapaho. One thing the beleaguered Ward Churchill (Creek—Cherokee Métis) gets right is how thoroughly popular culture has overwritten Native presences. "North American indigenous peoples," asserts Churchill, "have been reduced in terms of cultural identity within the popular consciousness—through a combination of movie treatments, television programming and distortive literature—to a point where the general public perceives them as extinct for all practical purposes" (*Fantasies of the Master Race*, 239). To counter this prevailing perception, the National Museum of the American Indian has made its main mission to prove that Indians "are still here." In their poems, Rose, Alexie, and Erdrich make similar, though more pointed, assertions.

That Indian writers might turn to culturally significant forms of resistance is not surprising. Natives have often eschewed the seemingly pragmatic options of public policy and law and opted instead to rely on language or performance as modes of resistance and cultural preservation. In her essay "Approaches to Native American Philosophy," V. F. Cordova echoes Churchill, arguing that Indians, despite everything done to them, have, remarkably, been able to keep their identities alive: "Many Native Americans, whether one wishes to believe it or not, have managed to survive the onslaughts of assimilation and outright eradications with an intact cultural identity" (30). One reason for this is the fact that Natives invest considerable capital in cultural practices and cultural expressions that contravene assaults on mediated sovereignty that law and policies cannot address.

In response to these assaults, Erdrich, Alexie, and Rose turn the lyric into what I see as a site of aesthetic activism: their poems reverse the imperial colonizing thrust of contemporary culture through participation in it. Their inventive use of the lyric transforms both public and private discourses and allows them not only to counter establishments of identity but also to tell who they are, in their own words. These authors withstand cultural erasure by attacking those armaments designed to annihilate their ability to speak themselves into being; yet, through the lyric poem, they recoup the performative energies of the oral tradition, pulling from the best traditions of both Anglo and Native discourse.

The remainder of this chapter examines how these Native writers turn to the lyric as a means of engaged resistance. I begin with Erdrich's "Dear John Wayne," in which she takes on the metanarrative of Wayne and the western by directly challenging his metonymic image. For her, Wayne's ubiquitous presence mirrors the totalizing gestures of Manifest Destiny. Wayne and his smile are also happy fodder for Alexie in "My Heroes Have Never Been Cowboys," as are Fred Astaire and Anglo entitlement in his hilarious poem "Owl Dancing with Fred Astaire." In these texts, Alexie defies Hollywood typecasting by contextualizing Indian reality and Hollywood fantasy. Wendy Rose takes a much different tone from that of Erdrich or Alexie. She situates her poems in an entirely different space: *Star Trek*'s holodeck. Here, Rose inverts media machinery, transforming it into a space that enables a kind of rejuvenating radicalism. My goal is to demonstrate that while each poet enters into his or her own form of creative continuance, they are united through their desires to inhabit both popular and Native culture. Thus, these moments become both enactions and reenactions of language's ability to transform the writer, the reader, and the mediated spaces that determine identity and cultural capital.

"Dear John Wayne"

Resistance comes in many forms, including poetry. For example, Simon Ortiz's *From Sand Creek*—a book-length poetic reenvisioning of the Sand Creek Massacre—is inexorably connected with the all too clearly written text of history and violence. Ortiz's text rewrites that event from a Native perspective by rooting each poem in the collection in a particular moment in history and a specific geographic place. In her poem to John Wayne, also a reenvisioning of the West and westerns, Erdrich picks up where Ortiz leaves off. If cultural imperialism and eradication in the nineteenth century occurred in places like Sand Creek, the twentieth century's correlative would have to be the media. No longer requiring physical invasion into Native spaces, America opted instead for virtual incursion. "Dear John Wayne" stands as a one-woman force against such projects. Perhaps the most well-known poem from her first book, *Jacklight*, "Dear John Wayne" may be the most famous poem by any Native writer.

The poem enjoys many strong components, but one reason it remains effective is its unique positionality. Through an alteration of perspective, our readerly gaze is reversed.

Erdrich orients herself as one of us; she becomes a member of the audience, approaching a John Wayne movie from the outside. Moreover, she collapses the boundary between reader and author, Indian and non-Indian, making the reader the conarrator: "August and the drive-in picture is packed. / We lounge on the hood of the Pontiac" (*Jacklight*, 12). Though a small move, this shifts the "Indian on the page" away from the reader's gaze, making the screen the reified target, not exoticized (or in the case of the car, commodified) Natives. Like Erdrich, we find ourselves waiting for the text before us to unfold, excited with anticipation. Soon we realize that we are on the reservation, about to watch a John Wayne western through the eyes of Erdrich—to be sure, an intense level of alterity. But the poem pulls us in. Written in the form of a letter, the text weaves dialogue from Wayne's character (in italics) into the text of the letter itself, perhaps indicating that not even Erdrich's thoughts escape Wayne's influence. The inability to ignore the culture and technology—the ravenous power—that Wayne's image embodies also evokes the impossibility of eluding the drive for cultural domination that brought the white settlers and, by extension, Wayne and the cinema to Ojibwe territory in the first place.

In short, his imposition into the poem metonymizes the larger Anglo intrusion onto Native lands:

> The drum breaks. There will be no parlance.
> Only the arrows whining, a death-cloud of nerves
> swarming down on the settlers
> who die beautifully, tumbling like dust weeds
> into the history that brought us all here
> together: this wide screen beneath the sign of the bear.
>
> —(9)

Troubled by the merciless arrival of both physical violence carried by the settlers and cultural violence carried by movies, Erdrich links the ontology of the western to its roots in Anglo domination and Native subordination. Stealthier and lovelier than the settlers, the film causes the spillage of beer only, not blood; still, it remains clear that the past is the present. The fight is never over:

> The sky fills, acres of blue squint and eye
> that the crowd cheers. His face moves over us,
> a thick cloud of vengeance, pitted
> like the land that was once flesh. Each rut,
> each scar makes a promise: *It is*
> *not over, this fight, not as long as you resist.*
>
> *Everything we see belongs to us.*
>
> —(9)

Like Rose in her poem about the holodeck and Alexie in his about Fred Astaire and the Owl Dance, Erdrich confronts troubling issues regarding the enigmatic relationship among mass communication, culture, and art. Here, for example, the words that Wayne speaks are words of eradication, removal justified by a higher calling. Of course, Erdrich's description of the wrath of the white settlers on the pagan Indians not only finds resonance in many biblical narratives, but is also seemingly justified by scripture. Laurence Goldstein makes a similar observation: "The phrase, 'His face moves over us,' adapted from the opening of Genesis, suggests a godlike figure of vengeance and wrath, punishing the infidels by firepower and by denial of the blessing needed for redemption in his new Zion" (*The American Poet at the Movies*, 204). Indeed, the elevated language in the poem and the finality of Wayne's phrases create a sense of Wayne's holiness and supremacy—even if it is invented.

Wayne's cultural apotheosis in America is not lost on Alexie either. In stanza eight of "My Heroes Have Never Been Cowboys," Alexie's brother seems to equate Wayne's cultural omnipotence with the cosmic equivalent: "Looking up into the night sky, I asked my brother what he thought God looked like and he said, 'He probably looks like John Wayne'" (*The First Indian on the Moon*, 102). Similarly, Victor and Thomas, the two main characters in Alexie's film *Smoke Signals*, also link Wayne with cultural notions of triumph. When they get kicked out of their seats and removed to the back of the bus, Thomas uses Wayne as an example of a cowboy who always wins. They even make up a song about him; ironically, Victor and Thomas's song focuses on the fact that he never smiles, whereas Erdrich is struck by his "horizon of teeth."[1] Indeed, the physical characteristics of Wayne's face remain all too indelible. The dark gaze of Wayne, a virtual panopticon of judgment and retribution, remains a force from which there is no escape, not even in the margins. For Erdrich, even humor is a placebo. The raucous behavior of Erdrich and her friends as they drive away—drunk, noisy, irreverent—is contrasted with Wayne's authoritative voice and demeanor, and his words, ringing in her ears, seem to justify further punishment. To resist is to resist redemption.

Though Erdrich and her friends laugh at the screen, in the final stanza, she acknowledges the difficulty of erasing Wayne's face from her eyes and his voice from her head:

> How can we help but keep hearing his voice,
> the flip side of the sound track, still playing:
> *Come on boys, we got them*
> *where we want them, drunk, running.*
> *They'll give us what we want, what we need.*
> Even his disease was the idea of taking everything.
> Those cells, burning, doubling, splitting out of their skins.
>
> —(10)

The inability to silence the voice of Hollywood hegemony also drives "My Heroes Have Never Been Cowboys," a poem for which "Dear John Wayne" serves as a likely source. In stanza six of this piece, a bodiless and seemingly omnipresent voice, also in italics, speaks to the audience in metaphors of conquest: "*Win their hearts and minds and we win the war.* Can you hear that song echo across history?" (*The First Indian on the Moon*, 102). The same voice echoes in the same ears. It keeps inscribing an ethos of domination and submission, arrival and removal, imperialism and colonialism. There is literally no deliverance from history or, for that matter, from destiny. Both Alexie and Erdrich seem to understand that, like the past, the future has also been written.

The italicized passages throughout reinforce the dialogic trajectory in the poem, but the "we" in the final stanza makes us wonder whom, exactly, Erdrich addresses and with whom she speaks. Even though the poem doubles as a letter written to John Wayne, the curious pronoun usage in the penultimate line, ("his" as opposed to "your") suggests that the speaker has turned to someone else, perhaps her friends, her community, perhaps herself. The poem accentuates that dual signification when we reread Wayne's comments in the same stanza. They, too, seem particularly personal, as though they are being spoken simultaneously by hundreds of white men from the past and future and are being aimed directly at the group of Indians on the hood of the Pontiac. That Wayne is an icon for a certain type of American goes unsaid; what he does say, though, on the large white screen that expands into the sky and into the wilderness becomes more significant than mere movie dialogue. His ubiquitous, even iconic, pale face speaks for America, and Erdrich is profoundly disturbed by what she hears.

This is not to say that the poem is anti-Anglo or even antitechnology; however, it is clear that for Erdrich and her friends, the pervasive presence Wayne commands on the screen embodies the equally pervasive entitlement that "Western" culture and the technology that deifies him commands both geographically and spiritually. No Ojibwe carries Wayne's cultural currency because no Ojibwe occupies the space of Wayne in contemporary visual culture. Even when the drive-in's screen goes blank, the audience knows that it is very unlikely a movie about Indians will inhabit that space. Thus, like Sand Creek, the screen becomes a place signifying Native absence, a site where Indians return again and again to see Apaches, Comanches, and Kiowas killed, vilified, demonized, and oppressed.

Erdrich understands Marshall McLuhan's key message about the technological age: the medium is the message. On a basic level, the fact that the projector and screen exist at all stands as a silent reminder (and a pretty clear message) of the power of the sleeping giant as well as of the value system that John Wayne (and the entire Manifest Destined sweep of the western) represents. As Goldstein notes, "[Wayne] has taken from them not only their land but their self-respect, their humanity" (*The American Poet at the Movies*, 204). At its core, Manifest Destiny is all about the dual projects of acquisition and eradication—projects that Wayne thoroughly embodied. As the final lines of the previous stanza indicate, "even his disease was the idea of taking everything." "John Wayne, a stand-in for American society, himself a 'great white father'," observes Janice Gould (Maidu), "not only has cancer, a disease whose moral equivalent is greed, but all that he stands for becomes a cancer in this poem as well" ("American Indian Women's Poetry," 804). Erdrich's recuperative, restorative act displaces the voraciousness of Wayne's and the western's appetite for domination with a different kind of cultural representation. The white guy becomes the savage, and Erdrich's dialogue, not Wayne's, ultimately creates identity in the poem.

Despite the text's thematic sorties, perhaps its most intriguing forms of aesthetic activism happen formally. "Dear John Wayne" is a case study in the use of a classic Western poetic technique—reversed. For instance, Erdrich creates a remarkable apostrophic moment that critics seem to have missed. The lyric poem has enjoyed a long history of the apostrophe, a poetic figuration in which the "speaker directly and often emotionally addresses a person who is dead or otherwise not physically present" (Murfin and Ray, *Bedford Glossary of Critical and Literary Terms*, 21). Here, Erdrich's speaker addresses the departed John Wayne, "*The eye sees a lot, John, but the heart is so blind*" (12); however, unlike most apostrophes, in which the speaker unburdens himself with a positive revelation, Erdrich's address doubles as a critique, turning poetic history on its head. She uses canonical Anglo literary history to destabilize a canonized Anglo American icon.

Along those same lines, the poem also serves an excellent example of a contemporary dramatic monologue. Without question, the moment on the Pontiac is a turning point for the poet, but not as significantly so as the moment of the poem. What I love about "Dear John Wayne" is that unlike most practitioners of the dramatic monologue, Erdrich does not silence the object of her address. She provides Wayne with dialogue, a gesture typical of Native discourse in general, but she uses Wayne's words against him, turning his language back on himself. Last, the poem is a fine example of what we might call an antielegy. Rather than celebrate or mourn Wayne's death, "Dear John Wayne" problematizes Wayne's life. Erdrich uses his manner of dying not simply as a metaphor for the system he symbolized, but also as a means of identity making—thereby inverting the film paradigm.

The cumulative effect here is cultural production in grand form. Erdrich deftly employs classic tropes and gestures of Anglo poetic form to help drive home the contextual and compositional resistance at work in her poem. On one hand, she creates a beautiful lyric whose architecture echoes that of Browning, Milton, and Shakespeare. On the other hand, she employs the machinery of established literary institutions to call into question the cultural machinery that could produce an icon like John Wayne, creating a provocative interplay of Native oral discourse and Anglo poetic strategies.[2] In other words, she uses the basic infrastructure of the Western canon to deconstruct an icon that mindset has canonized. Thus, in the ongoing battle of Native ethical codes and value systems versus traditional colonial capitalist systems, Native systems win. These are rare victories, but there are situations in which any victory is a big one.

Of course, one cannot help but realize, as Erdrich must, the discrepancy between the power and universality of Wayne's image—his putative audience—and the audience for Erdrich's poem. Which carries the greater cultural significance? The greater mass appeal? The small audience that will read Erdrich's poem is probably already aware of the cultural imperialism propagated and nostalgized by Wayne's hundreds of films. Still, the political impulse of the poem effectively discredits the public personae of Wayne and the western, for, after reading the poem, it is not Wayne's voice we hear in our heads, but Erdrich's. It is her words, her language that alter and allocate the sites of resistance within the contact zone of picture and poem.

"Owl Dancing with Fred Astaire"

Audience, mass appeal, and cultural imperialism are favorite topoi of Sherman Alexie. From his characters' jabs at westerns and Wayne in *The Lone Ranger and Tonto Fistfight in Heaven* to a poem like "Reservation Drive-In," in which he situates *Star Wars* and *Rocky* within the milieu of the reservation, Alexie loves both embracing and interrogating the machinery of the modern media. His humorous and captivating poem "Owl Dancing with Fred Astaire," in which Alexie imagines Astaire dancing at a powwow, is not his most politically charged poem, but it remains one of his most inventive. The poem begins with the absurd juxtaposition of traditional Native dancing and Hollywood dancing of the 1940s:

> I met the Indian woman who asked Fred Astaire to dance.
> He had politely refused her offer.
>
> "He was so charming," she said, "even when he rejected me.
> But I kept wishing it was an owl dance."
>
> —(*SUMMER OF BLACK WIDOWS*, 78).

At an owl dance, a woman asks a man to dance, an offer which he is not supposed to refuse; however, if he does, he must pay the woman any price she asks and explain to the crowd why he has declined her offer. Clearly, had Astaire been attending an owl dance when Alexie's speaker approached him, the power dynamic would have been slightly more complicated, but as it stands, that scenario, like many others in Alexie's world, exists in the world of the mediated hypothetical.

In section two of the poem, Alexie writes:

> There are Indian men who have never been asked to owl dance
> Alone in the powwow crowd, these men tap their feet lightly

along with the drums. They sing softly under their breath.
Perhaps they secretly wish they were Fred Astaire.

—(79)

The image of Astaire trying to acclimate to the unusual steps of an Indian dance gets a laugh every time. Would he step forward and backward along with the Indians? Or would he leap, glide, and pirouette, exhibiting dexterity and balance not required for the owl dance? Is his motivation to show up the Indians or to blend in? Would he become part of the community of the dance, or would he showcase his talents, as he does in his films? I like to think that his refusal of the Indian woman's offer reveals an insecurity about owl dancing, but more likely it suggests a lack of interest in blending Anglo and Native dance steps. But as Alexie muses in section four, perhaps not. Indeed, he is as puzzled by what Astaire might be thinking at a powwow as non-Indians are by the falsetto singing during the owl dance.

However, Alexie's subtext reveals yet another troubling instance of cultural colonization; for the Indian men never asked to dance, the object of desire becomes the other, the Hollywood icon. Alexie transforms Astaire into a symbol of what the Indian men think they lack or, more precisely, what Hollywood and television argue they lack. Suddenly, the beloved and comfortable image of Fred Astaire gamboling across the screen feels inappropriate. We don't like thinking of him at an owl dance. He belongs with other white people in suits and dresses and tuxedos, not in the middle of a powwow. But Alexie has a fondness for dissonant juxtaposition. Like several of his other poems about the media and media figures, such as "Going to the Movies with Geronimo's Wife," "Reading Harvey Shapiro's Poetry While Standing in Line to See Tom Hanks in *Apollo 13*," and "Tourists" (in which he places James Dean, Janis Joplin, and Marilyn Monroe on the reservation), Alexie's text is a poem of contextualization—as is Erdrich's. On the screen, Astaire and Wayne are at home. On the Ojibwe reservation or at a Coeur d'Alene powwow, their centrality becomes suspect.

Drawing its power from the ability of the reader to picture and comprehend the juxtapositions of class, privilege, and agency, Alexie's poem riffs on that image through intriguing twists of language and metaphor:

In my dream, Fred Astaire stumbles (yes, stumbles)
into the powwow and is shocked by the number of Indians

who have survived
the smallpox blankets, U.S. Cavalry, relocation, etc.

He smiles because, well, he is a good man prone to smiling.
(I must emphasize, however, that there are also bad men

who are prone to smiling.) Fred Astaire loves the drums.
He is pleasantly surprised by the quality of the singing.

Such pitch! and timbre! and range! and projection!
Fred Astaire taps his foot. He is wearing a tuxedo.

He is the skinniest white man in the history of the world.
Can you see him? He is not all that handsome

but he looks like a dancer. A great dancer.
In all cultures, women will choose a homely great dancer

> over a handsome non-dancer. Fred Astaire is confident.
> He waits for the next owl dance to begin.
>
> —(79–80)

When Alexie asks whether we can see Astaire, he wants to know whether we can picture him dancing among the Indians. We can. And he really does look like the skinniest white man in the world. Dreaming of a "stumbling" and "shocked" Fred Astaire offers insight into how Alexie frames this scenario. There is no question that Astaire is out of his element at the powwow, but note how quickly his confidence builds. He is happy, confident, sure—unlike his Indian companions.

Alexie contrasts the affluence and spectacle of Hollywood films with the baseball-cap-wearing dancers at the powwow, effectively marginalizing the Indians in their own space and at their own event. Even though he is the outsider, Astaire feels no alterity; otherness reverts back to the Indians. Indeed, while they muse over smallpox blankets and relocation, Fred Astaire smiles, trips lightly. While the Indians remember the cavalry and the westerns, Astaire revels in the drums. Why is it that a white man like Fred Astaire can be so confident at an owl dance, when (as in stanza two) insecure Indians sing under their breath at their own ritual? So powerful is Astaire's celebrity for Alexie, and so magical are his on- and offscreen images, that even within a traditional Native American dance, he displaces many Natives.

Whereas Erdrich's poem plays on the kinds of roles that John Wayne's character perpetually represented and the negative stereotype his films engendered about Native Americans, Alexie seems to bear no grudge against Astaire. However, it is this very distinction that makes Alexie's poem more complex and more troubling than Erdrich's, because it deftly illustrates how a benign media figure can supplant Native cultures simply as a result of his currency in the dominant culture and in the dominant media. By all accounts, Fred Astaire had a lot more to smile about than the Indians at the dance, and as Alexie suggests, a lot more reason to skip lightly across the floor than Indians in general. Eagerly awaiting the next owl dance to begin, he knows that when that dance and every dance after that one comes around, he will not be "alone in the powwow crowd." Even more important, Alexie implies, is the fact that because of the power his on-screen persona affords him, Fred Astaire, unlike his Native American counterparts, can refuse a woman's invitation to dance and still be charming. Of course, the larger implication is that the stark juxtaposition of Astaire and the Indians serves as a kind of metonym for the larger cultural and economic gap between whites and Indians in the United States. If Astaire represents affluence, cultural capital, and entitlement, then the Indians in the poem represent all the American Indians unable to gain access to these things. Every Indian is the woman denied access to Astaire at her own ritual, and every white person is Fred Astaire in the owl dance that is America.

While he does not seem directly critical of Astaire, Alexie uses Astaire's refusal to dance with the Native woman as a casual metaphor for America's benign neglect of Native issues and concerns. Not very many Americans advocate removal or eradication of Indians, a view embodied by Wayne, but many simply refuse to acknowledge Native issues. For Alexie, the visual translates into the political: the image of Astaire turning down the woman, the image of him at the dance, the image of him on the screen—white, rich, and oblivious—and the image of Indians watching him. According to Jennifer Gillan, Alexie remains frustrated at his inability to displace the images he has seen flickering across various screens throughout his life, despite the fact that these images have displaced his notions of his own culture: "Trapped in the 'reservation of his mind,' [Alexie] always experiences himself and his culture mediated through these television images. Through this mediation he has learned to see himself as an actor in an elaborately scripted drama, 'the same old story whispered on the television in every HUD house on the reservation'" ("Sherman Alexie's Poetry," 97). Gillan is on the mark here, for Alexie sees the dissemination of four hundred years of American history as a selective cinematic adaptation, a television movie of actual events. In "My Heroes Have Never Been Cowboys," Alexie claims that "in 1492, every Indian instantly became an extra in the Great American Western" (*The First Indian on the Moon*, 102), an observation that says as much about Indians as it does about Anglos.

It comes as no surprise, then, that even at the owl dance, an Anglo gets top billing, a pattern that seems to be in constant rerun in the network of Alexie's mind. Wayne, Astaire, James Dean, Marilyn Monroe: these figures were forced upon him and Erdrich as role models, as icons, as symbols of authority. Still, because they were ubiquitous and larger than life, and because there were few other options, one had no choice but to insert them into the landscape of one's imagined country. It is in that country of reality and imagination that Alexie and his characters experience the anxiety of simultaneously desiring the dream that American movies and television offer and rejecting its scripted version of what American life and culture must be and do. Gillan goes on to argue that the "Spokane characters in Alexie's poems must struggle to articulate the complexities of their circumstances as they confront legal, educational, and cinematic systems that attempt to define their experience for them" ("Sherman Alexie's Poetry," 103). If that is the case, and I think it is, then the project of Alexie's characters is the same as his, despite its apparent futility, as expressed in the final lines of "My Heroes Have Never Been Cowboys": "Arthur, I have no words that can save our lives, no words approaching forgiveness, no words flashed across the screen at the reservation drive-in, no words promising either of us top billing. Extras, Arthur, we're all extras" (*The First Indian on the Moon*, 104).

"Holodeck"

Perhaps because she deals with television and not films, or perhaps because she focuses on a theory of a more obvious fiction than "the West," Wendy Rose departs from Erdrich and Alexie in her reaction to a popular media invention. In "Holodeck," Rose transforms the holodeck of TV's *Star Trek: The Next Generation* into a metaphor for the ideal poetic space. On the holodeck, dream and desire become manifest. The person who enters or programs the holodeck functions as a sort of god, in that he or she orders the world and personal reality in it; however, Rose does not desire to make others (whites, for instance) do as she pleases. Her program for the holodeck is poetic; she simply wants people "to sit and listen. / The miracle is that they do" (*Bone Game*, 101). For Rose, the futuristic *Star Trek* offers a source of community because she can create a space in the holodeck entirely of her own making. At first glance, this poem seems to be an affirmation of language and the power of the imagination (à la Wallace Stevens); however, a closer reading suggests something more disturbing: that desire for a culturally cohesive audience (to invoke Bierhorst) can find its manifestation only in the twenty-second century on a big white spaceship. It would appear that her yearning for self-fulfillment and self-positioning necessitate turning to science fiction as opposed to reality—but then again, isn't this what television tells us to do all the time?

Rose's poem remains the most indeterminate of those under study here because she eagerly locates a site of community, exchange, healing, and holism within a futuristic technological space as opposed to a more tribal, pre-Columbian, pre-Anglo space, as one might expect. Not only does she refrain from criticizing television, but she actually apologizes for appropriating the concept of the holodeck from *Star Trek*. In what remains the most thorough reading of Rose's poetics to date, Karen Tongson-McCall argues that because

Rose refuses the binary discourse of same versus other, she perpetually navigates within the world of the liminal: "[Rose] achieves what the poststructuralist Emmanuel Levinas expressed the utmost desire for: 'a sociality of linguistic exchange [which] allows the self to open up to the other without assimilating the other [. . .]' In other words, it is a dialogue that frees the self from the entrapment of the 'double bind,' one that defies a tendency to define the self in relation to something else" ("The Nether World of Neither World," 7).

In "Holodeck," Rose never subsumes the holodeck's abilities for her own work, but neither is her vision defined by or assimilated into technology's fabula. Whereas Alexie perpetually defines himself against a backdrop of pervasive media screens, Rose carves out a niche for herself and her bicultural poetics among the same screens. Furthermore, this poem, indicative of many thematics, turns on the locus of difference without marginalization. Interestingly, Rose merely literalizes what both Erdrich and Alexie desire for their poems: an idealized space in which an audience of Anglos listen and change and Natives listen and respond. Just as Erdrich and Alexie use the confluence of visual and Native cultures as a public holodeck to enact change, so does Rose turn to the holodeck to create a space of exchange and interaction. The result is a provocative cyborg of a lyric that serves as a metaphor for larger notions of personal and cultural connections.

Additionally, Tongson-McCall's claim that Rose's poetry defies "a tendency to define the self in relation to something else" calls much of Alexie's work into question. Gillan's primary assertion is that Alexie cannot, for even a moment, conceive of the self without television or the movies interceding, forcing him to engender his own type of hybridized discourse in which he both incorporates and manipulates popular culture. In "Holodeck," Rose opens up to technology as a mode of invention rather than mechanization. The myth of technological progress sleeps side by side with the myth of Manifest Destiny, but here that technology is in service to dialogue.

Because of the poem's inward trajectory and its internal landscape, her text remains the most traditionally lyric of the poems under examination here. The space the poem inhabits is the space marked by the self. Whereas Erdrich and Alexie project their visionary gazes outward, Rose looks within. But even this gesture serves an important role in re-presenting Native identity, because it locates the self as part of a community. "Indian people are the ones my words are intended for," Simon Ortiz tells Joseph Bruchac, "That is partly because I am an Indian person and it's like I'm speaking to myself. I'm speaking *with* myself. Language is an important act which has to do with a reaffirmation of self" (Ortiz, "The Story Never Ends," 225). Because Rose's poem has feet in both the public and the private realms, her act of engaged resistance works on two levels. Personally, her work defies mainstream stereotyping that limits individual Native expression to reductive "Native American" discourses like shamanism, ecology, mysticism, and environmentalism. Rather than altering her voice to fit that of the culture that produced *Star Trek*, she forces *Star Trek* to collaborate with her voice; yet she does not subsume or appropriate Anglo expression. On a public level, she circumscribes tribal sovereignty through an articulation of difference that places her within both popular culture and Hopi-Miwok culture. In short, she creates dialogue based not on the benign imperialism of Star Fleet or the *Enterprise* but on dialogue that opens up to interaction and community. Whereas Wayne works as a symbol of destruction for Erdrich, and Astaire as a symbol of neglect for Alexie, the nonhuman holodeck becomes, for Rose, a symbol of sovereignty. It is a place without Anglo interference, where Indians make decisions for Indians. It is the Ghost Dance realized.

Despite their contrasting interpretations of visual media, these poems are ultimately linked by the tension between absence and presence. Rose's poem takes as its point of departure an absence without, so she retreats into the presence within: "I go into my head / private holodeck / so easy / like breathing" (*Bone Game*, 101). Missing is dialogue, audience.

She longs for voices "that beg [her] not to die" (101), so she embraces the metaphor of the holodeck and its eager, invented audience in order to subvert monologue and engage in dialogue. The desire for telling and listening is so great that the story ultimately invents a site for its own making. But who tells the story, and what story is finally being told? Erdrich addresses these questions in "Dear John Wayne." Like Rose's, Erdrich's poem responds to not only a personal but also a cultural absence. When Erdrich imagines Wayne speaking the line "Everything we see belongs to us" (*Jacklight*, 12), it marks an imperialist desire not only to possess everything in sight but also to take it away from the Indians. Thus, Erdrich's poem arises out of the space her desire creates, a desire for a cultural presence as captivating and as pervasive as Wayne's. Wayne's physical domination of the movie screen serves as a haunting metaphor for the geographic and cultural domination of the white world's push westward—a domination that Wayne and the entire genre of westerns embodied for nearly half a century. Erdrich's elegiac response mourns not the deceased Wayne but the deceased dreams that Wayne's celebrity signals. Perhaps her choice of media, the letter, an outdated and perhaps dying technology, serves as yet another metaphor for an outdated and dying perspective that Wayne represents. Conversely, Rose's choice of media, the highly technologized, futuristic holodeck, may represent the perspective of the future: dialogue, transformation, sovereignty.

Alexie's darkly comic poems fall somewhere between Erdrich's and Rose's. Less earnest and more ironic, his reading of the textuality of contemporary media participates in high postmodern play. He remains a more overtly political writer than either Erdrich or Rose, and he understands that like Wayne and Astaire, he can rewrite the text that is the modern media. He has become famous for his observation that only 1 percent of Indians have read *House Made of Dawn*, but 99 percent have seen *Powwow Highway* (Alexie, "Crossroads," 3). For Alexie, movies and television have become the new oral tradition, the new performative language. Because so many people see and interact with them, movies enact the kind of transformation today that was reserved for power songs 150 years ago. Perhaps more than any other Native writer, Alexie understands the power of the media. He recognizes that it is the new battlefield. His sophisticated internalization of films and television in these poems reveals the critical and cultural vision that eventually pushed him to turn the written narratives of *The Lone Ranger and Tonto Fistfight in Heaven* into the visual narrative of *Smoke Signals*. He knows how screens of culture and history can be manipulated. In this sense, his vision of a spliced celluloid self seems in concert with Rose's. Ultimately, for Alexie, and to a certain degree for Rose and Erdrich, movies and films—and the engagement between them and the lyric project—serve as the best opportunities for reinventing the enemy's visual language.

Tropes of Agency and Contingency

Laguna writer and scholar Paula Gunn Allen argues that true cultural colonization takes place within what Alexie calls "the reservation of the mind": the "wars of imperial conquest have not been solely or even mostly waged over the land and its resources, but they have been fought within the bodies, minds, and hearts of the people of the earth for dominion over them" (*The Sacred Hoop*, 214). As I have tried to demonstrate, these poems address and counter media attempts to win the hearts and minds of American Indians. They provocatively problematize the tension between the lyric space and the space of television and movies: even while engaging the media and the culture that creates the media, Erdrich, Alexie, and Rose resist being defined by media.

Perhaps because they presume that inhabiting the screen of popular imagination to the degree that Wayne and Astaire did is impossible, these writers work within the space of the linguistic screen.[3] Still, their project counters cultural canonization. They counter it by reminding their readers of the power of the poetic voice to undermine authority, to speak truth to power, to bear witness. As Joy Harjo asserts, "to speak, at whatever the cost, is to become empowered rather than victimized by destruction" (Harjo and Bird, *Reinventing the Enemy's Language*, 22). But writing and speaking do more than bear witness; they transform the means by which power is implemented. "These colonizers' languages," Harjo continues, "which often usurped our own tribal languages or diminished them, now hand back emblems of our cultures, our own designs. . . . We've transformed these enemy languages" (22). To confront the enemy is to remake and reinvent history.

Ultimately, these poems function as tropes of agency and contingency, for in the final scene, they empower Natives and Native culture. Each writer uniquely envisions alternative modes of being that do not define Indians in relation to Anglos, but establish Natives as independent and interdependent communities. By viewing their poems as positive engagements with an increasingly complex cultural matrix, we not only broaden our conception of Native discourse, but also cultivate a more inclusive vision of resistance.[4] In her book *Resistance Literature*, Barbara Harlow claims that "the role of poetry in the liberation struggle has thus been a crucial one, both as a force for mobilizing a collective response to occupation and domination and as a repository for popular memory and consciousness" (34).[5] These poems, these actions, these engaged resistances serve as important markers of cultural sovereignty because they are concurrently sites of struggle against a dominant discourse. As cultural texts, they mobilize Native linguistic reenvisionings. And while their aims may not be as absolute as those of the Ghost Dance, they are just as eminent, for rather than occluding or erasing one culture or another, the poems perform the most miraculous feat of all—they keep Native cultural identity not simply intact, but also alive and vibrant and present.

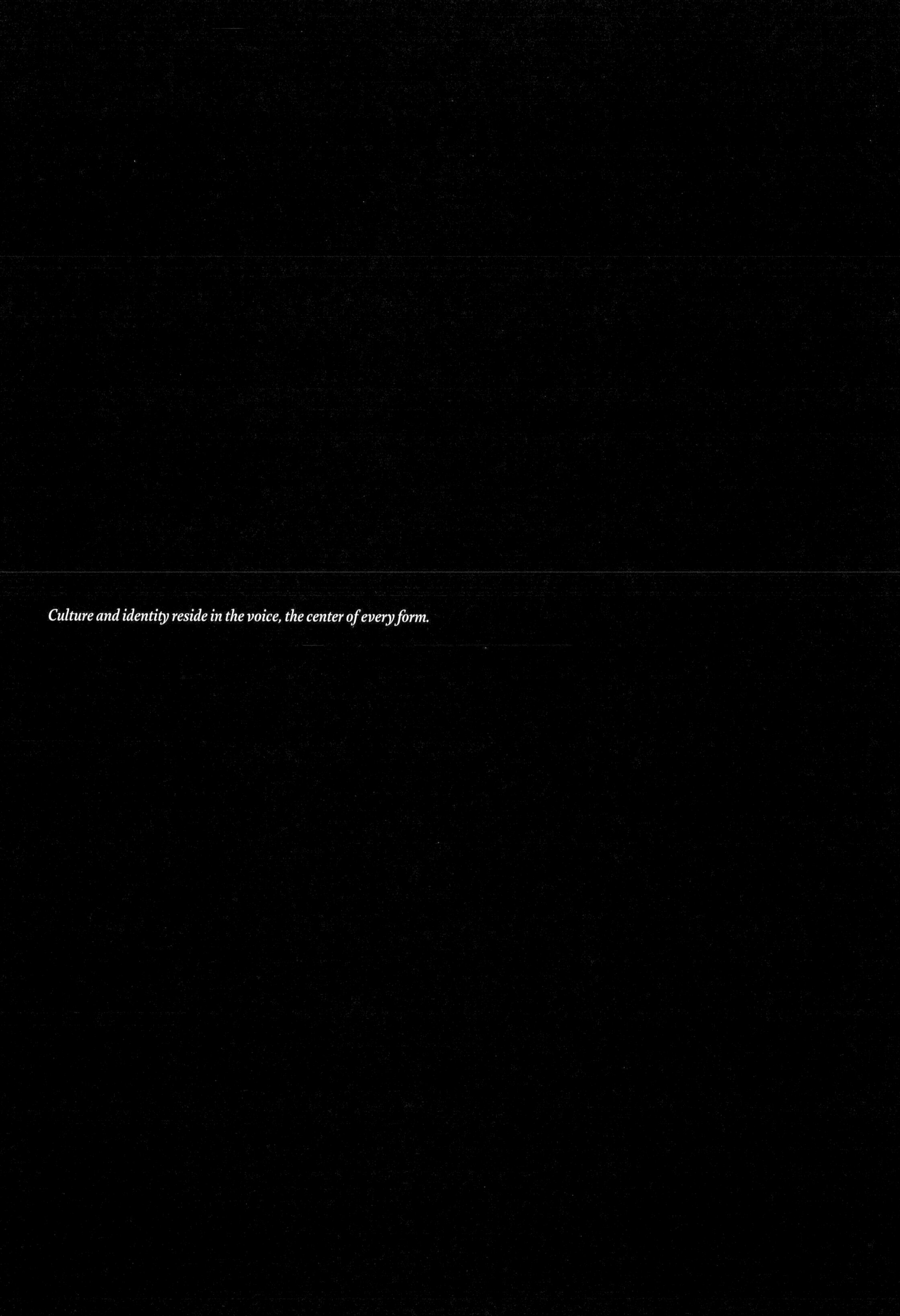

Culture and identity reside in the voice, the center of every form.

6.

COMPOSITIONAL RESISTANCE

GENRE AND CONTEMPORARY AMERICAN INDIAN POETRY

It does not have to dress up
in beads and feathers
in order to be powerful.

IN HER MINIMALIST but striking poem "Check One," Navajo poet Esther Belin has great fun playing with the dual notion of form:

Check One

☐ Diné
☐ Other

—(*FROM THE BELLY OF MY BEAUTY*, 12)

The above represents Belin's "poem" in its entirety, and I have tried as closely as possible to recreate its design. The word "poem" appears in quotation marks because even though "Check One" is printed in a book of poems, it doesn't look or sound like a poem. On the contrary, it resembles a government application document, which, for most of us, is about as far from a poem as is humanly possible. But even at that, it is not like any governmental document anyone has seen. For one thing, it is dreamily short, and for another, it gives only two options: "Diné" and "Other." Surely, it can't be a real form, nor can it be a real poem. What, exactly, is going on here?

A lot.

On the compositional level, "Check One" riffs on two different notion of form. On one hand, it reinvents traditional affirmative action "forms," and on the other, it reinvents standard poetic "form"—how a poem is composed and printed on the page. Just as it looks like no other governmental form, it also looks like no other poem. It reinvents on two distinct but omnipresent planes—governmental forms and poetic forms—both of which have long histories of generic expectations.

By making her poem resemble a standard governmental form, Belin seems to be making a comment about just how limiting both kinds of forms can be. Through its centralizing of "Diné" (the Navajo term for the Navajo people), "Check One" marginalizes all those applicants who are not Diné. A counternarrative to these forms, "Check One" reverses traditional notions of alterity, shifting otherness from Navajo to not-Navajo. For American colonizers and Spanish missionaries, the Diné were other, but Belin inverts the imperial model that denotes otherness; she tips hegemony on its head. Similarly, the poem also tips traditional poetic form on its head. It avoids rhyme and meter, line breaks and verses. Belin contextualizes it within other poems, but it doesn't mirror poetic texts in any way. There are boxes but no images, directions but no music. Neither lyric nor prose poem, neither essay nor memoir, her text about classification defies easy literary classification.

But what does it mean to classify identity? What if Belin could check both boxes simultaneously? Other poems from her collection *From the Belly of My Beauty* articulate how she feels both Diné and other, and this poem perhaps both literalizes and attempts to reconcile that bifurcation. Just as Belin's Diné identity does not fit into the formula of generic governmental documents, her poem does not adhere to generic expectations for poetic form. In fact, some traditional readers will not consider "Check One" a poem at all, since it does not contain even the most basic attributes of a lyric. But this may be the point of the poem. To resist expectations of form and genre is to resist larger Western imperial impositions that determine more than just how we read a poem—such as how we read an entire race of people.

Form, then, is about demarcation, borders, and boundaries. In "Ruby's Welfare," Belin once again plays with dual definitions of "form," this time equating it with rules and regulations:

> I smile
> place my forms in the box marked
> leave forms here
> black and bold
> welfare is a luxury
> place your form in our box
> play by our rules
>
> —(*FROM THE BELLY OF MY BEAUTY*, 43)

For Belin, form literally equals content. She warns against categorizing people based on the external signifiers of race or class, the signifiers of otherness. Profoundly aware that forms of cultural production like poems are a means of identity formation (both personal and tribal), Belin's work suggests that breaking out of the identity markers of poetic form also means liberation from larger notions of identity limitations that attempt to circumscribe and circumvent Native independence. Resistance to generic assimilation is neither futile nor fanciful; it is a means and a mode of sovereignty.

This chapter offers a reading of the many ways in which recent American Indian writers have interacted with genre and poetic form. It focuses on poems that subvert traditional expectations of genre, and it pays close attention to Native poetic strategies that engender self-determination, self-definition, and self-identification. Like a Silko narrative, mine takes many turns. I ask the reader's indulgence as I move back and forth between theoretical speculations and practical explications in an attempt to tease out the literary and cultural implications of these texts. I begin by talking about the very notion of genre and why we might see it as more than merely a descriptor, especially in regard to American Indian poetry. I turn most of my attention, though, to radically different examples of Native genre busting and genre bending, including prose poetry, experimental poetry, and the Native proclivity for the prose-poetry book. I am primarily interested in how these texts function as examples of compositional resistance—an intentional reluctance to make a text conform to the formulaic expectations of its genre. What interests me as a writer, scholar, and teacher is the ingenuity with which (and the degree to which) almost every Native poet practices some sort of compositional resistance, either through line breaks, capitalization, closure, fragmentation, play with poetic traditions, bilingualism, and even genre shifting. My goal is to initiate an interpretive strategy whose methodology is commensurate with the polygeneric work it engages.

In the world of literary studies, genre has become a metanarrative.[1] Writers and scholars may not think of it in those terms, but within the proscribed world of literature and literary form, genre absolutely functions as a controlling and totalizing structure. In their fascinating study *Retelling Stories, Framing Culture: Traditional Stories and Metanarratives in Children's Literature*, John Stephens and Robyn McCallum provide one of the clearest and most succinct definitions of this concept. For them, metanarrative "is a global or totalizing cultural narrative schema which orders and explains knowledge and experience" (x).[2] There is no question that genre orders and explains the experience of literature: how a poem appears on the page, how a book is shelved or marketed, or whether a prose piece is labeled *fiction* or *nonfiction* determines entirely how we approach the text, what the rules of the text are, and the norms and behaviors of the writing within the text. In general, genre is a signpost, a marker that prepares the mind to take in a certain kind of information. If the text before the reader is poetry, then he or she expects something serious, perhaps romantic or sentimental, certainly something lyrical and symbolic. But if it is prose, it is expected to be about people or be funny or have a plot. In genre lie the codes of a text's characteristics, meaning that at its core, genre is about identity.[3]

This simple but profound concept, so seemingly innocuous, sits at the center of literary classification and recognition. Indeed, once a generic identity has been established, it is often impossible to break out of it. You are the genre you write: Don DeLillo, fiction; Billy Collins, poetry; Toni Morrison, fiction; John Ashbery, poetry; Cormac McCarthy, fiction; and so on. How interesting that these rigid generic labels don't seem to apply to Native writers, as though the borders delineating mainstream literary publishing simply don't exist in Indian territory. In her fine study *The Heart as a Drum: Continuance and Resistance in Contemporary American Indian Poetry*, Robin Riley Fast makes a similar point about the range of Native poetry and the problematics of borders: "Border consciousness is consciousness of imposed definitions of distinctions that have contributed to the distortion of Native lives and voices—that is, awareness of the effects of what [Louis] Owens would call territorial intentions. Seen in this light, borders are impediments to be exposed, opened, crossed or blurred" (15). The ability of and the desire among so many Native poets to slip easily between genres underscore Native worldviews that often articulate the world in unifying, encompassing language rather than in the parlance of bifurcation or delineation. Furthermore, to impose a restrictive Western overlay like genre onto a non-Western bicultural discourse like Native poetry mirrors the most basic tenets of colonialism. Hegemonic to its core, genre, like the boarding-school project, promotes assimilation.[4] One cannot force Native poetry into generic classifications. It spills over into the margins, making the liminal central.

This is one reason, I would argue, that almost none of the major figures in American poetry criticism (Marjorie Perloff, Helen Vendler, Albert Gelpi, and others) ever write about American Indian poetry. Native poetry pulls from many domains, merging strains from oral, historical, tribal, and written sources. Because it signifies as both lyric and epic, and because Native writers problematize genre so frequently, most critics in the United States are simply at a loss when it comes to making sense of Native verse. There is so much going on, so many contexts—both poetic and cultural—that most critics find it easier to stick to

Native fiction. The truth is that contemporary Native poetry just doesn't look or sound like poems in the *New Yorker* or *Poetry*. It draws on different sources, operates on alternate frequencies. According to colleagues, fellow scholars, and my students, attempting to unpack Native poetry can often result in frustration, anxiety, and sheer cluelessness.

Robert Allen Warrior argues that Indian poets, rather than being ordered and enumerated by genre, have turned the confining tendencies of form against itself. "We could not," claims Warrior, "ask as critics how it is that these poets have taken a European written form thousands of years old and transformed it so easily to become a form of resistance against other European forms and systems. Poetry has provided a vehicle for such resistance because of the way it can unsettle prevailing ideologies and give voice to what is not being spoken within a culture" (*Tribal Secrets*, 117). Like Belin, Warrior picks up on the dual significance of form, suggesting that it can be both a limitation and a weapon. Native poetry works as a form of resistance precisely because of its ongoing resistance to form. That resistance, like the art of Alcatraz or the public art of Edgar Heap of Birds, doesn't exist outside of form; it merely converts, reinvents, indigenizes form.

Let me be clear: I am not suggesting that Native poets are the only writers to play with genre, nor am I suggesting that merging poetry and prose is an essentially Native project. I do not want to imply that Indian poets invented cross-generic strategies or that they are the first to use poetic form as a mode of resistance. Poets and painters and artists have been mixing and blending materials, structures, and genres for centuries. So I don't want this chapter to come off as an attack on Western literary history or the lyric poem—I am a huge fan of both. But I do want to urge readers to consider Native poetry from the perspective of genre and form. Native poetry excites and pleases in part because it operates both within and without the system, engaging useful Western literary traditions while simultaneously exploding them.[5] It resides neither inside nor outside the circumscribed space of genre, but rather, straddles that sphere, creating a bicultural poetics, a hoop of contingency and sovereignty. Indeed, it is Warrior who holds up American Indian poetry as a model of the autonomy of articulation that scholars of Native literatures should emulate. "In developing American Indian critical studies," Warrior claims, "we need to practice the same sort of intellectual sovereignty as many Native poets practice" (*Tribal Secrets*, 117). To my mind, the most provocative articulation of Native poetry's intellectual sovereignty lies in its refusal to be subsumed under or defined by the metanarrative of genre, making much of Native poetry fundamentally emancipatory.

A quick detour back to Belin provides a useful illustration of a poet moving both thematically and formally from limitation to liberation. In "Ruby in Me #1," Belin ruptures the traditional terrain of genre just as she ruptures traditional ideas of identity:

> middle child
> smart child
> ¼ Navajo
>   ¼ Navajo
>   ¼ Navajo
>   ¼ Navajo
> four parts equal my whole
> #311,990
>
> enrolled = proof
> 50
> 80

100 if you can stand
it

veiled
minority status
alcohol
resemblance

—(*FROM THE BELLY OF MY BEAUTY*, 39)

Traversing the borderlands of internal and external identity, Belin plays with the connotations of Native buzzwords like "proof" and the insane practice of partial tribal identification. Profoundly self-aware, Belin knows that notions of identity are informed not only by interior characteristics like a person's percentage of Indian blood but also by external characteristics like skin pigmentation or homeland. The poem operates in the realm of the dislocated so that what it signifies thematically, it mirrors in terms of tone, diction, meter, and typography. Note how Belin's poem resembles—in both form and content—Elizabeth Woody's wonderful "Translation of Blood Quantum," itself a pleasing taunt of genres:

31/32 Warm Springs-Wasco-Yakama-Pit River-Navajo
1/32 Other Tribal roll number 1553

thirty-second parts of a human being

—(*LUMINARIES OF THE HUMBLE*, 103)

Though this snippet is but an excerpt, even in its brevity, Woody's poem gets at many of the same issues at work in Belin. Both women feel fractured by issues of identity and blood quantum, and through the use of fragments and scattered lines, they depict visually what they experience personally. Exploiting the terminology of identity politics, both Woody and Belin offer a physical blueprint of the spiritual fragmentation engendered by BIA and governmental regulations. As Belin and Woody demonstrate, indigenous poetic compositional resistance foundationalizes Native epistemology through its resistance to Western notions of knowledge and classification.

In a gesture that both waves at and gives the bird to such methods of Western knowledge and classification, James Thomas Stevens's (Akwesasne Mohawk) "Alphabet of Letters" (Fig. 6.1) converts the traditional American schoolbook into a veritable collage of signifiers. Subtitled "A New Primer for the Use of Native or Confused Americans," this twenty-plus-page "poem" collates phonics, classical rhetoric, a 1766 inventory list, false and real headlines, instructions on diphthongs, snatches of correspondence, a short Mohawk-English dictionary, and even heroic couplets as an alphabet lesson ("K When KING Phillip, dead did lay, / the Puritans did Make their Way" (*A Bridge Dead in the Water*, 97). Part time capsule, part linguistic experiment, part experimental poetics, part historical bricolage, and part pedagogical sketchbook, Stevens's bizarre antipoem takes Belin's and Woody's fragmentation one step further. Suggesting the cornucopia of sources that have shaped Indian identity (both within and outside Native communities), Stevens utilizes the genres of knowledge making to assert the impossibility of compressing Indian and Mohawk identities into lessons, lists, and libraries. "Alphabet of Letters" divests the Western project of "letters" of its privilege of seeing Indians as its subjects. The forms of teaching and learning, the forms of identity arrangement, the forms of blood catalogue—these are the forms that poetic genres, through their ontology of exclusion, perpetuate. But

Oi and *Oy*, are generally hard; as in oil &c.

Let's speak of oil.
The import of brown children to learn
the word
of GOD & OIL.

The indigen as obstacle. You will be removed.

Oil springs used by the autochthon
for medicinal purposes only.
Lubricated, we bring you up.
At what cost?

25,000 civilian casualties today, September 2005. The Oi in
oil
is generally hard.

Alaska. Iraq. You will be removed.

10.

Oil	coin	joint	toil	groin	coy
boil	loin	point	ſpoil	void	ſoy
coil	join	ſoil	broil	Boy	joy

A coin slipped into an American Boy's joint
to pay his toil, the ſpoils of which, are Oil.

Teach us the words we need
for our limited rhetoric—
Popiſh plots and Quranic crimes.

[88]

Oil for the machine.

Spiritual Milk
For American BABES.

Brant, did those little books drag us
from Wheelock's *worse than Egyptian darkness*?

At first, your libraries
from across the sea.

Little books taking root
and raining down when ripe:

An Account of a Plan for Civilising the North American
INDIANS.
A PRIMER For The USE of The MOHAWK CHILDREN.

The Original RIGHTS of MANKIND, Freely to Subdue
and Improve the EARTH.

The Duty of Christians toward the Heathen.

The Knowledge and Practice of CHRISTIANITY Made Easy to
the Meanest Capacities: Or an Easy Essay towards an Instruction
for the INDIANS.

[89]

FIGURE 6.1. *Pages from James Thomas Stevens's funky fusion of forms, "Alphabet of Letters" (2007). Reprinted with permission of Salt Publishing.*

FIGURE 6.2. (facing page) *Pages from Joy Harjo's* The Woman Who Fell from the Sky *(1994). Poetry on the left, prose on the right. The prose serves as a kind of epilogue to the poem. Reprinted by permission of W. W. Norton & Company.*

Stevens, Woody, and Belin contravene; they advance their own modes of self-acculturation and self-narration, a practice endemic to Native cultural expression.

Eric Gary Anderson links the desire of Indian writers like Stevens, Woody, and Belin to "qualify, question, dismiss, leapfrog over, or revise Western notions and practices of literary genre" with more global desires to eschew Western practices of identity limitation: "For . . . Native critics, as well as for many other Native writers who work in various other Western-defined forms, the question or issue of genre does not loom large. Genres, after all, are forms of identity imported from outside Native cultures and at times imposed on them; by implication, genre identities come to be associated with other suspect methods determining Native identity, such as those that set out to calculate Indianness on the basis of blood percentiles" ("Situating American Indian Poetry," 35). Anderson does a good job of articulating what Belin and Woody dramatize in their poems via both form and content. Compositional resistance can often either reinforce or enable contextual resistance. In this case, how the poems abrogate genre goes hand in hand with thematic attempts to assert identity.

A concept I call "the trap of receptive determinacy," explained at length in Chapter 4, can be used to make a point about how non-Native-authored texts leave very little room for interpretation. Overly romanticized sculptures of primitive Indians, or Hollywood films that adhere entirely to generic formulas, determine how spectators encounter them; they provide their own interpretation through their allegiance to genre. Much the same can be said about poetry. Too often ignored as a visual genre, poetry's semiotics often indicate how it should be read. When an author like Belin or Woody denies the reader those semiotic cues indicative of poetry, it can create receptive indeterminacy. A text's identity—like a person's—can often locate freedom in malleability.

The Mixed-Genre Book

This kind of semiotic indeterminacy can occur within a poem or within a book. Anderson, as it happens, is the only other critic I have encountered who discusses a quite different but complementary form of compositional resistance: the tendency among American Indian writers to combine many genres in one book (see "Situating American Indian Poetry," 36). This minor observation may seem irrelevant, but within the long tradition of publishing, marketing, and genre identification, it goes against what most writing and publishing conventionally stands for. Think about how inviolate the rather precious "collection of poems" is; consider how inflexible the literary novel has been; think about the very structure of bookstores and how books are marketed and displayed. Even *The New York Times Book Review* arranges its texts by genre.[6] The inability to get out from under genre—either on the authorial end or the marketing end—metanarrativizes almost every aspect of the writing, publishing, marketing, selling, and reading of literature. How radical, then, to come across so many books by Native authors that stand up to generic profiling: Erdrich's *Baptism of Desire* and *Jacklight*, Luci Tapahonso's *Sáanii Dahataał: The Women are Singing* and *Blue Horses Rush In*, Simon J. Ortiz's *From Sand Creek*, Sherman Alexie's *The First Indian on the Moon* and *The Business of Fancydancing* and *Face*, and Esther Belin's *In the Belly of My Beauty*. These books blur boundaries, cross borders, fly in the face of restriction, and confront the most basic tenets of literary identity—tendencies seemingly endemic to Native writing. I am not saying that authors from other ethnic groups ignore the mixed-genre book, but nowhere is it as prolific as with American Indian literature. Or, put another way, it cannot be a coincidence, it cannot be random, that so many Native authors are drawn to this format.

Harjo's *The Woman Who Fell from the Sky* (an excerpt is shown in Fig. 6.2) and Ortiz's *From Sand Creek* (excerpt in Fig. 6.3) serve as perfect examples of how even the smallest publica-

A POSTCOLONIAL TALE

Every day is a reenactment of the creation story. We emerge from dense unspeakable material, through the shimmering power of dreaming stuff.

This is the first world, and the last.

Once we abandoned ourselves for television, the box that separates the dreamer from the dreaming. It was as if we were stolen, put into a bag carried on the back of a whiteman who pretends to own the earth and the sky. In the sack were all the people of the world. We fought until there was a hole in the bag.

When we fell we were not aware of falling. We were driving to work, or to the mall. The children were in school learning subtraction with guns, although they appeared to be in classes.

We found ourselves somewhere near the diminishing point of civilization, not far from the trickster's bag of tricks.

Everything was as we imagined it. The earth and stars, every creature and leaf imagined with us.

The imagining needs praise as does any living thing. Stories and songs are evidence of this praise.

The imagination conversely illumines us, speaks with us, sings with us.

Stories and songs are like humans who when they laugh are indestructible.

No story or song will translate the full impact of falling, or the inverse power of rising up.

Of rising up.

18

☆

The landscape of the late twentieth century is littered with bodies of our relatives. Native peoples in this country were 100 percent of the population a few hundred years ago. We are now one half of 1 percent. Violence is a prevalent theme in the history of this land.

I think of the death of the brother of a Dakota friend of mine who was killed recently in Oakland. When a program to inspire the creativity of Indian children lost funding and couldn't pay him for his services he kept working out of commitment and love for these children. His killing was a reckless act by other Indian men who were just over the legal definition of the age of childhood, who did not even know him.

As I write this I am interrupted by an Apache man who is passing by my table in a restaurant owned by his tribe. He asks me first about my portable computer, then tells me he has come home to bury his son, who was shot and killed because he intercepted some young men who were partying on the street in front of his home in a place not far from Oakland. He, his wife and daughter-in-law have brought him home to bury him.

Their grief is slick with tears that will be soaked up by this beautiful land.

If I am a poet who is charged with speaking the truth (and I believe the word poet is synonymous with truth-teller), what do I have to say about all of this?

19

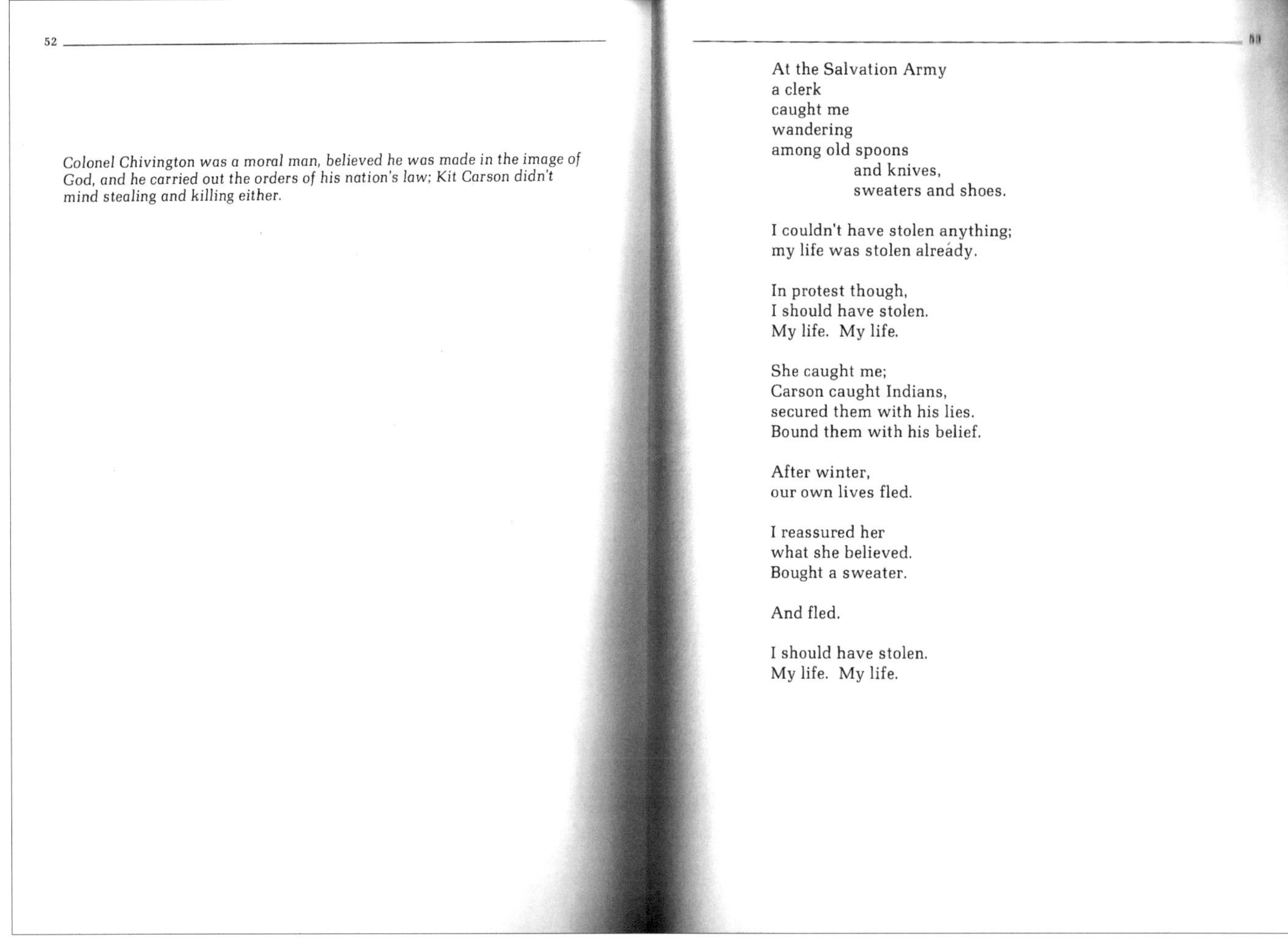
52

Colonel Chivington was a moral man, believed he was made in the image of God, and he carried out the orders of his nation's law; Kit Carson didn't mind stealing and killing either.

53

At the Salvation Army
a clerk
caught me
wandering
among old spoons
                and knives,
                sweaters and shoes.

I couldn't have stolen anything;
my life was stolen already.

In protest though,
I should have stolen.
My life. My life.

She caught me;
Carson caught Indians,
secured them with his lies.
Bound them with his belief.

After winter,
our own lives fled.

I reassured her
what she believed.
Bought a sweater.

And fled.

I should have stolen.
My life. My life.

FIGURE 6.3. *Pages from Simon Ortiz's* From Sand Creek *(1981). For Ortiz, the prose (*left*) functions as prologue to the poetry. Reprinted with permission of the author, Simon J. Ortiz.*

tion details undermine the long tradition of how books of poems are designed, composed, printed, and experienced. In both books, the poems are accompanied by prose explanations that help elucidate the work the poem does. For Ortiz, the prose introduces or sets up the poem, providing either historical or biographical context that the subsequent lyric poeticizes. In the case of Harjo, the prose segments follow her poems, rounding out and filling in the natural gaps that poetry engenders. In Harjo's text, the prose segments can be as long (or longer) than the poem itself, suggesting that the prose is as important as the poem. On one hand, this technique engages the long and accepted literary traditions of the preface and the epilogue, but on the other, their intrabook implementation resists the traditional utilization of them.

Ortiz and Harjo go off on both function and context, transplanting them from fiction and criticism to poetry, and inserting them within the books rather than at the beginning and end. Preface and epilogue intend linearity; a beginning and an end, point A and point B. But Harjo and Ortiz perform their own kind of removal, transplanting preface and epilogue from the lands where they normally reside to the community of text alongside the poems they border. Appropriating the commentary function of these techniques but mixing them into the flow of the poems not only challenges centuries of readerly expectations, but also undermines the poetry's nearly sacred autotelism. Part of the New Critics' project was to ensure that the poem exists outside of time, history, race, context, or genocide. For them, the poem was its own end; readers should ignore messy distractions like biography, gender, or, say, tribal affiliation. I was fascinated to discover that Womack makes a similar observation about the structure of *The Woman Who Fell from the Sky*: "Harjo's combination of commentary and poetry suggests an inherent argument against the formalist 'text-only' approaches that separate literature and criticism . . . Political discussion complements the aesthetics of the poem" (*Red on Red*, 248).

The effects of these gestures are subtle but important. From an aesthetic perspective, prose irrupts the linear reading pattern that is so much a part of the contemporary book of poems. However, these prose segments also stitch the poems together, creating a web of intrageneric connection and interaction. Rhetorically, the prose takes the exact opposite tack as the aims of the New Criticism; it makes the argument that contextualization is part of the ontology of poetics. These books also drive home the point that the line between oral and written discourse is imaginary. The call-and-response composition resembles a live poetry reading in which the poet introduces or explains the poem before reading it, but it also mimics the interactivity of a sacred telling in which the audience becomes part of the story. That component of oral performance—so absent from most of contemporary poetry—works its way into these two books, suggesting that poetry and prose, like the oral and the written, are two sides of the same coin.

Genre Bending and Blending in Silko and Howe

Blurring the boundaries of genre even further are Silko's *Storyteller* and Howe's *Evidence of Red*, both of which take Indigenous interdisciplinarity to new levels. In *Storyteller*, Silko suggests that pictures, poems, stories, myths, letters, and essays can each tell a story equally well—a rather radical concept. The intertextual trajectory of the book dramatically blurs the lines between poetry and prose, between the written and the oral, and between myth and fact. Silko shows that we construct identity, both personal and tribal, through a collage of multigenred narratives. In 1981, when *Storyteller* arrived in bookstores and in the narrow university curricula, the Western male literary establishment was not particularly accustomed to dealing with polyvocality, especially from a Native American woman. In the twentieth century, few female writers successfully negotiated their way among more than one genre in a lifetime, and yet this relatively unknown writer published a book from which no singular genre emerged. It was a revolutionary book—even down to its horizontally rectangular shape (which, I would argue, can be read as another form of compositional resistance).

What does emerge from *Storyteller* is an urgency to communicate. Even now, I am struck by the intimacy of the book, its revelatory voice, and its confessional envois. Though the book is entitled *Storyteller*, suggesting a prosaic structure and the sort of narrativity found in plot-based fiction, the book actually works more like a lyric poem. Traditionally, the lyric has been the most successful literary form for engendering a personal connection with its reader. From Shakespeare's sonnets to Keats's odes to Whitman's elegies to the confessionalist poems of the 1950s and 1960s, the lyric moment fundamentally intends a visceral reciprocity with the person who enters into its world. When one opens *Storyteller*, it is like walking into a lyric collage. Like a lyric poem, the book does not move in a linear fashion. Like a lyric, the book signifies on an associative level as opposed to a chronological one.[7] And like a lyric, the book evokes a sense of the author through a first-person poetic persona. The distancing mechanisms so frequent in contemporary American prose are alarmingly absent in much of Silko's text, and we are forced to come to terms with the fact that the book frustrates our expectations of genre. Jorge Luis Borges imagined God as a circular book—no beginning and no end. *Storyteller* operates like a circular poem, always transporting us between prose and poetry, autobiography and analysis.

The contemporary corollary to Silko's seminal book is Howe's award-winning *Evidence of Red*. Like Silko, Howe populates her polygeneric collection with myriad kinds of texts: poetry, drama, memoir, essay, and fiction. The book opens with a few lyric poems, but rather surprisingly, it moves quickly to a short one-act play (complete with stage directions). The next texts we encounter are a short story and, following that, an autobiographical essay entitled "How My Fever Broke," within which two poems are embedded. Thus, in the first thirty-five pages of her book, one finds a virtual anthology of Native genres—all penned by the same person and all asking to be read through the same lens. When I first taught *Evidence of Red*, my students were absolutely stymied by the domino effect of Howe's generic playfulness. They expected to find "poems," but quickly had to adjust to meet Howe's radical shifts in textual production. No contemporary writer is a better generic shape-shifter than Howe; many readers still find her book a bit of a mystery, especially when trying to determine which genre certain texts in the book actually belong to. This final text I mention above, "How My Fever Broke," serves as a remarkable instance of indigenous intrageneric work. Howe's autobiographical essay requires her to use two genres in order to best represent the rhythms and tonalities of the story to be told. Merging written and oral, historical and personal, and the remembered and the representational, Howe both problematizes and contextualizes what she asks of genre.

The best examples of genre blending, rather than genre bending, occur in Howe's Indian Mascot—Noble Savage "poems" that appear toward the end of *Evidence of Red*. This suite of eleven short poetic texts dramatizes a series of conversations and conflicts between Howe's two favorite stereotypes—the Noble Savage and the Indian Mascot. While some of the poems look and read like standard lyric poems, the most notable ones puree a virtual shopping list of genres into one smooth treat that is easy to swallow but confounds taste. Howe writes "Noble Savage Sees A Therapist," "The Indian Sports Mascot Meets Noble Savage," and "Noble Savage Confronts Indian Mascot" using dialogue, but they are printed on the page to resemble poems. Too short to be plays, too interactive to be a dramatic monologues, too conversational to be purely lyric poems, too kooky to fit easily

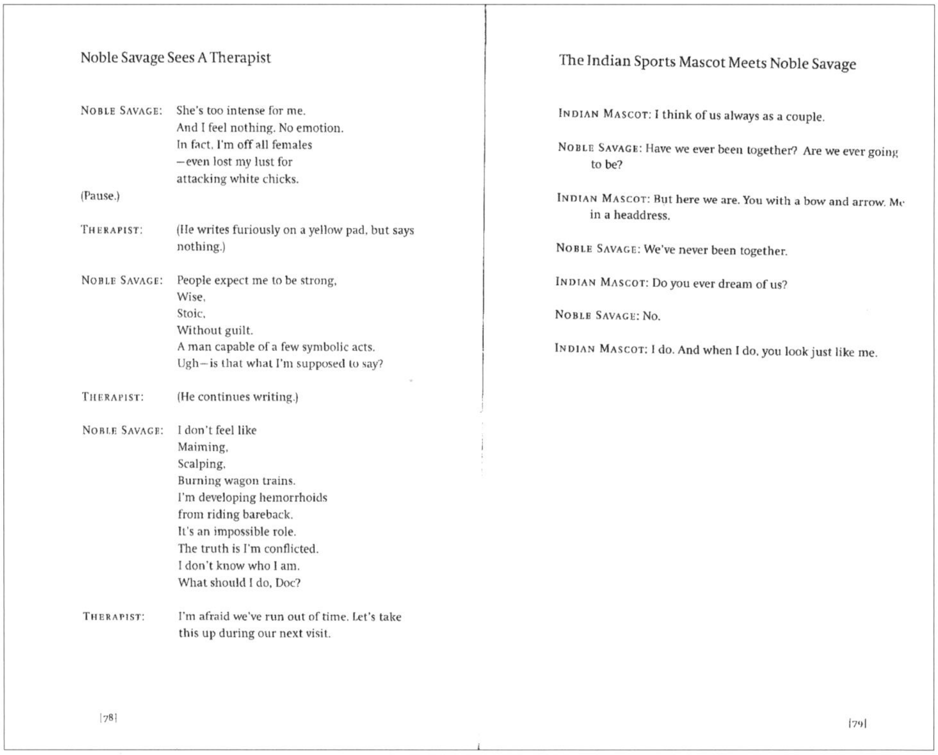

Noble Savage Sees A Therapist

NOBLE SAVAGE: She's too intense for me.
And I feel nothing. No emotion.
In fact, I'm off all females
—even lost my lust for
attacking white chicks.

(Pause.)

THERAPIST: (He writes furiously on a yellow pad, but says nothing.)

NOBLE SAVAGE: People expect me to be strong,
Wise,
Stoic,
Without guilt.
A man capable of a few symbolic acts.
Ugh—is that what I'm supposed to say?

THERAPIST: (He continues writing.)

NOBLE SAVAGE: I don't feel like
Maiming,
Scalping,
Burning wagon trains.
I'm developing hemorrhoids
from riding bareback.
It's an impossible role.
The truth is I'm conflicted.
I don't know who I am.
What should I do, Doc?

THERAPIST: I'm afraid we've run out of time. Let's take this up during our next visit.

|78|

The Indian Sports Mascot Meets Noble Savage

INDIAN MASCOT: I think of us always as a couple.

NOBLE SAVAGE: Have we ever been together? Are we ever going to be?

INDIAN MASCOT: But here we are. You with a bow and arrow. Me in a headdress.

NOBLE SAVAGE: We've never been together.

INDIAN MASCOT: Do you ever dream of us?

NOBLE SAVAGE: No.

INDIAN MASCOT: I do. And when I do, you look just like me.

|79|

FIGURE 6.4. *Pages from LeAnne Howe's* Evidence of Red *(2005). "Poems" written in both verse and dialogue, evoking a drama or screenplay. As much visual texts as lexical ones, these pieces underscore poetry's, and the stereotype's, semiotic quality. Reprinted by permission of Salt Publishing.*

into any classification system, they contain significant elements from pretty much every literary genre.

In "Noble Savage Sees a Therapist" (Fig. 6.4), for instance, the dialogic format asks us to read the text as a play. Even the parenthetical asides reinforce this approach. But the line breaks of the "dialogue" stop short of the right margin, indicating not prose but poetry. Similarly, Howe capitalizes the first word of each new line, also an indication of verse. And yet the poem's language resists the mythopoetic mysticism of so much contemporary poetry. In fact, it is chatty, almost to the point of parody. Moreover, since we have such strong images in our mind of both therapists and noble savages, we cannot help visualizing this intercourse as a television show or a short film. When I read the poem, I immediately cast Sigmund Freud in the role of the therapist and a loincloth-clad brave from the front cover of a romance novel as the noble savage. This performative aspect might, for some readers, shift the text from the poetic realm to the cinematic, but as many have argued, performative texts are part of the Native oral and ceremonial experience—as is role-playing and character embodiment. Alexie makes similar, though more specific observations about Howe's multigenred creativity:

> I am stunned by the beauty, humor, and originality of this book. It feels as new as the Garden of Eden, except Adam is really the Holy Trinity of the Three Stooges, and Eve is a genius Native woman poet-professor. For years, I've hoped that we Native writers will build a 21st century literary rocket and blast off into brand new space. LeAnne Howe (along with Adam, Eve, the Three Stooges, The Lone Ranger and Tonto, Crazy Horse and Custer, and the entire cast of Gilligan's Island, along with Emily Dickinson, Walt Whitman, and five or six smiling Indian elders) has done exactly that. This book is new.[8]

One reason Howe's work feels "new" is because she seems to have invented new genres. Nothing matches expectations or conventions. That newness, that freshness, doesn't come just from her thematics—those are actually topics she and others have explored before—it comes from how she stages her work, how we see her characterizations alter and shift. For me, Howe's texts stand as some of the best models of engaged resistance. She collects and collates threads and strands from diverse aesthetic and literary spools in order to weave a garment no one but she can wear. Her texts engage many literary traditions (both Anglo and Native), but resist being controlled or subsumed by any of them. Just as the Noble Savage has no interest in performing the prescribed duties of maiming and scalping written onto his identity by the master narratives of American culture, so too does Howe defy expectations of the prescribed duties of "poetry," "prose," and "poetry collections" written onto her identity as a "writer" by the master narratives of Western genre.

Tapahonso's Poetry-Prose Hybrids

An analogous genre bending and blending occurs frequently in Native literature—the combined book of poems and stories. Extinct in most publishing circles, this twinning of genres has come to characterize a surprising number of books by contemporary Native writers. In fact, some of the most important books published in the past twenty years contain both poems and stories under the same title, such as Hogan's *Red Clay*; Erdrich's *Baptism of Desire* and *Jacklight*; Tapahonso's *Sáanii Dahataał*, *Blue Horses Rush In*, and *A Radiant Curve*; and Alexie's *The First Indian on the Moon*, *The Business of Fancydancing*, and his most recent, *Face*.[9] I ask the reader to consider how many books written by mainstream Anglo poets—such as Robert Pinsky, Charles Wright, Jorie Graham, and Billy Collins—and published by major publishers have included both poems and stories. On the macro level, I remain fascinated by Native writing's resiliency in the marketplace, evidenced by these multiform books, given the dictates of publishing and generic colonialism. To move from poetry to prose and back again evinces Native nimbleness, an ability to navigate any terrain—even aesthetic ones.

In *Blue Horses Rush In*, for instance, Tapahonso (Navajo) traffics in both poetry and prose in order to deliver key observations about past and present, public and private. To my knowledge, only Silko's *Storyteller* and Howe's *Evidence of Red* match the multigenred design and intertextuality of *Blue Horses Rush In*. Though the book's major components remain poetry and fiction, Tapahonso punctuates these texts with various nonfiction essays, including four pieces that document the excavation of an ancient Hohokamki settlement and an autobiographical essay on language and storytelling. Furthermore, the mosaic structure of the collection underscores Tapahonso's techniques, her thematics, and her politics. Technically, Tapahonso deftly threads language—both English and Navajo—through myriad genres, forcing the genre to acclimate to her words instead of the other way around. At times, poetry sounds like prose, prose like poetry, fiction like autobiography, and anthropology like a dream. So seamless is her shift from lyric poet to minimalist fiction writer that one begins to wonder what lure genre holds for Tapahonso. It would appear, though, that her ability to inhabit both poetry and prose is linked to larger thematic concerns. In fact, I would suggest that Tapahonso's desire to speak through both poetry and prose is inexorably stitched to her desire to speak to both the public and the private spheres of human lives, and to both Navajo and Anglo audiences.

One of Fritz Scholder's most intriguing qualities is the innovative conflation of representation and abstraction in his paintings. Tapahonso's written texts work on similar planes. I have argued elsewhere that Tapahonso, perhaps more than any other American poet, combines critical elements of the lyric and epic forms, and the levels of diction and genres she manipulates in this book merely accentuate this claim.[10] For instance, in "Daané' Diné," one of the most compelling texts in the book, Tapahonso moves from a description of a Hohokamki excavation site to a description of a childhood dream that she has upon returning to her hotel. What makes this "poem" unusual is the form it takes. Consider this generic interplay: the analytical narrative of the site is rendered through poetry, but the more poetic dream sequence finds expression in prose. Already, our assumptions about genre are inverted. Below, stanzas two and three:

> We are witnesses to the excavation
> Of the old Hohokamki homes
> Where archaeologists are working
> At the Pueblo Grande site.
> A cache of clay animals was unearthed this afternoon,
> And a ripple of excitement swept through the work site.
> This is the most significant find to date.
>
> The archaeologists feel certain that the small figures
> Are ritual ceremonial images. The figures were in the center
> of a pithouse alongside a huge pot that had been shattered
> by centuries of dirt and layers of civilization
>
> —(*BLUE HORSES RUSH IN*, 27).

The first half of the poem is composed of five strophes similar to the two above, all containing four to seven lines. In short, the text looks like a poem. Yet the tone, the matter-of-fact voice, the lack of overt symbolism or imagery, give the text a prosaic quality. At times, the lines above read like journalism, as though the observations are being rendered objectively by a disinterested party. As readers, we wonder what goes unsaid; we speculate about the text behind the text.

But how the tone shifts when the poem moves from verse to prose. Suddenly, as Tapahonso dreams in her hotel room a few hundred yards from the site, her own past encroaches onto her present reality, just as the Hohokamki ruins are interposed onto the reality of the present world. Past and present, poetry and prose, dream and reality, fuse into one almost mystic expression: "The next morning, the eastern sky glowed clean yellow. The sun had not yet risen. From the hotel window, I could see the Pueblo Grande site. Thin wisps of fire smoke rose from the camps of those homeless who stayed nearby. I wondered if they heard noises from the excavation site at night or if they saw the spirits of the Hohokamki, who were being unearthed, walking about" (29).

Having just woken from a dream about her youth, Tapahonso wonders whether items or toys we use today will become ruins for ancient civilizations. More provocatively, she suggests that human energy and human spirits have been exhumed as she, the living, reenters the world of the dead: "And I wondered what had happened to the toys we had made as children. Had they been absorbed back into the soft dirt beside my parents' house? Had they been carried off by the wind, or by our children? Had they been buried by seasons of rain, leaves, and snow?" (29).[11]

Tapahonso plays with present and past tense so that in the dream, the Hohokamki excavation, the dream of childhood, and the present reality merge into one time and place, just as the forms of poetry and prose merge into one timeless utterance. Her fusion of the present and past further reveals how the temporal moves outside of the conventional Western linear model. Instead of time pressing "forward," for Tapahonso and most Navajo, time moves more like a circle or a spiral than an arrow. Thus, the fluidity of tenses in the poem further collapses binarisms like "present" and "past" into a uniquely situated moment.

By altering expectations and characteristics of poetry and prose, Tapahonso navigates like a seasoned sailor through the always-merging waters of lyric and epic and shows us how public and private experiences inevitably flow into each other. Tapahonso elicits an utterly original perception of how a geographic space becomes part and parcel of the language spoken within it and the people who live on it. Indeed, given the texture and levels of evocation, a poem like "Daané' Diné" begins to appear more and more like a canvas by Scholder or Georgia O'Keeffe, blurring the distinctions between landscape and symbolic process. But whereas Scholder arrives at his style through aesthetic means, Tapahonso's poetic gestures are inextricably linked to Navajo ontology. In short, her poem reflects Navajo linguistics, aesthetics, temporality, and culture, and in so doing, necessarily operates outside Anglo conceptions of these areas. What may seem like poetic transgressions to Anglo readers become poetic ingressions to her Navajo audience.

Ultimately, Tapahonso's poem, like the entire multigenred collection *Blue Horses Rush In*, performs a synthetic poetics in which conventional Western distinctions collapse onto one another, leaving an indigenous poetics standing among the rubble. Susan Berry Brill de Ramirez claims that Tapahonso's culminating gestures advance a fundamentally Navajo position on language and living: "In contrast to the Navajo perception of the interdependency of these worlds, a Western orientation posits sharply delineated distinctions between these worlds, often seen in a competitively fearful framework that opposes individual and group against each other. . . . Conversely, these poems speak and depict worlds that interact and overlap, not in competition, but in an open engagement unthreatened by the diversity inherent within conversive relations (be those between and among individuals, poems, or worlds)" (*Contemporary American Indian Literatures*, 82–83). In other words, Tapahonso's linguistic and poetic strategies open up her texts when they are read as embodiments of

Navajo modes of being. The interdependence of poetry and prose mirrors the interdependence of past and present, motion and stasis, body and spirit. And as is the case with Silko, Alexie, and Erdrich, these tropes allow Tapahonso to participate in important projects of tribal nationalism and expressive sovereignty.

Erdrich's Trickster Poetics

Nationalism and sovereignty are also at work in the beguiling prose poems of Ojibwe author Louise Erdrich. In both *Jacklight* and *Baptism of Desire*, Erdrich devotes space in her collections of poems to sections of writing that would appear to be "prose." I say this because the lines run all the way to the right margin. Nothing is in couplets. There is no rhyming. There are not even stanzas, but there is indention. According to all the rules, these pieces are prose. Yet they appear in a book of poems. It says so right on the cover. One finds the same thing on the front of *Baptism of Desire*.

Of course, on the *Jacklight* cover the word "poems" appears smaller than the title and Erdrich's name, but it is in capital letters. Similarly, the word "poems" figures prominently on the dust jacket of *Baptism of Desire*, as the final word on the cover, a last testament to the book's contents. I am having some fun with nomenclature, classification, and naming here, but dust jackets and covers tell us how to approach a book, and both of Erdrich's collections of poems indicate that when we open her book of poems, poems are what we will find.

However, both books contain prose texts about the rascally character Potchikoo, texts

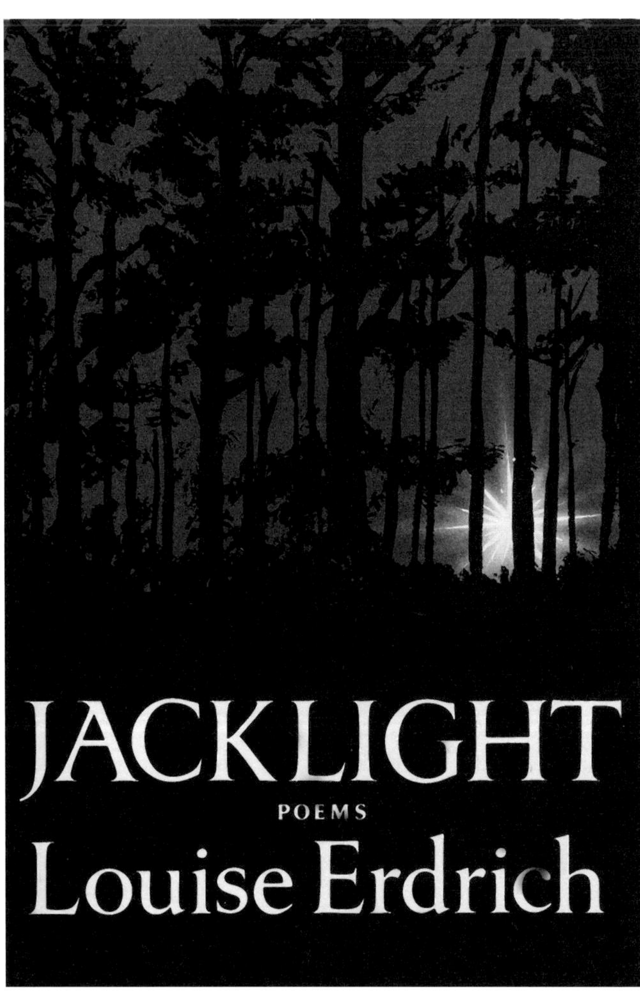

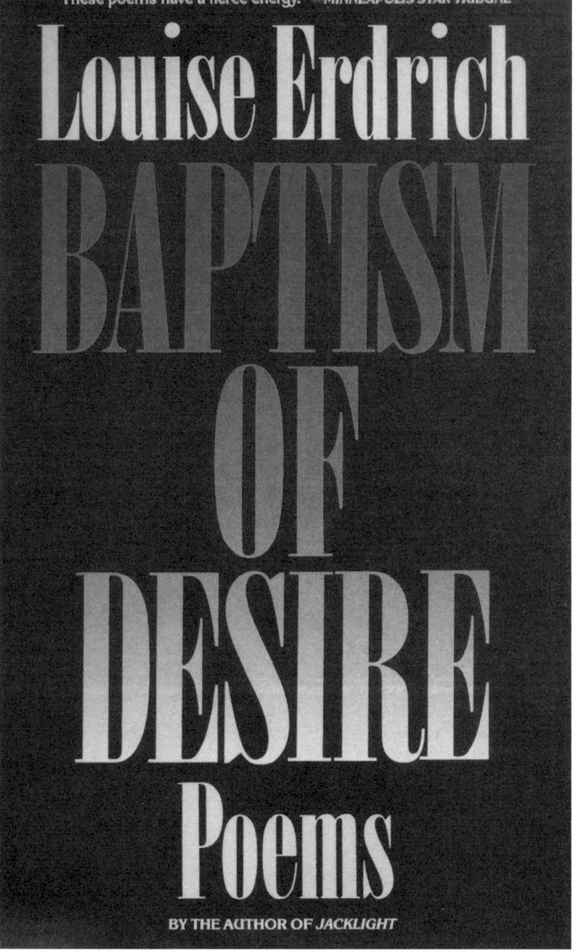

that are part short story and part folktale. Almost none of the Potchikoo texts are intuitively identifiable as poetry, despite the insistence of the publishers that the content of the books in question is poetry. The question remains: why does Erdrich include these prose pieces in her collections of poems? Certainly, she could make more money by publishing the Potchikoo stories together separately, and in the process secure a wider readership. Yet she places them toward the end of both books, surrounded by some of the most lyrical poems of the last twenty years. To me, her intent is clear. Erdrich's motivations resemble the structure of the pieces themselves—to fuse artistic, social, and political concerns in one formless form.

These segments, stories of the lovable trickster Potchikoo, further blur the boundaries between prose and poetry, personal and communal narratives, and public and private expression. In these texts, Erdrich plays with conceptions of genre on a number of levels. According to P. Jane Hafen (Taos Pueblo), Erdrich erases "the Western distinction between poetry and prose" ("Sacramental Language," 152). Hafen is on the mark here, and goes on to suggest that the pieces are a "linguistic reflection of tribal communities where sacred beliefs are expressed without regard to literary structure but with particular attention to ritual retelling and setting." (152). I like Hafen's reading of the seamlessness of Erdrich's form and thematics. She correctly notes that the forms of the Potchikoo pieces are not simply technical experimentations but manifestations of cultural forms of expression.

Both the forms and expressions Hafen refers to derive from histories of orality. By now, most readers of American Indian poetry understand that current poetry enjoys long ties to oral traditions. Womack argues that oral narratives rely on interdependence and that they serve in both literary and political capacities. In his chapter on Harjo, he proposes that her thematics and formal construction likely "flow more out of a natural connection to tribal culture than to an adherence to European poetic techniques," a claim that easily extends to Erdrich and her fluency in regard to genre and structure (*Red on Red*, 260). Indeed, in *The Woven Stone*, Ortiz reminds readers that oral traditions are more than means of locution and preservation—they are woven into notions of identity: "Oral tradition is inclusive; it is the actions, behavior, relationships, practices throughout the whole social, economic, and spiritual life process of people. . . . In this respect, the oral tradition is the consciousness of the people" (7). If oral traditions are the consciousness of a people, then like people, these traditions are always in flux. Orality and textuality flow into but do not subsume each other; such is the case for Erdrich's Potchikoo poems. As Brill de Ramirez argues: "Oral storytelling is a process, not a theory," a process by which, through the story's interactive organization, "all things are transformed" (*Contemporary American Indian Literature*, 13). Because so many Native texts open and unfold in unexpected ways, they do not fit into closed systems or categorizations. By their very design, these poems are not products, but processes, exchanges, conversations.

Right away, Erdrich establishes what Brill de Ramirez calls the "conversive element" in the text, the point of interaction between author and reader (1). In the very first piece, "Old Man Potchikoo," Erdrich begins with a telling: "You don't have to believe this, I'm not asking you to. But Potchikoo claims that his father is the sun in heaven that shines on us all" (*Jacklight*, 74). Unlike many of the lyrics in the collection, this text directly addresses an audience. It assumes an active audience, listening and thinking. Traditionally, the lyric poem is a private medium of expression, a gesture that seeks to explore the internal landscape of the self. On the other hand, a story is a more public maneuver, in which a speaker narrates events involving people to either an actual audience or an imagined one. And normally, one expects a tale to carry some sort of moral or theme, whereas a lyric poem might simply evoke an idea, emotion, or image. The Potchikoo pieces do both. They function as a lyric in that they interrogate individual tensions and desires in a tone that is unusually personal; however, they also carry important social implications for particular problems or concerns. Though there is no doubt that in both form and content the Potchikoo pieces maneuver through the choppy waters of prose more than the interior channels of poetry, they seem, like ships themselves, to inhabit the worlds of neither and both.

Like portions of Erdrich's *Love Medicine*, Susan Howe's *Grass Dancer*, and Momaday's *House Made of Dawn*, the world of Potchikoo moves back and forth between myth, dream, and reality. For instance, in "Potchikoo Marries," Potchikoo travels to the big city of Minneapolis for the first time, in search of a bride. What transpires has roots both in reality and fantasy: "He took the train to Minneapolis to find a wife and as soon as he got off he saw her. She was a beautiful Indian girl standing at the door to a little shop where they sold cigarettes and pipe tobacco. How proud she looked! How peaceful. She was so lovely that she made Potchikoo shy. He could hardly look at her" (75). Somewhere between the tragedy of cigar-store Indians, the magic of love, and the authenticity of a geographic place, the text signifies on levels that transgress the boundaries of any single genre. The text is simultaneously myth and poem, epic and lyric, prose and folk tale, fiction and autobiography.

In the last paragraph of "The Death of Potchikoo," the final Potchikoo text of *Jacklight*, Potchikoo is shattered by his daughters, who are made of stone. The daughters are born from a Whitman-like sexual experience in which Potchikoo "makes love to the slough"—that is, a pile of rising mud near some stones that Potchikoo finds erotic to the touch. When the slough rises to his crotch, Potchikoo enters into an ambisexual encounter with the mud and rocks. As most readers know, such sketchy sexual encounters rarely end well. And indeed, several years later, three women made of stone return to see Potchikoo, who, as it turns out, is their father. Conceived several years earlier when he planted his seed into the warm, smooth morass, they return now to tell their story. Potchikoo remembers and invites them to sit on his lap:

> The daughters moved slowly toward Potchikoo. As he saw their skin up close, he marveled at how fine it was, smooth as polished stone. The first daughter sank upon his knee and clasped her arms around him. She was so heavy the old man couldn't move. The others sank upon him, blocking away the sun with their massive bodies. The old man's head began to swim and yellow stars turned in his skull. He hardly knew it when all three daughters laid their heads dreamily against his chest. They were cold, and so heavy, that his ribs snapped apart like little dry twigs. (78)

What the daughters do to their father exemplifies what Erdrich does to genre—itself a kind of father. She smashes it. Her texts are heavy stones, weighty with significance. And the limits and illusion of genre are like an old, feeble man, crumbling under the shock of the new. To me, these segments function as metonyms for larger issues of hybridization and amalgamation. For Erdrich, Western history and theology have bifurcated Native culture, the body's relation to the natural world, perhaps even the relation of "prose" to "poetry." Erdrich wants to conflate the dualities of otherness into one voice, one genre-less articulation. These pieces work as lyrics and memoir because their subject is Erdrich herself. She is Potchikoo, the trickster, fooling us into thinking these texts are poems (or not) and teaching us lessons about the limits of institutions and the possibilities of utterance.

Alexie's Prose Sonnets

Like Erdrich, Sherman Alexie likes to move back and forth between poetry and prose in his books of poems. And like Erdrich, Alexie is himself a Potchikoo figure, tricking the reader into thinking his prose pieces are poetry and his poems, prose. One of the most salient examples of this occurs in his "Sonnet: Tattoo Tears." Unfortunately, the text is too long to reproduce here, but for readers who do not know the poem, it is important to grasp the formal and thematic interplay at work; so I ask for patience while I establish the setting. As most readers know, a sonnet contains fourteen lines; however, this "poem" by Alexie is structured not in lines but in paragraphs—fourteen paragraphs rendered in prose.[12] Thus, the poem is prose, but the prose is a poem. Even more interesting, each line is numbered, driving home the fact that the linear numerical criterion for the sonnet has been met. That said, "line" one is the following: "No one will believe this story I'm telling, so it must be true" (*Summer of Black Widows*, 56). Of course, most savvy readers are accustomed to prose poetry, and we are all familiar with the dramatic monologue and poems that tell stories, but rarely does one text contain so many mixed signifiers of its generic classification.

Alexie has fun toying with the sonnet—the most revered Western poetic form. Typically, classic Petrarchan and Shakespearian sonnets come in two parts, an octave (the first eight lines) and a sestet (the remaining six lines). The octave poses a question, asserts a problem, or proposes an idea, and the sestet answers the question, resolves the problem, or responds to the assertion. Line eight of Alexie's poem plays right along: "What kind of music do you play when drums aren't enough?" (58). Like any good sonneteer, Alexie devotes the final six units to answering this question, but at the risk of repeating myself, the answer comes not in heroic couplets or with an *abab* rhyme scheme, but in six paragraphs of varying length.

Line/paragraph eleven, however, is so lyrical, so beautifully cadenced and paced, that if it were read aloud, one would surely assume it had been rendered in verse:

> 11.
> If I begin this story with the last word, the last spark of flame left from the trailer fire, will you remember everything that came before? If I show you the photograph of my sister just emerged from the sweat house, steam rising from her body like horses, a single tear tattooed under the right eye, can you pretend to miss her? If I tell you her body was found in the ash, the soft edge of the earth, will you believe she attempted escape but couldn't lift her head from the pillow? If I show you the photograph of my sister in her coffin, hair cut short by the undertaker who never knew she called her hair *Wild Ponies*, will you imagine you loved her?
>
> —(*SUMMER OF BLACK WIDOWS*, 58)

Even though the passage asks us to read it as story, the text draws on a number of classic poetic tropes. First, the syntactic repetitions and parallelisms Alexie utilizes are the cornerstones of Western poetic language, particularly the notion of anaphora (the repetition of initial words, as with "If I . . . If I . . . If I . . . If I . . ."). Second, the text plays on the long poetic tradition of the elegy. In this case, the passage becomes an elegy for his sister. "Borrowing from oral traditions, elegiac conventions, and formal poetic structures," writes Laura Arnold Leibman, "Alexie creates a performative poetry in which words enact deeds. Because this performance requires the work of both writer and reader, Alexie's elegies . . . renounce readers who refuse to 'pay their way'" ("Bridge of Difference," 544). Leibman argues that this poem, like many others in *The Summer of Black Widows*, draws from typical Western strategies in order to solidify an activist impulse. She goes on to posit that the aim of *The Summer of Black Widows* is to "heal the community through storytelling," even though we don't normally think of an activist or storyteller as a sonneteer (544).

Yet, this section is a story, and it makes an argument to be read as prose fiction (just as its semiotic coding asks for it to be read as a sonnet). For example, section eleven pushes along the plot of the poem, advancing the sister as a protagonist, though a tragic one. The narrator continues describing the tearful aspects of the reservation and its toll on human life. The arc of the plot continues to rise. It also reiterates the story-ness of the text by echoing the opening line, indicating that there will be an end, a resolution to the account. A virtual disk jockey of genres, Alexie effectively samples poetry and prose, creating a dexterous blend of the best aspects of Native orality, storytelling, and poetic conventions—it is not either-or. It is both-and.

For some readers, these traits confuse because they create an untraversable gulf between the text, the reader, and the unfortunate gutter of genre. Take, for example, the following passage from Ron McFarland's essay "'Another Kind of Violence': Sherman Alexie's Poems":

> A strict formalist critic keen to classify Alexie's work as to genre would, in fact, be hard put, except when it comes to the twenty-two short stories that comprise *The Lone Ranger and Tonto Fistfight in Heaven*, and even those stories range from short-short, "sudden," or "flash" fiction of just three to five pages to more conventionally constructed stories that run nearly twenty pages. Alexie's other collections of poetry are even more problematic with respect to form (and he is a very conscious, though only rarely conventional, formalist). The forty-two items that make up *The Business of Fancydancing* (counting the four "Indian Boy Love Songs" as one poem, as it is listed in the contents) comprise twenty-eight poems and fourteen prose pieces, one of which is a nine-page story and eight of which run just a paragraph and could be considered prose poems, though I am inclined to regard them as sudden fiction. *Old Shirts & New Skins* consists of fifty items, as many as forty of which are obviously poems. But is "Snapping the Fringe" a prose piece consisting of about thirteen very short paragraphs, or a poem consisting of almost thirty lines (depending on the format) and using indentation in favor of stanza breaks? Although mixed genres like "prose poetry" always leave me feeling a bit uneasy, I am inclined to think it is his best effort in that mode. (260)

We can all sympathize with McFarland's stumbling with classification here. He is quite correct that Alexie consciously plays with genre and form, but McFarland never sees this trait as a strength, a fused power that taps into the energies of recitation, poetry, and narrative. I quote the long passage in full because it illustrates how painfully the critic gropes toward some kind of conclusion that will enable him, finally, to make sense of the prose-ness or poetry-ness of Alexie's texts—as though running through the myriad strategies on his ring will eventually enable him to stumble upon the skeleton key.[13] Looking to Western forms for the key to unlock Native poems remains a largely frustrating pursuit.

Genre Bending as Tradition and Resistance

Indeed, even the best scholars stumble. In his recent book on "classic" Native American writers, Kenneth Lincoln, one of Native poetry's most devoted readers, falls prey. In his preface, Lincoln says he "wants to come as close as possible to the translated Native literary classics and their tribal contexts," and later, in an attempt to arrive at that boundaryless realm, he acknowledges how "lyric pitch blends into narrative pace . . . and into many fusions of song and speech, poetry, and prose, orality, and literacy" (*Speak like Singing*, 3, 12). However, he spends nearly three pages scatting about the distinctions between poetry and prose:

- "Prose masters may try to nail their targets, poetry may feel more, know less about less and speak in tongues." (17)

- "Novelists know what they want from a character or scene . . . Poets don't edit or email action." (17)
- "The prose narrator reaches across the space between reader and writers; the poet reaches into reality through metaphor." (18)
- "Poetry is rhythmic, prose runs on." (19)

To be sure, Lincoln is a careful reader—his section on Sherwin Bitsui's *Shapeshift* rings with clarity and alacrity—so it is fascinating to see how fully immersed in generic bifurcation his critical stance remains.

At the other end of the spectrum, Eric Gary Anderson makes significant inroads in this regard, calling for different questions about Native poetics:

> I want to urge a shift away from Western questions of formal identity—*What* is Indian poetry? What shapes and forms does this poetry take?—and to encourage more attention to a different series of questions having to do with some of the various ways Native literature both grounds itself and travels—*Where* is this work of literature? Where does it come from (i.e., what culture or cultures and which physical places, not which literary-historical provenance)? Where is it going? Where do Native writings express this sense of mobility, this traveling sense of groundlessness?
>
> —("SITUATING AMERICAN INDIAN POETRY," 35)

Anderson's observations about Native poetry's "mobility" and "groundlessness" mirror my claim early in this chapter when I call for a Native poetic methodology that is mutable, compatible, and adaptable. My interest here, like Anderson's and Warrior's, comes from a desire to create a criticism in conversation with its subject.[14]

One way toward that conversation might involve asking what Native writers need from poetry, what they need from prose, and what linguistic, cultural, and political gestures each enacts. Instead of approaching Native poetic texts through their inability to fully wear the costume of a particular genre, it might be more useful to recognize that they sport different garments altogether. Second, trained readers of Native oral narratives know that the performance of a traditional Indian story requires the participation of many voices. In fact, when translating a performative telling, linguistic anthropologists like Karl Kroeber, Dell Hymes, and Jarold Ramey include the audience's contributions and reactions as part of the primary text.[15] The speaker often stops or pauses, awaiting the phrases, sounds, or gestures from the audience before continuing, making the process dialogic rather than monologic. When a poet moves from prose to poetry within a text, she re-creates an aspect of that dialogic component of Native expression. Third, the many instances in which Native writers engage in multiple genres reflects not an inconsistency or an uncertainty on their part but a fluency—a familiarity with Western genres, the way one might gain knowledge of an enemy. Incorporating aspects of the sonnet, Western rhyme schemes, or the elegy can be seen as a form of counting poetic coup, a symbolic but telling manifestation of triumph. Lastly, readers of Native texts might consider how Native fluency in many genres makes Indian writing more like Indian ways of being in the world—holistic, comprehensive, synthetic, and dialogic.

Again, I am not suggesting that Native writers do not believe in genres—merely that their reluctance as writers to be defined by them reflects larger modes of resistance to even more serious forms of cultural definition. I am also not suggesting the writers I refer to in this chapter are the only poets doing compositional resistance. Carter Revard, Phillip Carroll Morgan, Gerald Vizenor, and many of the poets in the special prose poetry issue of *Sentence* continue to push these boundaries.[16] Additionally, one of the greatest gifts Janet

McAdams and the Salt Earthworks Series has given us is a new showering of innovative Native poetry, much of which is redefining American poetic publishing and the role that Indian poets play within the larger genre of "poetry."[17]

Ultimately, the tendency for Native writers to destabilize terms like "poetry" and "prose" confirms literary and cultural sovereignty. Warrior's term has become a kind of catchall for issues of independence and contingency, but these writers' structural independence is indicative of larger cultural sensibilities. In this regard, Warrior is spot on: "Perhaps the greatest lesson of Indian poetry is that it has often shown us not only how tradition is able to live in new written forms, but that it does not have to dress up in beads and feathers in order to be powerful" (*Tribal Secrets*, 117). Native poetry will continue to see genre as just another metanarrative to deconstruct—one more strip mall, one more Hollywood western, one more treaty, one more sports mascot. Native poets go intrageneric because it is a revolutionary project that subverts the means by which cultural dominance is created and fostered. By resisting the dominant Western literary classifications, these writers send a message that they do not need categorization or apportionment. They have language and ritual and performance and pastiche. Just as they don't require beads and feathers, nor do they require the comfort, the security, the endorsement of genre.

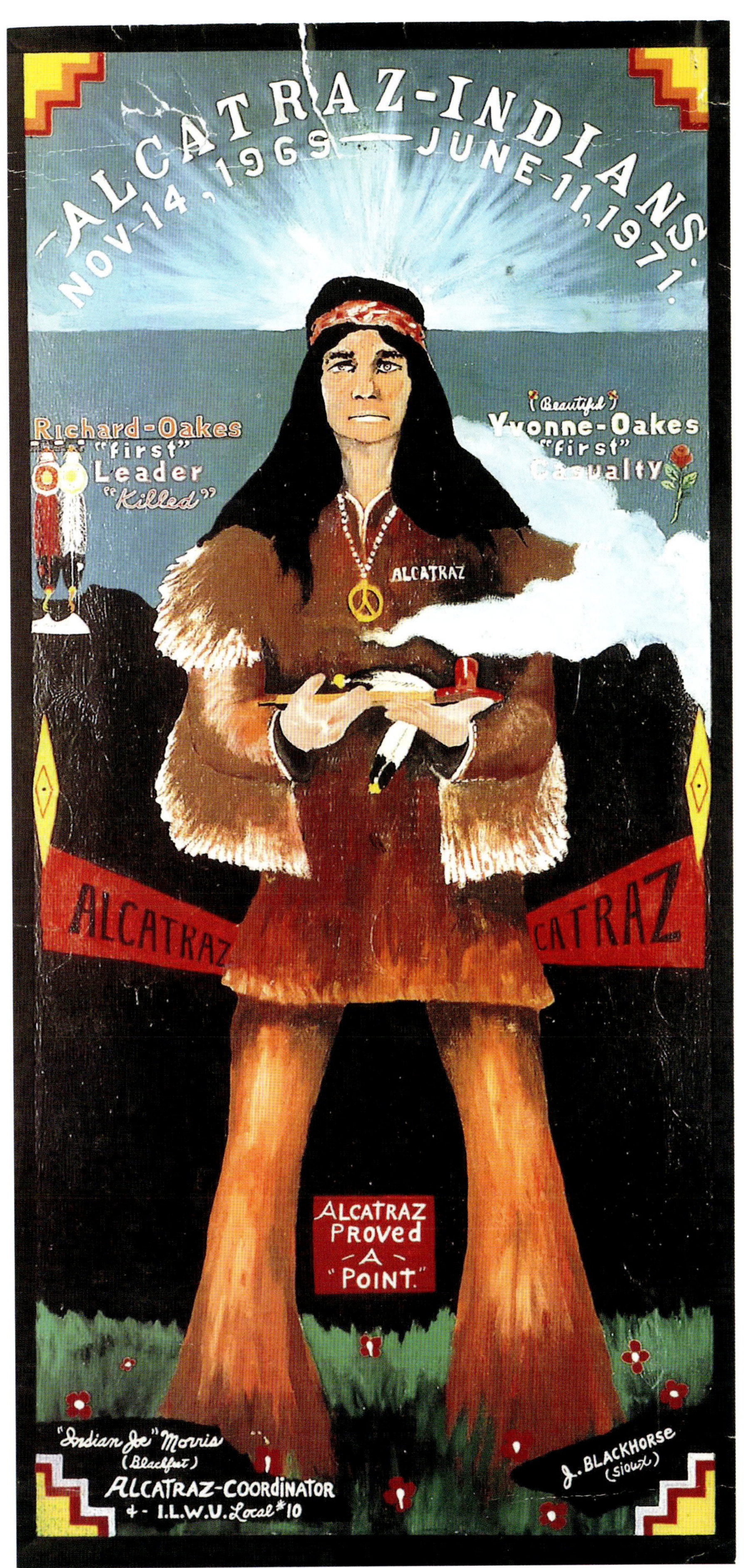

"Indian Joe" Morris, Modern Militant Indian, or Alcatraz Proved a Point, *1972. Oil on board, 48 × 108 in. An iconic painting. Courtesy of the U.S. Department of the Interior, National Park Service.*

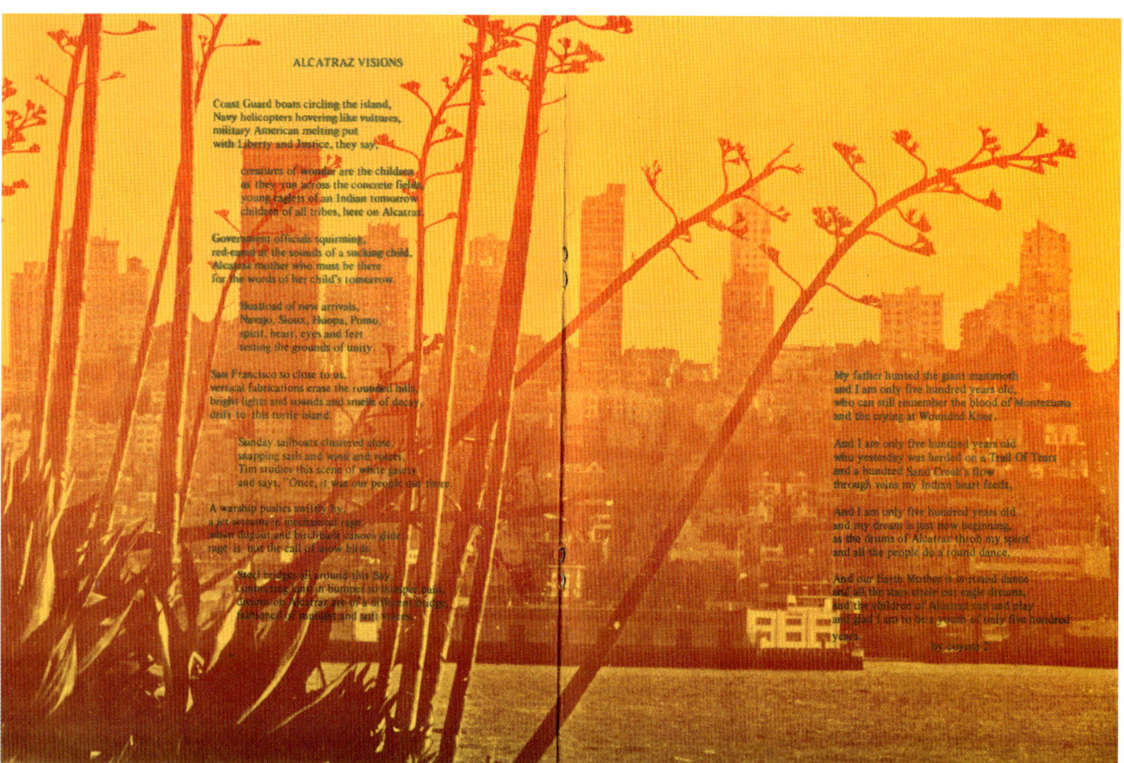

ALCATRAZ VISIONS

Coast Guard boats circling the island,
Navy helicopters hovering like vultures,
military American melting pot
with Liberty and Justice, they say,

creatures of wonder are the children
as they run across the concrete fields,
young eaglets of an Indian tomorrow
children of all tribes, here on Alcatraz.

Government officials squirming,
red-eared at the sounds of a sucking child.
Alcatraz mother who must be there
for the words of her child's tomorrow.

Boatload of new arrivals,
Navajo, Sioux, Hoopa, Pomo,
spirit, heart, eyes and feet
testing the grounds of unity.

San Francisco so close to us,
vertical fabrications erase the rounded hills,
bright lights and sounds and smells of decay,
drift to this turtle island.

Sunday sailboats clustered close,
snapping sails and wind and voices,
Tim studies this scene of white gaiety
and says, "Once, it was our people out there.

A warship pushes swiftly by,
a jet screams in mechanical rage,
when dugout and birchbark canoes glide,
rage is not the call of snow birds.

Steel bridges all around this Bay,
connecting land in bumper to bumper pain,
dreams on Alcatraz are of a different bridge,
fashioned of sunlight and soft voices.

My father hunted the giant mammoth
and I am only five hundred years old,
who can still remember the blood of Montezuma
and the crying at Wounded Knee.

And I am only five hundred years old
who yesterday was herded on a Trail Of Tears
and a hundred Sand Creek's flow
through veins my Indian heart feeds.

And I am only five hundred years old
and my dream is just now beginning,
as the drums of Alcatraz throb my spirit
and all the people do a round dance.

And our Earth Mother is in round dance
and all the stars circle our eagle dreams,
and the children of Alcatraz run and play
and glad I am to be a youth of only five hundred
years.

by [illegible]

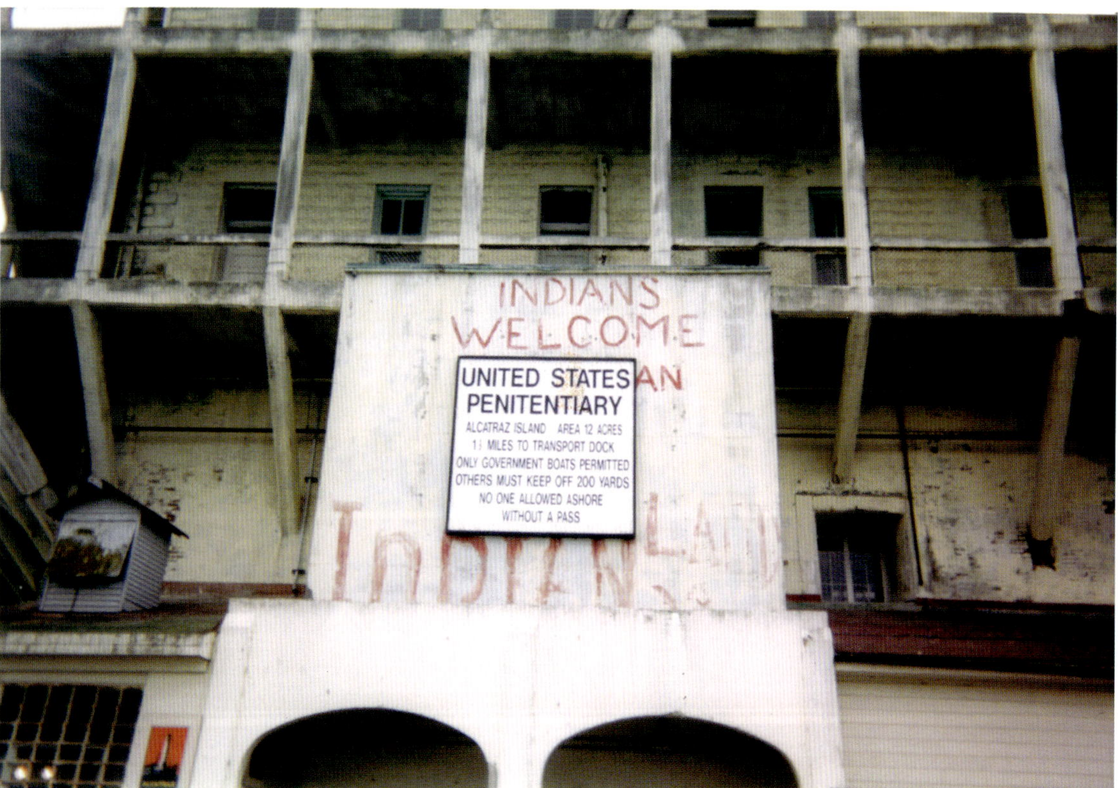

(top) *"Alcatraz Visions," as it appeared in one of the occupation newsletters. Courtesy of the U.S. Department of the Interior, National Park Service.*

(bottom) *The Alcatraz sign in 2003. Photo by the author.*

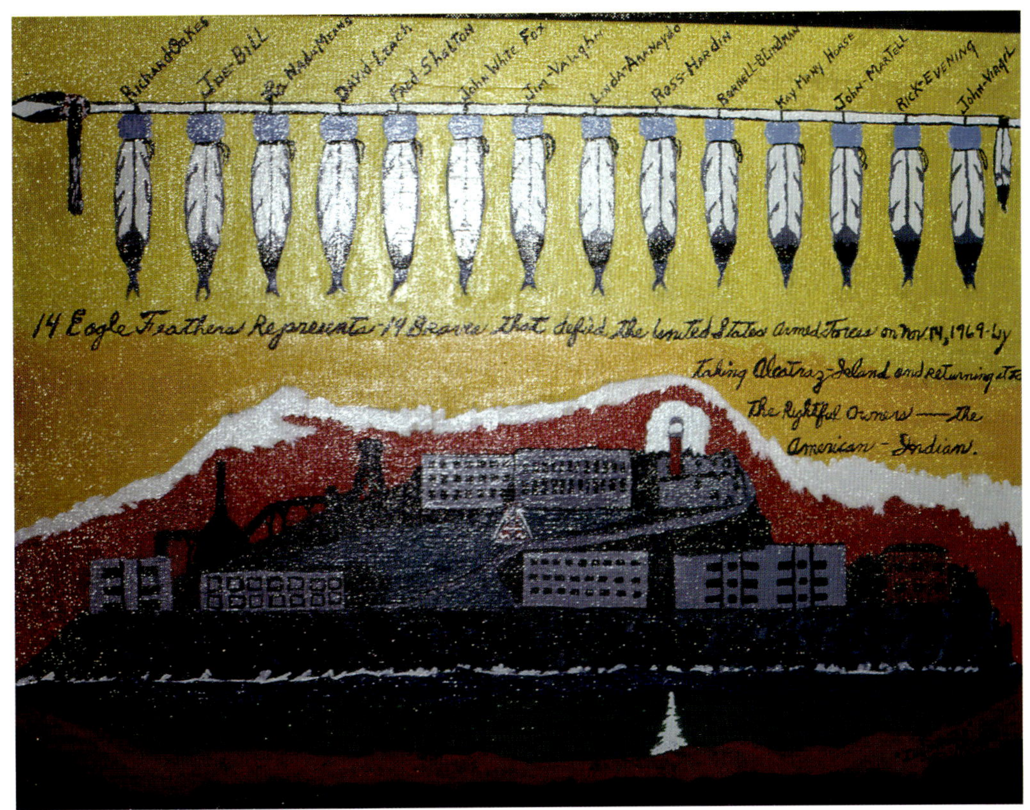

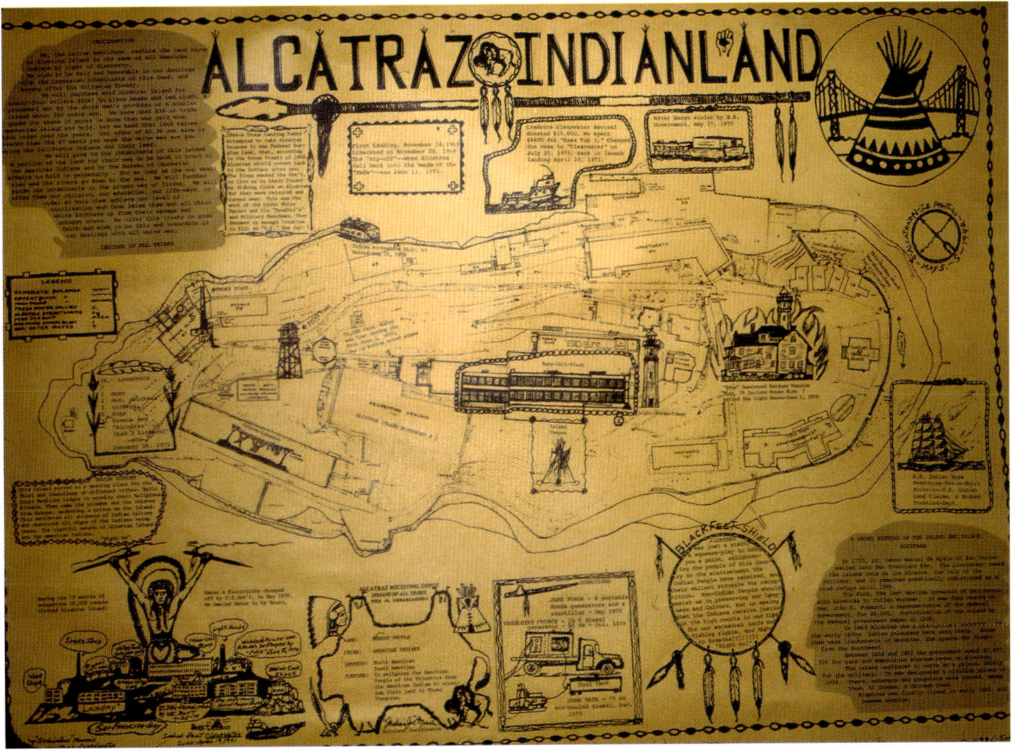

(top) *Joe Morris,* 14 Feathers over Alcatraz, *c. 1971. A tribute to the fourteen "braves" who dove into the water to claim Alcatraz. Courtesy of the U.S. Department of the Interior, National Park Service.*

(bottom) *Joe Morris,* Alcatraz Indianland, *c. 1971–1972. Less a map of place than experience, it tells many stories. Courtesy of the U.S. Department of the Interior, National Park Service.*

Jaune Quick-to-See Smith, Indian Map, *1992. Diptych. Oil and mixed-media collage on canvas. 64 × 96 in. Courtesy of the artist.*

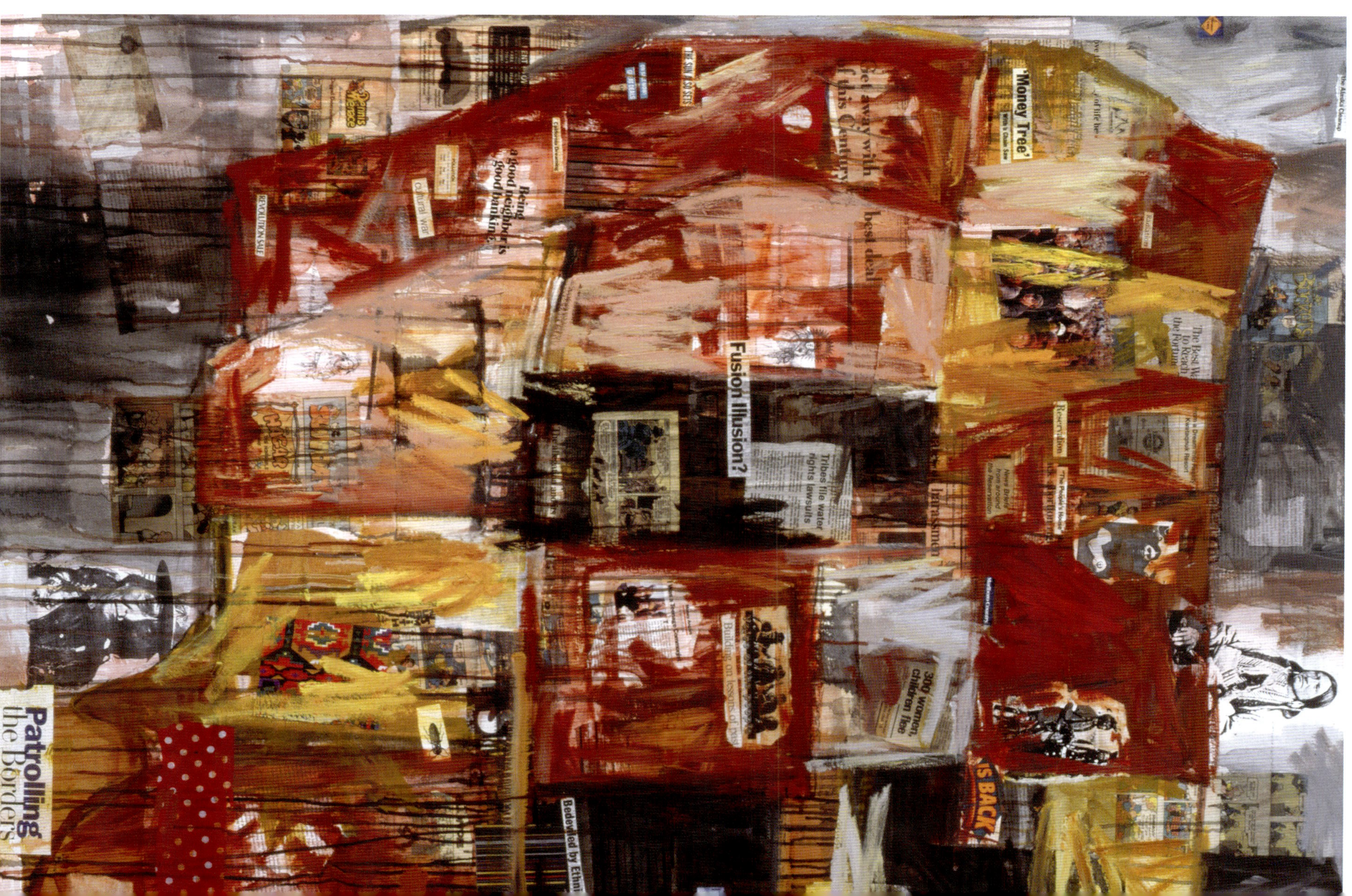

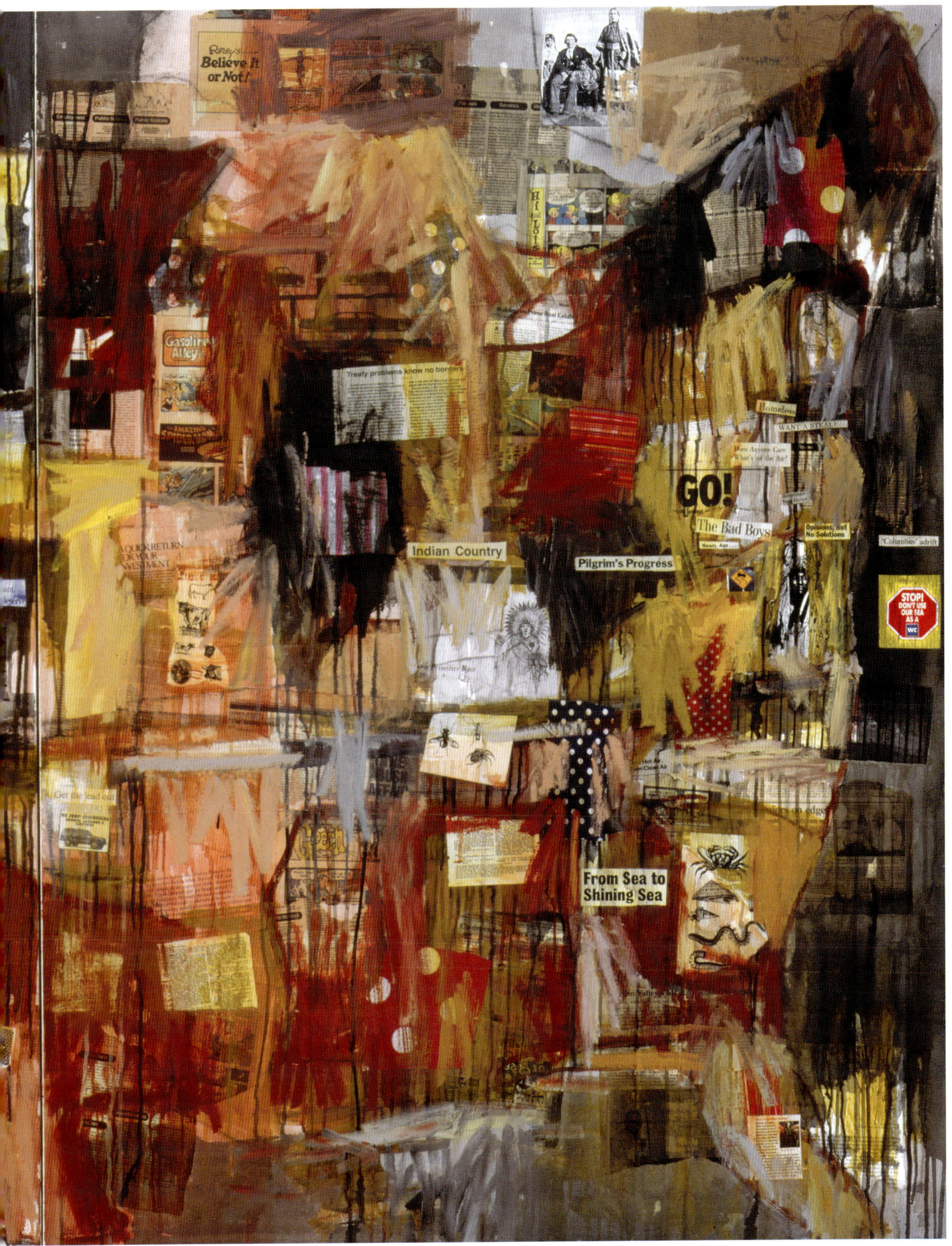
Believe It or Not!
Gasoline Alley
Treaty problems know no borders
Homeless
Does Anyone Care What's in the Air?
GO!
The Bad Boys
Opinions, but No Solutions
'Columbus' adrift
STOP! DON'T USE OUR SEA AS A WC
Indian Country
Pilgrim's Progress
A QUICK RETURN FOR YOUR INVESTMENT
From Sea to Shining Sea

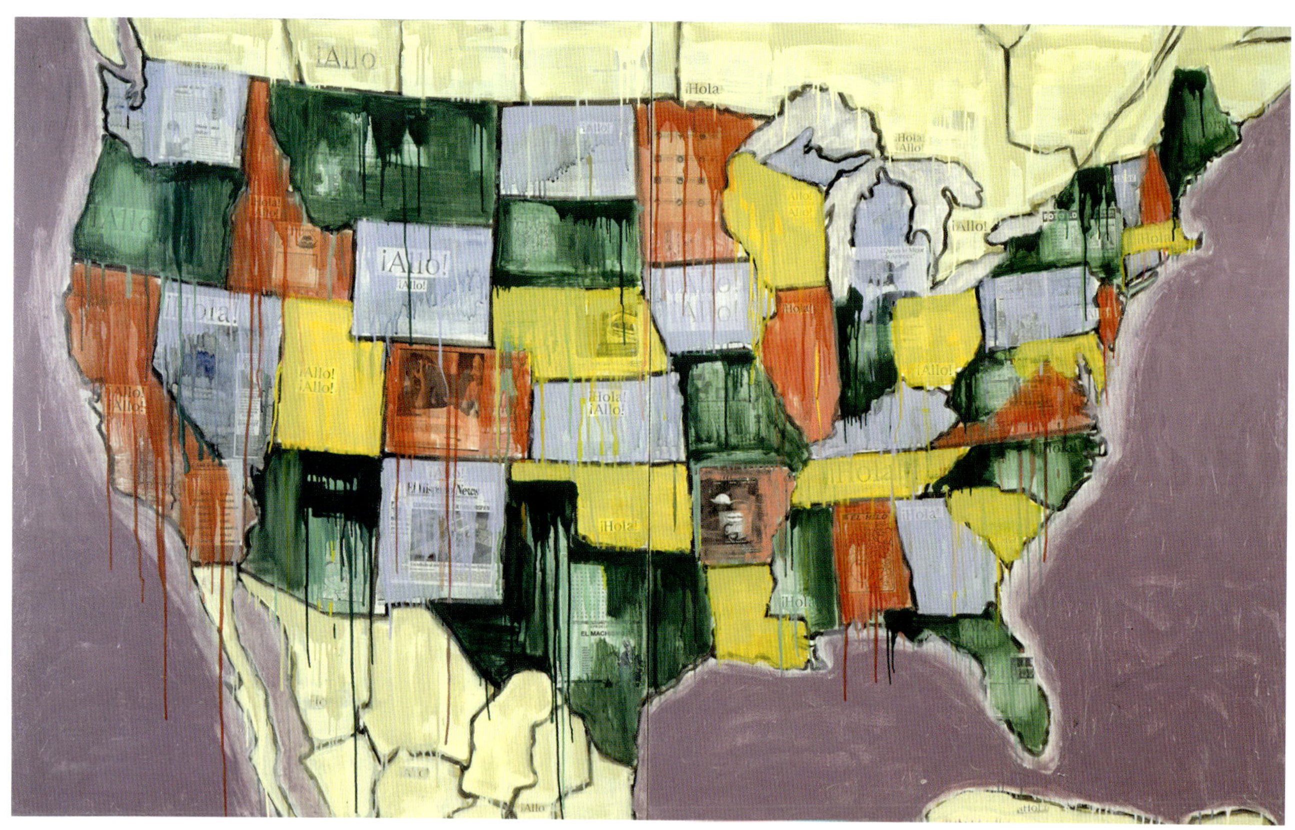

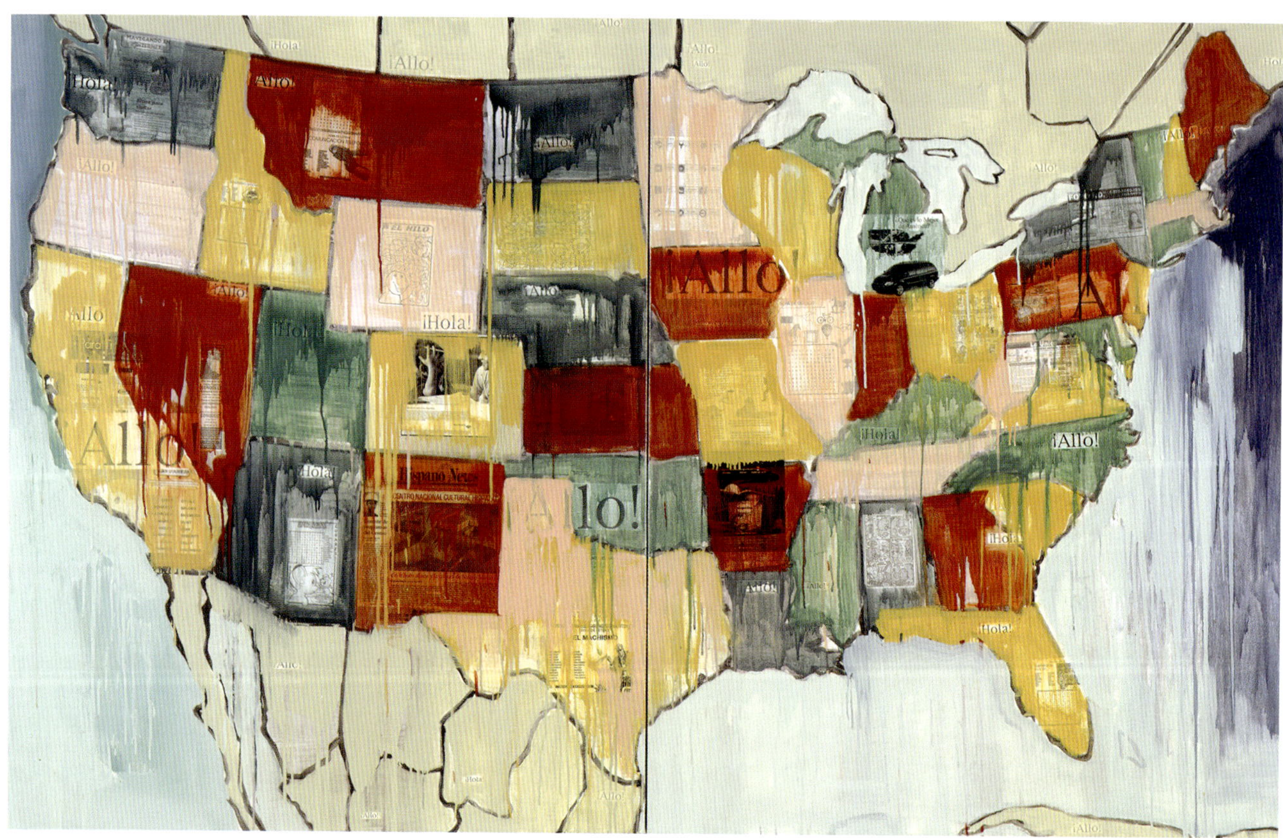

(top) *Jaune Quick-to-See Smith,* Echo Map I (Allo), *2000. Oil, collage, and mixed media on canvas. 60 × 100 in. Courtesy of the artist.*

(bottom) *Jaune Quick-to-See Smith,* Echo Map II (Allo), *2000. Oil, collage, and mixed media on canvas. 36 × 48 in. Courtesy of the artist.*

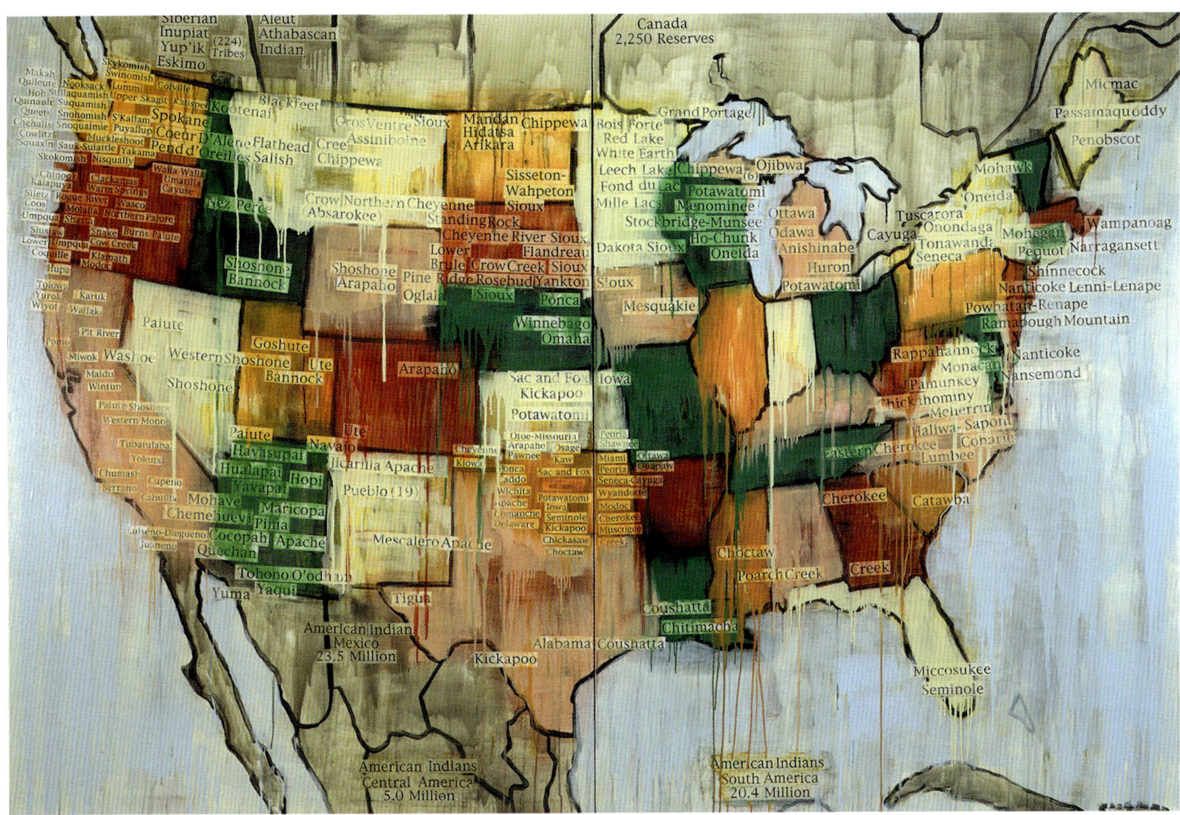

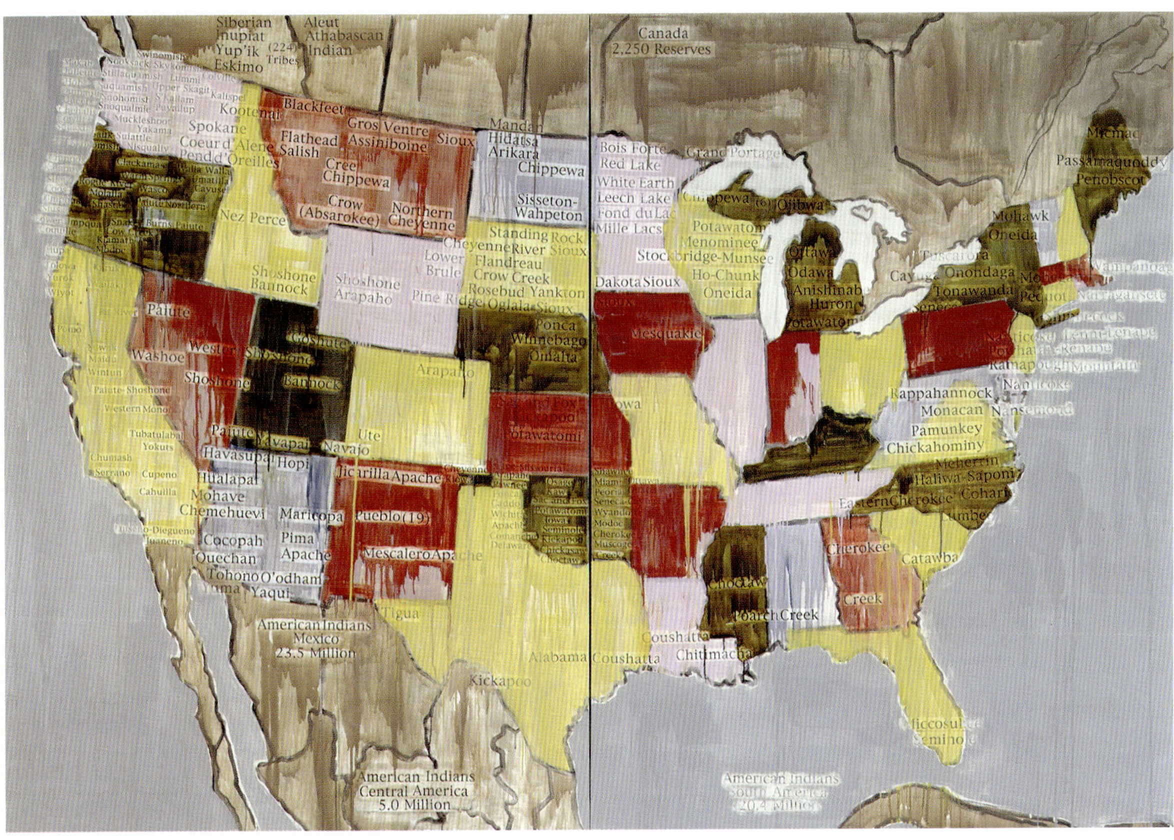

Jaune Quick-to-See Smith, Tribal Map *and* Tribal Map II, *2001, Oil, collage, and mixed media on canvas. 80 × 120 in. Courtesy of the artist.*

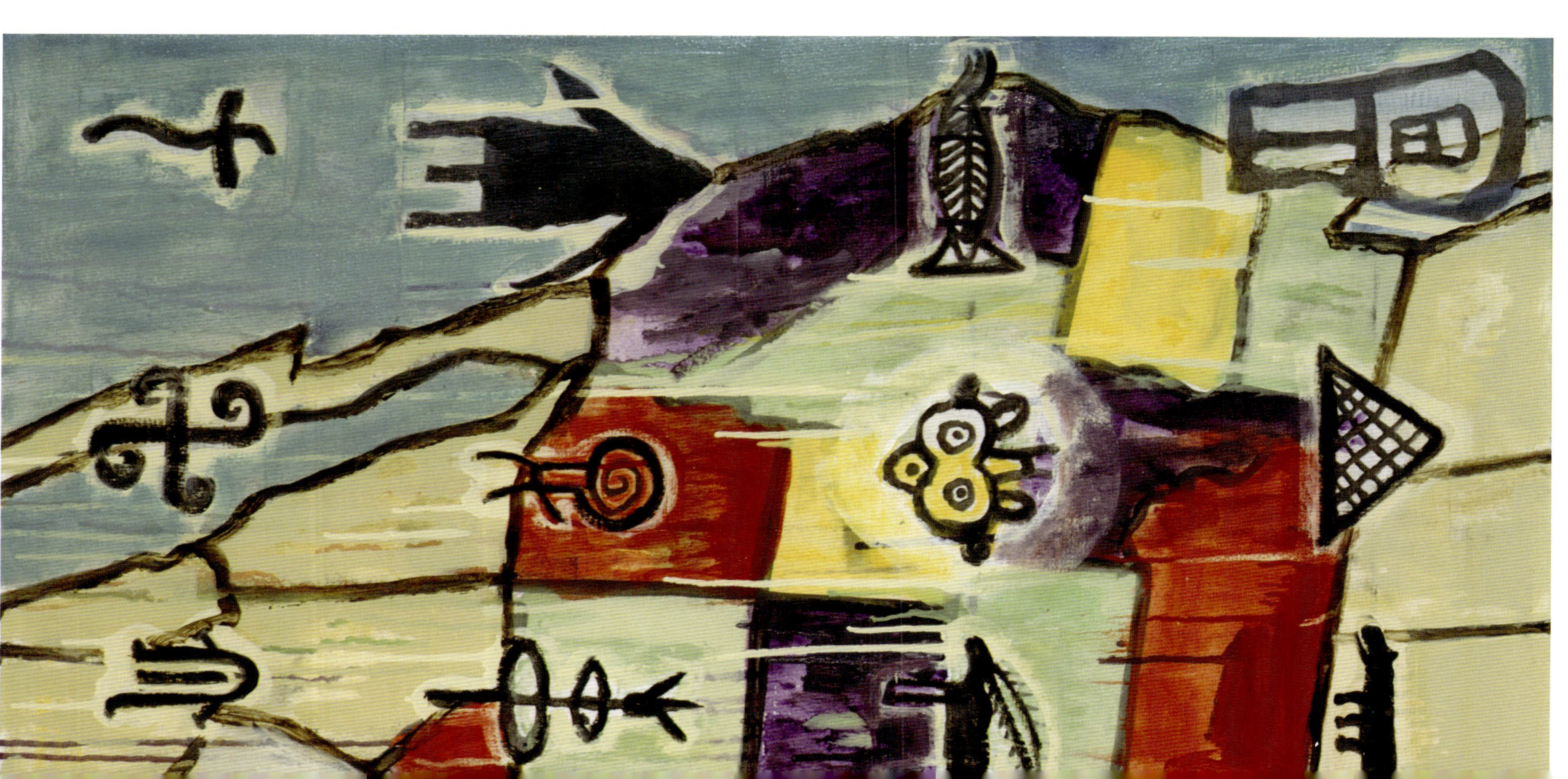

Jaune Quick-to-See Smith, (Untitled) Memory Map, *2000. Mixed media on paper. 46 × 34 in. Courtesy of the artist.*

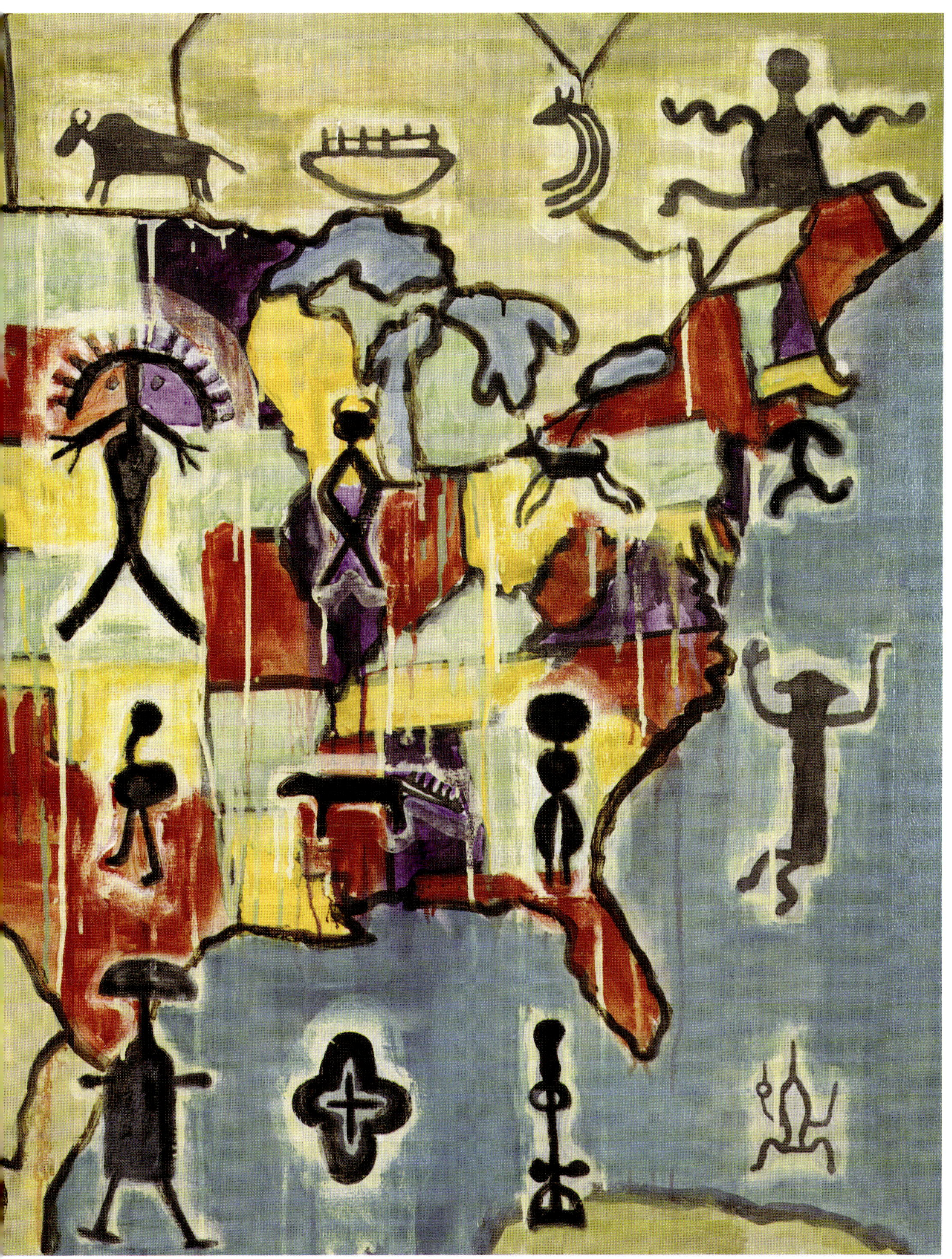

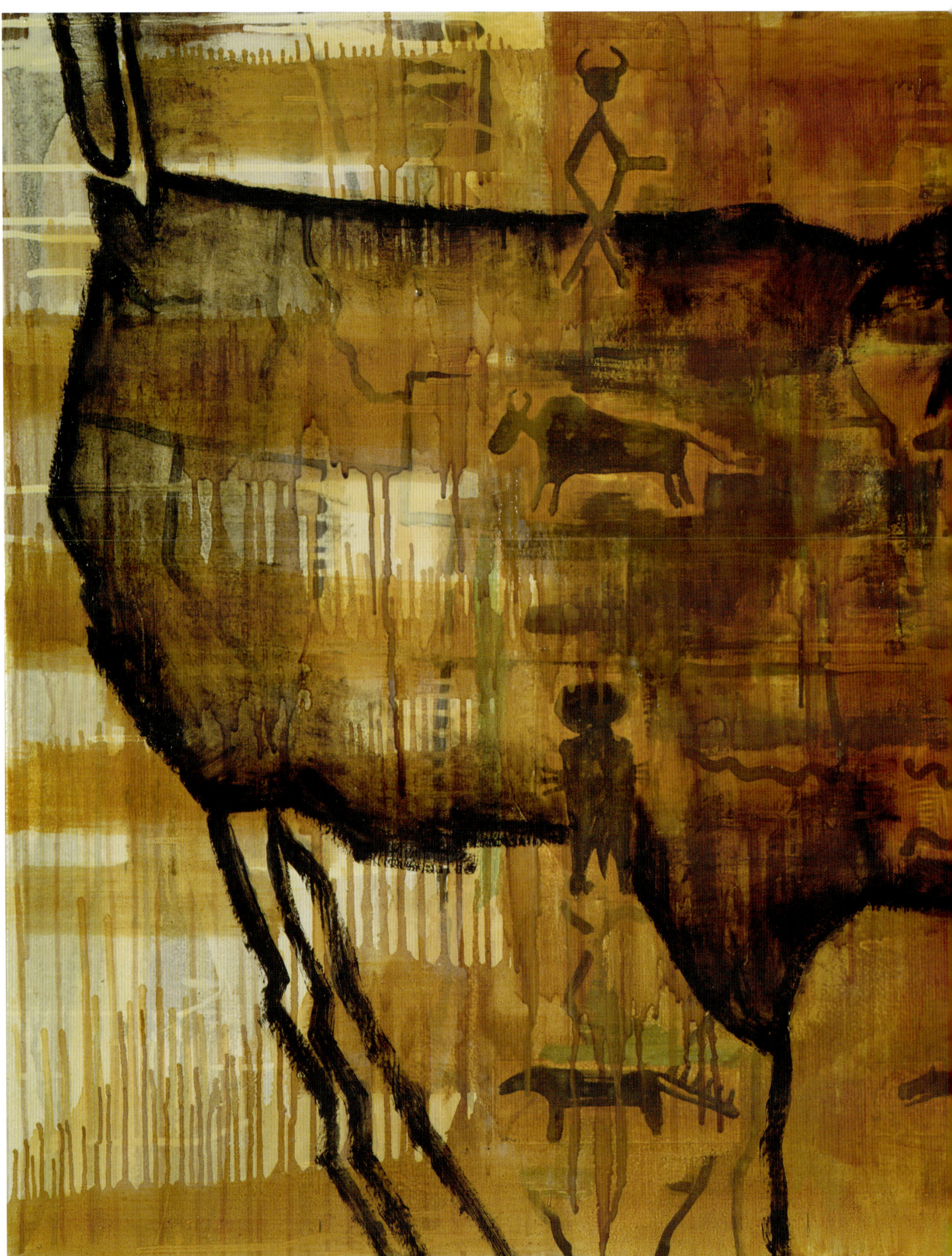

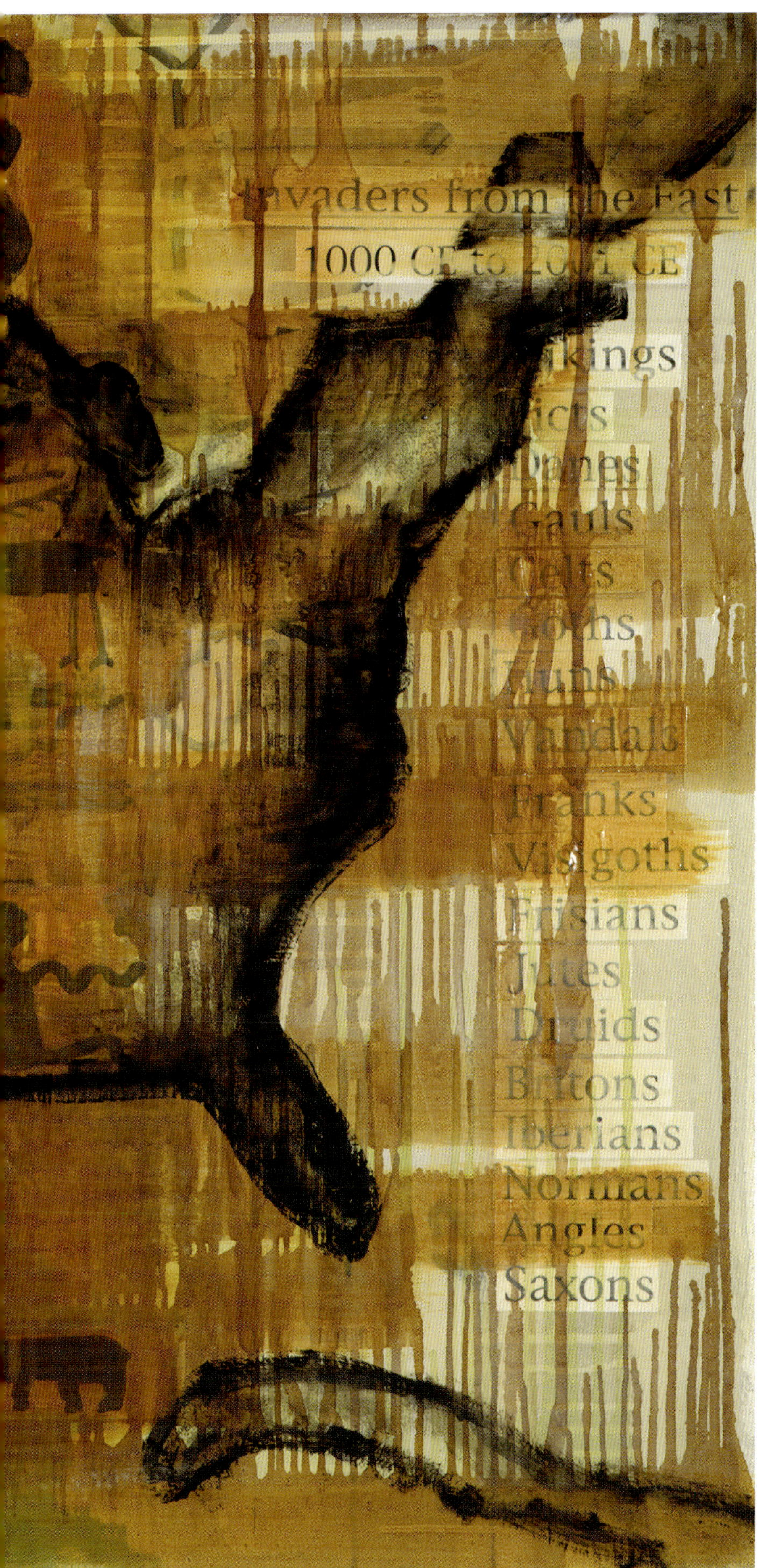

Jaune Quick-to-See Smith, The Browning of America, *2000. Oil, collage, and mixed media on canvas. 36 × 48. Courtesy of the artist.*

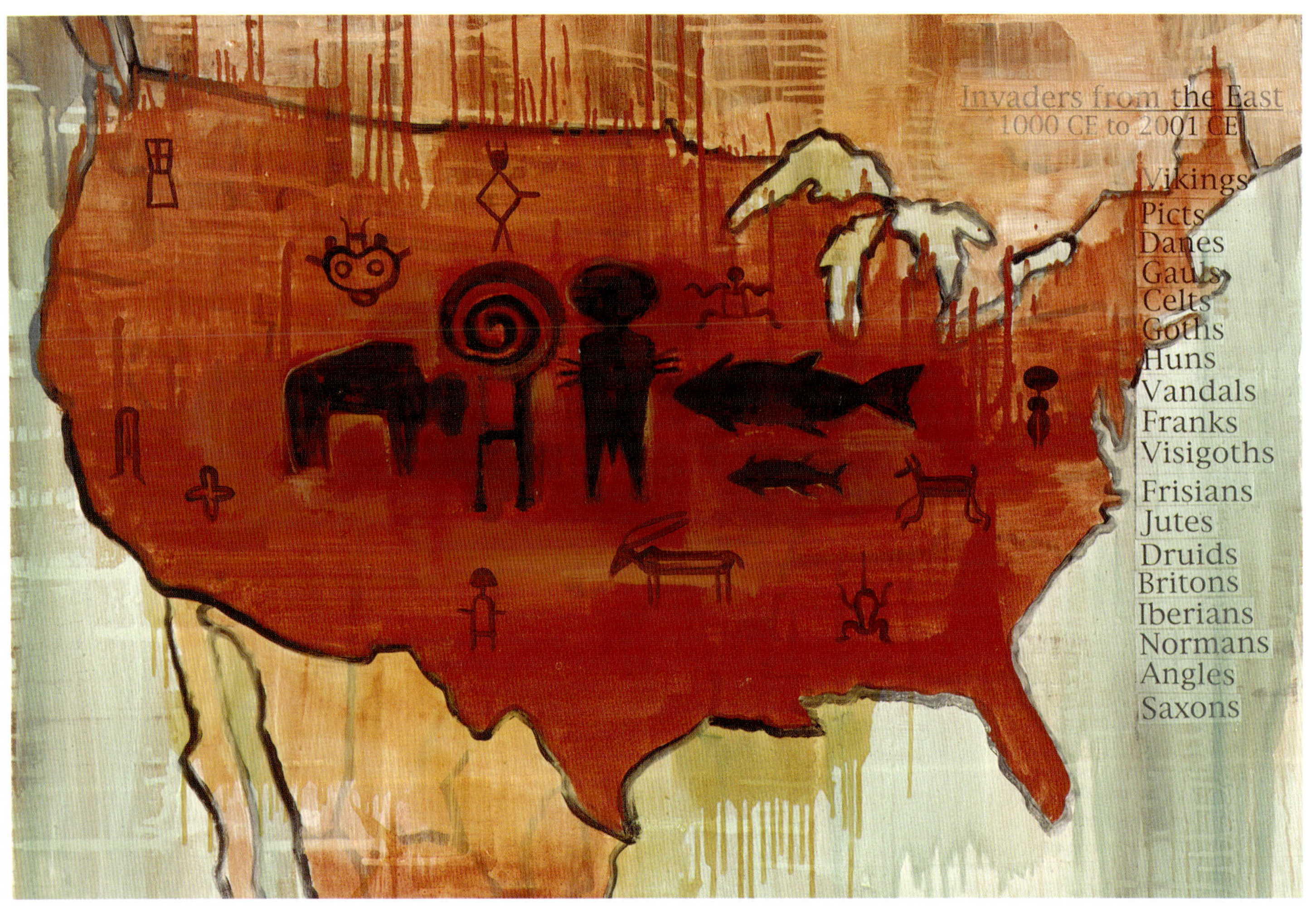

Jaune Quick-to-See Smith, The Browning of America II, *2000. Oil, collage, and mixed media on canvas. 36 × 48 in. Courtesy of the artist.*

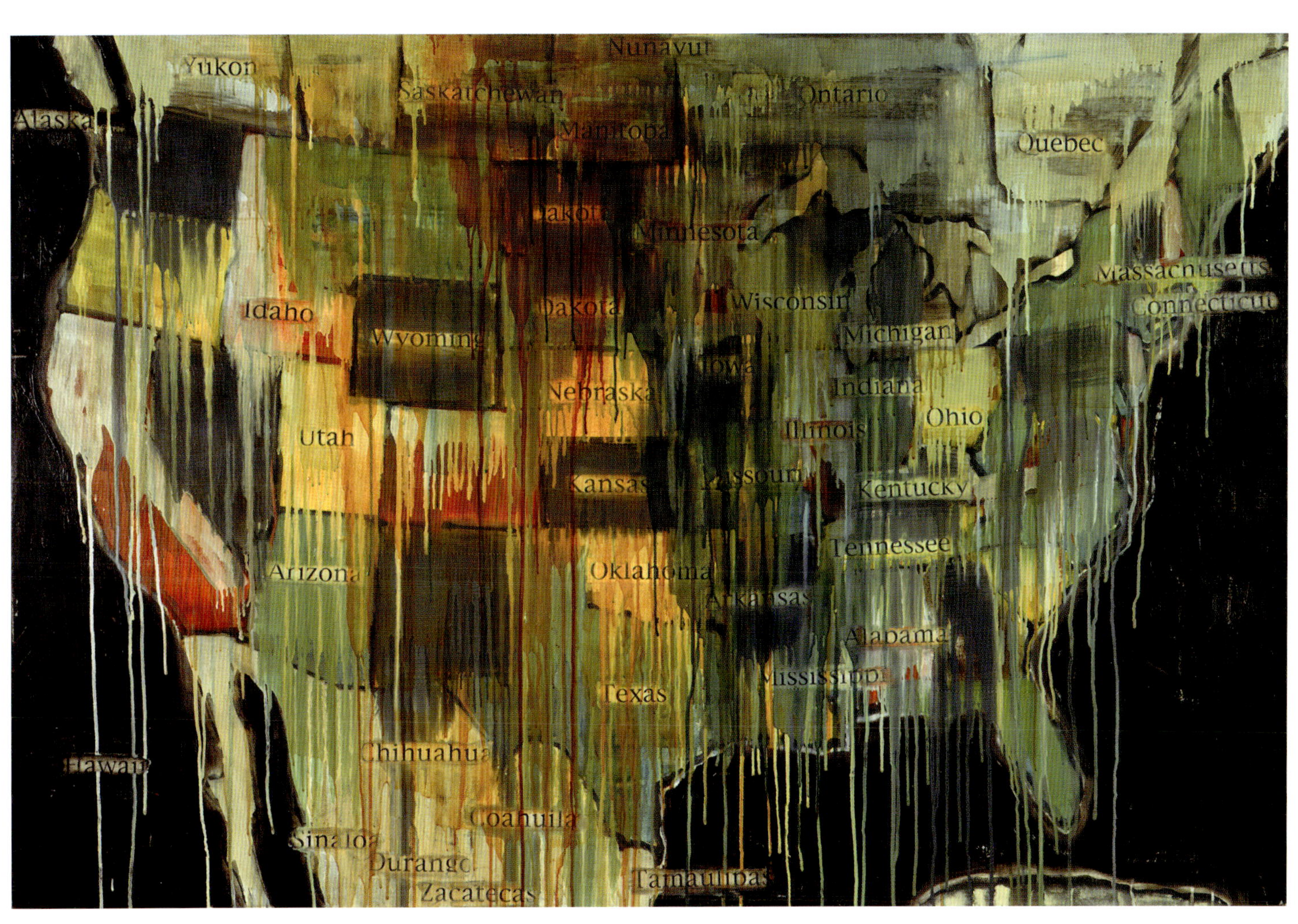

Jaune Quick-to-See Smith, State Names I, *2000. Oil and mixed media on canvas. 40 × 72 in. Courtesy of the artist.*

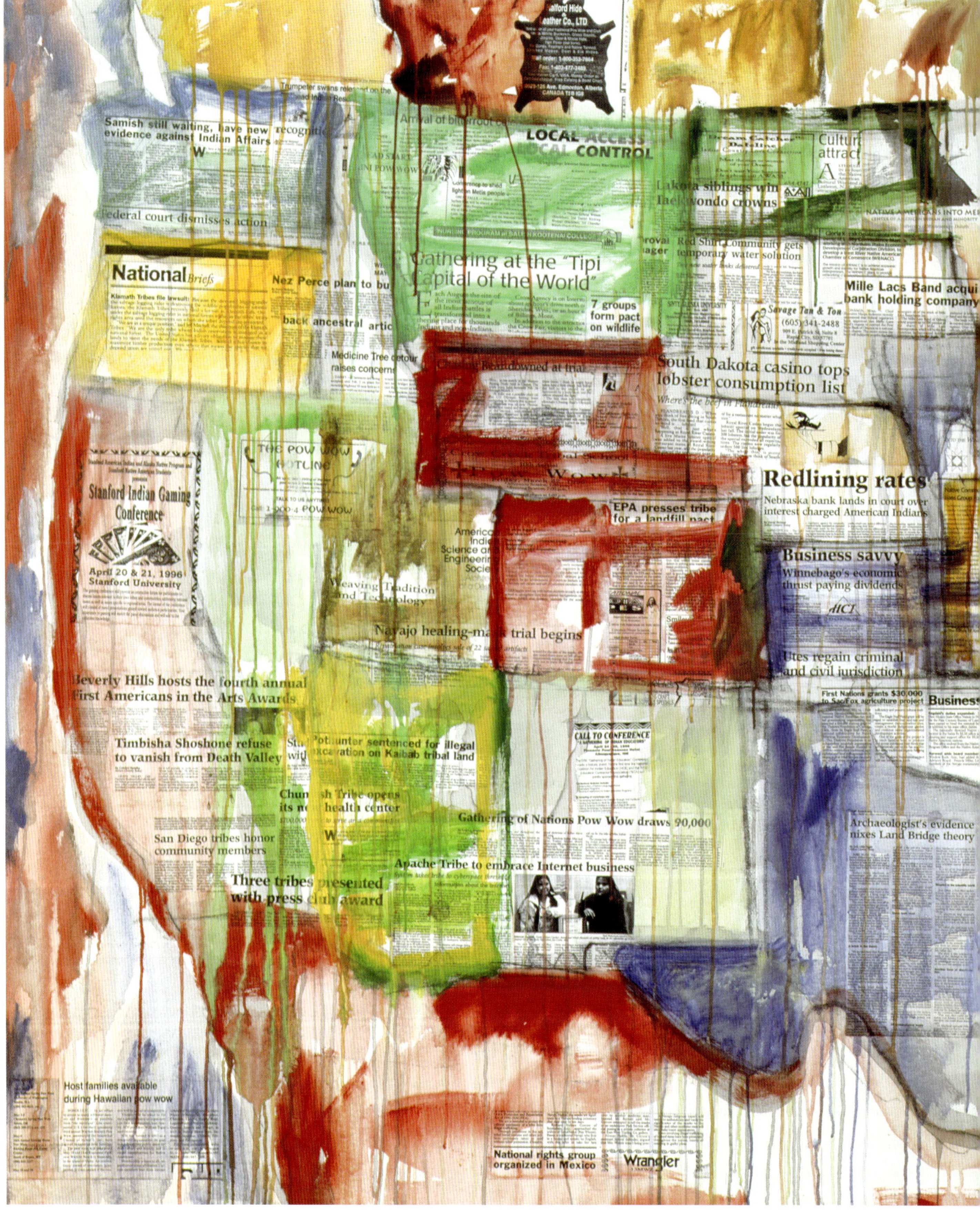
Samish still waiting, have new
evidence against Indian Affairs
Federal court dismisses action
LOCAL CONTROL
National Briefs
Klamath Tribes file lawsuit
Nez Perce plan to bu
back ancestral
Gathering at the "Tipi Capital of the World"
7 groups form pact on wildlife
Lakota siblings win
Red Shirt Community gets temporary water solution
Mille Lacs Band acqui
bank holding company
Savage Tan & Ton
Medicine Tree detour raises concerns
South Dakota casino tops lobster consumption list
THE POW WOW HOTLINE
Stanford Indian Gaming Conference
April 20 & 21, 1996
Stanford University
Redlining rates
Nebraska bank lands in court over interest charged American Indians
EPA presses tribe for a landfill pact
Business savvy
Winnebago's economic thrust paying dividends
Weaving Tradition and Technology
Navajo healing-ma trial begins
Utes regain criminal and civil jurisdiction
First Americans in the Arts Awards
First Nations grants $30,000 to Sac/Fox agriculture project
Timbisha Shoshone refuse to vanish from Death Valley
CALL TO CONFERENCE
Gathering of Nations Pow Wow draws 90,000
San Diego tribes honor community members
Archaeologist's evidence nixes Land Bridge theory
Apache Tribe to embrace Internet business
Host families available during Hawaiian pow wow
National rights group organized in Mexico
Wrangler

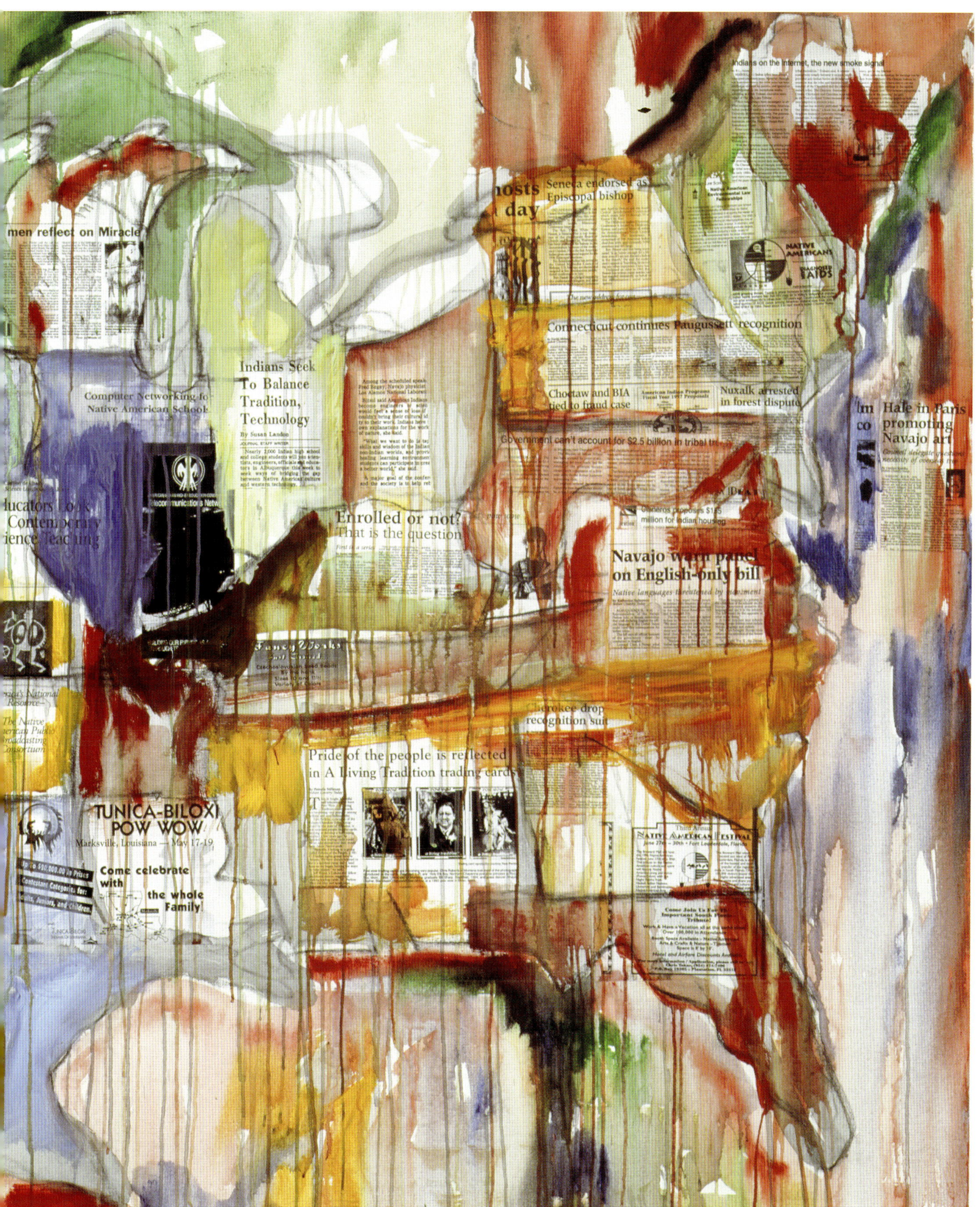

Jaune Quick-to-See Smith, Indian Country Today, *1996. Acrylic and collage on canvas. 60 × 100 in. Courtesy of the artist.*

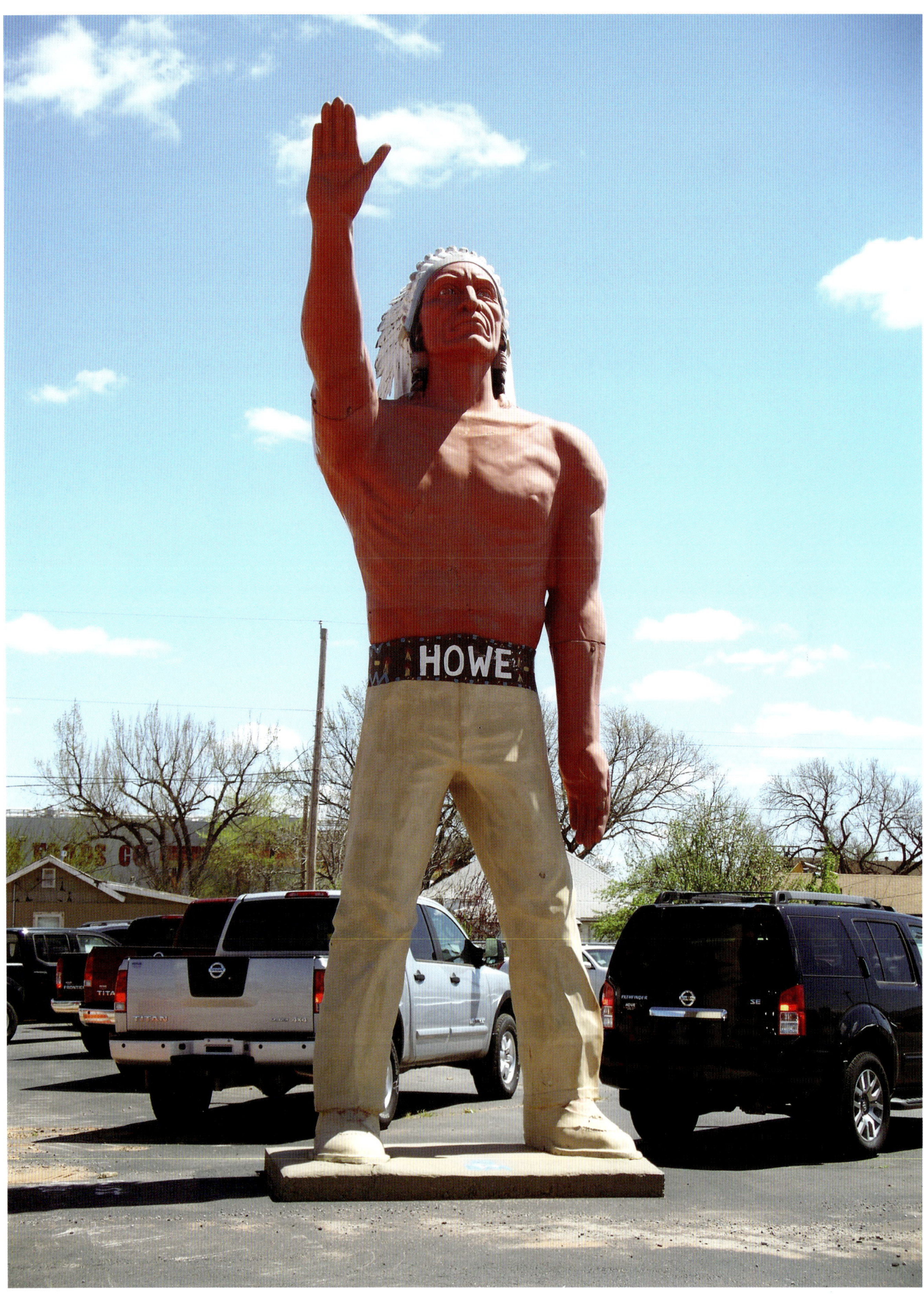
HOWE

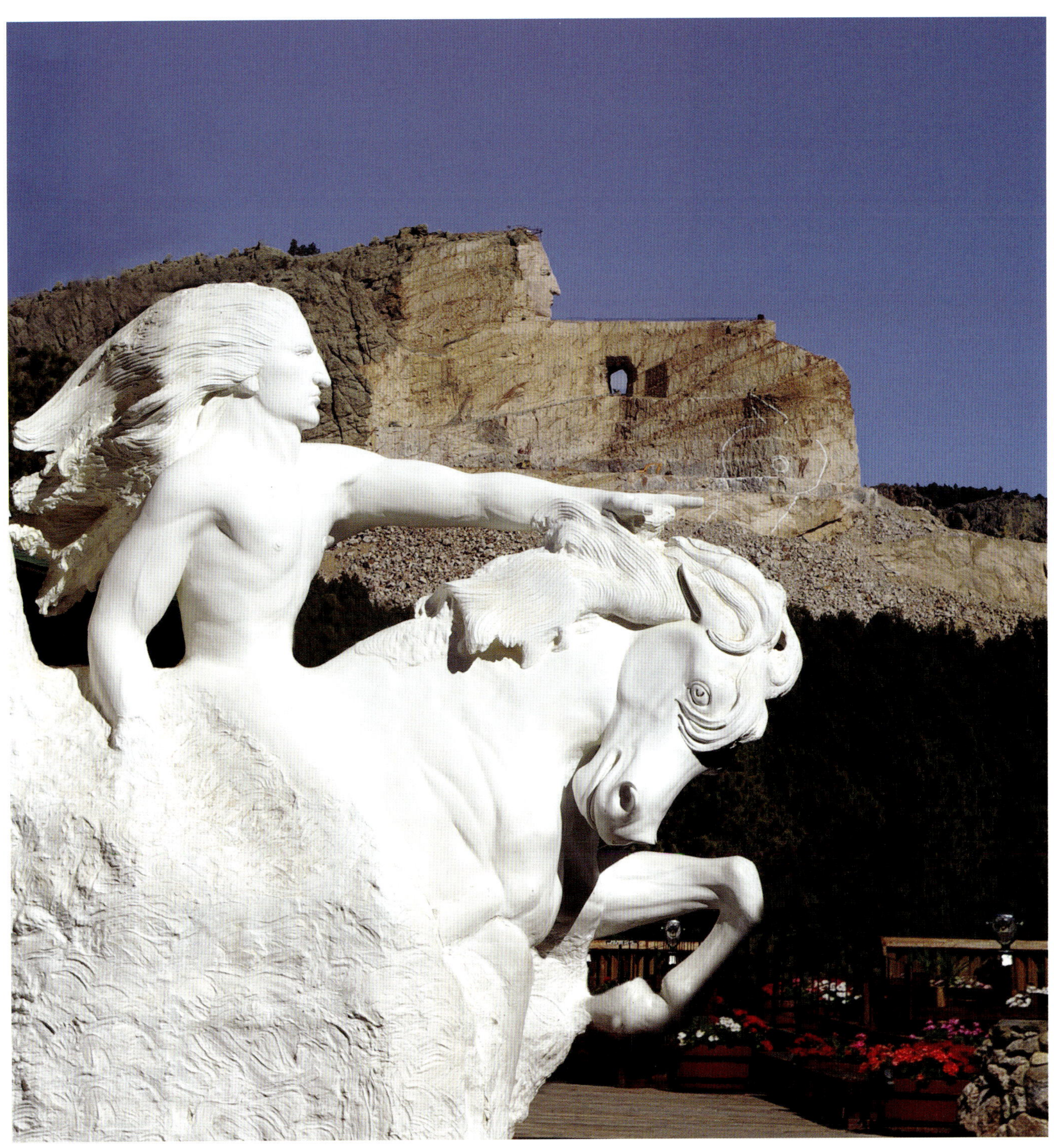

(facing page) *The Howe Chevrolet Nissan Indian in Clinton, Oklahoma, just off I-40. Photo by author, 2007.*

(above) Foreground*: The model for the Crazy Horse Memorial. The actual carving looms in the background. Situated near Mount Rushmore, the Crazy Horse Memorial is designed to offset and even over-write Mount Rushmore's more famous carvings of American presidents. Photo courtesy of the Crazy Horse Memorial.*

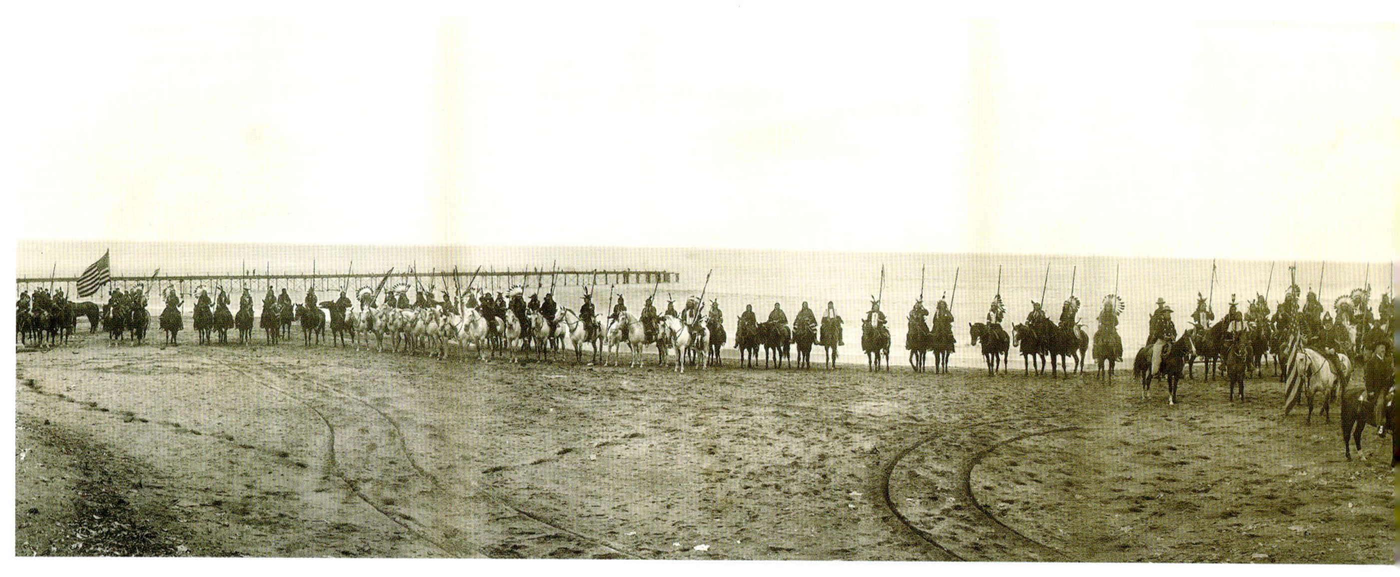

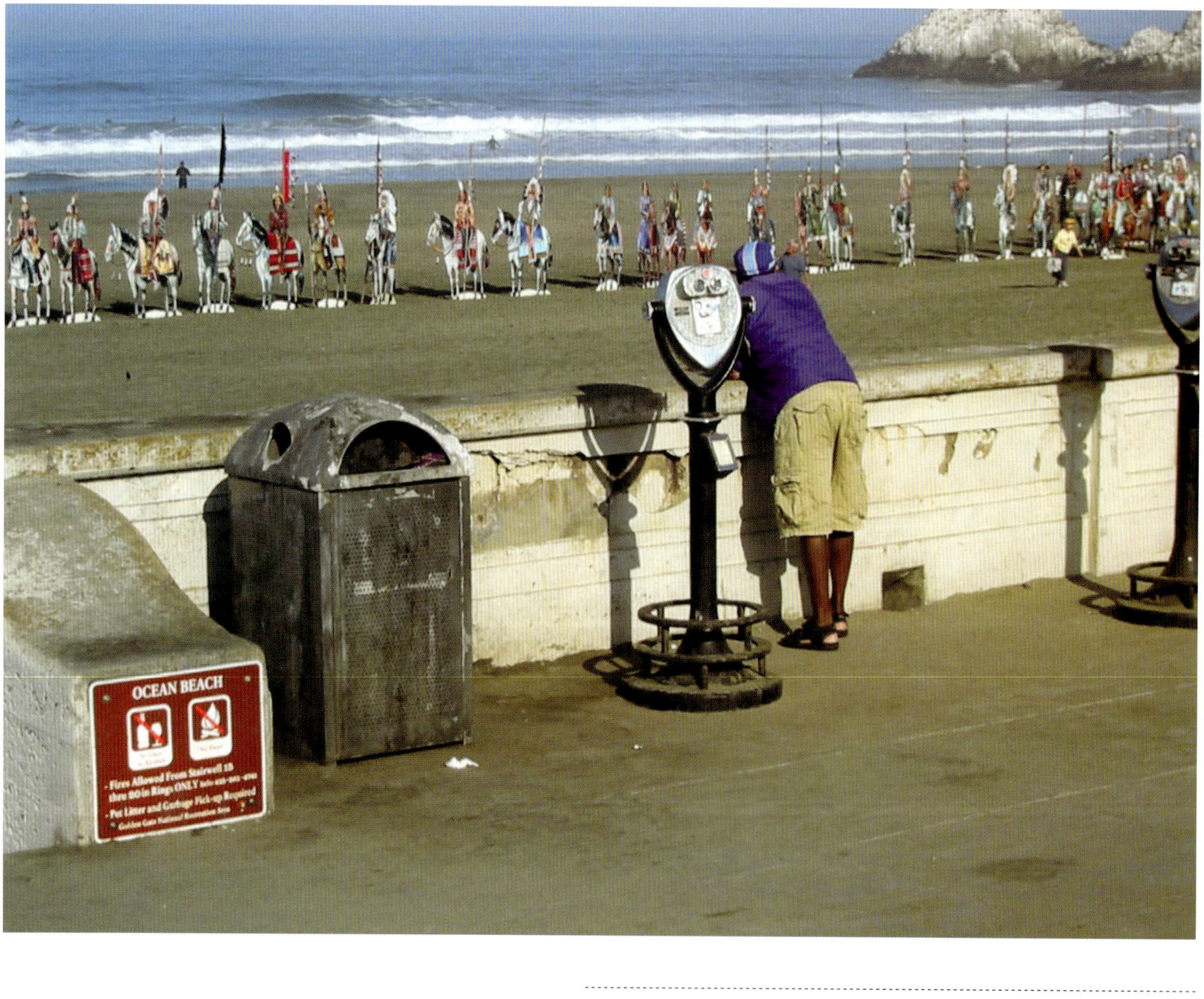

(top) *Buffalo Bill's Wild West show lined up along Ocean Beach, 1902. Courtesy of the Buffalo Bill Historical Museum.*

(bottom) *Panoramic view along Ocean Beach, California, of* Buffalo Bill and the Indians on the Beach, *by Thom Ross, 2008. Photo by author.*

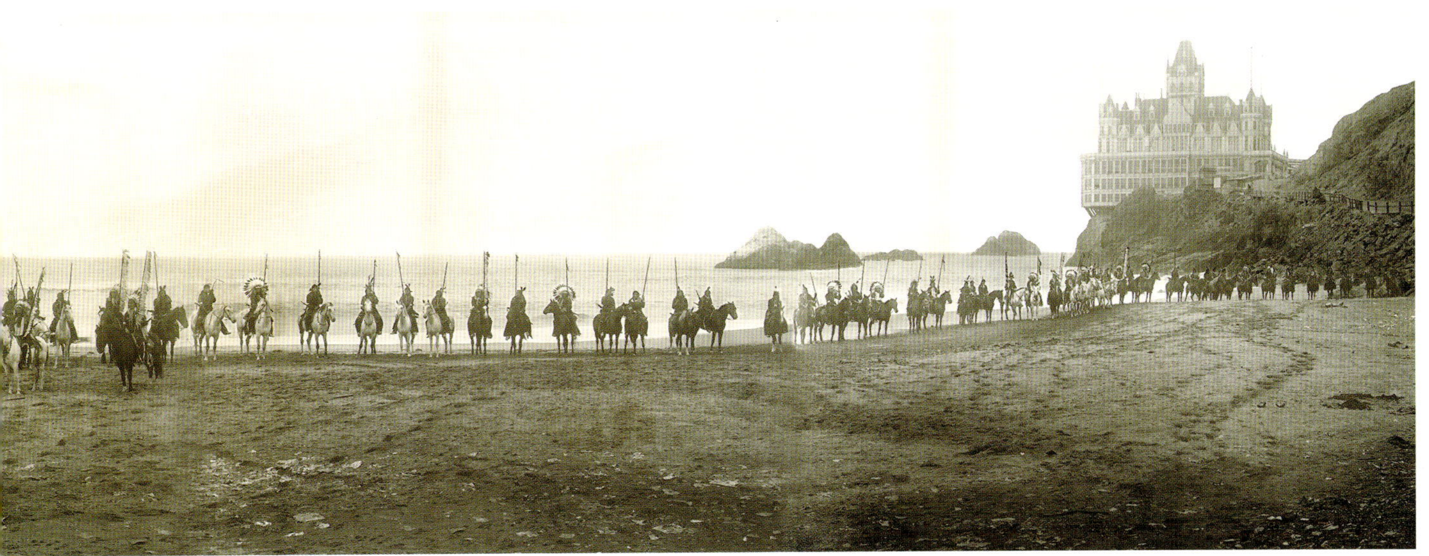

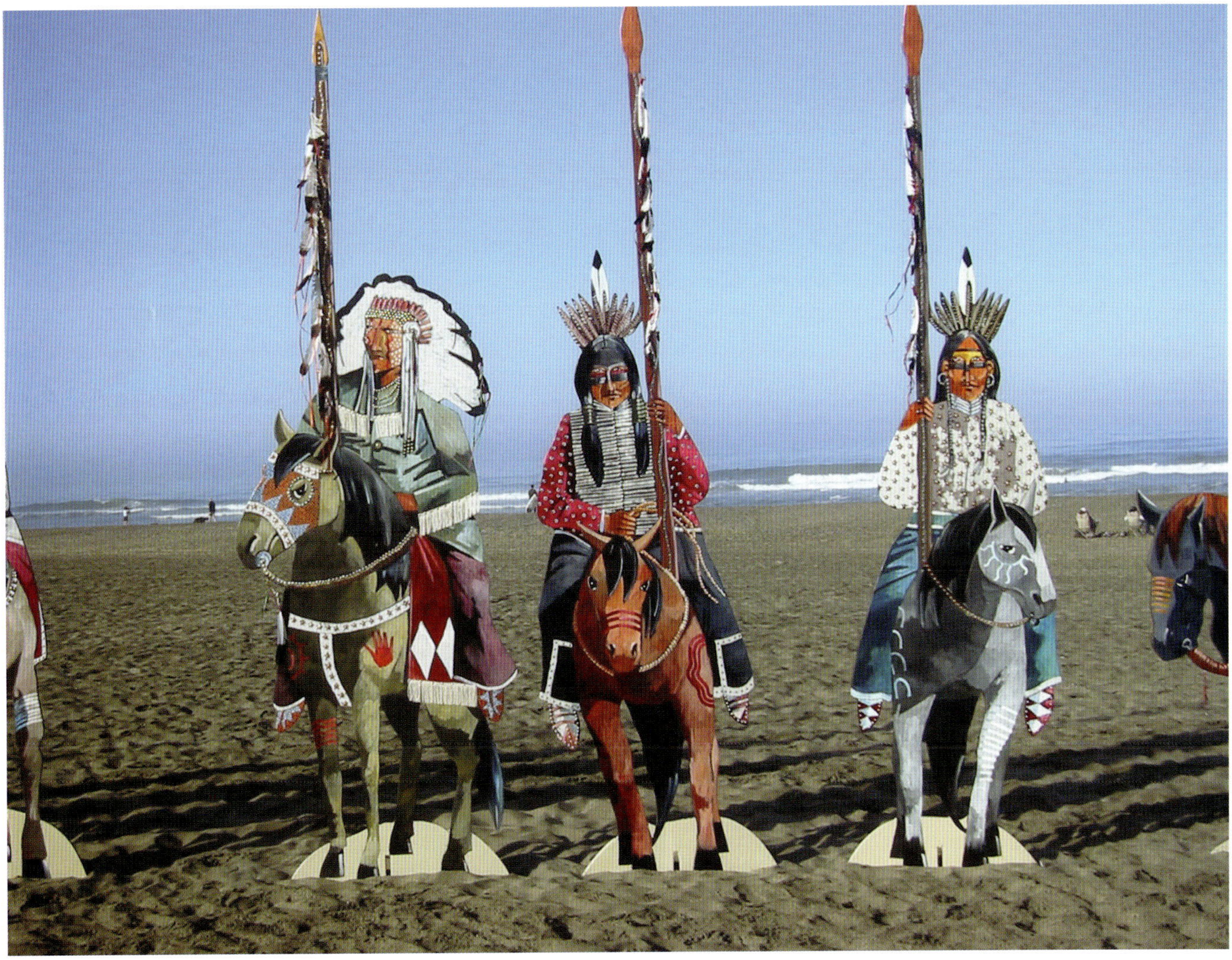

(**bottom**) *Three of the Indians in* Buffalo Bill and the Indians on the Beach, *by Thom Ross, 2008. Photo by author.*

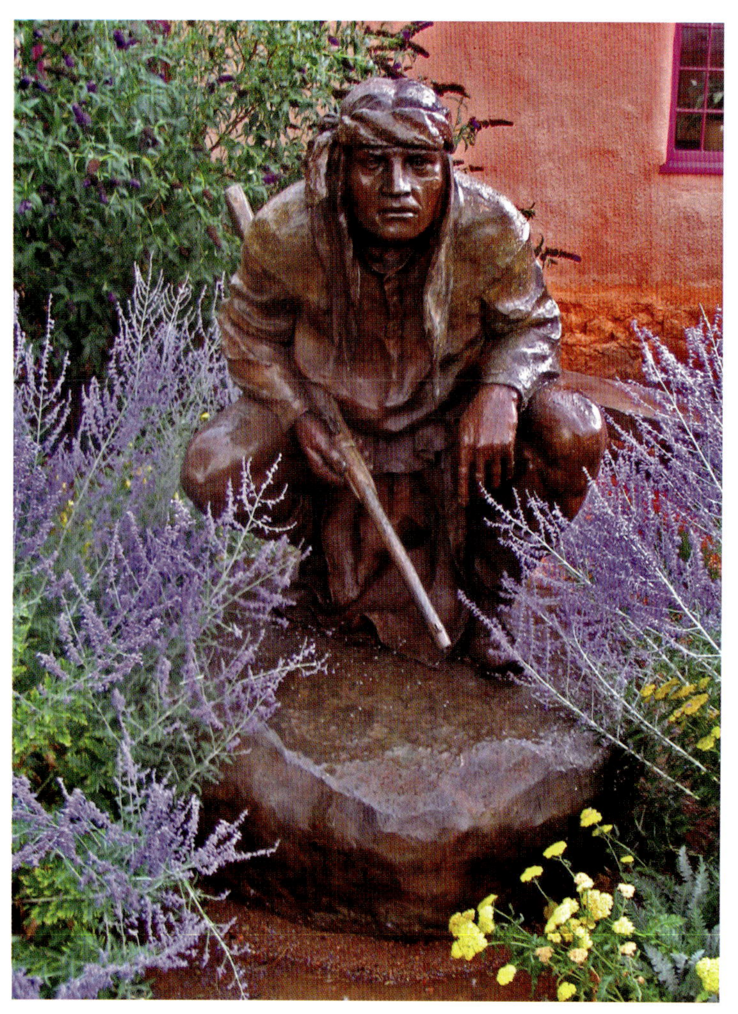

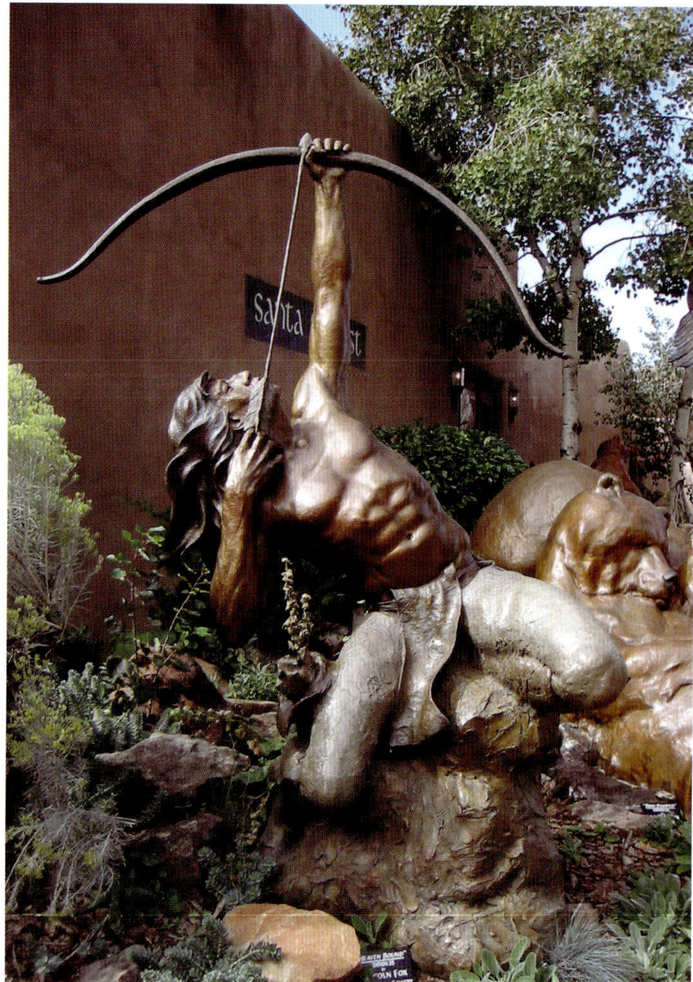

(left) *David Scott Rogers,* Chiricahua. *This sculpture is in a public courtyard in Santa Fe, New Mexico. Photo by author, 2008.*

(right) *Lincoln Fox,* Heaven Bound, *c. 2007. Bronze, 8 × 6 ft. This piece, one of an edition of thirty-five, by a sought-after Western sculptor retails for around $59,000. Photo by author.*

(facing page) *Allan Houser,* As Long as the Waters Flow, *1989. The sculpture stands outside the Oklahoma capitol. Photo by author.*

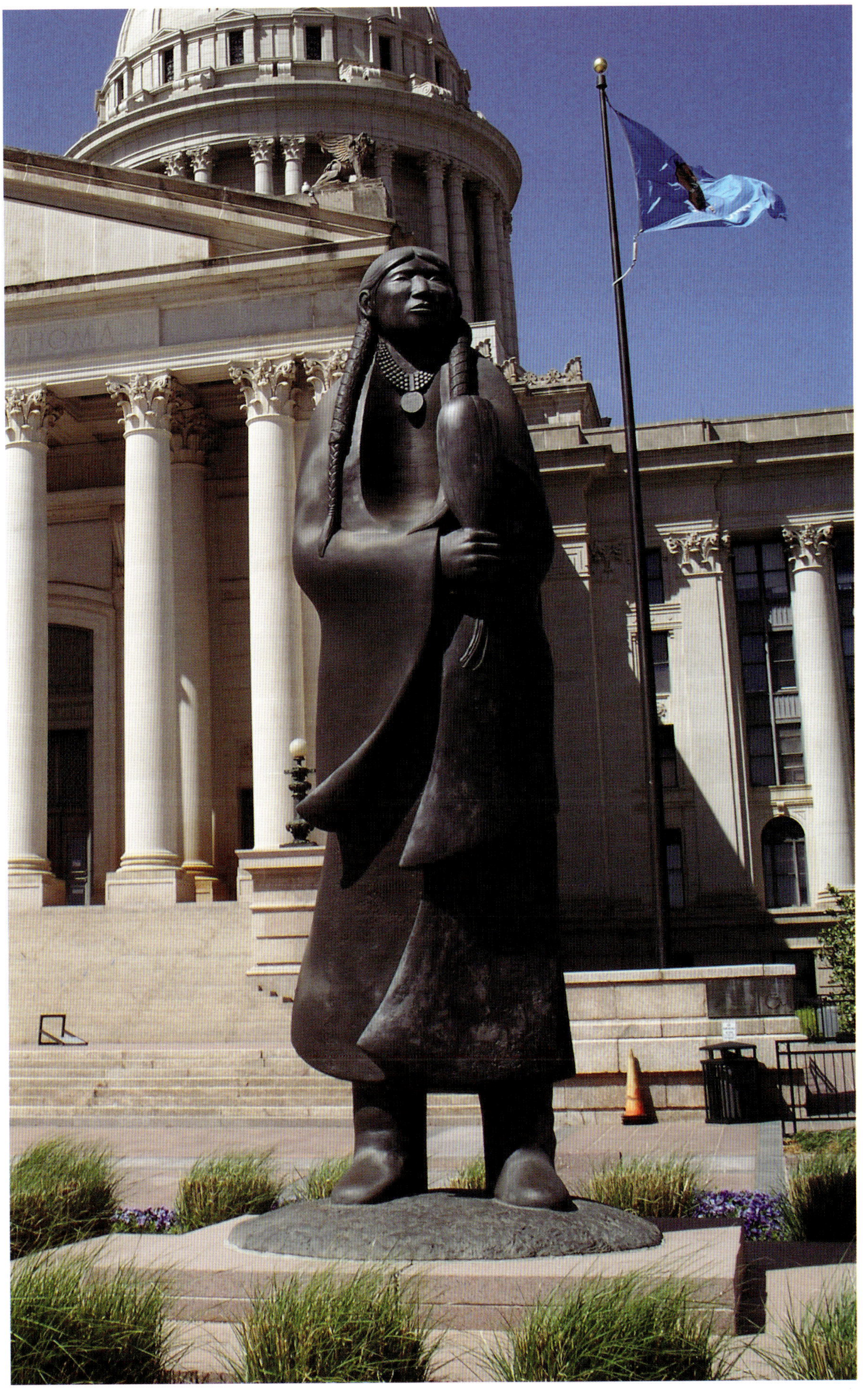
AHOMA

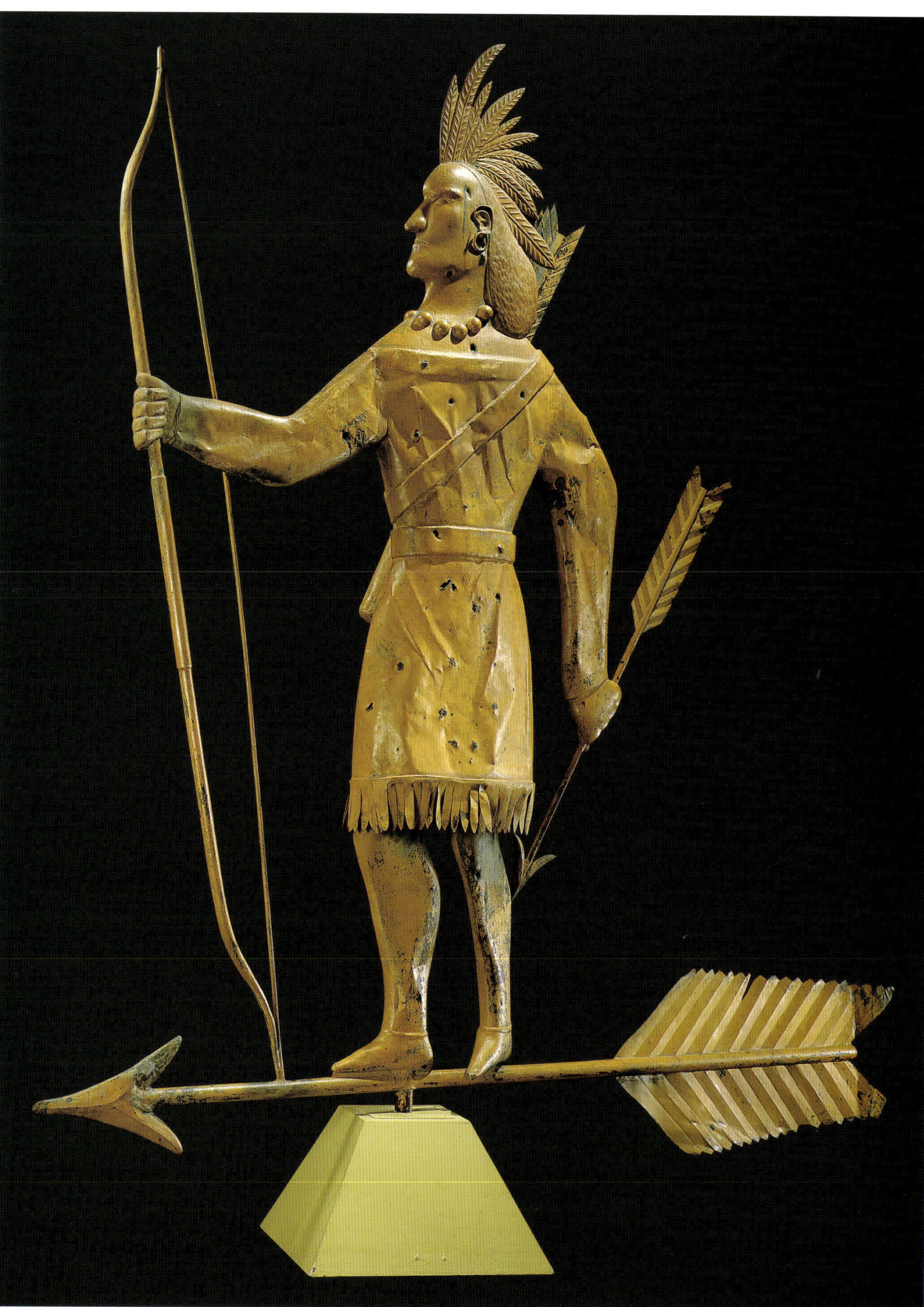

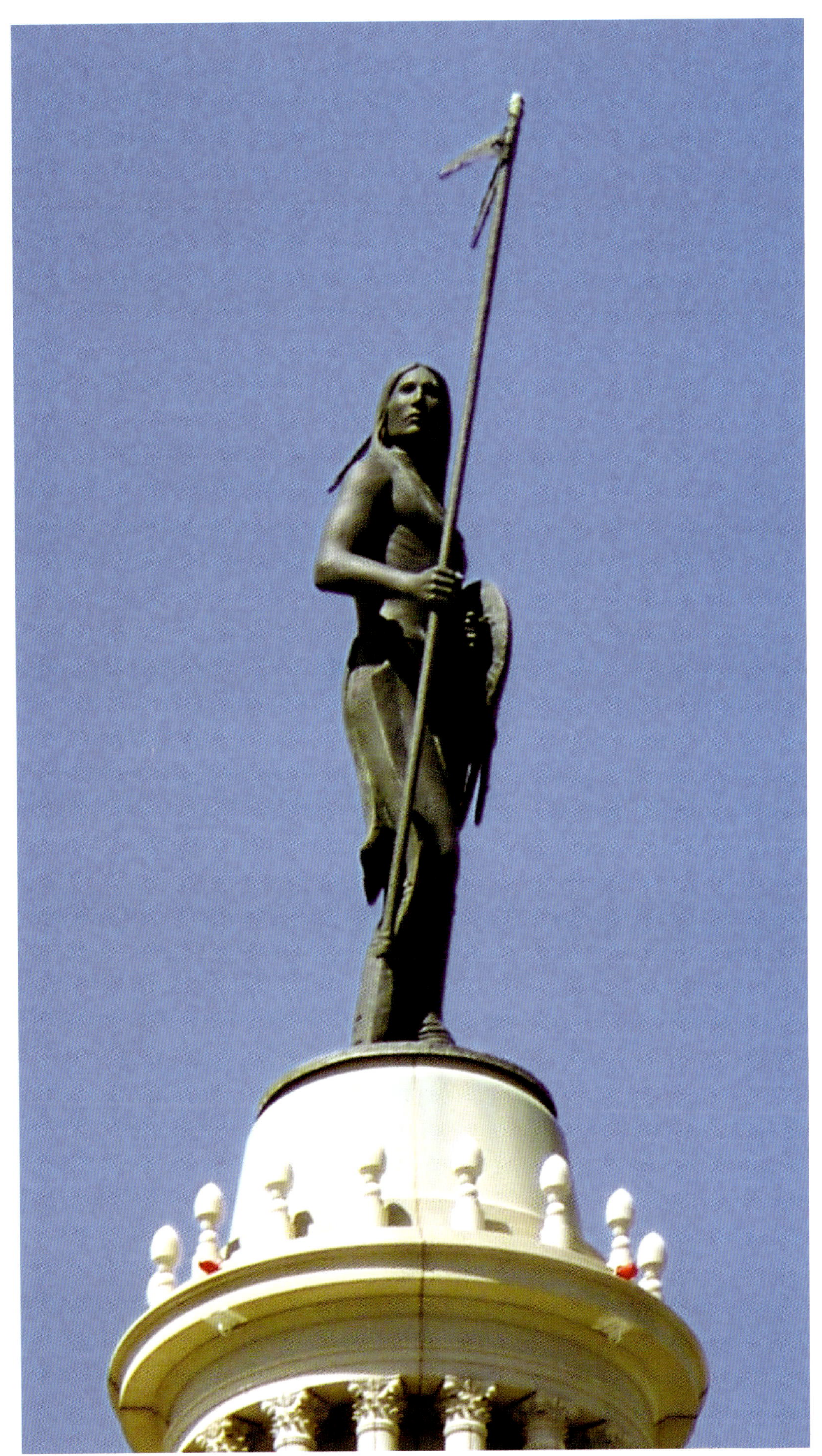

An Indian weather vane, left, *a common icon atop houses in colonial New England. From a formal perspective, there is a great deal of similarity between the weather vane (c. 1700) and* The Guardian, right. *Both figures are scantily clad, both hold weapons, both seem to stand at attention, both are more figural than abstract, and, of course, both were designed to sit on top of a structure. Weather vane image courtesy of the American Folk Art Museum. Author photo of* The Guardian, *2008.*

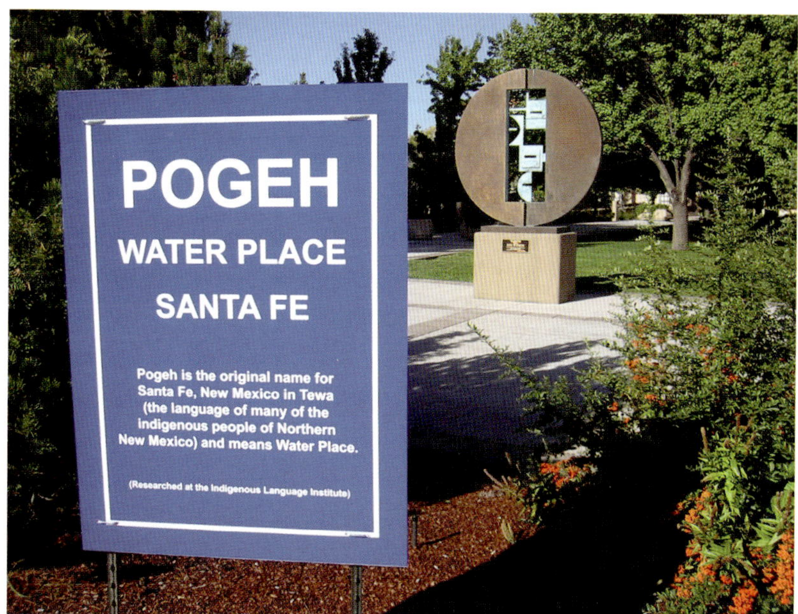

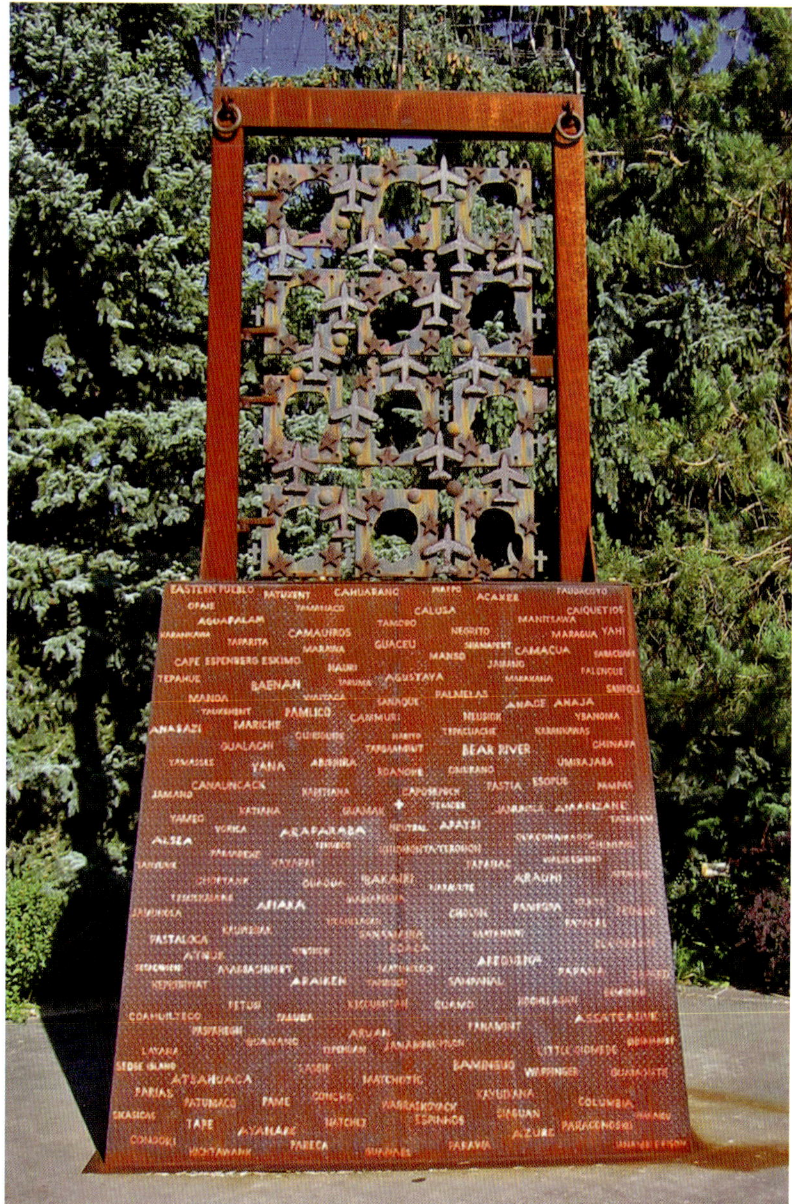

(top) Background*: Dan Namingha,* Passage, *1998. Bronze, 8 ft. in diameter. The sculpture is just outside the New Mexico capitol. Capitol Art Collection. Photo by author.*

(bottom) *Bob Houzous,* Gate/Negate, *2000. Steel and mixed media, 18 × 8 × 4 ft. The sculpture is in front of the capitol in Santa Fe. On loan to the Capitol Art Collection. Photo by author.*

(facing page) *Edgar Heap of Birds,* Walk to Oklahoma *and* Trail of Tears, 1836, *2005, part of the* Ocmulgee Sign Project, *Atlanta, Georgia. Metal sign panels, each 18 × 12 in. Photos courtesy of the artist.*

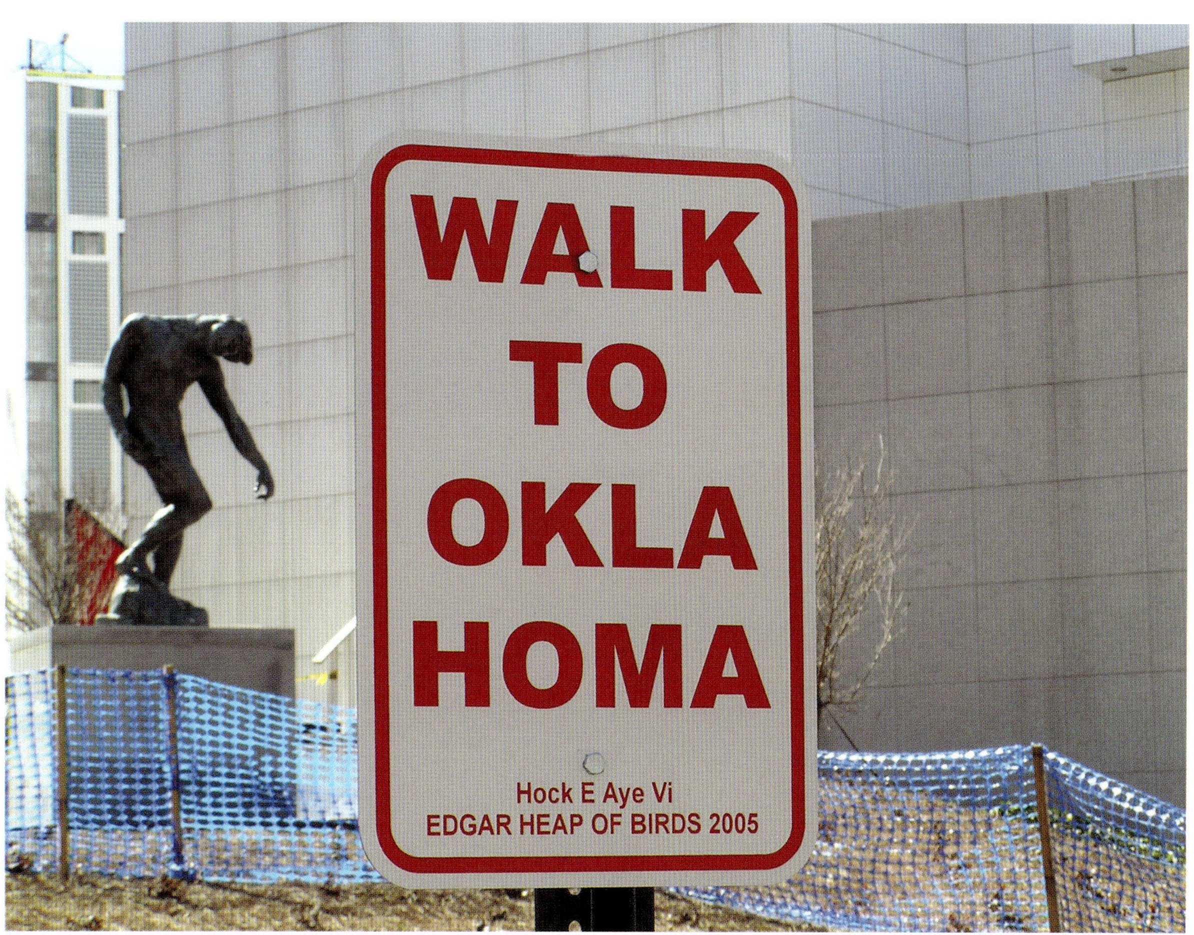
WALK
TO
OKLA
HOMA
Hock E Aye Vi
EDGAR HEAP OF BIRDS 2005

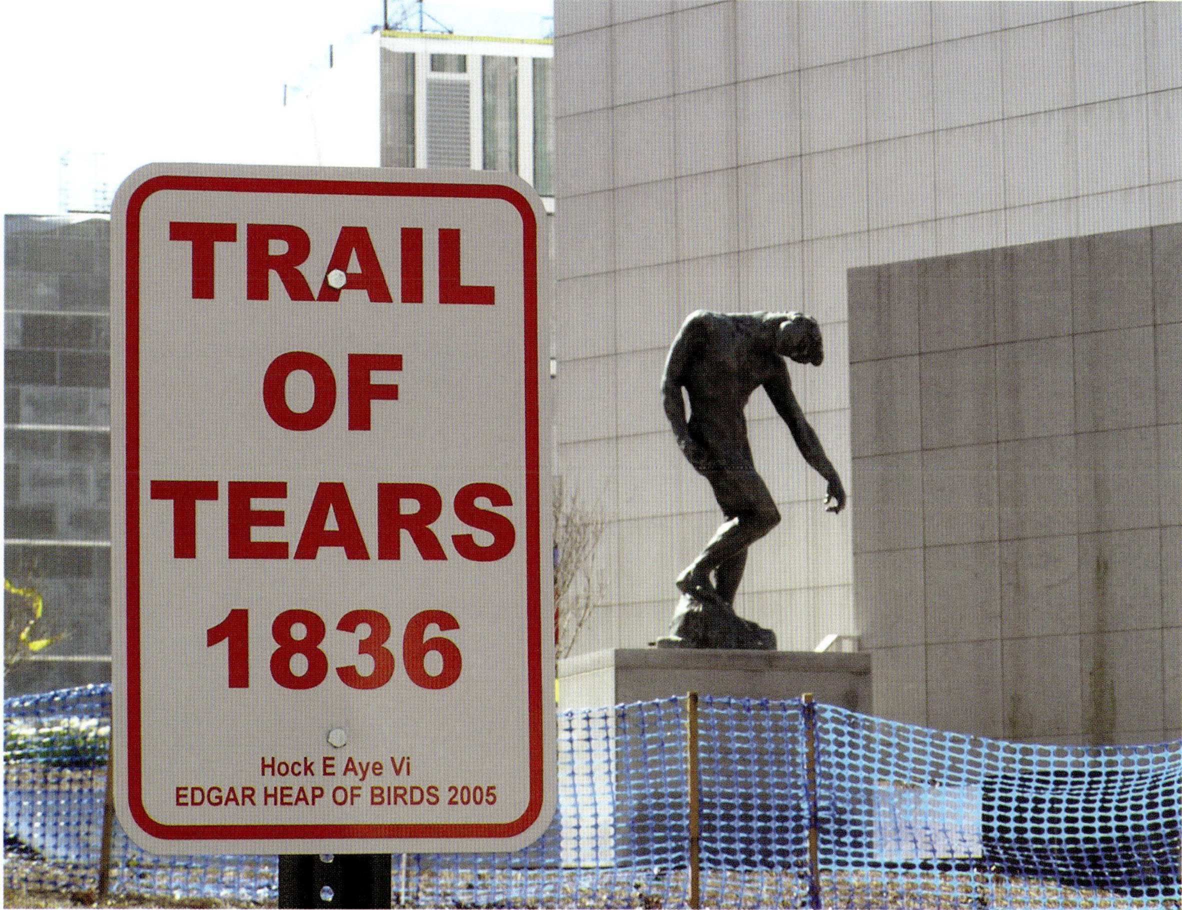
TRAIL
OF
TEARS
1836
Hock E Aye Vi
EDGAR HEAP OF BIRDS 2005

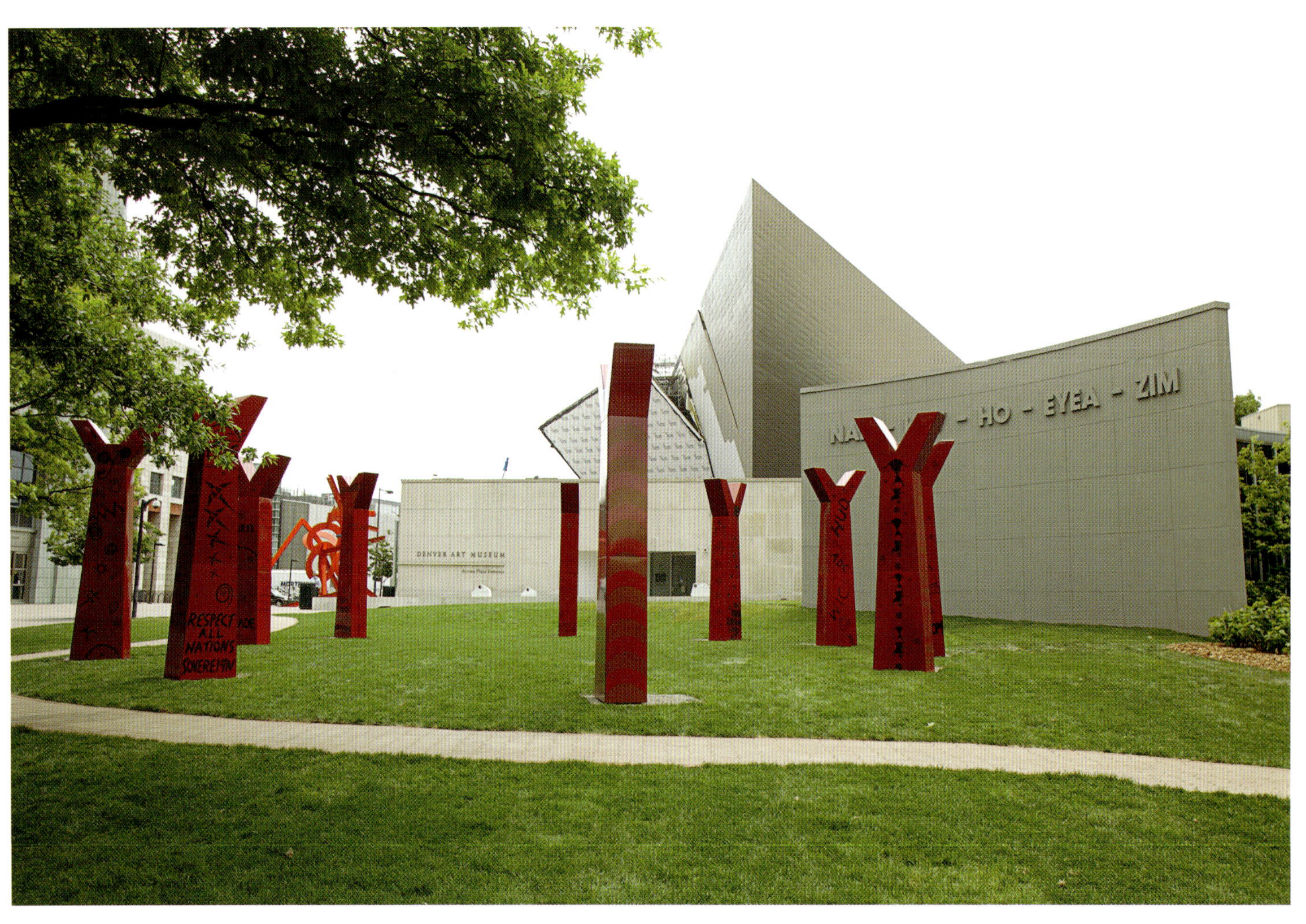

Edgar Heap of Birds, Wheel, *2007. Each "tree" is porcelain on steel, 144 × 24 × 12 in. The sculpture is installed outside the Denver Art Museum. Courtesy of the Denver Art Museum.*

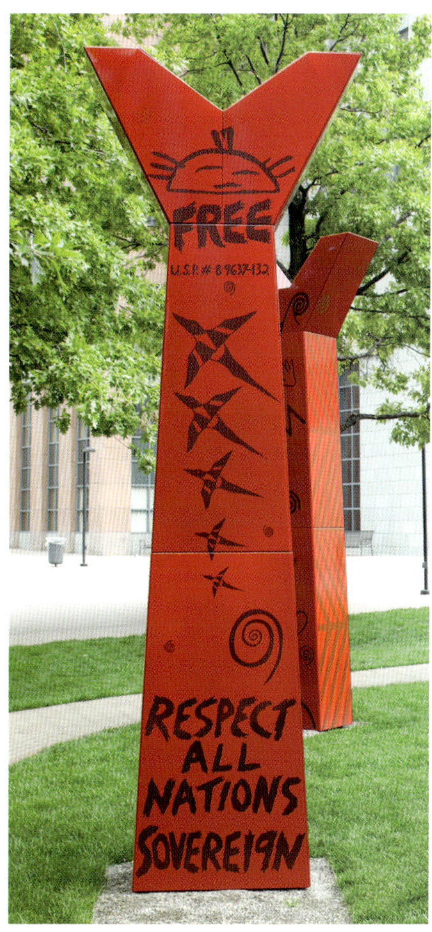
FREE
U.S.P. # 89637-132
RESPECT
ALL
NATIONS
SOVEREIGN

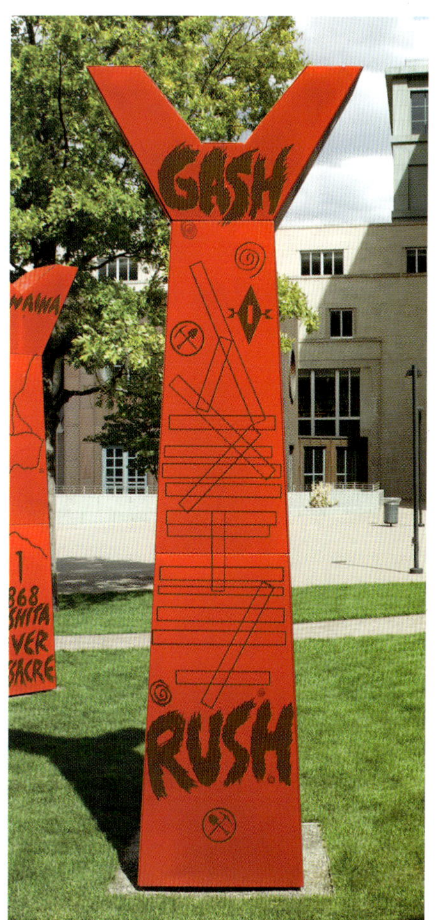
GASH
RUSH

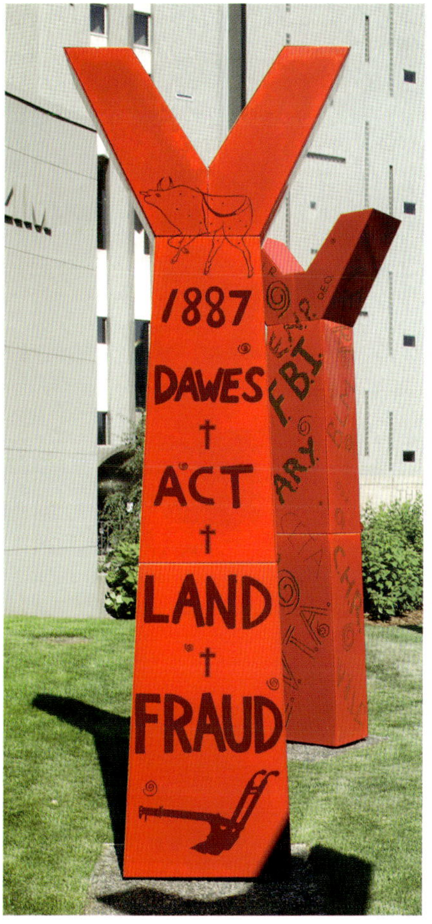
1887
DAWES
ACT
LAND
FRAUD
F.B.I.

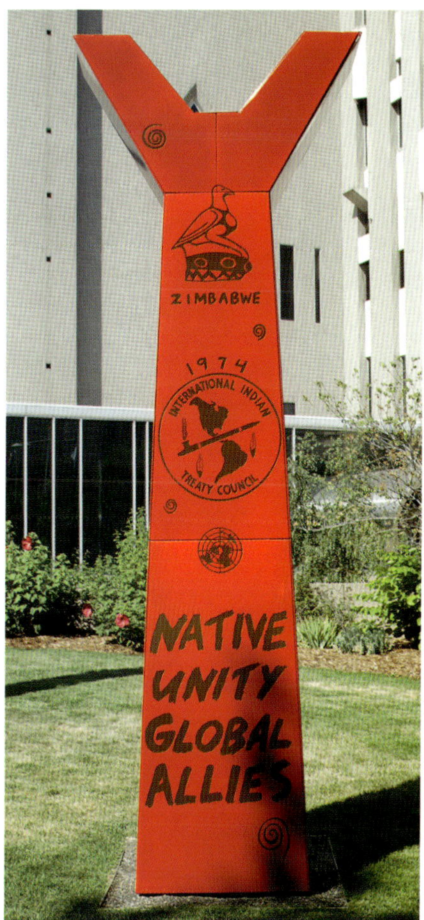
ZIMBABWE
1974
INTERNATIONAL INDIAN
TREATY COUNCIL
NATIVE
UNITY
GLOBAL
ALLIES

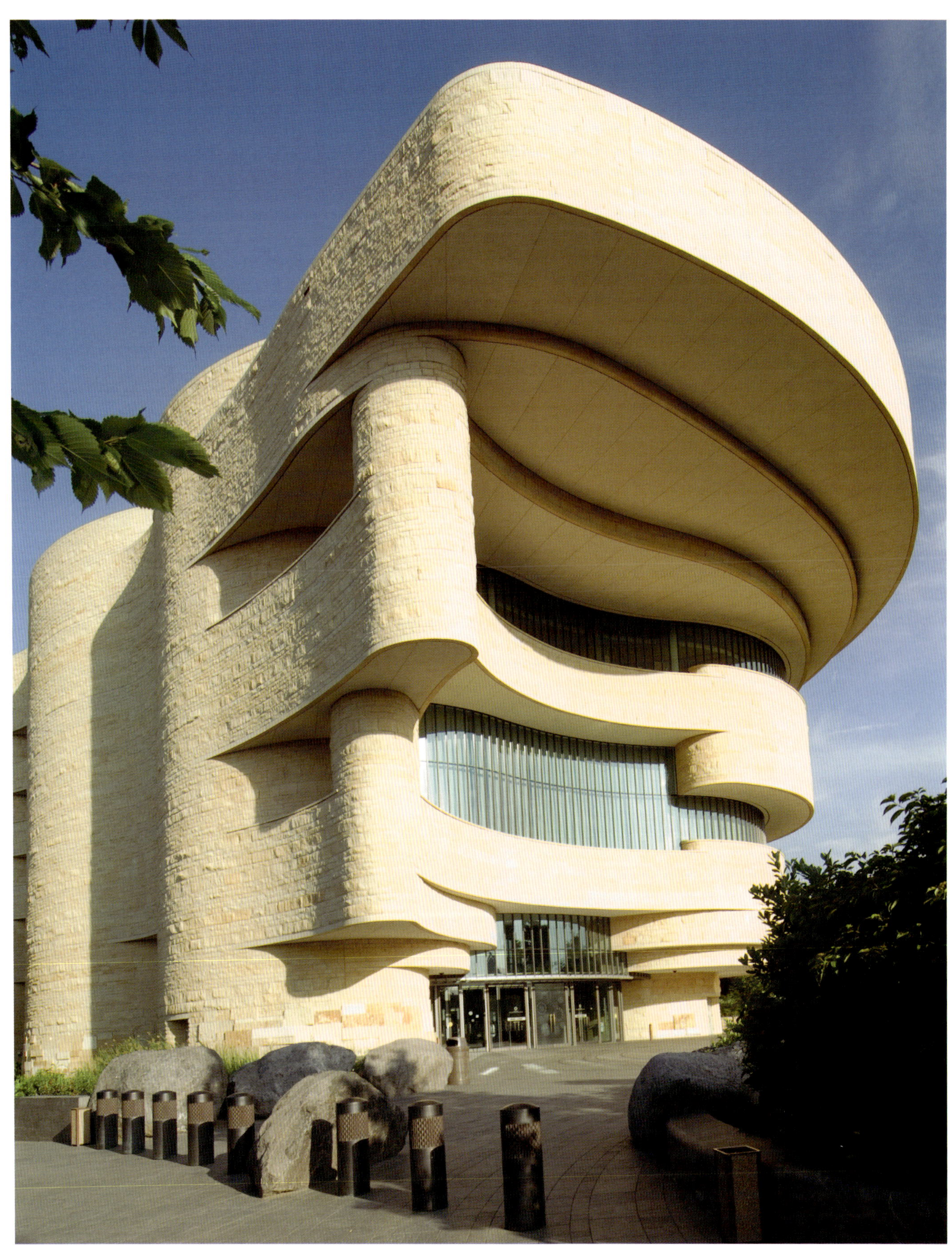

Main entrance of the NMAI with vertical tiers and a cantilevered roof. Courtesy of the National Museum of the American Indian, Smithsonian Institution. Photo by R. A. Whiteside.

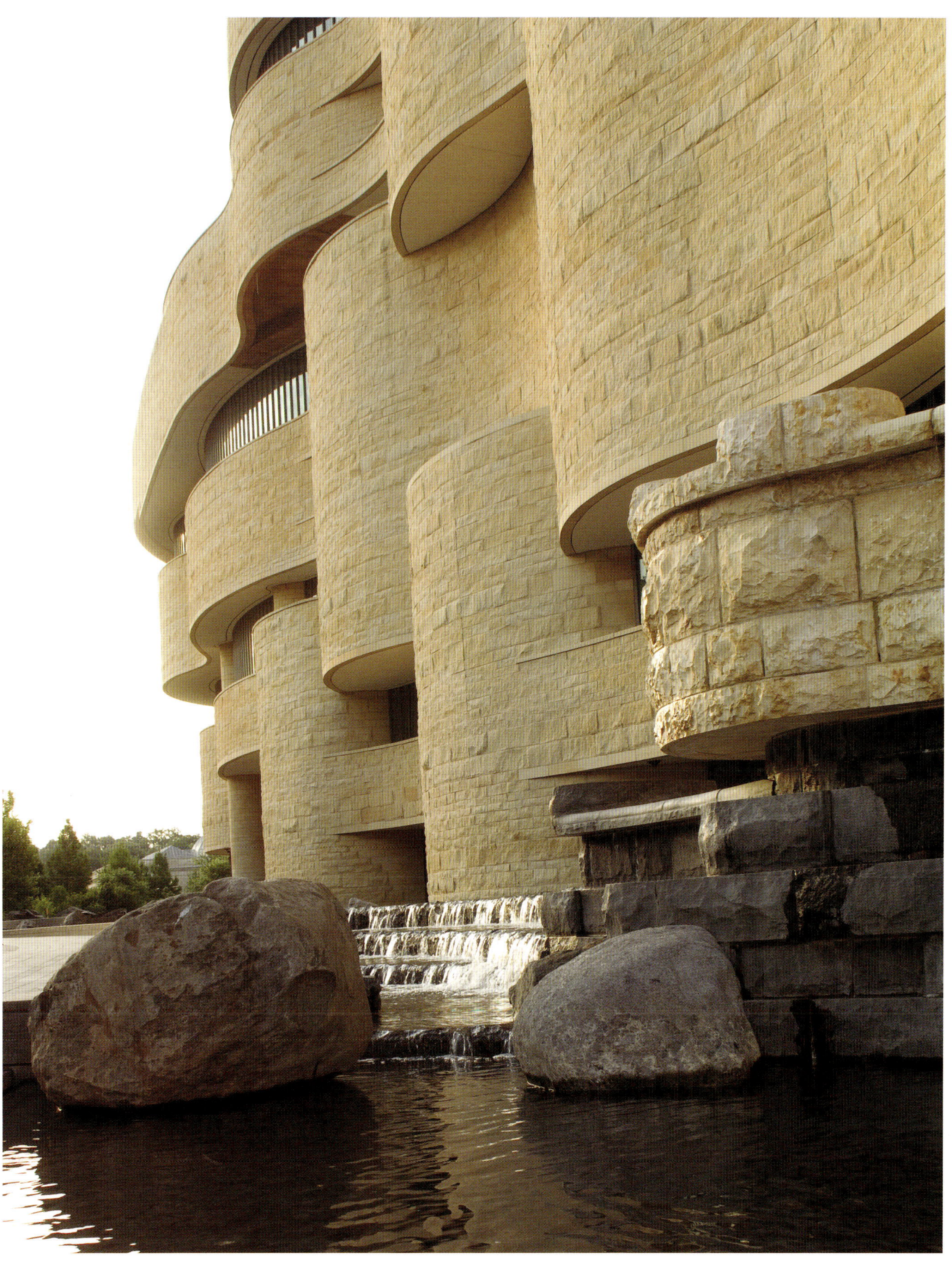

Curvilinear walls of the NMAI*, designed to resemble eroded rock carved by "wind and water." Courtesy of the National Museum of the American Indian, Smithsonian Institution. Photo by R. A. Whiteside.*

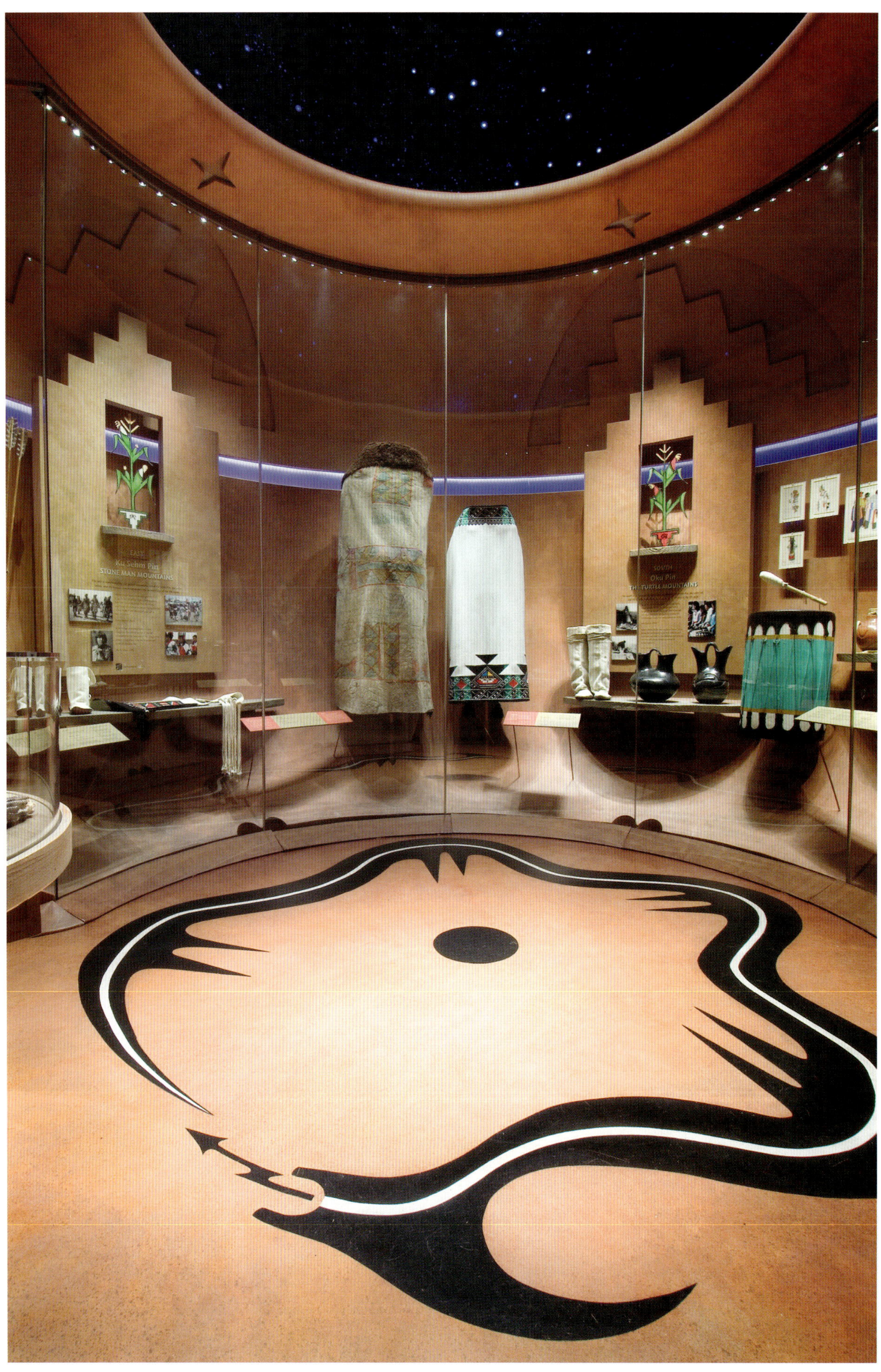
STONE MAN MOUNTAINS

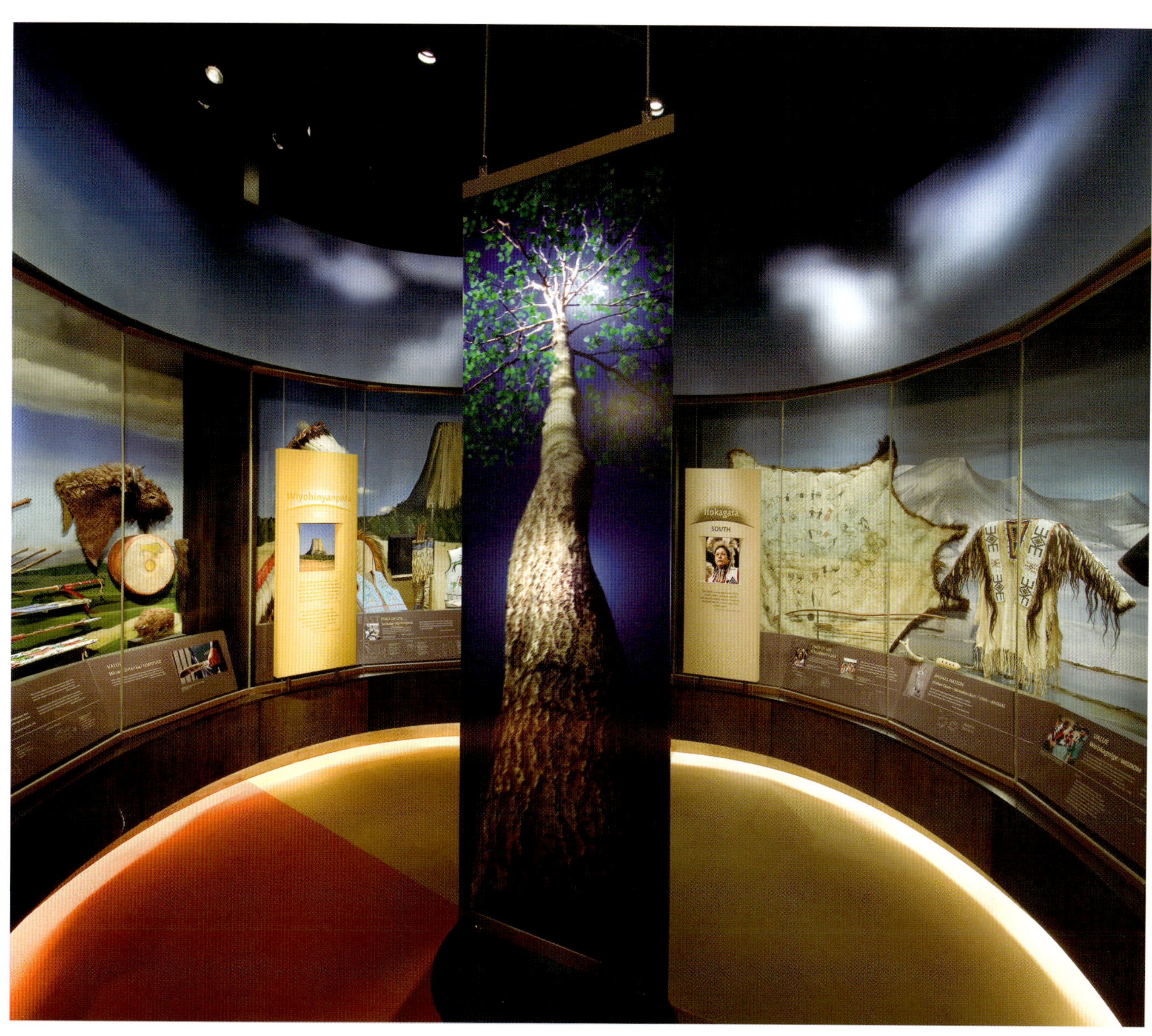

(facing page) *Santa Clara Pueblo Community section of "Our Universes." Courtesy of the National Museum of the American Indian, Smithsonian Institution. Photo by Walter Larrimore.*

(above) *Lakota Community section of "Our Universes." Courtesy of the National Museum of the American Indian, Smithsonian Institution. Photo by Walter Larrimore.*

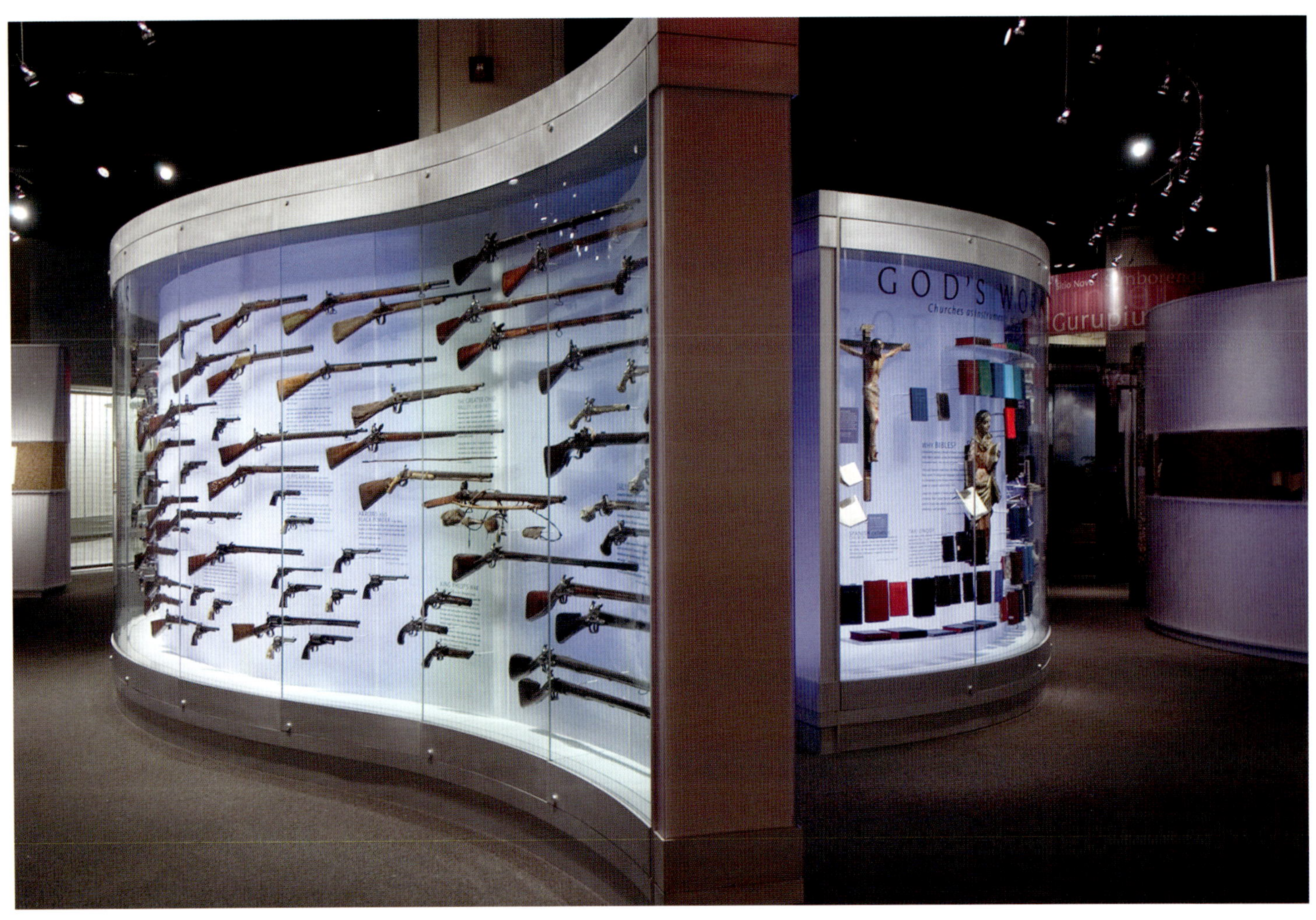

"Guns, Bibles, and Treaties," a three-paneled glass display in the "Our Peoples" exhibition. Courtesy of the National Museum of the American Indian, Smithsonian Institution. Photo by Katherine Fogden.

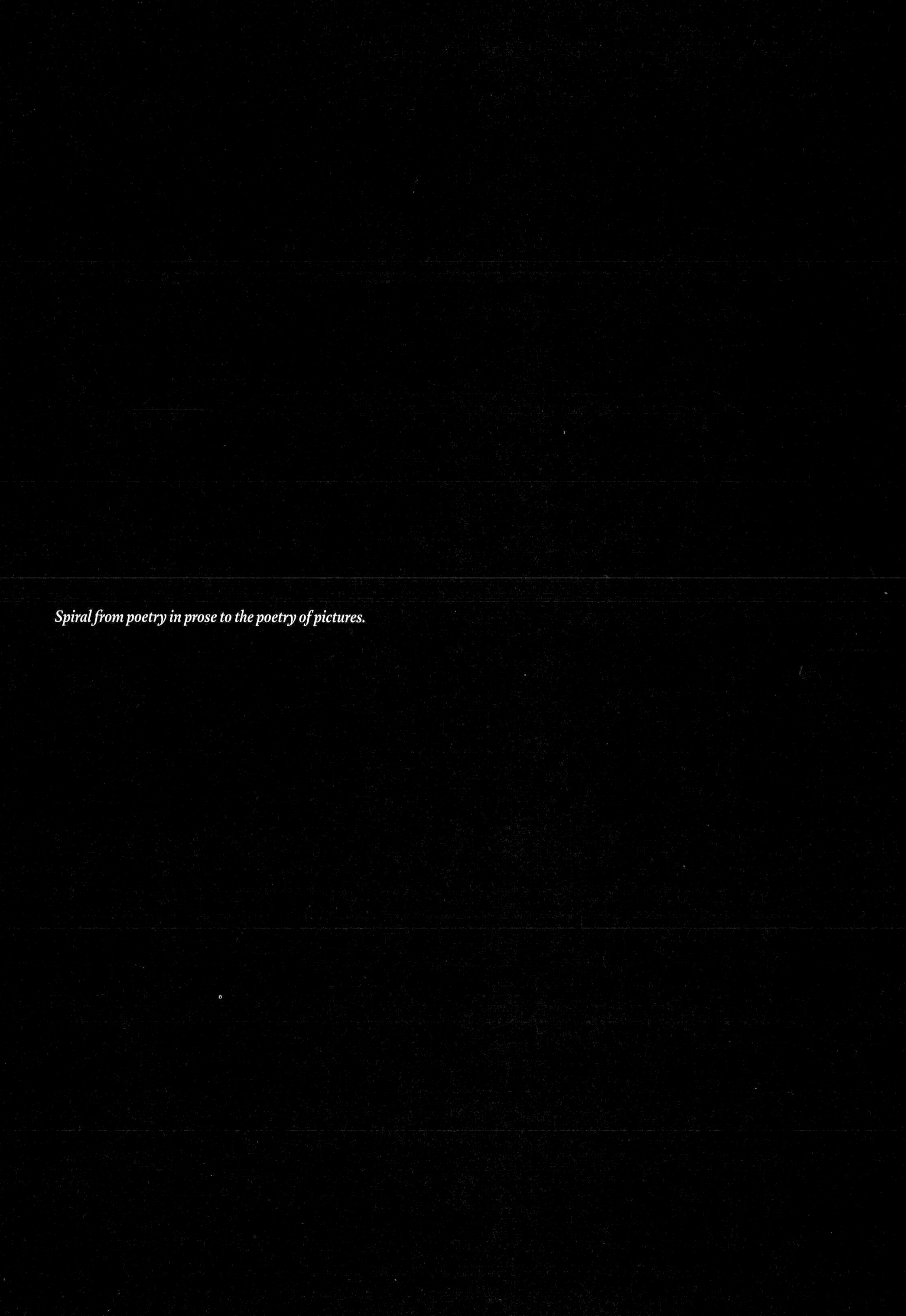

Spiral from poetry in prose to the poetry of pictures.

7. CELLULOID ALEXIE

POSTINDIANISM IN *SMOKE SIGNALS* AND *THE BUSINESS OF FANCYDANCING*

The only thing more pathetic than Indians on TV is Indians watching Indians on TV.

SHERMAN ALEXIE IS NOW, officially, an institution.

He is the most widely recognized Indian writer as well as one of the most visible figures in American Indian film. I write about him in three other chapters in this book; in fact, he may get more page time than anyone else. By no means is this intentional, but its reality speaks to the ubiquity of Alexie in the world of Native fiction, poetry, and film and to his importance in any discourse about indigenous aesthetics. His two film projects—*Smoke Signals* (1998), for which Alexie wrote the screenplay and served as coproducer, and *The Business of Fancydancing* (2002), for which Alexie was writer and director—both please and perturb, since they seem to embody two seemingly irreconcilable aspects of Native aesthetic discourse.

More than any other figure in Native literature and film, Alexie remains keenly aware of genre and generic forms; in fact, most of his work fits squarely within recognized genres: *Flight* (science fiction); *Reservation Blues* (historical fantasy); *Indian Killer* (murder mystery); and *The Absolutely True Diary of a Part-Time Indian* (young adult). Similarly, many of his short stories also fall within established genres, as do his poems, though in both cases, he riffs on those forms. His reworkings of the sonnet, for example, are among his most inventive texts, as are his tinkerings with what we might call a new subgenre—the Native American short story. Like his literary work, his cinematic work plays with genre in innovative ways. *Smoke Signals* puts an Indian twist on both the western and the road (or buddy) movie, while *The Business of Fancydancing* reads like a parody of what has become a genre that, almost predictably, appears once a month at every art house in the country: the "sensitive artist returns home" film. The movie also plays with the local-boy-makes-good genre and the ubiquitous coming-of-age love story. Participating in these genres is a form of engagement with their assumptions, techniques, and traditions, even though Alexie's refusal to succumb to their easy formulas, cultural predictability, and middle-class values remains a powerful form of resistance.

Alexie's interest in established genres, his eagerness to subvert those genres, and the aplomb with which he creates new Native narratives make him a model of what Gerald Vizenor calls a "postindian warrior." "Postindians," asserts Vizenor, "are the *new* storiers of conversions and survivance" (*Manifest Manners*, viii; emphasis added). Armed with the aesthetic arsenal of postmodernism, postindian warriors are those artists who replace tired, static, and reductionist representations of Indians with innovative, vibrant, self-determined versions of Indian agency. Whereas the traditional construct of "the Indian" remains, to Vizenor, an invention of the project of colonialism (what he dubs "manifest manners"), the postindian is the reinvention of Indianness as creative and alive. For Vizenor, these "postindian conversions are in the new stories of survivance over dominance . . . The postindian ousts the inventions with humor, new stories, and the simulations of survivance" (5). Though it takes different forms, a profound thematic connecting both films is the many ways, both large and small, Indians convert potential instances of dominance, as enacted by Hollywood formulas, into scenes of survivance. This chapter explores the ways Alexie incorporates and decommissions Hollywood's generic formulas as part of his larger postindian project of aesthetic activism.

Before I proceed, I should outline some terms and establish a critical context for the rest of this chapter. Throughout this chapter, I will use the term "genre." Though it shares both connotation and denotation with the genres I discuss in regard to poetry, here I refer specifically to movie genres. My working definition comes from Thomas Schatz's important book *Hollywood Genres*, which has become the keystone text for genre studies in film. For Schatz, "a genre film—whether a Western or a musical, a screwball comedy or a gangster film—involves familiar, essentially one-dimensional characters acting out a predictable story pattern within a familiar setting" (6). But that describes simply the mechanics of film genres. Tied up in the ideology of genres are larger implications about America, imperialism, race, class, high and low art, and what we might call a national narrative. "In their formulaic narrative process," writes Schatz,

> genre films celebrate the most fundamental ideological precepts—they examine and affirm "Americanism" with all its rampant conflicts, contradictions, and ambiguities. Not only do genre films establish a sense of continuity between our cultural past and present (or between present and future as with science fiction), but they also attempt to eliminate the distinctions between them. As social ritual, genre films function to stop time, to portray our culture in a stable and invariable ideological position. (31)

It is my contention that Alexie's films participate in generic formulas in order to interrogate Americanism's conflicts and contradictions and to comment on America's and Native America's cultural past and present.

However, Alexie's projects enact this not through stasis but through action—what I refer to as resistance in motion. Alexie's film projects move back and forth across genres, passing in and out of both public and private spaces. In his study *American Indian Literatures and the Southwest*, Eric Gary Anderson invokes the metaphor of migration to explore regional and cultural examples of resistance and displacement (3–9). My own notion of resistance in motion is influenced by Anderson, but whereas he focuses on geography, I focus on genre. In particular, I remain interested in the less terrestrial but equally well-mapped region of genre and how what Anderson would call a migratory resistance gets played out in the specific discipline of motion pictures. To me, Alexie's projects seek to subvert the positionality of traditional film genres by imploding their boundaries while exploiting their symbolic discourse. Through this participation in and rejection of movie genres, Alexie enacts his own brand of postindianism. "The postindian," according to Vizenor, "ousts the inventions with humor, new stories, and the simulations of survivance" (*Manifest Manners*, 5). For Vizenor and for Alexie, Indian aesthetic sovereignty advances survivance over dominance, autonomy over colonialism, and invention over incorporation. Let us be clear: Alexie did not make either movie with a copy of *Manifest Manners* on his lap, but if we read both films through the lens of postindianism, we can see the many provocative instances of new stories, the simulations of survivance, and especially the humor that characterize Alexie's projects.

One of Alexie's most convincing examples of autonomy and invention lies in his play with the book-to-film genre, the most beloved of all genres by English professors. *Smoke Signals* is the offspring of a short story from *The Lone Ranger and Tonto Fistfight in Heaven*, while *The Business of Fancydancing* was birthed from a collection of poems of the same title, with genes from other poems and short stories thrown in for good measure. It will not be the purview of this study to evaluate the success or failure of the book-to-film adaptation process; that seems to me only minimally rewarding or useful. However, I will discuss now and then how the books and the movies contribute to the larger notion of intertext. Another topic I try to avoid is the issue of representation, since that malady has been well treated by a number of studies.[1] In fact, my main criticism of such studies is that they do a fine job of talking about the transgressions of white directors, but they tend to ignore Indian directors. My goal is to take up the complicated and neglected project of making sense of films made by Indians. No other figure has been more successful in this regard than Alexie. Since his work projects Native storytelling on a wide screen, it deserves critical attention commensurate with its ambition. This chapter hopes not only to unpack Alexie's films but also to show why we might view them as activist texts within the larger frame of Native aesthetic discourse.

Humor, New Stories, and the Simulations of Survivance: *Smoke Signals*

Adapted and written by Alexie and directed by Chris Eyre, *Smoke Signals* (1998) marketed itself as the first feature film written, directed, and produced by American Indians. Though technically an independent film, almost everything about it was pitched to a mainstream audience, such as the decision to frame it as a comedy. Miramax, the film's distribution company, was petrified that audiences would be turned off by another dire Indian saga, à la *Dances with Wolves*.[2] For the most part, it worked. *Smoke Signals* grossed nearly seven million dollars, a huge success by the standards of art and independent films—especially since it cost just less than two million dollars to produce. The film won a special Audience Award at the Sundance Film Festival as well as prizes at the American Indian Film Festival, the Taos Talking Pictures Festival, and the Tokyo International Film Festival. The National Board of Review and the Florida Film Critics Circle also gave *Smoke Signals* awards. As Angela Aleiss notes, however, *Smoke Signals* garnered only a fraction of the viewers or attention attracted by Hollywood westerns.

It is worth asking, though, whether box-office receipts are truly the best barometer of success. If we judge films like *Smoke Signals* by the value system of Hollywood commercialism, aren't we situating the film within the very value system that Alexie's films challenge? When "placed in the context of the long and colonizing history of American Indians and film," observes Amanda J. Cobb (Chickasaw), *Smoke Signals* "is an achievement *because it exists at all*" ("This Is What It Means to Say," 206). For Cobb, *Smoke Signals* "is a masterstroke for Eyre and Alexie because they challenge popular culture by creating popular culture, using the very medium that has arguably threatened Native American sovereignty the most—the Hollywood film" (208). Cobb, like Vizenor, correctly identifies film (and in particular, the western) as a nefarious medium when it comes to Indian sovereignty.

Vizenor, in particular, is unequivocal here: "The Western movies, of course, are not cultural visions, but the vicious encounters with the antiselves of civilization, the invented savage" (*Manifest Manners*, 7). To be sure, the on-screen representation of Indians creates both a caricaturization and an absenteeism that makes it nearly impossible for non-Indians to see Indians as part and parcel of themselves, but by now, most viewers of cinematic texts have either been told that classic Hollywood portrayals of Indians are inaccurate, or they have come to realize it on their own.[3]

Worse, in my estimation, than the continued existence of westerns is the present absence of what Vizenor calls the "new stories," the narratives of survivance created by Indians and delivered by Indians. In her study of Indian film and video, Beverly Singer underscores the significance of self-determination. "What really matters to us," Singer asserts, "is that we be able to tell our own stories in whatever form we chose" (*Wiping the War Paint off the Lens*, 2). *Smoke Signals* works because it connects the opportunity and means of self-narration with self-determination; it explores how storytelling becomes a form of sovereignty. *Smoke Signals* is important not simply because it exists, but also because it stands as the most popular, most widely received example of Indians telling their own stories—all within the very genre that has sought for decades to diminish those stories.

Part of self-storytelling is un-storytelling. One of the things *Smoke Signals* does well is to undo popular notions of celluloid Indians while simultaneously calling attention to some of the contemporary issues noncelluloid Indians face. This film, then, does double duty: it expunges the traces of the western Indian while providing some insight into what motivates a few Indians on a particular reservation in Idaho. The Indians in question, Victor Joseph (Adam Beach [Salteaux]) and Thomas Builds-the-Fire (Evan Adams, [Salish]), are young Coeur d'Alenes who reside on the reservation. Probably around eighteen or twenty years old, the men don't seem to have any real problems—they don't drink, they are not criminals—but they don't really have much of a life either. Apparently, they don't have jobs, and they mostly just help out their guardians (for Victor, his mom; for Thomas, his grandmother). One day, though, they get word that Victor's father, Arnold, (Gary Farmer), who had abandoned Victor and his mother many years previous, has died outside of Phoenix. Full of confusion and questions and with virtually no money, the boys set out via bus to Arizona to retrieve Arnold and his effects. From here, the film turns into a classic buddy movie—road movie as their first real journey off the reservation becomes, for both Victor and Thomas, a larger journey of self-discovery and Indian identity. And, as I discuss later, *Smoke Signals* also plays with the semiotics of westerns—a genre ripe for the right kind of indigenous deconstruction—but for now, suffice it to say that as interested as Alexie might be in deconstructing the "simulations of dominance," he is just as interested in telling new stories, in helping construct some of the seminal visual simulations of Indian survivance.

As I suggested previously, one reason *Smoke Signals* connected with audiences was because of its mainstream appeal. The production qualities are first rate, the performances impress, and the movie engages its audience through charming self-deprecation and good humor. This last point distinguishes it from *Naturally Native* and *Skins*, especially in regard to Indian identity. Interestingly, the most serious subplots tend not to revolve around Indian-specific issues. Although alcoholism and poverty work their way into scenes now and then, the most intense parts of the film transcend race and class. Fathers leave in all cultures; there is abuse in all cultures; there is death in all cultures; there are quests for identity in all cultures; there is loss, there is renewal, and there is hope across classes, ethnicities, religions, and nationalities. Alexie builds the main thematic infrastructure of the film on a bedrock of universals. At the same time—and this remains the genius of *Smoke Signals*—it utilizes humor both to Indianize those universals and to poke fun at spe-

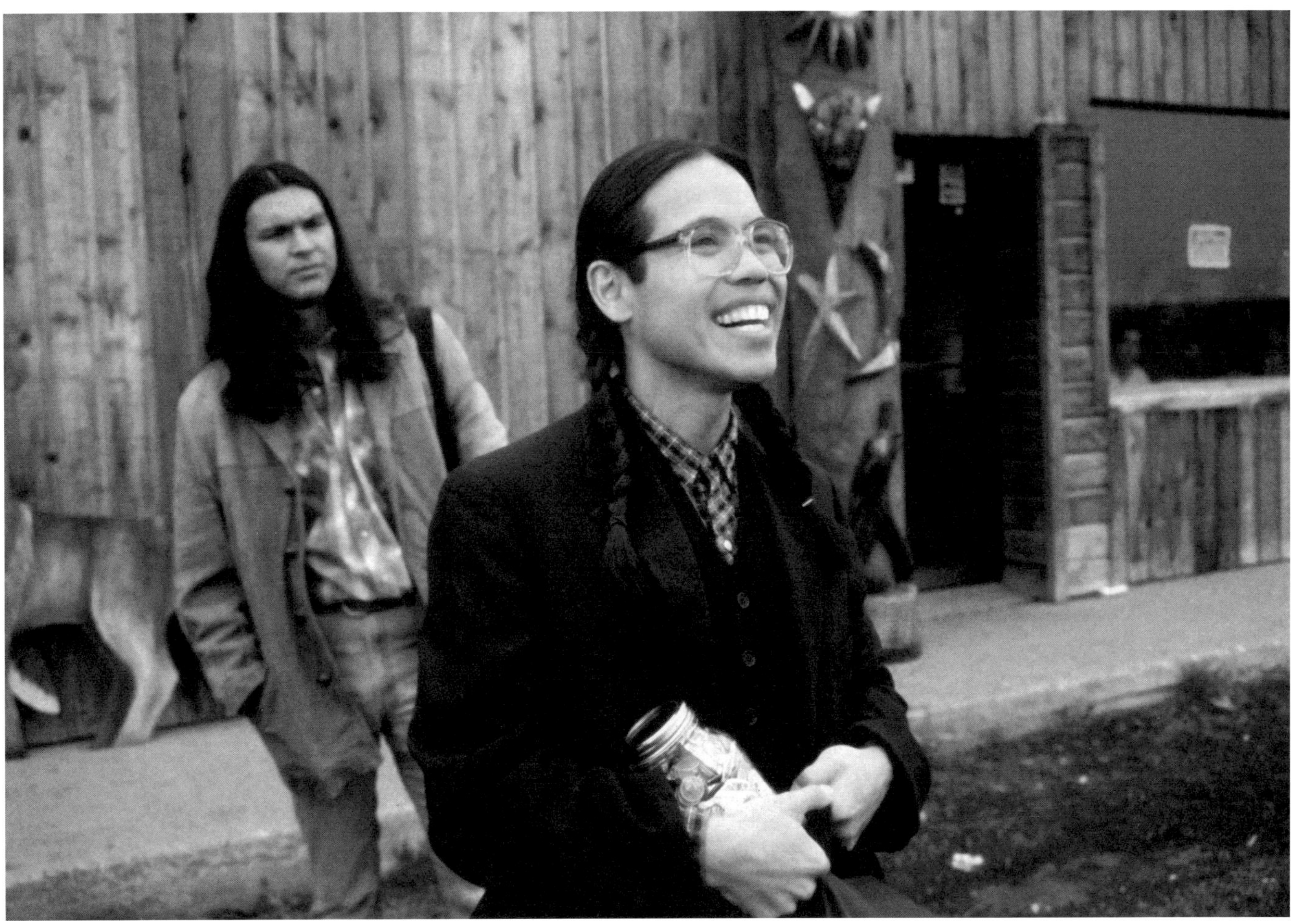

cific aspects of Indian identity. In so doing, it becomes a pedagogical text without being a didactic one; we laugh with Indians, rather than at them. To be sure, this is a new experience in American movies.

So, how does *Smoke Signals* subvert the manifest manners of the Hollywood Indian? A good example is through its send-up of "Today is a good day to die," the famous fatalistic phrase supposedly uttered by Crazy Horse and reified through film, television, and pop-culture lore.[4] This tagline, which all research suggests is apocryphal, underscores already prevalent stereotypes about Indians as defeatable. Whereas *Naturally Native* might see an opportunity to set the audience straight (as it does with Indian mascots) through a dramatized lecture, *Smoke Signals* pokes fun. And pokes again. Alexie sets up this joke early on, when Randy Peone (John Trudell), the disc jockey for KREZ, closes one of his morning monologues with a funny reversal: "It's a good day to be indigenous." Subtle, yes, but smart. That improvisation moves the aphorism from dying to living, and it places the steering wheel of the linguistic ship back in the hands of the Indians themselves.

From here, the film takes that line and sails with it. For instance, just a few minutes later, Victor and some friends take a break from playing pickup basketball to discuss the greatest basketball players and the physical stature of Apaches. After making a series of jokes, Victor slyly closes out the scene with his own comical turn of the phrase: "Some days it's a good day to die. Some days it's a good day to play basketball."[5] Later on, during a stopover for dinner en route to Phoenix, after Thomas regales Victor once again with a story about how Victor's father took Thomas to breakfast at Denny's, Thomas offers a response to Victor's earlier call: "Sometimes it's a good day to die. Sometimes it's a good day to

FIGURE 7.1. *Victor (Adam Beach,* left*) and Thomas (Evan Adams) preparing to leave the reservation in Idaho for a road trip to Arizona in* Smoke Signals. *© Photofest.*

have breakfast." To be sure, these are small moments, but they do some worthwhile work. First, the scenes let the audience know that Indians know their own stereotypes. They are aware not simply of their own world but also of the Indian myths that have become part of their identity. Second, it shows that Indians—Thomas and Victor at least—know how to dismantle those stereotypes on their own terms. If "Today is a good day to die" represents a philosophy inscribed in language, the boys can one-up that mystic fatalism with their own linguistic inscription. Third, and perhaps most importantly, that dismantling mechanism comes through good-natured humor. It is not gut-bustingly broad comedy or slapstick farce, but modest and incisive ridicule. Both Victor and Thomas take the bigness of that phrase and convert it to smallness—basketball and breakfast. They turn death day into every day; the infinite into the finite. We laugh, then, not just with the boys but also at the myth, the fiction of nostalgic invention.

In *Custer Died for Your Sins*, Vine Deloria, Jr., rightly quips, "One of the best ways to understand a people is to know what makes them laugh" (146). What makes Indians laugh is what makes everyone laugh—themselves and others. For Native writers, artists, and filmmakers, satire and self-satire remain useful tools because they take the power out of the hands of inventors of the primary source and place it in the hands of the satirists. Once you laugh at something, it no longer feels dangerous or powerful. This trait has long been a weapon of Native cultures. In his fine study of Indian humor, Kenneth Lincoln adroitly acknowledges the role of humor for Indian identity and survival. His task, he tells us, is "to fashion a new image of the surviving Indian as comic artist rather than tragic victim" (*Indi'n Humor*, 5), and though Lincoln's study succeeds on many levels, Indians have been fashioning that image on their own for some time.

Alexie and Eyre take it to the big screen in new ways, though, and when it works, it is a treat. One such instance occurs when Victor and Thomas have dinner with Suzy Song (Irene Bedard), Arnold's neighbor in Arizona and the one who finds his body. Though Victor wants to return immediately to Idaho, Suzy convinces them to stay for dinner. Over fry bread and Coke, the three half-talk and half-watch a black-and-white western on television. Thomas, after getting some more food, muses in passing: "The only thing more pathetic than Indians on TV is Indians watching Indians on TV." Indeed. The irony, of course, is that when *Smoke Signals* came out, thousands of Indians watched Indians in the movies watch Indians on TV. Note how Alexie forgoes easy comments here on representation, opting instead to have his characters provide a fine example of sarcastic semiosis. For Vizenor, that recognition signals the gap between Indians on television and the Alexie-Eyre Indians in *Smoke Signals*, because it means the difference between survivance and domination, colonialism and courage, warriors and westerns. Humor and its twin brother, insight, become cinematic catalysts for postindian praxis.

This praxis occurs most often in the blanket statements the various characters make about Indians, gestures that come across as overwrought at times, but ones that are clearly deployed to perform specific work. When, in *Smoke Signals*, Indians make generalizations about Indians, the intended audience is not, despite how it may appear, other Indians. For example, on their way to the bus station, Thomas and Victor encounter Lucy (Elaine Miles) and Velma (Michelle St. John) driving down the road in their car that only goes in reverse (the film's most often discussed metaphor). When Velma asks Thomas whether they need a ride, and he indicates that they do, Velma retorts, "What are you gonna trade for it? We're Indians, remember? We barter." The unnecessary phrase "We're Indians" functions as a gentle reminder to the audience that they are watching Indians on the screen, but it also makes the gentle point that Indians have their own internal jokes and know how to make them. Similarly, as Victor discusses with his mother, Arlene (Tantoo Cardinal), his impending trip to Arizona with Thomas, she makes him promise to return home. His response to

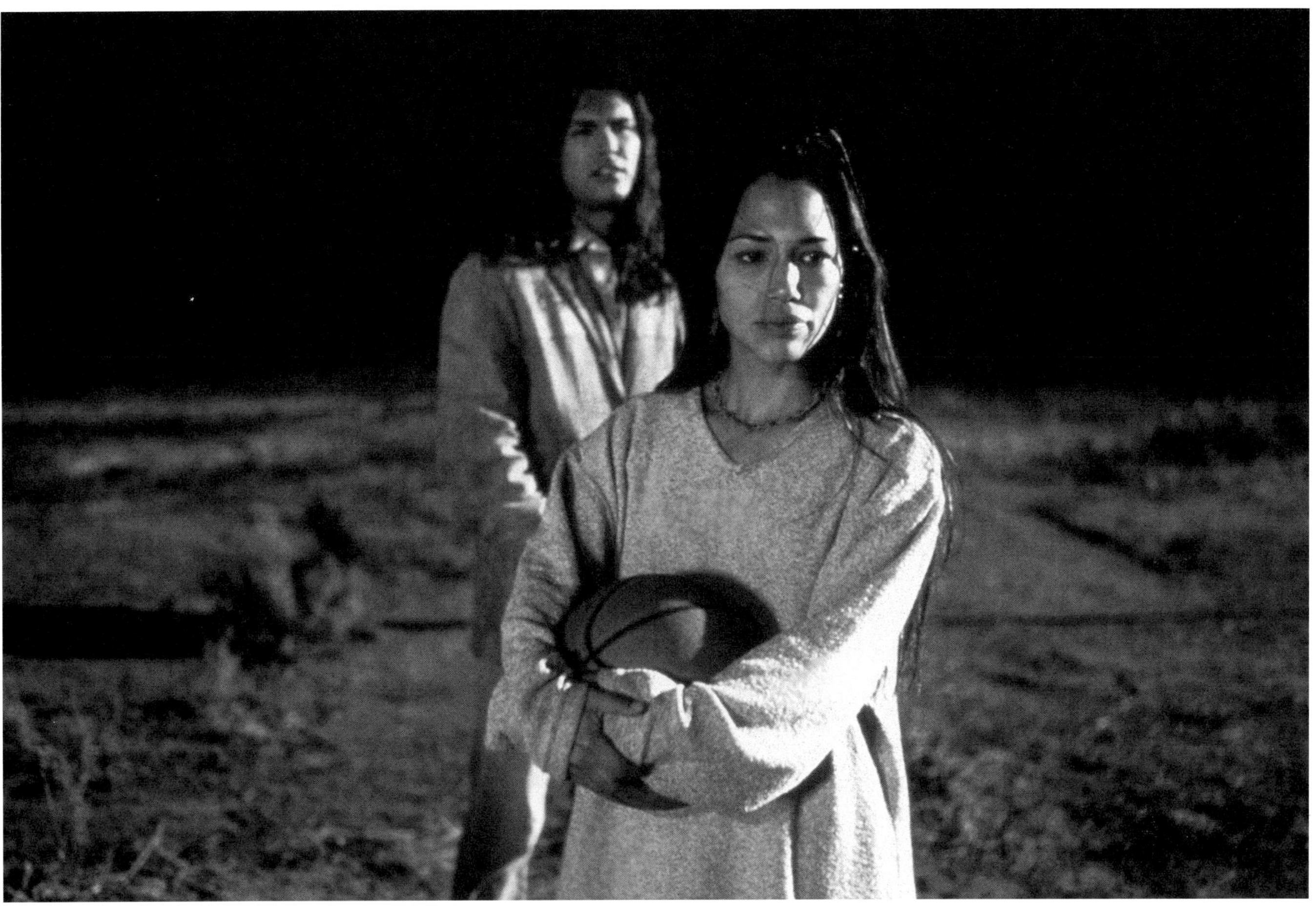

FIGURE 7.2. *Victor and Suzy Song (Irene Bedard) talking about Arnold Joseph, Victor's father, after his death.* © *Photofest.*

her is "Geez, you want me to sign a paper or something?" Her comeback, like Velma's, is funny but frank: "No way. You know how Indians feel about signing papers." More than the exchange with Velma, this interaction is forced. It is a crowbar trying to wedge into the script a dig about treaties, papers, and contracts. Still, these moments limn the self-reflexivity of Indian awareness and humor. They remind the viewer in the most charming, least threatening way possible that the people on-screen are, despite the transgressive and dispossessing past, human, alive, and vibrant. To those audience members accustomed to seeing Indian flatness on-screen, these small asides communicate that the filmmakers (and Indians in general) know history, culture, and popular culture. For me, these minute moments take back celluloid identity for Native peoples because Alexie and Eyre use the identity-encoding machinery of film against itself.

The best of these scenes is the famous series of exchanges between Thomas and Victor on the bus ride to Arizona. In his smart reading of *Smoke Signals*, Jhon Warren Gilroy astutely points out how the classic road trip—buddy movie provides an unusually roomy vehicle for conversation ("Another Fine Example," 25). In the case of *Smoke Signals*, the topics of the conversations deal less with the main plot (Victor and his father or even Victor and Thomas) than with Victor and Thomas and the rich topic of Indian identity. Thomas, bespectacled, braided, and suited, is, to Victor, Indian anathema—the geekiest friend's geekiest friend. And so a lesson transpires on how to be a "real Indian:"

VICTOR: First of all, quit grinning like an idiot. Indians ain't supposed to smile like that. Get stoic. You gotta look mean, or people won't respect you. You gotta look like a warrior. You gotta look like you just came back from killing a buffalo.

THOMAS: But our tribe never hunted buffalo. We were fishermen.

VICTOR: You want to look like you just came back from catching a fish? This ain't *Dances with Salmon*, you know. You gotta know how to use your hair. An Indian man ain't nothing without his hair.

The scene ends, and we cut to a shot of Victor and the bus driver waiting outside a truck stop. Thomas emerges from the bathroom without his glasses, his long hair blowing in the wind and sporting a "Frybread Power" T-shirt. Suddenly, Thomas is transformed.

Of course, the key word the above conversation hinges on is "real." Realness, Victor asserts, is essentially performance. Authenticity is facade—we are what we make people believe we are. Simulacra, representation, invention, colonialism, and an entire litany of poststructuralist concepts have their fingers in this pie, but that doesn't necessarily make Victor wrong. He is aware of the gap between how "real" (read performed) Indians are treated versus how "regular" (read regular) Indians are treated, and Thomas is a constant reminder, a walking totem of the non-Indian in need of an extreme makeover.

Though they are friends, that relationship exists in a constant state of tension, in part because Victor finds Thomas both annoying and embarrassing. But there is another reason. Thomas's parents were killed in a house fire on the Fourth of July when Arnold, Victor's drunken father, shot a bottle rocket into Thomas's house, setting the home ablaze. Arnold was the closest thing to a father Thomas ever knew; in fact, Arnold may have been a better father to Thomas than he was to Victor. Subsequently, Thomas worships Victor's father, and his constant revisionist tales about him only remind Victor of the fact that his father abandoned him. Victor's shame, layered and complex, gets outperformed by his belief that a real Indian must be stoic and warrior-like. Thomas's goofy, geeky lack of self- (and Indian) awareness constantly pokes holes in Victor's Indian mask.

But what Victor doesn't seem to understand is that Thomas is himself performing a form of Indianism—that of the storyteller. Victor knows that his realness is performed, and so does Thomas. In the same restaurant scene I mentioned previously, Thomas, who typically removes himself into a closed-eyed and clasped-handed reverie when telling a story, breaks his shamanic fourth wall during this particular telling to quickly open one eye, sneaking a peek to see whether Victor is listening to his narrative. Victor's real Indian is the Indian of manifest manners, the old simulations. His real Indian is the invented Indian. But oddly enough, so is Thomas's—just of a different generation. If Victor's notions of realness come from Indians like Scar in *The Searchers*, then Thomas's originates from the New Age storytelling shaman, à la Sedona, Santa Fe, and *Dances with Wolves*.

But here is where Alexie distinguishes himself from his characters. Even if Victor and Thomas are not always fully aware of the extent to which Indianness is a construct, Alexie is. *Smoke Signals* is, in part, an insider document made public, a quick tour inside the territory of Indian identity. For Vizenor, the power not only to reinvent representation but also to dramatize Indian self-situationalism is the enactment of the real, the true weapon of the postindian warrior: "The postindian warriors hover at last over the ruins of tribal representations and surmount the scriptures of manifest manners with new stories; these warriors counter the surveillance and literature of dominance with their own simulations of survivance. The postindian arises from the earlier inventions of the tribes only to contravene the absence of the real with theatrical performances; the theater of tribal consciousness is the recreation of the real, not the absence of the real in the simulations of dominance" (5). If, as Vizenor suggests, the postindian warrior obviates the antiselves propagated by Hollywood and the western, and if the western is the dominant text of dominance, the mass-produced method of manifest mannerism, then one might argue that a particularly effective new story might be one that inverts the semiotic and cinematic language of the

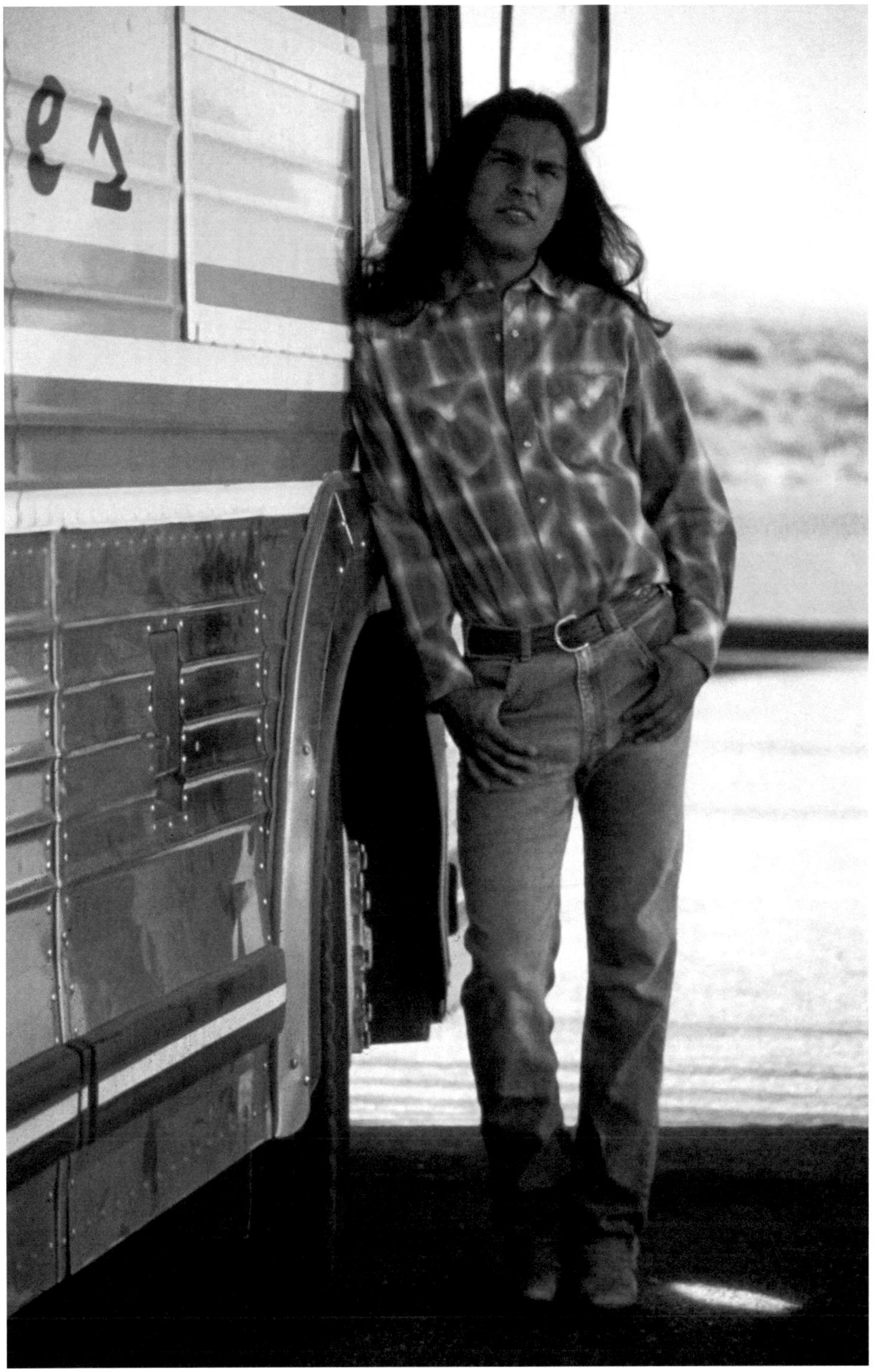

western as part of its larger project of advancing simulations of survivance (new stories of Indian sovereignty) within the framework of the simulations of dominance (Hollywood movies in general and the western in particular). Put another way, the most effective mode of sculpting and showing Indian sovereignty is through the language of the discourse that has been the most responsible for undermining that sovereignty. If decades of anti-Indian film have inscribed Indianness into the American psyche, it will take that many future decades of Indian film to edit out that inscription, to reshoot those scenes.

FIGURE 7.3. *Victor: stoic, decked out in a standard cowboy shirt and boots, and looking as though he could actually have just come from killing a buffalo. © Photofest.*

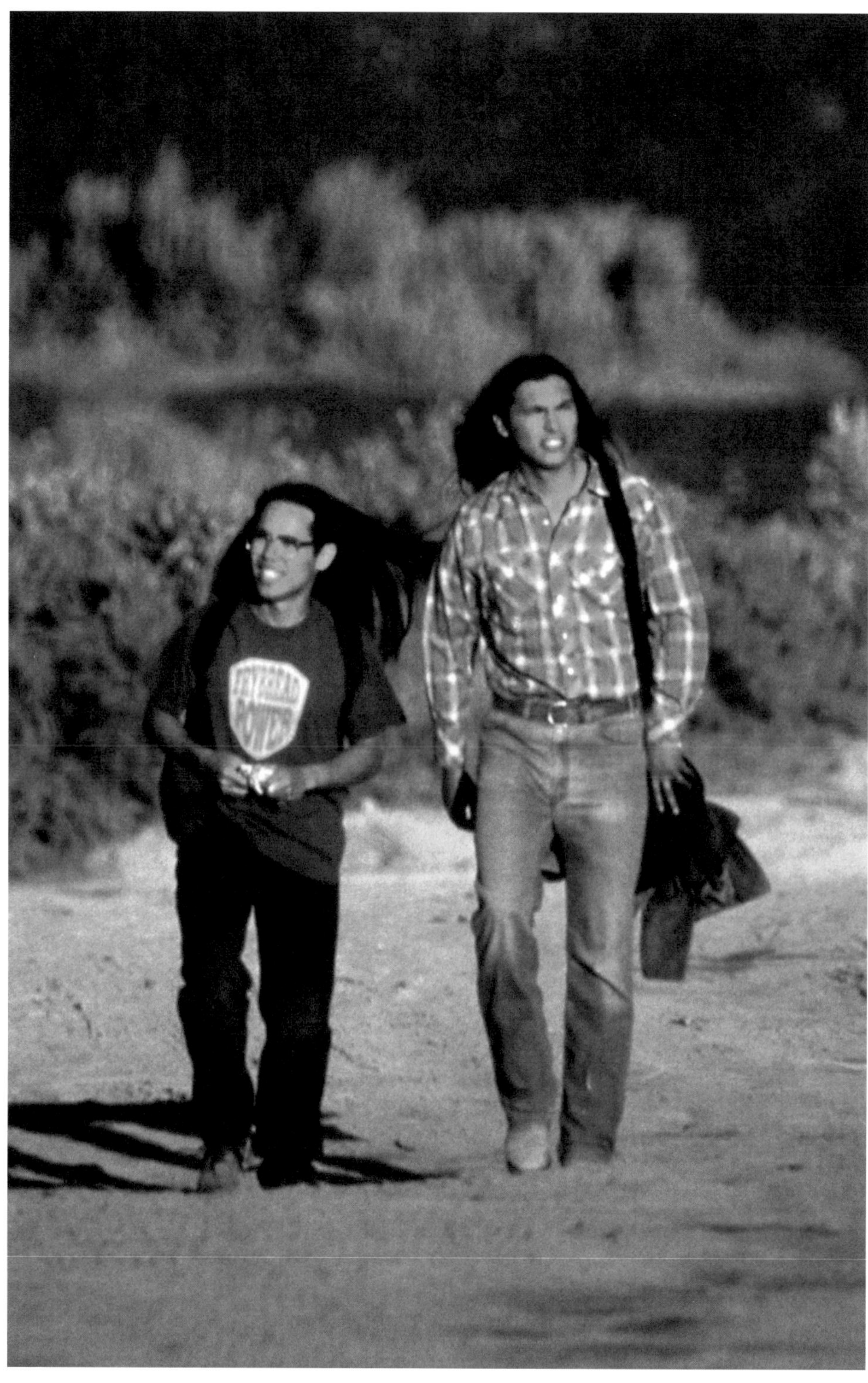

FIGURE 7.4. *Victor and Thomas out on the trail. Part of the semiotic work of* Smoke Signals *involves playing with western icons. © Photofest.*

Though the details are often quite subtle in the film, Alexie and Eyre play with the cinematic codes and icons of the western as way to undermine it, a cagey but useful form of engaged resistance. Details, including the clothes Victor wears on the trip to Arizona, an encounter with "cowboys" on the bus, and jokes about Tonto and Tonto, indicate to the viewer that he should view *Smoke Signals* through a western lens. The structuaralist journey, for example, from the upper West in Idaho to the iconic West of Arizona is both a historical and a visual echo of many classic westerns. Because of all the John Ford movies filmed around Monument Valley and the hundreds shot in the Tucson area, Arizona is, for most Americans, the semiotic setting of this genre. In fact, until *Smoke Signals*, if one saw a movie that showed two Native Americans traveling in or to Arizona, it could be nothing but a western. In semiotic terms, a clear formula emerged: Arizona + Indians = Western. So even if Eyre and Alexie are not intentionally playing with genre, it is happening nonetheless. Moreover, Victor and Thomas's means of transport—a "coach"—is also symbolic. It functions as a metonym for all the stagecoaches, on all the movie screens, that were attacked by all the savage Indians as the Anglos moved from civilization into the savage unknown. This motif finds unexpected inversion when Velma and Louise ask Thomas and Victor, who are about to leave the rez, whether they have had their shots, adding that America is as foreign as it gets.

Other signifiers do this work as well, like Victor's clothes on the drive back to Idaho—he wears a western shirt and cowboy boots. On one hand, this detail is merely a realistic portrayal of how many Indians dress; on the other, it is a small funny reversal of Hollywood costuming. Similarly, toward the end of the film, when the boys check on the young woman injured in a crash, her friend calls them heroes, like "the Lone Ranger and Tonto," indicating that basic heroism can be articulated only through western grammatology. Thomas's response, "more like Tonto and Tonto," is a doubly ironic play on the only notable Indian hero in classic westerns and a clever erasing of the cowboy with a new representation of Indianness and a new moment of postindian humor.

The now-classic encounter with the rednecks on the bus, though, stands as the most salient example of the western and its many devices, all Alexied up. In this scene, Thomas and Victor exit the bus at a standard rest stop, in part so Thomas can take down his hair and change from his suit into jeans and his "Frybread Power" T-shirt. When they board the bus and walk back to their seats, they discover two middle-aged white men have taken them. Thomas, recently liberated from his suit and braids, and Victor, fresh from his lesson on stoic strength, inform the men they are sitting in the wrong seats. To no one's surprise, they refuse to leave. Alexie and Eyre play this scene to the hilt; the men are as stereotyped and one-dimensionalized as Indians were for so many decades. One dons a camouflage cap that says "My Gun Cleaning Hat" across the front, and the other sports a white cowboy hat. Both sit plump and self-satisfied in spaces once occupied by two Indians. The tension, symbolism, and iconic history are palpable. In keeping with the long history of such encounters, the Anglos both dismiss and insult Victor and Thomas, saying, "Why don't you and Super Injun there find yourself someplace else to have a powwow?"

A slightly updated but still-classic cinematic showdown between cowboys and Indians clicks into place. We wonder what will happen next, what Alexie's comment on this turn of events will be. Ultimately, Thomas and Victor retreat to the back of the bus and have a conversation about whether cowboys always win and why, in all westerns, one never sees John Wayne's teeth. Rather than retaliate against the white men with anger, violence, or insolence, the boys sing their now-famous song about John Wayne's teeth, a sort of ceremonial mocking of Wayne and his spirit brothers a few rows up. A song of resistance that echoes back to the Ghost Dance and forward to a scene at the beginning of *The Plague of Doves*, it captures the attention of the passengers on the bus and returns the dialogic power back to Thomas and Victor.

In this loaded scene, one wonders whether there are intentional subtexts at work. For one, there are certainly overtones of Indian removal. Is the scene also a subtle comment on Anglos stealing, squatting on, and occupying Indian Territory? Perhaps. It is no coincidence that the closer they get to Arizona and the cinematic West, the more they bisect the great American frontier, the more that real life starts to feel like the movies. Schatz argues that even simple generic icons like western shirts, references to guns, and cowboy hats flick on some receptor in our brain that tells us we are watching a genre picture, and we react accordingly. Less interested in the characters' semiosis and more focused on the movie's thematics and geographics, Gilroy makes an argument about genre similar to mine, but for him, the key concept is the frontier: "The film plays off a viewer's familiarity with a form . . . It is at the subtextual or philosophical narrative level [that] there exists the potential for subversion of stereotypes, and mainstream viewers' implication in the fabula-making based upon them, becomes more noticeable. Here, the viewer finds herself not in the comfortable, well mapped-out confines of territory, but rather in a frontier space" ("Another Fine Example," 25).

For Gilroy, as for Louis Owens, a frontier space is a space where cultures collide and all things are unstable. While a frontier space is not exactly the same thing as the frontier, the former derives its meaning from the latter, and the frontier space of the film is entered when the boys cross the frontier itself. What distinguishes *Smoke Signals* from the traditional western, though, is Alexie's ability to transfer the metaphorics of the frontier, which are part and parcel of the standard western, onto the frontier space that is *Smoke Signals*, his antiwestern. In the world of Vizenor's postindianism, this inversion makes his project one of survivance: "The postindian warriors and the missionaries of manifest manners are both responsible for simulations; even that resemblance is a simulation that ends in silence, or the presence of an original referent to tribal survivance" (*Manifest Manners*, 13).

Smoke Signals, then, is a simulation of a western—that genre most thoroughly laced with manifest manners—that reconstitutes the ruins of representation in the frontier space of genre. And though I am not sure Gilroy would go quite as far as I do in arguing that Alexie inverts the genre, he does, like Vizenor, agree that Eyre and Alexie shift the heavy plates on which easy notions of celluloid Indians have been camping: "By replacing the film's underlying philosophical message with an American Indian cosmology, *Smoke Signals* creates a frontier environment—particularly for a mainstream Euramerican viewer—to build a bridge from which viewers can examine stereotypical assumptions about American Indians" ("Another Fine Example," 25–26). It is this bridge, this play with genre and expectation, this charming, humorous new storytelling, which feels like old storytelling, that enables viewers to engage Alexie's narratives of resistance and make *Smoke Signals* the most iconic and most revolutionary mainstream American Indian text.

Humor, New Stories, and the Simulations of Survivance: *The Business of Fancydancing*

No one really knows what to do with *The Business of Fancydancing* (2002). It is one of the few Alexie projects whose success was simply not commensurate with his talent and vision. The box-office numbers were tepid, the film got very little theatrical release or promotion, and the awards from film festivals were nearly nonexistent, though it did do well at the Durango Film Festival and the Victoria Film Festival, two powerhouses on the circuit. Worst of all was the lukewarm critical reception. "There are a few too many devices," writes Elvis Mitchell in the *New York Times*, finding the film, especially the beginning, "clumsy and a little hard to follow." He also laments some of the dialogue: "Steven (Kevin Phillip), is saddled with some unfortunate lines to broadcast his sympathy, like 'They're not your tribe anymore. I'm your tribe.'" Richard Curnutte, Jr., the editor of *The Film Journal*, makes Mitchell look like Leonard Maltin: "Trying to paint on such a vast canvas is often admirable, even if the process is not entirely successful. Here, though, the results are almost embarrassing." Accusing Alexie of both taking characters too seriously and ridiculing them, Curnutte argues that these approaches "collide and deliver a stunted story of supposed redemption and forgiveness. Neither homespun nor avant-garde, *Fancydancing* attempts to be all things for all people and winds up being nothing for anyone."

Despite these rough reviews, the film resonates with a certain kind of viewer. For example, in the summer of 2008, I was invited to give a presentation on American Indian film to the Department of Screen and Media Studies at the University of Waikato in Aotearoa (New Zealand). The audience was mostly faculty and graduate students who, clearly, knew a lot about film, even if not a great deal about Indian film. I showed clips from all four of the movies I write about in this book (*Smoke Signals*, *Skins*, *Naturally Native*, and *Fancydancing*), and out of all of them, *Fancydancing* was far and away the favorite. There were more questions about it than about all of the other films combined, and there was substantially more interest in teaching it in their courses. In fact, the very traits Mitchell decries in his review attracted the New Zealanders to Alexie's disjointed text. The film also does well among gay and lesbian groups, and, indeed, *Fancydancing* won audience awards at the Philadelphia International Gay and Lesbian Film Festival and at the San Francisco Film Festival, arguably the most gay-friendly major film festival.

Yet the film remains virtually unknown even in San Francisco. To illustrate, I ask the reader's patience with yet another personal anecdote. Having lent my copy of *Fancydancing* to a student and then never receiving it back, I was forced to get the film from my university library in preparation for this chapter. When I went to the University of San Francisco library, I discovered, to my astonishment, that it was already checked out. Both delighted and annoyed, I began calling every video rental store in the Bay Area in hopes of finding it, but no luck. Finally, I located one place in Potrero Hill that had a copy. Pleased that a visionary entrepreneur had had the foresight to purchase *Fancydancing*, I pictured, as I drove to the store, someone who knew and valued Indian film. An imaginary conversation took place in my head in which he might recommend movies that had flown under my radar. I was mistaken. When the store's owner checked out the film to me, he said that the movie had apparently never been rented before. In fact, he confessed that he had never heard of *The Business of Fancydancing* and had no idea how the movie wound up in his store. Was it a self-help video about investing in a dance studio?

Granted, this is one experience with one person, and so it cannot really give us any idea about how the film is received—and yet it does. Despite our best attempts to the contrary, we rarely escape the stranglehold of anecdotal evidence and personal experience. In my case, this exchange at the video store reinforced every other experience involving *Fancydancing*—that it is unknown and essentially ignored. The movie's floating signifiers and confusing plot structure can be blamed for some of this, but the real culprit is, ironically, *Smoke Signals*. It is already *the* Indian film, and right now there does not seem to be room in America's consciousness for another. It is impossible to discuss how many times people have asked—when they discover I teach and write about American Indian studies—whether I have seen *Smoke Signals*. More than any Silko or Erdrich novel, more than any painting, more, even, than *Dances with Wolves*, *Smoke Signals* is the single point of reference in American popular culture for contemporary American Indian cultural production. Even for Alexie himself. When he spoke at the Native American Literature Symposium in 2006, Alexie talked a great deal about *Smoke Signals*, its popularity, its grosses, and its importance for Indian communities, but he never mentioned *Fancydancing*.

The question remains what do we do with *Fancydancing*? Is it a success? Is it a good movie? Is it an important Indian text? Or, to the point of this chapter, to what degree is *The Business of Fancydancing* a postindian text? Does it, in Vizenor's vernacular, counter the contrivances of manifest manners with simulations of survivance? The answers to these questions, as well as a few unasked and unanswered others, construct the framing mechanism for the second half of this chapter. My contention is that *The Business of Fancydancing* is, in fact, an important and prescient postindian text that is worthy of close consideration, but less for what it accomplishes than for what it signals.

If *Smoke Signals* is the fry bread of Indian cinema, *The Business of Fancydancing* is bird brain stew—a dish hard to digest for some, but a real delicacy for those with the right palates. In fact, *The Business of Fancydancing* stands as a kind of anti–*Smoke Signals* project, a nonnarrative experimental film that eschews all the trappings of cinematic pleasure its predecessor enjoys. Whereas *Smoke Signals* seeks recognition, *Fancydancing* looks for distance; whereas *Smoke Signals* embraces convention, *Fancydancing* displays innovation; whereas *Smoke Signals* goes for universals, *Fancydancing* homes in on particulars; whereas *Smoke Signals* provides meaning and closure, *Fancydancing* enacts indeterminacy and open-endedness; whereas *Smoke Signals* ends on a note of optimism, *Fancydancing* closes on chords of indeterminacy and open-endedness. In short, one can argue that *Smoke Signals*, with its thematics of arrival, harmony, and renewal, is an utterly modernist text, while *Fancydancing*, with its fragmented narrative, its self-referentiality, and its metacommentaries, becomes one of the first—perhaps *the* first—postmodern Indian films. Indeed, it is through its postmodernity that the film most fully embodies Vizenor's notion of postindianism. "Postindian narratives," Vizenor argues, "observe natives, the chance of totemic associations, conversions, and reversions of tribal cultures, as postmodern survivance and vivancy" (*Manifest Manners*, viii). Alexie locates that "postmodern survivance and vivancy" in the character of Seymour Polatkin, the alter ego for his mixed feelings about his identity, his success, and his loyalty to the reservation. Whereas most reviewers and viewers find flaws in the film's representation of Indians, the reservation, and, most importantly, Indian aesthetic production, I argue that these very traits are what make *Fancydancing* a postindian simulation of survivance and a contextual collage of engaged resistance.

The plot of *Fancydancing* proceeds along a fairly conventional route; the truly interesting aspects of the film are directorial detours that take our expectations, not the narrative, in new directions. Seymour Polatkin (Evan Adams), a gay Indian (Coeur d'Alene) poet who has achieved uncommon literary celebrity, functions as the film's protagonist. The first part of the movie explores his writing life (fulfilling) and his love life (perhaps less so) as it traces his experimentations with heterosexuality in college to his present life as an out gay man. Living in Seattle and partnered with a white man, Steven (Kevin Phillip), Seymour feels far away from the reservation in every possible way. But news of the death of his childhood best friend, Mouse (Swil Kanim [Lummi]), jerks him back into the clutches of reservation life and its many tentacles. He returns to the reservation for Mouse's wake, where he also faces many of the people who see him as both a turncoat and a favorite son.

Although based as loosely as humanly possible on Alexie's collection of poems of the same name, the movie feels more like an adaptation of the text of Alexie's life as a writer turned celebrity city dweller. Shot in just about three weeks on a minimal budget, the film suffers from production values that are less sophisticated than those in *Smoke Signals* or *Skins*, but the acting and the script trump those of *Naturally Native*. In truth, the movie's weaknesses are also its strengths. The many devices that Mitchell decries distinguish it from every other Indian film, but for him (and others), they are more flash than felicitous; he does not (or cannot) see the film's postindian values, nor can he place it within the larger context of Indian aesthetic activism.

For me, the best feature of *Fancydancing* is its awareness of itself as a text—a classic tenet of postmodernism and a gesture at the heart of Vizenor's notion of postindian invention and simulation. At no point during *Fancydancing* does the viewer suspect he is watching a documentary (unlike a viewer's experience of *Skins*, for example). Alexie keeps reminding the viewer she is looking at a screen, not out a window. *Fancydancing* is not real life, though it is realistic; it is a construct, a simulation, a play on cinematic verisimilitude and the questionable history of ethnographic films. It locates authentic Indianness within its experimental, performative, antidiegetic design—a design reflective of Seymour Polatkin himself. As the film suggests, "Seymour Polatkin" is a text, a self-invention made necessary by his fame. Ironically, the idea of Seymour Polatkin is also an external construct, one concocted by those who want an image of the "Indian poet." Thus, most viewers don't know what to do with *Fancydancing* because they don't know what to do with Seymour; unlike Victor or Thomas, he bears no resemblance to any other iconic Indian. Some want to read Seymour as "Sherman Alexie," but that doppleganging doesn't fit either. It stands to reason then, that a film reflecting Seymour's aesthetic sensibilities and his complicated identity, and that also perpetually reminds the viewer of its own fictionality, might be difficult to decode. Indeed, its textuality problematizes expectations of fictional Indians, forcing viewers to rethink not just their notions of Natives, but all inventions by the left-wing bookstore set, like the "sensitive poet," the "passionate Indian," the "Indian writer," and the "sage scribe." Alexie takes on all of these stereotypes, suggesting that if they are easy to debunk, then seemingly stronger stereotypes about Indians can also be debunked.

Alexie loves hacking away at fictions, and *Fancydancing* wastes no time pulling out the ax. In the second scene of the film, only a minute into the movie, Alexie replaces mimetic scenes of reservation life and family interaction with a bizarre shot of someone who looks a lot like Thomas Builds-the-Fire: the figure is sitting in a bookstore window, facing the street like a mannequin, and reading a poem called "How To Write the Great American Indian Novel." A close-up of the book tells us its author is Seymour Polatkin, and almost immediately a black-and-white intertitle appears on the screen:

> "Seymour Polatkin's poetry is funny, angry, authentic, and ultimately redemptive."—*New York Literature Quarterly*, May 21, 2001."

At this point, the viewer has been prepared for an earnest portrayal of the Indian writer who chronicles the woes, magic, and dreams of his people. But as soon as the audience settles into this easy reading, Alexie irrupts with yet another intertitle:

> "Seymour Polatkin is full of shit"—Indianz.com, May 22, 2001.

The second intertitle brings the entire scene into focus and tells the audience how to read the film. All of a sudden, Seymour, perched in a bookstore window, ceases to be a poet giving a reading and instead looks like he is in an exhibit at the zoo—a live "Indian" on display, safely tucked away behind glass. A passer-by, a confused Anglo man, stops and looks quizzically at Seymour before entering the bookstore and ignoring him altogether. Then, almost as quickly, the film cuts to another odd scene: Seymour placing his hands on the cheeks of a famous statue of Chief Seattle in Pioneer Square, at which point Seymour gives the chief a long, passionate, open-mouthed kiss. While all this is going on, the audience listens to Seymour's voice reading a poem—an actual poem of Alexie's—that riffs on the readerly expectations of Indians, "Native Americans" stereotypes, and the stereotypes that some highly regarded Indian literature romanticizes. To be sure, it is an unusually rich scene. It is rare, for example, to see someone on film make out with a statue and even rarer to see an Indian French kiss a statue of another Indian. It engenders an entirely new image of the sacred and the profane.[6] In fact, the first three minutes of the film unnerve preceding and perceived expectations of what to expect from a "Native American film." It mocks not only itself but also the entire institution of earnest ethnic independent movies and the audiences who fetishize them.

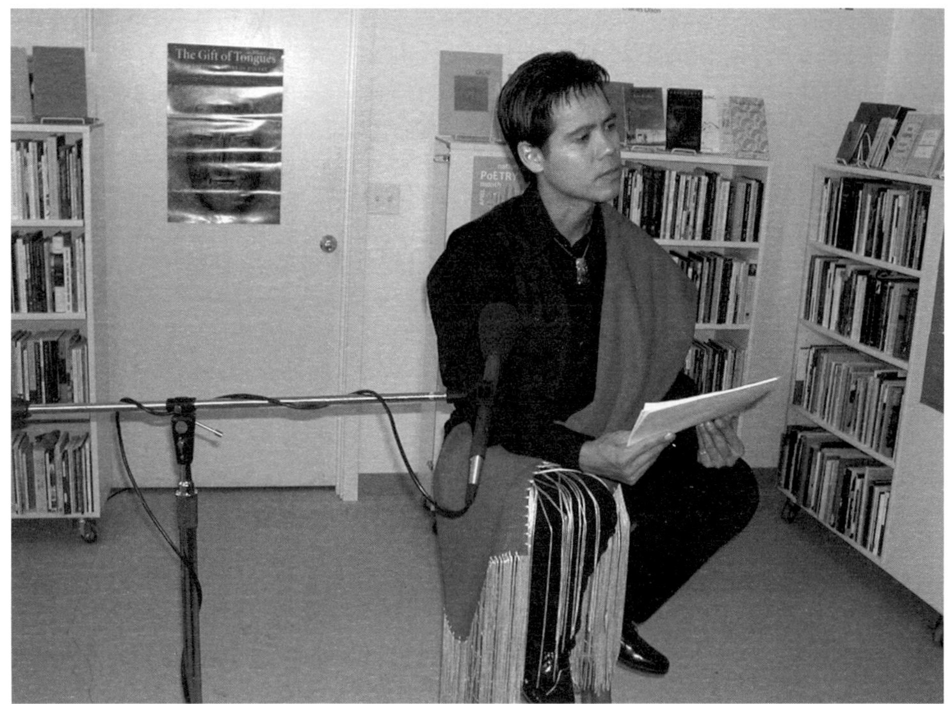

FIGURE 7.5. *Evan Adams in* The Business of Fancydancing *as Seymour Polatkin, a famous Indian poet, at one of his many readings. Photo by Larry Estes; used with his permission.*

This section I describe above, beginning with Seymour reading the Alexie poem, through the intertitles and the statue kiss, and ending with the final lines of the poem, is one of the most revolutionary three minutes in Native film. In that span of time, the movie moves from modern to postmodern, from earnest to ironic, and from predictable to performative like nothing before it. One of the great contributions of *Smoke Signals* is its ability to signify like a buddy movie or a western but ultimately to embody, better than any other text, a new genre we might call the American Indian independent film. *Fancydancing* picks up where *Smoke Signals* leaves off. *Fancydancing* begins as yet another seemingly depressing but ultimately uplifting American Indian independent film that audiences have been prepared to view, but Alexie's deep play with cinematic grammar in these scenes deconstructs the very genre he helped construct. "A genre's progression from transparency to opacity," writes Schatz, "from straightforward storytelling to self-conscious formalism—involves its concerted effort to explain itself" (*Hollywood Genres*, 38). The succession from *Smoke Signals* to *Fancydancing* reveals Alexie's desire to achieve in film what he accomplished in fiction—to move beyond what he calls "the expected idea" (Purdy, "Crossroads," 8). For Alexie, the expected idea undermines aesthetic and indigenous autonomy, relegating cultural production to what has been seen, as opposed to what can be imagined. In Vizenorian terms, it is precisely in that postmodern turn that we locate Alexie's postindianism. If *Smoke Signals* is about vision, *Fancydancing* is about revision. *Fancydancing* becomes a "reversion" of the version of Indian life that he and Eyre chronicle in *Smoke Signals*.

Fancydancing also stands as a bizarrely literal example of re-version through its unusual adaptation, in that the screenplay derives not from a novel but from a collection of verse. What is more, the self-reflexivity of Alexie's poetic persona within the character and performance of Seymour makes the film as much a commentary on Indian writing as on Indian living (and loving). As Schatz notes, the drift toward self-conscious formalism signals a desire on the part of the filmmaker to move beyond generic formulas. In the case of *Fancydancing*, that self-commentary manifests through an intentional textuality that calls attention to the film's awareness of itself as a construct, but also to Alexie's Alexie-ness—itself a construct.

The opening scenes exemplify the movie's complicated treatment of these issues in truly innovative ways, perhaps most obsessively with the poem Seymour reads. Almost no one I spoke with who saw the film knew that Seymour's poem is actually a published poem by Alexie.[7] In truth, the poem Seymour reads is a version of the original, just as Seymour is a version of the original Alexie, but in neither case is the new version less authentic than its predecessor. One of Alexie's better poems, "How To Write the Great American Indian Novel" excavates some of the same terrain as *Fancydancing* (the image of Indians, the nature of Indian writing, how Indians see non-Indians, how Indians are inscribed in American culture) and even enjoys a similarly ironic tone of weary but whimsical nihilism:

> All of the Indians must have tragic features: tragic noses, eyes, and arms.
> Their hands and fingers must be tragic when they reach for tragic food.
>
> The hero must be a half-breed, half white and half Indian, preferably
> from a horse culture. He should often weep alone. That is mandatory.
>
> If the hero is an Indian woman, she is beautiful. She must be slender
> and in love with a white man. But if she loves an Indian man
>
> then he must be a half-breed, preferably from a horse culture.
> If the Indian woman loves a white man, then he has to be so white
>
> that we can see the blue veins running through his skin like rivers.
> When the Indian woman steps out of her dress, the white man gasps
>
> at the endless beauty of her brown skin. She should be compared to nature:
> brown hills, mountains, fertile valleys, dewy grass, wind, and clear water.
>
> If she is compared to murky water, however, then she must have a secret.
> Indians always have secrets, which are carefully and slowly revealed.
>
> Yet Indian secrets can be disclosed suddenly, like a storm.
> Indian men, of course, are storms. They should destroy the lives
>
> of any white women who choose to love them. All white women love
> Indian men. That is always the case. White women feign disgust
>
> at the savage in blue jeans and T-shirt, but secretly lust after him.
> White women dream about half-breed Indian men from horse cultures.
>
> Indian men are horses, smelling wild and gamey. When the Indian man
> unbuttons his pants, the white woman should think of topsoil.
>
> There must be one murder, one suicide, one attempted rape.
> Alcohol should be consumed. Cars must be driven at high speeds.
>
> Indians must see visions. White people can have the same visions
> if they are in love with Indians. If a white person loves an Indian
>
> then the white person is Indian by proximity. White people must carry

> an Indian deep inside themselves. Those interior Indians are half-breed
>
> and obviously from horse cultures. If the interior Indian is male
> then he must be a warrior, especially if he is inside a white man.
>
> If the interior Indian is female, then she must be a healer, especially if she is inside
> a white woman. Sometimes there are complications.
>
> An Indian man can be hidden inside a white woman. An Indian woman
> can be hidden inside a white man. In these rare instances,
>
> everybody is a half-breed struggling to learn more about his or her horse culture.
> There must be redemption, of course, and sins must be forgiven.
>
> For this, we need children. A white child and an Indian child, gender
> not important, should express deep affection in a childlike way.
>
> In the Great American Indian novel, when it is finally written,
> all of the white people will be Indians and all of the Indians will be ghosts.
>
> —(*THE SUMMER OF BLACK WIDOWS*, 94–95)

One wonders whether Seymour becomes a kind of talking mannequin for Alexie here, a vehicle that delivers his poem to many more people than would normally consume it, or whether the poem functions more as a lens through which to best view the film (or a combination of both). But the scene also mocks the earnestness of poetry readings, their solemnity, and their fascinating ability to put writers on display. Of course, Alexie literalizes this by propping up Seymour in the store window. Is the poet a shaman or a showman, a prophet or an exhibit?

The two intertitles punctuating Seymour's reading reinforce this textuality, and they set the stage for the rest of the film. The first pokes fun at the discourse of white scholars writing about Indian writing, and in the seconds following that intertitle, the audience thinks it knows what kind of movie they are going to see and what kind of writer Alexie wants us to think Seymour is. There is no *New York Literature Quarterly*, but there is no shortage of observations in the publishing world about Indian discourse being authentic and redemptive. But before the film sutures itself too neatly to the audience, Alexie inverts the entire paradigm with the funny and irreverent quote from Indianz.com (an actual site). All of a sudden, the *NLQ*'s observation about Seymour's authenticity feels a lot less authentic and a lot stuffier. Tack on the subsequent scene of Seymour (Indian) making out with a bust of Chief Seattle (Indian, and by all accounts a straight one). Is the film making fun of Indianness? Is it making fun of artifice? Is the film suggesting that Seymour is full of shit? Since the poem Seymour has been reading is really a poem by Alexie, it stands to reason that, on at least some level, Alexie is arguing that Alexie is full of shit. One wonders, then, which intertitle Alexie thinks best describes his work; which one most accurately reflects Alexie's perception of Seymour and himself? Is it possible that Seymour is full of shit in a way that Alexie is not? Certainly, no Indian writer is more aware of his own persona than Alexie, and consequently, no Indian writer is more aware of the criticisms leveled against him.

In one of the best scenes in the film, Alexie makes a cameo appearance as an unnamed but cranky reservation Indian who has nothing but bad things to say about Seymour. Midway through the film, Seymour returns to the reservation for the first time in nearly a decade for Mouse's wake. As Seymour sits in his car outside the house where he knows everyone

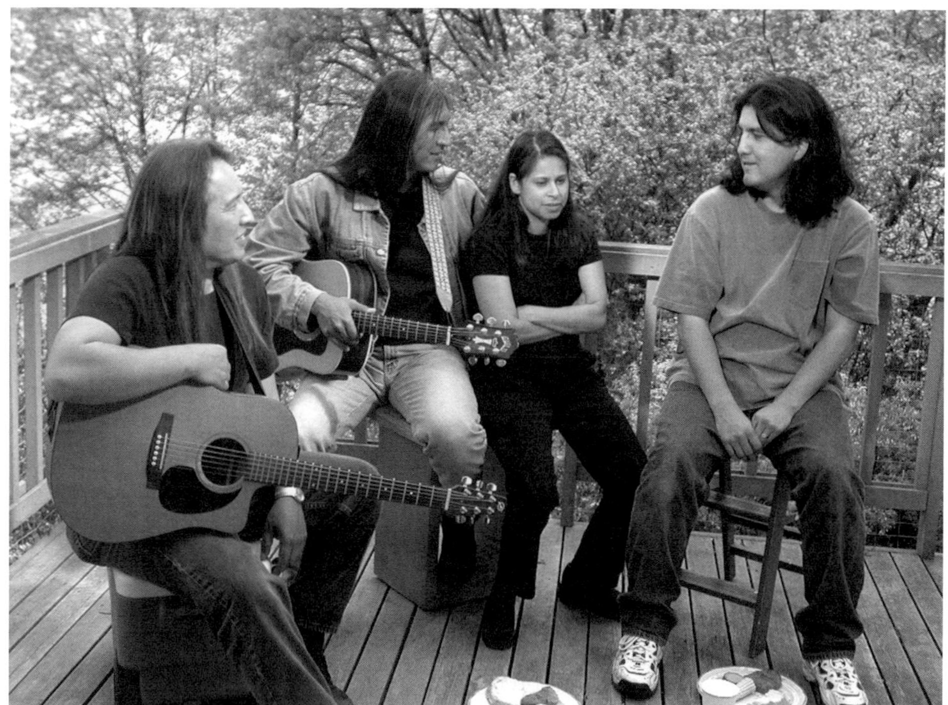

has gathered, a conversation ensues about Seymour. Alexie's character takes the first jab: "When was the last time Seymour talked to Mouse? Writin' all those poems, walkin' around here, thinking he's too good for us. He always did." Seymour's college girlfriend and closest friend on the reservation, Agnes Roth (Michelle St. John [Cree]), defends Seymour, suggesting that perhaps Seymour communicated to Mouse through the poems, reminding everyone that Mouse read Seymour's work. But that falls flat. Alexie's character immediately retorts, adding insult to injury, "And, I don't even like those poems! Do you?"

Wow! How much fun it must have been to make a cameo appearance in your own film, to use the film as a runway for your own poetry, then to turn around and make fun of the poems as they strut down that runway. This last scene allows Alexie to let everyone know that he is aware of the many criticisms leveled against him—the accusations that he is a sellout, that he abandoned the reservation, and that he exploits the difficulties of reservation life for his writing. It also reminds the audience that he knows he is himself a constructed text—the "successful but controversial Indian writer" so frequently invoked in interviews and news stories.

Much of *Fancydancing* is about deconstructing texts, regardless of the text or its author. For example, just as *Smoke Signals* enables its characters to participate in the revisioning process of "It's a good day to die," *Fancydancing* undermines the liberal stereotype of the mystical Indian poet-shaman at one with language, land, and the spirit world. It also shatters New Age images of Indians living in harmony with each other and nature. On Alexie's celluloid reservation, Indians fight, bicker, get high, and avoid work. But they also write poetry, play the violin, fall in love, and dance. In other words, like everyone else, Indians fully embody human contradictions, as do their writers (and filmmakers). To Alexie's credit, he does not use *Fancydancing* to take on his critics; rather, he provides an aesthetic infrastructure and cultural context so that viewers can better understand the provenance of Seymour's work (and his own). What emerges is a round portrayal of Seymour as a complicated, talented individual. Similarly, the film depicts his Indian friends and family as full, nuanced humans, not as totemized one-dimensional figurines in a Disneyland diorama. Sometimes, though, we live best in places when we live somewhere else. Seymour himself

FIGURE 7.6. Left to right: *Junior Two (Jim Boyd), Aristotle (Gene Tagaban), Agnes (Michelle St. John), and Junior Three (Sherman Alexie) discuss Seymour and his poems during Mouse's funeral on the Spokane Indian Reservation. Photo by Larry Estes; used with his permission.*

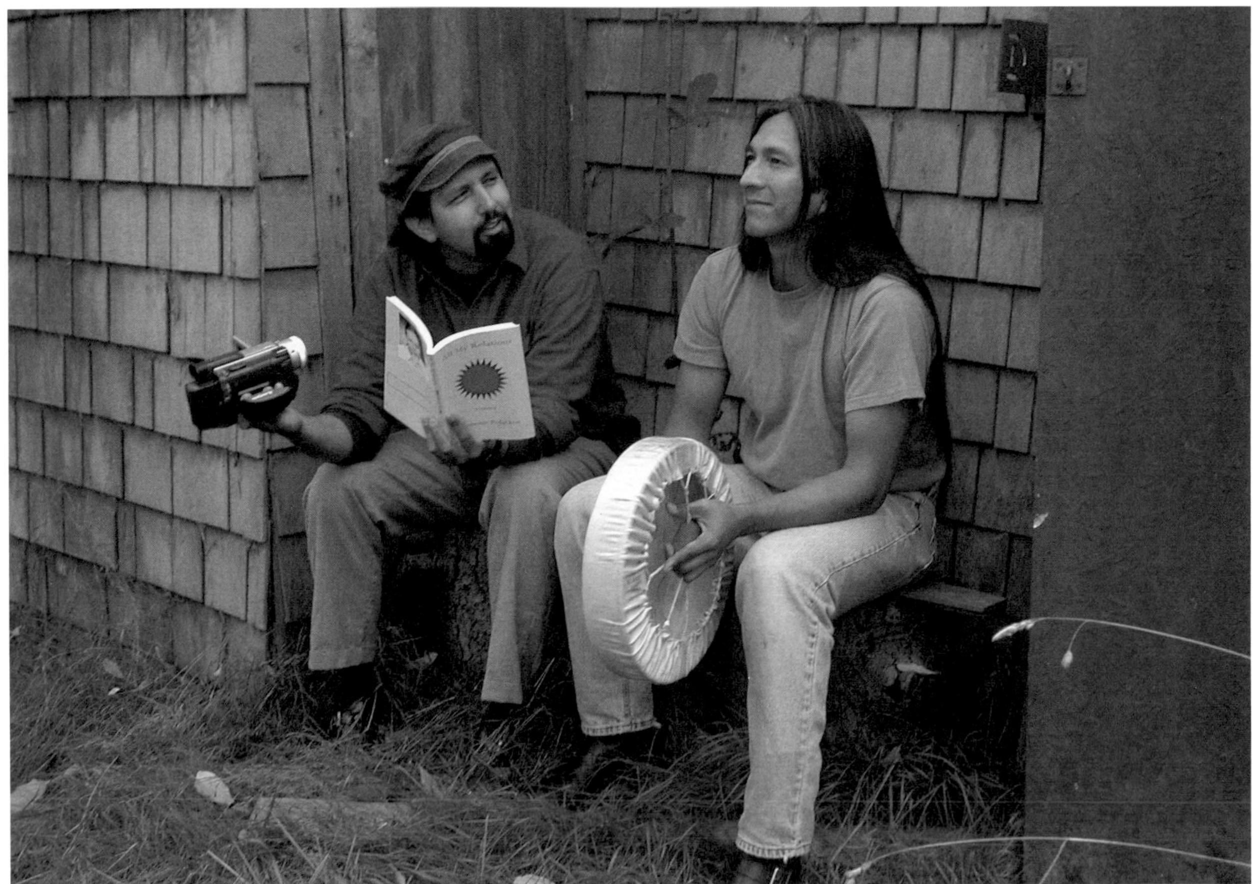

FIGURE 7.7. *Mouse (Swil Kanim,* left*) and Aristotle discuss a book of Seymour's poems. Photo by Larry Estes; used with his permission.*

acknowledges that even though he may have left the reservation long ago, it remains the one topic in his poetry he returns to time and again. It seems to be the one place where he can locate his Indianness. Provenance and figurations, positionality and memory—these are the regions of writing, the systems of survivance, and they are the tools, the implements of Indianness.

More than being about Seymour or Alexie, *Fancydancing* is about Indianness—about the presence of Indianness despite its absence in mainstream America, the parlor room of manifest manners. On one hand, this may not seem like one of the new stories Vizenor has in mind, but on the other, it is radical in its simplicity. The discourse of domination would lead you to believe that Indians and Indian cultural production are, at their core, irrelevant. But Alexie and Seymour have something to say about that. In the face of nearly totalizing cultural machinery programmed to quietly shuffle Indian aesthetic activism back behind the curtains and the props, people like Alexie are whipping out tools to construct a grand stage.

Even though *Fancydancing* didn't do as well with audiences and critics as *Smoke Signals*, for me it is the more interesting of the two movies, in part because it breaks all the rules. It doesn't worry about representation; it concentrates on innovation. It liberates indigenization from fetishization. On an aesthetic level, the film's collage structure, its full embrace of nonnarrativity, and its open-endedness imbue it with a sympathetic indigenous consciousness—what I think of as postmodernism with a heart. Another reason the movie works for me is that it never strives for metanarrativity. It aspires for neither comprehensiveness nor totality. It remains, even within its world of inclusion, acceptance, and tolerance, a version of Indian realities, a fragmentary and imaginative rendering of what is and what is not, a simulation of postindian ingenuity and determination.

Despite the fact that the film doesn't write Seymour as completely as Alexie writes himself, one can make an argument that Seymour is also engaged in a postindian project. He wants to reconcile himself to the reservation and the reservation to the present. Famous and successful, gay and urban, he knows he is both loathed and loved, misunderstood and martyred. But most importantly, he makes it his mission to advance Indian fortitude through Indian aesthetic values. In this regard, Agnes stands as the best reader of Seymour's work. After Alexie's character takes Seymour and his poems to task, Agnes retorts: "He's fightin' the war, you know? He's telling everybody that we're still here. He does it for all of us." Seymour, the postindian warrior; Seymour, the fashioner of new stories; Seymour, the manifestation of engaged resistance.

In his important book *The World in a Frame*, film critic Leo Braudy links the popularity of film formulas with audience desire: "Genre films essentially ask the audience, 'Do you still want to believe this?' . . . Change in genre occurs when the audience says, 'That's too infantile a form of what we believe. Show us something more complicated.'" (38). To be sure, Braudy is correct. But for the postmodern, postindian, self-reflexive film, the most important audience may be the filmmaker himself. *The Business of Fancydancing* stands as Alexie's most interesting, most complicated answer to Braudy's question.

Reading Alexie's cinema projects alongside each other and within the frame of postindianism makes for good intertext. At first, the movies seem wildly dissimilar—one a mainstream picture designed for a mainstream audience; the other an intentional frustration of every possible expectation and, simultaneously, a postmodern self-referential experiment—but if one imagines each completing the incompleteness of the other, if one imagines each filling in the other's lacunae, then, together, they out-Vizenor Vizenor. They provide the most accessible examples of postindianism because, despite their sense of humor, their sense of play, they migrate through pure theory. Like a savvy trickster, they dodge genres, they avoid the trap of receptive determinacy; they embody resistance in motion—a moving, changing praxis that merges process with populism, subversion with survivance. Perhaps most importantly, though, they demonstrate that postindiansim, like Indianism in general, is, at its core, funny.

You can really do no better work than that.

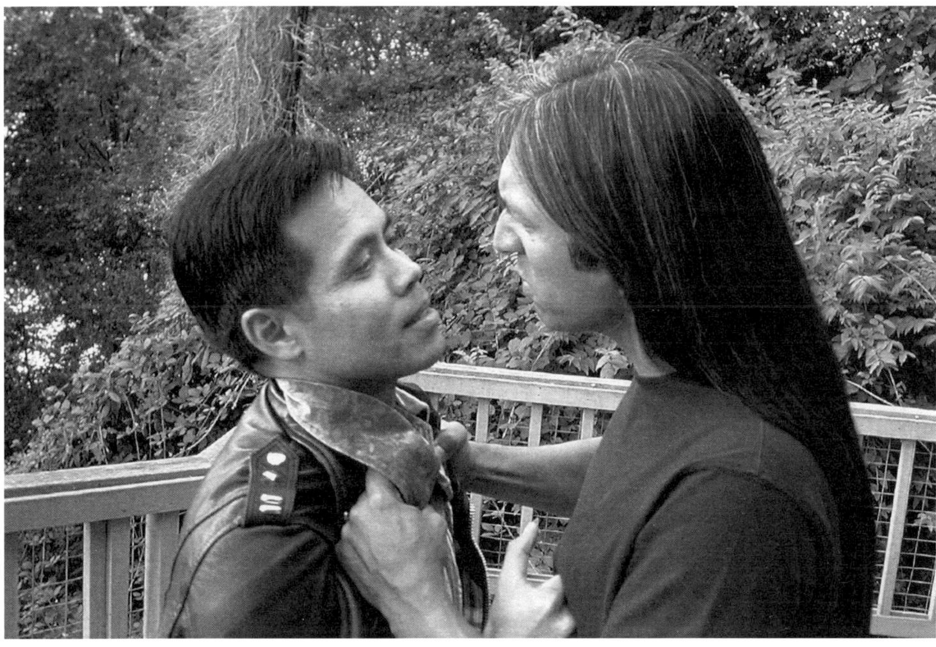

FIGURE 7.8. *Aristotle confronts Seymour about issues of love, loyalty, and identity. Photo by Larry Estes; used with his permission.*

Subversion and survivance: circle from one storyteller to another.

8.

NARRATIVE RESISTANCE

LESLIE MARMON SILKO'S "STORYTELLER"

She went on with the story,
and she never stopped.

IT MIGHT SEEM ODD in a monograph that moves across so many genres to devote an entire chapter to a single short story, but Leslie Silko's "Storyteller" is no ordinary story. It remains among the most frequently taught and anthologized short texts by an Indian writer, making it, for better or worse, a kind of rest stop on the highway of the American literature survey course. With its circular narrative, its emphasis on storytelling, its focus on landscape, and its exploration of Indian-white relations, it is the native short story used more often than any I know. In short, "Storyteller" has come to metonymize "Native American Literature."

Interestingly, the story also remains Silko's favorite.[1]

What makes the story attractive to anthology editors, professors, and general readers is probably not what makes Silko cotton to "Storyteller." But then again, we don't always know exactly why we are drawn to complex texts; there may be more at work in the story that bridges Silko, the editors who reprint her work, and the professors who teach it. Because of its popularity in the classroom, "Storyteller" has been the subject of pedagogical essays penned by some of the brightest scholars in the field, including Helen Jaskoski. The combination of "Storyteller"'s complexity and ubiquity make pedagogical aids almost a necessity. Though I hope all the chapters in *Engaged Resistance* prove to be teachable, this chapter looks at "Storyteller" through a straightforwardly pedagogical lens.

Most authors of monographs rarely consider the usefulness of their studies to the surly, confused sophomore who might stumble upon the books in the library or, more likely, on Google Books. Nor do they often take into account the even surlier, rushed, overworked instructor prepping at the last minute for a survey class of forty-plus students. It is even rarer for scholars to address the casual reader who has no interest in jargoned musings but just wants to know more about Native American writing. The aim of this short chapter is to offer a focused, accessible close reading of a text that resists close readings. My hope is that it will bring a potentially distancing text like "Storyteller" and a foreign (but relatable) concept like "engaged resistance" into the classroom. Or, for the general reader long out of college, this chapter seeks to make the concept of engaged resistance palatable enough to actually help a piece like "Storyteller" make more sense, so that the concept and the story might work their way into a conversation with what academics tend to think of as normal people.

This chapter is also a sort of apology for the close reading. The *explication de texte*, so out of fashion for the past twenty years, is poised to make a comeback with the popularity of semiotics and visual culture, which demand close attention to codes, symbols, and visual cues. Though "Storyteller" is never talked about in these terms, I find it a particularly visual text. Certain tenets of semiotics, then, can provide yet another tool to aid any close reading; so in addition to traditional literary terms and techniques, I hope to show how literary semiotics—the visual markings and cues a text gives—can help unpack a packed text.

My thesis here is that "Storyteller"'s narrative totality—its structure, language, theme, even its epistemology—embodies resistance. In and of itself, that claim is only partly useful. However, I hope to show how Silko's story also simultaneously asserts (and embodies) a narrative engagement that heretofore has gone either unnoticed or unexamined by critics. Though there are many different notions of "narrative," I am using it here in a relatively populist manner as a mechanism of organization and articulation. In her entry on defining "narrative" for the *Cambridge Companion to Narrative*, Marie-Laurie Ryan invokes Peter Brooks to make a similar claim for narrative's ability to make sense of human experience: "Narrative is one of the principal ways we organize our experience of the world—a part of our cognitive tool kit that was long neglected by psychologists and philosophers" (22). Similarly, in her essay on Silko and the narrative schematic, Dharma Thornton Hernandez argues, by way of psychologists Lynne Angus and Karen Hardtke, that a "narrative is not simply a story; it is a process that 'generates explanations of everyday events and organizes these experiences into a coherent self-identity or life-story'" ("*Storyteller*: Revising," 55). Narrative, then, synthesizes. It collects and organizes data so that we can understand it better—a virtual iPhone for literary interpretation. The reason this kind of synthesis aids in understanding is because the world comes to us in stories; we have practice organizing the effluvium of living into the stories of our lives. Whether we know it or not, we narrativize nearly all of the data we take in daily into a kind of account of who we are, what we believe in, where we are going, and what our place in the world might be. We are always writing and rewriting the story that is our existence; the story we tell ourselves about ourselves is our narrative.

This is especially so, avers Jace Weaver, for Indian writers: "Narrative is a means that colonized people employ to assert their own existence and identity. The struggle may be land and sovereignty, but it is often reflected, contested, and decided in narrative" (*That the People Might Live,* 41–42). In the case of "Storyteller," it is land, sovereignty, and narrative. In fact, so important is this concept to the text that two narrative processes take place: a micronarrative (the main character's collation and distillation of past, present, and future events) and a macronarrative (Leslie Marmon Silko's collation and distillation of past, present, and future characters and plotlines). The latter becomes the story, "Storyteller"; the former pushes the plot along and gives "Storyteller" humanity and meaning. My point is that the story's story—the narrative of "Storyteller"—is itself an organizing mechanism with its own identity and experience and, in particular, its own process.

The Story of "Storyteller"

Despite (or because of) its popularity, "Storyteller"'s story is an unusual one. First published in 1975 in the literary magazine *Puerto del Sol*, "Storyteller" was written after Silko took a trip to Alaska. As most stories do in little magazines with small subscriptions, it went virtually unnoticed until it appeared as the first short story in *Storyteller* (1981), Silko's fabulous collection of poems, photographs, letters, essays, and stories. As many have noted, "Storyteller" feels almost out of place in *Storyteller*, primarily because of its narrative placement-displacement.[2] Unlike everything else in *Storyteller*, which is set in or around Laguna and the other pueblos of New Mexico and Arizona, "Storyteller" takes place on the tundra of Bethel, Alaska, among the Yupik. Even more puzzling is the fact that while Silko was writing "Storyteller," she was also working on *Ceremony*, a book so fully ensconced in the Southwest that it is hard to imagine her relocating even her fictional structures to an almost completely opposite landscape. Still, even if the physical landscape feels alien, the compositional landscape of circumference, space, resistance, and distance is pure Silko.

In many ways, "Storyteller" is about distance, though it is also about proximity, or, to be more precise, the proximity of distance—how entities that are or should be close are actually leagues, centuries, and cultures apart. The story also explores the desire for proximity and distance (both personal and cultural) and how that desire can lead to colonization and death but also to narrative. And it is through narrative—its architecture, energy, and connection—that the story uses notions of distance and proximity to reach both teller and audience. At first, it might seem counterintuitive and counterproductive to employ distance as a controlling metaphor for a short story the author wants people to feel close to, but part of Silko's project is to help the reader understand the seemingly unbridgeable cultural expanse between the two ethnic groups in the story—the Gussuck and the Yupik.[3] So she creates both a geographic and an interpretive distance that simultaneously sets the stage for the story and puts the reader up on that stage, but, frustratingly for some, with no stage directions and virtually no script.

"Storyteller" is a difficult text because it is rendered in a manner that is difficult to parse. From a plot perspective, though, it is relatively straightforward. Silko's story follows the narrative and recollective spoor of a young Yupik woman through a series of tragic and bizarre events. Via flashbacks, cutaways, and cinematic edits of time and chronology, a web emerges that spirals out a series of interconnected events the reader is ultimately able to collage into concatenated, liminal meaning:

- An unnamed young Eskimo woman, whose parents died when she was young, is in prison for murder.
- Before her incarceration, she lived with her grandmother and a similarly unnamed "old man" (a local storyteller), who is on his deathbed.
- The woman engages in a disturbing sexual encounter with a white roughneck and has, in the past, been sexually involved with the old man.
- As he slowly moves toward death, the old man tells a long, detailed story about hunting a bear on a frozen river—a story that continues throughout "Storyteller."
- The woman discovers that a local shopkeeper is responsible for poisoning her parents with bad alcohol.
- She decides to enact revenge on the shopkeeper by luring him out onto thin ice over a river, the way the hunter kills the bear in the old man's story.
- Despite advice from her attorney, the woman refuses to lie about the manner of the shopkeeper's death or even to give any context whatsoever for the turn of events.
- The old man eventually dies.
- From her prison cell, the woman becomes a storyteller herself (which is also where the story begins).[4]

The chronology and factual details of the events are far less important than their narrative aggregate—that is, what kind of work is done by techniques like theme, structure, and characterization and how Silko pulls the nonlinear, nonchronological pieces together to create a holistic puzzle.

Characterization as Resistance

Silko's odd characterization in "Storyteller" serves as a good entrée to this discussion, since her characters frustrate easy assumptions about how literary characters should develop. Take, for example, Silko's figuration of the young woman, the old man, the roughneck, and the shopkeeper. None of these characters gets fleshed out; they remain, like the landscape, shadowy, liminal, hazy. The author endows none of them with names and provides them with only the most minimal, fragmented backstories, suggesting that what they stand for is more important than who they are. In fact, one could argue that what the characters signify becomes their identity. In the case of the old man, one finds no character development but infinite character connotation. His presence evokes both tradition and perception, past and performance. He is the storyteller incarnate, the one who knows land and people, whose language was part of the land before the Gussucks (Anglos) arrived to eviscerate both. Physically, Silko makes him a less than desirable character—he smells of fish and urine, he hates to leave his bed, and he comes off as more than a little creepy—but culturally he is the voice and vision of the community. As a storyteller, he is also the mentor for the woman, even if she doesn't know it yet. The important thing is that he does.

Standing in stark contrast to the Old Man are the shopkeeper and the roughneck. Silko links these two Gussucks not simply through their ethnicity but also through their disregard for the indigenous community and for their shared project of acquisition and accumulation. "They only come when there is something to steal" (22), the old man tells her. Though it seems he is referring to oil or land, as the reader and the girl discover, the old man has a wider net of theft in mind. Toward the end of the story, while standing in the shopkeeper's store, the reader sees the girl begin to put the pieces of a larger story together, drawing an intellectual line from the shopkeeper to the roughneck to the entire colonial enterprise: "He remembered how she had gone with the oil drillers, and his blue eyes moved like flies crawling over her body. He held his thin pale lips like he wanted to spit on her. He hated the people because they had something of value, the old man said, something which the Gussucks could never have. They thought they could take it, suck it out of the earth or cut it from the mountains; but they were fools" (29). The shopkeeper and his Anglo counterparts move to the tundra to strip land from the Eskimo, and the roughneck moves to the tundra to strip the land of oil and, at least in this story, to strip the protagonist of her clothes and her dignity. Neither have the best interests of the Yupik at heart because—like the Indians on the Plains and in the West and Southwest—they get in the way. Both literally and symbolically, indigeneity stands between land exploitation and land preservation.

As readers, we never get to know the roughneck or the shopkeeper, though we understand that we are not to like them, that their desires are antithetical to the young woman and the old man. Later, I go into more detail about what the characters might symbolize, but suffice it to say that as literary characters, they are more flat than round—an intentional design that says less about her ability to create three-dimensional people and more about Silko's nearly global metaphors.

Indeed, the shopkeeper and the roughneck serve largely to embody the metaphorics of erasure. Silko illustrates this on a communal level through eradicative drilling and land removal, which seem less about expansion than destruction. All indications point to the desire to wipe the Yupik off the map and be done with them. So overwhelming is this desire that it gets enacted on a personal level as well, seen most notably through the roughneck's bizarre sexual encounter with the young woman and the shopkeeper's intentionality in regard to the murder of her parents. Curious about what sex with someone other than the old man might be like, curious to know what the roughneck looks like beneath his heavy work clothes, she begins a short liaison with him that moves from the merely odd to the perverse. During the sexual act, the woman notices that the man tapes a picture up on the wall and that it becomes the focus of his attention. When he is done, he carefully removes it and folds it away. Curious about that as well, she sneaks a peak on what she knows will be her final visit to his room, only to discover the photo is of a dog. This scenario revels less about the roughneck's sexual predilections and more about the Gussucks' perception of the Yupik. It is easy to rob a people of land and humanity when they are not people. Again, the woman's inquisitiveness provides her with an accrual of clues that help her construct a narrative of her conscious landscape. For Jaskoski, this keen interest in synthesizing, enlarging, and building stands in sharp contrast to the Gussuck venture of obliteration (*Leslie Marmon Silko*, 14–15).

What's fascinating is the woman's ability to compose her narrative amidst a culture of erasure. "Her story," writes Cynthia Carsten, "is one of complete cultural disruption by the Gussucks . . . From the strange intrusive square buildings of the school and the Bureau of Indian Affairs to the oil drillers who exploit her sexuality, the landscape and her life are ravaged by the domination of the Gussucks" ("*Storyteller*: Reappropriation," 112). So complete is this destruction that it seems to have erased her personal identity as well. Despite the fact that she is the main character and we follow her story from the beginning of its telling to the end, we really never gain much information about her, other than facts of her life. Who she is as a person and what motivates her actions and her emotional spectrum remain largely mysteries. What we do learn is that she and her family have been victimized, and that she has retaliated. It also appears that after the old man passed away, she assumes the role of a storyteller. In fact, the turn of events suggests that it is precisely her inspirational defiance that generates the story—two acts connected by destiny and design. After she has been imprisoned, her attorney pleads with her to say the man's death was an accident, but she will have none of it. Silko writes: "She shook her head. 'I will not change the story, not even to escape this place and go home. I intended that he die. The story must be told as it is'" (31). The girl, then, embodies resistance. She is the characterization of the new generation of defiance.

Ultimately, Silko's characters operate in service to the story's thematics. Jaskoski goes so far as to suggest that the story is allegory: "The characters—the grandmother, the old man, the storeman (or men), the jailer, the dormitory matron, the village people, and the protagonist girl/woman—all have the archetypal anonymity of mythical personages" (*Leslie Marmon Silko*, 19). This observation is important because it suggests that Silko's characterization is rhetorical. This is not to say the characters don't have significance on their own, but their primary functionality lies within the story's thematic framework, much like a fable or a folktale. Rather than functioning as round characters with an arc and internal growth, the characters evince an argument; they are assertions toward a thesis.

Narrative Circumscription

It is worth asking, then, what exactly Silko argues in "Storyteller."[5] Though many critics have discussed the story's theme, it seems to me that such discussions deemphasize Silko's storytelling, especially when we consider the similarities between the young woman's project and Silko's. Indeed, both the woman's story and Silko's make the argument that telling your own story in your own way is both an act of resistance and an act of narrative circumscription. What I call narrative circumscription is a form of verbal articulation in which story making and storytelling simultaneously enact a circular identity that is both personal and communal. In the case of "Storyteller," the term's reciprocity will become particularly important when discussing the story's structure, but for now, suffice it to say that for the protagonist (and perhaps even for Silko), telling a story on one's own terms is about finding a voice, finding how one articulates one's identity in the world. Linked to that is the significance of survivance, the active practice of cultural endurance. Survivance is more than existence: it is the creative process of tribal making, community building through the maintenance of identity. These things can happen only through what Silko describes as the "telling which continues." Survivance and continuance are linked by their interactivity, their cumulative power of self-determination. It is not that the one speaks for the many; it is that the one speaks with, and with the voice of, the many.

In LeAnne Howe's *Shell Shaker*, a similarly unexplainable murder is at the center of the story. The mother of the main protagonist, Auda Billy, claims to have committed the murder, but midway through the novel, in the presence of a lawyer, the sheriff, and members of her family, Auda herself confesses to the murder when, "without warning her mother's voice roars out of her mouth, "*I killed Redford McAlester! I did it and I alone will stand trial for his murder!*" (87). Auda is somewhat surprised by her confession, but she owns it, much the same way the woman owns her story in "Storyteller." In both instances, the storyteller's voice seems to be spoken not by the putative speaker but by the previous generation. For the woman, her version of how she lured the shopkeeper out onto the ice was narrated by the old man as he told the story of the hunter and the bear; likewise, Auda's voice was that of her mother's, as if to suggest that individual autonomy defines tribal autonomy. Or, put another way, sovereignty is both an individual and a group effort. The storyteller never stands alone.

That notion, so central to indigenous communities, clashes with the value system of the Gussucks—a realization that also helps our protagonist frame her narrative. After the woman refuses to admit that the shopkeeper's death was accidental, Silko lets us peek into her head: "She laughed out loud when the jailer translated what the attorney said. The Gussucks did not understand the story; they could not see the way it must be told, year after year as the old man had done, without lapse or silence" (31–32). The woman's laugh echoes, literally, throughout the story, and up until now, the laugh was her only form of vocalized resistance. Neither English nor Yupik, it functions as a defiant exclamation of mockery, derision, refusal, and assertion. But now that a story has found her (and she, a story), she can more fully articulate these emotions and her story through language. And as Jaskoski rightly notes, language and identity are fundamentally intertwined: "'Storyteller' takes up language in two senses: the language of individual and communal self-creation that is storytelling, and the language—and silence—that creates boundary, identity, and personal power" (*Leslie Marmon Silko*, 14).

One of the forces that cannot be stripped by mining, drilling, or removal, language stands as the unifying web connecting past and present, internal and external, resistance and engagement. For John Big Bluff Tosamah (the Priest of the Sun) in N. Scott Momaday's *House Made of Dawn*, his grandmother Tai-Me's sacred relationship with the word distinguishes the Kiowa world from "the white man's world," in which "such things as words and literature [are taken] for granted" (95). Relying on the performative and transformative power of the word to move his congregation, Tosamah, like the young woman and Auda Billy, charges the speaking present with the voice of the past: "And be assured that her regard for words was always keen in proportion as she depended upon them. You see, for her words were medicine; they were magic and invisible. They came from nothing into sound and meaning. They were beyond price; they could never be bought nor sold. And she never threw words away" (96). In *House Made of Dawn*, as in "Storyteller," the Native association with language provides a cultural inoculation against the malady of avaricious conquest in which everything—bodies of land, bodies of people—can be devoured.

Along these same lines, Brewster E. Fitz maintains that "Storyteller" works against Western constructs of objectivity, justice, and Christian morality. For him, "Storyteller," like *Ceremony*, is a form of "healing writing." "This healing writing," Fitz argues, "indicts the narrative of Anglo-American Law, which Silko had studied for three semesters then abandoned in order to pursue graduate study in literature and writing, because she finally realized that 'injustice is built into the Anglo-American legal system'" (*Silko,* 60). One of the arguments this book makes is that Native writers, filmmakers, and painters turn to cultural production in the absence of political or legal options. As Silko discovered, there are alternatives to the courtroom or the police. She, like her protagonist, enacts justice outside the system; to the Western metanarratives, Silko constructs counternarratives. Magic and invisible, the word, language—these stories—are power.

In addition to personal power, the woman-cum-storyteller also enacts tribal power through her new role as storier. In her smart reading of "Storyteller," Kathryn W. Shanley correctly identifies not only how important the woman will be in her new role but also the sacrifice that role demands. Through her story, says Shanley, the woman "has successfully resurrected the native voice, the voice that speaks out of a connectedness to the land. The story hinges on an incredible irony: the survival of the girl and her people—survival, that is, in spiritual and cultural terms specific to them as people—depends on her ability to tell the story; yet in order for her story to be told, she must enter the terms of the dominant culture's discourse as categorically condemned—as murderer and fornicator" ("Devil's Domain," 176–177). If Shanley and Jaskoski are correct, and I think they are, Silko's ultimate argument in "Storyteller" is that the Native world—language, the individual, and the tribe—depends on telling the right story, at the right time, and in the right way, no matter the cost. If it means the woman or Auda goes to jail, prison confines only the body; culture and history and tradition slip through any bars.

To understand and mitigate that cost, it is worth spending some time on Shanley's first point—the Native voice's connection to the land. Both Shanley and Jaskoski are emphatic that land and language are not just important but interconnected. "The landscape is so crucial," writes Jaskoski, "that it comes to have the force of a character" (*Leslie Marmon Silko,* 14). And Silko herself has expressed how important setting is in "Storyteller": "Nowhere is landscape more crucial to the outcome than in my short story 'Storyteller'" ("Interior and Exterior Landscapes," 44). One wonders what outcome Silko has in mind here—the outcome of the shopkeeper or the outcome of the young woman. I suspect, as most readers do, Silko refers to both, since one leads to the other. But Silko hints toward this reading herself: "I love that story just because I like the characters *and* how she does the guy in" ("Stories and Their Tellers," 23; emphasis added).

Outcomes

But I am interested in the outcome of the woman—as are my students. As they often ask, are we to assume she spends the rest of her life (or a good portion of it) in prison? As teachers and scholars, we should be transparent in this regard—most current and future readers of "Storyteller" are going to be undergraduate students and the professors teaching the story to them. Undergraduates, who are likely around the same age as the main character, are often vexed by a story that is supposed to be "empowering," "pro-Indian," and "about resistance" but that closes with its protagonist in jail, her mentor dead, the destruction of her community all but impending, and, most confusingly, the young woman refusing to seek her own liberation so that she can be an active force in the community. Despite the proliferation of readings of "Storyteller," no one really answers the one question that students raised in a culture of *CSI* always ask: is the reader supposed to be satisfied that the woman—the village's new storyteller—is destined to remain behind bars indefinitely, even though there is no evidence she literally killed anyone?

This is a fair question and not as simplistic as it may sound. I believe we owe it to readers and students to explain the outcome of this story in terms other than those grounded in the often vague and detached jargon of postcolonialism, poststructuralism, or Bakhtinian dialogism. The answer, I believe, lies in her role as storyteller and to telling's connection to place—that is where we ultimately live, where we spend our days. We might call this place "landscape"; we might call it "home"; we might call it "milieu." Whatever term we use, it is connected to the place we build for ourselves, where we dwell, which may or may not have anything to do with where our bodies are incarcerated. As so many ceremonies in tribal cultures suggest, we are more than body: we are that which propels itself outward. In the case of Silko, Howe, and Momaday, storytelling can lift the teller out of time, into a place that is both internal and external.

Note how Silko prefaces her comment above by suggesting that in this story, inner and outer are one and the same: "The story is interesting to me and I like it because, perhaps because the landscape is different, because I find a common point where I can relate to the land, regardless of whether it's land I'm from or not. That's a big step for me, to go to a completely alien landscape. I managed. What I did in that story finally was to get the interior landscapes of the characters, and yet they are still related to the tundra and the river because that's how she does the guy in" (22–23). There is a potentially confusing circularity at work here that I hope the reader's patience will allow me to explain. As Jaskoski and others have noted (including Silko), language is fundamentally tied to landscape. The words one uses, the rhythms and topics of telling, the icons of storytelling are contingent upon the place out of which the story arises. Which is to say, if we take Silko at her word (and we have no reason not to), then "Storyteller" is as much about interior landscape as exterior. So if, on one hand, "Storyteller" emphasizes telling, and on the other it foregrounds interiority, then for this particular allegory, where the woman physically ends up is less important than the narrative place she creates. In other words, she ultimately resides not in the cell but in the interior space she speaks into being with the help of her grandmother and, in particular, the old man, who has provided her with a map of the internal terrain of telling.

Indeed, the old man models for the woman—as though he portends her fate—how one lives through story. Even though he is himself a prisoner in his own bed, he resides in his perpetual narration of land, animal, and hunter: "He had not fished or hunted with the other men for many years, although he was not crippled or sick. He stayed in his bed, smelling like dry fish and urine, telling stories all winter" (19). As the story accretes, the man never leaves his bed or stops telling the story except to use the toilet, though, as the passage above suggests, he may not always leave even for that. Still, even when robbed of his dignity, almost all of his cultural practices, and his rituals, he refuses to be imprisoned.

"We are what we imagine," writes Momaday in "The Man Made Out of Words," a point Bernard A. Hirsch uses to argue for a thematics of survival in Silko's work (39). For Hirsch, Silko's reworking of "the oral tradition" is a "self-renewing act of imagination/memory designed to keep storytellers as well as stories from so tragic a fate" ("'The Telling Which Continues,'" 4). Yes, the woman's fate is that she winds up in prison, but that is not her life. From the old man, the woman learns the cartography of narrative survivance. She follows his spoor of telling just as the hunter tracks the prints of the bear, and they lead her to a place where she dwells not in her cell but in the liberating space of narrative. In fact, it is through telling and truth telling that she buries the ghost truly imprisoning her. Even though she is in jail, she finds identity. Most importantly, she finds identity as a storyteller on her own terms. She resists the colonial machinations of the roughnecks and the sexual and capitalist omnivorousness of the other Gussucks. She resists saying what the attorney wants her to say. She resists speaking English with her jailer. She resists erasure.

For students and instructors still at odds with the story's ending, it may be useful to think of the woman's resolution as a combination of sacrifice and survivance. The Gussucks appear to be free, but are, in truth, prisoners to a cycle of eradication, destruction, and consumption. The young woman locates liberation through her role in the community; her position as truth teller and storier endows her with a moral authority the Anglos on the outside lack. In a profound moment of cultural reversal, it is only when she is a prisoner that her story gets heard by both Native and Anglo audiences. As Cynthia Carsten notes, through the translative actions of the jailer, her story makes its way into English: "She wants the truth of her story—the corruption of her world by the Gussucks—and her act of resistance to be heard. The only way she can regain control of her world is to stay in jail, narrating her story through her jailer, who has been assimilated to the culture and language of the whites" ("*Storyteller*: Reappropriation," 113). Thus, she recounts the transgressions of the enemy in the enemy's language. She finds liberation through telling, speaking truth about land and power. She is, in the words of Paula Gunn Allen, a "word warrior," a soldier of survivance.[6]

Native Narrativity and Compositional Resistance

"Storyteller"'s structure augments this reading because it plays with chronology and linearity in a way that undermines conventional Anglo notions of temporality. The woman's refusal to change her story is an act of resistance, and Silko's refusal to change her story or its telling to fit the conventions of literary narrative or linear time is a similarly liberating and identity-making act of what I have called in this book compositional resistance. As Hirsch, Linda Krumholz, and Toby C. S. Langen have all demonstrated, the structure of *Storyteller* proper reflects Pueblo and, in particular, Laguna systems of narrative and meaning making.[7] In the larger book, Silko jumps from photo to essay to poem to letter to short story, creating a collage of genres and texts. Like a web (Linda Danielson's metaphor) or a woven basket (Langen), Silko weaves together seemingly unrelated strands of signification. "This breakdown of generic boundaries," argues Krumholz, "challenges Western aesthetic categories and reading methods" ("Native Designs," 72).[8] Not surprisingly, the book's short-story namesake does similar work. Most who write about the story discuss in some form or another its design, and anyone who has taught "Storyteller" knows how that design can trip up students who expect a conventional plot and narrative arc. The text neither begins at the beginning nor ends at the end, and the middle is never really the middle. Though it is a mistake to call the story a circle, it is circular. Like Louise Erdrich's *Love Medicine*, "Storyteller" is more a spiral or a circle within a circle than a simple hoop. The narrative rivers do not flow into one another; rather, they start at one point and end at another, similar, proximate point. Throughout the story, the narrative jumps around, circling back on itself, shifting in time, ultimately becoming a structural metonym for the entire book. "Storyteller"'s design, then, becomes itself an act of resistance, a narrative refusal to capitulate to colonial or generic linearity and chronology—a point I make in Chapter 10, about the design of the National Museum of the American Indian. Native spaces, regardless of where they are built or what they are built out of, always speak back to an other.

That structure also reinforces the story's other main arguments—most notably, its aesthetic awareness and its recursive thematics of dwelling and residing. Despite the fact that Silko paints the town in broad, rather unattractive strokes, the characters on the story's canvas remain attuned to aesthetic issues, though they may not articulate it in quite that way. For the old man and the woman, the details of their stories are paramount. The old

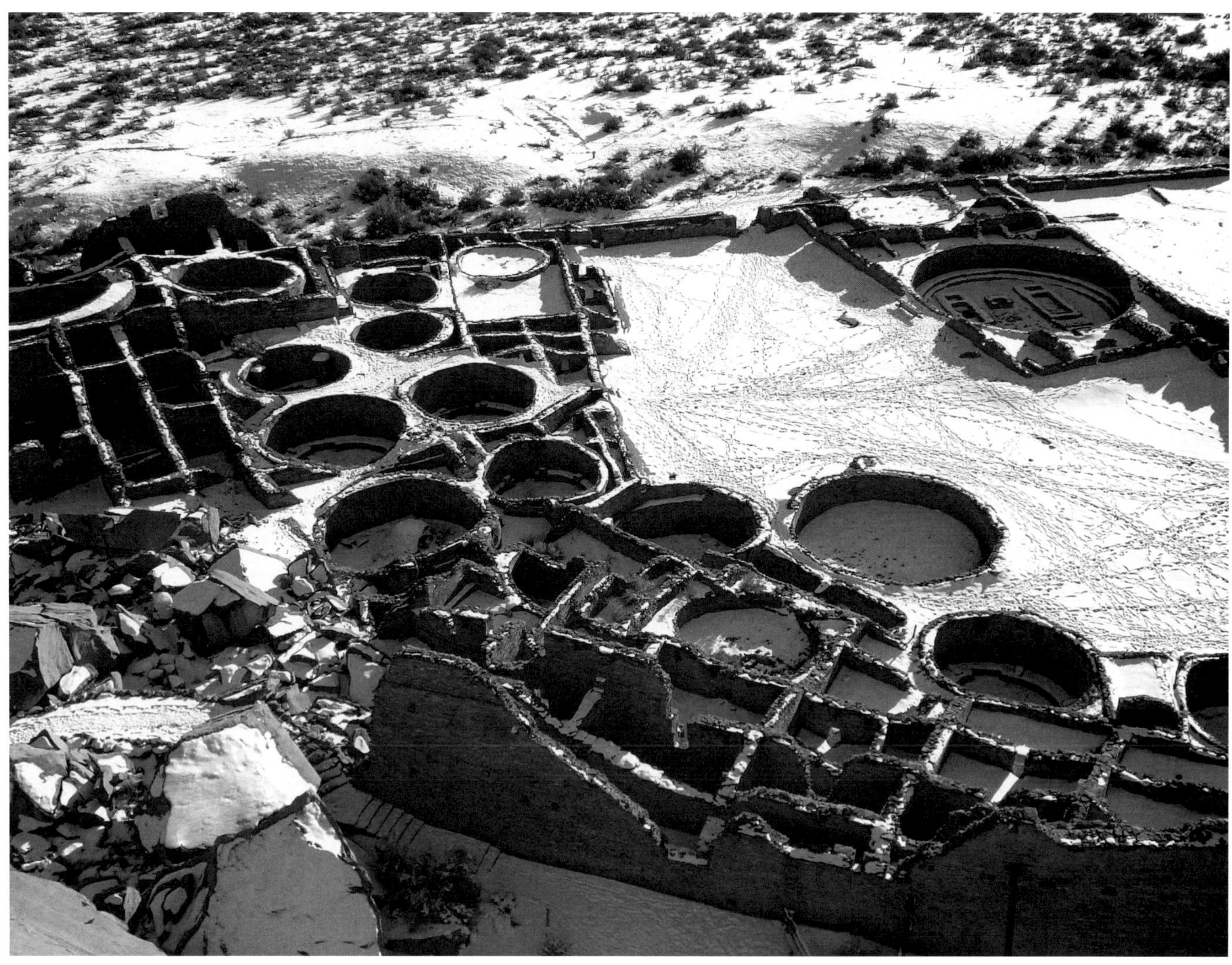

FIGURE 8.1. *Aerial shot of the Pueblo Bonito kivas, Chaco Canyon, New Mexico. The interconnected circles of the kivas mirror the interconnected circular foundation of Silko's narrative. Photo courtesy of Pueblo Bonito National Park.*

man's attention to detail goes beyond simply being accurate. He is aware not only of the beauty within his story, but also of the beauty *of* his story. Similarly, when the narrator describes how she lures the lusty shopkeeper out onto the ice, where he falls through to his death, her narrative spoor functions as a compass for the reader, a literal and cultural guide to justice, balance, and reciprocity. Like the trail of color and design on a basket, the symbolic action of aesthetic discourse reminds and reorients purpose and practice.

Just as the old man and the woman insist on telling their own stories at their own pace and on their own terms, so too does Silko encode that mode of telling for her story, which also becomes a kind of web, the starting point of which is Laguna telling. Langen's study of orality and concentrism in *Storyteller* links the circular pattern of the individual pieces back to "a Laguna oral-traditional device whose inherent traditional referentiality is not only being talked about, but also performed" ("*Storyteller* as Hopi Basket," 18). As with the Hopi basket referenced on the opening pages of *Storyteller*, story actuates both form and function. In the basket and the short story, a series of concentric compositional loops bind and intersect: first, the original Laguna stories that serve Silko as a model of concentrism; second, the collection *Storyteller*, which, as Langen shows, embodies this circularity; third, the metonymic text "Storyteller," whose architecture is also a series of circles; and fourth, the circular narratives of the old man and the woman, which embody indigenous patterns of storytelling themselves. This full-frontal engagement with Native oral narrative makes the text's resistance to Western infrastructure an assertion of tribal and individual author-ity.

The story's structure also reflects Laguna and Pueblo epistemology. "For those of you accustomed to a structure that moves from point A to point B to point C," Silko teases her Harvard audience in "Language and Literature from a Pueblo Perspective," "this presentation may be somewhat difficult to follow because the structure of Pueblo expression resembles something like a spider's web—with many little threads radiating from a center, criss-crossing each other. As with the web, the structure will emerge as it is made and you must simply listen and trust, as the Pueblo people do, that meaning will be made" (54). If we think of epistemology as a mode of knowing, a system that shapes and materializes meaning, then this web composes all facets of Pueblo life. From tales to baskets to poems to kivas, both structure and meaning process themselves through our self- and communal storytelling. "Storyteller"'s most comparable companion piece, the prosy poem "Storytelling," which appears about sixty pages later in *Storyteller,* evinces a similar structure.[9] Shifting not only from past to present and back again, it also shifts among voices. A model of polyvocality, "Storytelling" takes as its theme the importance of telling a good story, but also a more nuanced assertion that every story comprises a plurality of voices. To tell a Pueblo story right, you can't move in a linear fashion; that would be out of order, since no correlative to such compositionality exists in Pueblo modes of knowing.

The Telling Which Continues

Contrary to some of my students' assumptions, then, the nonlinearity of "Storyteller" is not a cruel collusion on the part of Silko and professors. It is not a text designed to flummox unprepared undergraduates who are already nervous that their inability to parse the story will lead to a failing grade in class. It is a complicated text to be sure, but then again, so is life. As both window and lens, "Storyteller" provides micro- and macroglimpses of how Native characters and a Native author write and right the world. Fitz makes the compelling argument that "getting to 'the interior landscape of the characters,' produces a disorienting and ambiguous depiction of an apocalyptic white otherness from which Silko returns not by telling stories to herself, like the old man, but by writing these stories for herself and for the Gussuck readers, who, like Silko cannot understand Yupik" (*Silko*, 67). Acting as both writer and translator, Silko helps readers navigate the circular terrain of her text's landscape, a text of which she is only a partial author.

"Storyteller" arrives as a story of land, borders, narrative circumscription, and outcome: land as borderless, land as language, language as borderless, telling as map, telling as identity, telling as knowing. In a world of erasure, in a world that locates nobody-ness in indigeneity, Silko demonstrates how, through telling, she and her character find somebody-ness. That act of location, though, is not an end in itself. It is a process, like story, like knowledge, and like those practices, there is no end. In the penultimate scene of the story—which happens to be, chronologically, the final scene—it is the day after the old man has died, and the village has brought to thc prisoner a split salmon, but "she did not pause or hesitate; she went on with the story, and she never stopped, not even when the women got up to close the door behind the village men." (32). The telling which continues, which continues long after doors and death, is the telling which saves, struggles, and sustains.

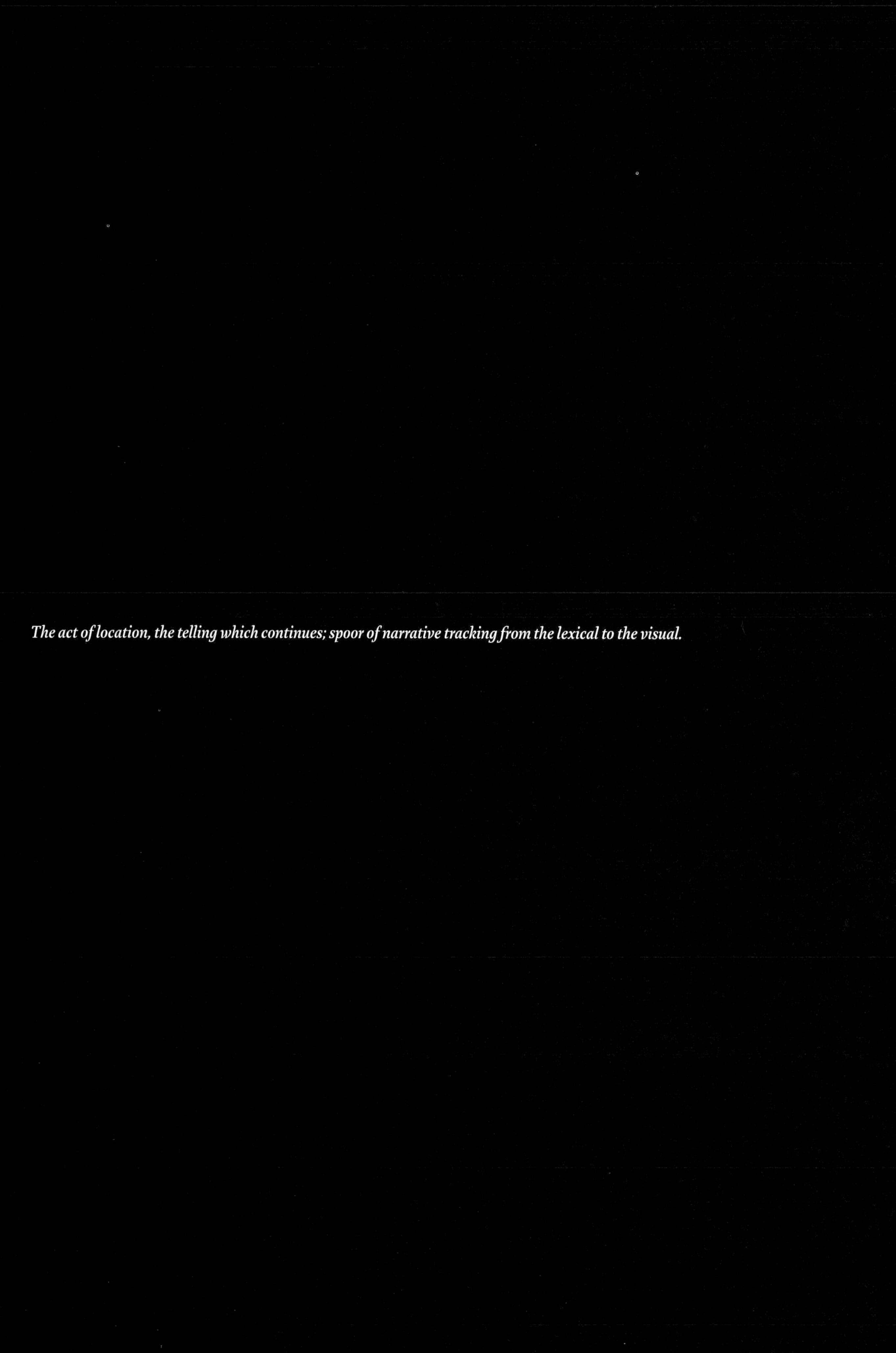

The act of location, the telling which continues; spoor of narrative tracking from the lexical to the visual.

9. ROOFS, ROADS, AND ROTUNDAS

AMERICAN INDIAN PUBLIC ART

They think you're just putting it out there, but no, you're spinning it around.

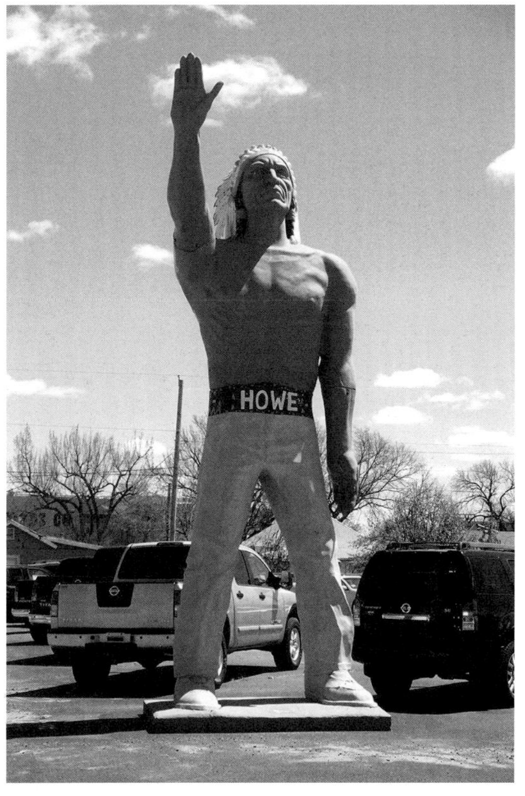

ONE OF MY EARLIEST memories is of the Howe Chevrolet Indian in Clinton, Oklahoma.

Howe Chevrolet Nissan, a large and popular car dealership, sits on the outskirts of Clinton, right off one of the main exits from Interstate 40. Any traveler who took this exit to head into Clinton would pass the Howe Indian (Fig. 9.1). Positioned out in front of the car lot is an iconic statue or sculpture of what we are to assume is a Plains Indian, complete with large headdress, buckskin pants, moccasins, and a big bare chest. Sternly visaged, his outstretched right arm with its palm facing the road, he looks at first like a Nazi saluting Hitler, but, because he is an Indian, we know he salutes not *der Fürher* but us—he is giving us the *howe* greeting. Of peculiar note is his belt buckle, which features "howe" emblazoned across it in white letters. A kind of subtitle for the semiotically impaired, the belt offers the linguistic version of the greeting that everyone knows all Indians give.

Every time we drove past the Howe Indian, I wondered why he wasn't wearing a shirt. I am sure there had been previous instances over the course of my childhood when I tried to deconstruct a complicated text, but in my mind, this image represents my first conscious engagement with semiotics. Even though I wasn't sure why the Howe statue had to be shirtless, I knew it wasn't random; I knew it was part of the overall package of the Howe Indian. Now, of course, it is clear that the bare, red-toned chest goes hand in hand with the buckskin, the moccasins, and the feathers as part of the semiotically stereotyped package: they tell us that we are in the presence of an Indian.

FIGURE 9.1. *The Howe Chevrolet Nissan Indian in Clinton, Oklahoma, just off I-40. Photo by author, 2007.*

This chapter concerns itself with what I call the coding of visual reception by addressing the semiotics of public sculptures, statues, and paintings of Indians, Indian symbolism, and Indian absence. The title of this chapter advances an uncommonly broad notion of "art," but as Esther Pasztory argues in *Thinking with Things: Toward a New Vision of Art*, "It is not possible to separate art from non-art; there are only things of various sorts, functions, forms, and meanings" (10). This is especially the case with public art. To be sure, some readers will take exception to my claim that pieces like the Howe Indian should be subsumed under the rubric of art, because such pieces, as capitalist icons of commerce, embody neither the aesthetic impulse of art nor art's tradition of truth and beauty. But I think that is naïve. Public art in this country carries with it—both intentionally and unintentionally—municipal, geographic, and cultural associations that extend beyond narrow notions of art and art history. In her excellent essay "Public Art and Its Uses," Rosalyn Deutsche says outright that "traditional art-historical paradigms cannot explicate the social functions of public art—past or present—since they remain committed to idealist assumptions that work to obscure those functions" (159). Context and backdrop, ideology and identity, all inform how we see public art. In fact, for some pieces there is more of an association with the municipality than with the artist. For example, many of the public statues and sculptures of Native Americans in Santa Fe now carry a meaning beyond themselves. They are woven into the tapestry of the town's landscape; they are part and parcel of the argument Santa Fe makes about itself. However, are these sculptures an homage to the Indians who once occupied the areas around Santa Fe, or are they part of the municipal semiotics that bring tourists and their credit cards to the plaza?

The inability to parse these two competing but complementary gestures is the impetus for this chapter. The icon of the Indian—especially the bare-chested male Indian warrior—transcends circumscription. Both public and private, both artistic and commercial, both primitive and sophisticated, this image blurs artistic intention and aesthetic reception. Employed as a mascot, a commercial brand, a logo of noble savagery, an image of lone natural Indian masculinity, and—like the nude female—a canonical subject for painters and sculptors, the image of the bare-chested Indian warrior seems both frozen in time and able to move fluidly through time itself. Indeed, has any ethnic image in America carried more diverse significations? This chapter will look closely at this image as manifest in public sculpture, but it will also pay attention to other forms of Indian iconography that, in some form or another, serve as metonyms for the Indian warrior, Indian savagery, Indian beauty, and Indian presence. Most importantly, though, in the second part of the chapter, I look closely at counterexamples of Native public art that challenge the kitsch aesthetic so much a part of Native statuary. By reading sculptures by Allan Houser, Dan Namingha, Edgar Heap of Birds, and others as countertexts of sculptural stereotypes, I show that there are two sides to the wooden nickel of Indian public art.

Almost all Indian public art trades on the same stereotypical ideas of what an Indian means. The difference between public sculptures like the Howe Indian and Edgar Heap of Birds's *Wheel*, for example, is that the former implies Indians are supernatural, primitive beings whom the audience should both marvel at and fear, while a text like *Wheel* grounds Indian identity not in Anglo nostalgia but in Native semiology. The former traffics in an invented iconography of the romanticized past, the latter in indigenous iconography of the lived past, the active present, and the visionary future.

Unlike other chapters in this book, this one will also address the tricky issue of Indian and non-Indian authorship and creativity. Who, after all, is the real "author" of the Howe Indian? Was there an "artist" behind it? Is it even Indian art? What about the sculptures of Indians around the plaza in Santa Fe that were crafted by non-Indians? Are they Indian art? I raise this issue because it affects how we see important examples of Indian public art like Enoch Kelly Haney's *The Guardian*, which sits atop the Oklahoma State Capitol rotunda, and the ambitious statue *The American*, by Osage artist Shan Gray. Larger than the Statue of Liberty, this sculpture of a bare-chested Indian brave was slated to appear outside Tulsa in 2011.[1] At 207 feet tall, it will be the largest stand-alone piece of American Indian sculpture. Neither project compares with the ongoing Crazy Horse Memorial, an enormous sculpture near Mount Rushmore, which it intends to both physically and symbolically eclipse (Fig. 9.2). The Crazy Horse Memorial is absolutely gigantic. According to the memorial's press kit, the carving will be 641 feet long by 563 feet high. The head alone, which has been completed, stands 87 feet 6 inches high. The horse's head, currently the focus of work on the mountain, is 219 feet, or 22 stories, high.[2]

At first glance, the reader might wonder what such an optimistic project as *The American* could possibly have in common with the fiberglass Howe Chevrolet Indian and its fleet of gas-guzzling cars. The answer is: more than one might think. Of course, the impetuses behind the projects might be entirely at variance with each other, but the semiotics of the two share a great deal: both deploy the bare-chested Indian male as magnet and icon. If, in fact, both are intended to get people to come to a specific site, then the fiberglass stereotyped Indian outside the car dealership might not be so different from the bronzed stereotyped Indian outside Tulsa. If, as some might argue, it is impossible for both to be art, they are, nonetheless, texts. And all texts ask to be read. All texts invite you toward them. I ask the reader's indulgence as I work through a series of sculptures and statues—none of which were carved by indigenous artists—in order to build an argument about

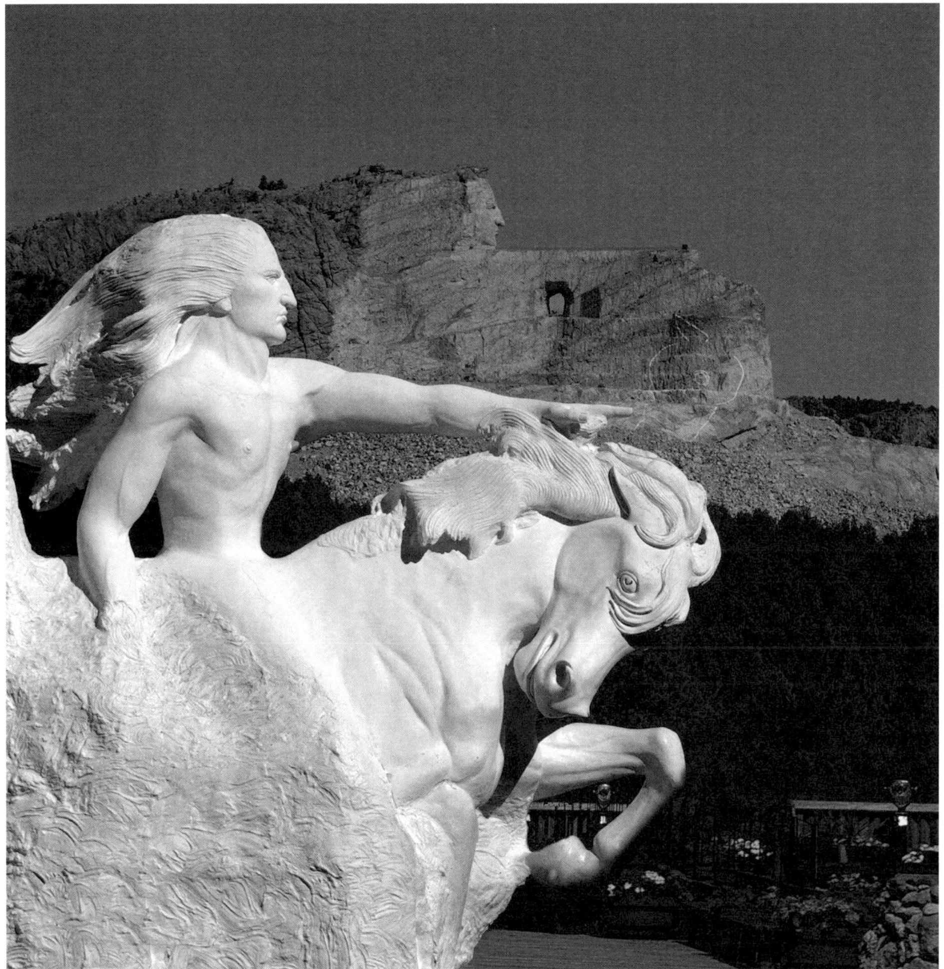

FIGURE 9.2. Foreground*: The model for the Crazy Horse Memorial. The actual carving looms in the background. Situated near Mount Rushmore, the Crazy Horse Memorial is designed to offset and even overwrite Mount Rushmore's more famous carvings of American presidents. Photo courtesy of the Crazy Horse Memorial.*

the complex condition of Indianness in American public art. Complicating these distinctions even further is the book's larger thesis of engaged resistance. Because this chapter deals with incendiary images, icons, and stereotypes that stretch broadly and deeply into high and popular culture, Native identity, and the long roots of semiotic racism, it seems to me among the most layered chapters in the book. My ultimate argument about engaged resistance hinges upon successfully working through what I see as a potential minefield of signification and a nuanced exploration of the cultural work sculptures and statues do. So I must ask for the reader's patience as I invoke the postmodern technique of deferral. In other words, I will get to it later in the chapter, but for now, back to the Howe Indian.

One of the great ironies of the twentieth century was the degree to which Indian semiotics came to symbolize the region of the country most notoriously colonized by white settlement, federal land policies, and missionary aggression. Without question, the West is one large, complicated text, ripe for any number of readings. With its mythology of "free" land, the promise of gold, virgin wilderness, and the vistas of the Rockies and the Sierras, the West (and in this term I also include the Southwest) has enjoyed decades of a kind of cultural free pass. For example, at the 2008 Republican National Convention, Cindy McCain, the wife of the Republican presidential nominee, John McCain, introduced her husband by way of autobiography. She talked openly about being raised in the West and seeing everything through the lens of western values. At one point, she referred to her father, who amassed millions, as a "true western gentleman" who embodied "western values." Ms. McCain made these pronouncements without any irony whatsoever. I kept waiting for one of the pundits to make some sort of observation about Native Americans, especially since the media had circled the wagons around the issue of race for the entire campaign. But this moment went by without comment. Nothing about the tension between Anglo acquisition of wealth in the West and Southwest; nothing about the "values" of colonialism; nothing about the ethics of Indian removal, land acquisition, and present Native realities. One of the great mysteries surrounding contemporary American discourse about western culture is the absence of Indian issues, despite the overwhelming presence of Indian semiotics.

To be sure, the main iconography of the Southwest's mythos—for better or worse—is all things Indian. On one hand, the pervasiveness of Indian imagery reminds Americans passing through Native lands that Indians are still here. On the other hand, the stereotyping—especially among roadside statues and sculptures—continues to rankle.[3] The Howe Indian has loomed over the used Pontiacs and Cherokees on its lot for close to five decades, thereby becoming a local attraction. But it also recalls, too painfully, the cigar-store Indian, which (even if unintentionally) evokes images of the stoic, "wooden," passive, and defeatable Indian reinscribed in films, comics, dime-store novels, and other illustrations of the West. Whether public art or public embarrassment, roadside Indians like the Howe version have been converted into capitalist icons, despite the fact that they originated in noncapitalist cultures.

Cigar Stores, Truck Stops, and Wild West Shows: The Semiotics of Stereotype

Though it is not a cigar store per se, the Cherokee truck stop along I-40 near Hinton, Oklahoma, asks its Indian mascot to perform similar semiotic work (Fig. 9.3). The cigar-store Indian functioned as an indicator of cigar and tobacco shops, much the same way the red, white, and blue pole indicates a barber shop (Fig. 9.4). The signifier (wooden Indian) stands in for the signified (cigar shop) and becomes not simply a visual motto but an icon.[4] In the case of the Indian, the choice of signifiers was not coincidental. Invoking the Indian tradition of tobacco is certainly part of the connection, but there are also cultural associations with bartering, trading, and even the positive attributes of getting a good deal. There is

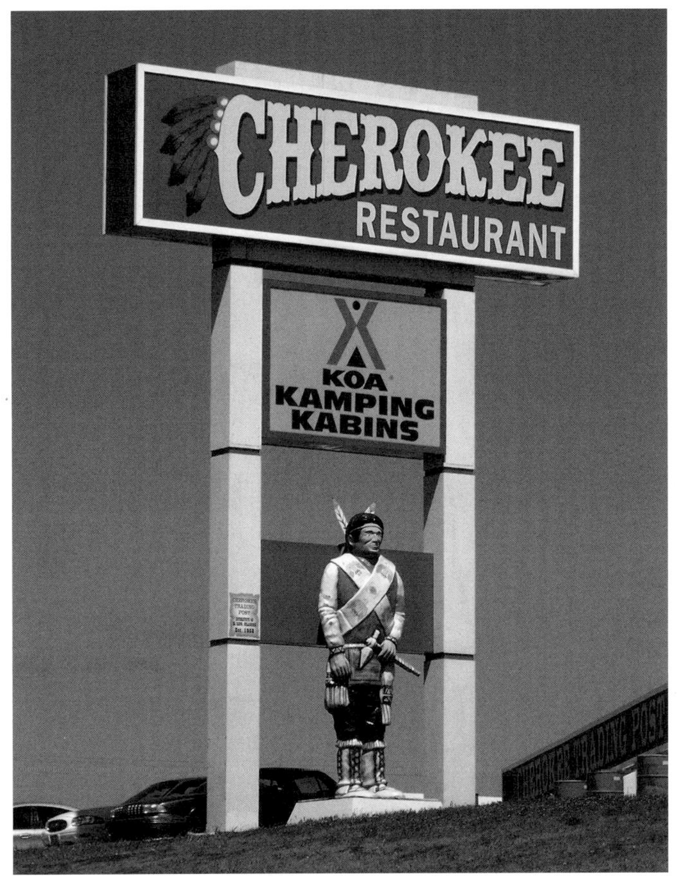

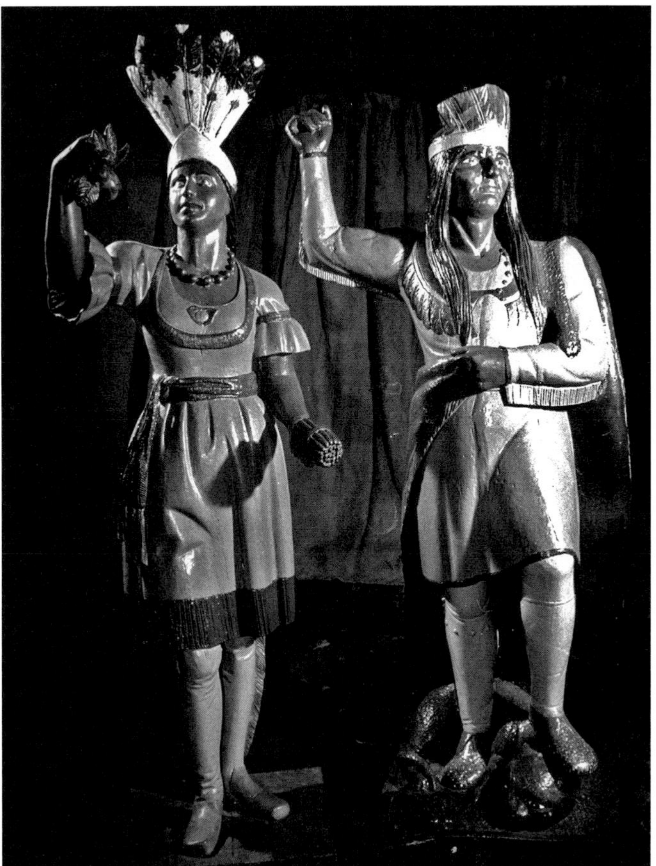

no doubt the Cherokee plays with this trading-post association. It even refers to itself as a trading post rather than a truck stop or convenience store, an association reinforced by the stocky Indian standing guard over the goods.

No one would mistake this figure for a sculpture or for art, but as the finely carved cigar-store Indians in Figure 9.4 indicate, there is not always a connection between aesthetic technique and aesthetic reception. Though it is a bit of a ridiculous comparison, the Howe Indian evinces more craftsmanship than the Cherokee Indian, though both traffic in similar modes of advertising. That said, the Cherokee warrior comes off as more respectfully adorned, with his crossed sashes, boots, and other decorative details. Even so, his shiny fiberglass exterior gives him a comic tone, as though he should be on the fourteenth hole of a miniature-golf course where players would have to time their swings correctly so that his tomahawk, going up and down, wouldn't block their shots. The Howe Indian—more earnest, more in line with Victor's notion of the stoic Indian that he outlines in *Smoke Signals*—does look like he could have just come back from killing a buffalo—an association of strength, endurance, durability, and aggression the car dealer no doubt cherishes. One must inquire, then, into the relationship between stereotype and commerce—a neither surprising nor innovative question—but also into the relationship between the semiotics of Native art and the semiotics of Native stereotype.

A 2008 exhibit in San Francisco by western artist Thom Ross problematizes this issue even further. Part nineteenth-century reenactment, part still-life painting, and part outdoor art installation, Ross's *Buffalo Bill and the Indians on the Beach* is a bizarre blend of history and high camp set against the dramatic backdrop of Seal Rock, Ocean Beach, and the Pacific Ocean (Figs. 9.5, 9.6, and 9.7). There are obvious differences in size and coloring, but on a fundamental level, not much distinguishes Ross's Indians from those in front of

FIGURE 9.3. (left) *The Cherokee Trading Post along I-40 near Hinton, Oklahoma. Photo by author, 2007.*

FIGURE 9.4. (right) *Two figurines from a tobacco shop in Minnesota, c. 1943. Both figures traffic in classic Indian stereotypes and semiotic signifiers, such as feathers, buckskin, and headdresses. © Getty Images.*

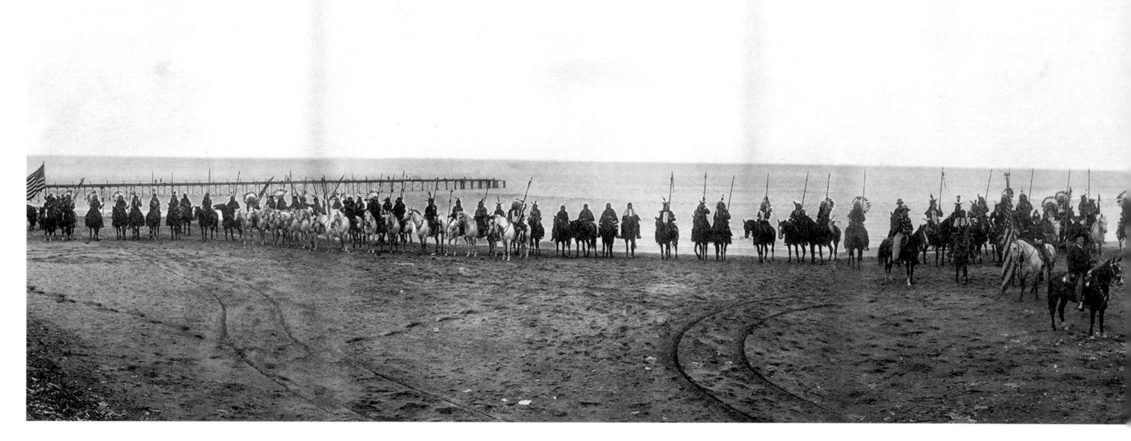

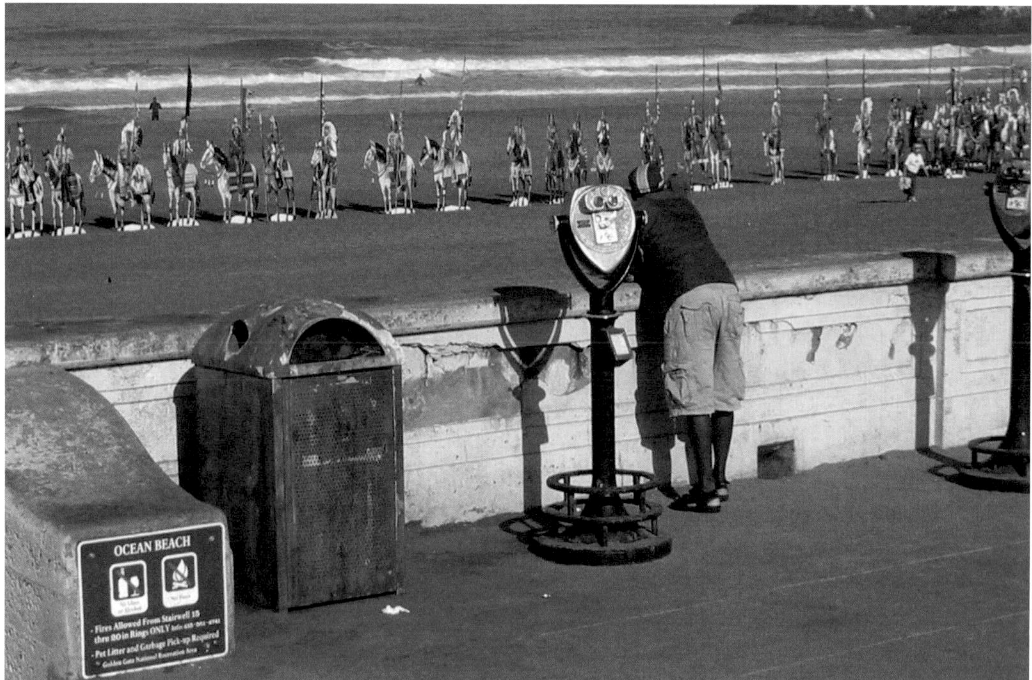

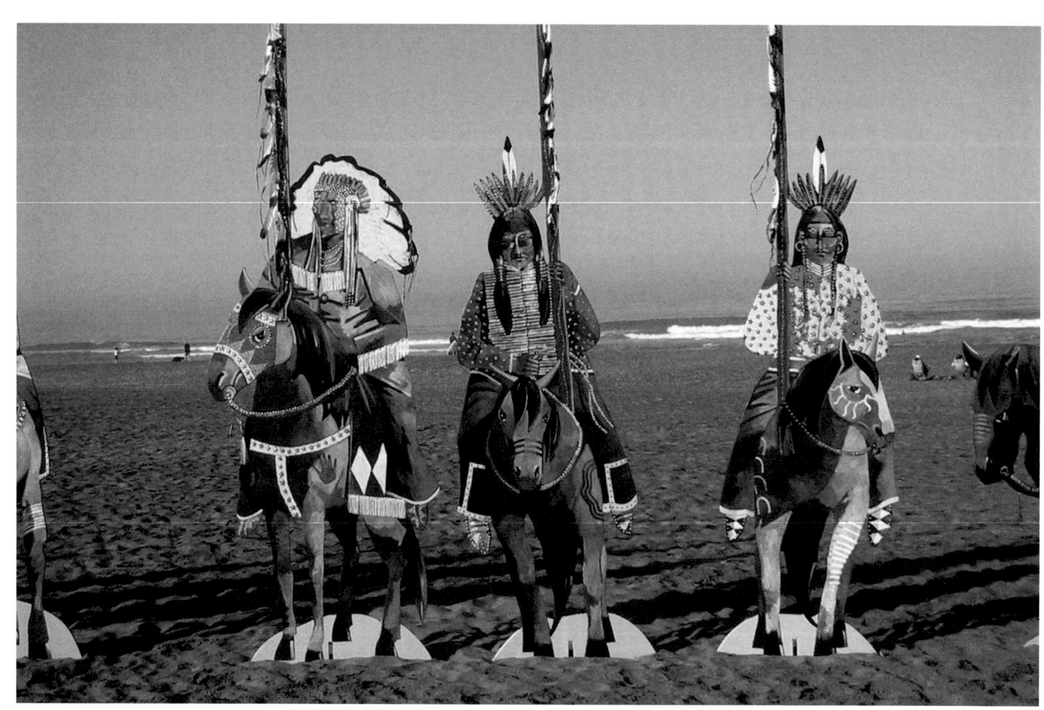

FIGURE 9.5. (top) *Buffalo Bill's Wild West show lined up along Ocean Beach, 1902. Courtesy of the Buffalo Bill Historical Museum.*

FIGURE 9.6. (middle) *Panoramic view along Ocean Beach, California, of* Buffalo Bill and the Indians on the Beach, *by Thom Ross, 2008. Photo by author.*

FIGURE 9.7. (right) *Three of the Indians in* Buffalo Bill and the Indians on the Beach, *by Thom Ross, 2008. Photo by author.*

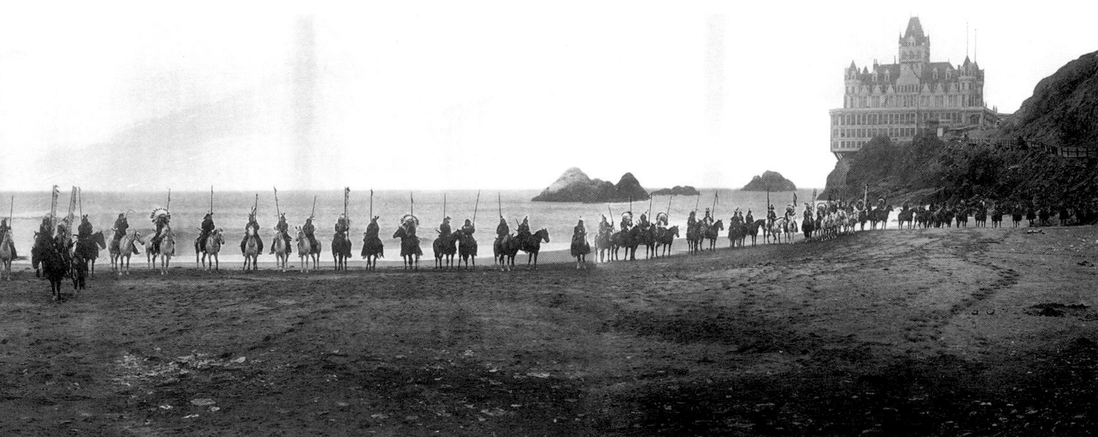

the trading post and the car lot. Yet from both an aesthetic standpoint and that of a collector, one is art and others are not.

Inspired by a classic photograph from Buffalo Bill Cody's Wild West show—snapped on the same spot on Ocean Beach in 1902—Ross re-creates the photo with life-sized cutouts that he and dozens of volunteers lined along the lumpy strand of sand just off the Great Highway. More than one hundred painted Indians and cowboys form an imposing but flashy phalanx that seems to be out of another time and place. From a distance, it appears as if the figures, mounted on horses, have ridden, like ghostly apparitions, out of the ocean's fog and foam to camp on the beach. Since each piece is close to fifteen feet tall, the veritable army casts an eerie but striking silhouette against the gray-green water. It was a strange, circus-like scene. I kept wondering whether I was looking at the relics of a pre-Disneyland Wild West ride that had gone awry.

From an art-historical perspective, Ross's renderings of western gunslingers and their Native counterparts owe more to murals and folk art than to the long history of portraiture. The faces of his Native Americans bear little or no resemblance to the museum-like photographs of Edward Curtis; rather, with their angular features, thick lines, and flat dimensionality, they evoke self-taught artists like Howard Finster or Mose Tolliver. Like these artists and contemporary crafters of Navajo kachina dolls, Ross accessorizes many of the Indian figures with real feathers, fabrics, and glass items in order to replicate decorated beading on both costumes and tack accoutrements. His artistic strength lies less in the microdetails of shading, perspective, and representation and more in the macronarrative.

What that narrative says about Indian identity leaves a great deal to be desired. In 2005, Ross completed a similar project when he memorialized Custer's Last Stand by erecting over 200 figures at Little Big Horn. Not surprisingly, Ross fancies himself a western artist, which typically means that he is more fascinated by the mythical West than the actual one. If the project itself doesn't tip you off, Ross himself may. For example, when I visited the exhibit, Ross was decked out in a cowboy costume that was clearly meant to resemble Buffalo Bill's but looked more like Teddy Roosevelt's during his Rough Rider days. His apparent sidekick was an Anglo woman sporting buckskin and a hairdo of braided pigtails. That intense and disturbing devotion to a western mythos, that heightened level of nostalgia, colors this particular art project more than Ross's paints. One wonders what sort of cultural work Ross wants his installation to do, since he seems most comfortable painting Indians performing as Indians, freezing them in time, re-presenting them as sideshow attractions rather than a living, changing people.

It was entertaining to watch surfers and tourists meander in and out of the cutouts, peering up at the decorated faces, and looking big fiberglass horses straight in the eye.

However, they would have been shocked to discover that it cost around $10,000 to take just one of the figures home. That is roughly $3,000 more than the U.S. government paid the Pawnee Indians in 1967 for land taken from them in the nineteenth century. Granted, Ross hasn't stolen Indian land, but I wonder if his projects steal some shred of Indian identity and dignity. "It is particularly important," writes Troy Lynn Yellow Wood (Oglala Lakota—Northern Cheyenne), "that a more accurate perception is expressed in public memorials that reference indigenous peoples and to dispel the stereotypes often found in sculpture and public art" ("Trauma and Memory," 32). For Yellow Wood, public art that misrepresents or misinvents Native peoples doesn't just summon trauma, it literalizes and memorializes it. I would put Ross's projects in this camp.

Imperialist Nostalgia and Indian Action Sculptures

Looking at the various sculptures of Indians in and around Santa Fe, New Mexico, through Yellow Wood's lens brings these issues of memorialization into even sharper focus. Indianness has come to be inexorably linked with Santa Fe's identity. Exotic for its connections to Indian history, culture, and, especially, art, Santa Fe has marketed itself as one of America's most indigenously embodied municipalities. Indeed, it remains the one city where Americans and Europeans travel to experience Indian creativity. Not surprisingly, sculptures and statues of and by American Indians adorn this "city different." They stand outside galleries, near walking paths, and in plazas around the city. There are exceptions, of course, but a vast majority of the representational sculptures of Indians were not carved by Indian artists. It is hard to imagine that many tourists notice the distinction, but one

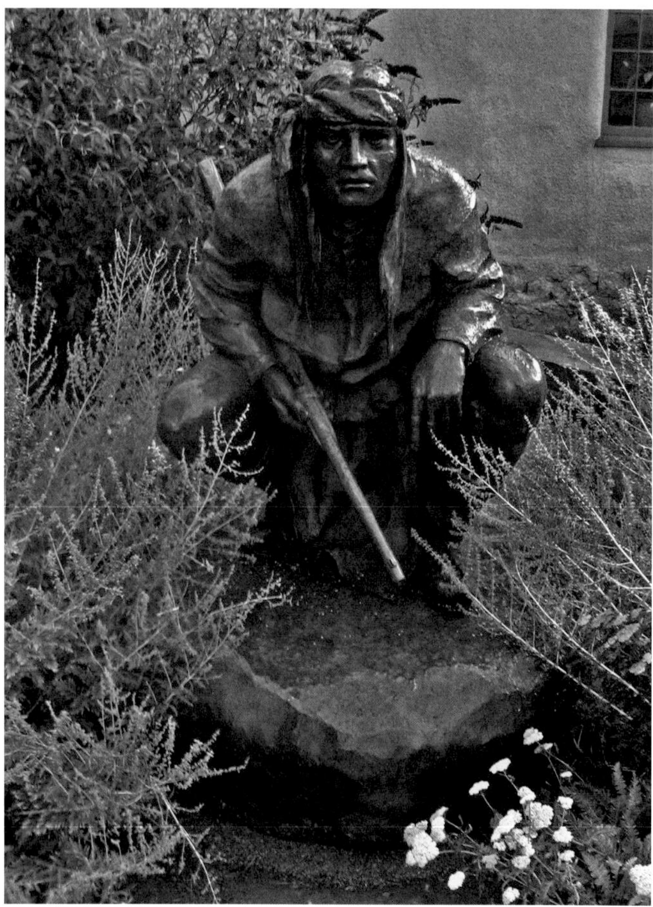

FIGURE 9.8. (left) *David Scott Rogers,* Chiricahua. *This sculpture is in a public courtyard in Santa Fe, New Mexico. Photo by author, 2008.*

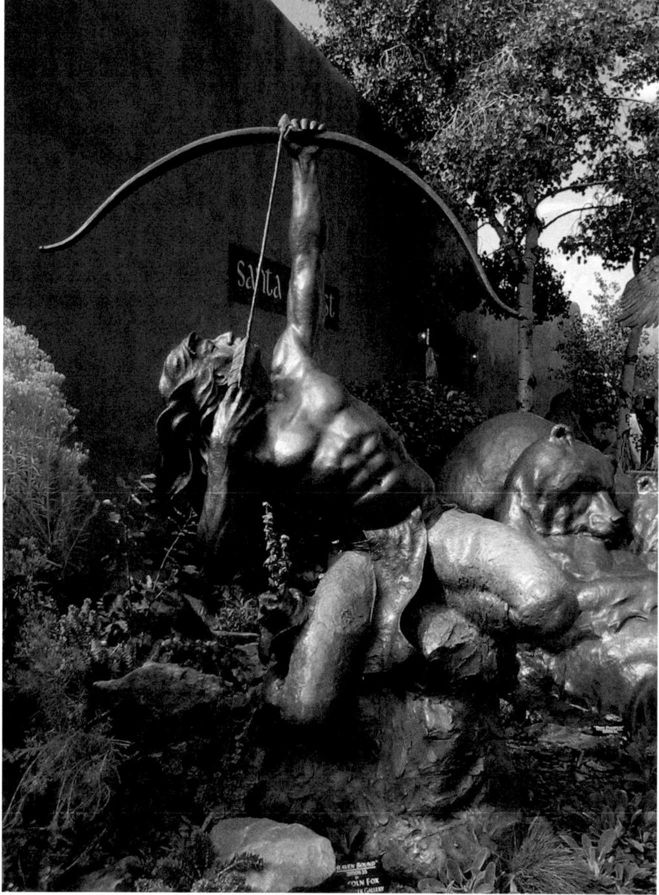

FIGURE 9.9. (right) *Lincoln Fox,* Heaven Bound, *c. 2007. Bronze, 8 × 6 ft. This piece, one of an edition of thirty-five, by a sought-after Western sculptor retails for around $59,000. Photo by author.*

emerges nonetheless. In general—and again, there are exceptions—sculptures in Santa Fe by Indian artists tend toward abstraction, whereas the pieces by non-Indians, like those by Ross, skew toward the mythic, the representational, and the invented. Often, these serve as fine examples of what I call "Indian action sculptures." They depict a nineteenth-century Plains Indian either poetically communing with some aspect of nature, fiercely grappling with a wild animal, or craftily preparing to lunge into battle.[5]

For example, in Figure 9.8, a stealthy Chiricahua warrior crouches in battle, clutching his .45-70 rifle (a detail mentioned on the explanatory plaque). Here, the landscaping adds to the intrigue of the scene, helping viewers imagine the realism and the drama of such activity during the 1880s. Though its intent was something more bellicose, in truth, this crouched Indian by sculptor David Scott Rogers shares a great deal with the cigar-store Indian. Both embody the stereotypical Indian traits of patience and stoicism. This piece sits in the courtyard of a small shopping and eating strip mall off San Francisco Street and has been part of the décor of the space for several years now.

On the other hand, Lincoln Fox's sculpture of the Indian archer takes action to a new level. Fox freezes a shirtless Indian warrior in time as he pulls back a large bow, magically, without a drawstring. Six-packed and loinclothed, this hunter-marksman evokes the wild romanticism of poised tension just before an arrow discharges into the air—at what, we are left to imagine. Oddly sexual, with ripped abs and thighs astraddle, the sculpture feels like a study in the kind of mythological behavior an Anglo imagines nineteenth-century Indians might have engaged in when not lurking behind prairie grasses. In her fabulous poem-in-dialogue "Noble Savage Confronts Indian Mascot," LeAnne Howe has fun with the latent sexuality associated with the visual grammar of the noble savage:

> *NOBLE SAVAGE*: What are you doing in my closet?
> *INDIAN MASCOT*: Sugar, can I wear your loin cloth to the big game tonight?
> *NOBLE SAVAGE*: No, and don't call me sugar.
> *INDIAN MASCOT*: C'mon. Besides you've outgrown it.
> *NOBLE SAVAGE*: No I haven't. Take off those feathers.
>
> —(*EVIDENCE OF RED*, 80)

Comically and brilliantly, Howe connects the coding of the visual reception of the noble savage (as embodied by sculpture) to that of the Indian mascot (as embodied by caricature). In both instances, she locates the finery of the noble savage as a site of play and critique: "INDIAN MASCOT: But, here we are. You with a bow and arrow. Me in a headdress" (79). Not surprisingly, many of these sculptures depict Indians thus, often with weapons at the ready. Regardless of the genre of the text, one almost always encounters some sort of semiotic indicator of the warrior spirit so that we know not only that we gaze upon an Indian but also that we know how to see that Indian.

Neither piece can compete with Vic Payne's sculpture though (Fig. 9.10). In this bizarre encounter, yet another shirtless (and pantless) Indian, this time in a headdress, holds off, miraculously, a lunging mountain lion with little more than an extended arm and drawn bow. A mix of high myth and high drama, there is no mistaking that this Indian action sculpture proves that Indians are masters of nature, much like Tarzan is master of the jungle. The primal battle of Indian, big cat, and deer horn confirms visually what many tourists no doubt imagine to be part of authentic Indian lore. The finely attuned realism of both the warrior and the cat are counterbalanced by the fantasy of the actual event. In a way, it evokes much hyperrealistic sci-fi—fantasy art in its explicit foregrounding of musculature, the threat of violence, and weaponry. It is animal versus animation.

Also balanced—compositionally at least—are the two figures, as though dually locked in

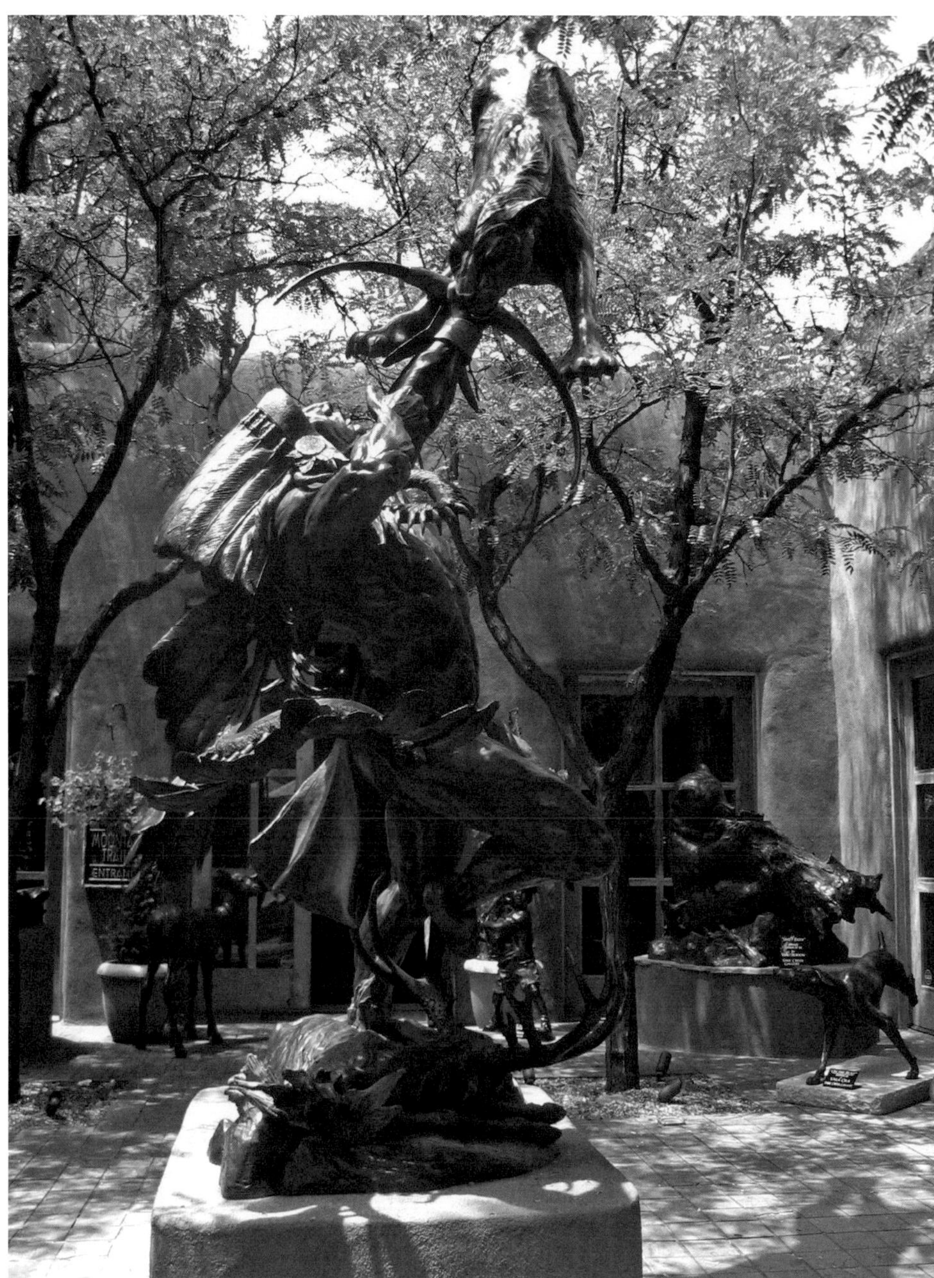

FIGURE 9.10. *Vic Payne,* The Hunter Becomes the Hunted, *2001 (one of an edition of thirty-five). Bronze, 12.5 × 5 × 4 ft. In this sculpture, a muscular warrior holds off a lunging mountain lion with one hand! Photo by author.*

a dance that violates both the laws of nature and the law of gravity. Thematically, perhaps the sculpture wrestles with the many ways in which Indians are or were under attack. Or it may stand as a musing on the long-lost masculine ways of the noble savage. Either way, the piece is rippled with fabricated nostalgia, which, for tourists, is almost as good as the real thing.

At work here is what Renato Rosaldo calls "imperialist nostalgia." For Rosaldo, imperialist nostalgia is a "particular kind of nostalgia, often found under imperialism, where people mourn the passing of what they themselves have transformed . . . In more attenuated form, someone deliberately alters a form of life, and then regrets that things have not remained as they were prior to the intervention" (*Culture and Truth*, 69, 70). In the case of these sculptures, one locates Rosaldo's observations in the mélange of iconic signifiers, the sexualized images, the overly romantic depictions, and, most saliently, in the unspoken but clearly encoded lamentation for the glory days of fabricated yesteryear. We fantasize about what we have destroyed, we embellish what we have broken, we replace what we have removed. In effect, we make more beautiful the memory of that which we have tried to forget.

All three of these sculptures are designed to evoke the Wild West, but not as Natives would have rendered it. My hunch is the Cherokee and Howe Indians are supposed to do similar work. Indeed, with the exception of the mountain lion, the posture of the Vic Payne Indian and the Howe Indian are not too different from each other. And from a narrative and thematic perspective, not much distinguishes the Cherokee Trading Post Indian from the crouching Chiricahua warrior, despite the fact that the former is considered by most to be mere signage and the latter, high art. And as I noted earlier, both stand in front of a place of business, so they carry semiotic codes similar to those of the cigar-store Indian. In short, these sculptures meet at the cultural trading post of kitsch and camp. As I was trying to shoot a photo of the Payne sculpture, two other tourists were doing the same thing, each commenting on the figure's muscles and calm demeanor. In a tourist destination where many of the products for sale are tchochkes of all kinds, these pieces fit into the commercial landscape—they are simply larger examples of memorabilia.

Capitol Indians and Receptive Determinacy

Though I love Santa Fe, it does read at times like a Disneyland of colonialism, as though it is always already performing indigeneity. This is in part because many of the art and design projects signify Indianness only through caricature. Much more interesting are instances of Native public art that are permanent, not for sale, and executed by Indian artists. In the remaining pages of this chapter I offer some examples of Native public art that function as counternarratives to the stories of imperialist nostalgia that so much public art about Native Americans seems condemned to tell. To that end, I'll look at abstract and representational public-art pieces on both public and private land.

Actual public art—as opposed to for-profit statues—initiates a more sophisticated conversation about self-selecting Native semiology. For example, I'm intrigued by Indian art that has become a fixed presence in public spaces like plazas, museums, and parks, and, in particular, government structures like state and federal buildings. Among such spaces, one often finds unusually provocative tensions between the indigenous aesthetic and the governmental ethic. The symbolic interplay between Indian art and capitols becomes an incredibly complex canvas on which historical, cultural, political, and racial issues get painted in big, broad strokes. This conflict of history (as opposed to the conflict of fantasy) actuates Native public art that facilitates both contextual and compositional resistance and also cultural and aesthetic engagement.

I began this chapter with a discussion about the semiotics of the West, and I return to that provenance now—specifically, the capitol grounds in Santa Fe and Oklahoma City—municipalities whose Indianness is often at odds with their West-ness. In the case of Oklahoma City, its western identity gets proudly canonized via the pro-land-rush, pro–Manifest Destiny murals that adorn the inside of the capitol rotunda. Contravening those murals are two major sculptures by Indian artists outside and, literally, on the capitol. The iconic but mellifluous *As Long as the Waters Flow* (Fig. 9.11), by Allen Houser (Chiricahua Apache) provides a soothing contrast to the triumphalist architecture of the capitol. The soft, round lines and their deep grey hues juxtaposed against the stark white of the building make for an unexpected visual interplay of light and dark, firm and delicate, structural and human. Against the ornate Doric columns of the building, the simple, almost primitive curves are an inviting entrée to the capitol's commons. Notable for her lack of weaponry or exposed limbs, this piece contrasts sharply with the lion-fighting, arrow-shooting figures in Santa Fe.

In his massive study of the artist, W. Jackson Rushing III rightly notes that *As Long as the Waters Flow* is a "towering, dignified image . . . neither bombastic nor kitschy, as many large-scale realist sculptures can be" (*Allen Houser*, 221). For him, the sculpture is "characterized instead by aesthetic and emotional substance" as well as "sincerity and heroism" (221). Another trait distinguishing Houser's piece is the sculpture's gender. Unlike the overtly masculine, nearly naked representations of warriors, the fully clothed female here evokes neither maidenhood nor overt sexuality. Where the exposed and detailed bodies of the male figures invite the viewer's gaze, Houser's Indian woman is less about narrative and more about form. On the Oklahoma capitol grounds, the gender distinction becomes political—a female Indian guards the statehouse that has typically been peopled by white men. Even though this piece also evokes a kind of stoicism, its absence of romantic and mythological feats makes it feel simultaneously precontact and political. "When you look at a Houser sculpture," writes Kiowa author N. Scott Momaday, "you see not only what the hand has wrought in the studio; you see also an ancient origin, something of cultural genesis, a profound mystery" ("The Testament of Allan Houser," 71). Similarly, Truman T. Lowe (Ho-Chunk) writes of *As Long as the Waters Flow* that even the most minute detail, such as "a wistful glance or the determined set of the jaw[,] speaks volumes about tragic and proud events in his tribe's history" (*Native Modernism*, 32). That ability to signify on two seemingly alternate planes makes this public sculpture part of public history and public discourse. And in the case of Oklahoma, a particularly profound example of the state's history and discourse.

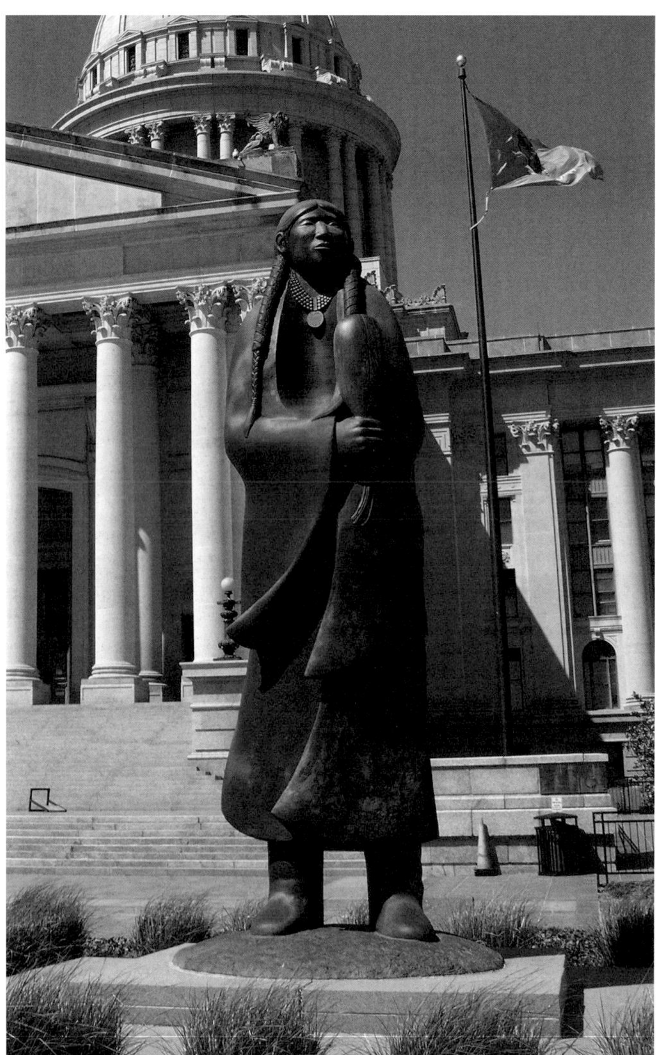

FIGURE 9.11. *Allan Houser,* As Long as the Waters Flow, *1989. The sculpture stands outside the Oklahoma capitol. Photo by author.*

That element of public-ness makes *As Long as the Waters Flow* simultaneously indigenous and democratic. When compared to pieces by sculptors like Ross and Rodgers—which come out of the traditions of romanticism and realism—Houser's draped and occluded bodies leave room for the imagination and, therefore, emerge as less determined and more inviting pieces of art. "The fifteen-foot bronze statue exudes Houser's artistic style," reads the Art of the Oklahoma State Capitol website. "Lacking intricate representative detailing," it goes on to say, "the large solid planes among the surface denote strength within an everlasting presence." Houser's appropriation of modernist techniques like the interplay of abstraction and representation creates space for the viewer to insert her own notion of self (and society). In the title, Houser plays with President Andrew Jackson's famous claim that Indians will get to keep their land "as long as the grass grows and the rivers run."[6] Similar to how the Alcatraz authors incorporated and indicted treaty language, so too does Houser appropriate governmental language as part of a governmental art project. By refusing to be inscribed by either governmental or visual grammars of restriction, Houser's sculptures provide a mode of engagement with democratic indigeneity. In a great and ironic feat, Houser reclaims land for Indians—in Oklahoma!

But as impressive and important as this sculpture is, it does not compare either in size or in placement to its counterpart—Enoch Kelly Haney's *The Guardian*—the wildly popular statue atop the new capitol rotunda (Fig. 9.12). In 2000, my home state of Oklahoma decided to convert its rotunda-less state capitol into one with a large, eye-catching rotunda of 155 feet. A public contest was held to pick a statue that would eventually adorn the top of the rotunda. The winning sculpture was *The Guardian* by Haney (Seminole), an Oklahoma artist and congressman, whose design depicts a Choctaw warrior holding a staff and a shield. With the statue itself standing at seventeen feet and the staff extending another five feet beyond that, the piece is monumental on its own right, but when positioned on the apex of the capitol of a state with as many past and present political issues involving American Indians as Oklahoma, *The Guardian* becomes more than a monument—it becomes a statement.

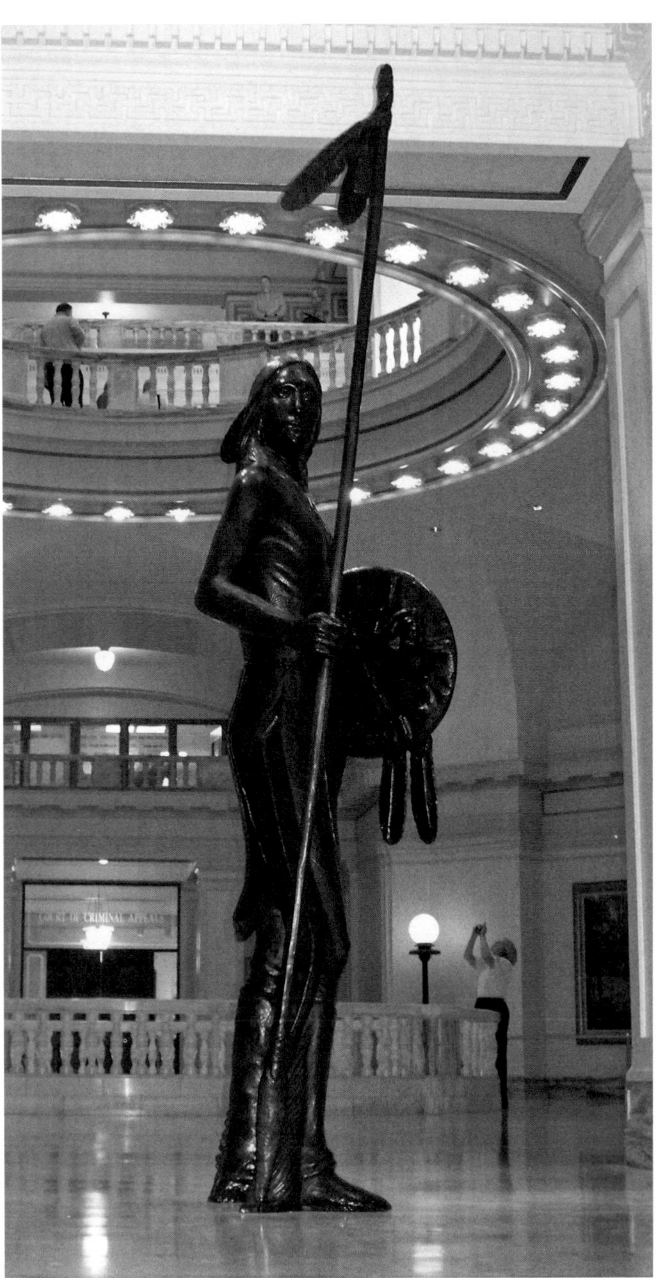

FIGURE 9.12. *Enoch Kelley Haney,* The Guardian, *2002. This six-foot-tall version sits inside the Oklahoma capitol, just beneath the rotunda, which supports its much larger doppelganger. Photo by author.*

That said, *The Guardian* is a strange text. Its mixed messages and cross-signifiers puzzle more than they illuminate. Festooned with a necklace of beads, hoop earrings, and feathers in his long, flowing hair, *The Guardian* looks unusually androgynous. But his staff and shield, his buff chest and abs, signify maleness in its rawest form. Not surprisingly, as an aesthetic statement, *The Guardian* hardly deviates from the norm. Like most other public statues, sculptures, and signage featuring American Indians, *The Guardian* is a shirtless male warrior whose muscled physique and accoutrements of war assert force, capability, and—remarkably, despite the fact that he is topless—dignity. Because of the popularity of photographs by people like Edward Curtis, a dignified portraiture genre has emerged as an acceptable mode of representing Indians. We have been trained to respond to oft-repeated visual signifiers in predictable ways so that when we see a certain profile, certain details (feathers, bare chest) we read *Indian*. Perhaps because Curtis was so aware of the many ways whites and the government had stripped Indians of that dignity, part of his project was to reencode dignity into the representations of Indian faces and Indian bodies. To be sure, this phenomenon is cultural, not aesthetic. It is hard to imagine, for example, a statue of a shirtless African American atop the statehouse in South Carolina.[7] A bare chest does not automatically connote bravery or dignity. It can connote "slave" or, in the case of Indians, "Indian."

The choice of this particular representation of Indians, its placement on the dome of the Oklahoma capitol, the history of Native representation in Oklahoma, and the history of sculptures of Indians on roofs of American structures raise a number of provocative questions about Native representation, Native public art, and the contact zone of resistance and assimilation. Is the Haney sculpture a positive advancement for Oklahoma Indians? What are the historical and political implications of a sculpture of an eighteenth- or nineteenth-century brave on top of the capitol of the state that was the terminus of Indian removal? Is *The Guardian* a suitable way of honoring Oklahoma Indians? Is the statue a symbolic gesture toward Indians that lets the Oklahoma legislature off the hook in regard to Indian policies?[8] Does it matter that the sculptor is Seminole but the guardian is Choctaw?

My reading of the politics of *The Guardian* is similar to my reading of the statue's aesthetics—it is all a little old-fashioned.[9] There is really nothing wrong with it. It is executed competently, nothing is exaggerated, and, unlike the Howe Indian, it connotes reverence. In my mind, the most intriguing detail of the statue is the guardian's lance, which has been driven through a strap tied to his leggings—effectively staking him to the ground. According to Haney, this echoes a classic strategy of Indian warriors facing insurmountable odds. Though subtle, this detail imbues the piece with elements of resistance that the more public aspects of the sculpture lack. This engagement both with the military armature and structures of Native warrior history and with the architecture and infrastructure of Anglo government is the one component of the sculpture that flies in the face of easy monumentalization and reification.

Indeed, despite a subtext of resistance, I might also argue that in some subtle way, *The Guardian* literally and figuratively assimilates the Indian into the body of the government, into its vast bureaucratic whiteness. It slips in silently next to all of the other representations of eighteenth- and nineteenth-century Indians that do not challenge the past, the present, or the future. It is a conservative text.

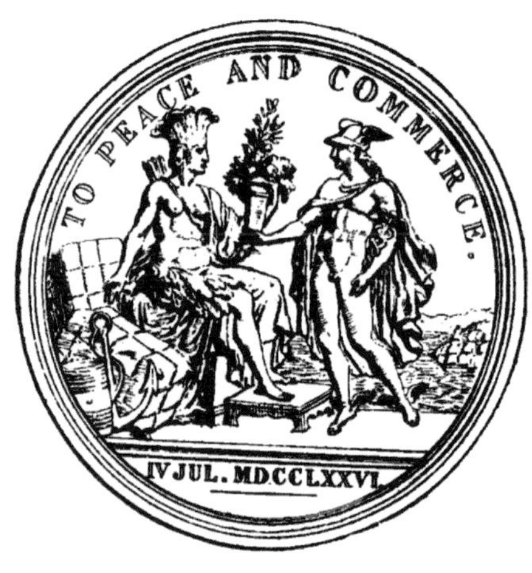

But then again, when are governmental monuments not? Lest the viewer misinterpret Haney's work, the good folks at the Oklahoma State Capitol explain what everything stands for. According to the official state website, *The Guardian* is saddled with a great deal of symbolic work: "*The Guardian* embodies the diversity within the proud and strong population of Oklahoma while serving as a reminder of our tumultuous times. The sculpture signifies the thousand[s] of Native Americans that were forced from their homes during the 1800s and the sons and daughters that survived the devastating Dust Bowl. The towering statue exemplifies the valor of Oklahomans and their ability to overcome the most horrific catastrophes such as the bombing at the Murrah Building in Oklahoma City."[10] The state gets around the representation issue by claiming the Indian is not really an Indian, or at least is not just an Indian.

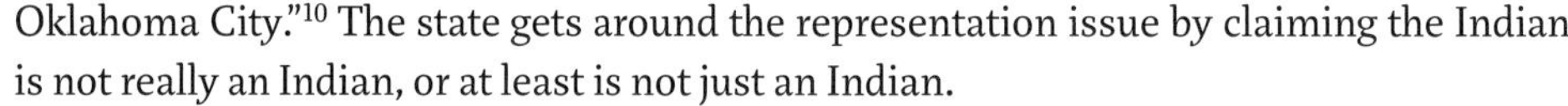

In Oklahoma, the argument seems to be, the placement of public art can be just as important as a piece's narrativity. I suspect that *The Guardian*'s many exemplifications have less to do with the content of the sculpture than with its positioning on the dome of the capitol. How a Choctaw warrior stands in for those afflicted by the Dust Bowl or those murdered in the Murrah Building bombing is nearly unexplainable except through mythology, stereotype, and the familiarities of semiotics. In the case of *The Guardian*, Haney packs his subject with all of the symbolism of nobility (proud profile), strength (ripped abs), protection (shield, staff), endurance (youth, vitality), and even defiance (stance, positionality, posture) that the legacy and representations of conquest have inscribed onto physical representations of Indians. We know what to feel because we have been taught how to see. We have been taught to see Indians as embodiments of Anglo ideals, and we have been taught to see Indians on top of buildings not as symbols of Indians but as symbols of all that is not Indian.

FIGURE 9.13. *The Indian queen on an American diplomatic medal. Note the similarities between the Indian represented here and the cigar-store Indians in Figure 9.4.*

For years, the enduring icon of American ideals was the Indian queen, which adorned many early American medals (Fig. 9.13).[11] In the United States Mint catalogue, the Indian queen, like *The Guardian*, is asked to wear many headdresses: "America, personified as an Indian queen, holds in her left hand the cornucopia of abundance (Peace) and welcomes

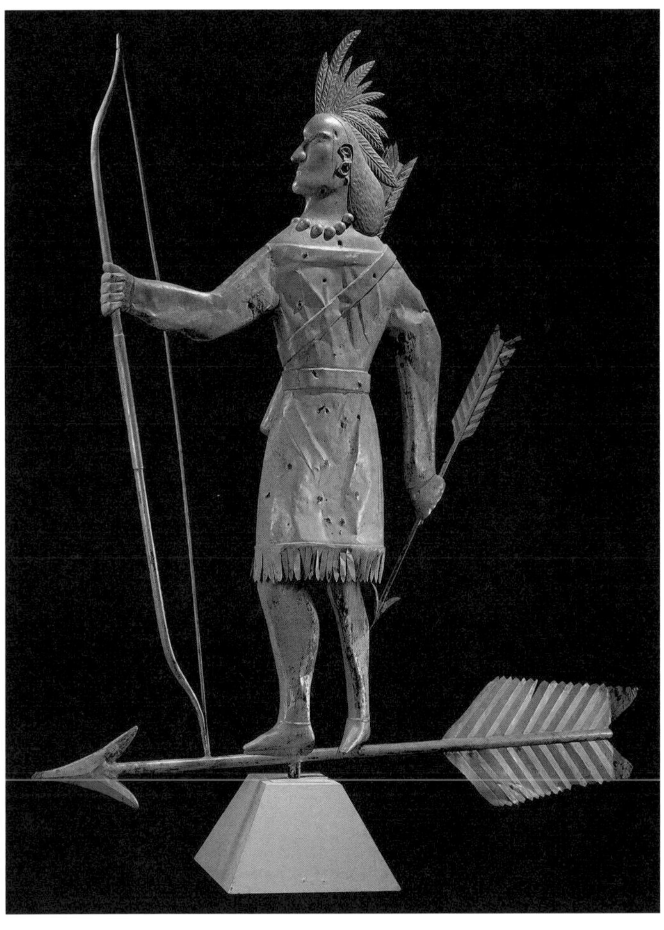

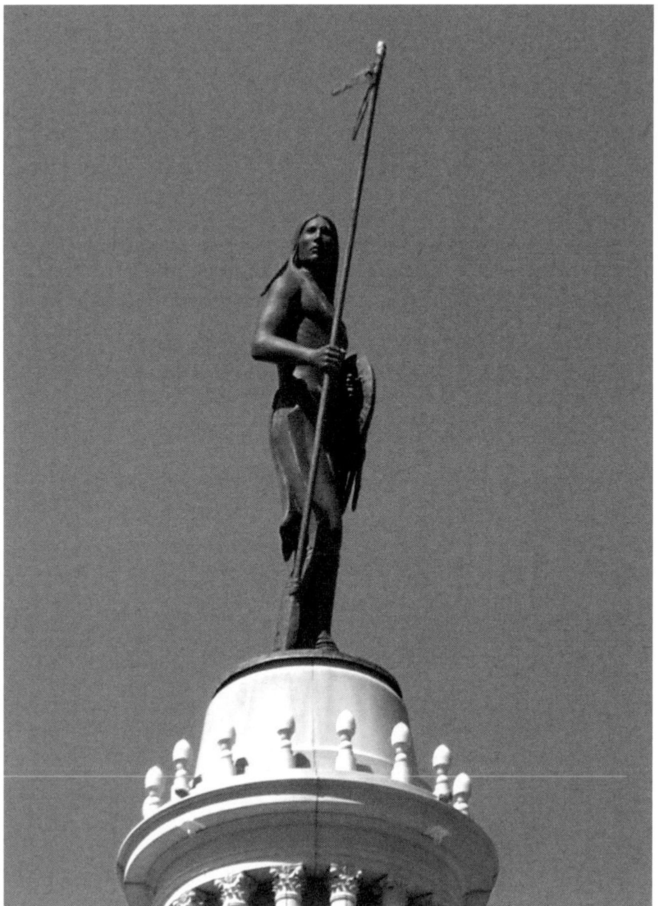

FIGURES 9.14 and 9.15. *An Indian weather vane,* left, *a common icon atop houses in colonial New England. From a formal perspective, there is a great deal of similarity between the weather vane (c. 1700) and* The Guardian, right. *Both figures are scantily clad, both hold weapons, both seem to stand at attention, both are more figural than abstract, and, of course, both were designed to sit on top of a structure. Weather vane image courtesy of the American Folk Art Museum. Author photo of* The Guardian, *2008.*

Mercury (Commerce) to her shores. Her right hand directs attention to American products, packed ready for export."[12] More capitalist than resistant, more corporate than tribal, more commercial than democratic, the Indian queen actually has little to do with Indians at all. The uncanny semiotic ability of Indians to signify cigars, trade, commerce, peace, diversity, antiterrorism, football teams, and automobiles is partly the reason that Indians have long been signifiers emptied of meaning, relegated to whimsy. One recalls Patricia Limerick's astute observation at the beginning of *The Legacy of Conquest*: "The legacy of slavery was serious business, while the legacy of conquest was not" (18). And so it is: the proliferation of wooden Indians, Indians on coins and medals, and Indian weather vanes (Fig. 9.14). It is the last that comes to mind when I see *The Guardian* on top of the Oklahoma capitol (Fig. 9.15)—a potential site for truly provocative, engaged resistance undermined by the trivial history of flat representation, the ease with which stereotype masquerades as monument, and the eagerness to two-dimensionalize (and therefore dematerialize) race and culture.

New Mexicans, on the other hand, may see Indians, the West, and government a little differently from Oklahomans—at least if their capitol statues and sculptures are any indication. Unlike the Oklahoma capitol grounds, the New Mexico capitol has been liberated of sculptures of cowboys or mythologizations of the Wild West. To be sure, you can find such pieces in New Mexico—in fact, in most galleries in Santa Fe—but not often as public art and not on the capitol complex. A plurality of sculptures by Indian artists graces the grounds of the capitol, but I am going to spend time on two in particular—a piece by Allan Houser's son Bob Houzous and another by Hopi artist Dan Namingha. These two sculptures stand in sharp contrast to much of the other American Indian public art in Santa Fe, since they foreground aesthetic technique and semiotic ambiguity over discursiveness.

Namingha's beguiling sculpture *Passage* (Fig. 9.16), for example, locates Indianness not through figuration but through iconography. Positioned just off the main entry sidewalk leading into the capitol, this large but inviting piece has become part of the visual landscape of the capitol complex. The sculpture's circular shape echoes the circularity of the state capitol as well as canonical recurrences in Native spirituality, worldviews, and aesthetics. More abstract than Houser's *As Long as the Waters Flow*, Namingha's sculpture locates its Native semiotic resonance in an evocative symbology whose internal narratives try to reconcile opposing forces. Like petroglyphs and cave paintings, *Passage* works on associative levels. For example, the central squares suggest both Indian jewelry (through their turquoise palette) and the heads and eyes of the masks of Hopi kachina dolls. Those squares also evoke the four cardinal directions, the four sacred mountains of the Navajo, and the four natural elements—all of which are circumscribed by a sacred hoop that is sun, moon, stars, earth, teepee, and tribe. But, like Houser, Namingha incorporates gestures of modernism and postmodernism. The circle is bifurcated; the squares are fragmented and askew. A sort of primal struggle between positive and negative space reveals classic postmodern tropes of presence and absence vying for both centrality and invisibility. "The grand and subtle forms evoke duality," notes Thomas Hoving of *Passage*, "the colors refer to land textures, the concept of passages, and reminiscences of rituals. But, above all, the work simply and purely offers a series of shapes and the interplay of negative and positive spaces holding together in perfect harmony" (*Art of Dan Namingha*, 148). Hoving sees more symmetry in the sculpture than I do. I see balance and counterpose; I see verticality; and I see the presence of absence. But I am not convinced that the colors refer to passages. In fact, to my eye, the earth tones and the heavy bronze, weighted at its center, evoke stones, the New Mexico desert, and terrestrial unending.

In that disagreement, though, lies the value of the piece, especially as an object of Native American art. Whereas the more figural sculptures of Indians fighting mountain lions leave little interpretive space, Namingha's sculpture opens up to interpretation, which I see as an important metaphor for Native aesthetics and Native culture. As dramatic as a shirtless

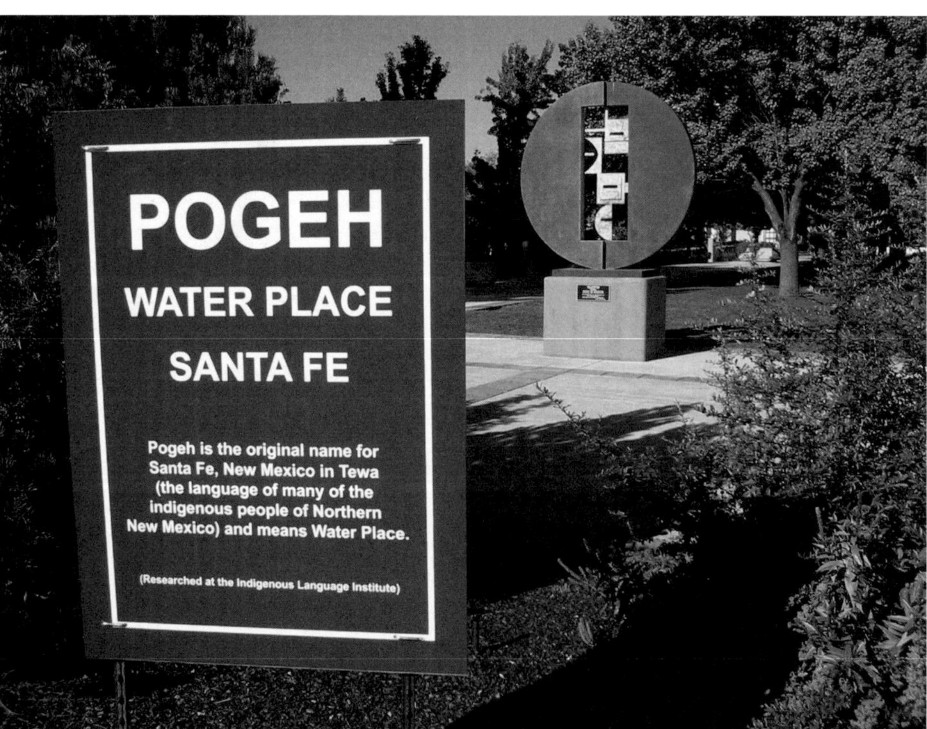

FIGURE 9.16. Background: *Dan Namingha,* Passage, *1998. Bronze, 8 ft. in diameter. The sculpture is just outside the New Mexico capitol. Capitol Art Collection. Photo by author.*

feathered warrior wrestling a bobcat might be, it closes off viewer participation because of its autotelism—it has connected all the dots. It is its own end. The crouching Indian and the mammal-fighting Indian fall into what I refer to as the trap of receptive determinacy. How we see the sculpture, its culture, and the history the sculpture embodies have already been determined for us. It leaves no room for difference, no room for negative space, no room for internal tension. In the trap of receptive determinacy, those human elements are overwritten by an overdetermined linearity of form, narrative, and purpose. Namingha's *Passage*, then, resists receptive determinacy through an engagement with cultural plurality, aesthetic open-endedness, and historical semiotics. If it is a gate, we walk ourselves through it; if it is a passage, we find our own way along it.

If Namingha's *Passage* eschews the lure of receptive determinacy, Bob Houzous's *Gate/Negate* (2000) shatters it (Fig. 9.17). Neither overtly Native nor overtly New Mexican, Houzous's (Warm Springs Chiricahua Apache) sculpture resists both easy access and easy interpretation. In fact, when I was at the capitol in August 2008, the employees couldn't answer any questions about it except to say that it was not a "monument." They handed me a half-page printout that navigates between an artist's statement and a press release.

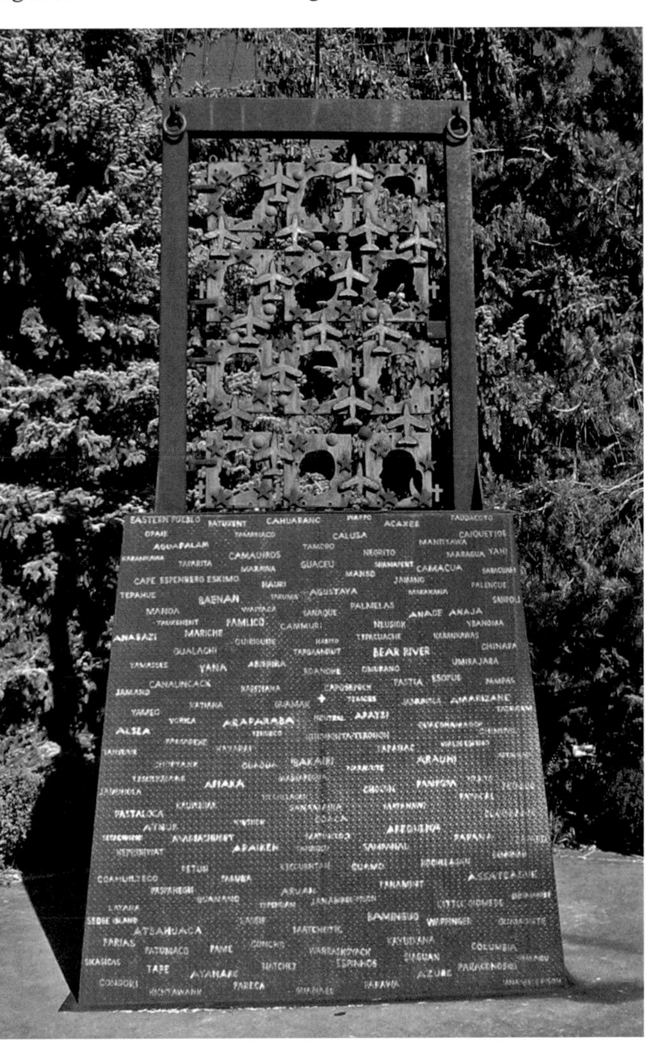

FIGURE 9.17. *Bob Houzous,* Gate/Negate, *2000. Steel and mixed media, 18 × 8 × 4 ft. The sculpture is in front of the capitol in Santa Fe. On loan to the Capitol Art Collection. Photo by author.*

Standing eighteen feet tall, the imposing bronze structure confronts just about anyone who approaches the capitol complex from the main parking lot. Planes fly upward toward barbed wire; behind them are silhouetted profiles of different ethnicities, all of which are supported by a large terra cotta base inscribed with mysterious names. At first glance, it looks like a World War II memorial, but the piece lacks the celebratory aura so common to such works. Moreover, the words don't correspond to infantry units or locations of military incursions during the war. Ironically, not even the large bronze gate framing the planes provides much entry into the piece, nor do the little stars and crosses affixed to the profiles like so many *milagros* help decode a seemingly disorderly text. Most intriguing is the lack of any obvious Native American signifier.

Except for those names.

For pretty much anyone who does not work in the field of Native American history or Native American studies, the names on the base will remain a mystery. The small group of tourists puzzled by the sculpture when I visited could make neither heads nor tails of the sculpture's heads and tails. They were most confused by the dozens of names that they decided must have been "made up." What the sculpture doesn't make clear but the printout does is that the "prominent base of the work highlights a partial listing of the Native Nations that did not survive the invasions of 1492–1992" (*Gate/Negate 2000*). Like Namingha, Houzous sees the sculptural site as one not of declaration but of exploration. According to the capitol's document, Houzous "does not believe in dictating the meaning of his work for any one person, but instead believes strongly in the viewer bringing her/his individual associations and experiences to the work." In the military-heavy state of New Mexico, in the largely Native- and Chicano-populated state of New Mexico, and in the art-heavy city of Santa Fe, those associations are going to be wildly diverse—especially given the pre- and post-9/11 associations Americans have with planes, crosses, and stars.

What's particularly fascinating about this piece is the absence of Indian iconography but the presence of Indian text. Houzous uses, as part of his literal and thematic foundation, information most Americans do not have about Indians, but withholds the visual devices that do the most obvious cultural work of indicating Indianness. By so doing, he denies access to overly simplistic interpretations and representations of indigeneity, making his sculpture of a gate a barrier. The capitol's explanation of the sculpture goes on to say that for Houzous, "the barrier symbol 'has always represented an antiquated obstacle that is easily removed and replaced by open dialogue untainted by race or economics.'" Open dialogues "untainted by race or economics" are nearly impossible on the topic of indigeneity; so, for me, that notion of apoliticism undermines Houzous's claim that he wants his pieces to provoke discourse and "encourage discussion." I am not sure what sort of discussion images of planes, crosses, and the names of vanquished Native nations can engender if it needs to be free of race and economics, nor am I sure what the purpose of such a discussion would be if it were to avoid those topics.

Even so, I admire how the sculpture's formal and thematic barriers engage through resistance. Like Namingha's *Passage*, *Gate/Negate* participates in Indian history through re-presenting the past. In the case of the former, as I have suggested, it is done through iconic references to petroglyphs; in the latter, Houzous rewrites the present by unerasing the past. Just as the occupiers of Alcatraz forged both personal and spatial identity through names and naming, so too does Houzous inscribe into the foundation of his gate the tribal names that colonial history has attempted to negate. Jaune Quick-to-See Smith does something similar in her *Tribal Map* (page 59). Both she and Houzous fuse the textuality of names with the visual capital of eternal symbols (the map of the United States, planes, the cross) as a way of defying history to ignore Natives. They ask the reader to induct the names of peoples, nations, and tribes rarely spoken in mainstream American discourse into the commons that has become visual culture. In short, both Smith and Houzous place text in context.

How radical to refuse to allocate words to a discourse of potential silence—a discourse of the mute. How inventive to enter the names (and faces) of the invisible into the pantheon of the visible. In fact, both *Passage* and *Gate/Negate* participate in the poetics of entrance. As sculptures, they ask, literally, to be walked up to, and as fields of symbols, they ask to be invited in. Not only do the sculptures open up avenues of appreciation through unique geometries of expression, but they also seek an interaction and engagement with the viewer in which interpretation happens by collapsing the distinction between subject and object. These pieces stand in opposition to most of the works this chapter has discussed thus far because they resist the false engagement of objectification. Objectification is the antithesis of engagement; to objectify is to silence.

FIGURE 9.18. (facing page) *Hock E Aye Vi (Edgar Heap of Birds),* New York: Purchased, Stolen, Reclaimed, *1998. Metal sign panel. The artwork sat along an actual roadway. Photo courtesy of the artist.*

FIGURES 9.19 and 9.20. (facing page) *Edgar Heap of Birds,* Walk to Oklahoma *and* Trail of Tears, 1836, *2005, part of the* Ocmulgee Sign Project, *Atlanta, Georgia. Metal sign panels, each 18 × 12 in. Photos courtesy of the artist.*

Edgar Heap of Birds and the Semiotics of Resistance

No Indian public artist resists silence and objectification more than Hock E Aye Vi (Edgar Heap of Birds), a painter and sculptor of Cheyenne-Arapaho descent. For me, Heap of Birds is to Native public art what Jaune Quick-to-See Smith is to Native gallery art: its most promising and practiced visionary. Heap of Birds isn't just working in the field of public art; he is defining it. Just as Native poets have altered the genre of lyric poetry, Heap of Birds has changed the genre of public Native aesthetic discourse. From his political street signs to his installation *Wheel*, Heap of Birds asks Natives and non-Natives alike to reexamine how they see Indians and Indian semiotics, particularly within the realm of American semiotics.

Take, for example, his sign *New York: Purchased, Stolen, Reclaimed* (Fig. 9.18) from the 1998 Reclaim New York project. Posing as a standard Department of Transportation mileage sign, this piece inverts the expected information such signs disseminate. Motorists rely on such signs to give them objective information, data, to help them with their travels, but here, Heap of Birds offers a different kind of objectivity. "Signs do not just 'convey' meanings," claims Daniel Chandler in his study of semiotics, "but constitute a medium in which meanings are constructed" (*Semiotics*, 217). In this case, the medium is brilliantly rendered, and it turns a sign that is largely about distance into a sign that is largely about resistance. There is no artist signature, no plaque denoting authorship, no gallery or frame that would indicate the sign is a work of art. It fully embodies the design of nameless, faceless highway signs and therefore carries with it a putative authority.[13] Free of overt political markings but still overtly political, this piece also enacts subtle resistance by withholding the critical information most drivers seek—the objective data the right column of the sign is supposed to provide. As is the case with Houser and Houzous, the viewer must fill in his own answer; she must complete the incompleteness of the text. The piece also reorients the viewer's assumptions at seeing the words "NEW YORK" emblazoned on a highway sign. Rather than signifying merely entry into the state and distances yet to be traveled, this piece signifies the acquisition of the state and the ethical questions such attainment raises, including have we actually come far at all?

Heap of Birds poses similar questions in *Ocmulgee Sign Project* (2005), a series of signs that appeared along Peachtree Street in Atlanta (Figs. 9.19 and 9.20). Where the New York piece references mileage, these reference parking. One of the many tensions Heap of Birds plays with is the darkly comic variance between parking a car on the street and walking the nine hundred miles from Georgia to Oklahoma along the Trail of Tears. Heap of Birds understands how passively we react to the semiotics of authority and law, and he uses that reaction to gnaw away at our passivity about other forms of authority and law, like textbooks, treaties, place-names, and even executive orders. Here, the subtlety of the small red and white sign becomes an ironic symbol for the colossal removal of nearly fifty thousand souls, as though such a paltry marker could encompass that project.

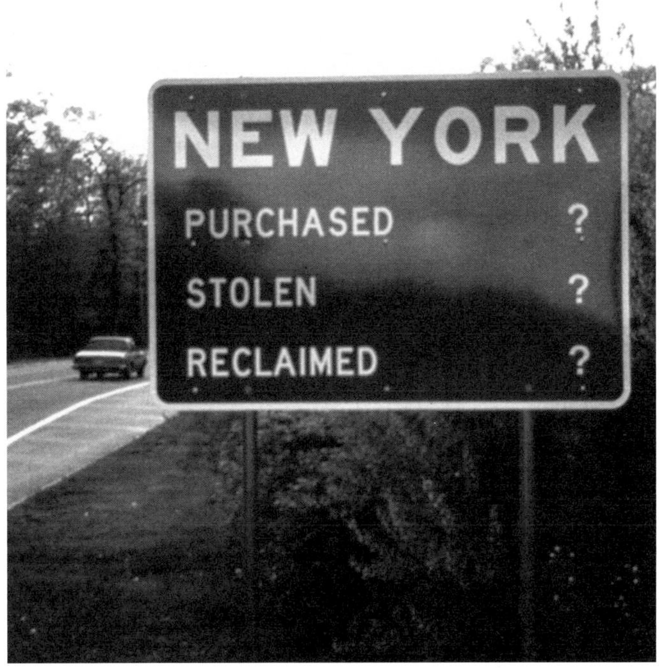

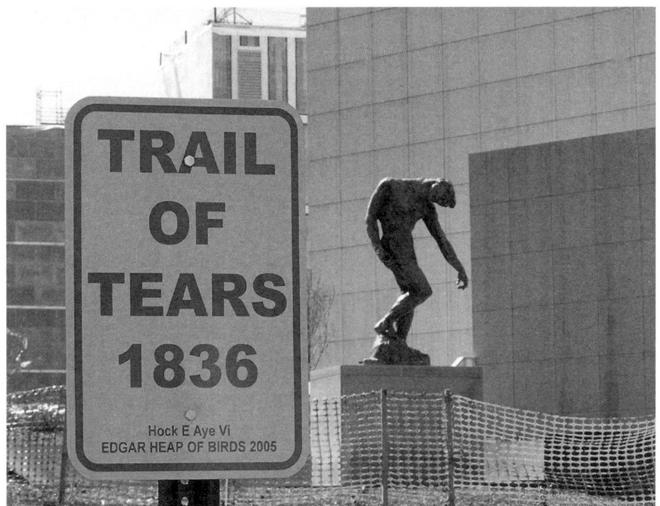

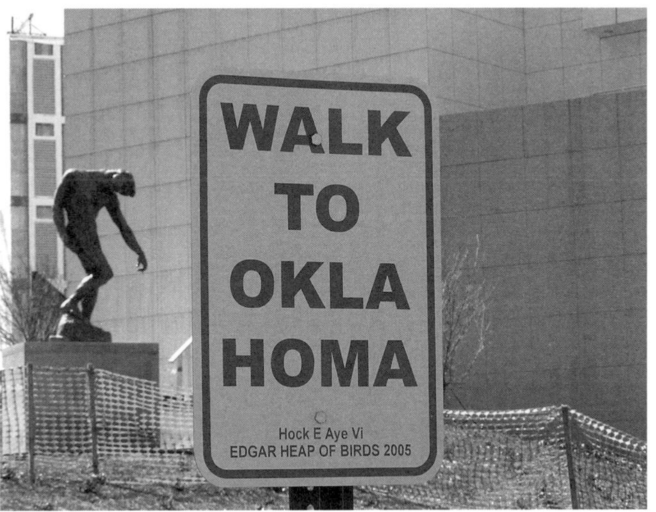

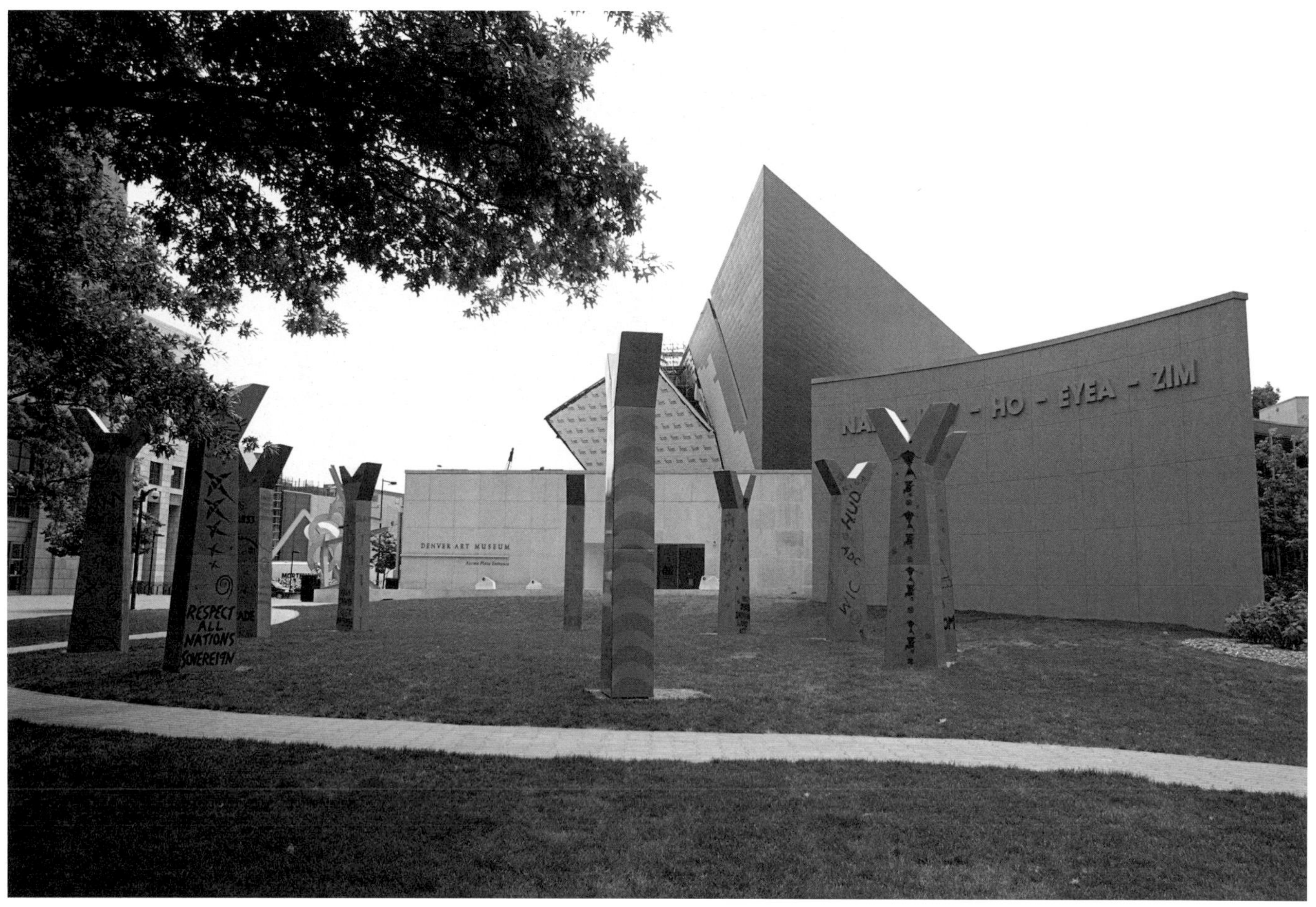

These signs also call attention to how the discourse of authority, whether a parking code or Indian removal, assumes an inviolable power; ultimately, though, they play with that assumption. Robert Allen Warrior correctly notes that in this project, Heap of Birds uses the semiotics of the state "as a means of public interrogation and intervention" that calls "into question . . . the legitimacy of names and signs" ("Liberating Words," 5). By turning governmental signifiers on themselves, Heap of Birds simultaneously undermines governmental discourse and its social symbolism of legality and authenticity. The occupiers of Alcatraz performed a similar kind of symbolic inversion when they transformed the symbol of the American penal system into a sign that both reclaimed Indian land and sported a photo of Geronimo (p. 42). In both instances, the artists strip authority from those governmental signifiers and replace that signification with Native presences.

Like Quick-to-See Smith, Heap of Birds remains interested in the relationship between text and context. In his case, pieces of art are also pieces of written text. Of course, they derive their power from how fully they mimic common signs, but their political message is conveyed through text. In *Wheel*, text also plays a crucial role in the piece's aesthetic context, both as medium and as message (Fig. 9.21). Heap of Birds deploys words and symbols because they spell and signify. They also establish a dialogue between the lexical and the visual, the connotative and the denotative. Just as many Native poets fuse elements of the lyric and the epic, in *Wheel*, Heap of Birds attempts to fuse these two modes of signification into what he calls "text drawings." In the street-sign projects, Heap of Birds doesn't get the opportunity to imbue his "canvas" with gestural brushstrokes—the artist's flair, his identity, disappears into the background of the flatness of the sign—but in *Wheel*, he juxtaposes authorless native symbology with texts of his own hand. This detail enables Heap of Birds

FIGURES 9.21–9.25. *Edgar Heap of Birds,* Wheel, *2007. Each "tree" is porcelain on steel, 144 × 24 × 12 in. The sculpture is installed outside the Denver Art Museum. Courtesy of the Denver Art Museum.*

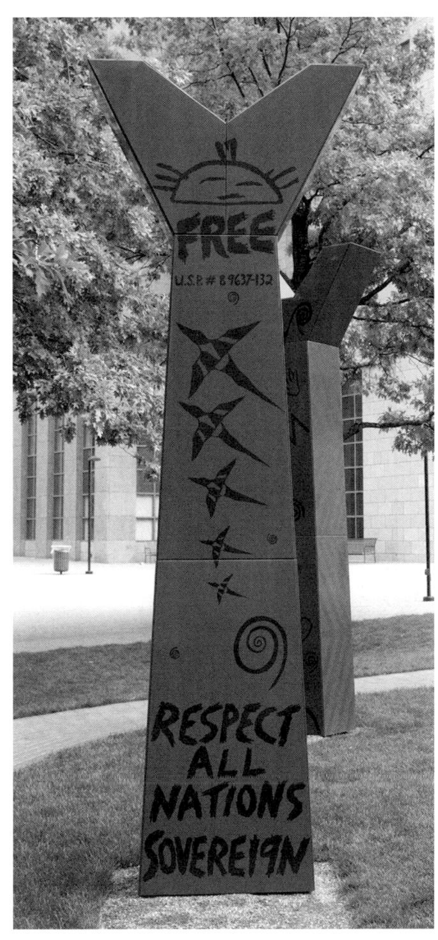

9.22

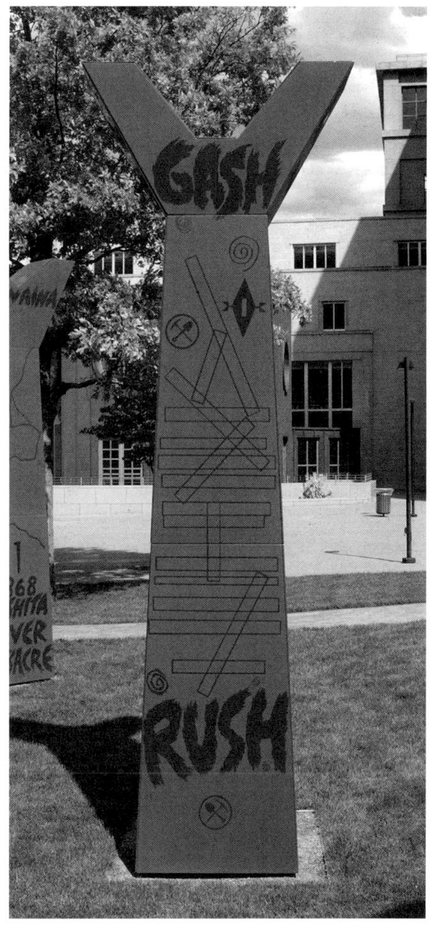

9.23

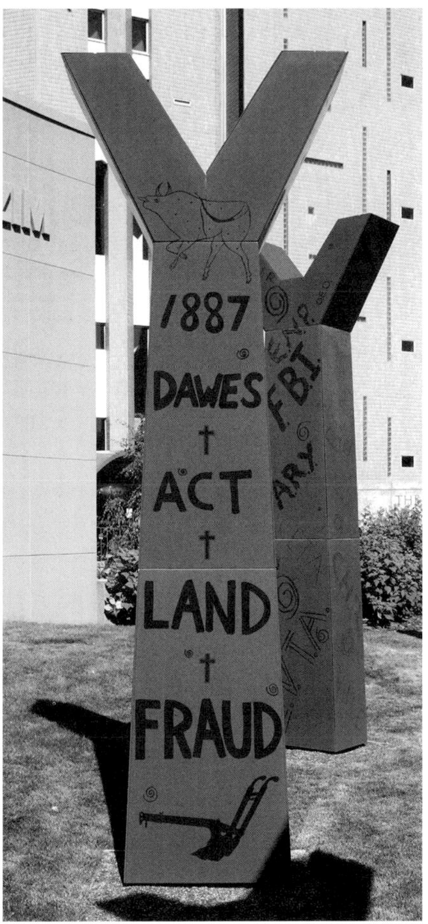

9.24

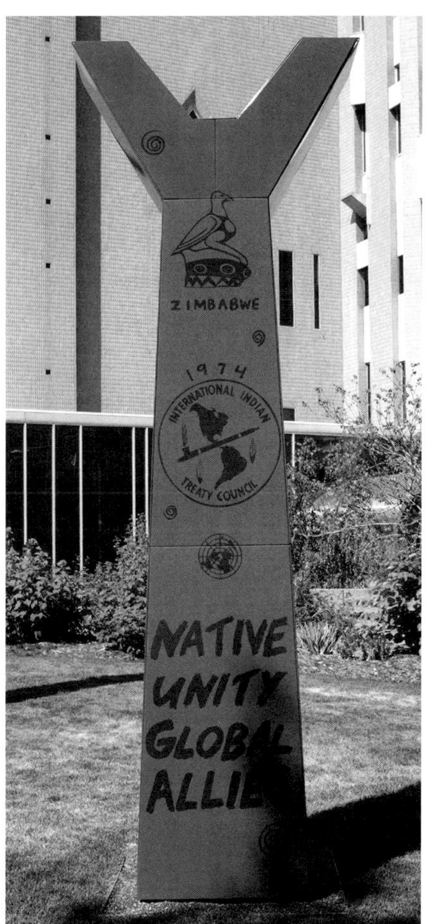

9.25

to shift *Wheel* from the realm of the nearly objective into a world in which subjective and objective interpenetrate, facilitating personal indications of defiance through participation in pan-Indian motifs.

As an artistic text, *Wheel* dazzles. A permanent fixture at the Denver Art Museum, *Wheel* is a fifty-foot circle composed of ten Y-shaped monoliths, or "trees," each of which stands more than twelve feet tall.[14] (Figures 9.21–9.25) Shaped from galvanized steel and painted a deep, nearly blood red, each tree appears to have "carved" on its trunk words, symbols, and patterns that either connote or denote historical aspects of the Cheyenne and Arapaho in and around the Colorado Plateau. One of his major influences, according to Heap of Birds, was the "earth renewal solstice lodge," in which Y-shaped trees help construct an arbor roof. Another influence was the designs on pottery and petroglyphs found in the southwestern part of the United States. Still another was the Big Horn Medicine Wheel. This multilevel, multihistorical design connects present, past, and future through the circular, progressive structure of the wheel. Moveable and mobile, fluid and flexible, the wheel embodies return, renewal, and revolution. Ultimately, as Warrior smartly recognizes, *Wheel* is primarily about engagement: "The research for the sculpture, significantly, involved not only engagement with historical scholarship and visits to historic sites, but also meetings with tribal leaders and community members. That process has culminated in a sculpture that brings together provocative social engagement with deeply elemental features of human experiences of land and place" ("Liberating Words," 4).

Although the trees signify engagement, they also signify resistance. Like the Alcatraz occupiers, Heap of Birds tends to rely on text to express themes of resistance, saving image and symbol for the different but complementary motifs of holism and balance. In the trunks of these trees, Heap of Birds encodes the incitive language of defiance and repudiation. Decrying the Dawes Act and celebrating AIM undermines one and undergirds another. The messages on these trees reflect how resistance is rooted to Indian identity and how that spirit of survivance can branch out across the great abyss of contemporary America. At the same time, their place on the wheel, the hoop of indigenous America, reinforces Indian survivance as transnational transmotion. *Wheel* provokes and preserves, defies and defends. For Heap of Birds, this is part of his duty as an artist and as an Indian. "Indian artists are in a public arena, an international arena," he says. "And we've got to think about what that arena is all about and how we're going to work with that. . . . You've got to beat it . . . outsmart it. It's subversive, where they don't think you're doing that, they think you're just putting it out there, but no, you're spinning it around" (quoted in Abbott, *I Stand in the Center*, 50). *Wheel* spins it around. *Wheel* spins it all around.

If the text of *Wheel*'s trees points to the present and future, then the petroglyphic images connect Heap of Birds's performance with indigenous origins. One of the great absences in the already-meager discourse about Native public art is any consideration of the first forms of indigenous public art—petroglyphs, pictographs, and geoglyphs. Though there is widespread debate about what various forms of cave painting, rock art, and mounds actually mean, most thoughtful scholars agree that one of the functions of this early symbolic action was to express something specific about a culture and a place. In *Hero, Hawk, and Open Hand: American Indian Art of the Ancient Midwest and South*, Richard F. Townsend acknowledges that one of the projects of the book and the accompanying exhibit was to understand how forms of cultural continuity get embedded in the art and architecture of these early societies. He is interested, in particular, in knowing "the way different societies defined themselves and their environment through the symbolism and expressive power of art, architecture, and ritual performance. Our intention," he continues, "is to identify and interpret the dominant forms of symbolic and aesthetic expression, outlining patterns of thought and the determining force of ideas and visual imagery in the formation and maintenance of ancient societies" (19).

No random graffiti, no prehistoric tagging, these instances of aesthetic communication are coded messages about how these people thought, how they saw the world and their surroundings, and, perhaps most significantly, what mattered to them. Even the earliest artists intended an audience; at its most basic level, aesthetic practice is primarily about communication. What makes Heap of Birds such an important and enduring artist is the fact that his pieces both push the boundaries of contemporary art and participate in the long tradition of Native public aesthetic communication. The force of his ideas helps us maintain our society, and we are the richer for it. Jackson Rushing, one of the most prolific readers of Native sculpture, agrees. For him, *Wheel* continues Heap of Birds's interaction with history to potentially alter the future: "Familiar also [in *Wheel*] is the commingling of ancient belief systems, awareness of colonial history, and hope for healing and renewal" ("In Our Language," 384). Indeed, flowing both circuitously and vertically, *Wheel* seems to stretch in all directions, an aesthetic compass, a map of both historical and interior landscapes leading us concurrently outward and inward.

If public art operates as anchor and catapult—connecting us to place and transporting us to other places—it is worth asking what forms of symbolic discourse we want along our cultural roadways, our intellectual and emotional plazas and parking lots, and our sites and seats of power. If our culture, as Townsend says of the ancient Mississippian, defines itself and our environment through symbolism and expressive art, I am going to drive on past the Howe Indian. In fact, I am going to forgo buying his cars altogether. That's not the way I roll.

All I need is a wheel.

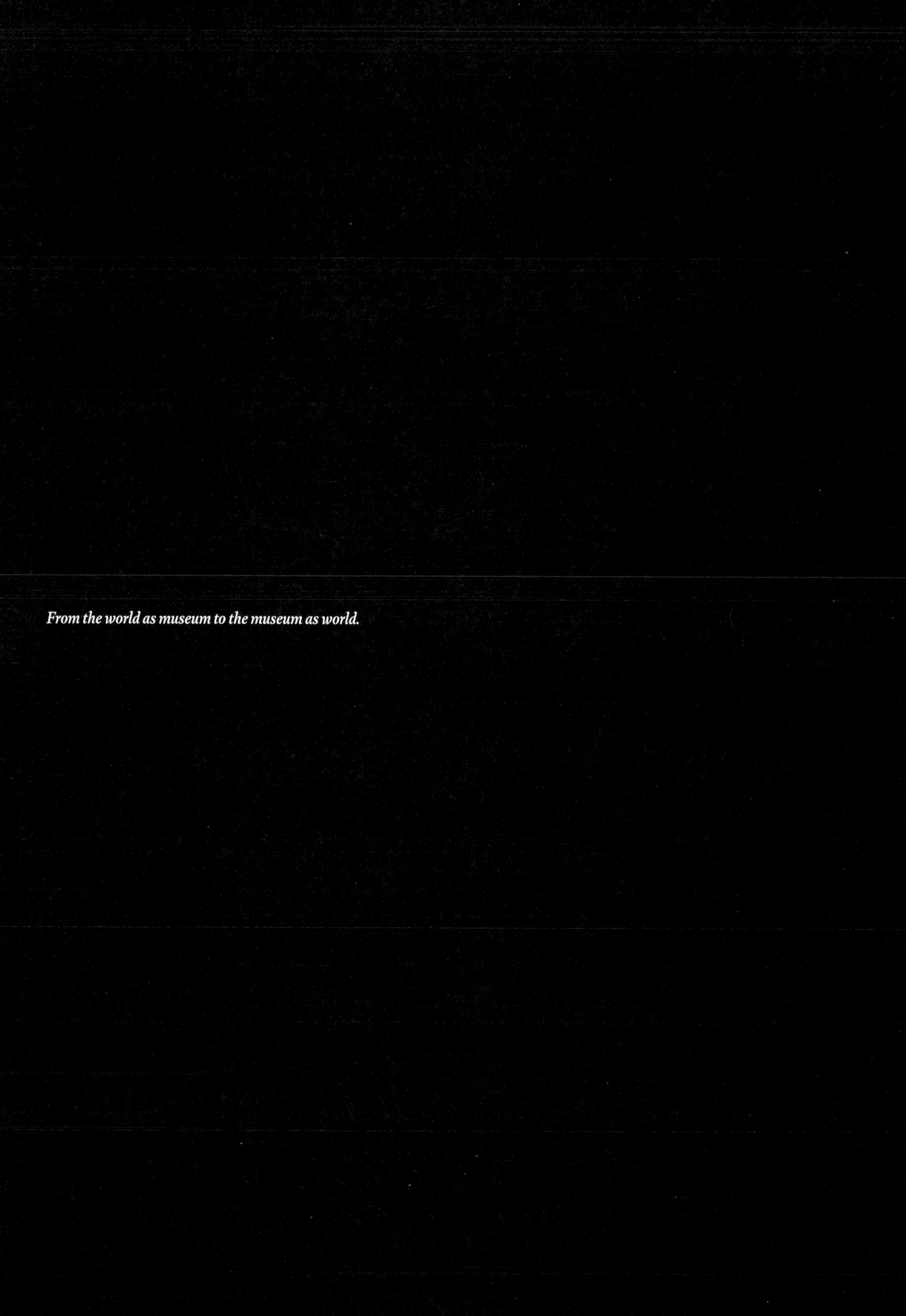

From the world as museum to the museum as world.

10.
ENGAGED RESISTANCE

THE NATIONAL MUSEUM OF THE AMERICAN INDIAN

We wanted to write ourselves back into history.

NACOCHTANKE, 1612. John Smith charts an area called Nacochtanke along the Potomac River. This Algonquin settlement is one of two communities located on the very spot that will become the capital city of the United States of America. It is a thriving place. There are several commercial sites along the Potomac and also along a tributary that will come to be known as Tiber Creek. In addition, several locations exist around the area where members of many tribes will meet and trade. In 220 years, one such location will come to be known as the Smithsonian Mall.

PHILADELPHIA, PENNSYLVANIA, JULY 1, 1790. The Residence Act of 1790 makes it official: the new capital of the United States will be located along the Potomac River near Georgetown. Plans commence for moving the capital from Philadelphia to the District of Columbia. Though the Indian Removal Act is still forty years away, the Algonquin are pushed out of Nacochtanke and other nearby communities to make way for Washington, D.C.

LONDON, 1826. James Smithson, a scientist from Great Britain, leaves $500,000 to the U.S. government to endow an American museum to "facilitate and enhance knowledge." The government finds out about the bequeath almost ten years after Smithson passes and spends nearly another decade deciding what to do with the money.

WASHINGTON, D.C., 1841. City planner Robert Mills draws up what will come to be known as the "Mills Plan," which lays out the Smithsonian and the U.S. Botanic Garden. In 1846, part of the Mall is set aside and identified as the future site of the Smithsonian Museum.

KINGMAN, ARIZONA, 1897. George Gustav Heye, the son of a German immigrant, finds himself supervising the construction of a railroad outside Kingman, Arizona. An engineer trained at Columbia University in New York, Heye is fascinated by Indians and the Indian cultures he encounters in Arizona. He purchases a Navajo deerskin shirt. It becomes his first Indian acquisition. The Heye collection is born.

MANHATTAN, NEW YORK, 1916. On the corner of 155th and Broadway, the Heye Foundation's Museum of the American Indian breaks ground. Eight years later, the museum opens to the public. It houses the largest privately held collection of American Indian items and artifacts in the world.

WASHINGTON, D.C., 1989. An act of Congress decrees that a national museum for American Indians is to be built. It will reside in three locations—New York City; Suitland, Maryland; and on the Mall in Washington, D.C.

ALEXANDER HAMILTON U.S. CUSTOM HOUSE, LOWER MANHATTAN, 1994. The George Gustav Heye Center of the National Museum of the American Indian replaces the museum in Hamilton Heights as the new location in New York City for American Indian education and exhibition within a preservation context.

SUITLAND, MARYLAND, 1998. The National Museum of the American Indian Resource Center opens in suburban Maryland.

WASHINGTON, D.C., September 21, 2004. Fifteen years in the making, the National Museum of the American Indian (NMAI) debuts on the Mall, not far from the very spot where, in 1612, John Smith watched the Tiber Creek flow into the Potomac.

This book begins and ends with explorations of multifaceted Indian occupations of federal land. In the first instance—Alcatraz—the occupation no doubt appears more overtly radical than the sanctioned occupation of a parcel of land on the National Mall in Washington, D.C. One was illegal, the other legal; one was acquired by an act of defiance, the other by an act of congress. In fact, some readers may find my comparison of the Alcatraz occupation and the NMAI cheeky at the very least and, at worst, wrongheaded and critically irresponsible. But I ask the reader's indulgence as I tease out the Venn diagram that allows for both overlap and interplay between the Indian occupation of Alcatraz and the NMAI as important instances of interdisciplinary activism—cross-disciplinary, cross-genre forms of aesthetic activism. For me, Alcatraz and the NMAI stand as ambitious, fascinating, and controversial sites of engaged resistance, and they deserve closer reads, not just alongside each other, but also as comprehensive assertions of Indian sovereignty always and already in conversation with each other.

Controversy, as it happens, is one of many facets connecting Alcatraz and the NMAI. Just as people like Vine Deloria have questioned the value of Alcatraz, so too have critics taken issue with the NMAI. "Many of the reviews of the museum," writes Amy Lonetree (Ho-Chunk), "have been glowing, others ambivalent, and many have been downright scathing" ("Guest Editor's Remarks," 507).[1] Much of the discourse surrounding the NMAI and Alcatraz focuses on the same question: are they successful? Linked to that question is a host of others. Do they advance Indian awareness and Indian causes? Are they our best efforts at sovereignty and survivance? Do they tell Indian stories accurately? The NMAI and Alcatraz remain two of the most divisive issues among Indians today, but they remain also two of the most provocative and, it would appear, most enduring. Ironically, though the Alcatraz occupation ended around forty years ago, it functions like the NMAI—as a living museum.

In the opening chapter of this book, I note that I am not primarily interested in whether the Alcatraz occupation "worked" or "succeeded." Rather, I pose different questions, all of which involve exploring interdisciplinary indigenous activist practices like poems, proclamations, and painting. Not surprisingly, similar notions underpin my queries in regard to the museum. I am interested in reading the NMAI through the lens of Alcatraz, but in interpreting it on its own terms. Both the Alcatraz project and the NMAI mobilize text, image, and rhetoric to establish a new level of discourse about Indian issues and Indian identity, and both can be read as large-scale projects of Indian resistance. To that end, I ask a number of questions: What cultural work does the museum do? What is the interplay of word, image, artifact, and architecture there? How does it assert itself as a place? How is the NMAI about identity? And does it provide a kind of cultural bookend to Alcatraz? Just as I am interested in the poems, paintings, and proclamations of Alcatraz, so too am I intrigued by the various discourses of and in the NMAI that make it a project of survivance and an example of aesthetic activism.

Not surprisingly, this chapter considers the NMAI in much the same way that Chapter 1 regards the totality of the documents of the Alcatraz occupation—as a rhetorical text. Just as the occupiers of Alcatraz wrote poems, drew up proclamations, and painted buildings as means of articulated defiance, so too do the occupants of that parcel of land on the Mall enact a kind of engaged resistance through poems, artifacts, photographs, documents, stories, and paintings. In the case of Alcatraz, these texts tell multiple stories: stories of the occupation, stories of Native survival, stories of the desire for Native autonomy, stories of the reservation experience, and stories of Native anger. Similar (even if not the same) stories also get told through the various displays, exhibitions, and curatorial devices at the museum. In both instances, the sites function as locations of indigenous narration and scenes of identity formation. The overarching argument made by Alcatraz is the same as the one made by the NMAI—Indians are still here—but the ancillary arguments underpin and augment the main point, adding context and contour: Indians are self-governing, Indians participate in active forms of survivance, Indian culture is alive and well, and creative expression is part and parcel of Native activism. The goal of the rest of this chapter is to examine how the NMAI makes those arguments. For better or worse, the NMAI is one large, complicated, but intentional text. And like any complex text, it has yielded a dizzying number of misreadings. My project is to reduce that number by one.

I should say at the outset that the NMAI does not advertise itself as an activist text. On the contrary, it insinuates itself as a site of acclimation, accomplishment, and, most importantly, Native authorship. In her essay "Making Our World Understandable," Ramona Sakiestewa (Hopi) provides a quotation that kept her focused on the task at hand during the early design phases of the museum. For her, this guiding principle "summarizes some of the hopes people had for the museum during the early consultations: 'The architecture, design, and atmosphere of the spaces in mind must reflect a deep understanding of Native values, sense of place, and cultural symbolism'" (80). The book in which this passage appears, *Spirit of a Native Place*, serves as an encapsulation of this concept, suggesting that the museum's main purpose is to embody Nativeness. Note the similarities to the following passage, which appears in the foreword to the NMAI's guidebook and was written by W. Richard West (Southern Cheyenne), the museum's founding director, to lay out what he hopes the museum accomplishes: "We define a moment of reconciliation and recognition in American history, a time for Indian people to assume, finally, a prominent place of honor on the nation's front lawn. It is our most fervent hope that we will be an instrument of enlightenment, helping our visitors learn more about the extraordinary achievements of the indigenous people of the Western Hemisphere. We also hope that Native people will look upon the museum as a truly Native place, where they are welcomed as honored guests" (*Welcome to a Native Place*, 7).

I am struck by much of the language here. Immediately, the discourse of recognition asserts itself, both overtly and covertly ("prominent place of honor" and "extraordinary achievements"). These are the words of a man not at all interested in defining Indians by what has been done to them but rather by that which Indians have themselves done and, even more importantly, are actively doing. Though West hints at this notion of action, there is precious little here about activism. Indeed, one word you don't expect to see in regard to activism is "reconciliation." One expects a more forceful, more vigorous assertion of Indian dynamism. Instead of making the museum sound revolutionary, he makes it sound residential. There is something about the metaphor of "placement" on the "nation's front lawn" that evokes lawn jockeys, cigar-store Indians, weather vanes, and other figures of passive decoration that are at variance with the unending struggle of Native tribes. For some, then, the museum is flawed because the vision behind its inception is more about recognition than agitation, more about acceptance than resistance.

Different Visions of the NMAI: Contextual versus Compositional Resistance

Indeed, most of the criticisms of the museum come from those in museum studies and Native studies, who feel the NMAI's narrative intentionally whitewashes the history of resistance, colonialism, and the past struggles of Native communities. Lonetree and fellow scholar Sonya Atalay (Ojibwe) both level relatively harsh critiques at the NMAI on these very grounds. For Atalay, who sees the museum as an educational text and a rare opportunity to tell Native stories on a grand stage, "the messages about colonization and its devastating and continual effects on Native communities [are] benign" ("No Sense of the Struggle," 601).[2] Similarly, Lonetree cites the NMAI's "failure to discuss the colonization process in a clear and coherent manner" as a "notable absence" and a "missed opportunity to truly challenge the American master narrative—a narrative that has silenced or even erased the memory of genocidal policies of America's past and present" ("Missed Opportunities," 636–637). But Lonetree, a historian, and Atalay, an archeologist, are also sympathetic to the museum's goals and its unbelievably difficult task. Less sympathetic, though, is the American Indian Movement's statement in 2004—which Lonetree cites—decrying the museum for falling "short in that it does not characterize or does not display the sordid and tragic history of America's holocaust against the Native Nations and peoples of the Americas" (637).

To these criticisms, West (now rather famously) responded with what some have called the 5 percent rule. West intentionally distances the NMAI, which is about the present, from traditional museums with dioramas and artifacts, which are, to him, about the past—as is colonialism: "As much and as important as that period of history is—the centuries of war, disease and exile—it is at best only about 5 percent of the period we have been in this hemisphere. We do not want to make the National Museum of the American Indian into an Indian Holocaust Museum . . . You have to go beyond the story of the tragedy and the travesty of the past 500 years. What we are talking about in the end is cultural survivance. We are still here" (quoted in Achenbach, "Within These Walls").

To be sure, White and the entire curatorial staff face an insurmountable dilemma. How does one create a living museum that comprehensively, inclusively, and accurately tells the stories of Native Americans for, say, the past thousand years? Though that question is largely rhetorical, it is worth taking a moment to consider the impossibility of the task before West and his team: the vast numbers of tribes, their languages, their stories, their landscapes, their systems of belief, their journeys, their architecture, and their art. I cannot even begin to imagine how one contextualizes any of it in one museum with any real success. Then take into account the politics of historical identity, the semiotics of representing and re-representing disease and treachery and genocide and removal. As I have tried to suggest in this study, the power of semiotics is not to be underestimated, and in my mind, West and his staff understand better than most what damage the museum could do to contemporary notions of Native identity if the authoritative version of Native history foregrounds conquest over creativity, removal over recovery, and slaughter over survivance.

For those who have not read the previous chapters, I would like to make an important distinction between contextual resistance and compositional resistance, specifically in regard to the NMAI. Lonetree, Atalay, AIM, and a host of others are rightfully angry over the lack of curatorial evidence devoted to Indian resistance, what we might call contextual resistance. By this I mean information in displays, exhibitions, and curatorial signs that both explain and depict instances of Native resistance. There is no question that the NMAI could do more in this regard; in fact, part of their charge should be to deliver to the world the best examples of this both historically and currently.[3] As many other writers, artists, filmmakers, and even museums have shown, it is possible to portray Indian resistance in a way that doesn't freeze Indians in the past. In fact, as this book demonstrates, there are infinite examples of creative contemporary resistance that are positive, progressive, and present. That said, part of the project of the museum is to facilitate contemporary tribes' telling of their own stories in their own way, and if the mission of the museum is to help send the message that Indians are still here, continually reinscribing the narratives of conquest and Manifest Destiny might be at loggerheads with the narratives of contextual resistance. When faced with a choice of depicting the Massacre at Wounded Knee or giving exhibition space to the practices of a contemporary tribe, the museum almost always comes down on the side of present process. For example, if the Tohono O'odham are primarily interested in highlighting their 240-mile walk from Tucson to Mexico in an attempt to raise awareness about diabetes, or if the Kiowa want to describe how they are retaining cultural traditions and advancing educational programs, it might be difficult—perhaps impossible—to seamlessly marry present programs to depictions of past transgressions.

Where the NMAI may come up short on contextual resistance, it excels in the arena of compositional resistance. Compositional resistance implies macroresistance. By this, I mean resistance on the structural level as opposed to the micro- or descriptive levels. In other words, how the museum is put together. Examples include the building's architecture, the design of the museum's exhibits, its internal layout, how exhibitions are curated, and its placement on the Mall. These forms of resistance are less sexy; they don't do as well in the take-home story. Yet they contribute to the overall experience of the museum and the work it does. They create an aura, and they shape not just the exhibits but how those exhibits give voice. If contextual resistance is text, then compositional resistance is subtext, and if postmodernism teaches us anything, it is sensitivity to text and subtext. The occupiers of Alcatraz knew this as well. Many of their public statements were engaging, funny, and charming, despite the fact that the fire driving the occupation's engine was one of roiling anger, atomic resentment, and deep despair.

Put another way, the NMAI may not be revolutionary in its story, but it is revolutionary in its structure—what experts in the field call "museological procedures." As mentioned in Chapter 2, Michel de Certeau makes the argument that human practices can function as modes of resistance. For Certeau, "procedures of everyday creativity" are self-generating tactics to resist the consuming forces of colonialism, commercial machinery, governmental regulations, and political structures. "These 'ways of operating,'" writes Certeau, "constitute the innumerable practices by means of which users reappropriate the space organized by techniques of sociocultural production" (*The Practice of Everyday Life*, xiv). Indians have proved themselves masters of everyday creativity, whether weaving or speaking or

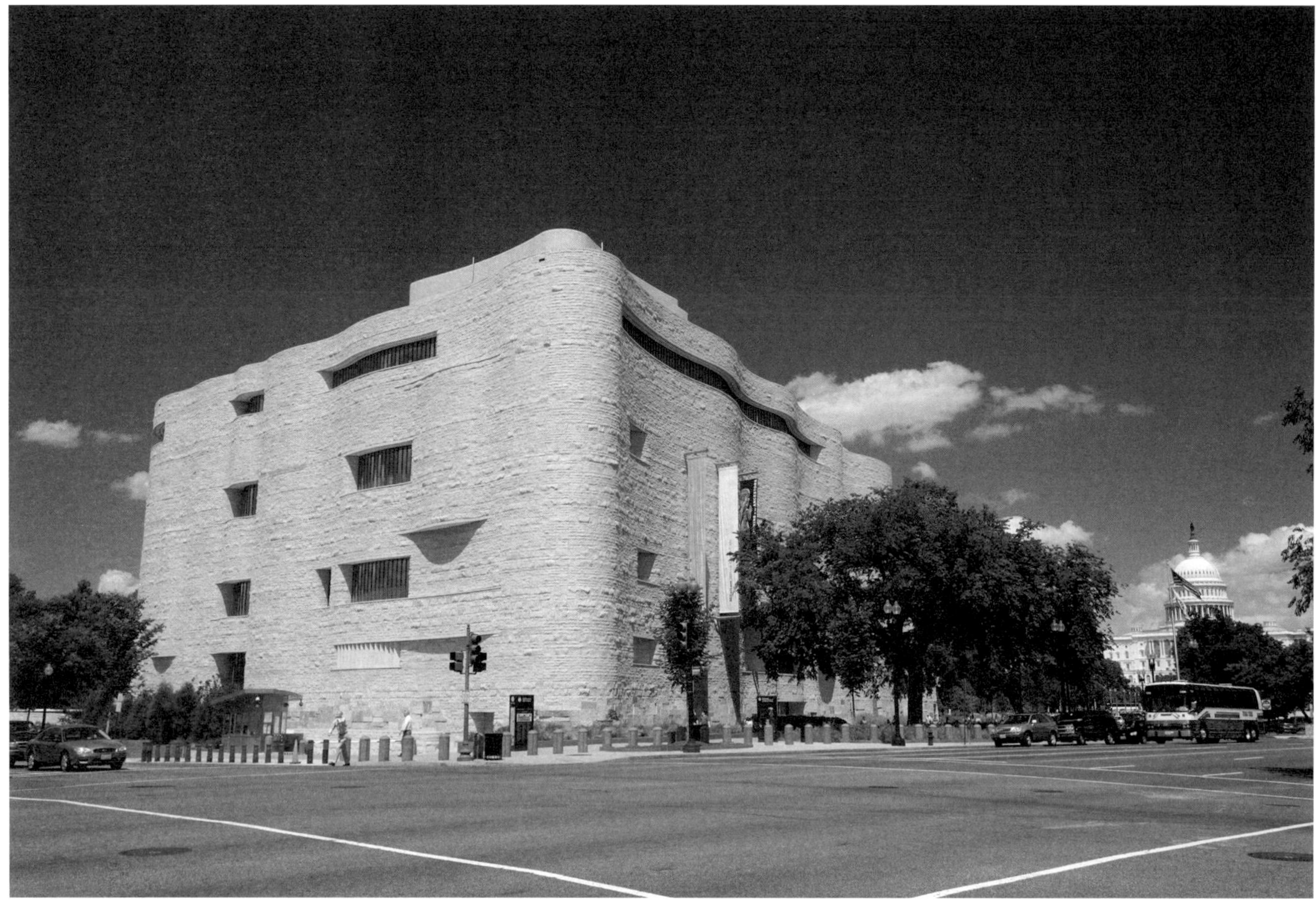

FIGURE 10.1. *National Museum of the American Indian, Washington, D.C. The U.S. Capitol is in the background. The NMAI is the closest museum to the Capitol on the south side of the Mall. Courtesy of the National Museum of the American Indian, Smithsonian Institution. Photo by Katherine Fogden.*

cooking or merely surviving. Moreover, it is hard to imagine a place more governed by the techniques of sociocultural production than the Mall, where nationalism meets exhibition. Despite its shortcomings, the NMAI has instituted—consciously or not—museological procedures of everyday creativity that in my mind serve as important and engaging (even if not always visible) forms of compositional resistance, and it is these ways of operating that make the NMAI an activist text.

The Architecture of Compositional Resistance

The most obvious examples of this compositional resistance lie in the building's architecture, design, and location. Insinuated into the cultural lineup of the heavy-hitting museums on the National Mall, the NMAI occupies an enviable position at the foot of the Capitol, as it was described by one curator (Evelyn, "Most Beautiful Sight," 183; see Fig. 10.1). One of the great ironies, lost on almost no Native visitor, is the fact that Indian land sits right next door to the building where most of the decisions were made to move Indians from their land. Andrew Jackson, who signed the Indian Removal Act in 1830, would be astonished to learn that Indians had come back 174 years later and set up shop in his front yard. So for many—me included—it is a sign of cultural and aesthetic perseverance, arrival, and even triumph that an Indian museum even exists in D.C. "The District of Columbia," writes Elizabeth Archuleta (Yaqui-Chicana), "is a city dominated by marble and granite and neoclassical styles that are reminiscent of the United States' transplanted European heritage and reminders of a government that has tried desperately to assimilate Indians, transforming them into white Americans. The NMAI's presence in space largely occupied by the federal government challenges this heritage and history and asserts Indigenous peoples' survival" ("Gym Shoes," 434). Washington, D.C., the National Mall, and the Smithsonian are themselves institutions of Americanness, repositories of master texts and precious documents, square one for the most important American historical, cultural, and ideological concepts. It is both fitting and radical that the space on the Mall closest to the U.S. Capitol be occupied by Indians.

While few would argue the significance of that symbolism, they would (and do) take issue with the form that symbolism takes. In this case, that form would be the building itself, which, like most aspects of the NMAI, has been both praised and pilloried. The original design team consisted of Douglas Cardinal (Blackfoot), Jonpaul Jones (Cherokee-Choctaw), Donna House (Oneida-Navajo), and Sakiestewa, who traveled all over the United States and Canada, talking to elders, gathering information, taking notes, and consulting with dozens of tribes. The unusually collaborative consultation process was lengthy, but everyone involved believed strongly that the process had to be as inclusive as possible. Even so, like the interior exhibits, the exterior structure stymies expectations. For some, the building comes off as too flashy, too southwestern, and too corporate to authentically embody Indian values. Some criticize the rotunda, the building's attempts at grandeur, its enormous size, and even its color. But for others, the building has emerged as a living monument to Indian ingenuity. Everything about the building's design—the circular floor plan, the landscaping of natural flora and fauna, the domed roof, the windows running like a horizontal river across the facade—is supposed to suggest a Native place. The structure, designed to look as though it had been carved by wind and water, mimics the ancient patterns of riverbeds and sandstone walls, so the entire building appears to have been eroded out of a giant rock outcropping, not erected with steel and concrete (Fig. 10.2).

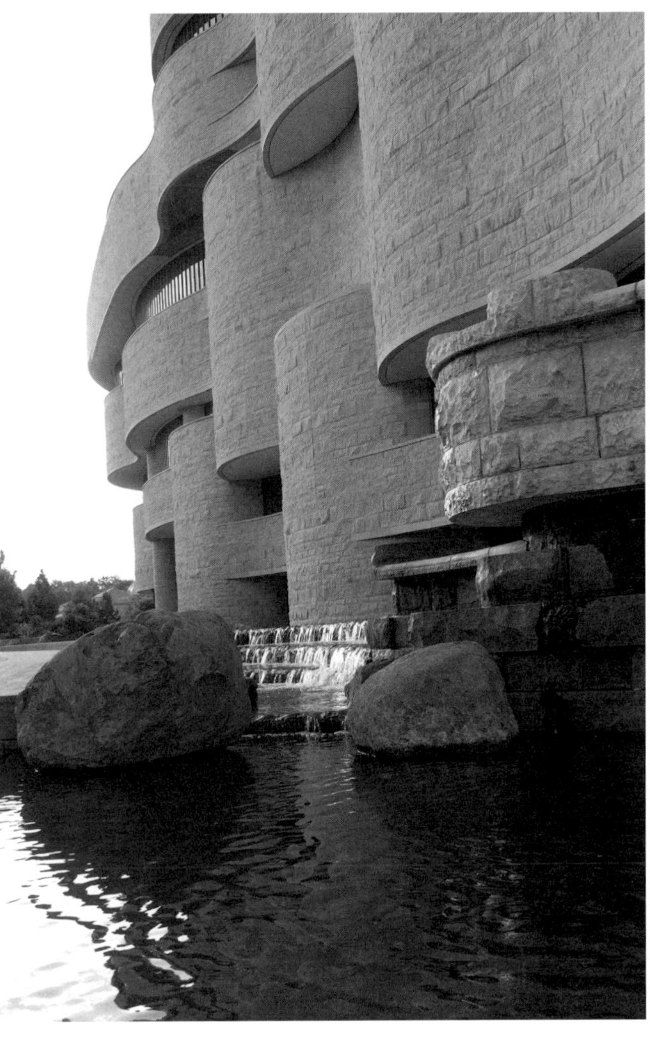

FIGURE 10.2. *Curvilinear walls of the NMAI, designed to resemble eroded rock carved by "wind and water." Courtesy of the National Museum of the American Indian, Smithsonian Institution. Photo by R. A. Whiteside.*

Evoking soil, natural grasses, and sand, the Kasota stone, quarried in Minnesota, feels more alive, more natural, than the ubiquitous polished marble and granite around the nation's capital. Whereas other buildings in the District find inspiration in the columns, pillars, and sharp lines of man-made structures, the NMAI goes terrestrial. The dialogue of form and function, design and material, results in a space that is, at its core, both indigenous and celebratory. For Amanda J. Cobb, Cardinal and his team pull off the perfect marriage of indigeneity and modernity: "The structure's curved lines, tiers, and dome call to mind the very best of contemporary architecture, thus underscoring that Native cultures are both ancient and thoroughly present in the here and now" ("National Museum of the American Indian," 491). Whereas Anglo architects looked to past iconic structures in order to imbue their buildings with the values of that era, the architects of the NMAI looked to nature in order to encode their building with the value-laden icons of movement, reciprocity, beauty, and interconnectedness (Fig. 10.3).

As an architectural text, the NMAI is a fun read. Inserted into the culturally rich, hal-

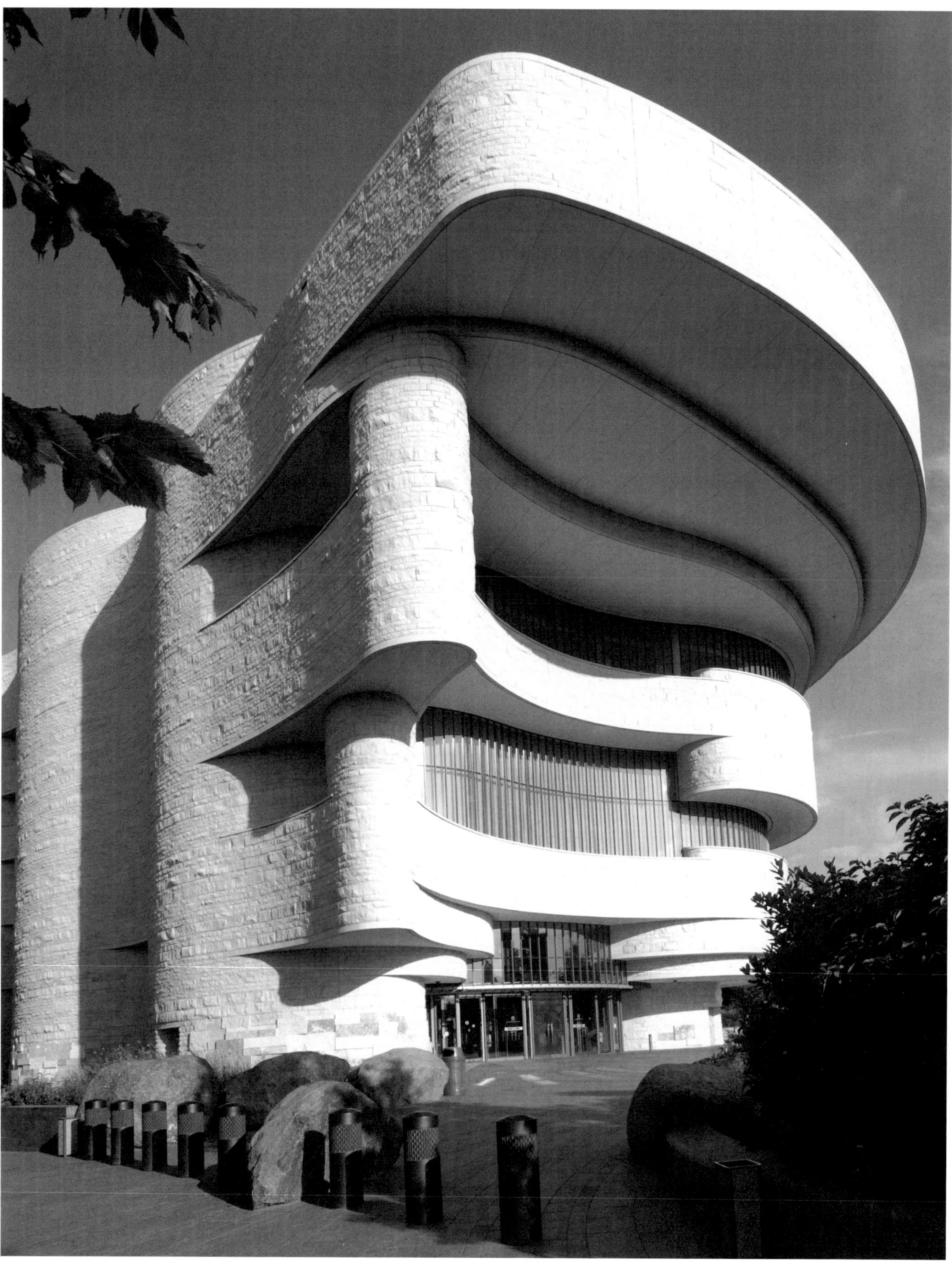

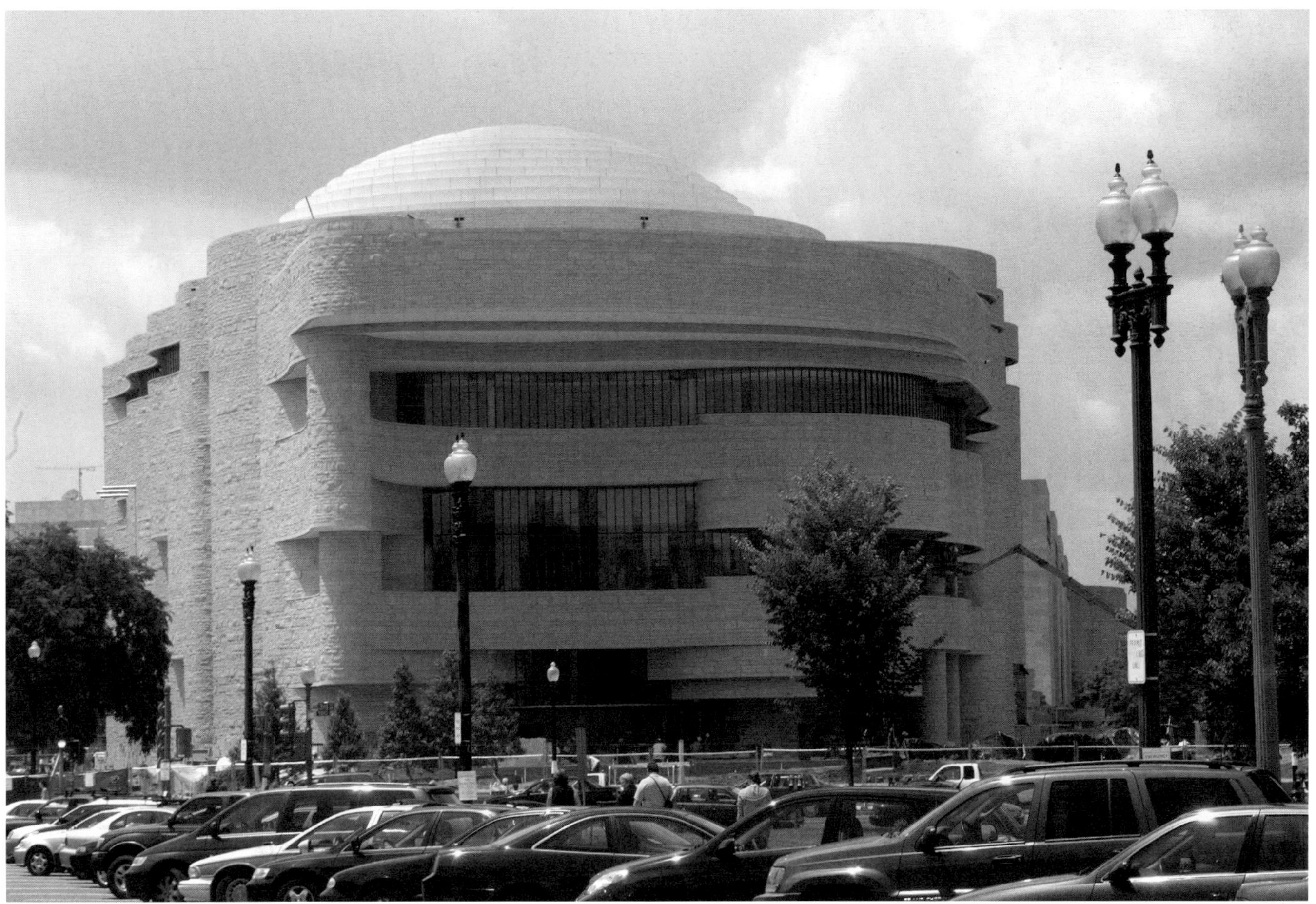

lowed hall of the Mall, it holds its own. The building's curvilinear walls oppose the hard edges and intense linearity of many of the other buildings on the Mall, and its creamy beige stone stands in stark contrast to the whiteness of the Capitol, the Washington Monument, the Lincoln Memorial, and most of the other neoclassical structures identified as American, classic, and stately. For me, that absence of whiteness so close to the Capitol does important work in the arena of race. It sends a strong semiotic message about what colors belong on the mall. Perhaps to savvy visitors, the indigenous local landscaping will remind them that these very plants, like Indians themselves, occupied the land long before Thomas Jefferson, George Washington, and Abraham Lincoln. Cobb's observation about the present and past is on point in this regard. Even the rotunda—so much a part of Western authoritarian architecture, especially in D.C.—gets downplayed in the NMAI (Fig. 10.4). More horizontal than the Capitol's rotunda, it recalls the smooth curve of a kiva or the gentle slope of a burial mound or sand dune. While the rotunda interacts with others like it around town, because of its infrastructure it resists being subsumed under their cultural rubric. As a visual marker, the NMAI cuts its own path on the Mall. It refuses to conform to the Mall's narrativity, its nostalgia, or its colonial commemoration. As an attraction on the country's map, it asserts Native presence; as a story in the country's imagination, it narrates Native survivance.

The circularity that characterizes the external footprint also informs the internal space. Immediately upon entering the museum, visitors are ushered into a large circular room—called the Potomac Atrium—vertically capped by the four-story rotunda and terrestrially grounded by a hundred-foot-diameter circle called the Potomac (Fig. 10.5). Like the building itself, the Potomac is oriented to the cardinal directions, and its subtle markings

FIGURE 10.3. (facing page) *Main entrance of the NMAI with vertical tiers and a cantilevered roof. Courtesy of the National Museum of the American Indian, Smithsonian Institution. Photo by R. A. Whiteside.*

FIGURE 10.4. (top) *View of the NMAI with the curved walls in the foreground and the rotunda in the background. Courtesy of the National Museum of the American Indian, Smithsonian Institution. Photo by R. A. Whiteside.*

denote both ceremony and symbolic communication. The large open design resembles the circular spaces used for rituals and dances by most North and South American indigenous communities.[4]

Created to host powwows, dances, demonstrations, and other ceremonies, the Potomac encodes the entry space of the museum with the semiotics of participation. Upon entering the museum, visitors are not greeted by long wooden canoes, figures behind glass, or any item on display. The first thing seen is open space, a circle in which interaction takes place.[5] On one of my visits, there was a cooking demonstration taking place in the Potomac, followed later by a musical performance. This realm of interactivity adds both ritualistic reverence to the museum's ingress and a kind of bustling energy of human engagement. I see this design aesthetic as fundamentally rhetorical and somewhat radical. It turns the classic museum experience on its head. Typically, museums position themselves as being about objects, whereas the NMAI makes the argument that it is first and foremost about people. Whereas most art museums encourage a hushed solemnity, the NMAI breaks that mold by facilitating an interpenetration of ceremony and celebration, inverting the classic museum paradigm of passivity into one of activity that prepares the visitor for how the vast, globular text of the museum should be read.

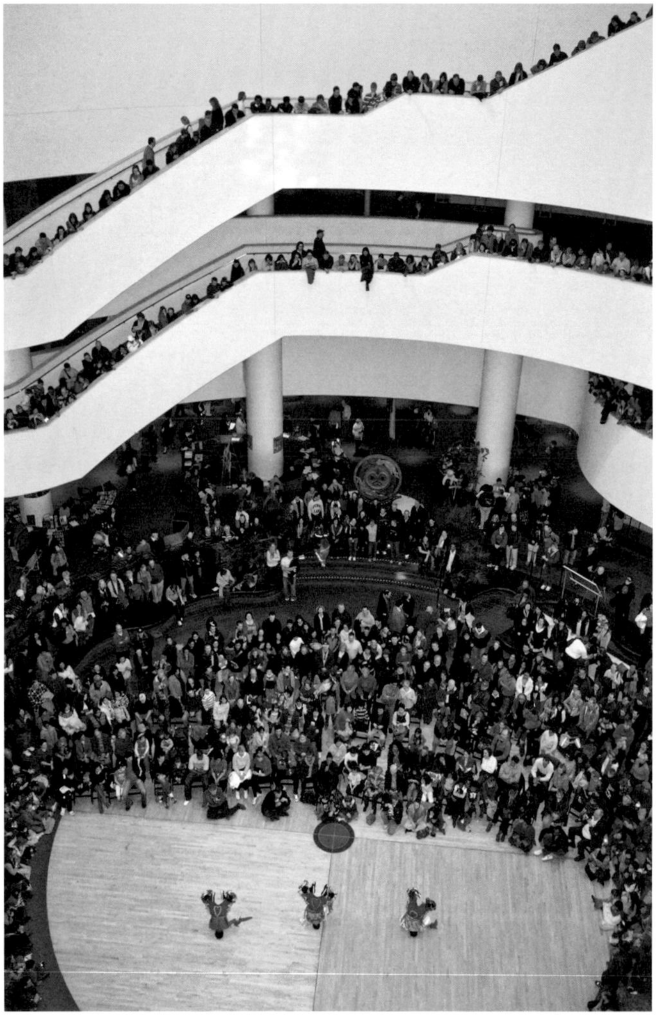

FIGURE 10.5. *The Potomac circle within the Potomac Atrium. The space functions as a site for demonstrations, ceremonials, dances, and performances, as seen here. Courtesy of the National Museum of the American Indian, Smithsonian Institution. Photo by Katherine Fogden.*

Curatorial Clashes

Just as the external and internal architecture connotes activism, so too does the curatorial architecture. Controversial as the architecture may be, the most contentious debate has been over the displays and exhibitions (or lack thereof). Here, more than anywhere else, the museum challenges traditional notions of contextual resistance by including very little information about genocide, colonialism, or the history of Indian resistance. Instead, the museum mixes dashes of contextual information in a notoriously circular exhibit space that serves as a textbook example of compositional resistance. Determined to rewrite the classic anthropological-museum text, West and his team intentionally created an exhibition space that flies in the face of conventional anthropological presentation. The deputy assistant director of cultural resources, James Henry, links that stance to the museum's impudence toward standard museology: "We're not an anthropology museum. We're a museum of living culture . . . This is a venue for native peoples to tell their own story. You're not going to get the anthropological perspective" (quoted in "Within These Walls").

And indeed you don't.

So, why, one might ask, is this such a hot-button issue?

Much of this book concerns itself with how Native writers, filmmakers, and artists undermine conventional forms of authority, whether they are street signs, literary genres, historical landmarks, or maps of the United States. An often-unexplored genre of authority is museum curation and its putative unassailability. Like poetic genres, like maps, like governmental structures, the museum has for ages functioned as a master text, a metanarrative canonized by the preciousness of its relics. The NMAI takes as its main mission the unenviable task of completely rewriting the curatorial text. Gone are the anthropological underpinnings. Gone are the historical time lines and linear modeling. Gone are the dioramas. Gone are the "Start Here" and "End Here" chronological exhibits. And gone is the notion that museums tell stories primarily about that which has already happened. In short, past has been replaced by place. "The result is something triumphant for the people who trace their lineage to the first Americans," writes Joel Achenbach in the *Washington Post*. "Many people, when they visit the National Museum of the American Indian, will enter a world they know little or nothing about. This is not a typical government museum full of artifacts. It's not a scientific, secular enterprise that speaks in an anonymous institutional voice. It has many voices, and they are native voices. It feels more like a cathedral than a museum. Walk inside and you enter Indian Country" ("Within These Walls").

How you feel about the NMAI will have everything to do with how you feel about what Achenbach characterizes as the museum's cathedral-ness as opposed to its museumness. The museum's celebratory tonality is a result of what Gerald McMaster calls its "new Indian museology" (Lonetree, "Missed Opportunities," 636).[6] Lonetree herself, one of the museum's most displeased critics, describes this as a "complicated, nuanced, and ultimately effective presentation of Indigenous philosophy, history, and identity as told from the perspective of Indigenous communities" (636). Those who want the exhibition and curatorial experience to be historical, linear, artifact laden, and angry, will find the museum sorely lacking, perhaps even negligent in its duty as a public document of Native resilience. But for those interested in polyvocality, the possibilities of the indigenous present, and the potential for contemporary Native storytelling on a grand stage, the NMAI may not merely pass—it may prevail. Those of us who spend our days decoding semiotic, visual, and literary texts tend to love that which surprises, upends expectation, and flies in the face of predictability. One would think that appreciation of virtuosity would extend to museums, but for many, a museum is not a museum unless it memorializes. However, as so many novelists, critics, and poets have stated over the past thirty years, Indian country is a place out of time, a place in which linear notions of temporality, Western conceptions of knowing and being, are suspended. When we consider that the NMAI takes as its project the depiction and articulation of Native survivance and indigenous epistemology, should we really expect this Native place to feel non-Native?

As it happens, it doesn't. In fact, the museum feels very much like a Native place, and the stories it tells feel like Native stories—perhaps for some, a little too much. The museum's lack of explanatory material has proved confusing for some visitors, just as its ambling, meandering circularity can come off as both aimless and repetitive. Similarly frustrating are the exhibitions themselves. Given the number of artifacts collected by Heye, the NMAI features surprisingly few iconic Native collectibles, opting instead for text-heavy displays that highlight present projects of Native tribes rather than past remnants of "wilder," more "savage" Indian times. For better or worse, the curators opt for large colorful displays with photographs, sounds, moving images, and lots of text to tell three different stories—the story of "Our Universes," the story of "Our Peoples," and the story of "Our Lives." Though the museum features a theater, a gift shop, a restaurant, temporary exhibition space, and, of course, the Potomac, these three distinct sections function as the main narrative and curatorial exhibitions in the museum. Each spotlights tribally specific items, projects, policies, and practices of eight indigenous communities from North, Central, and South America. It is these exhibits that have angered so many, for such different reasons, since no matter who you are, none of these exhibits is going to contain what you want. Visitors expecting exhibitions on "Our Arrowheads" or "Our Teepees" will be disappointed (and

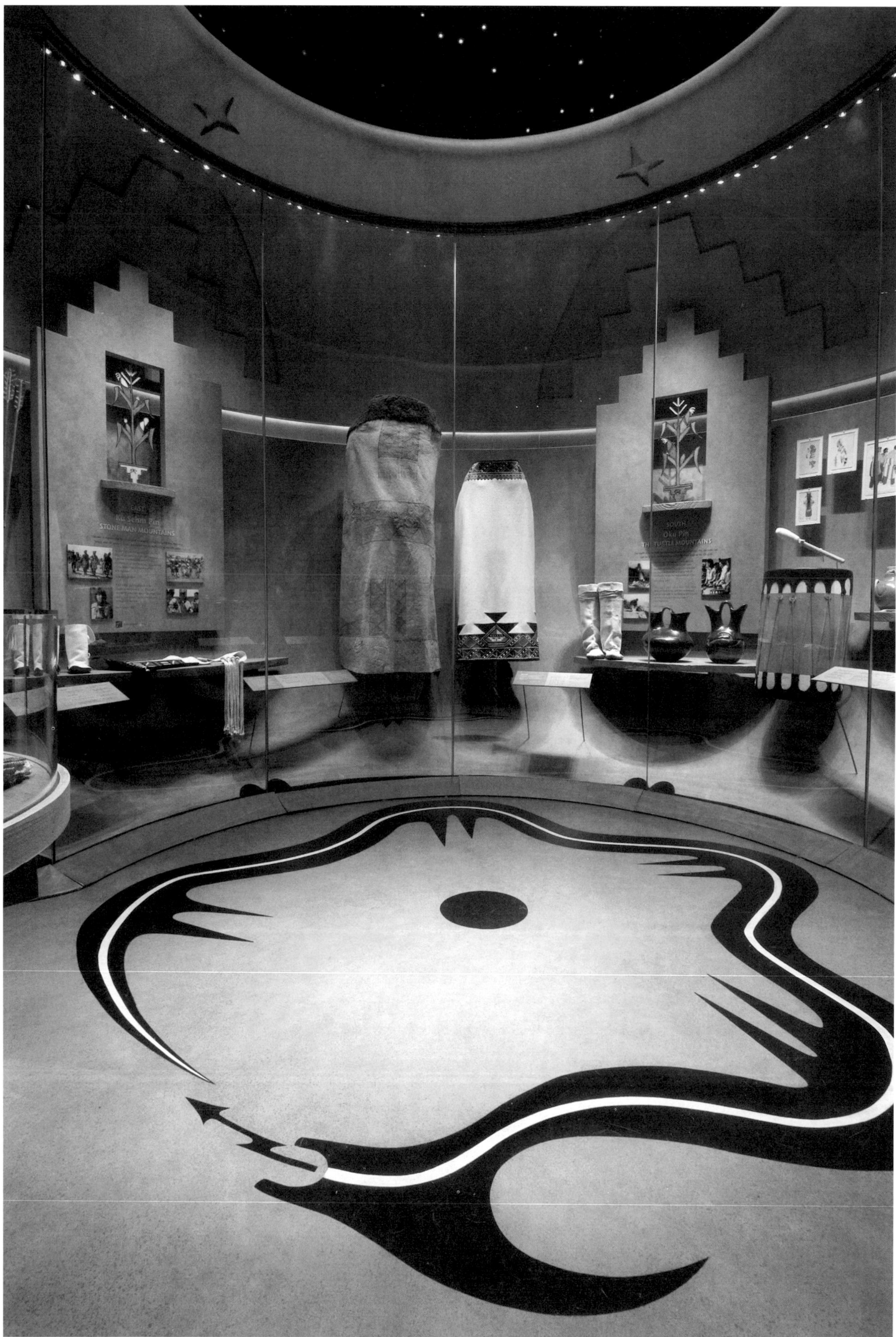
STONE MAN MOUNTAINS
SOUTH
Oku Pin
TURTLE MOUNTAINS

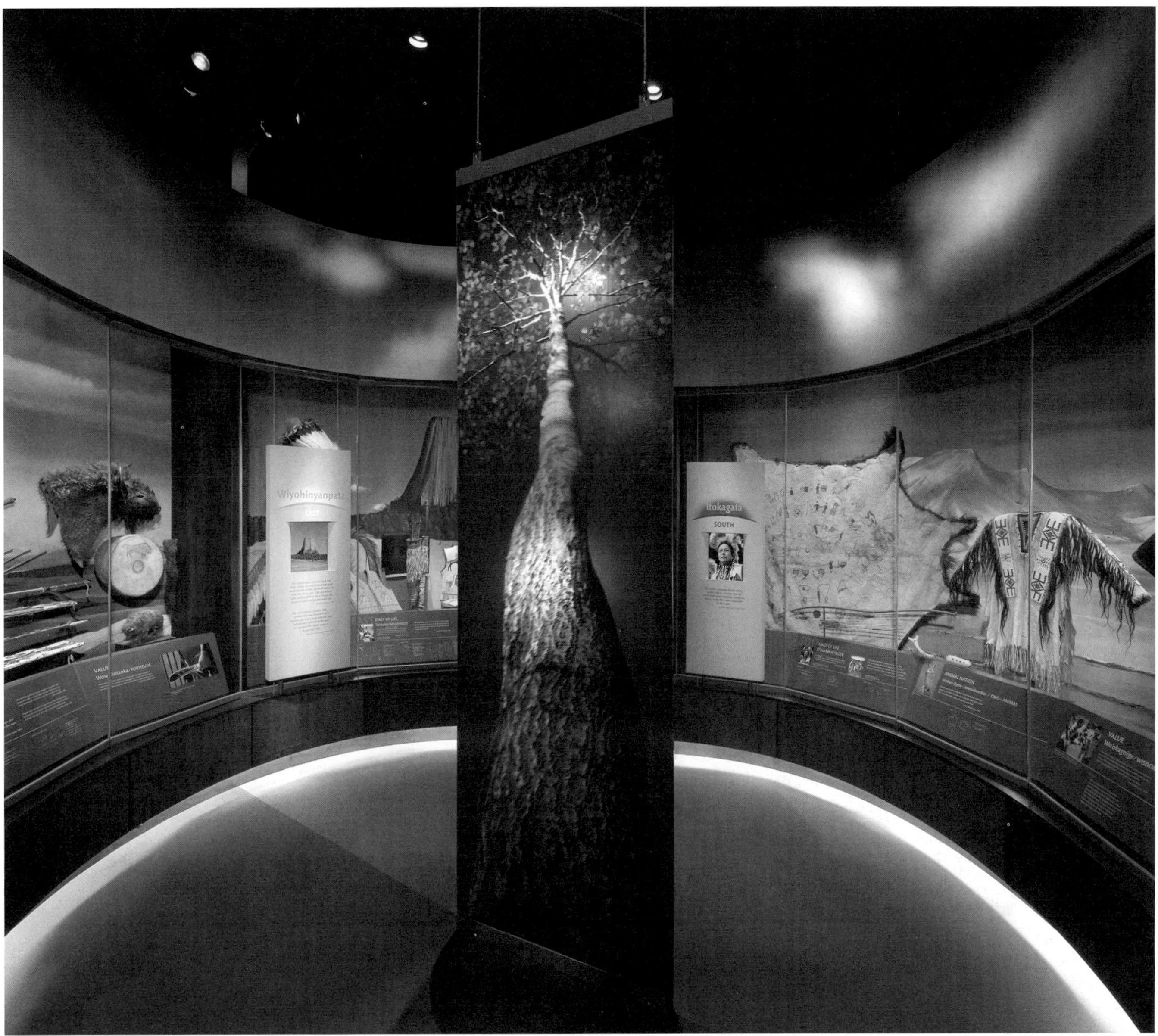

frustrated); equally frustrated will be scholars and activists looking for "Our Genocide" and "Our Resistance." What you get is something in the middle, something new, something you don't expect to find in a museum.

"Our Universes: Traditional Knowledge Shapes Our World" tries to connect creation stories, traditional knowledge, and indigenous cosmologies through artistically designed rooms and exhibit halls devoted to eight different tribes (Figs. 10.6 and 10.7). Here, visitors won't find actual war shirts, but paintings of shirts; they won't see pre-Columbian pottery, but examples of work of the best contemporary Santa Clara ceramicists. Mostly, they will find stories, myths, films, and illustrations that exemplify the spiritual-historical arcs of the featured communities. To be sure, these are educational exhibits, designed to teach as opposed to exoticize. For example, tourists making a beeline for the Lakota section and hoping to walk in and out of teepees routinely get perturbed when instead of teepees they find drawings and videos. To many, this perceived bait and switch can be baffling, and no doubt such absences can make the museum feel ahistorical, but these absences are actually presences—present forms of defiance. They suggest that what is more important than the

FIGURE 10.6. (facing page) *Santa Clara Pueblo Community section of "Our Universes." Courtesy of the National Museum of the American Indian, Smithsonian Institution. Photo by Walter Larrimore.*

FIGURE 10.7. (top) *Lakota Community section of "Our Universes." Courtesy of the National Museum of the American Indian, Smithsonian Institution. Photo by Walter Larrimore.*

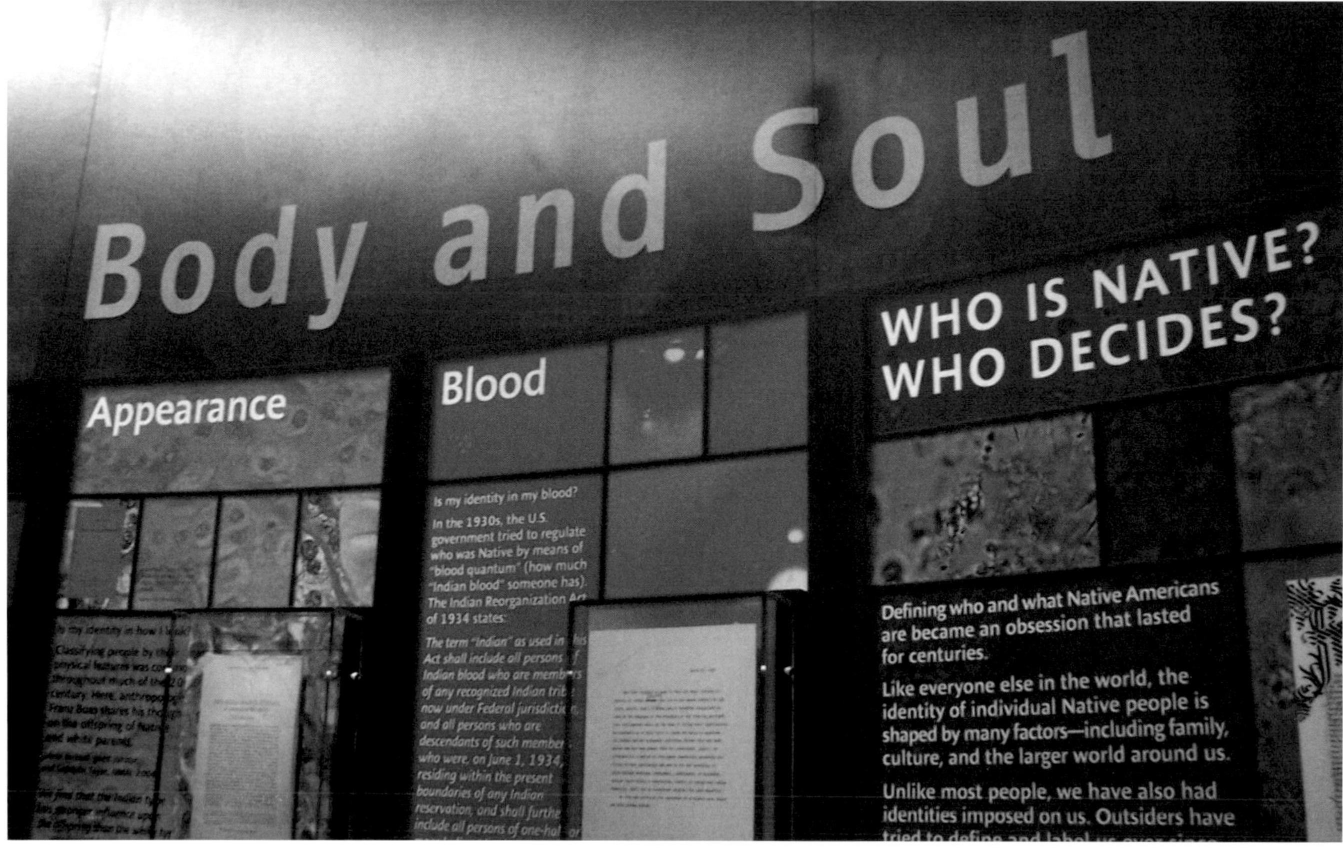

FIGURE 10.8. *The "Body and Soul" section of "Our Lives," an unusual mélange of data, images, cultural theory, history, and identity politics. Photo courtesy of Elizabeth Archuleta.*

objects themselves is how the tribes interpret objects, symbols, and community. Attempting to tell who the Lakota are rather than who they were counters prevailing stereotypes, not just about how the Lakota have been seen, but also about how the Lakota want to be seen right now.

The bookend to the "Our Universes" is "Our Lives: Contemporary Lives and Identities," which demonstrates through images, words, film, and sound how eight communities—the Campo Band of Kumeyaay Indians (California), the urban Indian community of Chicago, the Yakama Nation (Washington State), the Igloolik (Nunavut, Canada), the Kahnawake (Quebec, Canada), the Saint-Laurent Métis (Manitoba, Canada), the Kalinago (Carib Territory, Dominica), and the Pamunkey Tribe (Virginia)—live, work, create, celebrate, and survive in the twenty-first century. Though all of the tribal galleries entertain and educate, the most interesting aspect of this exhibition is "Body and Soul," which focuses on Indian identity (Fig. 10.8). Taking the touchy issues of blood quantum and skin color head-on, this display challenges archaic notions of who Indians are—notions that have, in part, been created and perpetuated by museums. Just as Esther Belin and Elizabeth Woody take on CDIBs and the blood quantum in their poems (see pages 128, 130–131), so too the NMAI rather forcefully problematizes these issues, going so far as to spotlight them in the city of their inception and perpetuation.

One reason this exhibition intrigues is because we tend to look to museums to confirm identity, not to challenge it. Indians are not, the NMAI asserts, tomahawks, moccasins, and peace pipes. Identity cannot be mapped onto entire nations. Identity cannot be created by movies. Identity cannot be determined by sports mascots. Identity cannot be taught by looking at reconstructed papooses. Were those exhibits to exist, the NMAI would have to call them "Our Deaths" as opposed to "Our Lives," meaning it would traffic in the same veneratory business as any other museum. In this manner, this exhibition confronts the cultural work of museums in much the same way the entire museum challenges the cultural work of mainstream American history.

As noted earlier, the NMAI has been criticized for ignoring the struggles of conquest and colonization. The NMAI's attempt to address this issue is "Our Peoples: Giving Voice to Our History," which integrates important events in the evolution of American Indian communities. The official museum description of this exhibition, given on the NMAI website, is fascinating:

> Historically, Native people have been portrayed in textbooks in narrow or inaccurate ways. In *Our Peoples*, Native Americans tell their own stories—their own histories—and in this way the exhibition presents new insights into, and different perspectives on, history. . . .
>
> The main story of *Our Peoples* focuses on the last 500 years of Native history and shows how the arrival of newcomers in the Western Hemisphere set the stage for one of the most momentous events in human history. In the struggle for survival, nearly every Native community wrestled with the impact of deadly new diseases and weaponry, the weakening of traditional spirituality, and the seizure of homelands by invading governments. But the story of these last five centuries is not entirely a story of destruction. It is also about how Native people intentionally and strategically kept their cultures alive.

Without question, this remains the most controversial display hall in the museum. The problem stems from the historical work the section tries to do—its representation of the "struggle for survival." Rather than chronicling the genocidal policies of the U.S. government, offering a time line of the Trail of Tears, or detailing the slaughters at Wounded Knee and Sand Creek, the NMAI chooses to display pre-Columbian artifacts from South and Central America, a beaded Blackfeet dress from 1890, a wall of gold items from the Americas, an Apache hide painting from around 1900, and, most notoriously, a glass triptych of weapons used against (and by) Indians—guns, Bibles, and treaties.

For many scholars like Lonetree and Atalay, the NMAI gets this story all wrong, a stance with which I sympathize.[7] As I note above, there is no doubt that the curatorial staff could have done something creative to honor the millions who died through the various effects of contact and still foregrounded specific instances of survival in the face of extinction. What exactly was it, some visitors may ask, that the Indians survived? For curators, scholars, historians, and archaeologists, that kind of information could very well be context, but for others, the very same information would be read as trauma, and for others still, it would be little more than cultural inscription.

On a small scale, many of these disputes would exist only in the rarefied air of the academic ether, but on the gigantic scale of the NMAI, they are the sine qua non. Nothing disappears, nothing is random, and nothing is small; the often-ignored totality of Native experiences is writ large. Indeed, of all the texts in this book—the films, the art exhibitions, even the Alcatraz occupation—none received as much media attention as the opening of the NMAI. This meant that in a world in which American Indians get little press and American Indian aesthetics even less, it was a rare moment in September 2004 when an Indian-based project was splashed across America's front pages. As interesting as the press coverage was how consistent were the observations made by those involved with the project:

- *People Magazine*: "In other museums 'our dead relatives were on display and lies were being told,' says Suzan Shown Harjo, 59, a Cheyenne who helped conceive the project. 'We wanted to write ourselves back into history. This is a dream come true.'" ("Tribal Tribute," 149)

- *U.S. News and World Report*: "While the exhibits are steeped in history, the focus here is not on the European conquest of the Americas. 'The encounter was tragic for us, yes, but what we really want visitors to understand is that we survived that,' says West. 'We are still here, making vital contributions to contemporary American culture.'" (Ulrich Boser, "A New Museum," 52)

- *Newsweek*: "'This museum is about the empowerment of native people to tell their story,' said Bruce Bernstein, the museum's assistant director. 'We're not trying to revise history—but write a history that is more inclusive.'" (Pat Wingert, "Return of the Native," 48)

- *Time*: "Would it be useful somewhere to have that old-fashioned timeline too? Jolene Rickard, a professor at the University at Buffalo and a Tuscarora Indian, who is a guest curator, doesn't think so. 'There are other places where you can learn the exact dates of the Trail of Tears,' she says. 'It's less important to me that someone leave this museum knowing all about Wounded Knee than that they leave knowing what it takes to survive that kind of tragedy.' The 'tremendous "before"' is still part of this place. But the 'tremendous "after"' is what the people here care about most." (Richard Lacayo, "A Place to Bring the Tribe, 68)

In all these quotes, we see this notion of before and after. Refusing to obsess on the before means the after carries a big burden, because it is responsible for "writing [Indians] back into history." Clearly, those at the NMAI believe that through film, one-sided textbooks, and hegemonic narratives, Indian persistence, creativity, and contributions have been written out or simply subsumed by the larger American narratives of triumph, arrival, and conquest. The ridiculousness of the titles of these articles aside, what emerges from the passages is the pressing need to tell new stories, to reinvent the enemy's language, and to insert a new model of Indigenous semiotics into the media mix. Note also how nearly all the people involved in the museum pit history's inability to tell the right story against the more inclusive, more authoritative story of survivance that the museum embodies.

One of those stories is told in "Guns, Bibles, and Treaties," which remains one of the more memorable displays in the museum, in part because it is the most problematic (Fig. 10.9). Atalay in particular takes the curatorial staff to task for giving over a "large space in the gallery to a group of objects that were not made by Native people but were used to control them" ("No Sense of the Struggle," 606). That said, part of the NMAI's new Indian museology seems to be predicated on inversion. The museum likes taking visitors' expectations and vexing them. To that end, this display does double duty. On one hand, it provides stark visual examples of how Anglos forcibly murdered, converted, removed, abused, threatened, and disabused American Indians. In many ways, the display's bleakness, its lack of context, is its greatest strength. On the other hand, carefully (and minimally) worded texts explain the many ways in which Indians turned these objects against Anglo forces, indigenizing the armaments of white power and authority.

In one of the smartest, most nuanced readings of the NMAI, Cobb argues that this display is not encoded in the semiotics of dispossession but of resistance:

> The accompanying wall text argues that the three major forces of colonization were warfare, churches, and government, and through the display of literally hundreds of guns, Bibles, and treaties, the exhibit demonstrates how all three served as instruments of dispossession. But, the exhibit goes on to say that these same objects—in the hands of Native Americans—served also as instruments of resistance, resilience, and survival. Armies

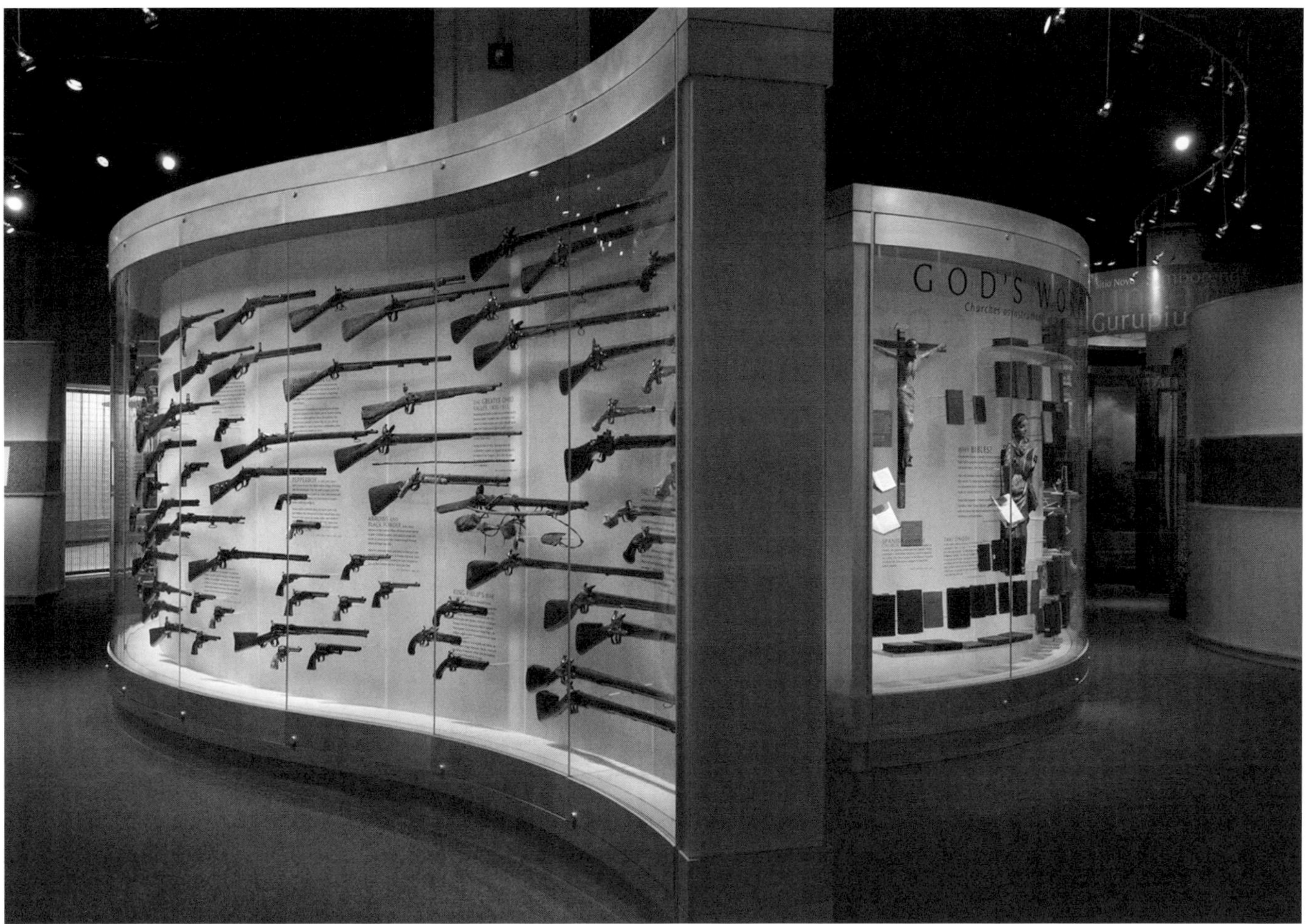

FIGURE 10.9. *"Guns, Bibles, and Treaties," a three-paneled glass display in the "Our Peoples" exhibition. Courtesy of the National Museum of the American Indian, Smithsonian Institution. Photo by Katherine Fogden.*

> may have used guns and warfare to seize land and conquer tribes, but Native peoples used guns to protect their communities and fight back. Missionaries and schoolteachers may have used churches and Bibles to "civilize" Native individuals in their attempt to destroy elements of Native cultures, but Native Americans, in an exercise of profound cultural agency, either rejected the imposed religion or adapted elements of it into existing religious and spiritual traditions, using religion as a common thread to bind the community together. Government officials may have used treaties to forge alliances and force the cession of land, but Native nations learned to use these documents to fight for the continued federal recognition of their sovereign status . . . I was therefore struck by the fact that in creating the NMAI, Native Americans have *again* turned an instrument of colonization and dispossession into something else—in this case, into an instrument of self-definition and cultural continuance. ("National Museum of the American Indian," 486)

I quote Cobb's lengthy interpretation here because it demonstrates her working through the complexities of the gallery's semiology. It also serves as a how-to guide for reading the exhibits through the lens of engaged resistance. What I like about Cobb's decoding is her ability to see through the veneer of the items on display. In the NMAI, guns, Bibles, and treaties are transformed into antiartifacts through the museum's curatorial reversals. This book examines the many ways Indians have seized the armaments of American authority and transformed them into their own instruments of self-articulation and self-preservation. Even with their contextual shortcomings, these displays literalize (and canonize) this uniquely Indian trait of participatory defiance, which has characterized (and continues to characterize) American Indian self-fashioning. Rather than reading this trinity of objects as symbols of disgrace, we might instead consider them symbols of dissent.

As with the structure of the museum, the prominence of the Potomac, and the hooplike footprint of the gallery spaces, this display signifies not literally but symbolically—again, a master shock to standard museum scaffolding. So much of the modern museum depends upon the actual that it has forgotten the symbolic. But as Sakiestewa notes, a guiding principle for the museum was a generative cultural symbolism. Thus, in its spaces, the NMAI isn't so much missing things as reframing them.

Indeed, the main reason this gallery and many of the other exhibitions disappoint some visitors and critics is because the museum refuses to be a museum in the traditional sense. Most museums are passive systems. They are all about stasis. Museums freeze items behind glass; they fix artifacts to walls and columns; they place objects in history. Standard anthropological museums are not too far from dioramas in that they function as three-dimensional visual aids to help imagine past realities. With an emphasis on excavated and restored visual texts, museums encourage the fetishization of objects, the primacy of the gaze, and what it means to look upon relics. Moreover, museums resemble malls. Consumers window-shop in the curatorial halls and literally shop in the ubiquitous stores. The NMAI tries very hard to resist this model. It doesn't wholly succeed—in places it, too, feels like a mall, and I found some of the spaces far too sterile—but its main museological trajectory eschews the expected path in favor of a new mode of museum making. Whereas traditional museums emphasize product, the NMAI emphasizes process.

Ultimately, that process is narrative. Put more plainly, the NMAI is structured more like a novel than a museum.[8] Instead of pointing out linear paths that chronologize history, the NMAI ushers you onto the winding road of Native narrative. Its circular galleries resemble the circularity of a Louise Erdrich novel or, for the purposes of this study, Silko's "Storyteller." The museum is a Native place in part because it re-creates the internal experience of storytelling. Its text-heavy exhibitions, its photos of present-day tribal projects, and its prioritization of ancient stories over ancient artifacts nudge the visitor out of the pattern of passive museum shopping and into the active world of the participatory present. The museum is its own exhibit. It asks its visitors not to obsess over the static object or the fixed artifact. It invites visitors instead to embrace the museum's true exhibit—the recuperative, regenerative power of language. Archuleta makes a similar observation in her piece on the NMAI, the epigraph of which comes from Silko.[9] For Archuleta, the museum's structure presents

> multiple stories structured like the spider web that Silko uses to explain the process of Pueblo storytelling. Rather than structure the exhibits in a way that guides visitors and "teaches" them about Indians, leading them from point A to point B to point C, museum curators structured them like the "many little threads" of a spider web with each strand adding to the larger picture. This method of organization means that visitors have to set aside notions they previously held about museums and Indians, "listen" to the stories being told in the exhibits, and trust that meaning will be made if they become involved in the storytelling process.
>
> —("GYM SHOES," 429–430).

Archuleta also notes the importance of process in regard to the museum's curatorial design, and she correctly articulates the important work the museum does in asking its visitors to rethink assumptions about Indians and about how museums historicize Indians. Like the Alcatraz occupiers, who often turned to text over image—even when painting—the NMAI relies on the interplay of text and image as dual storytelling mechanisms deployed to infiltrate uninformed perceptions about Native America. As a text, the NMAI's curatorial narrative also rewrites how museums merchandise Indians. It destabilizes the putative cultural inscriptions that claim Indians, Indian accoutrements, and Indian identities can be bought, sold, discounted, excavated, fixed, frozen, displayed, commodified, and consumed.

Nationalisms: When Semiotics Meets Politics

This is radical work that moves traditional museology from the archeological to the political. It also perfectly demonstrates how Native interdisciplinarity blurs the boundaries between the aesthetic and the activist. Without realizing it, we think of museum exhibits as authoritative texts—like street signs and maps—and we tend not to question them. But the NMAI, like Heap of Birds and Quick-to-See Smith—undermines the manifest manners of such master texts. Archuleta again: "The NMAI's decision to challenge traditional museum modes of exhibition is political in that the outcome confronts stereotypes created by museums and other knowledge-producing institutions" ("Gym Shoes," 431). Maps and signs produce knowledge; sculptures and genres produce knowledge; films and exhibitions also produce knowledge. What matters, though, is how the various forms of Native aesthetic activism attack those fortresses of identity formulation.

One final mode of activism almost completely ignored by critics is how the NMAI confronts Washington D.C.'s and the National Mall's metanarrative of nationalism. Just about every museum and monument in the District of Columbia tells an ethnocentric story of how America became America. Through the power of triumphalist semiotics, through the design and structure of national iconography, and through the kinds of institutions positioned along the nation's main cultural artery, Washington and its overt monumentalism frames a story of American history and American identity that has, for decades, ignored Indian nations and transnational indigenous identities. Both compositionally and contextually, the NMAI serves as a corrective to Washington's symbolic metanarrative about America's Americanness. Along these same lines, although the NMAI embraces pan-Indianism on the macroscale, on the microplane it also endorses American Indian nationalism, foregrounding twenty-four distinct, tribally specific exhibits. Much of Washington's classification system of Indians assumed a monoculture, a generic race of subalterns indistinguishable from one another. On the nation's front lawn, at the right hand of the Capitol, a text of Indian pluralism and polyvocality suggests otherwise.

When viewed from these vantage points, the NMAI feels closer to the Alcatraz occupation than one might expect. And, indeed, it is. Two important figures for the NMAI—George Horse Capture (A'ani') and Paul Chaat Smith (Comanche)—also have strong connections to Alcatraz. Horse Capture, a consultant to the NMAI, was one of the first occupiers on the island. In fact, in the NMAI's main history text, *Spirit of a Native Place: Building the National Museum of the American Indian*, Horse Capture makes a symbolic link between Alcatraz, which "awakened us and set us on a new course," and the NMAI: "While I was at Alcatraz, my friend and colleague Rick West was at Stanford Law School. . . . When Rick was named the first director of the National Museum of the American Indian, he embarked upon a course of action unheard of then in the museum world. In a peaceful yet profound revolution, Rick and his associates realized that the only proper way to create a museum representative of Native people was to hear from those people themselves" (36). For Horse Capture, both Alcatraz and the NMAI are revolutionary projects that have at their heart the affirmation of Indian sovereignty. Even more interesting is the fact that, for him, the projects are also important forms of public service—local and global Indian communities benefited from Alcatraz in much the same way that they stand to benefit from the NMAI. Like the Alcatraz documents, the NMAI's exhibits seek to educate "the world about the ways of Indian people" (31). Horse Capture's time on the island, his participation in the documentation and assertion of Indian aesthetic autonomy, actually shaped his career as a museum professional.

Though he wasn't on Alcatraz, Paul Chaat Smith has emerged as one of the best and most articulate advocates of American Indian activism in general and Indian Alcatraz in particular. His coauthored book, *Like a Hurricane: Alcatraz to the Longest Walk*, remains the single best study of the precise manner in which Indian activism shaped Indian and American cultures. Smith is also one of the main curators at the NMAI; in fact, a great many of the exhibits reflect his influence, including the contentious "Guns, Bibles, and Treaties" display. He is also the author of many of the curatorial panels. Indeed, it is through Smith that one can draw a direct intellectual line from the critical discourse of Alcatraz and Indian activism to the textual infrastructure of the NMAI. What contextual resistance exists in the NMAI comes largely from Smith.

It is Smith who is ultimately responsible for the museum's most theoretically sophisticated articulation of curatorial sovereignty—the survivance panel. Located in the "Our Peoples" exhibition, this explication of survivance (first laid out by Gerald Vizenor) serves as the compass for the entire curatorial ship. Vizenor, who has used his notion of survivance judiciously in his critical work, defines it as "more than survival, more than endurance or mere response; the stories of survivance are an active presence . . . The native stories of survivance are successive and natural estates; survivance is an active repudiation of dominance, tragedy, and victimry" (*Fugitive Poses*, 15). Provocatively, the concept gets an entire panel near the notorious "Guns, Bibles, and Treaties" display. Smith does a fine job of taking Vizenor's primary argument and applying it to this diabolical trinity:

> Survivance: Native societies that survived the firestorm of Contact faced unique challenges. No two situations were the same, even for Native groups in the same area at the same time. But in nearly every case, Native people faced a contest for power and possessions that involved three forces—guns, churches, and governments. These forces shaped the lives of Indians who survived the massive rupture of the first century of Contact. By adopting the very tools that were used to change, control, and dispossess them, Native peoples reshaped their cultures and societies to keep them alive. This strategy has been called survivance.

A model of engaged resistance, this panel functions as both explanation and epistemology. It not only fuses the items in the display case to an ideology, but also roots that ideology to a fundamental process of regenerative practices that have sustained Native communities.

If, as West suggests, the NMAI is first and foremost a living testament to survivance, then it is through the notion of survivance that the museum operates as an active presence, or, to put it less theoretically, as an activist presence. Those presences are the sustaining processes of ongoing self-fashioning, self-authoring, and self-storytelling. They are the presences that animated Alcatraz, that transformed the rock into Indian Land, and they are the same forces that turn the Mall into a Native place. "By focusing on use or process over object or product in its own form and function," Cobb argues, "the NMAI highlights the vitality and dynamism of Native peoples—agents engaged in acts of self-definition and cultural sovereignty, living cultures modeling the survivance strategies that have enabled their cultural continuance. . . . For Native Americans, the National Museum of the American Indian not only announces, 'We Are Still Here,' but it also demonstrates the process that made this fact possible" ("National Museum of the American Indian," 499, 502). As Cobb notes, at its core, the NMAI's thematic hardly wavers from that of a Silko story, an Eyre film, or an Alexie poem—all are about defiance and assertion, repudiation and regeneration, resistance and engagement. Like the poets who cross poetry and prose, the artists who merge image and text, the filmmakers who blend form and function, and like the occupying liberators who lent both voice and vision to the Indian cause, the NMAI seeks to activate and educate.

Scholars who write about either the NMAI or Alcatraz tend to gloss over the final request of the occupiers, as elucidated in the Proclamation: "Some of the present buildings will be taken over to develop an American Indian Museum which will depict our native food and other cultural contributions we have given to the world. Another part of the museum will present some of the things the white man has given to the Indians in return for the land and life he took." The District of Columbia is a long way from Alcatraz, and the NMAI is not exactly what Nordwall and Oakes had in mind for the American Indian Museum, but yet, here it is. Even in 1969, standing before the long shadow of protest, the first thing the occupiers ask for their museum is an acknowledgment of Native contributions.

Despite their shortcomings, the Alcatraz occupation and the NMAI still do important work, and despite history, they seem destined to circle back on each other, completing each other's political, social, and aesthetic incompleteness. Through these texts, we are reminded of the ways that impassioned forms of aesthetic activism both resist and engage; through these texts, we are reminded of the people who created them and the people, tribes, and communities for whom the consummatory power of indigenous aesthetic expression really matters.

EPILOGUE

"IT DOESN'T END," writes Simon Ortiz in *Going for Rain*, and indeed, here we are back at the beginning with Alcatraz's intergeneric announcement to America that Indian aesthetic activism was here to stay and with the request for a museum to ensure that it does. In the museum of our consciousness, the great bookstore of culture, the vast movie house of history, Native creative expression does what it has always done—enervate the manifest manners of America's rough beast and catalyze emotion into action.

The texts in this book try to populate, articulate, and narrate the cultural and aesthetic history of American Indians over the last four decades. That history—one of interrogation, resistance, participation, and engagement—is also the future, the map to the imagined, the envisioned.

In the face of overwhelming forces that seem to be on a collision course with Native modes of being, the decolonized, liberated vision of Native America—as exemplified by the many texts in this book—don't simply show but also remind us where we came from, where we are going, and, most importantly, where we are.

Compass and beacon, voice in the darkness. Image and imagination, picture and poem. Alcatraz, Washington. Symbol and song, circle and spoor.

"Go ahead," says Silko in "Story from Bear Country,"

> turn around
> see the shape
> of your footprints

NOTES

Prologue

1. Howe singles out, for example, Navajo writer Irvin Morris's ability to fashion a tribal history and a personal memoir that connect with both the Navajo and "the glittering world of the highways of the *bilagaanaa*, or white people" ("The Story of America," 43). Howe's example of multigenre synthesis and bicultural engagement has shaped my own thinking.

2. "These colonizer's languages," writes Harjo, "which often usurped our own tribal languages or diminished them, now hand back emblems of our cultures, our own designs: beadwork, quills if you will. We transformed these enemy languages" (*Reinventing the Enemy's Language*, 22). In the chapters on Alcatraz and the NMAI, I invoke and reinvent Harjo's language.

3. A concept similar to survivance is Mary Louise Pratt's theory of "autoethnography." Though I do not rely on this term in *Engaged Resistance*, I do want to mention it as a partial correlative to engaged resistance. Pratt defines autoethnography as "instances in which colonized subjects undertake to represent themselves in ways that *engage with* the colonizer's own terms" (*Imperial Eyes*, 7). Though her theory also calls attention to forms of engagement, it does not quite apply to many of the artists, writers, and filmmakers I discuss. Her concept of "colonized subjects" renders those subjects as too flatly colonized for my purposes. In fact, my project makes the opposite argument—the artists I write about not only have agency but also act it out, and they seek to preserve it.

4. When I first began using this term several years ago, I was under the impression that it was, in fact, a term I had manufactured. I was not aware that it had already been born, and I have since come to know its parents and siblings. The first instance of the term seems to be a single appearance in Christian Lenhardt's 1984 translation of Theodor Adorno's *Aesthetic Theory* (356), though my version of *Aesthetic Theory*, translated by Robert Hullont-Kentor in 1997, renders the phrase as "aesthetic actionism" (251). That said, Adorno's usage differs slightly from mine in that it describes artists who continue to produce art despite attempts to ban it. The term also crops up in Charles Russell's *Poets, Prophets, and Revolutionaries* (1985) in regard to the avant-garde. Russell avers that modernists turn to art for a "self sustaining activity." For him, aesthetic activism is not about social issues or political protest but about self-conscious art that brings about new ways of knowing and acting.

While I acknowledge its prior denotations, my own deployment of the term "aesthetic activism" arises out of indigenous traditions of survivance, resistance, and performance. *Engaged Resistance* moves this concept away from mere action to encompass the ability of creative texts to function as dramatizations of social and political activism. "The collective struggle for indigenous self-determination," Mohawk scholar Taiaiake Alfred asserts, "is truly a fight for freedom and justice" (*Peace, Power, Righteousness*, xi). As chronicled in the present work, the artists' and writers' collective struggles toward indigenous self-determination are only aesthetic activities—they activate art in order to fight for freedom and justice.

Chapter 1

1. As it turns out, no such provision exists in the original treaty. See Deloria, "Alcatraz, Activism, and Accommodation," 47, for a longer explanation.

2. For one of the more interesting vantage points in this regard, see Deloria, "Alcatraz, Activism, and Accommodation."

3. See Lake's "Enacting Red Power: The Comsummatory Function in Native American Protest Rhetoric" and "Between Myth and History: Enacting Time in Native American Protest Rhetoric."

4. The notion of the right of discovery is itself a child of proclamation—in particular of two papal orders. The first, the infamous *Romanus Pontifex* of 1455 by Pope Nicholas V, granted Portugal the right to claim non-Christian lands. *Inter Caetera*, issued by Pope Alexander VI in 1493, entitled Columbus to conquer and subdue all lands and people he had "discovered" and would "discover." Not surprisingly, the United States converted the latter decree into U.S. law, via the Supreme Court's decision in *Johnson v. M'intosh* (1823). Writing for a unanimous court, Chief Justice John Marshall claimed the United States inherited the right of discovery and supremacy over Native Americans. See Davenport, *European Treaties Bearing on the History of the United States and Its Dependencies*; Pranzer, *The Popes and Slavery*; Gottschalk, *The Earliest Diplomatic Documents on America*; and Utter, "The Discovery Doctrine, the Tribes, and the Truth."

5. Powell talks also about the importance of Winnemucca coming off as "civilized," a trait the authors of the witty proclamation were also quite aware of.

6. See page 194 in Chapter 9. Sculptor Allan Houser incorporates this phrase into the title of a sculpture of his that stands in front of the Oklahoma state capitol.

7. As Troy Johnson, Paul Chaat Smith, and Robert Allen Warrior note, Adam Nordwall was the primary architect of the proclamation. Smith and Warrior recount a great moment when Nordwall read the proclamation aloud at the end of a fund-raiser, just a couple of weeks into the occupation (Smith and Warrior, *Like a Hurricane*, 28–29).

8. See Momaday, "An American Land Ethic."

9. During a press conference in May 1970, a day before a supposed evacuation, the occupiers placed the declaration front and center.

10. For a fuller discussion of this point, see Rader, "The Epic Lyric: Genre and Contemporary American Indian Poetry."

11. Very few of the poems written on the island were widely accessible outside of San Francisco until the publication of Johnson, *Alcatraz: Indian Land Forever*, an anthology of poetry and photographs from the occupation.

12. See Kristeva, *Revolution in Poetic Language*, 2, 64–65, 80–84.

13. In his cranky apology for prose, the Russian critic M. M. Bakhtin admits that poetry is an "extrahistorical language" that is "a language of the gods" ("Discourse in the Novel," 331).

14. See Silko on the connection between language and landscape also in "Language and Literature from a Pueblo Indian Perspective."

15. See Nöth, *Handbook of Semiotics*; Bouissac, *Encyclopedia of Semiotics*.

16. Capone and Preucel go on to explain that the "*Sign* is something that is understood by the mind as a sign to represent something else, namely the *Object*, or the physical thing or process that exists in the world. The *Interpretant* is thus the semiotic formulation of what the mind has come to know, whether that be some further action or a mental representation" ("Ceramic Semiotics," 101).

17. The barracks proved to be a fabulously interesting contact zone of Indianism and Pan-Indianism.

18. In a troubling mode of linguistic and political prescience, the word "free" scrawled across the penal seal affixed to the prison predicted the "Free Leonard Peltier" sloganing that framed his imprisonment.

19. In "California Indigenous Storytelling," a talk given at the 2008 Modern Language Convention in San Francisco, Acoma writer Simon Ortiz referred to the occupation as "the liberation of Alcatraz."

Chapter 2

1. Smith shares this interest in words and images with Edgar Heap of Birds. See pages 200–205 for more on his blending of the semiotics of text and context.

2. See the introduction of *Tribal Secrets*, in which Warrior outmaneuvers the denotative dragon: "I have consciously employed a large set of terms without defining them in detail. Categories such as sovereignty, self-determination, tribal and process appear without much detailed specification of how I am using them . . . This is perhaps most true of sovereignty" (xxi).

3. Vizenor defines "transmotion" actively: "The connotations of transmotion are creation stories, totemic visions, reincarnation, and souvenance [presence in remembrance]; transmotion, that sense of native motion and an active presence, is *sui generis* sovereignty. Native transmotion is survivance, a reciprocal use of nature, not a monotheistic, territorial sovereignty" (*Fugitive Poses*, 15).

4. Despite the hunger for American Indian art among collectors, virtually none of the pottery, rugs, dolls, or paintings sold in Santa Fe, Phoenix, or Sedona take on political or social issues. In fact, the most desired pieces are those that evoke a romantic, wispy, almost ghostly Native past in which Indians are frozen in time. Like Jasper Johns and Robert Rauschenberg, Smith believes that art has the potential and the responsibility to help make sense of the current, but the current and the political are two distinct spheres. In fact, I would argue that critics and collectors are drawn to Johns's and Rauschenberg's work because of its accessibility, collectability, and apolitical content. This is not to say that their art lacks meaning or significance; however, not even Rauschenberg's *Persimmon* really confronts the viewer with the disturbing realities of race, class, and violence in contemporary America. Nothing in Johns, however aesthetically arresting and visually pleasing, pushes collage over the precipice into history.

5. In *The Practice of Everyday Life*, Michel de Certeau argues that common "practices" of daily life can often be seen as modes of resistance—slacking at work, ambling in a park, choosing a particular vocabulary. One wonders how much conscious and unconscious resistant practice takes place every time someone says "Oklahoma" or "Illinois."

6. Warhus explores this tension brilliantly in *Another America*, a collection of mostly older Native maps of America and tribal lands. What is fascinating about the maps Warhus uncovers is how the artists define and project space and reality via the map, how it does not restrict space but opens it up. For me, Smith's paintings do the same work. Also, see Hugh Brody, *Maps and Dreams*.

7. Stott defines documentary's goals thus: "To right wrongs, to promote social action, documentary tries to influence its audience's intellect and feelings. It persuades in either or both of two ways, directly and by example" (*Documentary Expression*, 26). "This is what documentary must do," he continues, "if it is to work social change: talk to us, and convince us that we, our deepest interests, are engaged" (28).

Chapter 3

1. I am referring, of course, to Kenneth Lincoln's book *The Native American Renaissance* (1983) and his now-famous claim that the works of Momaday, Simon Ortiz, Louise Erdrich, Leslie Marmon Silko, and James Welch caused a "rebirth" of inventive, important Native writing. While Lincoln's terminology has come under fire by some for downplaying the significance of early oral literatures, the purpose of this chapter is not to debate the usefulness of the term.

2. See the introduction to Rader and Gould, *Speak to Me Words: Essays on Contemporary American Indian Poetry* (4–5). A good deal of my own scholarly work has been an attempt to combat what I see as a dearth of attention paid to Native poetry in favor of the novel.

3. See Howe, "The Story of America," for her reading of *Grass Dancer* as a tribalographic text (44–45).

4. There is not the space here to go into a discussion of the breadth and depth the topic warrants, but readers interested in the two-spirit tradition in indigenous communities are encouraged to consult the many good sources on this topic, including Sabine Lang's *Men as Women, Women as Men: Changing Gender in Native American Cultures*.

5. For a longer discussion of Womack's preference for the term "queer," see his final chapter on Lynn Riggs in *Red on Red* (273–274 in particular).

6. A strategy perhaps also influenced by Harjo through the anthology she coedited with Gloria Bird, *Reinventing the Enemy's Language*.

Chapter 4

1. And almost all are devoted to *Smoke Signals* (Chris Eyre, 1998).

2. Viewers familiar with *Smoke Signals* will recognize the similarities between Rudy's exultation here and Victor's after he throws his father's ashes into the river.

3. See Churchill, "The Bloody Wake of Alcatraz," 245.

Chapter 5

1. For a close reading of the significance of Wayne's body in film, see Thomas, "John Wayne's Body."

2. For more information on teaching this poem and Erdrich's poetry in general, see Rader, "Sites of Unification: Teaching Louise Erdrich's Poetry."

3. Gillan adroitly picks up on the power of the blank screen in her reading of Alexie. Referring to the final line of the *Star Wars* segment of "Reservation Drive-In," in which "Indian boys cheer, rise up, and fall out of car windows, honk horns, flash headlights, all half-anger, until the movie ends and leaves us with the white noise of an empty screen," (*The First Indian on the Moon*, 17) she writes: "Although Alexie's characters can reject the film's assumed spectator position and refuse to cheer for Skywalker, they will pay the price for this rejection. When the movie ends, they discover that the white noise of the empty screen is scarier than the barrage of sound and light that preceded it" ("Sherman Alexie's Poetry," 102).

4. My own image for this study is also a form (although archaic) of visual culture: a triptych. I envision "Dear John Wayne" on the left panel, "Holodeck" on the right, and Alexie's collage of poems in the middle, a kind of Janus-faced text gazing to either side. Each panel represents a unique but complementary form of engaged resistance, and as viewers, we are drawn in by the texts but unable to fully inhabit them. But then the figures on the panels begin to move, and it is clear that the triptych is not wood but a giant monitor on which a documentary of American history unfolds, in real time, edited for content.

5. While Harlow's study focuses on Third World literature, primarily in Latin America and the Middle East, her claims for resistance poetry can be extended to American Indian texts.

Chapter 6

1. My use of the term "metanarrative" here comes from Jean-François Lyotard's classic text *The Postmodern Condition: A Report on Knowledge*: "Simplifying to the extreme, I define postmodern as incredulity toward metanarratives. This incredulity is undoubtedly a product of progress in the sciences: but that progress in turn presupposes it. To the obsolescence of the metanarrative apparatus of legitimation corresponds, most notably, the crisis of metaphysical philosophy and of the university institution which in the past relied on it. The narrative function is losing its functors, its great hero, its great dangers, its great voyages, its great goal" (xxiv–xxv).

2. Though it is not a major part of this discussion, Stephens and McCallum make the implicit argument that genre in children's literature functions as a kind of metanarrative, particularly in what they describe as "reversions"—new versions of old stories: "To a great extent, such reversions are constituted by motifs; by narrative structures isomorphic with those visible in generic pre-texts; and/or by a shared habitus—that is a conjunction of physical and social spaces where sociality is organized by social distances and hierarchies, and where a system of schemata (that is social codes) organizes action and practice, and thought and perception" (*Retelling Stories, Framing Culture*, 5).

3. According to Jace Weaver (Osage), "the majority of Indians live their lives as if . . . definitions were largely irrelevant, living out their own Indianness without a great deal of worry about such contestations over identity" (*That People Might Live*, 4). This notion of personal identity carries over into the world of literary identity as well, most saliently manifest in a rather remarkable interest and ability for Native writers to move back and forth between genres. For example, N. Scott Momaday, Louise Erdrich, LeAnne Howe, Sherman Alexie, Simon Ortiz, Luci Tapahonso, Linda Hogan, Eric Gansworth, and Leslie Marmon Silko all publish both fiction and poetry.

4. Womack puzzles over the criteria used to establish what is good literature and who does the establishing: "My point is this: I was dismayed at just how little formal discussion there was among Indian writers concerning who controls Indian literature, what is the purpose of Indian literature, what constitutes Indian literatures of excellence, how such criteria should be determined, what set of ethical issues surrounds being a Native writer, and what role should tribes play in the whole process. What happens, it seems to me, is that when we abandon such a discussion, we give away all our power to a group of outsiders who then determine our aesthetics *for* us, and this happens without even a fight!" (*Red on Red*, 10).

5. See Kimberly Blaeser's (Anishinaabe) excellent essay "Native Literatures: Seeking a Critical Center."

6. Again, I want to acknowledge books like Jean Toomer's *Cane*, some of Ezra Pound's writing, and even Walt Whitman's—all of which merge poetry and prose in individual collections.

7. Robert Nelson argues that Silko develops the trajectory of *Storyteller* in concert with Laguna storytelling patters. According to Nelson, the book is "concentric rather than linear, associational rather than chronologically determined" ("He Said/She Said," 47).

8. This "unpublished endorsement" is on the website of Salt Publishing: http://www.saltpublishing.com/books/ewk/1844710629.htm.

9. *Face* came out too late in 2009 to be adequately addressed in this study, but I did include it in my top five books of poems for the year (*San Francisco Chronicle*, December 20, 2009). The collection contains the fewest overtly Indian-themed poems of any of his books, and it is the most formal. He employs traditional rhyming stanzas and, in more than one instance, composes entire poems in heroic couplets. It is a fascinating blend of Native and Western discourses.

10. See Rader, "Simon Ortiz and Luci Tapahonso."

11. Though this is not the place to enter into a discussion of the Navajo relation to death, it might prove fruitful to think of life and death as genres themselves, in that the Navajo believe that some can more easily move back and forth between them.

12. Alexie's poem "Red Blues" is also a prose poem with fourteen numbered paragraphs, though it is not labeled a "sonnet" (see *Old Shirts and New Skins*, 85–87).

13. This is a delicate area, and I do not want to be confused with critics who essentialize. But to understand the complicated interplay of language and culture, scholars of Native literature will be better served by reading Native poetry first and foremost through a Native lens, rather than through the refracting prism of genre. Even a problematic book like James Nolan's *Poet-Chief: The Native American Poetics of Walt Whitman and Pablo Neruda* goes to great lengths to chronicle the many ways in which common poetic techniques like repetition, catalogues, circularity, incantatory language, and orality find origins in Native discourse. These indigenous techniques—which Alexie, Tapahonso, Erdrich, Ortiz, and Harjo love to use—can often provide a better entrée to the poem than non-Native passageways.

14. This claim is not particularly radical. Craig Womack, Robert Allen Warrior, Jace Weaver, Susan Berry Brill de Ramirez, Kimberly Blaeser, and others have made similar observations, but less in terms of language and more in terms of culture.

15. See Kroeber, *Traditional American Indian Literatures*; Swann, *Smoothing the Ground*; and Hymes, *Now I Know Only So Far*. Also, see Hymes's controversial but provocative claim that traditional Native poetries rely on lines, verses, and stanzas that reflect "the pattern numbers of the culture" ("Tonkawa Poetics," 22).

16. See Rader, "When Form Invents Function," and the prose poems in *Sentence* 7.

17. For more on this series' contribution to American publishing, see Rader, "British Publisher Touts American Indian Poets."

Chapter 7

1. See Aleiss, *Making the White Man's Indian*; Kilpatrick, *Celluloid Indians*; Rollins and O'Connor, *Hollywood's Indian*; Hilger, *From Savage to Nobleman*; and Singer, *Wiping the War Paint off the Lens*.

2. See Aleiss, *Making the White Man's Indian*, 159, 161.

3. See Mihelich, "Smoke or Signals?" 129–130. Mihelich experiments on his students, and they are quite easily able to list negative stereotypes of Indians with the clear knowledge that they are constructed caricatures.

4. While trolling the Internet, I came across this blog entry, which pretty much encapsulates much of the anxiety many feel about the Hollywood Indian and the degree to which people believe: "I think a common native american saying (if I've learned anything from Hollywood) is 'Today is a good day to die.' I think warriors said this to themselves and to the Great Spirit before heading into battle. Well the more I think about it the more I believe that was true of yesterday; 80 degree temperatures, warm offshore breeze, big swell pumping" (http://www.santabarbarasurfing.com/2003_01_01_archive.html). I do not detect irony in the first two sentences.

5. There is a fabulous (and perhaps intentional) moment of intertext with Vine Deloria, Jr., here. "Living cannot be postponed," Deloria quips, "It is the solitary acknowledgement that the question of man's life and identity is to let the bastards know you've been there and that it is always a good day to die. We are therefore able to live" ("Good Day to Die," 65).

6. For a more detailed reading of this scene, see Youngberg, "Interpenetrations," 65. As this book goes to press, Youngberg's essay, which is a reading of the film as a queer text, stands as the only scholarly article devoted to *Fancydancing*.

7. In yet another interesting self-referential moment, Alexie admits, on the DVD version of the film, that he wrote poems especially for Seymour but made sure not to make them better than his own.

Chapter 8

1. See Silko, "Stories and Their Tellers," 22–23.

2. See, for example, Jaskoski, *Leslie Marmon Silko*, 13.

3. In the story, "Gussuck" refers to any non-Yupik. Derived from the word "Cossack," it has its etymological and cultural roots in the early attempts of white Russians to colonize Alaska.

4. Paul H. Lorenz offers a useful time line of the various scenes in the story ("The Other Story," 65).

5. I think this is a more useful tack—asking what Silko argues—rather than asking what "Storyteller"'s "theme" might be.

6. See "The Word Warriors" (a short introduction) and the accompanying chapters in Allen, *Sacred Hoop* (51–165).

7. See Krumholz, "Native Designs" and Langen, "*Storyteller* as Hopi Basket."

8. I expand on this notion of genre as metaphor for larger notions of classification and conscription in Chapter 6 (on poetry and genre) and Chapter 7 (on Alexie's films).

9. For an interesting comparative reading of the two texts, see Vizenor, *Narrative Chance*, 62–63.

Chapter 9

1. As this book goes to press, the website for *The American* has come down, indicating a problem with the extraordinary stream of funds this project would require.

2. An interesting side note is that the memorial refuses governmental funding, a move I see as a not-so-subtle act of resistance.

3. For more on some of the fiberglass Indians along roadsides, including the Red McCombs Indian outside of San Antonio, visit RoadsideAmerica.com: http://www.roadsideamerica.com/tip/4390.

4. For more on Indian stereotypes, mascots, and icons, see Raymond William Stedman, *Shadows of the Indian: Stereotypes in American Culture*; Robert F. Berkhofer, Jr., *The White Man's Indian: Images of the American Indian from Columbus to the Present*; Shari M. Huhndorf, *Going Native: Indians in the American Cultural Imagination*; and Phillip Deloria, *Playing Indian*. For more explorations of stereotypes in popular and Web culture, see Rob Schmidt's Blue Corn Comics site: http://www.bluecorncomics.com/stertype.htm.

5. In writing of Fritz Scholder's (Luiseño) paintings, Adelyn D. Breeskin acknowledges his ability to break out of the two main schools of Indian painting prevalent at that point—the "Waters of the Minnetonka School" and "Bambi art." "It has been popular," writes Breeskin, "with a large tourist public eager to glamorize the figure of 'the noble savage' and to salve its conscience for the treatment this segment of the American people has received" (*Scholder/Indians*, 1). These sculptures, I would argue, participate in a combination of these two traditions.

6. According to Arrell Morgan Gibson, President Jackson promised the Creek Nation in the 1830s "permanent prosperity, and to sit down where no bad white men will trouble you, where no ardent spirits will tempt you, and where the land will be yours as long as the grass grows and the rivers run" (*Oklahoma*, 60).

7. I will, however, call the reader's attention to a well-known statue of a shirtless Joe Louis in Detroit, executed by Ed Hamilton. See Donna Graves, "Representing the Race: Detroit's Monument to Joe Louis."

8. This notion of a symbol doing reparational work is a theme in Sherman Alexie's "The Museum of Tolerance": "The Museum of Tolerance / has opened its doors / and, as agreed, we forgive all sins" (*Summer of Black Widows*, 133). Also, see note 5 above.

9. I have been unable to see other finalists for the competition. I would hazard a guess that more experimental, more contemporary designs were submitted and rejected.

10. See the Art of the Oklahoma State Capitol website: http://www.ok.gov/~arts/capitolart/permart/sculpture/haney/guardian.html.

11. For a lengthier exploration of this topic, see E. McClung Fleming, "The American Image as Indian Princess, 1765–1783."

12. See the United States Mint Online Catalog: http://catalog.usmint.gov/webapp/wcs/stores/servlet/ProductDisplay?catalogId=10001&storeId=10001&productId=10965&langId=-1&parent_category_rn=10051.

13. The artist-occupiers on Alcatraz engaged in similar aesthetic practice, particularly in regard to the "official" signs on the governmental buildings. See Chapter 1 for more on this.

14. In Troy Lynn Yellow Wood's essay on Indians and public art, she identifies Preston Powers's sculpture *The Closing Era*, which depicts a victorious Indian standing, admiringly, on a buffalo he just killed, as a negative example of Native public art, arguing it "exhibits only arrogance" and is "sacrilegious" ("Trauma and Memory," 34). Located in Denver on the east capitol lawn, it stands in contrast to *Wheel*, which is not so far from the capitol, at the Denver Art Museum. The intracity and intrastate dialogue between these two pieces of "Indian" public art is fascinating though disturbing.

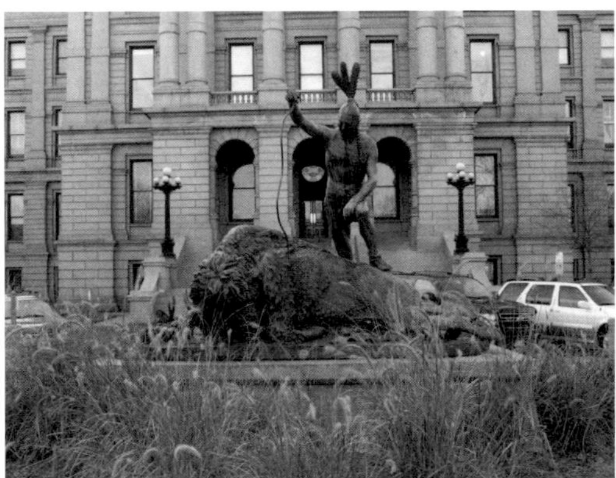

FIGURE N.1. *Preston Powers,* The Closing Era, *1893. Bronze. Photo by the author.*

Chapter 10

1. See Deloria, "Alcatraz, Activism, and Accommodation."

2. In 2006, the *American Indian Quarterly* devoted an issue to the NMAI. It was essentially edited and expanded into Lonetree and Cobb, *The National Museum of the American Indian*.

3. I have been told that some of the recent and future art exhibits are going to try to address these issues better.

4. See Nabokov and Easton, *Native American Architecture*, pp 40–60.

5. The NMAI's main brochure, for example, includes a photograph of children performing a winter round dance in the Potomac.

6. See also Lonetree, "Missed Opportunities," 644n16.

7. In the interest of full disclosure, I should say that in the course of researching this chapter, I spoke with a few people who found the "Guns, Bibles, and Treaties" display "offensive," "disturbing," "violent," and "anti-Indian."

8. Oddly enough, the NMAI embodies the original etymological notion of a museum—a place to worship the muse, a place that celebrates the arts.

9. Archuleta's essay begins with this epigraph from Leslie Marmon Silko's "Language and Literature from a Pueblo Indian Perspective": "For those of you accustomed to a structure that moves from point A to point B to point C, this presentation may be somewhat difficult to follow because the structure of Pueblo expression resembles something like a spider's web—with many little threads radiating from a center, criss-crossing each other. As with the web, the structure will emerge as it is made and you must simply listen and trust, as the Pueblo people do, that meaning will be made."

WORKS CITED

Abbott, Lawrence. *I Stand in the Center of the Good: Interviews with Contemporary Native American Artists*. Lincoln: Univ. of Nebraska Press, 1994.

Achenbach, Joel. "Within These Walls, Science Yields to Stories." *Washington Post*, September 19, 2004.

Adorno, Theodor W. *Aesthetic Theory*. Translated by Christian Lenhardt. London: Routledge, 1984.

——. *Aesthetic Theory*. Translated by Robert Hullont-Kentor. Minneapolis: Univ. of Minnesota Press, 1998.

Alcatraz Manifesto. San Francisco, 1970.

Alcatraz Reclamation Proclamation. San Francisco, 1970.

Aleiss, Angela. *Making the White Man's Indian: Native Americans and Hollywood Movies*. Westport, Conn.: Praeger, 2005.

Alexie, Sherman. *The Business of Fancydancing*. DVD. Directed by Sherman Alexie. FallsApart Productions. New York: Wellspring Media, 2003.

——. "Crossroads: A Conversation with Sherman Alexie." By John Purdy. *SAIL: Studies in American Indian Literatures* 9, no. 4 (1997): 1–18.

——. *The First Indian on the Moon*. Brooklyn: Hanging Loose Press, 1993.

——. *Flight: A Novel*. New York: Black Cat, 2007.

——. *Indian Killer*. New York: Warner Books, 1996.

——. *Old Shirts and New Skins*. Los Angeles: American Indian Studies Center, 1996.

——. *Smoke Signals*. DVD. Directed by Chris Eyre. ShadowCatcher Entertainment. Burbank, Calif.: Miramax Home Entertainment, 1998.

——. *The Summer of Black Widows*. Brooklyn: Hanging Loose Press, 1996.

Alfred, Taiaiake. *Peace, Power, Righteousness: An Indigenous Manifesto*. Don Mills, Ont.: Oxford Univ. Press, 1999.

Allen, Chadwick. *Blood Narrative: Indigenous Identity in American Indian and Maori Literary and Activist Texts*. Durham, N.C.: Duke Univ. Press, 2002.

Allen, Paula Gunn. *The Sacred Hoop: Recovering the Feminine in American Indian Traditions*. Boston: Beacon Press, 1986.

Anderson, Eric Gary. *American Indian Literature and the Southwest: Contexts and Dispositions*. Austin: Univ. of Texas Press, 1999.

——. "Situating American Indian Poetry: Place, Community, and the Question of Genre." In *Speak to Me Words: Essays on Contemporary American Indian Poetry*, ed. Dean Rader and Janice Gould, 34–55. Tucson: Univ. of Arizona Press, 2003.

Archuleta, Elizabeth. "Gym Shoes, Maps, and Passports, Oh My! Creating Community or Creating Chaos at the NMAI?" *American Indian Quarterly* 29, no. 3–4 (2005): 426–449.

Atalay, Sonya. "No Sense of the Struggle: Creating a Context for Survivance at the NMAI." *American Indian Quarterly* 30, no. 3–4 (2006): 597–618.

Bakhtin, M. M. "Discourse in the Novel." In *The Dialogic Imagination: Four Essays*, ed. Michael Holquist, trans. Caryl Emerson and Michael Holquist, 259–422. Austin: Univ. of Texas Press, 1981.

Bazin, André. "On the *politique des auteurs*." In *Cahiers du Cinema, the 1950s: Neo-Realism, Hollywood, New Wave*, ed. Jim Hillier, 248–263. Cambridge, Mass.: Harvard Univ. Press, 1985.

Belin, Esther. *From the Belly of My Beauty*. Tucson: Univ. of Arizona Press, 1999.

Berkhofer, Robert F., Jr. *The White Man's Indian: Images of the American Indian from Columbus to the Present*. New York: Random House, 1978.

Bierhorst, John, ed. *The Sacred Path: Spells, Prayers, and Power Songs of the American Indians*. New York: Quill, 1984.

Bitsui, Sherwin. *Shapeshift*. Tucson: Univ. of Arizona Press, 2003.

Blaeser, Kimberly. "Native Literatures: Seeking a Critical Center." In *Looking at the Words of Our People: First Nations Analysis of Literature*, ed. Jeannette Armstrong, 51–62. Penticton, B.C.: Theytus Books, 1993.

Blue Spruce, Duane, ed. *Spirit of a Native Place: Building the National Museum of the American Indian*. Washington, D.C.: National Geographic Society, in association with the National Museum of the American Indian, 2004.

Boser, Ulrich. "A New Museum: Finally, a Place to Honor America's Native Peoples." *U.S. News and World Report*, October 4, 2004, 52.

Bowles, K. Johnson. "Stop. Look. Listen." In *Jaune Quick-to-See Smith: A Journey through Tribal Lands*, an exhibition catalogue. Longwood, V.: Longwood Center for the Arts, 2001.

Breeskin, Adelyn D. Introduction to *Scholder/Indians*, ed. Doris Monthan. Flagstaff, Ariz.: Northland, 1976.

Bouissac, Paul, ed. *Encyclopedia of Semiotics*. New York: Oxford Univ. Press, 1998.

Braudy, Leo. *The World in a Frame: What We See in Films*. Chicago: Univ. of Chicago Press, 1976.

Brill de Ramirez, Susan Berry. *Contemporary American Indian Literature and the Oral Tradition*. Tucson: Univ. of Arizona Press, 1999.

Brody, Hugh. *Maps and Dreams: Indians and the British Columbia Frontier*. New York: Pantheon, 1981.

Capone, P. W., and R. W. Preucel. "Ceramic Semiotics: Women, Pottery, and Social Meanings at Kotyiti Pueblo." In *Archaeologies of the Pueblo Revolt: Identity, Meaning, and Renewal in the Pueblo World*, ed. R. W. Preucel, 99–113. Albuquerque: Univ. of New Mexico Press, 2002.

Carsten, Cynthia. "*Storyteller*: Leslie Marmon Silko's Reappropriation of Native American History and Identity." *Wicazo Sa Review* 21, no. 2 (2006): 105–126.

Certeau, Michel de. *The Practice of Everyday Life*. Translated by Steven Rendall. Berkeley and Los Angeles: Univ. of California Press, 1988.

Chandler, Daniel. *Semiotics: The Basics*. London: Routledge, 2002.

Churchill, Ward. "The Bloody Wake of Alcatraz: Political Repression of the American Indian Movement during the 1970s." In Johnson, Nagel, and Champagne, *American Indian Activism: Alcatraz to the Longest Walk*, 242–284.

——. *Fantasies of the Master Race: Literature, Cinema, and the Colonization of American Indians*. Monroe, Me.: Common Courage, 1992.

Cobb, Amanda J. "The National Museum of the American Indian as Cultural Sovereignty." *American Quarterly* 57, no. 2 (2005): 485–506.

——. "This Is What It Means to Say *Smoke Signals*: Native American Cultural Sovereignty." In *Hollywood's Indian: The Portrayal of the Native American in Film*, expanded ed., ed. Peter C. Rollins and John E. O'Connor, 206–228. Lexington: Univ. Press of Kentucky, 2002.

Cordova, V. F. "Approaches to Native American Philosophy." In *Native American Thought*, ed. Anne Waters, 27–33. Malden, Mass.: Blackwell, 1988.

Curnutte, Rick. Review of *The Business of Fancydancing*, directed by Sherman Alexie. *Film Journal*, 2002. http://www.thefilmjournal.com/issue3/fancydancing.html.

Davenport, Francis Gardiner, ed. *European Treaties Bearing on the History of the United States and Its Dependencies*. 2 vols. Washington, D.C.: Carnegie Institute of Washington, 1917.

Declaration of the Return of Indian Land. San Francisco, 1970.

Deloria, Philip. *Playing Indian*. New Haven, Conn.: Yale Univ. Press, 1998.

Deloria, Jr., Vine. "Alcatraz, Activism, and Accommodation." In Johnson, Nagel, and Champagne, *American Indian Activism: Alcatraz to the Longest Walk*. 45–51.

——. "It Is a Good Day to Die." *Katallagete* 4, no. 2–3 (1972): 62–65.

——. *Custer Died for Your Sins: An Indian Manifesto*. New York: Macmillan, 1969.

Deutsche, Rosalyn. "Public Art and Its Uses." In *Critical Issues in Public Art: Content, Context, and Controversy*, ed. Harriet F. Senie and Sally Webster, 158–170. Washington, D.C.: Smithsonian Institution Press, 1998.

Earling, Debra Magpie. *Perma Red*. New York: Blue Hen, 2002.

Ebert, Roger. Review of *Skins*, directed by Chris Eyre. *Chicago Sun-Times*, October 18, 2002. http://rogerebert.suntimes.com/apps/pbcs.dll/article?AID=2002210180310.

Erdrich, Louise. *Baptism of Desire*. New York: HarperCollins, 1990.

——. *Jacklight*. New York: Holt, 1984.

——. *The Last Report on the Miracles at Little No Horse*. New York: Perennial, 2002.

——. *The Plague of Doves*. New York: HarperCollins, 2008.

Evelyn, Douglas E. "'A Most Beautiful Sight Has Presented Itself to My View': The Long Return to a Native Place on the Mall." In Blue Spruce, *Spirit of a Native Place*, 151–183.

Fast, Robin Riley. *The Heart as a Drum: Continuance and Resistance in American Indian Poetry*. Ann Arbor: Univ. of Michigan Press, 1999.

Fitz, E. Brewster. *Silko: Writing Storyteller and Medicine Woman*. Norman: Univ. of Oklahoma Press, 2004.

Fleming, E. McClung. "The American Image as Indian Princess, 1765–1783." *Winterthur Portfolio* 2 (1965): 65–81.

Foucault, Michel. *Discipline and Punish: The Birth of the Prison*. Translated by Alan Sheridan. New York: Pantheon, 1977.

Gates, Henry Louis, Jr. *Thirteen Ways of Looking at a Black Man*. New York: Vintage, 1998.

Gathering of All Indian Tribes, Round Table Discussion: Design and Lay-Out. Minutes, December 1969. File 32, box 1, San Francisco Public Library.

Gibson, Arrell Morgan. *Oklahoma: A History of Five Centuries*. Norman: Univ. of Oklahoma Press, 1981.

Gillan, Jennifer. "Sherman Alexie's Poetry." *American Literature* 68 (March 1996): 91–110.

Gilroy, Jhon Warren. "Another Fine Example of the Oral Tradition? Identification and Subversion in Sherman Alexie's *Smoke Signals*." *SAIL: Studies in American Indian Literatures* 13, no. 1 (2001): 23–42.

Goldstein, Laurence. *The American Poet at the Movies*. Ann Arbor: Univ. of Michigan Press, 1997.

Gottschalk, Paul. *The Earliest Diplomatic Documents on America: The Papal Bulls of 1493 and the Treaty of Tordesillas*. Berlin: Gottschalk, 1927.

Gould, Janice. "American Indian Women's Poetry: Strategies of Rage and Hope." *Signs* 20, no. 4 (1995): 797–817.

——. "Poems as Maps in American Indian Women's Writing." In *Speak to Me Words: Essays on Contemporary American Indian Poetry*, ed. Dean Rader and Janice Gould, 21–33. Tucson: Univ. of Arizona Press, 2003.

Graves, Donna. "Representing Race: Detroit's Monument to Joe Louis." In *Critical Issues in Public Art*, ed. Harriet F. Senie and Sally Webster, 215–227. Washington, D.C.: Smithsonian Institution Press, 1992.

Hafen, Jane. "Sacramental Language: Ritual in the Poetry of Louise Erdrich." *Great Plains Quarterly* 16, no. 3 (1996): 147–155.

Harjo, Joy. "Creation Story: The Jaune Quick-to-See Smith Survey." In *Subversions/Affirmations: Jaune Quick-to-See Smith: A Survey*, ed. Alejandro Anreus. Jersey City, N.J.: Jersey City Museum, 1996.

——. Introduction to *Reinventing the Enemy's Language: Contemporary Native Women's Writings of North America*. Edited by Joy Harjo and Gloria Bird. New York: Norton, 1997.

——. *The Woman Who Fell from the Sky*. New York: Norton, 1996.

Harlow, Barbara. *Resistance Literature*. New York: Methuen, 1987.

Heidegger, Martin. *Poetry, Language, Thought*. Translated by Albert Hofstadter. New York: HarperCollins, 1976.

Henry, Michelle. "Canonizing Craig Womack: Finding Native Literature's Place in Indian Country." *American Indian Quarterly* 28, no. 1–2 (2004): 30–51.

Hernandez, Dharma Thornton. "*Storyteller*: Revising the Narrative Schematic." *Pacific Coast Philology* 31, no. 1 (1996): 54–67.

Hilger, Michael. *From Savage to Nobleman: Images of Native Americans in Film*. Lanham, Md.: Scarecrow, 1995.

Hirsch, Edward. *How to Read a Poem and Fall in Love with Poetry*. New York: Harcourt, Brace, 1999.

Hirsch, Bernard A. "'The Telling Which Continues': Oral Tradition and the Written Word in Leslie Marmon Silko's *Storyteller*." *American Indian Quarterly* 12, no. 1 (1988): 92–111.

Hogan, Linda. *The Book of Medicines*. Minneapolis: Coffee House, 1993.

Hollrah, Patrice E. "Decolonizing the Choctaws: Teaching LeAnne Howe's *Shell Shaker*." *American Indian Quarterly* 28, no. 1–2 (2004): 73–85.

Horse Capture, George. "The Way of the People." In Blue Spruce, *Spirit of a Native Place*, 30–45.

Hoving, Thomas. *The Art of Dan Namingha*. New York: Abrams, 2000.

Howe, LeAnne. *Evidence of Red: Poems and Prose*. Great Wilbraham, UK: Salt, 2005.

——. "An Interview with LeAnne Howe." By Golda Sargento. http://www.auntlute.com/h-interview.html (link discontinued).

——. *Miko Kings*. San Francisco: Aunt Lute Books, 2007.

——. "My Mothers, My Uncles, Myself." In *Here First: Autobiographical Essays by Native American Writers*, ed. Arnold Krupat and Brian Swann, 212–219. New York: Modern Library, 2000.

——. *Shell Shaker*. San Francisco: Aunt Lute Books, 2001.

——. "The Story of America: A Tribalography." In *Clearing a Path: Theorizing the Past in Native American Studies*, ed. Nancy Shumaker, 29–50. New York: Routledge, 2002.

Huhndorf, Shari M. *Going Native: Indians in the American Cultural Imagination*. Ithaca, N.Y.: Cornell Univ. Press, 2001.

Hymes, Dell. *Now I Know Only So Far: Essays in Ethnopoetics*. Lincoln: Univ. of Nebraska Press, 2003.

——. "Tonkawa Poetics: John Rush Buffalo's 'Coyote and Eagle's Daughter.'" In *Native American Discourse: Poetics and Rhetoric*, edited Joel Sherzer and Anthony Woodbury. Cambridge: Cambridge Univ. Press, 1987.

Iglesias, David Claudio. Review of *Naturally Native*, directed by Valerie Red-Horse. *Native Peoples* 14, no. 3 (March–April 2001): 60.

Jaskoski, Helen. *Leslie Marmon Silko: A Study of the Short Fiction*. New York: Twayne, 1998.

Johnson, Troy R., ed. *Alcatraz: Indian Land Forever*. Berkeley and Los Angeles: Univ. of California Press, 1994.

——. *The Occupation of Alcatraz Island: Indian Self-Determination and the Rise of Indian Activism*. Urbana: Univ. of Illinois Press, 1996.

Johnson, Troy, Joane Nagel, and Duane Champagne, eds. *American Indian Activism: Alcatraz to the Longest Walk*: Urbana: Univ. of Illinois Press, 1997.

Jones, Patricia. "The Web of Meaning: Naming the Absent Mother in *Storyteller*." In *Yellow Woman*, by Leslie Silko, ed. Melody Graulich, 213–232. New Brunswick, N.J.: Rutgers Univ. Press, 1993.

Kakutani, Michiko. "Unearthing Tangled Roots of a Town's Family Trees." Review of *The Plague of Doves*, by Louise Erdrich. *New York Times*, April 29, 2008. http://www.nytimes.com/2008/04/29/books/29kaku.html.

Keenan, Deidre. "Unrestricted Territory: Gender, Two Spirits, and Louise Erdrich's *The Last Report on the Miracles at Little No Horse*." *American Indian Culture and Research Journal* 30, no. 2 (2006): 1–15.

Kilpatrick, Jacquelyn. *Celluloid Indians: Native Americans and Film*. Lincoln: Univ. of Nebraska Press, 1999.

Kristeva, Julia. *Revolution in Poetic Language*. Translated by Margaret Waller. New York: Columbia Univ. Press, 1984.

Kroeber, Karl. *Traditional American Indian Literatures*. Lincoln: Univ. of Nebraska Press, 1981.

Krumholz, Linda. "Native Designs: Silko's *Storyteller* and the Reader's Initiation." In *Leslie Marmon Silko: A Collection of Critical Essays*, ed. Louise K. Barnett and James L. Thorson, 63–86. Albuquerque: Univ. of New Mexico Press, 1999.

Lacayo, Richard. "A Place to Bring the Tribe: The Guiding Vision at a Major New Museum Is Entirely Native American." *Time*, September 20, 2004, 68.

Lake, Randall A. "Between Myth and History: Enacting Time in Native American Protest Rhetoric." *Quarterly Journal of Speech* 77 (1991): 123–151.

——. "Enacting Red Power: The Consummatory Function in Native American Protest Rhetoric." *Quarterly Journal of Speech* 69, no. 2 (1983): 127–142.

Lang, Sabine. *Men as Women, Women as Men: Changing Gender in Native American Cultures*. Austin: Univ. of Texas Press, 1998.

Langen, Toby C. S. "*Storyteller* as Hopi Basket." *SAIL: Studies in American Indian Literatures* 5, no. 1 (1993): 7–24.

Leibman, Laura Arnold. "A Bridge of Difference: Sherman Alexie and the Politics of Mourning." *American Literature* 77, no. 3 (2005): 541–561.
Leuthold, Steven. *Indigenous Aesthetics: Native Art, Media, and Identity*. Austin: Univ. of Texas Press, 1998.
Lewis, Peter. Review of *Perma Red*, by Deborah Magpie Earling. *San Francisco Chronicle*, July 7, 2002.
Liggett, Lori. "The Wounded Knee Massacre." In *1890s America: A Chronology*, American Culture Studies Program, Bowling Green State University, 1998. http://www.bgsu.edu/departments/acs/1890s/woundedknee/WKghost.html.
Limerick, Patricia Nelson. *The Legacy of Conquest: The Unbroken Past of the American West*. New York: Norton, 1988.
Lincoln, Kenneth. *Indi'n Humor: Bicultural Play in Native America*. Oxford: Oxford Univ. Press, 1993.
——. *Native American Renaissance*. Berkeley and Los Angeles: Univ. of California Press, 1985.
——. *Speak like Singing: Classics of Native American Literature*. Albuquerque: Univ. of New Mexico Press, 1997.
Lonetree, Amy. "Guest Editor's Remarks." *American Indian Quarterly* 30, no. 3–4 (2006): 507–510.
——. "Missed Opportunities: Reflections on the NMAI." *American Indian Quarterly* 30, no. 3–4 (2006): 632–645.
Lonetree, Amy, and Amanda J. Cobb, eds. *The National Museum of the American Indian: Critical Conversations*. Lincoln: Univ. of Nebraska Press, 2008.
Lorenz, Paul H. "The Other Story of Leslie Marmon Silko's *Storyteller*." *South Central Review* 8, no. 4 (1991): 59–75.
Lovell, Glenn. Review of *Naturally Native*, directed by Valerie Red-Horse. *Variety* 369 (February 9, 1998), 73.
Lowe, Truman T., ed. *Native Modernism: The Art of George Morrison and Allan Houser*. Seattle: Univ. of Washington Press, 2004.
Lynn, Andrea. "Baseball Novel Explores Role of the Game in American Indian Life." Review of *Miko Kings*, by LeAnne Howe. News Bureau, University of Illinois at Urbana-Champaign, November 8, 2007. http://news.illinois.edu/news/07/1108baseball.html.
Lyotard, Jean Francois. *The Postmodern Condition: A Report on Knowledge*. Minneapolis: Univ. of Minnesota Press, 1984.
Marubbio, M. Elise. *Killing the Indian Maiden: Images of Native American Women in Film*. Lexington: Univ. Press of Kentucky, 2006.
McFarland, Ron. "'Another Kind of Violence': Sherman Alexie's Poems." *American Indian Quarterly* 21, no. 2 (1997): 251–264.
Mihelich, John. "Smoke or Signals? American Popular Culture and the Challenge to Hegemonic Images of American Indians in Native American Film." *Wicazo Sa Review* 16, no. 2 (2001): 129–137.
Mihesuah, Devon A. "Finding Empowerment through Writing and Reading, or Why Am I Doing This?: An Unpopular Writer's Comments about the State of American Indian Literary Criticism." *American Indian Quarterly* 28, no. 1–2 (2004): 97–102.
Mitchell, Elvis. "A Poet Finds His Past Is Just Where He Left It." Review of *The Business of Fancydancing*, directed by Sherman Alexie. *New York Times*, October 18, 2002. http://movies.nytimes.com/movie/review?res=9E04EFD7153DF93BA25753C1A9649C8B63.
Momaday, N. Scott. "An American Land Ethic." In *The Man Made of Words*, 42–49. New York: St. Martin's, 1997.
——. *House Made of Dawn*. New York: Harper and Row, 1968.
——. *The Man Made of Words: Essays, Stories, Passages*. New York: St. Martin's, 1997.
——. "Native American Attitudes to the Environment." In *Seeing with a Native Eye: Essays on Native American Religion*, ed. Walter Holden Capps, 79–85. New York: Harper and Row, 1976.
——. "The Testament of Allan Houser." In *Native Modernism: The Art of George Morrison and Allan Houser*, ed. Truman T. Lowe. Seattle: Univ. of Washington Press, 2004.
Mooney, James. *The Ghost Dance Religion and the Sioux Outbreak of 1890*. Chicago: Univ. of Chicago Press, 1965.
Morris, Charles E., III, and Stephen Howard Browne, eds. *Readings on the Rhetoric of Social Protest*. State College, Penn.: Strata, 2006.

Murfin, Ross, and Supryia M. Ray. *The Bedford Glossary of Critical and Literary Terms*. Boston: Bedford, 1998.

Myerhoff, Barbara G. "Return to Wirikuta: Ritual Reversal and Symbolic Continuity on the Peyote Hunt of the Huichol Indians." In *The World Upside Down: Studies in Symbolic Inversion*, ed. Barbara Babcock, 225–239. Ithaca, N.Y.: Cornell Univ. Press, 1978.

Nabokov, Peter, and Robert Easton. *Native American Architecture*. New York: Oxford Univ. Press, 1989.

National Museum of the American Indian. "Exhibitions" listings. http://www.nmai.si.edu/subpage.cfm?subpage=exhibitions&second=dc&third=current.

Nelson, Robert M. "He Said/She Said: Writing Oral Traditions in John Gunn's 'Ko-pot Ka-nat' and Leslie Silko's *Storyteller*." *SAIL: Studies in American Indian Literatures* 5, no. 1 (1993): 31–50.

Nolan, James. *Poet-Chief: The Native American Poetics of Walt Whitman and Pablo Neruda*. Albuquerque: Univ. of New Mexico Press, 1994.

Nöth, Winfried. *Handbook of Semiotics*. Bloomington: Indiana Univ. Press, 1995.

Oklahoma Arts Council. Description of the sculpture *As Long As The Waters Flow*, by Allan Houser (Hauzous). Art of the Oklahoma State Capitol. http://www.arts.ok.gov/capitolart/permart/sculpture/houser/waters.html.

——. Description of the sculpture *The Guardian*, by Enoch Kelly Haney. Art of the Oklahoma State Capitol. http://www.ok.gov/~arts/capitolart/permart/sculpture/haney/guardian.html.

Ortiz, Simon. "California Indigenous Storytelling." Paper presented at the Modern Language Association Convention, San Francisco, California, December 29, 2008.

——. *From Sand Creek: Rising in This Heart Which Is Our America*. New York: Thunder's Mouth, 1981.

——. *Going for the Rain*. New York: Harper and Row, 1976.

——. "The Story Never Ends: An Interview with Simon Ortiz." By Joseph Bruchac. In *Survival This Way: Interviews with American Indian Poets*, ed. Joseph Bruchac, 211–230. Tucson: Univ. of Arizona Press, 1987.

——. "Towards a National Indian Literature: Cultural Authenticity in Nationalism." *MELUS: Multiethnic Literatures of the United States* 8 (1981): 7–12.

——. *Woven Stone*. Tucson: Univ. of Arizona Press, 1992.

Owens, Louis. *Other Destinies: Understanding the American Indian Novel*. Norman: Univ. of Oklahoma Press, 1994.

——. "'The Song Is Very Short': Native American Literature and Literary Theory." *Weber Studies* 12, no. 3 (1995): 123–146.

Pasztory, Esther. *Thinking with Things: Toward a New Vision of Art*. Austin: Univ. of Texas Press, 2005.

People Magazine. "Tribal Tribute." October 4, 2004, 148–149.

Peterson, Nancy J. "Introduction: Native American Literature: From the Margins to the Mainstream." *Modern Fiction Studies* 45, no. 1 (1999): 1–9.

Powell, Malea. "Princess Sarah, the Civilized Indian: The Rhetoric of Cultural Literacies in Sarah Winnemucca Hopkins' *Life Among the Piutes*." *Rhetorical "Woman": Roles and Representations*, ed. Hildy Miller and Lillian Bridwell-Bowles, 63–80. Tuscaloosa: Univ. of Alabama Press, 2005.

Pranzer, Joel S. *The Popes and Slavery*. New York: Alba House, 1996.

Pratt, Mary Louise. *Imperial Eyes: Travel Writing and Transculturation*. New York: Routledge, 1992.

Rader, Dean. "British Publisher Touts American Indian Poets." *San Francisco Chronicle*, September 7, 2008.

——. "The Epic Lyric: Genre and Contemporary American Indian Poetry." In *Speak to Me Words: Essays on Contemporary American Indian Poetry*, ed. Dean Rader and Janice Gould, 123–142. Tucson: Univ. of Arizona Press, 2003.

——. "Simon Ortiz and Luci Tapahonso: Symbol, Allegory, Language, Poetry." *Southwestern American Literature* 22, no. 2 (1997): 75–92.

——. "Sites of Unification: Teaching Louise Erdrich's Poetry" In *Approaches to Teaching the Works of Louise Erdrich*, ed. Greg Sarris, Connie Jacobs, and James Giles, 102–113. New York: Modern Language Association, 2004.

——. "When Form Invents Function: Contemporary American Indian Prose Poetry." *Sentence* 7 (2009): 84–96.

Red Corn, Charles H. *A Pipe for February*. Norman: Univ. of Oklahoma Press, 2002.

Red-Horse, Valerie. "Production." http://www.naturallynative.com/filmmakers.html.

RoadsideAmerica.com. "San Antonio, Texas—Muffler Man—Native American." http://www.roadsideamerica.com/tip/4390.

Robinson, Douglas. "The Translator as Lover." Review of *The Translation of Dr. Apelles: A Love Story*, by David Treuer. *California Literary Review*, April 24, 2007. http://calitreview.com/174.

Rollins, Peter C., and John E. O'Connor, eds. *Hollywood's Indian: The Portrayal of the Native American in Film*. Lexington: Univ. Press of Kentucky, 1998.

Rosaldo, Renato. *Culture and Truth: The Remaking of Social Analysis*. Boston: Beacon Press, 1986.

Rose, Wendy. *Bone Game: New and Selected Poems, 1965–1993*. Tucson: Univ. of Arizona Press, 1994.

Ross, Thom. "Artist Thom Ross." http://www.thomrossart.com/Thom_Ross_Art_Biography.html.

Rundstrom, Robert A. "American Indian Placemaking on Alcatraz, 1969–71." In Johnson, Nagel, and Champagne, *American Indian Activism: Alcatraz to the Longest Walk*, 186–204.

Rushing, W. Jackson, III. *Allan Houser: An American Master (Chiricahua Apache, 1914–1994)*. New York: Abrams, 2004.

——. "In Our Language." *Third Text* 19, no. 4 (2005): 365–384. http://www.ingentaconnect.com/.

——. *Jaune Quick-to-See Smith: A Journey through Tribal Lands*. Washington, D.C.: Anton Gallery, 2001.

Russell, Charles. *Poets, Prophets, and Revolutionaries: The Literary Avant-Garde from Rimbaud through Postmodernism*. Oxford: Oxford Univ. Press, 1985.

Ryan, Marie-Laurie. "Toward a Definition of Narrative." In *The Cambridge Companion to Narrative*, ed. David Herman, 22–35. Cambridge: Cambridge Univ. Press, 2007.

Sakiestewa, Ramona. "Making Our World Understandable." In Blue Spruce, *Spirit of a Native Place*, 80–85.

Santa Barbara Surfing. Blog. http://www.santabarbarasurfing.com/2003_01_01_archive.html.

Sasse, Julie. *Jaune Quick-to-See Smith: Postmodern Messenger*. Tucson: Tucson Museum of Art, 2004.

Schatz, Thomas. *Hollywood Genres: Formulas, Filmmaking, and the Studio System*. Austin: Univ. of Texas Press, 1981.

Schmidt, Rob. Blue Corn Comics. "Stereotype of the Month Contest." http://www.bluecorncomics.com/stertype.htm.

Shanley, Kathryn W. "The Devil's Domain: Leslie Silko's 'Storyteller.'" In *Leslie Marmon Silko: A Study of the Short Fiction*, ed. Helen Jaskoski, 170–179. New York: Twayne, 1998.

Silko, Leslie Marmon. *Conversations with Leslie Marmon Silko*. Edited by Ellen L. Arnold. Jackson: Univ. Press of Mississippi, 2000.

——. "Interior and Exterior Landscapes: The Pueblo Migration Stories." In *Yellow Woman and a Beauty of the Spirit: Essays on Native American Life Today*, 25–47. New York: Simon and Schuster, 1997.

——. "Landscape, History, and the Pueblo Imagination." *Antaeus* 51 (Autumn 1986): 83–94.

——. "Language and Literature from a Pueblo Indian Perspective." In *Yellow Woman and a Beauty of the Spirit: Essays on Native American Life Today*, 48–59. New York: Simon and Schuster, 1997.

——. "Stories and Their Tellers: A Conversation with Leslie Marmon Silko." By Dexter Fisher. In *The Third Woman: Minority Women Writers of the United States*, ed. Dexter Fisher, 18–23. Boston: Houghton Mifflin, 1980.

——. *Storyteller*. New York: Arcade, 1989.

Singer, Beverly. *Wiping the War Paint off the Lens: Native American Film and Video*. Minneapolis: Univ. of Minnesota Press, 2001.

Smith, Andrea. *Conquest: Sexual Violence and American Indian Genocide*. Brooklyn, N.Y.: South End Press, 2005.

Smith, Jaune Quick-to-See. "Subversions/Affirmations: A Conversation with Jaune Quick-to-See-Smith." By Alejandro Anreus. In *Jaune Quick-to-See Smith: Subversions/Affirmations*, ed. Alejandro Anreus, 108–113. Jersey City, N.J.: Jersey City Museum, 1996.

Smith, Paul Chaat, and Robert Allen Warrior. *Like a Hurricane: The Indian Movement from Alcatraz to Wounded Knee*. New York: New Press, 1996.

Stedman, Raymond William. *Shadows of the Indian: Stereotypes in American Culture*. Norman: Univ. of Oklahoma Press, 1986.

Stephens, John, and Robyn McCallum. *Retelling Stories, Framing Culture: Traditional Story and Metanarratives in Children's Literature*. New York: Garland, 1998.

Stevens, James Thomas. *A Bridge Dead in the Water*. Great Wilbraham, UK: Salt, 2007.

Stott, William. *Documentary Expression and Thirties America*. Chicago: Univ. of Chicago Press, 1973.

Strange, Carolyn, and Tina Loo. "'Holding the Rock': The Indianization of Alcatraz Island, 1969–1999." *Public Historian* 23, no. 1 (2001): 27–54.

Swann, Brian, ed. *Smoothing the Ground: Essays on Native American Oral Literature*. Berkeley and Los Angeles: Univ. of California Press, 1983.

Tapahonso, Luci. *Blue Horses Rush In*. Tucson: Univ. of Arizona Press, 1997.

——. *Sáanii Dahataał: The Women Are Singing*. Tucson: Univ. of Arizona Press, 1993.

Teuton, Sean Kicummah. *Red Land, Red Power: Grounding Knowledge in the American Indian Novel*. Durham, N.C.: Duke Univ. Press, 2008.

Thomas, Deborah. "John Wayne's Body." In *The Book of Westerns*, ed. Ian Cameron and Douglas Pye, 75–87. New York: Continuum, 1996.

Tompkins, Jane. *Sensational Designs: The Cultural Work of American Fiction, 1790–1860*. Oxford: Oxford Univ. Press, 1985.

Tongson-McCall, Karen. "The Nether World of Neither World: Hybridization in the Literature of Wendy Rose." *American Indian Culture and Research Journal* 20, no. 4 (1996): 1–40.

Townsend, Richard F., ed. *Hero, Hawk, and Open Hand: American Indian Art of the Ancient Midwest and South*. Chicago: Art Institute of Chicago, 2004.

Treuer, David. *Native American Fiction: A User's Manual*. Saint Paul, Minn.: Graywolf, 2006.

——. *The Translation of Dr. Apelles: A Love Story*. Saint Paul, Minn.: Graywolf, 2006.

Turnbull, David. *Maps Are Territories: Science Is an Atlas*. Chicago: Univ. of Chicago Press, 1993.

U.S. Department of Treasury. United States Mint. "United States Diplomat Presentation Bronze Medal 2–13/16 (635)." https://catalog.usmint.gov/webapp/wcs/stores/servlet/ProductDisplay?catalogId=10001&storeId=10001&productId=10965&langId= 1&parent_category_rn=10051.

University of New Mexico. *Jaune Quick-to-See Smith: Made in America*. Albuquerque: Univ. of New Mexico Art Museum, 2005.

Utter, Jack. "The Discovery Doctrine, the Tribes, and the Truth." *Indian Country Today*, May 24, 2000. http://www.indiancountrytoday.com/archive/28219599.html.

Vizenor, Gerald. *Fugitive Poses: Native American Indian Scenes of Absence and Presence*. Lincoln: Univ. of Nebraska Press, 1998.

——. *Manifest Manners: Narratives on Postindian Survivance*. Lincoln: Univ. of Nebraska Press, 1999.

——, ed. *Narrative Chance: Postmodern Discourse on Native American Indian Literatures*. Norman: Univ. of Oklahoma Press, 1993.

Warhus, Mark. *Another America: Native American Maps and the History of Our Land*. New York: St. Martin's, 1997.

Warrior, Robert Allen. "Liberating Words: Texts and Contexts in Edgar Heap of Bird's 'Wheel.'" Paper presented at the Modern Language Association Convention, Philadelphia, December 30, 2004.

——. *Tribal Secrets: Recovering American Indian Intellectual Traditions*. Minneapolis: Univ. of Minnesota Press, 1994.

Weaver, Jace. *That the People Might Live: Native American Literatures and Native American Community*. New York: Oxford Univ. Press, 1997.

West, Richard A. Foreword to *Welcome to a Native Place*. Guidebook for the National Museum of the American Indian. Washington, D.C.: National Museum of the American Indian, 2004.

Wingert, Pat, "Return of the Native: The First Americans Get a Museum to Call Their Own." *Newsweek*, September 20, 2004, 48.

Womack, Craig S. *Drowning in Fire*. Tucson: Univ. of Arizona Press, 2001.

——. *Red on Red: Native American Literary Separatism*. Minneapolis: Univ. of Minnesota Press, 1999.

Woody, Elizabeth. *Luminaries of the Humble*. Tucson: Univ. of Arizona Press, 1994.

Yellow Wood, Troy Lynn. "Trauma and Memory: The Importance of Imagery to Native Peoples." *Sculpture Review* 55, no. 4 (2006): 32–34.

Youngberg, Quentin. "Interpenetrations: Re-encoding the Queer Indian in Sherman Alexie's *The Business of Fancydancing*." *SAIL: Studies in American Indian Literatures* 20, no. 1 (2008): 55–75.

INDEX

Page numbers in *italics* refer to pages with illustrations.